Alvah Hovey

Commentary on the Gospel of John

Volume 3

Alvah Hovey

Commentary on the Gospel of John
Volume 3

ISBN/EAN: 9783337285555

Printed in Europe, USA, Canada, Australia, Japan

Cover: Foto ©Lupo / pixelio.de

More available books at **www.hansebooks.com**

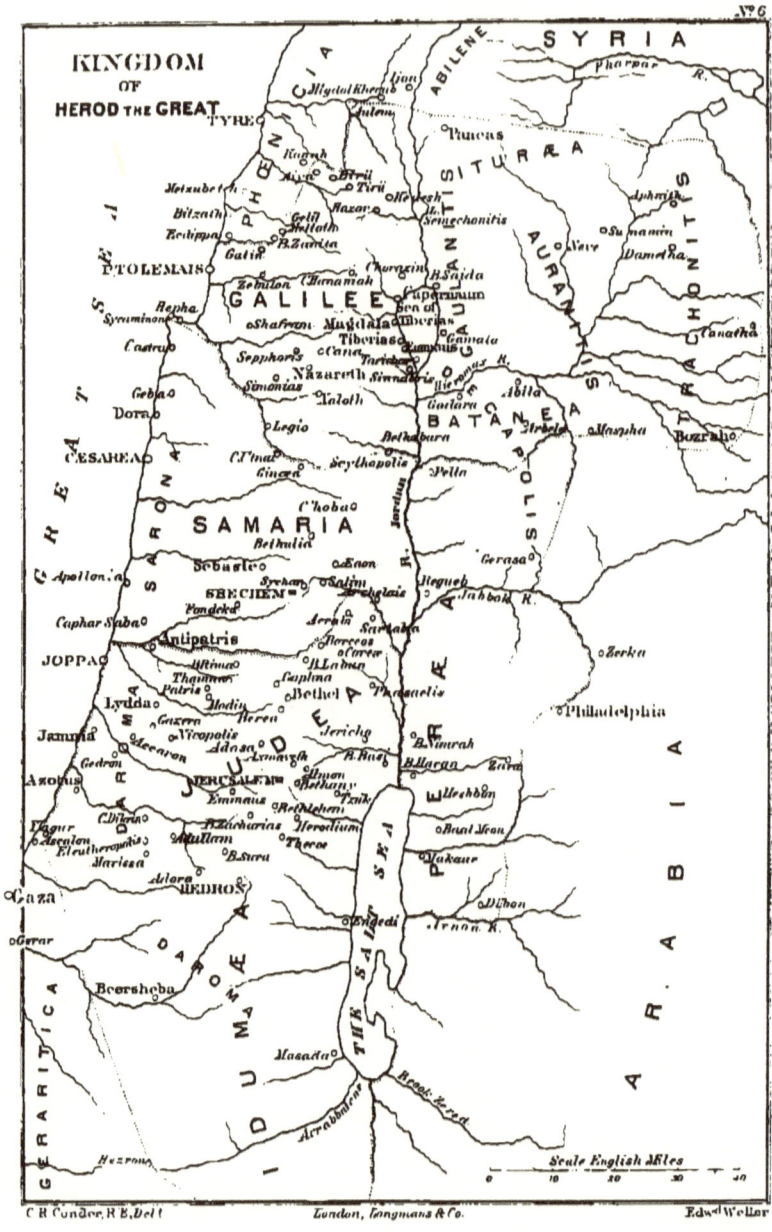

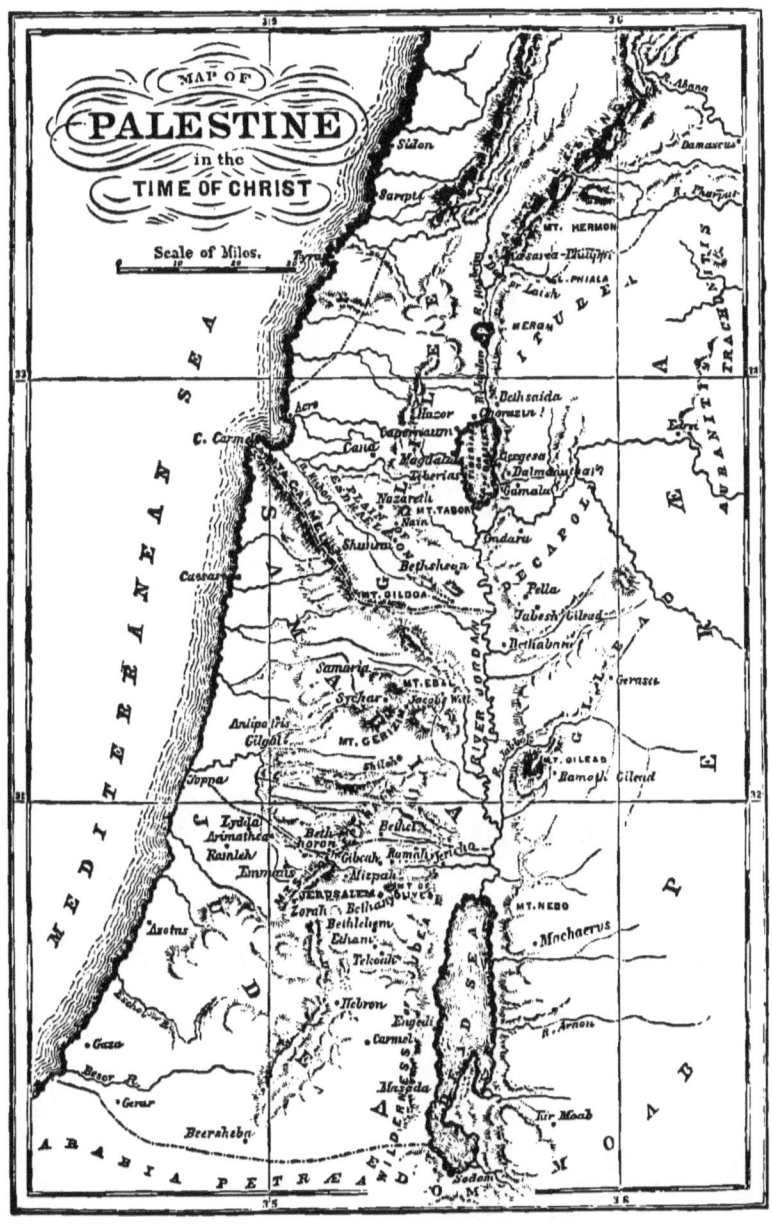

AN

AMERICAN COMMENTARY

ON THE

NEW TESTAMENT.

EDITED BY
ALVAH HOVEY, D.D., LL.D.

PHILADELPHIA:
AMERICAN BAPTIST PUBLICATION SOCIETY,
1420 Chestnut Street.

PREFACE.

For a statement of the purpose and plan of this series of Commentaries on the New Testament, the reader is referred to the last part of the General Introduction, published in the volume on the Gospel of Mark, and for a more particular account of the sources of the present volume, to the last part of the following Introduction. Two or three remarks are all that seem to be required in the way of further explanation.

Whenever the words of another writer are employed, his name is given, though it has not always been thought advisable to mention the volume and page from which the words are taken. In a great majority of cases they are from Notes on the particular passage under examination. Sentences are sometimes put in quotation marks, not because they are borrowed from another, but because they are meant to represent in paraphrase the words of Christ, or of the Evangelist, in the text explained.

For critical notes upon the text in several important passages, the writer is indebted to the kindness of Prof. John A. Broadus, D. D., who is preparing the volume on the Gospel according to Matthew. These Notes have been inserted in the margin, followed by the letter B. They are uncommonly clear and discriminating, and the conclusions which they reach are believed to be, in every instance, correct. The judgment of one who has given special attention to textual criticism will be highly valued by the reader.

To the preparation of this Commentary, the writer has given all the time at his command for such labor, during many years. And though the work produced is very imperfect, when compared with his own conception of what it should be, he cannot repress the hope that it will be useful to some who love "the spiritual Gospel." Often has this Gospel appeared to him, while exploring it, like the land promised to the Israelites by the Lord—"a good land, a land of brooks of water, of fountains and depths that spring out of valleys and hills; a land of wheat, and barley, and vines, and fig trees, and pomegranates; a land of olive oil and honey; a land wherein thou shalt eat bread without scarceness, thou shalt not lack anything in it." (Deut. 8:7–9.) Wells of purest truth, deeper than Jacob's well at Sychar, are in this Gospel, and the interpreter may let down his tiny cup a thousand times, with perfect confidence that it will always return filled to the brim.

May the Son of God, whose person is so fully revealed in this Gospel, accept the humble effort which has been made to expound his words, and by means of it bring a blessing to the hearts of his people! And to this end, may the reader fervently pray to the Father of lights, "Open thou mine eyes, that I may behold wondrous things out of thy law." (Ps. 119:18.)   ALVAH HOVEY.

NEWTON THEOLOGICAL INSTITUTION, *Nov. 26, 1885.*

ON THE

GOSPEL OF JOHN.

BY
ALVAH HOVEY, D. D., LL. D.

PHILADELPHIA:
AMERICAN BAPTIST PUBLICATION SOCIETY,
1420 Chestnut Street.

Entered, according to Act of Congress, in the year 1885, by the
AMERICAN BAPTIST PUBLICATION SOCIETY,
In the Office of the Librarian of Congress, at Washington, D. C.

INTRODUCTION TO THE GOSPEL OF JOHN.

For reasons, which will readily occur to every one who is familiar with Biblical criticism during the present century, an Introduction to the Fourth Gospel must treat with some fullness the question of its authorship. If the Gospel is believed to have been written by the Apostle John, the grounds of this belief should be clearly stated, even though they cannot be elaborately defended; and if this ancient belief is impugned and rejected by any one, the grounds for such rejection should be carefully explained. We propose therefore to consider (1) the authorship of the Fourth Gospel; (2) its trustworthiness as a historical record, especially as a record of the discourses of Jesus; (3) the time and place of its composition; (4) the occasion, object, and plan of the work; and (5) the aim and sources of this commentary.

I. AUTHORSHIP OF THE FOURTH GOSPEL.

It has been the common belief of Christians from the second century until now that the Fourth Gospel was written by John, the brother of James, an apostle of Jesus Christ our Lord. This belief has rested upon certain indications of authorship which the Gospel itself affords, and upon certain passages in Christian writings of an early age which point to the same authorship. *First.* While the name of the writer is not mentioned in the Gospel, he that "beareth witness of these things, and wrote these things," is plainly declared to be "the disciple whom Jesus loved," and who "also leaned on his bosom at the supper" (ch. 21 : 20-24). But "the disciple whom Jesus loved," and to whom he committed his mother from the cross as to a son, must have been one of that inner circle of three—Peter, James, and John—whom Jesus honored with his special confidence. Now Peter is distinguished from "the disciple whom Jesus loved" in the passage just cited (ch. 21 : 20-24), as well as in others (*e. g.*, 13 : 23 sq.; 20 : 2 sq.); and James, the brother of John, was slain by the sword at the command of Herod, about A. D. 40 (see Acts 12 : 2), long before this Gospel was written. Interpreters are therefore generally agreed in saying that, if the Fourth Gospel was written by an apostle, the words of the Gospel itself point clearly to John as that apostle. *Second.* The references of early Christian writers to this Gospel prove that they either knew, or at least supposed, it to be a work of the Apostle John. These references are so conclusive that nearly all who admit the Gospel to have been written before the close of the first century hold that the Apostle John was its author. But certain modern scholars of much learning and acuteness have denied its origin in the first century, and have attributed it to some unknown writer of the second century. Indeed, nearly all the arguments by which the authorship of John have been assailed are meant to prove that it could not have been written by any immediate follower of Christ. We propose to look first at the external testimonies relating to the authorship of the Fourth Gospel, and then at the internal evidences.

In examining the external evidences, it will be important to bear in mind two facts.

First, that the early Christian writers, who were contemporaneous with the apostles during a part of their lives, make use of the New Testament in a very informal way, often quoting its language inexactly, and generally neglecting to mention the writer or book from which they quote; and, *second*, that they quote from the first three Gospels and some of the Epistles more frequently than from the Fourth Gospel. These facts are accounted for by the practical necessity of quoting largely from memory, and by the earlier and wider circulation of the writings more frequently used. Yet there are traces of the use of the Fourth Gospel in the writings ascribed to the Apostolical Fathers.

For if, with many of the best scholars, we assume that the Shorter Greek recension of the Seven Epistles of *Ignatius* is, for the most part, genuine, there are passages in those letters which are so similar to certain expressions in the Fourth Gospel, or the first Epistle of John, that it is difficult to account for them without supposing that Ignatius had seen the latter. Thus, in his letter to the Ephesians (ch. 7), he speaks of Christ as both "originated and unoriginated, God incarnated, true Life in death, both from Mary and from God, first passible, and then impassible." Yet the reminiscence is not absolutely certain. But, in his Epistle to the Romans (ch. 7), he writes: "I desire the bread of God, the heavenly bread, the bread of life, which is the flesh of Jesus Christ, the Son of God, who was afterwards made of the seed of David and Abraham; and I desire the drink of God, his blood, which is incorruptible love and perennial life." This language seems to be founded on the sayings of Jesus preserved in the sixth chapter of our Gospel (vs. 41-59). So, too, in his letter to the Church in Smyrna, after asserting that Christ had suffered in the flesh (ch. 2), he adds these words: "For I know that soon after the resurrection he was in the flesh, and I believe that he is so still. And when he came to Peter and those about him, he said unto them: 'Take hold of me, handle me, and see that I am not an incorporeal spirit, or demon'" (ch. 3). With this compare John 20: 20-27, and 1 John 1: 1, and the probability that Ignatius had seen both the Gospel and the First Epistle will appear strong. Other reminiscences might be adduced from this writer, who died not later than A. D. 115; but while the genuineness of the epistles attributed to him is still in doubt, the value of their testimony is uncertain.

In the Epistle of *Polycarp* to the Philippians, written about A. D. 116, there occurs the following passage: "For every one who does not confess that Jesus Christ has come in the flesh is antichrist" (ch. 7). And we readily perceive that it is borrowed from 1 John 4: 2, 3. But it is generally admitted that whoever wrote the First Epistle of John was also the writer of the Fourth Gospel. Hence, if one of these writings belongs to the first century, and could be used by Polycarp in A. D. 116, just as he used the Epistles of Paul, it is extremely probable that the other belongs to the same early age. Indeed, Canon Lightfoot regards the First Epistle of John as a sort of postscript to the Fourth Gospel (see "Contemporary Review" for 1875, p. 835, sq.). Polycarp was probably not less than thirty years old when the Apostle John died at Ephesus. Irenæus represents him as one who had known the apostle, and enjoyed his instruction. Thus he was a living link, connecting the apostolic age with that of Justin Martyr and Irenæus (Irenæus "Adv. Hær.," III. 3, and Euseb. "H. E.," V. 20, 24).

The five books of *Papias*, entitled, "Interpretation of the Oracles of the Lord," have all perished except a few brief extracts made by Irenæus and Eusebius, or Christian writers of a later age. Of Papias himself Irenæus speaks with uniform respect, calling him in one place, "Papias, a man of the olden time, the hearer of John and companion of Polycarp" ("Adv. Hær," III. 33. 3). Eusebius thinks that his "understanding was

INTRODUCTION TO THE GOSPEL. 9

very small" ("II. E." III. 39), probably because of his adhesion to Chiliastic views, rejected by the father of church history. In his "Chronic. Ad. Olym." 220, he states that "Irenæus and others relate that John the theologian and apostle continued in life until the times of Trajan" (A. D. 98), and that "Papias, Bishop of Hierapolis, and Polycarp, Bishop of Smyrna, were well known as his hearers " (comp. "II. E." III. 40). In view of all the facts accessible to scholars, it is safe to say that Papias lived from about A. D. 70 to about A. D. 150, and that any use of the New Testament writings, or reference to them, which he makes, is worthy of close examination. But Eusebius, who had read his "five books," affirms that "he made use of testimonies from the First Epistle of John, and likewise from that of Peter" ("II. E." III. 39), which shows the existence of John's First Epistle in the first part of the second century. It also shows that Papias considered the words of the Epistle "testimonies" (μαρτυρίαις) to the truth by a proper witness. Moreover, as we have remarked, the existence of the Epistle at this early date must be accepted as probable evidence of the existence of the Fourth Gospel also; for they were both written by the same man.

But if Papias had the Fourth Gospel, he probably made use of it in his four books entitled, "Interpretation of Dominican Oracles"; perhaps he took from it many of the Oracles which he explained. Why then did Eusebius fail to mention his use of the Gospel? Because the purpose which he sought to accomplish did not require him to do this. By a critical study of the prefatory statements of Eusebius concerning his citation of early testimonies relating to the books of the New Testament, Prof. Lightfoot has established the following propositions: (1) "His main object was to give such information as might assist in forming correct views respecting the Canon of Scripture. (2) He was indifferent to any quotations or references which went towards establishing the canonicity of those books which had never been disputed in the church. Even when the quotation was direct and by name, it had no value for him. (3) To this class belonged (i) *The Four Gospels;* (ii) the Acts; (iii) the thirteen Epistles of St. Paul. (4) As regards these, he contents himself with preserving any anecdotes which he may have found illustrating the circumstances under which they were written . . . (5) The Catholic Epistles lie on the border-land . . . between the universally acknowledged and the disputed books," etc. ("Contemporary Review" for 1875, p. 179, sq.). Hence the circumstance that Eusebius reckons the Four Gospels among the books universally received is a sufficient reason why he should not have called attention to the use of them by Papias—to say nothing of the probability that the whole work of Papias was an exposition of them.

Again, Westcott refers to a passage in Irenæus where the testimony of "the elders" is adduced, and then, a little after, the same testimony is said to be from the fourth book of Papias. He therefore supposes it probable that another citation from "the Elders" by Irenæus, containing a part of John 14: 2—viz., *"in my Father's house are many mansions"*—is taken from the work of Papias. (See Irenæus "Adv. Hær." V. 36.)

About the middle of the second century *Justin Martyr,* who, in his journeys, visited Ephesus, Alexandria, and Rome, refers many times to certain writings which he calls "Memorabilia of the Apostles" ("Dial. with Trypho" cc. 100, 101, 103, 104, 106, 88), "The Memorabilia of the Apostles which are called Gospels" ("Apol." I. c. 66). and "Memorabilia which were composed by his apostles, and by those who followed with them" ("Dial. with Trypho" cc. 103, 106). This last expression may be compared with the words of Tertullian: "We have established this, first of all, that the Gospel Instrument has for its authors apostles, on whom this office of promulgating the Gospel was imposed by the Lord himself; and if also apostolic men, yet these not alone, but with apostles and after apostles" ("Adv. Marc." IV. 2). It is observable in both these passages that the word referring to apostles, as well as the word referring to their companions, is plural; and it cannot be reasonably doubted that by the former were intended Matthew and John, by the latter Mark and Luke. It may also be noticed that, according to Justin, these Memorabilia or Gospels were read in his day, along with the writings of the prophets, in the public worship of God ("Apol." I. 67).

But the following passage in his description of the rite of Christian baptism deserves particular attention: "After this they (*i. e.*, the candidates) are led by us where there is water, and are regenerated after the same manner in which we were regenerated: for upon the name of the Father of all and Sovereign God, and of our Saviour Jesus Christ, and of the Holy Spirit, they there receive the bath in the water; for Christ also said: *Except ye be born again, ye shall not enter into the kingdom of heaven.* But it is evident to all that those who have been once born cannot enter into the wombs of those who bore them," etc. ("Apol." I. 61; compare John 3: 3 sq.). Justin, it is true, does not quote the precise words of Christ as recorded in the Fourth Gospel; but, from his customary method of citing passages from Scripture, there is ample reason to believe that he had read the Fourth Gospel, and that he intended to give the words of Christ to Nicodemus. Especially evident is this from the reference which he makes to the language of Nicodemus. For an elaborate and conclusive examination of this passage, the reader is referred to Dr. Ezra Abbot's "Authorship of the Fourth Gospel" (pp. 29–41). His conclusion is stated in the following moderate, but unhesitating, terms: "It has been shown, I trust, that in this question of the language of Christ respecting regeneration, the verbal differences between Justin and John are not such as to render it improbable that the former borrowed from the latter. The variations of phraseology are easily accounted for, and are matched by similar variations in writers who unquestionably used the Gospel of John. The positive reasons for believing that Justin derived his quotation from this source are, (1) the fact that in no other report of the teaching of Christ except that of John do we find this figure of the new birth: (2) the insistance in both Justin and John on the necessity of the new birth in order to an entrance into the kingdom of heaven; (3) its mention in both in connection with baptism; (4) and last and most important of all, the fact that Justin's remark on the impossibility of a second natural birth is such a platitude in the form in which he presents it, that we cannot regard it as original. We can only explain its introduction by supposing that the language of Christ which he quotes was strongly associated in his memory with the question of Nicodemus as recorded by John."

Moreover Justin's doctrine of the Logos presupposes a knowledge of the Fourth Gospel. A careful comparison of his doctrine with that of Philo, will reveal a very important difference. For Justin teaches the *incarnation* of the Logos in a great number of passages (*e. g.* "Apol" I. 32, 66; "Dial. with Trypho" 45, 84, 87, 100; also "Apol." I. 5, 23, 42, 50, 53, 63; "Apol" II. 13; "Dial. with Try." 48, 57. 64, 67, 68, 76, 85, 101, 125), while this doctrine is inconsistent with the teaching of Philo. Besides, it has been clearly pointed out that the doctrine of the Logos in Justin is not so simple as that in the Fourth Gospel—a circumstance which proves that Justin borrowed from the Gospel, and not the Gospel from Justin. Still further, it is noticeable that Justin refers to the "Memorabilia" as teaching that Christ as Logos was the *only-begotten* Son of God, a title which is applied to him by the Fourth Gospel only (see

INTRODUCTION TO THE GOSPEL.

"Dial. with Try." 105). For other passages which confirm the view that Justin was familiar with this Gospel, reference may be made to the work of Dr. Ezra Abbott, cited above. The first Apology of Justin is now supposed to have been written about the year 146 or 147, and his other writings a few years later.

Here we may also speak of *Tatian*, the Assyrian, who was for a time a disciple of Justin, and whose literary activity has been assigned to the period between A. D. 155–170. In his "Oratio ad Græcos," we find these words: "Do not hate us being such persons, but dismissing the demons, follow the only true God. 'All these things are by him, and without him not one thing has been made'" (p. 158). "And this, then, is that which is said: 'The darkness comprehendeth not the light. The Word indeed is the light of God'" (p. 152). With these and other passages must be combined the testimony of Eusebius ("H. E." IV. 29). Speaking of the Severians, he uses this language: "These indeed make use of the Law and Prophets and *Gospels*, giving a peculiar interpretation to the passages of the sacred writings, but they abuse Paul the Apostle, and set aside his Epistles; neither do they receive the Acts of the Apostles. But their chief and founder, Tatian, having formed a certain body and collection of Gospels, I know not how, has given it this title, 'Diatessaron,' that is, the 'Gospel of the Four,' or, the Gospel formed of the Four; which is in the possession of some even now." The expression, "I know not how," only implies that the plan of the work seemed strange to Eusebius, but does not mean, as some have thought, that he had never seen it. Tatian's work was [either] a harmony of the Four Gospels, or a single Gospel uniting in itself the statements of the Four. Theodoret, in his work on Haereses (Fab. i. 20), says that " he found more than two hundred copies of the book, held in esteem in his diocese, and substituted for it copies of our own Gospels." Theodoret was Bishop of Cyrus in Syria, from about A. D. 420, until his death, in A. D. 457. "His objection to Tatian's book is founded on the absence of the genealogies; and he seems to have known no other fault" (Charteris). There is no *evidence* that any other Gospels than the four which we now have, were in circulation among the churches about the middle of the second century, unless we except the so-called Gospel according to the Hebrews, "which, in its primitive form, may have been the Hebrew original from which our present Greek Gospel, ascribed to Matthew, was mainly derived." (Ezra Abbot). And the hypothesis that the Gospel according to the Hebrews was used by Tatian, instead of our Fourth Gospel, is destitute of any historical foundation. As to the Apocryphal Gospels, they were not occupied with the public ministry of Jesus, and were justly rejected from the first as unworthy of confidence.

Athenagoras, "an Athenian, a philosopher, and a Christian,"offered his "Embassy" or Apology to the Emperors Marcus Aurelius Antoninus, and Lucius Aurelius Commodus, in A. D. 176 or 177. In this Apology he says: "But the Son of God is the Logos of the Father in idea and energy; for of him and through him were all things made, the Father and the Son being one. But the Son being in the Father and the Father in the Son, by the oneness and power of the Spirit, the Son of God is the Father's Reason and Word." (Compare John 1: 1–3; 17: 21–23). Again, "For from the beginning God himself, being eternal Reason, had in himself the Logos, since he was eternally rational." (John 1: 1 sq.) This attempt to express in a semi-philosophical way the doctrine of the Trinity, or at least the relation of the eternal Word to the Father, is evidently founded on the language of John.

Contemporary with Athenagoras was *Theophilus*, bishop, or pastor, of Antioch from A. D. 169, onward. Writing to Autolychus he uses these words: "Whence the

Holy Scriptures, and all those moved by the Spirit teach, [one] of whom, John, says: 'In the beginning was the Word; and the Word was with God'; showing that at the first God was alone and in him was the Word. Then he says: 'And the Word was God. All things were made by him, and without him was not anything made.'" (See John 1 : 1–3). Jerome informs us ("*De viris ill.*," XXV., and "*Ep. ad Algasiam*") that he wrote a harmony of the Four Gospels with a commentary on the same, and Bleek justly observes : "Now this fact, merely, that soon after the middle of the second century more than one Christian scholar undertook the task of treating our Four Gospels synoptically and in a Harmony, shows that these Gospels must already have been held in high repute in the church, as distinguished from and above other writings of a similar kind ; and the Fourth Gospel, in particular, could not have been thus esteemed, if it had not already been recognized by the church for a considerable time as a genuine and apostolical work."

To the same period belongs the *Muratorian Fragment on the Canon*, which has the following passage : "Of the Fourth of the Gospels John, one of the disciples [is author]. Entreated by his fellow-disciples and his bishops, John said : 'Fast with me three days from this time, and whatever shall be revealed to each one of us let us relate to one another.' On the same night it was revealed to Andrew, one of the apostles, that John should relate all things in his own name, subject to the revision of all," etc. (See the "Canon Muritorianus, the earliest Catalogue of the Books of the New Testament, edited with Notes and a Facsimile of the MS. in the Ambrosian Library at Milan," by S. P. Tregelles, 1867). How much of truth or error may be in the circumstances here related, we may find it difficult to decide; but the testimony of the Fragment as to the authorship of the Fourth Gospel is unambiguous, agreeing with all other indications of the second century.

Prof. Lightfoot has examined, with great care, the brief extracts which have been preserved from such writers as *Melito*, Bishop of Sardis, and *Claudius Apollinaris*, Bishop of Hierapolis, who flourished in the last part of the second century; but we must content ourselves with only a reference to his instructive article ("Cont. Rev." for 1876, pp. 471–496). His concluding paragraph may be quoted in part, as it describes the evidence gleaned by him from "The School of St. John in their Asiatic home." "Out of a very extensive literature, by which this school was once represented, the extant remains are miserably few and fragmentary; but the evidence yielded by these meagre relics is decidedly greater, in proportion to their extent, than we had reason to expect. As regards the Fourth Gospel, this is especially the case. If the same amount of written matter—occupying a very few pages in all—were extracted accidentally from the current theological literature of our own day, the chances, unless I am mistaken, would be strongly against our finding so many indications of the use of this Gospel. In every one of the writers, from Polycarp and Papias to Polycrates, we have observed phenomena which bear witness directly or indirectly, and with different degrees of distinctness, to its recognition. It is quite possible for critical ingenuity to find a reason for discrediting each instance in turn. . . . By a sufficient number of assumptions, which lie beyond the range of verification, the evidence may be set aside. But the early existence and recognition of the Fourth Gospel is the one simple postulate which explains all facts." (Id. p. 495).

Irenæus, who flourished in the last quarter of the second century, speaks *in extenso* of the Four Gospels, naming their writers, and affirming that they were received as authoritative documents by heretics as well as orthodox Christians. Thus "the

Ebionites," he says, "made use of the Gospel by Matthew, and Marcion of that by Luke, though with some omissions, while those who separate Jesus from Christ, saying, that Christ remained impassible, though Jesus suffered death, prefer the Gospel by Mark, and the followers of Valentinus use that of John." (Quoted *ad sensum*). Indeed, he argues, fancifully yet strenuously, that in the fitness of things the gospel record must be fourfold. "For as there are four quarters of the earth over which the church is scattered, and also four universal winds, so the gospel which, with the Spirit, is the pillar and support of the church, ought to have four pillars, breathing from all directions immortality, and vivifying men" ("Adv. Haer." iii. 11, 7 sq.).

Clement of Alexandria, who was a contemporary of Irenæus (flor. A. D. 192), writes concerning a saying ascribed to the Lord, that "we do not have it *in the Four Gospels that have been handed down to us*, but in that according to the Hebrews" ("Strom." iii, 553). In another work, as quoted by Eusebius ("H. E." VI. 14), Clement states the tradition of the ancient presbyters concerning the order of the Gospels containing the genealogies, which is as follows: "They were wont to say that the Gospels containing the genealogies were written before the others . . . but that John, last of all, perceiving that what had respect to the natural [or bodily life of Christ] had been made manifest in the Gospels, and being encouraged by his familiar friends, as well as divinely moved by the Spirit, made a spiritual Gospel." This statement has distinct points of resemblance to the one cited above from the "Fragment on the Canon" discovered by Muratori.

Tertullian, of North Africa, another contemporary of Irenæus, remarks as follows in his treatise against Marcion (IV. 2): "We maintain, first of all, that the Evangelical Instrument has for its authors apostles, on whom this office of promulgating the Gospel was imposed by the Lord himself: if also apostolic men [*i. e.*, associates of apostles], yet not these alone, but with apostles and after apostles. For the preaching of disciples might have been suspected of a desire for glory, if the authority of masters, yea, of Christ, who made the apostles masters, did not support it. In fact, John and Matthew, who were apostles (lit. *of the apostles*), implant in us faith; Luke and Mark, who were apostolic men, renew it." Again, having shown that the Gospel according to Luke was received by all the principal churches, Tertullian proceeds thus: "The same authority of apostolic churches endorses also other Gospels which we receive through them and on account of them—I mean those of John and Matthew; while that also which Mark published may be ascribed to Peter, whose interpreter Mark was. Moreover, they are accustomed to ascribe the Digest of Luke to Paul" ("Adv. Marcionem" IV. 2, 5).

Origen, the greatest Biblical scholar of the Ante-Nicene Church, began his work as a teacher in Alexandria, about A. D. 203. A part of his extended commentary on the Fourth Gospel has come down to us in the Greek original; and in it he says: "For one may also venture to say that the Gospel is the first-fruits of all the Scriptures. . . . But we must know that the first-fruits and the first product are not the same. For the 'first-fruits' are offered after all the fruits, but the first product before all. Therefore of the Scriptures in circulation, and believed to be divine in all the churches, one would not err in saying that the law of Moses was the first product, but the Gospel the first-fruits; for, after all the fruits of the prophets who were until the Lord Jesus, the perfect Word sprang up" (Tomus I. 4). Again, speaking of the Four Gospels and their distinctive aims, he says that Luke "keeps for him who leaned upon the bosom of Jesus, the greater and more perfect words concerning Jesus. For no one of those (viz., the first three Evangelists) manifested clearly his deity, as did John, who introduced him saying:

INTRODUCTION TO THE GOSPEL.

'*I am the Light of the World; I am the Way and the Truth and the Life; I am the Resurrection; I am the Door; I am the Good Shepherd;*' and in the Apocalypse: '*I am the Alpha and the Omega, the Beginning and the End, the First and the Last.*' One may therefore venture to say that the Gospels are the 'first-fruits' of all the Scriptures, and that according to John, the 'first-fruits' of the Gospels, the mind (or meaning) of which no one is able to receive who has not leaned on Jesus' breast" (Tom. I. 6). Again, referring to the language of Luke's preface, that many had taken in hand to set forth the events of Christ's life, he remarks that "Matthew did not 'undertake,' but *wrote*, being moved by the Holy Spirit. In like manner also Mark and John; and similarly Luke" ("Hom. in Luc." Tom. iii). Here we have the clearest evidence that Origen regarded the Four Gospels as written by inspired men, Matthew, Mark, Luke, and John, and as the only Gospels then known to the churches as the work of inspired teachers.

It would be superfluous to adduce further evidence from Christian writers of this period, that our Fourth Gospel was received by the churches as authentic and divine. It was reckoned with the undisputed books, and was believed to be the work of John, the brother of James. This is freely admitted by scholars who themselves suppose it was written by some unknown Christian near the middle of the second century. To bring forward the opinion of later times would, therefore, be of no avail. Yet the testimony of *Eusebius*, who was familiar with many writings of the second century that have since perished, deserves a moment's consideration. The Christian writings to which he refers as produced in the period reaching from the death of John to the death of Irenæus, would form a respectable library; and, if in our possession, would answer a multitude of perplexing questions. With many of these books in his hands, Eusebius undertook to write a history of Christian faith and life down to his own time (before and after A. D. 325). Making free and careful use of sources of knowledge since lost, he testifies that the "Gospel of John was well known in the churches throughout the world," and must "be acknowledged as genuine." He includes it in what he calls "the holy quaternion of the Gospels," and remarks that "besides the Gospel of John, his first Epistle is acknowledged, without dispute, both by those of the present day, and also by the ancients" ("H. E." iii. 24, 25). Nowhere does he express any doubt concerning the apostolic origin of the Fourth Gospel. And it is incredible that he should have stated the case as he has, making no qualifications, if he had discovered in any early Christian writings doubts respecting that spiritual Gospel. His testimony is, therefore, of singular importance, and must not be treated as that of a man speaking for the men of his own generation only. His voice repeats the united testimony of many witnesses, and there is no reason to suspect that it is not faithful and true.

Again, the presence of the Fourth Gospel in the *earliest versions* of the New Testament proves that it was received by the authors of those versions, and by the churches for which they were made, as an authentic and inspired document; moreover, if authentic and inspired, written by the Apostle John. For there exists no shadow of reason to suppose that the Christians of the second century would have accepted any writing as authentic or inspired, which they did not believe to have been written in the first century by an apostle, or by a companion of apostles. And if they believed the Fourth Gospel to have been written by one of the apostles, or by one of their companions in the first century, there is everything for, and nothing against the view, that they held the writer to have been the Apostle John. This will scarcely be denied by the assailants of the Gospel. The *Old Syriac* and the *Old Latin* are the two earliest

INTRODUCTION TO THE GOSPEL. 15

versions of the New Testament which are known to scholars; and both these contain the Fourth Gospel, as well as the first three.

Of the *Old Syriac*, Westcott remarks: "The history of this Syriac Version offers a remarkable parallel to that of the Latin, but with this difference, that of the Old Syriac one very imperfect copy only, the Curetonian Version of the Gospels, has been preserved. But this is sufficient to show that the Old Syriac was related very nearly to the later revision of the Peshito, as the Old Latin was to the Hieronymian Latin." Again: "If a conjecture may be allowed, I think that the various facts of the case are adequately explained by supposing that versions of separate books of the New Testament were first made and used in Palestine, perhaps within the apostolic age, and that shortly afterwards these were collected, revised, and completed at Edessa." For a statement of the grounds of this conjecture, we refer the reader to Westcott's "History of the Canon of the New Testament: Fifth Edition;" p. 238 sq. We have not been able to find any valid reason for assigning the Old Syriac to a later date than the middle of the second century (A. D. 150), and it may have been completed much earlier, possibly near the beginning of the century.

The *Old Latin* Version appears to have been made in North Africa, where the Greek language was not understood by the common people as it generally was in Italy. Hence, Tertullian, though having himself a knowledge of Greek, wrote in Latin, and employed, in his quotations from the New Testament, a Latin Version with which the people of North Africa were familiar. This version he sometimes criticised as unsatisfactory, but it was afterwards improved by revision, and at length superseded the original Greek in all the Western Church. As to the date of the Old Latin, Westcott says: "If the version was, as has been seen, generally in use in Africa in his [Tertullian's] time, and had been in circulation sufficiently long to stereotype the meaning of particular phrases, we cannot allow less than twenty years for its publication and spread; and if we take into account its extension into Gaul and its reception there, that period will seem too short. Now the beginning of Tertullian's literary activity cannot be placed later than 190 A. D., and we shall thus obtain the date 170 A. D., as that before which the version must have been made. How much more ancient it really is, cannot yet be discovered."

As to the use which *heretics* living in the second century made of the Fourth Gospel, reference may be made in the first place to the testimony of Irenæus. Speaking of the Four Gospels, he says in his work against *Hæresies* (Lib. iii. 11. 7): "So firm is the ground upon which these Gospels rest, that the very heretics themselves bear witness to them, and, starting from these [documents], each one of them endeavors to establish his own peculiar doctrine." And after mentioning certain errorists who rely, some on this and some on that Synoptic Gospel, he proceeds thus: "Those, moreover, who follow Valentinus, making copious use of that according to John to illustrate their Conjunctions, shall be proved to be totally in error by means of this very Gospel, as I have shown in the first book. Since then, our opponents do bear testimony for us, and make use of these [documents], our proof derived from them is firm and true."

According to Hippolytus, whose "Refutation of all Hæresies" is accepted as one of the best sources of knowledge concerning the earliest perversions of Christian truth, the *Naassenes*, or *Ophites*, must have begun to disseminate their speculations near the close of the first century. He represents them as making use of sayings found in the Gospels or in the Epistles of Paul. Those from the Fourth Gospel are quoted freely, as, *e. g.*, "I am the true gate" (John x. 9); and, "No one can come unto me, except my heavonly Father draw some one unto me" (John 6 : 44); again, "by whom all things were made, and nothing was made without him" (Id. 1 : 3); and, "For God, he says, is spirit; wherefore, he affirms, neither in this mountain do the true worshippers worship, nor in Jerusalem, but in spirit" (Id. 4 : 21); also, "This," he says, "is the water that is above the firmament," concerning which, he says, the Saviour has declared, "If thou knewest who it is that asks, thou wouldst have asked from him, and he would have given you to drink living, bubbling water" (Id. 4 : 10) ; and, "If any one is blind from birth, and has never beheld the true light 'which lighteneth every man that cometh into the world' (Id. 1 : 9 ; 9 : 1), by us let him recover his sight."

The *Peratæ* are described by Hippolytus as another early class of heretics, akin to the Ophites, whose leader made use of the Fourth Gospel, thus: "This, he says, is that which has been declared : ' In the same manner as Moses lifted up the serpent in the wilderness, so also must the Son of man be lifted up' (John 3 : 14, 15); also, "Concerning this, he says, it has been declared : 'In the beginning was the Word, and the Word was with God, and the Word was God. This was in the beginning with God, all things were made by him, and without him was not one thing that was made. And what was formed in him is life'" (Id. 1 : 1–4); again ; "When, however, he [Jesus] remarks, 'Your father is a murderer from the beginning,' (Id. 8 : 44), he alludes to the Ruler and Demiurge of matter," etc. ; and, "I am the door" (Id. 10 : 7).

Basilides flourished in the reign of Hadrian, A. D. 117–138, and was the author of a Gnostic theory of the universe. He appears to have accepted the writings of the New Testament as of divine authority, but to have interpreted them according to a religious philosophy of his own. He is represented by Hippolytus (VII. 22) as saying : "This [viz., the Word, "Let there be light,"] is that which has been stated in the Gospels : ' He was the true light, which lighteth every man that cometh into the world'" (John 1 : 9). "Now this," remarks the translator of Hippolytus in the "Ante-Nicene Christian Library," "is precisely the mode of reference we should expect that Basilides would employ ; whereas, if Hippolytus had either fabricated the passage or adduced it from hearsay, it is almost certain he would have said ' in the Gospel of John,' and not indefinitely, ' the Gospels.' " It is certainly far more natural to suppose that Basilides is here quoted as interpreting a passage of Genesis by one in John, than to suppose that any unmentioned disciple of this heretic is thus quoted.

Valentinus was a contemporary of Justin Martyr. Irenæus says that he "came to Rome in the time of Hyginus, flourished under Pius, and remained until Anicetus." "The date A. D. 140–160 represents the close of his life" (Charteris, p. 413). According to Irenæus (L. I. 8, 5) the Valentinians "teach that John, the disciple of the Lord, has revealed the first Ogdoad," etc., and that " he expresses himself thus : 'In the beginning was the Word, and the Word was with God, and the Word was God.' Having first of all distinguished these three—God, the Beginning, and the Word—he again unites them, that he may exhibit the production of each of them, that is, of the Son and of the Word, and also at the same time show their union with one another, and with the Father . . . ' The same was in the beginning with God '—this clause discloses the order of production. 'All things were made by him, and without him was nothing made' ; for the Word was the author of form and beginning to all the Æons that came into existence after him. But ' what was made by him,' says John, ' is life.' " It will be seen that the Valentinians " made copious use " of the Fourth Gospel, and the only doubt concerning the value of this fact arises from the possibility that Irenæus quotes from later adherents of the heresy, instead of the founder. But it is well to remember that Irenæus was probably born about A. D. 135-140; that in early life he was a contemporary of Polycarp, Justin Martyr, Basilides, and Valentinus; and that he writes as if the whole Valentinian sect perverted the Gospel of John in order to commend their extraordinary speculation. That the Fourth Gospel, borrowed from the teaching of Valentinus, is a wild conjecture, resting upon no testimony, and contradicted by his followers, if not by himself; that it was written after his demise, and was laid hold of by his followers to bolster up his system, is no less unhistorical and absurd. That it was cited as an authoritative Christian document, likely to have great influence with the men of that generation, is perfectly obvious. And that it had such an influence because, and only because, it was believed to have been written by "John, the disciple of the Lord," is equally obvious to one familiar with Christian literature of the second century. How impossible, then, to believe that it had just seen the light, being foisted upon the Christians of that age, and received by them, without evidence of apostolic authority! An age, be it remembered, when heresies were breaking out in every quarter, and the churches were being warned against them by such men as Polycarp and Irenæus and Tertullian.

Finally, it may be well to observe the manner in which Tertullian refers to Valentinus. In his treatise, "De Præscript. Hæreticorum" (ch. 37), he maintains that heretics have no right to employ the Scriptures, adding: "To whom it should properly be said: 'Who are ye? When, and whence have you come? What are you doing in my [domain], not being mine? By what right, Marcion, dost thou cut down my forest? By whose permission, Valentinus, *dost thou turn away my fountains?* By what power, Apelles, dost thou remove my boundaries? Why do ye, aliens, here sow and feed according to your own will? This is my possession; from of old I possess it. I have firm titles from the authors to whom it belonged. I am heir of the apostles." Again (ch. 38): "One perverts the Scriptures by his hand; another, by his explanation of the meaning. For if Valentinus seems to use the entire Instrument [*i. e.*, Bible], he raises his hand against the truth with as prompt a mind as Marcion. For Marcion plainly and openly made use of a sword, not a pen, since he slaughtered the Scriptures for his material. But Valentinus spared them, since he did not invent Scriptures for his material, but material for the Scriptures. And yet he took away more, and added more, by removing the proper meanings of single words, and by inserting combinations of things discordant." It appears from this testimony of the great African, that Valentinus in his day accepted the entire Canon of Scripture received by orthodox Christians in the time of Tertullian; and this, we know, included the Fourth Gospel.

This unvarnished statement of the external evidence in favor of the belief that the Fourth Gospel was written by the Apostle John, is sufficient to prove the correctness of that belief, unless there is something in the Gospel itself inconsistent with such authorship.

Passing to the internal evidence, we discover many things in this Gospel which confirm the view that it was written by the Apostle John, rather than by some unknown Christian of the second century. And this is the alternative advanced by modern criticism. Whoever believes that it was written by a personal follower of Christ, *i. e.*, by a witness of much that is here said to have been done or taught by him, will concede that its writer was John; and whoever disbelieves that it could have been written by John, will be sure to assign it to some unknown Christian of the second century.

Attention may *first* be given to the *bearing of certain differences between the Fourth Gospel and the other three upon the question of authorship, as stated above*. One of these differences pertains to the *localities* in which Christ is said to have fulfilled his ministry. If a reader had the first three Gospels only, he would be apt to conclude that Jesus did very little teaching in Jerusalem before his final visit to that city—a visit which, after two or three days of public service, was terminated by his arrest and trial and crucifixion. A microscopic scrutiny might reveal to him a few traces of the Lord's earlier presence and influence there (Matt. 23 : 37; Luke 13 : 34; 10 : 38, 39), but even such scrutiny would not discover any trace of a previous ministry of Jesus in the *province* of Judea, or in that of Samaria. According to these Gospels, Galilee appears to have been the almost exclusive theatre of the Saviour's ministry. But, on the other hand, the Fourth Gospel represents the Lord as going up to Jerusalem at a passover which occurred soon after his baptism, as expelling the money-changers from his Father's house, as doing signs for several days in the holy city, and as continuing his ministry for a considerable period, perhaps for months, in the province of Judea. (See "Outlines of the Life of Christ," by E. R. Condor, pp. 62–4); also as preaching two days, with remarkable effect, in Sychar, near the ancient Shechem, on his way through Samaria to Galilee; then, at the next passover, as returning from Galilee to Jerusalem (John 5 : 1), where he healed the infirm man on the Sabbath and afterwards boldly preached to the Jews; and as coming once more after a long period of service in Galilee, to Jerusalem at the Feast of Tabernacles, six months before his death, that he might remain there off and on, teaching and doing wonderful works for another indefinite time ; and finally, as returning, after an absence in Ephraim, through Jericho, to spend the last days of his public life in the holy city.

It would then be not far from correct to say that the first three Gospels appear to assign about sixty-four out of sixty-five parts of the Saviour's public ministry to Galilee and its neighborhood, while the Fourth Gospel appears to assign not far from one hundred and seventeen out of one hundred and sixty-nine parts to Galilee, and perhaps fifty-two parts to other regions, especially Judea. The difference is striking. But it is a *difference*, not a contradiction. And there is no evidence that the writer of the Fourth Gospel was conscious of any difference requiring explanation between his Gospel and the first three ; for had he been conscious of such a difference, he would have given the requisite explanation, as was his custom in other instances where explanation was needful. These are the facts : A great difference; a difference that involves no contradiction ; a difference that was unperceived, or, at least, unfelt by the writer; in other words, a harmony in diversity which is remarkable and apparently unsought. How then can these facts be most naturally accounted for ? By supposing that the Fourth Gospel was written by John, a personal attendant of Jesus, or by supposing that it was written by a *falsarius* of the second century?

It does not appear to be at all improbable that a perfectly honest writer, as John is presumed to have been, who is relating what he has seen or heard, should fearlessly put down events as he remembers them, being sure that it is his duty as a first witness to declare the truth without change, and equally sure that the truth which he declares cannot be inconsistent with any other truth. This, I say, would be a natural state of mind in a conscientious writer, who was relating what he distinctly remembered seeing or hearing. And if, in this state of mind, he should intentionally omit much that he remembered, either because it had been already put in writing by others, or because a complete record would be too voluminous for use, he would do this without feeling it necessary to adjust his own narrative, minutely, to other narratives ; he would simply omit what his plan required him to omit, and describe the rest as he remembered it. A sense of reality would control his pen. But this could not be the case with a *falsarius* of the second century. In his own mind he could not be as independent of the Synoptic Gospels as the writer of the Fourth Gospel appears to have been. He could not have assigned so large a part of the Saviour's public ministry to new places, without feeling that there was great danger of contradicting the well known and approved Gospels. In a word, it seems quite improbable that he would have ventured to differ in this respect so widely from the Synoptists; improbable that, having ventured to do this, he would have escaped the danger of actual contradiction between his record and theirs; and improbable, if he accomplished this at all, that he could have done it, without betraying the slightest apprehension of the danger to which he was exposed, or the slightest attempt to adjust his narrative to theirs, or the slightest wish to correct what he might regard as inaccurate in their narratives. It is clear to me, therefore, that the difference between the Fourth Gospel and the other three, as to the localities of Christ's ministry, is best accounted for by ascribing the last of the Gospels to John.

Another difference relates to *the duration* of our Lord's ministry. If we had the first three Gospels only, we should probably think that the period from Christ's baptism to his crucifixion comprised about one year and a third; but with the Fourth Gospel in our hands, we should probably infer that this period comprised three years and a third. Even if it could be shown that the *feast of the Jews*, spoken of in John 5: 1, was not the passover, the Fourth Gospel would prove that the public life of Jesus filled a period of two years and a third. Now this difference between the first three Gospels and the fourth, is readily explained if the fourth was written by an apostle, familiar with the public life of Christ. For such a writer would see no difficulty in the case. It would probably never occur to him that any of his readers might be puzzled to ascertain which of the Jewish feasts he meant in John 5: 1, or that there could ever be any difficulty in reconciling his account of the duration of Christ's ministry with that of the Synoptical writers. The very clearness and certainty of his knowledge would prevent explanation. But it would have been far otherwise with a Christian of the second century in attempting to write as an eye-witness concerning events that he knew only by report, or that he imagined for a purpose. Too much boldness would have led to contradiction between his story and the earlier documents; while too much caution would have betrayed itself in minute adjustment or explanation. Marvelous indeed would have been the genius of any man of the second century, who could have written the Fourth Gospel! I do not hesitate to say that he would have been far greater than any of the apostles, and the task which he performed far more difficult than any that has been achieved by writers of history or of story since the world was.

Another difference relates to *the miracles of Jesus*. As to those recorded in the Fourth Gospel, four remarks may be made: 1. That, with two exceptions, they are not the same as those described in the other Gospels. The two exceptions are Christ's walking on the sea and his feeding the five thousand. 2. That several of them are singularly conclusive when studied as evidences of divine power. Such are the changing of water into wine, the feeding of the five thousand with five loaves and two small fishes, the giving of sight to one who had been born blind, the raising to life of one who had been dead four days, and, perhaps, the healing of the nobleman's son from a distance. But the same cannot be said of the other two, viz.: walking upon the sea, and helping the disciples to take an extraordinary draught of fishes. Hence, six out of the eight miracles recorded in the Fourth Gospel may be pronounced remarkable even as miracles, affording the strongest proof possible, from such a source, of supernatural power wielded by Christ. 3. That they seem to have been selected for narration, because of their fitness to beget faith in Christ in the minds of those who believed the record. For not without a measure of reason has the Fourth Gospel been described by certain scholars as a *Tendenzschrift*; i. e., a treatise composed with a definite aim, or to accomplish a given purpose. The writer himself authorizes this view of his work: "So also did Jesus many other signs before the disciples, which are not written in this book; but these have been written that ye may believe that Jesus is the Christ, the Son of God; and that believing, ye may have life in his name" (20: 30, 31.) A better statement of the object which moved the writer of this Gospel to select for insertion the particular miracles which are described in it, need not be sought. 4. That with the miracles are also related their obvious consequences. Indeed, the consequences are so manifestly important as to furnish an ample justification of the miracles. A thoughtful reader will observe the words of the Evangelist in John 2: 23: "Many believed in his name, beholding his signs which he did" (Rev. Ver.); and the similar words of Nicodemus, 3: 2: "We know that thou art a Teacher come from God, for no one can do these signs which thou doest, except God be with him"; also, the kindred statement of the Evangelist respecting the miracle at Cana, 2: 11: "This beginning of his signs did Jesus in Cana of Galilee, and manifested his glory; and his disciples believed on him" (Rev. Ver.); and his notice of the consequence of Christ's next miracle in Galilee, namely, the faith of the nobleman (βασιλικός) and his house, ch. 4: 53: "The father knew therefore that it was in the same hour in which Jesus said unto him: Thy son lives; and he himself believed, and all his house" (Bible Union Version). More at length are the consequences of the cure of the infirm man in Jerusalem described in the fifth chapter of this Gospel, as well as the consequences of feeding the five thousand, in the sixth chapter, the consequences of giving sight to the man who was born blind, in the ninth chapter, and the consequences of raising Lazarus to life again, in the eleventh chapter. The Fourth Gospel differs then from the first three in the four respects mentioned, in the particular miracles which it describes, in the greatness of these miracles, in their eminent fitness to inspire belief on the name of Jesus, the Son of God, and in their important consequences at the time. Not that the miracles of the earlier Gospels are entirely wanting in the three characteristics last named, but that these characteristics are more distinct and pronounced in the miracles of the Fourth Gospel. It is a difference of degree only, yet a difference so clearly marked as to need explanation.

What bearing, then, has the difference in question on the authorship of the Fourth Gospel? Is it best explained by considering the writer an apostle who selected his materials without fear from the life of Christ with which he was familiar, or by considering him a post-apostolic Christian, who shaped or invented materials to suit his purpose? Unless there is something really incredible in the miracles of the Fourth Gospel, something which compels us to assign them to the realm of fable, I see no good reason for supposing that an apostle may not have chosen to insert just these, and no others, in his narrative. Writing after the Synoptical Gospels had come into use, and writing for a definite and Christian purpose, it is easy to believe that he may have chosen them, chiefly because they were fitted to accomplish the object of his Gospel, but also because most of them were not recorded in existing Gospels. But I cannot see how a wise and good man of the second century could have learned or invented the simple, but perfect, story of these miracles, unrecorded by the other Evangelists; nor can I easily believe that the Fourth Gospel was written by any man who was not both wise and good. It does not bear the marks of folly or of craft. It seems a very bold and straightforward writing, and, looking simply at its record of miracles, I think the probabilities are as ten to one in favor of its Johannean authorship.

Before leaving this point we may recur to the object of the Fourth Gospel, as declared by the author himself, viz.: to lead its readers to "believe that Jesus is the Christ, the Son of God, and that believing" they "might have life in his name." Assuming the truth of this statement, can we doubt the sincerity of the author's faith in Christ as the Saviour of men? If not, and we admit the sincerity of his Christian faith, can we doubt his belief of the truth of what he was writing? Could he, being an honest believer in Jesus on grounds satisfactory to his own powerful mind, resort to fictions of the most extraordinary kind in persuading others to share his faith? Could the man who truly honored the Saviour, and desired to have others honor him, ascribe to him, falsely, such words as, "I am the way, and the truth, and the life," or such a prayer to the Father as this: "Sanctify them in the truth, thy word is truth?" (Revised Version.) There is a psychological absurdity involved in this view. But if we assume that the author of the Fourth Gospel did not himself truly believe in Jesus as the Christ, the Son of God and the Saviour of men, and did not seriously aim to lead others to this belief, how shall we explain the moral and spiritual elevation of this Gospel? "By their fruits ye shall know them." An evil tree cannot bring forth good fruit. But here certainly is good fruit.

Another difference relates to *the parables of Jesus*. The Fourth Gospel does not contain the word "parable" (παραβολή), or any discourse of Jesus that exactly corresponds with the beautiful illustrations of truth which bear that name in the Synoptical Gospels. His representation of himself as the door of the sheepfold, and then as the good shepherd that giveth his life for the sheep, in John 10:1-17, reminds one of the perfect parables reported by Matthew and Luke, but does not fill the mould in which they are cast. Yet, though there are no perfect parables in the Fourth Gospel, there are many passages which may be said to breathe the spirit of parables. Nature is made to utter the profoundest lessons of religious truth. Jesus represents himself as the way, the truth, and the life, as the light of the world, as the true bread from heaven, as the true vine, and as the king of all those who are of the truth. Moreover, the writer calls some of his sayings "proverbs" (παροιμίαι). Now it is easy to believe that Jesus made use of *dark sayings* (παροιμίαι) as well as of *parables* (παραβολαί), and that in some parts of his ministry he employed the former, while in others he employed the latter, skillfully adapting his method of instruction or appeal to the spiritual condition of those addressed. Nor is it difficult to believe that an apostle, who had often listened to both forms of teaching, might be led by his deeper interest in one form than in the other, or by his wish to record the truths which his Lord had taught in that form, but not in the other, to insert in his narrative of Christ's ministry the teaching which had been given in that form. But it is not so credible that a *falsarius* of the second century could have originated the metaphorical teaching of the Fourth Gospel, or could have received it in so perfect a form through oral tradition, or would have ventured to put so much teaching of this form in his Gospel, without even saying that Jesus sometimes taught in parables.

Another difference is found *in the events* related. Perhaps it may be suggested that a difference of locality and of duration in the ministry of Christ would account for this difference of events, whoever may have been the writer. To some extent it would; but nothing short of an examination of cases will show whether it is or is not a sufficient explanation of the actual narrative. Take the following instance : The Fourth Gospel not only asserts that Jesus was preaching and making disciples for a considerable period in Judea before the imprisonment of John the Baptist, but also that, by the hands of his first disciples, he was baptizing disciples in that region. Now as the work of Jesus in baptizing led to the debate about purification, to the consequent appeal to John the Baptist, and so to the testimony which he gave in respect to Christ, it evidently fell in with the purpose of the Evangelist to insert the whole story in his Gospel. If the events were actual, there is no reason why an apostle should not have made use of them in his narrative. But I think it far less probable that a writer of the second century, knowing the Lord's ministry through the earlier Gospels or oral tradition, would have been acquainted with these events, if they really occurred, or that he would have dared to relate them without historical warrant. For I need not pause to show that the writer of this paragraph in the Fourth Gospel (3 : 22–30) has come very near, apparently, to a contradiction of the earlier accounts which seem to represent the ministry of Jesus as beginning *after* the imprisonment of John the Baptist, and not in Judea, but in Galilee. Matt. 4 : 12, 17, 24 ; Mark 1 : 14, 28 ; Luke 4 : 14. Speaking of seeming contradictions, reference may also be made to the words which this Gospel ascribes to the Baptist : "And I knew him not," etc., (John 1 : 31). Would it have been natural for a writer of the second century, familiar with the first three Gospels, to put these words into the mouth of the Baptist? Would he not have inferred just the contrary from Matthew's account of John's words when Christ applied to him for baptism : "I have need to be baptized of thee, and comest thou to me" (3 : 14)? But, on the other hand, if the writer was one who had heard the Baptist, a great prophet and his revered teacher, utter these words, might he not have recorded them without fear of contradiction ? He would not have been carefully and laboriously working up a case, but simply stating what he remembered. But to return from this digression : I do not think it at all probable that there was any Christian in the second century who could have put into the mouth of John the Baptist these beautiful and magnanimous words: "A man can receive nothing, except it have been given him from heaven. Ye yourselves bear me witness, that I said, I am not the Christ, but that I am sent before him. He that hath the bride is the bridegroom ; but the friend of the bridegroom, who standeth and heareth him, rejoiceth greatly because of the bridegroom's voice : this my joy therefore is made full. He must increase, but I must decrease " (Rev. Ver). If any Christian of the second century originated such a response, I would join with all my heart in calling him the *Great Unknown* of New Testament writers ; but I have an impression that the theory of great unknown writers of Scripture has been stretched to the utmost, and even carried at times beyond the limits of sober reason.

Again, according to the Fourth Gospel, Jesus, when seized and bound in the garden, was "led to Annas first," because "he was father-in-law of Caiaphas, the high-priest." But the first three Gospels do not mention the fact that Jesus was led to Annas before he was taken to Caiaphas and the Sanhedrin. Precisely what was accomplished by leading him to Annas first is not stated in the Fourth Gospel ; nor is it perfectly clear how the record of this fact contributed to securing the object sought by the Evangelist in writing this Gospel. We are therefore unable to imagine any reason for the insertion of this statement, if it is not true ; and if what is stated was done, who so likely to mention it as one who followed Jesus from the garden that night ? Its insertion by a *falsarius* of the second century would be simply unaccountable ; especially as any one who was adjusting his narrative to earlier Gospels must have seen that the introduction of this event would be crowding an already crowded period, and would be likely to produce confusion in the reader's mind. Only one supposition, namely, that the statement is erroneous, can justify the view that it was made by some unknown writer of the second century; and that supposition cannot be proved correct.

Again, the Fourth Gospel seems to place *the supper in Bethany*, at which Christ was anointed by Mary, *six* days before the passover, while the other Gospels seem to place it *two* days before the passover. The language is not such in either case as to make the date perfectly certain against other testimony; but if we had only the Fourth Gospel we should doubtless put the supper on Saturday, while if we had only the Synoptical Gospels, we should put it on Wednesday. In this instance, also, I believe that an apostle, writing from the springs of personal knowledge, would scarcely think of a possibility of contradiction between his record and any other; but I cannot easily imagine that a *falsarius*, who had learned from others all that he knew of these events, would have failed to shun such a difference as the one in question—especially as there appears to be no assignable motive for giving the feast an earlier date than it seems to have in the Synoptists.

Another difference arises from *omissions*. There are a few things omitted in the Fourth Gospel which are recorded in the first three, and which John would have been more likely than a *falsarius* to omit. One of these is the *name of the Apostle John*. This does not once occur in the Fourth Gospel. And it is conceivable that a truly modest man might never refer to himself by name, though he had filled an important place among the disciples. But it is impossible to discover any motive that would have led a Chistian of the second century to omit the name of John, the companion of Peter.

A similar remark may be made concerning the omission of the *name of his brother James*, who was the third member of the inner group of three, so highly distinguished by Christ. Andrew, Peter, Philip, Nathanael, Thomas, even Judas Iscariot, are frequently mentioned, but neither James nor John. And the same may be noticed in regard to *Salome*, who was probably the *mother of James and John*. Compare, on this point, John 19:25, with Matthew 27:56, and Mark 15:40. "It is very unlikely," says Conder ("Outlines of the Life of Christ," p. 55, Note), "that Mary, the mother of Jesus, had a sister of the same name; and it quite accords with St. John's suppression of his own name that he should refer to his own mother in the same manner. This view throws a beautiful light both on the special love of the Master for this one disciple, and on John 19:26, 27," where Jesus commits to John the care of his mother.

Again, the Fourth Gospel never adds the epithet *Baptist* to the name of John, the harbinger of Christ. If the modest author was himself the only other John who was closely connected with Jesus, it is quite conceivable that he would speak of the forerunner as John—*the* John who needed no epithet to distinguish him from the writer—the only person, in fact, whom the writer, in his oral reminiscences, had any occasion to denominate John, since if he referred to himself at all it would naturally be done by means of the pronoun I. In such circumstances, I say, it is by no means improbable that the apostle would uniformly call his great namesake simply John. But this would not have been a natural thing for any one else to do, certainly not for a Christian of the second century.

The force of the argument from these omissions in favor of the view that the Fourth Gospel was written by the Apostle John rather than by some unknown Christian of the second century, depends in part upon the assumption that this apostle was a truly modest man. If there were good evidence that he was a forward, conceited, self-asserting man, the force of this consideration would be greatly weakened. And two facts have been supposed to favor the idea that he was the reverse of modest or self-forgetful, namely : *First*, that he sometimes refers to himself as *the disciple whom Jesus loved* (viz., in 13 : 23 ; 19 : 26 ; 20 : 2 ; 21 : 7, 20). But in estimating the bearing of this fact, we ought to ask ourselves : first, how this way of referring to himself was modified in his own feelings by withholding his name ; secondly, how it was modified by the warmth of his nature which may have made him peculiarly grateful to Christ for tender love, and inexpressibly eager to utter in some strong, though impersonal way, his profound appreciation of that love ; and, thirdly, how he bore himself, though a powerful and ardent soul, when afterwards he was associated with Peter and the other apostles in Christian service. If we answer these questions, as they ought to be answered in justice to the life and character of John as they appear in the sacred record, the argument from the omissions noted above will lose none of its force. The *second* fact which is alleged to be inconsistent with genuine or at least peculiar modesty on the part of John, is the request which he joined with his brother James in making, through their mother, that they two might sit, one on his right hand and the other on his left, in his kingdom. But in estimating the value of this fact, as an objection to the modesty of John, we may properly bear in mind, (*a*) that these two brothers were expecting that Jesus would establish an earthly kingdom, (*b*) that they were probably cousins of Jesus, and were certainly honored with his special intimacy, (*c*) that they presented their request through their mother, if not by her advice, and (*d*) that they appear to have quietly dropped the matter as soon as the Master's will was known. Beyond question they were among the ablest as well as the best beloved of the disciples, and this one request does not, in view of all the circumstances, prove that they were specially forward, or in any respect conceited men. The presentation of their request through their mother, points rather in the opposite direction.

We have now briefly considered the bearing of certain *differences* between the Fourth Gospel and the other three on the question as to the authorship of the former, namely : (*a*) a difference as to the localities in which Christ fulfilled his ministry, (*b*) a difference as to the duration of that ministry, (*c*) a difference as to the miracles ascribed to Jesus, (*d*) a difference as to parables or method of teaching, (*e*) a difference as to events related, (*f*) a difference occasioned by a definite class of omissions,—and have found them all to be favorable to the Johannean authorship of the Fourth Gospel.

Attention may be given, *secondly, to certain narratives of the Fou th Gospel which are rendered peculiarly graphic by means of unimportant circumstances*—meaning by unimportant circumstances those which are not essential to the expression of religious truth.

One of these is the circumstantial way in which *the Evangelist describes the gathering to Jesus of his first disciples* (1 : 29-42). After giving an account of an interview between John the Baptist and a deputation of Pharisees from Jerusalem, he mentions the place where this deputation was received, viz.: Bethany (or Bethabara), beyond Jordan, where John was baptizing, and then proceeds to relate how on the morrow the Baptist saw Jesus coming unto him, and said : "Behold the Lamb of God," etc.; how on the following day he was standing with two of his disciples and, looking upon Jesus as he walked, said again : "Behold the Lamb of God !" how the two disciples heard him saying this, though it may not have been addressed particularly to them, and therefore followed Jesus ; how Jesus having turned and seen them following, said unto them : "What seek ye ?" And when they answered, "Rabbi, where dwellest thou ?" invited them to "come and see"; how they complied with this invitation ; and, it being about the tenth hour, abode the rest of the day with him, though one of them, meanwhile, whose name was Andrew, found his more distinguished brother and brought him to Jesus; and how Jesus looked upon that brother, and, perceiving what he was to become, said: "Thou art Simon, the son of Jona; thou shalt be called Cephas" (i. e., Peter).

Does not this narrative declare itself to be the work of an eye-witness, by almost every line? For so brief a paragraph, the number of particulars mentioned is very great. And they are such particulars as a deeply interested witness might be expected to remember. If the writer was the Apostle John, the day when these events took place was a day never to be forgotten by him—a veritable turning-point in his life, to which he would look back with peculiar gratitude as the beginning of his fellowship with Christ. It is not therefore a matter of surprise that he should be able to sketch so bold and distinct and perfect a picture of it. Nor is it strange that he should have ventured to differ, as he seems to do, without a word of explanation, from the earlier Evangelists, both as to the time when the four leading disciples began to follow Jesus, and as to the time when the Lord gave to Simon his new name. I do not say or believe that there is any real contradiction between the Fourth Gospel and the first three on either of these points; but I think there is a difference of representation that cannot readily be accounted for, without supposing the Fourth Gospel to be true, and the testimony of an original witness. Everything is credible and, indeed, natural, if this Gospel be received as the work of the Apostle John; but much is surprising, if it be ascribed to some unknown Christian of the second century. The picture before us is too simple and vivid, too minute in detail, and independent in character, to be the work of a *falsarius*.

Equally graphic is the next paragraph, which relates what was done on the following day, viz.: how Philip was found by the Lord as the latter was about to go forth into Galilee, and then how Nathanael was found by Philip. Especially fresh and spicy is the conversation between Philip and Nathanael, while that between Nathanael and Christ is more striking and original still. It will also be observed that the native place of Philip is mentioned, with an added notice that it was the native place of Andrew and Peter as well. With no less particularity does the Evangelist describe the events of the next day—the marriage and miracle in Cana of Galilee. All these paragraphs appear to be the story of an eye-witness, of one who was present when the deputation questioned John the Baptist on the first day, when the Baptist pointed out Jesus as the Messiah on the second day, when he pointed him out again, on the third day, and two of his own disciples followed Christ to his abode, when Jesus went to Galilee on the fourth day, and when he turned the water into wine on the fifth day.

Another portion of the Fourth Gospel may be studied from the same point of view— namely, *the conversation of Jesus with the Samaritan woman at Jacob's well* (4: 5–45). But our study of it must be brief. Reference may, however, be made in a single paragraph to several particulars. Here are allusions to *scenery*—e. g., to the deep well, the adjacent mountain, the neighboring city, the fertile plain; to *historic facts*—as the connection of Jacob with the well, the non-intercourse of Jews and Samaritans, the worship of the former in Jerusalem and of the latter in Gerizim; to *social customs*—for the disciples, it is said, "marvelled that he was speaking with (*a*) woman," and, notwithstanding their non-intercourse with Samaritans, went into the city and mingled with the people enough to buy food of them; and, perhaps, to *the season of the year*—"Say ye not, there are yet four months, and then cometh harvest?" In all these respects the narrative appears to be remarkably true to place, age, and circumstances.

But the question of the woman, addressed to the men in the city, seems to bear the stamp of originality in a peculiar degree. According to the narrative the woman evidently believed that Jesus was the Christ; would not a writer of fiction have made her intimate this belief in her question?—even as the Common English Version: "Is not this the Christ?" intimates it? But according to the Greek narrative she did not. For some reason she saw fit to speak as if she were herself in doubt, and even a little inclined to think that he was not the Christ,—(μήτι οὗτός ἐστιν ὁ Χριστός),—though she was nevertheless anxious to have the judgment of her neighbors on the point. Says Godet: "She believes more than she says; but she does not venture to assume even as probable so great news. Nothing could be more natural than this little trait." Possibly it would be right to say that because she was a woman, and because she was *such* a woman, she felt that the people to whom she spoke would be more influenced by the facts she reported if she did not seem to draw, with too great confidence, the highest possible inference from them.

Men are sometimes too proud to be guided in their judgment, especially by women, and women are sometimes keen-sighted enough to perceive this. If this woman had known human nature perfectly, I question whether she could have made a report of Christ's words better calculated to lead the men of Sychar to consider fairly the claims of Jesus. But it seems to me that a writer of fiction in the second century would scarcely have had so subtle a perception of the workings of a woman's mind as to put into her mouth this form of question.

But how, it may perhaps be asked, could the Apostle John have learned the precise form or purport of this woman's question to the men of the city? We answer, from the men themselves, as he met and conversed with them during the two days spent by Jesus and his disciples in Sychar or Shechem. Or how, it may again be asked, could John have learned the substance of the remarkable conversation of Christ with the woman at the well? We answer, by hearing it, as he remained at the well with Jesus; for it is unnecessary to suppose that all the disciples went into the city to buy food. At the same time we must likewise admit that Jesus himself *may* have given an account of the conversation to the disciple whom he loved, or that this disciple may have learned it from the woman. The first supposition, however, seems to be more probable than either of the others.

As another instance of graphic narrative we may refer to the ninth chapter, which contains *the story of the Lord's giving sight to a man who had been blind from his birth, together with a sketch of the transactions springing out of that miracle.* Perhaps no person ever read the chapter without a feeling of admiration at the firmness, the honesty, the good sense, and the quickness of retort displayed by the man whose congenital blindness had been removed, or without a feeling of regret, if not of shame, at the timid and evasive answer of his parents, when they were questioned by the Pharisees, or without a feeling of deep indignation at the malicious and unscrupulous enmity of the Jewish leaders to Jesus. The whole narrative is powerful—instinct with reality and life. Especially do we admire the man who washed in the pool of Siloam and returned seeing, when he was brought before the rulers. As he stands there and answers, at once for himself and for his Benefactor, he is in our judgment a model witness. He clings to the simple truth with a lion's grip. His insight is as clear as his new-found sight. With only a beggar's education, his logic is sharp and strong as reason itself, and his attack on the position of his judges terrible as the stroke of a catapult. While his heart is singing: "Hail, holy light, offspring of heaven, first-

INTRODUCTION TO THE GOSPEL. 27

born," his intellect and conscience and purpose are unshaken by the deadly scowl of fanaticism armed with power. But there is one touch of nature in this narrative, which has long seemed to me inexplicable if the Fourth Gospel was written by a *falsarius* of the second century. For such a writer must be presumed to have filled in the details of the narrative by his own imagination, since it is scarcely possible that they could have reached him in this form by means of oral tradition. The touch of nature to which I allude is the way in which his neighbors describe the man whose eyes had now, for the first time, been opened to see the sun. For they ask, not as the thought of his blindness and its miraculous removal would naturally shape their question: Is not this he that was *born blind?* but rather: "Is not this he that *sat and begged?* (ὁ καθήμενος καὶ προσαιτῶν). And I do not think it uncharitable to suspect that these "neighbors and they who saw him aforetime that he was a beggar" (Rev. Ver.), had been more troubled by the man's begging than by his blindness; and therefore the fact that he was wont to ask an alms was more deeply impressed on their minds than the fact that he could not see. Hence, it was perfectly natural for them to employ the designation here reported. But I doubt whether any writer of the second century would have put these words into the lips of "the neighbors," any sooner than he would have put them into the lips of Jesus, or of the Jewish rulers. In describing this great miracle, *the giving of sight by Jesus to one born blind* would have been the absorbing idea; and a perfect side-stroke in his picture, like the one here introduced, would have been beyond the skill of any writer of that age. If not, this writer must have been, as I have intimated, more than once, a *great unknown*, a *prodigy* in his generation.

Another portion of the Fourth Gospel which is rendered peculiarly graphic and lifelike by the insertion of circumstances non-essential in a doctrinal respect, *is the narrative of the resurrection of Lazarus*, in the eleventh chapter. Meyer remarks that "the narrative is distinguished for its thoughtful tenderness, certainty, and truthfulness." Let us notice a few particulars which are best accounted for by supposing that this chapter was written by an apostolic witness, and therefore by John, the brother of James. 1. It is difficult to believe that a writer of the second century would have dared to ascribe this miracle to Christ without having any evidence that he wrought such a miracle, near the close of his ministry, in Bethany; and it is equally difficult to believe that he could have had satisfactory knowledge of the miracle in question. But if Lazarus was raised from the dead, and if John was present when this occurred, it is perfectly credible that the aged apostle may have been led by the Spirit and providence of God to insert an account of it in his Gospel. 2. It is difficult to believe that a writer of the second century either knew through oral tradition, or invented without the help of tradition, the striking particulars of this narrative. These particulars are too numerous for separate examination, but upon close scrutiny they will be found entirely self-consistent and wonderfully interesting. And they are withal such particulars as a loving disciple might be expected to remember with satisfaction and to put on record with his account of the miracle itself. 3. The impression which this narrative gives of the distinctive traits of Martha and Mary exactly accords with the impression which Luke's account of another scene gives (10 : 38 sq). For Luke says that "a certain woman, named Martha, received him [*i. e.*, Jesus] into her house. And she had a sister called Mary, who also sat at the Lord's feet, and heard his word. But Martha was distracted about much serving; and she came up to him, and said: Lord, dost thou not care that my sister did leave me to serve alone?" etc. (Rev. Ver.). To judge the sisters by this account, Martha was probably older than Mary, and likewise more energetic, practical, and pains-taking in domestic affairs, bearing the chief burden of care and service; but at the same time not afraid to speak her mind, even to a guest; while Mary was more gentle, docile, appreciative, spiritual, and eager to catch every word that fell from the lips of their divine Teacher. It may also be conjectured from the language used by Luke that they were in easy, if not in affluent circumstances. Now, without reproducing a phrase or incident from this earlier narrative, the impression made by the eleventh chapter of the Fourth Gospel concerning the traits of character and the circumstances of these sisters, is the same as that made by Luke. Thus, when Martha heard that Jesus was coming, she went and met him, entering at once into conversation with him, and expressing her confidence that if he had been with them her brother would not have died; but not accepting readily the Lord's intimation that Lazarus might even now be recalled to life. Moreover, when Jesus commanded the stone to be taken away from the door of the tomb, it was Martha who promptly raised an objection to this act. On the other hand, Mary remained at home until sent for by Jesus, when she rose quickly and went unto him. Seeing him, she fell down at his feet, saying unto him: "Lord, if thou hadst been here, my brother had not died." This was the only word that she is reported to have spoken. What more she did was to weep in silence, and we know that her weeping went to the heart of Jesus. Perhaps it will not be making too fine a point, if I call attention to the first sentence uttered by Martha, and the only one uttered by Mary upon meeting Jesus, as substantially identical. This identity may be taken as an indication that the words had been often on their lips during the last four days—a sorrowful refrain as the sisters communed together: "If *He* had been here, our brother would not have died." In this, then, the substantial identity of their first word to Jesus, I perceive a very delicate note of truth, an echo or reminiscence of private and sisterly converse, expressing the deepest feeling of their hearts. There is, indeed, a slight difference between the Greek sentence used by Mary and the one used by Martha. According to Meyer, the pronoun *my* (μου) is a little more noticeable in Mary's remark than it is in Martha's. In other words, it is slightly emphatic. This, however, the position of the pronoun *my* in the Greek sentence, is the only difference between the expression used by Mary and that used by Martha; and it is too slight to require explanation.

Very beautiful and trustful was the message which these sisters sent to Christ beyond the Jordan: "Lord, behold he whom thou lovest is sick." Perhaps they knew that Jesus could not visit them without extreme peril to his own life, and therefore would not ask him to come, though they could not refrain from letting him know of their brother's sickness. Perhaps they had learned that his Messianic work had claims upon his time more sacred even than those of personal friendship. At any rate their message was never surpassed in delicacy and appropriateness, and we instinctively imagine that it was dictated by the younger sister.

Again, in harmony with the respectable standing of the family, suggested by the account of Luke, is the representation that "many of the Jews had come to Martha and Mary to console them concerning their brother" (Rev. Ver.). For the writer of this Gospel commonly intends by "the Jews" the leaders of the people, and especially those in office, as members of the Sanhedrin. The fact that "many of the Jews" had come to console the mourning sisters, renders it probable that some of them were enemies of Christ (see v. 46), while a knowledge of this on the part of the sisters accounts for the circumstance that Martha spoke to Mary "secretly," saying: "The Master is here, and calleth thee" (Rev. Ver.). For evidently she wished her to go to Jesus without being followed by the company—showing thereby a wise and friendly interest in Christ. For she probably feared, as the event proved, that nothing which Jesus might do or say would diminish their hatred, or change their purpose to work his ruin.

Another point may be noted. The writer of this Gospel gives a certain precedence to Mary, thus: "Now a certain man was sick, Lazarus of Bethany, of the town of Mary and her sister Martha. And it was that Mary who anointed the Lord with ointment, and wiped his feet with her hair, whose brother Lazarus was sick" (Rev. Ver.). Two remarks are suggested by these verses: (1) That in spite of the precedence assigned to Martha by the passage in Luke, and, in some respects also, by the narrative under consideration here, Mary, at the time when the Fourth Gospel was written, had the first place in the mind of the writer, and, as he appears to assume, in the minds of those who would read his Gospel. (2) That the reason for this greater prominence of Mary is alluded to by the writer's saying, that this Mary was the one "who anointed the Lord with ointment, and wiped his feet with her hair," as if there had been something peculiar in the service thus performed which had given distinction to Mary. And, according to the description of the anointing, which is afterwards given in this Gospel, there had been something very remarkable connected with it; namely, the murmuring of Judas Iscariot and the approval of Jesus.

If now, looking at these features of the narrative, we ask whether it reads like the story of an eye-witness, or like that of a person living a hundred years later, I think the answer will not be doubtful. There are too many delicate harmonies, obviously natural, to allow of hesitation. They belong to the class of undesigned coincidences. To account for them we must either suppose that the story is true, which is an adequate explanation of all, or that it is the work of a consummate artist whose genius has never been matched. And by those who adopt the latter hypothesis, we are asked to believe that this great but unknown literary artist was a contemporary of Justin Martyr! that he was a man who never saw Jesus or felt the inspiration of intimate communion with him! and withal, that he was a man who could solemnly testify that his fiction was a record of actual words and deeds! The demand is too great. To believe this surpasses our credulity. At least we cannot believe it while the other alternative is offered to our acceptance.

In the thirteenth chapter we find another piece of historic description remarkable for its particularity and vividness. Jesus and his disciples are represented as about to partake of the paschal supper, in fact, as having taken their places in a reclining posture about the table. Jesus, then, as we are told, before the supper actually began, "riseth from supper, layeth aside his (outer) garments, taketh a towel and girdeth himself, poureth water into the basin, and began to wash his disciples' feet, and to wipe them with the towel" (literally). What could be more minute or graphic than this? Does it not read like the account of a deeply interested spectator or witness? But the question rises to our lips: With what emotions did the disciples see all this? Why did they not spring to their feet to take their Lord's place in the service which he was evidently preparing to render? Were they overawed by something in his look or bearing which forbade remonstrance? Or were they so filled with a spirit of rivalry as to who should be greatest that no one of them was ready to take the place of a servant? There is some reason, found especially in the Gospel of Luke, 22: 24 sq., to suspect that the latter may have been the case, though nothing in this narrative directly affirms it. To proceed: Now as Jesus was thus washing and wiping his disciples' feet, "he cometh," we are told by the Evangelist, "to Simon Peter," and was met by the question: "Lord, dost thou wash my feet?" [Note the position of "my" ($\mu o v$) in the Greek sentence: is it only slightly emphatic?] This question of Peter implies that he clearly perceived the indecorum of his being thus served by his Master, though it does not show that he was willing to take his Master's place and complete the menial service, which was doubtless suitable to the occasion, if not required by it. Then Christ answered him: "What I do thou knowest not now, but thou shalt understand hereafter" (Rev. Ver.). This answer would probably have silenced any other disciple than Peter. But he, the rash and positive, replied: "Thou shalt never wash my feet." O headstrong man, unwilling to trust the Son of God! Thy voice will soon be changed; for Jesus now answers: "If I wash thee not, thou hast no part with me." Peter did not look for this, and his next words reveal a sudden and complete revulsion of feeling: "Not my feet only, but also my hands and my head"! Yet the reaction has carried him too far. He asks for something that Jesus had neither done nor proposed to do. Peter's frank, bold, impulsive nature, as we see, is not easily trained to follow the will of another. But he is in the hands of a wise and patient Teacher, and is certain to learn submission at last. In the next paragraph we read: "So when he had washed their feet, and taken his garments, he said unto them"—going on to explain and enforce by his words the lesson of his significant action in washing their feet. This surely is the record of a loving disciple who delights to recall every look and act of his Lord.

And it is followed by a wonderfully graphic sketch of the scene in which the betrayer of Jesus was pointed out and sent away from the supper. "When Jesus had thus said, he was troubled in the spirit (*his spirit*), and testified, and said, Verily, verily, I say unto you, that one of you shall betray me. The disciples looked one on another, doubting of whom he spake. There was at the table reclining in Jesus' bosom one of his disciples, whom Jesus loved. Simon Peter therefore beckoneth to him, and saith unto him, Tell us who it is of whom he speaketh. He leaning back, as he was (or, *thus*), on Jesus' breast, saith unto him, Lord, who is it? Jesus therefore answereth, He it is, for whom I shall dip the sop, and give it him. So when he had dipped the sop, he taketh and giveth it to Judas, the son of Simon Iscariot. And after the sop, then entered Satan into him. Jesus therefore saith unto him, That thou doest, do quickly (or, *more quickly*)! Now no man at the table knew for what intent he spake this unto him. For some thought, because Judas had the bag, that Jesus said unto him, Buy what things we have need of for the feast; or, that he should give something to the poor. He then having received the sop went out straightway: and it was night" (Rev. Ver.). This life-picture deserves careful study. The first words of Jesus, so direct and unequivocal; the surprised and questioning look of the twelve into the faces of one another; the description of the exact position and posture of the disciple whom Jesus loved; the beckoning gesture of Peter to that disciple and the *sotto-voce* question which followed; the leaning back of that disciple until his head touched the breast of Jesus; the substance of Peter's request conveyed by him in a low voice to the Lord and the Lord's answer addressed to that disciple's private ear; the giving of the sop to the betrayer, thus pointing him out to the disciple whom he loved; the open word to Judas as the sop was given to him; the conjectures of some of the disciples as to what that word signified, casting suddenly a flash of light upon the duties of Judas as treasurer of the chosen band; the prompt exit of the traitor from the room and the house; and the terse comment picturing the out-side darkness into which the betrayer went: *it was night*:—all these particulars betoken the pen of an eye-witness who was at least a warm friend of Jesus. And a great part of them could be of no logical use in a *Tendenzschrift*, such as the school of Baur has proclaimed this Gospel to be. It would also be easy to show that

INTRODUCTION TO THE GOSPEL.

this narrative is very different from those in the Synoptic Gospels, though all may be true. The difference, however, is greater than any writer save an eye-witness would be likely to venture upon, if he were acquainted with the earlier Gospels. And if not acquainted with those Gospels, it is surprising that no real contradiction between his narrative and theirs appears.

Another passage which sparkles with evidence, derivable from unimportant circumstances, that it was written by a spectator of the events related, is a paragraph of the eighteenth chapter (ver. 15-27). Simon Peter is said to have followed Jesus when the latter was led from the Garden of Gethsemane to his trial in the city; which statement was preliminary to a record of Peter's denials, and these were important events, fulfilling the words of Christ. But the writer of the Gospel also inserts the following interesting particulars, which do not seem to be essential to the substance of the narrative, viz.: another disciple followed Jesus also, and that other disciple, being known to the high priest, and therefore no doubt to the portress and servants, was allowed to enter without remonstrance into the court of the high priest with Jesus. But Peter, being unknown to the high priest's household, could not thus enter, but stood without for a time. Therefore the other disciple went out and, speaking to the maid who was door-keeper, brought in Peter. But, as Peter was entering, the door-maid asked him, doubtfully: "Art thou also one of this man's disciples?" (Rev. Ver.) And Peter's first denial was uttered—an essential part of the history. Then follows a statement that "the servants and officers were standing there, having made a fire of coals, for it was cold; and they were warming themselves; and Peter also was with them, standing and warming himself" (Rev. Ver). This picture is perfect, and it represents a scene in the central court awhile after Peter was introduced; but it cannot be considered essential to the history in the same sense as the record of what next occurred in that group is essential to it. For, as Peter was standing there, some of the group said to him: "Art thou also one of his disciples?" (Rev. Ver.) The question being so framed, perhaps in courtesy, as to suggest that a negative answer was expected (Buttmann, p. 248, 1st P.). It came, and was probably, as in the preceding instance, heard by the writer of this Gospel. Next a very exact specification occurs. "One of the servants of the high priest, being his kinsman whose ear Peter cut off, saith: 'Did not I see thee in the garden with him?'" And in this case the question, as one might conjecture beforehand, is so framed as to anticipate, or perhaps, if we could hear the tone of voice, to demand an affirmative answer (Buttmann, p. 247). But it came not; for "Peter denied" the third time, "and immediately the cock crew."

Now this is to me, on the very face of it, a truthful as well as a very graphic narrative, and I cannot suppress the conviction that it is far more reasonable to ascribe it to the Apostle John, as "the other disciple," and an eye-witness of the events described, than to ascribe it to an unknown writer of the second century, who drew upon his imagination for his facts, or at least for the side-touches, which give life and naturalness to his picture.

Another sketch in this Gospel may be associated with the one just considered, viz.: *the story of the running of Peter and another disciple to the tomb after Christ had risen* (ch. 20: 3-8). It reads thus: "Peter therefore went forth, and the other disciple, and they went toward the tomb. And they ran both together; and the other disciple outran Peter, and came first to the tomb; and stooping and looking in, he seeth the linen cloths lying; yet entered he not in. Simon Peter therefore also cometh, following him, and entered into the tomb; and he beholdeth the linen cloths lying, and the napkin that was upon his head, not lying with the linen cloths, but rolled up in a place by itself. Then entered in therefore the other disciple also, who came first to the tomb, and he saw and believed" (Rev. Ver.). Can we suppose that these details are the fruit of imagination or of oral tradition? Or, granting that such a supposition is not strictly incredible, is it the fairest, the most rational account which can be given of their origin? I am willing to submit the case to the judgment of any impartial reader—sure that his verdict will be favorable to the apostolic authorship of the sketch. And the same result would follow a study of the next paragraph (ver. 11–18), which describes the Lord's first appearance to Mary Magdalene.

Other parts of the Fourth Gospel, especially the scene described in chapter twenty-one, might be examined under this head; but these are enough for our present purpose. They all point in one direction, towards the Johannean authorship of this Gospel, and their testimony is so clear and positive that we do not expect it will ever be set aside.

Attention may be paid, *thirdly,* to the fact that *names and facts are mentioned in the Fourth Gospel which would not probably have been known to a writer of the second century.* We have already referred to the fact, stated by this Gospel, that another disciple followed Peter on the evening after our Lord's betrayal, and that the other disciple *was known* to the high priest, and that he was therefore suffered to enter freely into the court of the high priest. This agrees with the circumstance that the name of the high priest is mentioned repeatedly, together with the fact that Annas was his father-in-law. The writer was, therefore, somewhat familiar with the high priest's family. But this familiarity is thought to be improbable. Would Caiaphas have allowed himself to be on friendly terms with a disciple of Christ? Would he have consented to recognize such a man as an acquaintance? Must we not rather pronounce this acquaintance a fiction of the writer, and conclude that he could not have been an apostle? I am unable to do this. It does not seem to me probable that the rulers were as yet greatly embittered against the *disciples* of Christ. For some reason, the Lord himself was so prominent, so principal and towering an object, that his followers were deemed of little account. Their time had not yet come. They were still pupils, not champions. Jesus stood practically *alone* in all his great encounters with the Jews. And so I think it altogether credible that John was known to the high priest—more credible than that a skillful writer should have imagined this without cause.

Again, the writer of the Fourth Gospel mentions the name of the high priest's servant whose right ear was cut off by the impetuous stroke of Peter in the garden, and this notice agrees with the supposition that the unnamed disciple who was known to the high priest was the writer of this Gospel. It is quite natural that one who was so well known to the portress as to be admitted without question, knew the names of other servants of Caiaphas, or would be likely to learn them. But is it probable that a writer of the second century would have known that the name of the wounded servant was Malchus? Or, if not, that he would have assigned him a name, when there was no necessity for his doing it? Instead of pursuing this enumeration of instances further, we will show the importance which others have seen in the line of inquiry adopted by us in the preceding pages. In 1865, Dr. Otto Thenius, an eminent Biblical scholar of Germany, addressed an open letter to Dr. David F. Strauss, in which he defends the Johannean authorship of the Fourth Gospel against the assaults of that famous critic. In one part of the letter he enumerates the following circumstances as bearing the stamp of reality, and as furnishing proof that the Gospel was written by one who knew whereof he

INTRODUCTION TO THE GOSPEL. 33

affirmed; viz.: "That Jesus had observed Nathanael under the fig tree (1 : 48); that his brothers did not believe on him, while officers of the Jews were impressed by his discourses; that Nicodemus took his part, and the Sanhedrists in their passion falsely asserted that no prophet cometh out of Galilee (7 : 5, 46, 50, 52); that during the rainy season Jesus taught in a sheltered place (10 : 22, 23); that Mary rose and went to Jesus only when called by Martha (11 : 20, 28, 29); that Judas had the common purse, and Jesus said unto him : "That thou doest do quickly" (12 : 6 ; 13 : 7); that a Roman cohort assisted in taking Jesus ; that the servant wounded at his capture was named Malchus, and that it was Peter who cut off his ear (18 : 3, 10, 26); that one of the servants who was standing by at the examination struck Jesus with his hand (18 : 22); that Pilate sought to excite sympathy for Jesus in the hearts of his accusers by crying : "Behold the man!" that he sat down on the judgment-seat at a place called the Pavement, or in Hebrew, Gabbatha ; and that he refused the request of the chief priests that he would change the superscription on the cross (19 : 5, 13, 21, 22); that the place of crucifixion was near the city; that four soldiers performed the dreadful deed, and that his *mother* was present as a beholder (19 : 20, 23, 25); that the grave was in a garden (19 : 41); and that Peter saw the napkin lying by itself (20 : 7)." With this extract from Thenius may be profitably compared the words of Sanday, in his able work on the "Authorship and Historical Character of the Fourth Gospel," (p. 163 sq.): "The author of the Fourth Gospel stands out a single isolated figure, with a loftiness and intensity to which there is hardly a parallel to be found in history ; with a force of character that transmutes and transforms all the more ductile matter that comes within its range, and yet with a certain childlike simplicity in the presence of external facts. This is not the personality of great writers of fiction in any community or time ; least of all is it the personality of one writing under a feigned name, and asseverating all the time that he records nothing but that which he has heard and seen. It must be remembered too that, if it is a fiction, it is not merely a fiction that would fit in equally well to any point of space or time. It is a fiction which is laid in definite localities, and in the midst of circumstances and a circle of ideas that are remarkably definite. It is written after a series of tremendous changes had swept away all the landmarks to which it might have been affixed. The siege and destruction of Jerusalem, together with the rapid progress and organization of Christianity, caused a breach between the ages before and behind it, which could be crossed only by memory, not by imagination. Those who deny the Johannean authorship of the Gospel require the supposed author of it to transgress the conditions of his age and position, and to throw himself back into another set of conditions entirely different from his own. They do not indeed do this in words; but this is, as I have tried to show, and as I think we cannot but see, because they have failed to take in, by far, the larger part of the phenomena. The hypothesis of apostolic and Johannean authorship satisfies these, while it satisfies also, as I believe, all the other phenomena as well. It gives a consistent and intelligible account of *all* the facts, and I venture to say that no other hypothesis as yet propounded has done so."

II. TRUSTWORTHINESS OF THE FOURTH GOSPEL AS A RECORD OF THE DISCOURSES OF JESUS.

A study of this Gospel brings to light, as we have seen, many indications that it was written by one of the apostles, and therefore by John, the brother of James. But these indications are found principally in the narrative parts of the Gospel, as distinguished

C

from the discourses of Jesus. An examination of the latter reveals the fact that they differ materially in style and thought from the discourses preserved in the Synoptical Gospels. Two questions are therefore suggested, viz.: (1) Is the difference referred to of such a nature as to make the Johannean authorship of the Fourth Gospel improbable, in spite of evidence from other sources in its favor? (2) Is the difference of such a nature as to disprove the substantial correctness of that part of the record?

(1) An argument against the Johannean authorship of the Gospel, founded on a difference of style and thought between the discourses ascribed to Jesus in that Gospel and the discourses ascribed to him in the Synoptical Gospels, must rest upon one or more of the following assumptions: (*a*) That the Synoptical report of Christ's discourses is trustworthy in respect to style and thought; for if it is not, the report of the Fourth Gospel may be correct, though it furnishes a type of discourse differing from any in the Synoptical record. (*b*) That if John wrote the Fourth Gospel he must have reproduced the discourses of his Master with substantial correctness; for if he can be supposed to have changed, either consciously or unconsciously, the style or substance of Christ's teaching, he may have been the author of the Fourth Gospel, though it does not represent correctly the words of Jesus. (*c*) That the Synoptical report contains ample specimens of every kind of discourse which the Lord ever employed; for if it does not, the report of the Fourth Evangelist may furnish a variety of teaching not distinctly represented in the first three Gospels.

To the first of these assumptions, that the Synoptical Gospels furnish a trustworthy report of Christ's teaching, no valid objection can be made. Jesus of Nazareth certainly did teach, much of the time, after the manner represented by the first three Gospels. To deny that the Sermon on the Mount, the numerous parables, and the discourse about the overthrow of Jerusalem and the final coming of the Son of Man, as read in those Gospels, preserve faithfully certain parts of the Lord's teaching, would be to disregard the rules of historical evidence. Again, much may be said in support of the second assumption, that if John wrote the Fourth Gospel he must be presumed to have reported the discourses of his Master with substantial accuracy. For the circumstance that he had been a disciple of Jesus and a hearer of many or all of the discourses reported in the Fourth Gospel, must be regarded as favorable to the general accuracy of that report. It would be unreasonable to suppose that Christ's language and teaching had made so little impression on the soul of John that he could ascribe to him thoughts which he never uttered, and a style of teaching which he never employed. If then the third assumption were certainly correct, if it were a case made out by just criticism that the discourses of Jesus in the Synoptical Gospels furnish ample specimens of every kind of discourse employed by him, so that it is safe to affirm that those ascribed to him in the Fourth Gospel were never uttered by him, it would undoubtedly be easier to believe that the latter were composed by some person not a hearer of Christ, than to believe them composed by John, who heard him so often.

But to this final assumption there are grave objections. For it is worthy of remark, in the *first* place, that the Synoptical Gospels nowhere pretend to furnish a complete record of Christ's teaching. Indeed, nothing is more evident from the Gospels themselves than the fact that they contain only a small part of what he said (see Matt. 4:23; 9:35; 11:1). The passages referred to are but samples of the Lord's preaching, a great part of which the Evangelists do not profess to record. It would probably be safe to affirm that not more than one discourse out of fifty which he delivered during the years of his public ministry is preserved by the Synoptists. This rough estimate, however, includes frequent repetitions of the same essential truth to different persons in nearly the same terms, and to the same persons in different terms. For why should not the same truth be repeated to different persons in nearly the same terms, and to the same persons in varied forms of speech? Is not this done more or less by every great teacher?

It is worthy of remark, in the *second* place, that there is no evidence in the Synoptical Gospels that they were meant to furnish illustrative specimens of every kind or style of discourse which the Saviour employed. The authors do not appear to have been guided in their selection of materials by any such purpose. If an inference may be drawn from the prevailing character of their narratives, it would be that they inserted some of the most striking parts of certain discourses which were addressed to the people of Galilee during the Lord's ministry there, together with a few of his impressive utterances in Jerusalem shortly before his death. Whether they made use of an earlier record which has since perished, or rather put in writing each for himself such special portions of the Saviour's teaching as were most frequently repeated by the apostles, may always be a matter of doubt, but certainly there is in their writings no trace of a plan to give a complete picture of the diversified work of Christ as a teacher of truth. And, apart from such a plan, what sufficient reason is there for thinking that the Synoptical Gospels furnish examples of every kind of discourse employed by Jesus? Is it safe for us to decide that One who delivered the Sermon on the Mount, the parables of Matthew and of Luke, the warnings and predictions of the last passover week, the answers which silenced by their sagacity Pharisee and Sadducee and lawyer, and indeed the right word to every man whom he met, was nevertheless restricted to just those ranges of thought and styles of expression which may be found illustrated in the first three Gospels? May it not rather be assumed that the truly marvelous insight and sympathy of Jesus were complemented by an equally marvelous power of adapting his thought and style to the minds before him? Is it not reasonable to suppose that his great nature, which represented mankind rather than any one type of humanity, was able to express itself in manifold ways, some adapted to deep and mystical souls, and others to sharp and practical intellects, some to men of spiritual vision and fervor, and others to punctilious observers of law and precedent? This is surely a credible hypothesis.

Furthermore, it is admitted by competent critics that the language and thought of Jesus in Matthew 11 : 25-30, are strikingly similar to his discourses in the Fourth Gospel. But is any scholar justified in pronouncing that paragraph unhistorical, because it differs thus from many, or from all other utterances of Christ preserved in the First Gospel? If not, let us suppose that Matthew had ascribed to Jesus a dozen such paragraphs; would a critic then have had any better ground for thinking the dozen unhistorical than he has for thinking the one to be so? If Jesus could have spoken on one occasion after the manner reported by John, as Matthew testifies, who can prove that he could not have spoken thus on a dozen occasions? Moreover, if a Johannean style in the First Gospel does not discredit the record, why should it do this in the Fourth Gospel? This question can be answered in only one way.

A hundred examples might be adduced to show the remarkable changes of thought and style in different addresses of the same man—changes occasioned sometimes by the moods of the speaker, sometimes by the themes discussed, and sometimes by the moral conditions of those addressed. Let a reader compare the Epistle to the Galatians with that to the Ephesians or Colossians, and he will perceive a vast difference between them. Or let him compare Paul's discourse to the Jews in their synagogue at Antioch of

Pisidia (Acts 13 : 17–41), with his discourse to the men of Athens on Mars' Hill (Acts 17 : 22–31), or with his address to the Elders of Ephesus in Miletus (Acts 20 : 18-35), and he will observe such differences of method and tone as will make it seem probable that Jesus spoke sometimes after the manner represented by the Synoptical discourses, and sometimes after the manner represented by the discourses of the Fourth Gospel. For surely in this matter of variety and adaptation, it would be inconsiderate to imagine the servant greater than his Lord.

Enough has been said to show that the difference between the discourses ascribed to Jesus in the Fourth Gospel and those ascribed to him in the first three, is not inconsistent with a Johannean authorship of the former. "But even the Johannean authorship of the record of Christ's discourses in the Fourth Gospel does not, it has been further said, prove them to be substantially correct, much less does it prove them to be strictly accurate. For sixty years may have elapsed between the time when they were spoken, and the time when they were put in writing, and the memory of one man can hardly be trusted to bear the words of another over so vast a period. Is it not extremely probable that John, revolving in his mind through the years of a long life the teaching of his Master, had, unconsciously to himself, changed more or less the substance and form of that teaching? Is it not almost *certain* that he had recast and remoulded in the laboratory of his own great spirit the doctrine of Jesus, adding to it much that was foreign to the original discourses, and impressing upon it everywhere the stamp of his own genius? And is not this the true and sufficient explanation of the difference in style and thought between the Fourth Gospel and the first three?" Thus we come to the second question to be answered in this part of our introduction, viz.: Is the difference referred to so great, or of such a nature as to disprove the substantial correctness of John's record of his Master's teaching?

The *first* reason for answering this question in the negative has already been noticed. It is the marked resemblance of the words of Christ in Matt. 11 : 25-30 to his teaching in the Fourth Gospel. It would surely be rash to deny that One who delivered the Sermon on the Mount, and the last paragraph of the First Gospel, could have uttered the sublime words: "I thank thee, O Father, Lord of heaven and earth, that thou didst hide these things from the wise and understanding, and didst reveal them unto babes : Yea, Father, for so it was well-pleasing in thy sight. All things have been delivered unto me of my Father : and no one knoweth the Son, save the Father; neither doth any know the Father, save the Son, and he to whomsoever the Son willeth to reveal him. Come unto me, all ye that labor and are heavy laden, and I will give you rest : Take my yoke upon you, and learn of me ; for I am meek and lowly in heart : and ye shall find rest to your souls : For my yoke is easy, and my burden is light " (Rev. Ver.). But it would be no less rash to deny that One who uttered the words just cited could have spoken as follows : " I am the good Shepherd ; and I know my own, and mine own know me, even as the Father knoweth me, and I know the Father ; and I lay down my life for the sheep. And other sheep I have which are not of this fold : Them also I must bring, and they shall hear my voice ; and there shall be one flock, one shepherd. Therefore doth the Father love me, because I lay down my life, that I may take it again. No one taketh it away from me, but I lay it down of myself. I have power to lay it down, and I have power to take it again. This commandment received I from my Father " (Rev. Ver.). The same authority, dignity, simplicity, and sweetness pervade the two paragraphs. Are we not then warranted in saying that Jesus sometimes spoke after the manner represented in the Fourth Gospel? And if he spoke thus on a

INTRODUCTION TO THE GOSPEL. 37

few occasions, it seems difficult to assign any conclusive reason why he may not have spoken thus as often as John affirms.

A *second* reason for answering the question before us in the negative is that John, as well as the other apostles, was assisted in his work of teaching the truth by the inspiration of the Holy Spirit. Unless we approach the Fourth Gospel with unwarrantable suspicion, refusing to allow its testimony any value, it will be impossible for us to deny that the Holy Spirit, as a revealer of truth, was promised by the Lord himself to his disciples just before his death. And if we admit that such a promise was given, and that it began to be fulfilled on the day of Pentecost, there will be no reason to doubt the specification, distinctly stated, that the Spirit of truth would bring to their remembrance all that Christ had said unto them (14 : 26). The Spirit of God was therefore to assist John, by what process we need not inquire, to recall the words and deeds of his Master, whenever he had occasion to use them in preaching the gospel or building up the churches. Unless this extraordinary assistance of the Spirit be taken into account, the *whole* reason for our confidence in the record of John is not grasped. Nay, this is the strongest pillar of our faith in the testimony of the apostles. They are to be believed, not only because there is abundant evidence of their intelligence and integrity, as witnesses to the works and words of Jesus, but also, and especially, because they were illuminated by the Spirit of God, and enabled by his quickening power to recall the sayings of their Lord. When therefore it is asked, "Could John have retained the teaching of Jesus in his memory fifty or sixty years?" it may be answered in the affirmative, (1) because the Holy Spirit was, in a very special sense, his Helper; and (2) because he was called by his work as an apostle to repeat more or less of this teaching every week, if not every day, dwelling no doubt with peculiar satisfaction upon those parts of it which were most congenial to his spirit and refreshing to his faith.

These considerations would probably be sufficient to satisfy almost every one that the difference in style and thought between the discourses ascribed to Jesus in the Fourth Gospel and those ascribed to him in the first three, is not so great or of such a nature as to disprove the substantial accuracy of John's record, were it not for a single circumstance, viz.: the striking resemblance of the style of the other parts of this Gospel to the style of the Saviour's teaching recorded in it. In other words, the style of John is said to be identical with the style of his Master, as reported by him. And this circumstance suggests the thought that John has not given us the teaching of Jesus pure and simple, but rather some of that teaching recast and recolored by its passage through his own mind. The suggestion is a natural one, but there is danger of allowing it to pass for more than it is worth.

For, in the *first* place, it might be conceded that John has not given us the precise words and style of Jesus, without conceding that his report is incorrect as to the meaning of what Jesus said. Especially easy would it be to justify this proposition in case of a report which is also a translation. And this is probably true of all the reports of our Lord's discourses in the Fourth Gospel, if not of all that are found in the Synoptical Gospels. We may then safely believe that John's report of his Master's teaching is no more unlike the original than any faithful and fluent version is apt to be. John's report must be looked upon as his own conscientious rendering of what he had heard the Master say; for these discourses do not appear in the earlier Gospels and are not supposed to have been among the "common places" of apostolic preaching. But if they are translations made by John himself from the Aramæan into the Greek language, the translator may have put the impress of his own style upon them, though the sentiments of Jesus are correctly reported. There is a plain difference of style between Pope's translation of the Iliad and Cowper's, even in passages where the Homeric thought is fairly reproduced by both. The same may be said of Prof. Torrey's translation of Neander's "History of the Christian Religion and Church," when compared with any other translation that I have seen. Many years ago the writer of this Introduction was associated with a friend in translating Perthes' "Life of Chrysostom." The first half of the volume was translated by the writer, and the second half by his friend; and the former did not feel himself flattered by observing that the second part was said by competent critics to "be done into better English than the first, though the sense of the original appeared to be reproduced with equal fidelity in both." From such instances it appears that a translation may closely resemble the translator's style and yet be faithful to the meaning of the original. Hence, if it were certain that John had given his own style to his Master's discourses, it would not follow that any part of the thought, or any particular illustration, ascribed to Jesus, was contributed by John; it would not follow that we have in the Fourth Gospel an unreliable report of the Lord's teaching. It might in fact be just as reliable as any of the "common places" preserved in the other Gospels; for they too must be regarded as versions of the more popular and striking parts of his teaching.

In the *second* place, the memory of John appears to have been singularly tenacious. As we have already seen, his narrative is remarkable for its accuracy in the representation of accompanying circumstances. Times and events were so deeply engraved on his memory that years could not erase them. There is no one of the Evangelists, not even Mark (virtually Peter), for whom events and the occasions of them had a profounder significance, no one who saw in them more clearly the purpose and hand of God. Plainly then he must have pondered these things in his heart, as he did the words of his Master. Yet they do not seem to have been transfigured by the action of his imagination. They retained their simple and real character, although subject, for more than half a century, to the influence of his brooding meditation. This fact deserves consideration. For it is scarcely probable that John gave more earnest heed, in the first instance, to any thing else than he gave to the *words* of Jesus. And, other things being equal, it is a law of the mind, that the closer the attention in the first instance, the better the memory ever after. If then his memory of events, occasions, and circumstances was singularly exact, there is much reason to suppose that it was equally clear and firm in its hold on the teaching which fell from the lips of his gracious Lord, and which must have made a deep impression on his mind. And if his brooding over events, and his growing apprehension of their meaning, did not change his view of them as objective realities, it would be somewhat surprising to find that his meditation on the words of Christ, and his growing insight into their meaning, unconsciously modified his recollection of those words as objective realities. Nor is this remark at all affected by the view we entertain of the help afforded by inspiration to the apostle. Whatever may be the true explanation of his vigorous memory, it is very certain that he possessed it, so far as scenes and events are concerned, and therefore probable that he possessed it, so far as the teaching of his Lord is concerned. And this raises a certain presumption against the theory proposed, and moves us to ask whether the phenomenon in question can be accounted for in any other way.

√ Is it then too much to assume, (1) that, beyond any other disciple of Jesus, John had a profoundly loving and spiritual nature, and that by reason of such a nature he was peculiarly susceptible to the influence of his Lord's words when they related to the Lord's person, or to the higher and mystical aspects of Christian truth? (2) That this extraordinary susceptibility to the sayings and sermons of Jesus which related to the Saviour's own person, or to the more vital and spiritual aspects of religion, led him to recall such sayings and sermons with peculiar interest, to meditate upon them with intense satisfaction, to use them frequently in his preaching, and thus to keep them ever fresh and distinct in his memory? And (3) that all this tended to bring the loving disciple's style of thought and of expression into closer and closer accord with a certain part of his Master's teaching, so that in fact his language was unconsciously modeled after *that part* of Christ's language which was dearest to his heart and oftenest on his tongue?

In favor of these assumptions is the fact that they recognize in the Founder of our religion One greater than any or all of his disciples. They represent his spiritual being as large enough, many-sided enough, to match and move and inspire the capacities of every man with whom he had to do. Yet they are also consistent with the view that each one of his twelve disciples had some eminent qualification for the work of an apostle,[1] some single faculty lifting him above the dead level of mediocrity and giving promise of valuable service in a certain direction, but they insist that no one of them equaled his Master, even in the faculty which had led to his selection as an apostle. And this estimate of Jesus agrees with his definite claims to pre-eminence in knowledge and authority, with his disciples' recognition of those claims and life-long devotion to his service, and with the place which many modern scholars give to his person and influence.

Especially does this estimate accord with the tone of the Fourth Gospel in speaking of Jesus. If John, as we have shown, was the writer of that Gospel, he certainly believed that Jesus had unparalleled knowledge of God and man, and also that, by union with Jesus, he himself had come into possession of new spiritual truth and life. Notice the following expressions: "But Jesus did not trust himself unto them, for that he knew all men, and because he needed not that any one should bear witness concerning man; for he himself knew what was in man" (John 2: 24, 25. Rev. Ver). "Of his fulness we all received, and grace for grace. For the law was given by Moses: grace and truth came by Jesus Christ" (1: 16, 17. Rev. Ver). "Many other signs therefore did Jesus in the presence of the disciples, which are not written in this book: but these are written, that ye may believe that Jesus is the Christ, the Son of God; and that believing ye may have life in his name" (20: 30, 31. Rev. Ver). It is perfectly evident that the author of such testimonies looked up to Jesus with reverence as well as love, counting him Master even though he were also Friend, and prizing his words as a legacy no less precious and divine than his works. How susceptible, impressible, plastic, his soul was to the influence of Christ may be partly inferred from his writings; and in view of their tone and testimony it is reasonable to assume that his habits of thinking and speaking must have been greatly influenced by those of his Lord, but especially by the discourses of Jesus that satisfied the deepest tendencies of his own spirit. These it is, that he has preserved in his Gospel. For the time came, in the history and ferment of Christian inquiry, when the churches were in need of that part of the Lord's instruction which had been welcomed with the greatest satisfaction by the soul of John, and which could be put on record in the best manner by him. He therefore, in obedience to the call of Providence, wrote his Gospel and gave it to the churches.

But though it is in itself credible, and indeed probable, that John's style was greatly influenced by that part of his Master's teaching which was peculiarly adapted to his

---

[1] Save Judas Iscariot, who appears to have had no moral qualification for the apostleship. But it was known to Jesus from the beginning that this unworthy disciple would at last betray him to his foes (see Notes on 6: 64, 70, 71; 13: 11, 18) and then perish, before entering upon the proper work of an apostle.

spiritual nature, this explanation of the resemblance between his style and that of Jesus in the discourses recorded by him, cannot be accepted unless satisfactory answers can be given to the following questions, viz. : (1) Is there any reason to suppose that the discourses reported by John were identical with discourses reported in other language by the Synoptists? For if there were reason to suppose this, the probability that John's record has been colored by his own thought and style, rather than his style derived from that of Christ, would be very strong, and the explanation proposed would deserve little favor. But the question may be confidently answered in the negative, leaving the explanation undisturbed. (2) Do the persons addressed in the discourses of John's Gospel furnish any argument against this explanation? The answer to this question should be carefully made. For if the persons addressed in the discourses of the Fourth Gospel were the same, and in the same mental condition, as those addressed by the discourses of the other Gospels, the change of style would be surprising and an argument against the theory; but if they were different, there may be no argument from this source against the theory, inasmuch as difference of hearers might account for difference of manner in addressing them. Now it will be found, upon close examination, that the words of Jesus reported by John were, most of them at least, addressed to hearers who differed in important respects from those to whom his words in the first three Gospels were addressed. Let the record of John be read with an eye to this difference as accounting for its character.

This record first gives the words of Jesus to Andrew and John, as they were following him, viz. : *What seek ye?* and next, his response to their question : "Rabbi, where abidest thou?" *Come, and ye shall see.* Then follow in rapid succession his saying to Peter : *Thou art Simon, the son of John; thou shalt be called Peter;* his commendation of Nathanael : *Behold an Israelite indeed, in whom there is no guile;* his answer to Nathanael's question : "Whence knowest thou me?" *Before Philip called thee, when thou wast under the fig-tree, I saw thee;* and his response to Nathanael's confession of him as the Son of God, the King of Israel : *Because I said unto thee, I saw thee under the fig-tree, believest t'ou? Thou shalt see greater things than these. Verily, verily, I say unto you, Ye shall see the heaven opened, and the angels of God ascending and descending on the Son of Man.* Only this last verse can be called Johannean, and this does not differ in tone or spirit from Christ's response to a similar confession of Peter, as recorded by Matthew (16 : 16–19). In both instances it was called forth by the spiritual attitude of the person addressed.

Three brief remarks of Jesus at the marriage in Cana of Galilee are preserved by John ; one to his mother : *Woman, what have I to do with thee? Mine hour is not yet come;* and two to the servants : *Fill the water-pots with water,* and, *Draw out now, and bear unto the ruler of the feast.* But none of these remarks would strike a reader as peculiar if found in the Synoptic Gospels. In John's account of Christ's purifying the Temple, the only sayings attributed to Jesus are two, viz. : *Take these things hence; make not my Father's house a house of merchandise;* and, *Destroy thi' Temple, and in three days I will raise it up;* both of which find support as to fact and style in the other Gospels. (See Matt. 21: 13 ; Mark 14: 58). And it is noticeable that when John, as in these instances, gives any sayings of Christ to which reference is made in the earlier Gospels, the character of his report agrees with their reference.

Passing on to the third chapter, and the Lord's conversation with Nicodemus, we meet for the first time with a type of thought and expression rarely appearing in the Synoptical Gospels. But it is also true that the person addressed differs from any one

INTRODUCTION TO THE GOSPEL.

addressed by Jesus in the discourses of the first three Gospels. For Nicodemus was "a ruler of the Jews," that is, probably, a member of the Sanhedrin (7 : 50). He was also called by Jesus in this conversation, if it is correctly reported, *the teacher of Israel* (Rev. Ver.), meaning at least one who belonged to the learned class in the Council, an expounder of the law. Besides, and this is a chief point, he was evidently a thoughtful man, fully persuaded by miracles or "signs" wrought in Jerusalem, that Jesus was "a teacher come from God," and half-convinced, it is probable, that he was the expected Messiah. Well might the Lord, in a quiet, confidential interview, turn the eye of such an inquirer to the necessity of a radical inward change, of his entering upon a new spiritual life, as indispensable to real discipleship. This was clearly the one thing that Nicodemus needed to know, and there is no solid ground for doubting that he was in a state of mind to profit by it more than he would have profited by any other teaching. Still further, if the words of Jesus close with the fifteenth verse, it is worthy of remark that they abound in figurative language. The spirit of parables is in them. Thus we have the figure of a new birth as expressive of the moral change experienced by those who enter truly upon the service of Christ, the figure of the wind moving unseen as an emblem of the Holy Spirit renewing the hearts of men, and the figure of the brazen serpent lifted up in the wilderness as a symbol of the Lord himself to be lifted up as an object of saving faith. To say that the Jesus of the Synoptical Gospels could not have conversed in this manner with such a man, would be to speak unadvisedly.

But it may perhaps be asserted that John meant to ascribe the six following verses also to Jesus, that these verses contain a much smaller proportion of figurative language than was generally used by him, and that they seem to be an explanation, repetition, and expansion of thoughts already expressed. From these considerations it is inferred that John has here put his own words into the mouth of Jesus. On the other hand it may be said that explanation, iteration, expansion, are more or less characteristic of every wise teacher, especially in the freedom of conversation; and, further, that the expansion of these verses is in perfect keeping with the germinal thoughts previously uttered. There is, then, no conclusive evidence that these verses could not have been spoken by Jesus; yet it is equally true that there is no conclusive evidence of John's intention to ascribe them to Jesus. Only this may be strongly affirmed, that the difference between Christ's style and thought in conversation with Nicodemus, and his style and thought in many discourses of the Synoptical Gospels, may be accounted for without ascribing it to John the Evangelist. It is sufficiently explained as a result of adapting truth to the mind of the hearer.

The next passage to be noticed is Christ's conversation with a Samaritan woman at Jacob's well. Of this conversation it may be remarked that it was held with one person only, that her spiritual condition was evidently divined by the Lord, that apt and free use was made of illustration, and that the truth gradually imparted appears to have been suited to the woman's spiritual state. To be sure, our knowledge of this woman is restricted to what may be learned from the narrative in question. But this at least may be inferred from it, that she was neither stupid nor thoughtless. She had a bright intellect, a ready wit, and a conscience still alive. Indeed, she was better prepared to receive the truth than were many of the Jews; and, perceiving this, the great Teacher gave himself earnestly and skillfully to the task of infusing it into her soul. The first hint of his religious mission was given in the words, *If thou knewest the gift of God, and who it is that saith unto thee, Give me to drink; thou wouldest have asked of him, and he would have given thee living water.* And the next was similar, continuing the same metaphor:

Every one that drinketh of this water shall thirst again: but whosoever drinketh of the water that I shall give him shall never thirst; but the water that I shall give him shall become in him a well of water springing up unto eternal life (Rev. Ver.). This use of imagery taken from objects at hand and familiar, is characteristic of the Christ of the Synoptists. *Consider the lilies of the field, how they grow; they toil not, neither do they spin: yet I say unto you, that even Solomon in all his glory was not arrayed like one of these. But if God doth so clothe the grass of the field, which to-day is, and to-morrow is cast into the oven, shall he not much more clothe you, O ye of little faith?* (comp. Luke 10 : 41, 42, and 14 : 7–24 ; Matt. 7 : 28–30. Rev. Ver.). Is there not the same divine skill and insight revealed in both passages? The same matchless use of natural objects in conveying religious truth? Do the writings of John, any more than those of Matthew, prove that *he*, the disciple, could have put such teaching into his Master's lips? Jesus now approaches the woman's conscience. *Go, call thy husband, and come hither;* and, in answer to her evasive reply, says, *Thou saidst well, I have no husband: for thou hast had five husbands; and he whom thou now hast is not thy husband* (Rev. Ver.). The woman, perceiving from this reply that he was a prophet, introduces the mooted question as to the proper place of worship, and he responds : *Woman, believe me, the hour cometh, when neither in this mountain nor in Jerusalem shall ye worship the Father. Ye worship that which ye know not: we worship that which we know: for salvation is from the Jews. But the hour cometh, and now is, when the worshippers shall worship the Father in spirit and truth: for such doth the Father seek to be his worshippers. God is a spirit: and they that worship him must worship in spirit and truth* (Rev. Ver.). Thereupon the woman expressed her belief that the coming Messiah would explain and settle all things now in debate between the Jews and Samaritans, and Jesus saith unto her plainly : *I that speak unto thee, am he.* Can any one affirm that a word of this is far-fetched or improbable ? That what Christ is here reported to have said was any less fitting than what he said, according to Luke, in his own village Nazareth, *To-day hath this Scripture been fulfilled in your ears?* Or what he said at the ruler's table, according to Luke 14 : 7–24? Plainly, the woman was better prepared to hear his final word than were his neighbors in Galilee to hear what he said to them. She was a part of the field which he looked upon as *white already for the harvest*, while the people of Nazareth promptly rejected him when he spoke of mercy for the Gentiles, though a moment before they had wondered at the words of grace which fell from his lips. The Samaritans were better prepared to hear spiritual truth than most of the Jews, and it is quite probable that no one of them was more conscious of needing divine grace, and so in a more suitable moral condition to welcome such truth, than the woman whom Christ met at the well. On the whole, therefore, this conversation bears internal evidence of being truly reported. It is Christ-like, rather than Johannean.

And the same is equally true of the language which he is said to have employed in speaking to his disciples on their return from the city. There is nothing like it in the known writings of John, so figurative and yet so condensed. *My meat is to do the will of him that sent me, and to accomplish his work. Say not ye, There are yet four months, and then cometh the harvest? behold, I say unto you : Lift up your eyes, and look on the fields, that they are white already unto harvest. He that reapeth receiveth wages, and gathereth fruit unto life eternal ; that he that soweth and he that reapeth may rejoice together. For herein is the saying true, One soweth and another reapeth. I sent you to reap that whereon ye have not laboured; others have laboured and ye are entered into their labour* (Rev. Ver.). Thus speaks the Christ of John to his disciples, and in every sentence we seem to hear the familiar voice of the Synoptical Master. In no sentence do we catch the faintest echo of words indubitably original with the author of the Fourth Gospel.

Up to this point, then, there is no sufficient reason to suppose that the record of Christ's teaching found in this Gospel is impaired by infusions of any sort from the writer's theology or style. And the writer's correctness thus far is a very considerable argument for his trustworthiness in the remainder of his work. Two other sayings, addressed to the nobleman from Capernaum, whose son was sick, complete the record which John gives of the Saviour's words during the first and tranquil period of his ministry, and these sayings—*Except ye see signs and wonders, ye will in no wise believe*, (Rev. Ver.), and, *Go thy way, thy son liveth*—are manifestly appropriate to the Christ of the earlier Gospels.

In the same manner it can be shown that all the sayings ascribed to Jesus by the Evangelist in the last four chapters of his Gospel, are such as the Christ of the Synoptists may be supposed to have uttered in perfect consistency with the style of speech attributed to him. Let the reader test for himself the correctness of this statement by carefully reading those chapters. With equal confidence we invite him to apply the same statement to the ninth and eleventh chapters of this Gospel, which contain the remarkable narratives concerning the giving of sight to a man who had been blind from birth, and the raising of Lazarus after he had been dead four days. The remaining chapters (viz.: the 5, 6, 7, 8, 10, 13–17), contain discourses or discussions addressed to influential companies of Jews who denied his Messianic authority and charged him with blasphemy, or to his chosen disciples on the evening before his arrest. Before looking at these discourses, it may be well to study for a moment the character and style of John.

The notices of John in the Four Gospels and the first part of the Acts are scarcely sufficient to reveal his character with distinctness. But in the impression which they make respecting him, they agree with the Fourth Gospel, the Epistles, and the Book of Revelation. And we can hardly be mistaken in saying, with Meyer, that love was the central principle of his renewed nature, and his fellowship with the spirit and life of Christ most true and deep and vital. In the words of Plumptre (Smith's "Dictionary of the Bible"): "The truest thought that we can attain to is still that he was 'the disciple whom Jesus loved' (ὁ ἐπιστήθιος) returning that love with a deep, absorbing, unwavering devotion. One aspect of that feeling is seen in the zeal for his Master's glory, the burning indignation against all that seemed to outrage it, which runs, with its fiery gleam, through his whole life, and makes him, from first to last, one of the sons of thunder. To him, more than to any other disciple, there is no neutrality between Christ and Antichrist. The spirit of such a man is intolerant of compromises and concessions. . . . He is the Apostle of Love, not because he starts from the easy temper of a general benevolence, nor again as being of a character soft, yielding, feminine, but because he has grown, ever more and more, into the likeness of him whom he loved so truly."

But where shall we go to learn the style of John? To his Gospel alone? Or to his Gospels and his Epistles, especially the first? Or to all these together, with the Book of Revelation? It will be safe to limit our examination to his First Epistle and his Prologue to the Fourth Gospel : for his Second and Third Epistles are very short, while the narrative parts of the Gospel and much of the Revelation would not require the same style as discourses would naturally take. As seen in the Prologue and First

Epistle, the literary style of John is uncommonly simple. Very rarely does the reader find an involved sentence. In point of grammatical accuracy, these portions of the New Testament are superior to many others. But in the structure and connection of sentences, there is almost nothing to remind one of classic Greek literature. Looked at from this point of view, John's style, is through and through Hebraistic. Every thing is cast in a Hebrew mould, though expressed in Greek words. In this respect it is impossible to perceive any difference between Matthew and Mark, on the one hand, and John, on the other, or betweeen either of these Evangelists and the Lord himself. Thus John's habit of presenting the same truth, after the manner of Hebrew parallelism, in both a positive and a negative form, is very noticeable. For example: "All things were made by him, and without him was not anything made." "God is light, and in him is no darkness at all." "We lie, and do not the truth." This antithetic parallelism is a most obvious and pervasive characteristic of the style of John's First Epistle; but it is less prominent in the prologue, though we find three or four instances of it in the latter. With it may be associated his habit of presenting two slightly different aspects of the inner life in successive clauses. "Love not the world, neither the things that are in the world." "Whosoever sinneth hath not seen him, neither known him." "Whatsoever is begotten of God overcometh the world; and this is the victory that hath overcome the world, even our faith" (Rev. Ver.).

Again, with a certain Hebraic simplicity of style, John is wont to express an idea in its absolute, unqualified form: "Whosoever is begotten of God doeth no sin, because his seed abideth in him; and he cannot sin, because he is begotten of God" (Rev. Ver.). "If any man love the world, the love of the Father is not in him." Any qualification of such a statement will generally be found in some other passage which, taken by itself, is equally unqualified. "If we say that we have no sin, we deceive ourselves, and the truth is not in us." Such a style betokens one who looks at the nature of things, and sees the perfect whole in the smallest part—one who bears witness of what he perceives, instead of appealing to argument in support of what he believes. To him truth is an atmosphere of light, vast, limitless, covering the whole face of the sky, rather than distinct lines of light, piercing the darkness here and there. Moreover, the light is golden, full of heat as well as splendor.

This great, yet simple, way of enunciating truth is, however, accompanied by a certain uniformity of style and a somewhat persistent repetition of the same thought. Every sentence is deep, intense, powerful. But now and then the light which gleams from the apostle's page without interruption, and spreads itself over a boundless sky of truth, concentrates its energy at a single point and dazzles the soul with its brightness. When we read such expressions as the following (in Rev. Ver.): "He that doeth sin is of the devil; for the devil sinneth from the beginning," "Every spirit which confesseth not Jesus, is not of God," and "Who is a liar but he that denieth that Jesus is the Christ? This is Antichrist," we understand why this disciple was surnamed "son of thunder." (Comp. John 8: 47; 8: 42; 8: 44.) Yet the style of John, as a whole, gives the reader a sense of elevated uniformity as one of its prominent characteristics. It is like a sunset sky, covered with golden clouds that overlap and gradually melt into each other. It reminds one of a "solemn music," with variations of the same theme, until the spirit of it penetrates the whole being of the listener. It deals with a few all-embracing conceptions in almost mystical language, but with simple grandeur of expression. There is progress, ascent, but, as has been said, by a kind of spiral movement, which brings the mind round to the same view again and again, though in every

INTRODUCTION TO THE GOSPEL. 45

instance at a higher point of observation. Another trait of John's style appears in the use of cardinal ideas and words, such as Life and Death, Light and Darkness, Truth and Falsehood, Love and Hatred, Believing and Disbelieving, Righteousness and Sin, Propitiation and Forgiveness, the World, Antichrist, etc. Many of these terms are figurative, some of them elastic, all of them rich in meaning.

Thus the style of John differs from that of any other New Testament writer. And the study of Christ's longer discourses preserved in his Gospel will bring to view a marked resemblance in style between the Master and his disciples. Let us now return to the beginning of the second, stormy period of the Lord's ministry for the purpose of looking at some of these discourses. That period was initiated by *healing an infirm man* in one of the five porches of the Pool of Bethesda, which was by the Sheep-gate. (Notice the particularity of the description). The words of Jesus to the man were few. *Wouldest thou be made whole?* (Rev. Ver.), and, *Arise, take up thy bed and walk*. But the cure was wrought on a Sabbath day, and the leading Jews of the holy city, who were looking for a charge against Jesus, reproved the man who had been healed for taking up his bed on the Sabbath. He excused himself for the act by referring to the command of Jesus; and afterwards Jesus, finding him in the Temple, said: "*Behold, thou art made whole: sin no more, lest a worse thing befall thee* (Rev. Ver.). For some reason the man then informed the Jews that it was Jesus who had made him whole; and they began to persecute Jesus because he did these things on the Sabbath. And his response to their accusation was: *My Father worketh even until now, and I work*. "Therefore the Jews sought the more to kill him, because he not only brake the Sabbath, but also called God his own Father, making himself equal with God" (Rev. Ver.), and he proceeded to vindicate his course in truly remarkable terms. This vindication is, however, too long to be quoted, though a brief analysis of it may be given. It naturally falls into two parts, the first reasserting and amplifying his claim to be in a special sense the Son of God, doing his Father's work and will, and the second bringing forward the witnesses that attested his claim, but were stubbornly rejected by his persecutors. In the *first*, while passing by the charge of desecrating the Sabbath, and replying only to the graver charge of blasphemous assumption in claiming to be the Son of God, and thus, as the Jews conceived, setting himself in sharp antagonism to God, he affirms the closest union between himself and the Father, he declares himself the Son of God in so true and absolute a sense that it is morally impossible for him to start from himself as the source and end of his action, impossible for him to do anything save as he sees the Father engaged in doing it; and at the same time he declares himself to be so loved by the Father that the Father shows him all his work, and indeed performs it all in and by him, imparting spiritual life, raising the dead in the last day, and judging all mankind through the agency and person of the Son, to the end that men may honor the Son even as they honor the Father. In the *second*, he briefly re-affirms his inseparable union with the Father, and then brings forward in support of his claims the witness of John the Baptist, who was a lamp kindled and shining, the witness of the Father which had been given in his own Godlike works, and the witness of the Jewish Scriptures, which his enemies professed to revere as a source of life, but which they could not understand because of their self-seeking spirit.

Now it will be observed (1) that this defense and vindication of his claims is addressed to leading Jews, many of them probably scribes and lawyers belonging to the Sanhedrin, and therefore capable of understanding the drift and tenor of such a discourse. They were men familiar with the Scriptures, who could be reached and convinced in their present mood, if at all, not by parables, but by the boldest assertion of the highest truth concerning himself. (2) It relates to his own person and office. The scope of it from first to last agrees with the occasion of it. True, it is very bold in its reproof of his adversaries, but not bolder or sharper in this respect than much that is recorded in the other Gospels as having been said by him to the same class (*e. g.*, Matt. 21 : 31 ; 23 : 13-36). (3) It teaches with authority, and appeals to testimony in the same way as do some of Christ's discourses in the Synoptic Gospels (Matt. 7 : 29 ; 15 : 4). There is in it no subtle argumentation, no attempt to make everything clear to the logical understanding, no misapprehension of the character of his assailants, or persuasion that all they needed was light for the reason. Their moral bias was clearly perceived : " How can ye believe, who receive glory one of another, and the glory that cometh from the only God ye seek not ? " (Rev. Ver.). (4) It is a discourse well suited to the mind and heart of John, for it is a luminous assertion and vindication of his Master's divine Sonship and work. If the Jews were not moved by it to greater reverence for the Lord, this disciple, we may be certain, was. It is impossible to read his writings without perceiving in him a capacity for such instruction. His loving spirit would drink in every word of it. From it he may have first learned the lesson that Christ is our life. " Verily, verily, I say unto you, He that heareth my word, and believeth him that sent me, hath eternal life, and cometh not into judgment, but hath passed out of death into life. . . . For as the Father hath life in himself, even so gave he to the Son to have life in himself " (Rev. Ver.). Bearing in mind all these facts, it is evidently unnecessary to ascribe to John any influence modifying the style or thought of this discourse.

The next considerable discussion of Jesus recorded in the Fourth Gospel took place in Capernaum, the day after the feeding of the five thousand. In a certain way it grew out of that miracle, and its figurative language was connected with it. For some of the thousands who had been miraculously fed in a desert place on the northeast shore of Gennesaret, and had wished thereupon to take Jesus by force and make him king, found him the next day on the west side of the lake, and said : " Rabbi, when camest thou hither ? " As often, the Lord took no notice of their question, but adapted his word to their spiritual condition. " Ye seek me, not because ye saw signs, but because ye ate of the loaves, and were filled. Work not for the meat which perisheth, but for the meat which abideth unto eternal life, which the Son of man shall give unto you, for him the Father, *even* God, hath sealed " (Rev. Ver.). Thus Jesus announces himself as the *Giver* of true and abiding food for the souls of men. The people, however, catch at the idea of "working," and ask : "What must we do that we may work the works of God?" And the answer came : "This is the work of God, that ye believe on him whom he hath sent" (Rev. Ver.). But in response to this demand for faith in himself, they ask for a sign from heaven to justify such faith, reminding Jesus of the manna which was given to their ancestors in the desert. To this Jesus replies by denying that the manna was given by Moses, as they appear to have been thinking, and by affirming that his Father was now giving them the true bread from heaven—a bread that giveth life to the world. Scarcely comprehending this, and doubtless associating it with the long continued supply of manna, they cried : " Lord, evermore give us this bread " ; and Jesus answered : " I am the bread of life : he that cometh unto me shall never hunger, and he that believeth on me shall never thirst." The Jews were naturally offended at this saying, and pronounced it inconsistent with their knowledge of his earthly parents ; but he repeated and amplified it, declaring, among other things, that the fathers who ate manna in the wilderness died, while any man who should eat of himself, the living bread that had come down out of heaven, should not die. And to this he added: "Yea, and the bread that I will give is my flesh, for the life of the world" (Rev. Ver.); an expression which led to still further debate. "How can this man give us his flesh to eat?" But Jesus persisted in his form of teaching, and even carried the representation a little further. "Except ye eat the flesh of the Son of man and drink his blood, ye have not life in yourselves. He that eateth my flesh and drinketh my blood abideth in me, and I in him" (Rev. Ver.),—thus affirming that divine life could only be secured by a vital union with himself as one who had suffered death.

Such is a brief sketch of what the Saviour said to the Jews at Capernaum, and the question to be considered is this: Has John reported his Master correctly? Or has he unintentionally changed the substance or form of that Master's teaching? In favor of John's report may be mentioned: (1) The obvious connection between the figurative language of Jesus and the circumstances of the hour. Nothing can be more natural than the way in which Christ introduces the idea of spiritual food, and then represents that it had been sent from heaven in his own person. This finally leads him to speak of his death, of his flesh and blood, as the one source of true life to men. And according to the first three Gospels, as well as the Fourth, Jesus was accustomed to make use of natural objects or passing events to set forth in a striking manner the facts or laws of his kingdom. (2) Those parts of the Gospel in which John uses his own language, do not possess all the qualities of paragraphs here ascribed to Jesus. They make, *e. g.*, less abundant use of illustration. I may be mistaken, but these paragraphs seem to me to approach much nearer the manner of teaching ascribed to Jesus by the Synoptical Gospels than do the First Epistle of John and the prologue. (3) The subsequent remarks of Jesus on this occasion bear the stamp of historic truth. Jesus, knowing that his disciples were murmuring at his final saying, added: "Doth this cause you to stumble? What then if ye should behold the Son of man ascending where he was before? It is the spirit that quickeneth; the flesh profiteth nothing: the words that I have spoken unto you are spirit, and are life. But there are some of you that believe not" (Rev. Ver.). And when he saw many of his disciples leaving him, he said to this twelve: "Will ye also go away?" The noble answer of Peter did not deceive the Lord, who, foreseeing the unfaithfulness of Judas, remarked, sadly: "Have I not chosen you twelve, and one of you is a devil?"

The next conversation of Jesus which requires notice is preserved in the seventh and eighth chapters. The scene of it was Jerusalem, at the Feast of Tabernacles, and the persons with whom it was held were "the Jews" who had sought to kill him for healing a man on the Sabbath, and yet more for "making God his own Father." It is clear from the colloquy between Jesus and his brothers before the latter went up to the feast, from his manner of going up at a later day, *i. e.*, "not publicly, but as it were in secret," and from the way in which he was received, that "the Jews" had lost none of their hostility to him. Naturally enough, therefore, what he said to them was very similar in tone and substance to what he is represented in the fifth chapter as saying to them. And if that could be rationally accounted for by supposing the language of Christ to have been adapted by him to the persons addressed, this can be accounted for in the same way.

The ninth chapter contains an account of the giving of sight to a man who had been born blind, and of the deadly enmity of "the Jews," which was rendered more intense by that great miracle. In the first part of the tenth chapter Jesus speaks of himself as the Good Shepherd that giveth his life for the sheep, and in the last part he asserts once more his divine Sonship. The raising of Lazarus from the dead is narrated in the eleventh chapter, and the triumphal entrance of Jesus into Jerusalem, with the brief sayings or discussions which followed that exciting event, are reported in the twelfth.

The next four chapters (13–16) are filled with a narrative of Christ's last passover with his disciples, and a record of his incomparable words to them in view of his impending crucifixion. It should not be an occasion of surprise that this discourse differs in style and thought from any other attributed to Jesus by the Evangelists. How could it have failed to be different? The occasion had no parallel in his ministry. If we say that this discourse is more unlike his denunciation of the Pharisees in Matthew's Gospel than David's elegy over Saul and Jonathan is unlike the Second Psalm, it is only necessary to observe that the contrast between the occasions was more marked in the former instance than in the latter. The words of Jesus were in both instances, as far as we can judge, perfectly suited to the occasion. Here it was his last interview before the crucifixion with his dearest and truest followers—men whom he knew far better than they knew themselves, and whom he loved with more than a brother's affection. Before himself were shame, agony, torture, and death. Before them, a trial too great for the strongest to bear, a blow so terrible that by it they would all be stunned. Yet with what matchless forecast, tenderness, and love does he speak to them of the many mansions in his Father's house, of his oneness of spirit with the Father, of their vital union with himself, of the divine Advocate whom he would send to abide with them forever, and of other blessings equally precious, until the reader who enters somewhat into the spirit of the record is lost in wonder at the "sweetness and light" which flow in his words. And now, having communed as never before with his disciples, Jesus offers to the Father a prayer which, while it seeks for himself and for them and for believers in all times just that which the holiest most crave as the highest good, completes the impression which he desires to make on their hearts.

From this rapid glance at the principal discourses of Jesus in the Fourth Gospel, it appears that the mental conditions or special circumstances of those addressed were such as might lead him to speak much of himself, of his Sonship to the Father, of his doing the Father's will, of his relations to believers, of his sacrificial death for mankind, of the deeper personal and vital aspects of union with himself, and of the Spirit's work in days to come. And if it is rational to believe that Nicodemus, an educated, thoughtful, half-convinced, but over-cautious or timid ruler of the Jews,—that a woman of Sychar, having a sense of sin smouldering in her soul, and with it an expectation of the Messiah as a religious teacher, without the disturbing influence of looking for him as a civil ruler, —that Jewish leaders who had resolved to kill Jesus, because he had violated their regulations as to keeping the Sabbath by doing cures on that day, and their ideas of reverence to Jehovah by claiming to be the Son of God,—that a multitude who had set their hearts on making Jesus an earthly king, while they were indifferent to his kingship in the realm of truth and eternal life,—and that the eleven faithful disciples, just after his last passover with them, and just before his betrayal, were each and all in spiritual conditions that called for such teaching as John has recorded, we may certainly believe that it was uttered by Christ, and merely reproduced by the Evangelist. For precisely this part of the Saviour's teaching was suited to the nature of John, and likely to sink down into his spirit. And that which attracts the soul will influence its character

INTRODUCTION TO THE GOSPEL.   49

and action. The type of thought and expression which awakens the deepest response within, will re-appear in language, and send its echo out into the world.

Hence, the resemblance between the style of John and that of Jesus in the discourses reported by John, is partly due to the influence which Christ's deeper teaching had upon the thought and style of his devoted follower. John was not great enough to supplement or change the teaching of his Master; but he was great enough to be moulded in an extraordinary degree by that which was highest in the personality and teaching of that Master. Again, this resemblance is partly due to the mental constitution of John, which was doubtless predisposed to the peculiar type of thought and expression found in his First Epistle. And, therefore, if Jesus had always spoken as the Synoptists lead us to suppose that he generally spoke, the style of John would doubtless have resembled in some degree that which we see in his First Epistle. But if Jesus had always spoken after the Synoptic pattern, it may be doubted whether John would have been chosen by the Spirit of God to write a Gospel, or, indeed, have been drawn to Jesus as powerfully as he manifestly was. Once more, the resemblance of John's style to that of certain discourses of Christ preserved by him, may be closer than it would have been if he had given all the words spoken by Christ in those discourses. No doubt his reports are but epitomes, and it may therefore be presumed that he has omitted sentences and illustrations that were less significant and impressive to his mind than those which are given. For the Holy Spirit avails himself, as far as possible, of the special powers and tendencies of those whom he inspires. Finally, the resemblance in question may be closer than it would have been if John had given us, in all cases, the *ipsissima verba*, instead of the essential thoughts of his Master. But it was impossible for him to do the former, unless he had written his Gospel in the Aramaean dialect used by Jesus. And it was likewise unnecessary; for it is the facts, the principles, the thoughts, expressed by Christ, rather than the particular words employed in doing this, which reveal to men their moral ruin and the way of recovery. The words may be changed by translation, by paraphrase, by condensation, by repetition, without serious loss, provided the essential thoughts are neither mutilated nor distorted. Many illustrations and applications of truth may be omitted without harm to the reader, if only what is given be given with substantial accuracy. For "the heavens," though we see but a part of them, "declare the glory of God." John himself calls attention to the fact that his record is incomplete, but he nowhere intimates that it may be incorrect. Yet the fragmentary character of a record, though it be correct as far as it goes, is likely to make it appear abrupt, disconnected, and perhaps in some degree obscure. It is not therefore surprising that imperfections of such a nature are found in the Fourth Gospel. All history, in proportion to its veracity, contains them. Any alleged record of human life on a large scale that shows in full the connection of events, so that all the reasons for the actions narrated are manifest, must be fictitious—ideal instead of real. Hence, the broken connections, the obscure passages in the Gospels, are in reality signs of their veracity, marks of historical trustworthiness. Bearing in mind these considerations, we are unable to discover any solid grounds for withholding our confidence from John's record of the Lord's discourses. That record we receive as the testimony of an honest, intelligent, inspired witness, giving us the essential truth without admixture of real error.

We do not forget that Biblical scholars have often denied to John the authorship of the Fourth Gospel, on the ground that he wrote the Book of Revelation. For it is incredible, they aver, that the same man could have written two books so unlike each other in thought and expression as these. The difference asserted, and its bearing on the question of authorship, have been briefly discussed by Dr. Smith, in his Introduction to the Book of Revelation ; but a few remarks may be added in this place : (1) The difference of thought between the two books is not doctrinal but practical. The object of the Gospel is not the same as that of the Apocalypse. For the former aims to produce belief in Christ as the Saviour of individual men who trust in him, while the latter aims to strengthen confidence in Christ as One who is able to do battle with organized sin, and overcome the world at last. But, in so far as the person and work of Christ are concerned, the doctrinal basis of the two books is identical. (2) The difference of expression may be partially explained. *First*, by the fact that one of the books is historical, and the other apocalyptical. While writing the former, the author's mind was engaged in a deeply interesting, but calm review of the past, and in a careful statement of familiar events ; but while writing the latter, it was "in the Spirit," rapt, entranced, and filled with wondrous visions of glory or terror. Even if the act of writing or dictating followed after the last vision was seen, it must have been performed before the ecstatic condition and illumination had entirely passed away. *Secondly*, by the fact that the two writings were not probably composed in the same period of John's life. An interval of fifteen or twenty years may lie between them. If the Gospel was written as early as A. D. 80, and the Revelation as late as A. D. 98 or 100, John had passed from the age of about seventy-five, to the age of about ninety-five, and it is certainly credible that his use of an acquired language may have been less careful at the greater age than it was at the less. When a man reaches an advanced period of life, he sometimes falls back in his forms of speech to the habits of youth. *Thirdly*, by the possible circumstance that the language of John, in the Apocalypse, was taken down by a less scholarly amanuensis than the one by whom his Gospel was written out. For an amanuensis may be supposed to mend or mar the language of his principal, in a grammatical respect, without failing to give every word dictated. Especially if the Gospel is supposed to have been dictated to an intelligent Greek, can we account for its grammatical correctness ; for by his aid the Hebrew thought of John might have been expressed in grammatical Greek ; while this might not have been always the case with a less Grecian amanuensis. (3) The similarity of style in the two books should not be overlooked. For this is marked and undeniable. In both the construction is simple and Hebraistic, perhaps equally so. The narrative parts of the Gospel remind us of the story of Joseph in Genesis ; the symbolical descriptions of the Apocalypse recall the style of certain passages in Ezekiel and Daniel. In neither do we meet with anything that is suggestive of Greek habits of thought or expression. Indeed, the difference of vocabulary between the books is sufficiently accounted for by the difference of themes, while the similarity is such as to favor the tradition of a single author. (4) The evidence of John's authorship of the Apocalypse is not really equal to that for his authorship of the Fourth Gospel and the first Epistle. For Eusebius, who had access to a large amount of early Christian literature, since lost, reckons the Gospel and the Epistle among the undisputed books ; and his treatment of the Gospel, shows that he felt it wholly unnecessary to cite testimonies in its favor. But the same cannot be said of the Book of Revelation. Its apostolic authorship had been questioned before that time by certain Christians, and Eusebius himself, perhaps on doctrinal grounds, entertained doubts respecting it. As a matter of fact, therefore, if Eusebius is to be trusted, the testimony of the early church is stronger in support of the Gospel than it is in support of the Apocalypse. And if the question were to be answered by an appeal to the judgment of Irenæus,

INTRODUCTION TO THE GOSPEL. 51

Clement of Alexandria, Origen, and Tertullian, who flourished a hundred years earlier, the same conclusion would be reached. We believe, however, that both writings are genuine, and the work of the same apostle; but if either were to be denied him it should not be the Gospel.

III. TIME AND PLACE OF ITS COMPOSITION.

No external or internal evidences are conclusive as to the precise date of this Gospel. But ecclesiastical tradition points to a time after the other genuine Gospels had been written, and indeed after the destruction of Jerusalem by Titus in the year 70. Irenæus, whose early life was spent in Asia Minor, and who must have been familiar, through Polycarp, with the work of John in Ephesus, speaks of the first three Gospels as prepared by Matthew, Mark, and Luke, and then says: "Afterwards John, the disciple of our Lord, the same that lay upon his bosom, also published the Gospel whilst he was yet at Ephesus in Asia" ("Adv. Hær." III. i. 1). Clement of Alexandria states that: "Last of all, John, perceiving that what had reference to the body in the Gospel of our Saviour was made known in the Gospels [already extant], and being encouraged by his familiar friends and moved by the Spirit, made a spiritual Gospel" (Euseb. "H. E." VI. 14). Jerome repeats the same tradition, adding to it several particulars. Moreover, the character of the Gospel favors the view that it was the last of the four, and especially does the way in which "the Jews" are spoken of imply that the writer had been absent many years from his land and people. Westcott assigns the origin of this Gospel without hesitation to "the last quarter of the first century," and thinks that it may belong "in its present form to the last decennium of that period." He also remarks that "this late date of the writing is scarcely of less importance than its peculiarly personal character, if we would form a correct estimate of the evidence which establishes its early use and authority."

There is a similar lack of indubitable testimony as to the place where this Gospel was written. Yet the best evidence within our reach points clearly to Ephesus. For early tradition represents John as making that city his residence and the centre of his apostolic ministry during the last part of his long life; and, as we have just seen, Irenæus declares that he wrote the Gospel there. Polycrates, Bishop of Ephesus about A. D. 190, testifies that "John, who leaned on the bosom of our Lord and was a priest that bore the sacerdotal plate, as well as a martyr and teacher, rests also at Ephesus" (Euseb. "H. E." III. 20). According to Irenæus, he lived until the time of Trajan (A. D. 98). He also speaks of his meeting with Cerinthus the heretic in a bath, and of his rushing out of the place, declaring that he dare not remain under the same roof with this enemy of the truth ("Adv. Hær." III. 3, 4). Clement of Alexandria has placed on record the story of a young man whom John in his old age recovered from a course of robbery and sin into which he had fallen after conversion. (See *Quis dives salutem consequi possit*, c. 42). And Jerome relates that, when very old and feeble, so that he could not walk, he had himself carried to the meetings of the church, and there, when he could say no more, repeated the words: *Little children, love one another* (In "Epist. ad Galatos," VI. 10). We may, therefore, rationally hold that this Gospel was written between the years A. D. 75 and A. D. 85, in the city of Ephesus.

IV. THE OCCASION, OBJECT, AND PLAN OF THE WORK.

In the Fragment on the Canon discovered by Muratori, it is said that John was exhorted by his fellow-disciples and bishops to engage in writing the Gospel, and that he asked them to fast with him three days, for the purpose of obtaining from the Lord a message in relation to the apostle's duty. It is also said that Andrew, one of the apostles, received the same night a revelation that John should describe all things in his own name, though all should review it. Jerome appears to have given credit to a similar tradition, for he relates that "John last of all wrote a Gospel, when asked to do so by the bishops of Asia, against Cerinthus and other heretics, and especially against the rising dogma of the Ebionites, who asserted that Christ did not exist before Mary" ("Catal. Script. Eccl." c. 9). It is therefore possible that the external occasion for this Gospel was a request of his fellow-disciples who were serving the churches of Asia Minor. This, perhaps, is all that can be safely affirmed; for some have urged that the story may have been invented to account for the last verse of the Gospel. Yet we detect in it no features of extravagance, and believe it may be true.

But the religious purpose or object of the Gospel is of far greater interest to us than its external occasion. What was there at that time in the state of the churches, or in the thought of the world, which called for another Gospel, presenting new aspects of the Saviour's teaching? The early Christian writers do not perfectly agree in their answers to this question. Irenæus declares that John wrote his Gospel "to remove from the minds of men the error which Cerinthus had sown therein, and still earlier, the Nicolaitans .... also to establish in the church the rule of truth, that there is one God Almighty, who, by his Word, created all things, visible and invisible," etc. ("Adv. Hær." III. 11. 1). Different from this is the statement of Clement of Alexandria, to which reference has already been made, namely, that "John last, perceiving that the bodily things [relating to Christ] had been made manifest in the Gospels [previously written], being also encouraged by his intimate friends and moved by the Spirit of God, made a spiritual Gospel," ("H. E." VI. 14). Eusebius himself defends another view, namely, that John wrote his Gospel to supply the deficiencies of the first three, particularly their omission of any narrative of Christ's ministry before the imprisonment of John the Baptist. "For these reasons the Apostle John, it is said, being entreated to undertake it, wrote the account of the time not recorded by the former Evangelists .... giving the deeds of Jesus before the Baptist was cast into prison .... It is probable, therefore, that John passed by, in silence, the genealogy of our Lord, because it was written by Matthew and Luke, but commenced with the doctrine of the divinity, as a part reserved for him, by the Divine Spirit, as if for a superior" ("H. E." III. 24).

There may be some truth in every one of these representations. The erroneous teaching of that period may have led the Evangelist to select for his Gospel such words and deeds of the Lord as would be likely to counteract and eradicate that insidious teaching. Again, the circumstance that the earlier Evangelists had put on record many of the parables and more popular sayings of Jesus, may have led John to see the need of preserving some part of his deeper instruction concerning his union with the Father, and the spiritual nature of his reign. And precisely this instruction may have been better fitted than any other to meet the errors which were at that time beginning to sap the foundations of faith in Christ. And lastly, the apostle may have remembered that Jesus began to assert his divine origin and power in Judea during the period of his ministry that had not been described by the earlier Evangelists, and their silence may have been an additional reason for including in his narrative some account of that period. But, while this must be admitted, the question may arise whether any of these statements rest upon tradition reaching back to the time of John. May not all of them have been inferences from the character of the Book itself? Possibly; though the relation of Irenæus to the Elders of the School of John in Asia Minor leads us to regard his testimony of some historical value. Besides, the narrative concerning John and the young robber, which Clement of Alexandria relates, renders it probable that he was familiar with some of the Asiatic disciples; and the reference which Eusebius makes to common report, by "it is said," forbids us to suppose that he is giving a mere conjecture of his own.

Yet we find no clear evidence in the Gospel itself that it was written with a distinct purpose of supplying deficiencies in earlier narratives, or of resisting the beginnings of error, or of giving to Christians the more spiritual aspects of their Lord's life. If the apostle had any of these things in mind, they must have been altogether subordinate to the one comprehensive aim which he avows near the close of his narrative: "Many other signs therefore did Jesus in the presence of the disciples, which are not written in this book: *but these are written, that ye may believe that Jesus is the Christ, the Son of God; and that believing, ye may have life in his name.*" Here we have a definite statement of the object for which the Gospel was written. With this key in his possession, the interpreter may unlock the rooms of this divine treasure-house, and bring out of it stores of truth and grace. It is needless to attempt any explanation of this key, any restatement of that which has been so clearly and powerfully expressed.

But how did the writer accomplish, or seek to accomplish his object? What is the plan of his great argument? Apparently, a very simple one. The Evangelist first gives his own view of the Lord Jesus, and then justifies that view by a recital of such passages from the history of Jesus—including his death and resurrection—as prove it to be correct. Possibly it would be more exact to say that he justifies the truth of his own view, given in the prologue, by a selection and recital of certain words and deeds and events in the history of Jesus which had been principal sources of his own belief and spiritual life. In doing this, he generally follows the order of time, and testifies of what he has himself seen or heard.

A. *During the first and peaceful period:* (1 : 19 ; 4 : 54). (1) The witness of John the Baptist, (*a*) before the deputation of Pharisees from Jerusalem, to the priority and superiority of Jesus (1: 20 : 27) ; (*b*) before his own disciples, to his being the Lamb of God (1 : 36), the Son of God (1 : 34), the Christ, and the Bridegroom of God's people (3 : 28-30). (2) The witness of Jesus as to himself by works and words ; (*a*) by miraculous signs, as at the wedding in Cana of Galilee (2: 1-11), in the expulsion of traders from the Temple (2: 13-22), in miracles at Jerusalem (2: 23; 3: 2), and in healing the nobleman's son from a distance (4:47-54) ; (*b*) by words manifesting or claiming that he had superhuman knowledge as to Peter (1: 42), and Nathanael (1: 48), that he was the Son of God and King of Israel (1: 49, 50), that he had special communion with heaven (1: 51), that he possessed power to raise his dead body to life again (2: 19, 21), that he had direct knowledge of heavenly things, because he had been in heaven (3: 12, 13), that belief in himself as "lifted up" on the cross, was the condition of eternal life (3: 14, 15), that he was the giver of the water of life (4: 10, 14), and, indeed, the expected Messiah (4: 25, 26).

B. *During the second or controversial period* (5: 1-12 : 50). (1) The further witness of Jesus as to himself, (*a*) by healing the infirm man on the Sabbath (5: 2–9), by feeding the five thousand men (6: 5–14), by giving sight to a man who had been blind from birth (9: 1–7), and by raising Lazarus from the dead (11: 3–44); and (2) by asserting, after the first miracle, his special Sonship to the Father, and unity in knowledge and action with him (5: 17, 19–30); by asserting, after the second miracle, that he was, himself, God's bread out of heaven, and so the source of eternal life to those who should believe in him (6: 27–40), and, indeed, that only such as received him as slain for them could have that life (6: 51–58), also that he was the Light of the world (8: 12), and One who had a timeless existence like God's (8: 58); by affirming, after the third miracle, that he was the Son of God (9: 36, 37), and, still later, that he was the Door of the sheep, and the good Shepherd, giving his life for the sheep (10: 7, 11, 15), having power, by virtue of his oneness with the Father, to keep all the flock (10: 28–30); and by affirming, in connection with the last miracle, that he was himself the Resurrection and the Life to those who should believe in him (11: 25), and, soon after, that, by being lifted up from the earth at death, he would draw all men unto himself (12: 32). This is only a brief sketch of his answers and discussions pertaining to his nature and work.

C. *During the third and final period* (13: 1; 21: 25). (1) By exhorting his disciples to belief in him as well as in God (14: 1), by declaring that he was the Way and the Truth and the Life (14: 6), a knowledge of whom was a knowledge of the Father (14: 7), also that he was the true Vine, in whom they must abide as branches, in order to have spiritual life (15: 1–6), that he would send them the Holy Spirit to be their Advocate (14: 16, 17; 15: 26; 16: 7–15), and that a knowledge of the Father and the Son was eternal life (17: 3), also by testifying before Pilate that he was King in the realm of highest truth (18: 37, 38); (2) finally, by rising from the dead on the third day (20: 1 sq.): by breathing upon his disciples, and saying : " Receive ye the Holy Spirit " (20: 22), by accepting divine homage from Thomas (20: 28), and by reinstating Peter in the apostleship (21: 15 sq.). In connection with all these claims to a divine nature and office, there is a plain recognition of his human nature, with all its normal limitations.

V. AIM AND SOURCES OF THIS COMMENTARY.

The writer's aim in preparing this volume has been to ascertain, if possible, the exact meaning of the sacred text, and then to state that meaning with the utmost clearness consistent with suitable brevity. Yet in doing this it has been deemed important to keep always in view the practical bearing of the Saviour's words, and to call attention frequently to that bearing. Not critical processes, but simply the results of such processes, have been thought to be entitled to any considerable space in a work designed for the people. And, in so far as this aim of the writer has been realized in the Commentary, will it be found, he is confident, useful as an explanation of Holy Scripture to readers of every class. But owing to the exceeding riches of the Fourth Gospel in the deep things of God and of his Son Jesus Christ, the work must fail to correspond in all respects with the ideal contemplated. Of this the writer is profoundly conscious. Yet the study of the Gospel has been delightful and quickening, even though the attempt to express the thoughts of the Master in words different from those chosen by himself, or by the disciple whom he loved, has often seemed to be ineffectual, if not irreverent. For, verily, beneath the tranquil surface of this Gospel, which is filled to so great an extent with what the Lord himself said, are deep and fervid ocean-currents of holy

INTRODUCTION TO THE GOSPEL.

life and love, which no one can undertake to explore and describe without being made to feel the dimness of his vision and the feebleness of his speech.

But while the text of the Gospel itself has been studied with special and principal care, the writer has made constant use of the best commentaries and monographs within his reach, and has derived from them important aid. Not unfrequently have citations been made from some of these works, but their helpfulness has been greater than would be inferred from the passages borrowed from them. Among the books that have been consulted with reference to the authorship of the Gospel may be named the anonymous work entitled, "Supernatural Religion," (6 ed.); especially Vol. II., and the article on the "Fourth Gospel," in the ninth edition of the "Encyclopædia Britannica," besides a great number of volumes or articles by German scholars who deny that this Gospel was written by the Apostle John. In favor of the Johannean authorship may be named Westcott "On the Canon of the New Testament," (5 ed.); Bleek, "Introduction to the New Testament," S. 71 ; Sanday (W.), "Authorship and Character of the Fourth Gospel"; Abbot (Ezra), "The Authorship of the Fourth Gospel"; several articles in the "Contemporary Review" for 1875, by Lightfoot ; also Luthardt, "St. John, the Author of the Fourth Gospel," which gives in the Appendix a list of the most valuable works on the subject published between 1792 and 1875. To these may be added, "Canonicity, A Collection of Early Testimonies to the Canonical Books of the New Testament," by Prof. Charteris, of Edinburgh. Among the commentaries which have been used most freely, the following deserve to be mentioned, viz.: those of Gill, Alford, McClellan, Westcott, Watkins, Abbot, Clark, Milligan and Moulton, in English; those of Lücke, De Wette, Luthardt, Meyer, Hengstenberg, Ewald, and Weiss-Meyer, in German; those of Calvin, Lampe, and Bengel, in Latin ; and that of Godet, in French. In the examination of the Greek text the critical labors of Tischendorf, Tregelles, Westcott and Hort, Scrivener, Burgon, Abbot, and McClellan, have been consulted; also Schaff's "Companion to the Greek Testament and English Version."

THE GOSPEL ACCORDING TO JOHN.

CHAPTER I.

IN the beginning *a* was the Word, and the Word *b* was with God,*c* and the Word was God.

1 In the beginning was the Word, and the Word

a Prov. 8: 22, 23, etc.; Col. 1: 17; 1 John 1: 1; Rev. 1: 2; 19: 13....*b* Prov. 8: 30; ch. 17: 5; 1 John 1: 2....*c* Phil. 2: 6; 1 John 5: 7.

The object for which John wrote the Fourth Gospel is stated by himself in the following words: "These are written, that ye may believe that Jesus is the Christ, the Son of God; and that believing ye may have life in his name" (20: 31, Rev. Ver.). For, though the term "these" refers only to "the signs" narrated by the Evangelist, it may be certainly inferred from the uniform tendency of the Gospel that the writer's choice of "the sayings," as well as of "the signs" to be recorded by him, was influenced greatly by the object which is here named.

Ch. 1: 1-18. THE PROLOGUE.

With this the prologue agrees; for it introduces the narrative which is to prove that Jesus is the Christ, the Son of God, by a statement concerning his being and work which, for simplicity, completeness, and depth, has never been approached. By this remarkable statement the reader is furnished beforehand with an interpretation of all that follows, and is invited, as it were, to compare the evidence with the interpretation—if it would not rather be more correct to say, that by it the reader is prepared, in some measure, to interpret aright the subsequent narrative of the wonderful words and works of Jesus.

This introduction to the narrative embraces eighteen verses, and may be divided into three parts. The *first* (ver. 1-5) speaks of the original being and the permanent offices of the Word; the *second* (ver. 6-13), of the treatment of the God-revealing Word by men; and the *third* (ver. 14-18), of the incarnation of the Word, by which God was most clearly revealed to men.

1-5. ORIGINAL BEING AND PERMANENT OFFICES OF THE WORD.

In this part of the introduction the apostle speaks with absolute certainty of the original existence, condition, and nature of the Word, of his agency in the creation of all things, and of his work in revealing God to men.

It will be observed that the Being of whom the writer speaks in this paragraph is called *the Word;* and from ver. 14 it appears that this expression is used to denote the higher nature of Christ before that nature "was made flesh." Why this designation was applied to that nature in its pre-incarnate state, is not explained; yet it may be safely assumed that, whatever else recommended it to the apostle, its own proper meaning was the principal reason for his choice of it.

In human intercourse, it is the proper office of "the word" to reveal thought, feeling, purpose, character. By "rational speech," the natural and best medium of expression, the spirit of man, itself invisible, makes known its being and will to others. And therefore, if the existence and perfection of God were revealed from the beginning by the higher nature of Christ which, in the fullness of time, became flesh, no other designation of that nature could have been more appropriate than the one selected by John for this paragraph. But the Evangelist affirms, in his own way, that the being and character of God *were* thus revealed. "In him was life, and the life was the light of men." With the utmost propriety, then, this Being is called "The Word," that is to say, the One through whom God made himself known to mankind.

But how did John know that the Being who was made flesh in the person of Jesus Christ, was the medium of divine revelation from the first? He knew this doubtless by the inspiration of the Holy Spirit, who had been sent, according to the Saviour's promise, to guide the apostles "into all truth" (16: 13). But in what way did the Spirit of Truth impart a knowledge of divine things to the apostles? He appears to have done this chiefly by such action upon their spiritual

57

powers as enabled them to recall and comprehend the instructions of Christ, and also those of the ancient Scriptures. In other words, the truth which he revealed was, for the most part, evolved from what had been said or done before. Its roots were in the past; it was old as well as new; and we may therefore expect to find germs of it in the Jewish Scriptures, as well as in the sayings of the Lord.

Now, in the first chapter of Genesis, which could not well have been absent from the mind of John when he wrote the opening sentences of his Gospel, the word of God is represented, by a ninefold repetition, as the medium of his creative energy. By the sole agency of his word, he originated the cosmos —the world of order, beauty, and life, of which man is the crown. But there is here no personification of this word. It is powerful, simply because it is spoken by God. It originates order and beauty, simply because it is the vehicle of divine wisdom. Yet in one expression of this chapter: "Let us make man in our image," there is a mysterious hint of Divine Society, a passing glance at some plurality of a personal nature in the Godhead, though the hint does not represent the word of God as having any part in that Divine Society which is suggested by the pronouns "us" and "our."

But the ancient Scriptures offered more than this to the inspired understanding of John; for they spoke of a Being who was called the Angel of Jehovah, or of God, the angel that wrestled with Jacob and redeemed Israel from all evil, the angel of his presence, and the angel in whom was God's name, as if he were a special messenger of God, representing his authority and glory; while he was also called God, or, his Presence, Jehovah, or, I am that I am, as if he were the true God manifesting himself to men. And these various designations point to a Being who is in some respects identical with the invisible God, and in other respects distinguishable from him—to a Being through whom the true nature of God is revealed to men, and who may, therefore, be called, in the highest sense, the Word.

But the mind of John, quickened and guided by the Holy Spirit, would readily connect these suggestions of the Old Testament with many references that were made by Christ himself to his existence and state before the incarnation. For the Saviour had spoken, in the presence of his disciples, of the glory which he had with the Father before the world was; of himself as the only being who knew the Father and could reveal him to men; of his knowledge of heavenly things; of his coming into the world from above; and of his being the Life, the Light, and the Truth, in a pre-eminent sense: and these wonderful sayings, when added to the significant intimations of the Old Testament, and interpreted by a mind full of the Spirit of Truth, may have sufficed to give the Evangelist his surprising knowledge of the Divine Word; or, at least, may have prepared him for the direct illumination of the Spirit as to the office of the higher nature of Christ before the incarnation.

It is, therefore, unnecessary to suppose that the knowledge in question was imparted to John by the Spirit as a wholly new revelation, foreshadowed by nothing in the past, or that it was borrowed from any philosophical or Rabbinical source. Divine revelation is itself progressive; "first the blade, then the ear, then the full corn in the ear." The fountain from which the apostle drew, in writing the prologue, was neither the doctrine of Philo concerning the Logos, nor the doctrine of the scribes concerning the Memra or the Bath-Kôl, but it was the teaching of the prophets and of Christ, unfolded and complemented by the work of the Spirit. We do not, however, deny that the religious speculations of Philo, and other Jews, may have prepared the minds of Christian people, in some measure, to understand John's use of the term Logos. Never before, it may be, would the meaning which he put into this word, as a designation of the higher nature of Christ, have been so readily apprehended by those for whom his Gospel was written. Yet the doctrine of Philo as to the Logos is, in many respects, very different from that of John, and it is impossible to discover in his writings the source of John's Christology.

1. In the beginning was the Word. (Compare Gen. 1:1; 1 John 1:1, 2; John 17:5; Eph. 1:4; Rev. 3:14; Prov. 8:23.) This expression affirms the existence of the Word at the time referred to in the opening verse of Genesis, when God created the heavens and the earth. He, the Word, was already in being when that which before was not began to be. His existence, therefore, is without beginning, or eternal. This is a logical inference from the statement of John, and it is also suggested by the verb (ἦν) which he employs. For there are two Greek verbs by means of which he is wont to express the idea of existence, one of them signifying existence with an implication of origin, and the other signifying existence with no such implication. The latter word is used in this place, and in the last part of the declaration, "before Abraham was, I am" (8:58); while the former is used in verse 6, below: "There was (arose, appeared,) a man sent from God," and in the first member of the saying, "before Abraham was (came to be), I am." The eternal existence of the Word is, therefore, logically implied and verbally suggested in the first sentence of this Gospel. —And the Word was with God. (Compare 1 John 1:2; John 17:5; 1:18.) An expression which brings to mind the words of Genesis: "Let us make man in our image." For the preposition here used points to intimacy, and so to distinction of a personal nature between the Eternal Word and the God revealed by him. If the Evangelist had said "*in* God," it might have been supposed that he had in mind some attribute of God, *e. g.*, reason; if he had said *from* God, it might have been supposed that he had in mind something impersonal, issuing from God, as creative energy; but he has used a preposition which "expresses, beyond the fact of co-existence, or immanence, the more significant fact of perpetuated intercommunion."—*Liddon.* According to Godet, this preposition "expresses *proximity;* but, combining with this notion that of drawing near, it indicates an active relation—a felt and personal communion." (Compare Mark 6:3; 9:19; Matt. 13:56; 26:55; 1 Cor. 16:6 sq.; Gal. 1:18; 4:18.) And Westcott, commenting on the passage, remarks that "the idea expressed by" the phrase **was with** (ἦν πρός), "is not that of simple co-existence, as of two persons contemplated separately in company (εἶναι μετά 3:22), or united under a common conception (εἶναι σύν, Luke 22:56), or (so to speak) in local relation (εἶναι παρά 17:5), but of being (in some sense) directed towards and regulated by that with which the relation is fixed (5:19). The personal being of the Word was realized in active intercourse with and in perfect communion with God."

... "This life (1 John 1:2) 'was with the Father'; it was realized in the intercommunion of the Divine Persons when time was not." "This expression, as in 1 John 1:2, also denotes the presence of the Logos with God from the point of view of intercourse. ... So in all the other passages where it appears to mean simply *by* or *with.* Mark 6:3; 9:19; Matt. 13:56; 26:55; 1 Cor. 16:6 sq.; Gal. 1:18; 4:18."—*Weiss.*

The Word knows and loves the Father whom he reveals; his relation to God antedates and conditions his relation to man. With this proposition may be compared the words of Christ: "And now, Father, glorify thou me with thine own self with the glory which I had with thee before the world was" (17:5), and, "No one knoweth the Son, save the Father; neither doth any one know the Father save the Son, and he to whom the Son willeth to reveal him" (Matt. 11:27, Rev. Ver.); for these two sayings are a sufficient foundation for the statement that "the Word was with God." (See also 1 John 1:2.)

Having asserted the eternal existence and communion of the Word with God, the Evangelist adds another fact of supreme interest to his account of that Being, viz.—**And the Word was God.** This is the only correct translation of the clause; and it would have been difficult for John to construct a more definite and emphatic assertion of the proper deity of the Word. For the terms of this clause are so arranged in the original that, according to the laws of the Greek language, the emphasis falls upon the term God. Hence the Evangelist pronounces the pre-existent Word to be strictly and fully *Divine.* Although distinguishable in a personal respect from the Father, in essence and nature he was truly God. The construction of the sentence is precisely the same as that of John 4:24: "God is a Spirit," where by virtue of its position the term "spirit" is emphatic, and is used to define the nature and essence of God. (See also 1 John 1:5, "God is light," and John 3:29, "He that hath the bride is the bridegroom.") Meyer quotes from Luther the pithy remark, "The last proposition, *the Word was God*, is against Arius; the other, *the Word was with God*, against Sabellius."

2 ᵃThe same was in the beginning with God. 2 was with God, and the Word was God. The same 3 ᵇAll things were made by him; and without him 3 was in the beginning with God. All things were was not any thing made that was made. made through him; and without ¹him ²was not any-

a Gen. 1:1....*b* Ps. 33:6; ver. 10; Eph. 3:9; Col. 1:16; Heb. 1:2; Rev. 4:11.—1 Or, by....2 Or, was not anything made. That which hath been made was life in him: and the life, etc.

2. The same (or, *This one*) **was in the beginning with God.** The three propositions of the first verse are here reduced to one, and solemnly re-affirmed. For the pronoun (οὗτος), translated **The same,** appears to represent the Word as he is described in the last and highest assertion of that verse, an assertion which, on account of its meaning and position, must hold the first place in the mind of writer or of reader. This Being, himself by essence and nature God, was in the beginning with God, which emphatic repetition of the first verse prepares the way for the statement that follows in verse third. And the practice of repeating an important truth for the sake of emphasis, or of preparing the mind for some connected truth, is characteristic of this Evangelist's style.

3. All things were made by him. The Greek word translated **All things** (πάντα), means every object in the universe; not the universe as a great whole, made up of numberless parts, but all the parts, however numerous and dissimilar, that exist in the wide universe. All these owe their existence to the agency of the Word. Through him they *came to be* (ἐγένετο). For the term which is rendered **were made,** signifies in itself *became* or *came to be,* and only by virtue of its connection with an agent does it take the meaning **were made.** The preposition *by,* or *through* (διά), represents the Word as the mediating and proximate cause of the existence of all things, and, interpreted by other statements of Scripture, suggests the will of the Father as the first cause of their existence. By the agency, therefore, of the Word, the being and power of the invisible God were expressed in things created.—**And without him was not anything made that was made** (lit., *has been made*). The same thought is here repeated in a negative form. Not one of all the objects that have been brought into being and now exist, was made without him. Look abroad, O man, over the universe, and consider all its parts, great and small! There is not one of them which does not owe its existence to the agency of that Divine Word who was in the

beginning with God. With this declaration should be compared the language of Paul to the Colossians: "Who is the image of the invisible God, the first-born of all creation; for in him were all things created, in the heavens and upon the earth, things visible and things invisible, whether thrones or dominions or principalities or powers: all things have been created through him and unto him; and he is before all things; and in him all things consist" (1:15-17, Rev. Ver.).

It may be added that the statement of John in this verse appears to affirm the creation of everything that exists save the Godhead. For to say that "all things came into being" through the agency of the Word, is tantamount to saying that the entire reality, the substance as well as form of things, was due to the Word. This, to say the least, is the most obvious interpretation of the phrase, and there is nothing in the context which fairly suggests a different one. That Grecian philosophy pronounced matter eternal is no sufficient reason for supposing that the Evangelist believed it eternal, and, on that account, would not speak of it as created. It must now be added that many editors and interpreters close the third verse with the words, **without him was not anything made,** and begin the fourth verse thus: *That which hath been made was life in him.* But the early authorities are not conclusive; and if *that which hath been made* had been intended by the writer to go with what follows, he would surely have written "*is* life," instead of "**was** life"; or if, for any reason, the past tense had been here preferred, the previous verb would have been, *was made* (ἐγένετο), rather than *hath been made* (γέγονεν). Indeed, several manuscripts and versions have *is,* instead of **was**; but the evidence for **was** decidedly outweighs that for *is,* though *is* would have been more readily substituted for **was,** than **was** for *is,* by the early Fathers who generally connected *which hath been made* with what follows. We adhere then, with Weiss and a majority of modern scholars, to the ordinary punctuation as correct, even though we do

CH. I.] JOHN. 61

4 *In him was life; and *the life was the light of men.
5 And *the light shineth in darkness; and the darkness comprehended it not.

4 thing made that hath been made. In him was life;
5 and the life was the light of men. And the light shineth in the darkness; and the darkness ¹ appro-

a ch. 5: 26; 1 John 5: 11....b ch. 8: 12; 9: 5; 12: 35, 46....c ch. 3: 19.——1 Or, overcome. See ch. 12: 35 (Gr.).

not insist on the fact that the other punctuation introduces a mystical and unintelligible expression.

4.. In him was life; *i. e.*, life in the highest sense, spiritual life, springing evermore, in his case, from direct vision of God and perfect fellowship with him (compare 17: 3, and 1 John 1: 2). This seems to be the idea of true life from the religious point of view taken by the Evangelist. And the object of this sentence is to assert that life, in the truest and deepest sense of the word, belonged to the Logos from the beginning, thus preparing the reader's mind for what the Evangelist was about to state as the second office or work of the Word. This clause, therefore, stands in the same relation to the next as the second verse stands to the third. —**And the life was the light of men;** *i. e.*, **the life,** as it was realized in the Divine Word, spiritual, holy, blessed, consisting in perfect knowledge of the Father and communion with him. All true knowledge of God on the part of men has come from the Word. Through him, and through him alone, have men been enabled to see and know the Father of lights. All revelation of the Divine Being, whether to Israel or to the nations, has been mediated by him. This interpretation will be confirmed by a careful study of the Evangelist's use of terms and by the end for which his Gospel was written. But two questions may be asked: Why is life conceived of as the source or principle of light? And why is light made the symbol of divine revelation? If we can answer these questions, we shall be prepared in some degree to understand the Fourth Gospel. In answering the second question, it may be said that, in the natural world, light is the means of sight, and that so much of human knowledge depends on sight, and therefore on light, as to make it suitable to use the word light to denote any means of knowledge. To see is to know, and to know is to see, in the language of common life. We see an argument as clearly as we do a mountain, and we know a color as well as we do an axiom. Hence if divine revelation brings to men a knowledge of God, it is light, that is, a means of spiritual vision; and inasmuch as this knowledge is the highest and only satisfying knowledge, he who brings it, is pre-eminently "*the* light of men." But the Divine Word is the One Being through whom God is made known to men, and he is therefore most fitly called **the light of men.** (Compare 1: 17, 18; 8: 12; 14: 6; Matt. 11: 27.) In answering the first question: Why does the Evangelist start with **life,** as if this were the source or principle of **light**—as if the Word could be the light of men only because there was in him the true and perfect life?—we may say, that all knowledge presupposes life. Intuition, perception, experience, are functions of life. A teacher must know what he teaches; a revealer must be acquainted with him whom he reveals. The highest life of which the Saviour speaks in this Gospel consists in knowing God; and he himself had possessed that life from eternity. Fellowship with the Father—a life which had been identified with the Father's in knowledge, feeling, and purpose, so that the whole fullness of the divine mind was his—qualified him to be the light of men. Out of this perfect life came the light which enlightens every man (ver. 9). Attention may also be called to the universality of the term **men.** As, in ch. 8: 12, Jesus is represented as having said: "I am the light of the world"—that is, not of the Jews only, but of all mankind—so in this place the Evangelist declares that the life of the Word was **the light of men.** Nothing, indeed, is said concerning the process by which the knowledge of the Eternal Word had been imparted to men before his incarnation; but the fact that he was the source of their knowledge of God is broadly affirmed. And this affirmation is in harmony with his own sayings. (See the last three passages referred to above).

5. And the light shineth in (*the*) **darkness.** According to Meyer, the emphasis falls upon the expression **in** (*the*) **darkness.** This expression introduces the new thought of the verse, and in the original precedes the verb **shineth,** an order of words which calls

6 *There was a man sent from God, whose name was John.
7 *The same came for a witness, to bear witness of the Light, that all men through him might believe.

6 hended it not. There came a man, sent from God, 7 whose name was John. The same came for witness, that he might bear witness of the light, that all

a Mal. 3:1; Matt. 3:1; Luke 3:2; ver. 33....b Acts 19:4.

special attention to the new thought. Moreover, the emphasis is increased by the use of an abstract instead of a concrete term to denote the sphere in which the light shines; for **the darkness** evidently means sinful humanity, or the world as it lies in "the wicked one." But why is the present tense employed? Many have answered: Because the Evangelist wishes to characterize this action of the light as constant, continuous, through all time. The light always shines, because it is its nature to shine. But it is, perhaps, equally natural to suppose that the present tense was selected because the Evangelist wished to say that in his own time the light was shining still, in spite of all that had been done to obscure it. This view is favored by the change of tense in the next sentence. —**And the darkness comprehended it not.** Better, with Westcott, Schaff, Weiss, and the Greek Fathers, *overcame it not.* John uses the verb in but one other passage (12:35), where the meaning is to "come down upon, to enwrap." "As applied to light," remarks Westcott, "this sense includes the further notion of overwhelming, eclipsing." The darkness had indeed, according to its nature, re-acted against the light, in order to suppress it; Calvary had witnessed this conflict; but it did not succeed in quenching the light. And because in that crucial attempt of moral darkness to overcome the true light, it signally failed, the light shines on even now. This interpretation is preferable to the one which is suggested by the word "comprehended"; especially if this word be equivalent to "understood."

6-13. TREATMENT OF THE GOD-REVEALING LIGHT BY MEN.

6. There was a man sent from God, whose name was John. The word (ἐγένετο) translated **was,** signifies primarily "became," and is sometimes used with reference to birth, as in Gal. 4:4. But it may also denote such an event as the historical appearance of John to the people as a messenger of God; and this seems to be its import here. The added expression, **sent from God,** characterizes John as a true prophet,

one entrusted with a special message or mission from God. (See 3:2, and Mal. 3:1.) The writer of this Gospel, here and elsewhere, calls the harbinger of Christ simply John, as none but the Apostle John would be likely to do. Any other writer would have distinguished him from the apostle by calling him John the Baptist. See Introduction, p. 23.

7. The same came for a witness (or, more briefly, *for witness*). The chief end for which John the Baptist appeared, is here expressed by a single word, "testimony," or "witness" (μαρτυρία). This was the highest and immediate, if not the only, object of his mission to the people. And the difference between teaching or preaching, and bearing witness, should be borne in mind. (Compare 3:11, 32; 15:27; also 1:19; 8:13, 14; 19:35; 21:24.) One bears witness of what he knows by personal observation, or by revelation from God.—**To bear witness of the Light.** (Compare 1:33, 34.) Literally, *that he might bear witness concerning the light.* This clause repeats the idea of the foregoing, together with a statement of the person concerning whom the testimony was to be given. That person is here called **the Light,** because in and through him divine truth was offered to the souls of men. John was indeed "the lamp kindled and shining" (5:35), but he was in no proper sense "the Light." His light was borrowed and dim, but Christ was light, self-revealing and God-revealing, the original and perfect light. This clause depends on the verb **came.—That all men through him might believe.** The word him refers to John; and the belief meant is belief in Christ, the true light. (Calvin, Bengel, Lücke, Olshausen, Tholuck, Lange, Luthardt, Alford, Meyer, De Wette, Godet, Weiss, Abbott, Clark.) The direct object of John's mission was to bear witness concerning the Word, or Light, who is the Revealer of the Father; and the remoter object to be secured by this witnessing, was belief in the Word made flesh, the Saviour of the world. "The person of John is in itself of no importance, because it is

8 He was not that Light, but *was sent* to bear witness of that Light.
9 *That* was the true Light, which lighteth every man that cometh into the world.
10 He was in the world, and *b* the world was made by him, and the world knew him not.

8 might believe through him. He was not the light, but *came* that he might bear witness of the light.
9 ¹There was the true light, *even the light* which lighteth ²every man, coming into the world. He was in the world, and the world was made through him,

a ver. 4; Isa. 49: 6; 1 John 2: 8....*b* ver. 3; Heb. 1: 2; 11: 3.—1 Or, *The true light, which lighteth every man, was coming*....2 Or, *every man as he cometh.*

human; its importance lies only in the testimony it has to give."—*Luthardt*.

8. He was not that (*the*) Light, but was sent to bear witness of that Light. The first three words are emphatic. This may be inferred from their position in the Greek sentence, and from the pronoun selected by the Evangelist (*i. e.*, ἐκεῖνος). After the conjunction **but** (ἀλλά), some expositors (Meyer, Schaff) would supply the word "came," to complete the sense; others would supply "was sent," and still others "was"; while yet others maintain that the thought of the writer is fully expressed. The third of these views is probably correct. The form of expression is one by which the writer hastens to the positive and principal thought contained in the second clause, carrying with him the idea of the verb "was" from the first. Such elliptical and slightly irregular expressions are very forcible, and are common to all languages.

9. That was the true Light, etc. The construction and interpretation of this verse are difficult. It has been variously translated: (1) "*There was the true light, which lighteth every man that comes into the world*" (Bible Union); (2) "*Present was the true light which lighteth every man that cometh into the world*" (Meyer); (3) "*The true light, which lighteneth every man, came into the world*" (Alford); (4) "*The true light which lighteneth every man, was coming into the world*" (Noyes, Davidson, Lücke); (5) "*That was the true light which lighteth every man* (by) *coming into the world*" (Godet, 2d ed.). The third and fourth versions (Alford, Noyes) may be regarded as virtually one; for Alford interprets the words, "came into the world," as meaning, "was in process of manifesting himself." That is to say, the true Light was already making its appearance when John was testifying of it. This seems to be a more exact translation than any save the first, and the meaning which it offers is satisfactory.—The Light of which John was to bear witness, and which was already ap-pearing in the world, is characterized, in the first place, as being the *true* Light (τὸ ἀληθινόν, see Trench's "N. T. Synonyms," 7th ed., p. 25 sq.), that is, the genuine, original Light, answering to the perfect idea of light, and used here in contrast with the imperfect and borrowed light of John; and in the *second* place, it lighteth every man—an expression which has been variously understood. It cannot, however, mean that every man is, in fact, spiritually enlightened by the Word, so that he has a true knowledge of God; for this is forbidden by the immediate context—unless we assume, with Bengel, that by "every man" is here meant "every one who is spiritually enlightened," which seems to be a scarcely justifiable restriction of the language. But it may signify that some knowledge of God is given to every man by the Word. We understand it, however, as a description of the normal relation of the Word to the world of mankind, as an affirmation that, if any one fails of true and saving knowledge, it is because he closes the eye of his soul to it, and not because the Word has failed to offer it to him.

10. He was in the world, and the world was made by him, and the world knew him not. Three questions have been raised concerning this verse, viz.: (1) At what point does the writer pass from the neuter and impersonal idea of the ninth verse to the masculine and personal idea of the eleventh, from the Light to the Word? (2) To what time does he refer in the several clauses, especially the first and the last? (3) What is the meaning of **the world** in the several clauses? In answer to the first, it may be said that though the Evangelist used a term in the ninth verse which is neuter in form (τὸ φῶς), it is by no means certain that it was used by him in an impersonal sense. Indeed, when saying that John was not the Light, he must have been thinking of One who was the Light, that is, of **the Light** as a person; and therefore it may be assumed, that as soon as the gender of the word light ceased to rule,

11 a He came unto his own, and his own received him not.
12 But bas many as received him, to them gave he power to become the sons of God, *even* to them that believe on his name;
11 and the world knew him not. He came unto his own, and they that were his own received him not.
12 But as many as received him, to them gave he the right to become children of God, *even* to them that

a Luke 19: 14; Acts 3: 26; 13: 46....b Isa. 56: 5; Rom. 8: 15; Gal. 3: 26; 2 Pet. 1: 4; 1 John 3: 1.——1 Gr. *his own things.*

in a merely *formal* way, the gender of relative words, the writer, had he used a pronoun, would have employed the masculine form. (Compare 14: 26; 15: 26; 16: 7-13.) In answer to the second: At what time does the writer mean to affirm that the Light, *i. e.*, the Word, was in the world? it may be said: In the time of his public ministry, when he was manifesting himself to the world, and John was bearing witness of him. "*He was in the world*—and therefore the world should have known him—*and the world was made by him*—so much the more should it have known him—*and yet the world knew him not*" (DeWette). "The world (ὁ κόσμος) is repeated three times with tragical emphasis, the noun instead of the pronoun. This makes the contrast between what should have been and what was the more affecting."—*Luthardt.* In answer to the third question: What is meant by **the world** in the several clauses? we remark, that in the last clause it must mean the world of mankind, or the world as represented by mankind; for only men could know the Word. But in the previous clauses the term may have a less restricted meaning. And it is characteristic of John to use words of comprehensive signification, leaving their exact reference to be inferred from the context. He teaches much with but few words.

11. He came unto his own, and his own received him not. In the first sentence of this verse, the words rendered **his own** (τὰ ἴδια) are neuter, and serve to fix the mind on the Jewish nation as the Messiah's heritage or possession; but in the second sentence, the words so translated (οἱ ἴδιοι) are masculine, and serve to fix the mind on the same people as *persons* who belong to the Messiah, and are subjects of his government, or members of his household. The simple idea of *ownership* is more forcibly expressed by the neuter form; but this form gives place to the masculine, because only *persons* can receive or reject. The Messiah, the Light of the world, was rejected by his own people, the members of his own family. Compare the language of the Old Testament in Ex. 19: 5; Deut. 7: 6; Psalm 135: 4; Isa. 31: 9, with that of the New Testament in 1 Peter 2: 9; Matt. 8: 12; John 4: 22; Rom. 1: 16. "In the negative form of expression, verses 10, 11, there is a profoundly elegiac and sorrowful tone."—*Meyer.* The beloved disciple felt a holy grief at the rejection of his Lord. Yet while the people, as a whole, rejected Christ, there were individuals who believed in him, and the Evangelist now turns to the manifestation of Christ in relation to them. He has spoken of unbelief, and he now speaks of belief.

12. But as many as received him, to them gave he power to become the sons of God, even to them that believe on his name. Compare the Revised Version. Following the order and emphasis of the Greek words, the verse may be rendered: *But as many as received him, he gave them right* (or *power*) *to be children of God, to them who believe in his name.* Gave, rather than *them,* is emphatic in the second clause. This verse, in connection with the next, taxes the wisdom of an interpreter severely. Yet one thing is evident, viz., that the first and last clauses refer to the same class of persons, and to the same kind of action; hence the receiving was effected by believing, and the last clause explains the first. This appears to us certain, though Weiss decides that the act of receiving Jesus, as the true Light, preceded belief in his name. Does, then, the second clause refer to regeneration? so that, according to John, faith precedes and conditions regeneration? This is assumed to be his teaching by Meyer, De Wette, Godet, and many others. But the objections to this assumption are very grave. (a) The next verse appears to teach that those who believe in the name of Christ have been begotten of God. (b) The same thing is clearly taught by John in his First Epistle, *e. g.*, 5: 1. (Compare 4: 7; 2: 29.) (c) Faith in Christ appears to be as truly a fruit of divine grace as any other Christian act.

If, then, we reject the assumption that faith precedes regeneration, the words of our

13 ᵃ Which were born, not of blood, nor of the will of the flesh, nor of the will of man, but of God.
14 ᵇ And the Word ᶜ was made ᵈ flesh, and dwelt among us, (and ᵉ we beheld his glory, the glory as of the only begotten of the Father,) ᶠ full of grace and truth.

13 believe on his name: who were born, not of ᵃblood, nor of the will of the flesh, nor of the will 11 of man, but of God. And the Word became flesh, and ᵈdwelt among us (and we beheld his glory, glory as of ᵉthe only begotten from the Father),

a ch. 3 : 5 ; James 1 : 18 ; 1 Pet. 1 : 23....*b* Matt. 1 : 16, 20 ; Luke 1 : 31, 35 ; 2 : 7 ; 1 Tim. 3 : 16.....*c* Rom. 1 : 3 ; Gal. 4 : 4....*d* Heb. 2 : 11, 14, 16, 17....*e* Isa. 40 : 5 ; Matt. 17 : 2 ; ch. 2 : 11 ; 11 : 40 ; 2 Pet. 1 : 17.....*f* Col. 1 : 19 ; 2 : 3, 9.—1 Or, *begotten*....2 Gr. *bloods*....3 Gr. *tabernacled*....4 Or, *an only begotten from a father*.

second clause must either refer to what Paul calls "adoption" (υἱοθεσία), or must represent regeneration as due to a gift of grace from Christ. In the former case the word translated **power** (ἐξουσία) means "privilege," "right," or "title," and the word translated **to become** (γενέσθαι), means "to be"—of course with an implication of origin. Against this the use of "children" (τέκνα), instead of "sons" (υἱοί), has been urged ; but without the fullest right, for John nowhere uses the latter term to denote sons by adoption, and Paul's style is not decisive as to the use of words by John. (Compare John 11 : 52 ; 1 John 3 : 1.) But why not accept the second view, according to which the word rendered **power** means the moral ability of men, under the renewing influence of the Spirit, to receive Christ and become thereby children of God? In favor of this interpretation may be alleged the position of **gave,** which makes this verb, instead of the pronoun **them,** the emphatic word of the clause. Had John meant to emphasize the human act alone as decisive, he would probably have placed the word **them** before the word **gave,** *i. e.,* to *them,* because they received him when others did not. Nor is this interpretation inconsistent with the use of a present participle in the last clause, while an aorist verb is used in the first. For this change may have been due to the intervening thought. The meaning would then be this: "Many did not receive him ; but some did ; and, as to all who received him, he *gave* them grace by which they were enabled to do this, and so to become God's children." This emphasizing of the grace of God in Christ perfectly accords with the general tone of the prologue.

13. Which (or *who*) **were born** (*begotten*) **not of blood, nor of the will of the flesh, nor of the will of man, but of God.** The main purpose of the Evangelist in this verse is to deny that regeneration owes its origin to man, and to affirm that it is effected by the power of God. Most interpreters suppose that the three negations are essentially one, in

that they all deny the production of a spiritual life by natural generation, or, in other words, that a state of grace is ever inherited from one's parents or ancestors. But is not this fully expressed by the first negation? And do not the second and third deny that this state is ever originated by an act of human will or choice? This is certainly the most obvious meaning of the words. Yet, if this be the meaning, why, it may be asked, is **will of the flesh** distinguished from **will of man?** Possibly because the writer would first reject a notion which is very plainly absurd **(of blood),** then one that is apparently less absurd **(of the will of the flesh),** and, finally, one that appears to many persons even probable **(of the will of man).** Thus faith in Christ is not transmitted from parents to children in the elements of physical life ("bloods" for blood). Nor is this faith originated by an act of will springing from a nature ruled by flesh and sense. Nor yet is it a product of **man's** will, although **will of man** signifies all that is highest and noblest in merely human power. The origin of this new life of faith is divine; it is implanted in the soul by God. If this interpretation is correct, the word **man** is here used (and Lücke maintains this view) as the antithesis of God, and not of woman, though the term here employed is generally used in the latter sense. At all events, the last clause distinctly affirms that believers have a life which owes its origin to God—that the new birth is effected by God, and that all believers in the name of Christ have experienced it. But it does not say that the grace of God for regeneration is resisted equally by those who are, and by those who are not, renewed. The positive, efficient agency is divine; but whether this divine agency is conditioned on any particular state of the human soul or not, the Evangelist does not explain.

14-18. INCARNATION OF THE WORD BY WHICH GOD WAS MOST CLEARLY REVEALED TO MEN.

14. And the word was made (*became*) **flesh.** This sentence is at once simple and sublime, unsurpassed by any in the sacred record. With it should be compared 1 John 4: 2; 2 John 7; 1 Tim. 3: 16; Gal. 4: 4; Rom. 1: 3; 8: 3; Phil. 2: 7; Col. 2: 9; John 8: 58; 17: 5; 3: 11-13. A careful study of these passages will lead one to hesitate long before concluding with Gess, Godet, and others, that the verb **became** (ἐγένετο) includes a surrender of his divine consciousness, or mode of existence, by the Word, and an entrance upon a simple human mode of existence. For this term does not assert that the Divine Word was converted into **flesh**, or human nature. It only declares that he became one of whom true humanity could be affirmed. If the order of the Greek original marks any word as emphatic, it is the word **flesh**. And this word is generally conceded to be a designation of human nature, taken from its lower and visible side. The meaning would have been nearly the same if John had said: *The Word became man.* Yet the word **flesh** serves to bring forward a little more distinctly the fact that he was visible, and had a human body, as well as a rational soul. (Compare John 17: 2.) If John had meant to say that the Word took to himself a human body simply, he would have said that he came in a body, or at least "in flesh." The expression which he has employed naturally signifies that the Word, though divine, became human. Beyond this, his language scarcely warrants our going. "In Jesus Christ," says Meyer, was "the absolute synthesis of the divine and the human." Meyer's exposition of this verse is, in most respects, admirable, while that of Godet, though extremely interesting and positive, is scarcely justified by the language of the Evangelist. **And dwelt among us—full of grace and truth.** The verb translated **dwelt** (ἐσκήνωσεν) signifies, literally, "pitched his tent," "tented," "tabernacled"; and "this word was chosen," Meyer holds, "for the purpose of fixing attention on the appearing of the incarnate Word, whose human nature became his holy tent (2 Pet. 1: 13) in fulfillment of God's promise that he would dwell among his people. Ex. 25: 8; 29: 45; Levit. 26: 11; Joel 3: 21; Ezek. 37: 27; Hag. 2: 9, cf. Sir. 24: 8; Rev. 21: 3. The context, **and we beheld his glory**, etc., authorizes this assumption." A similar thought underlies the statement of John in 2: 21: "But he spake of the temple of his body."

There is nothing in the context favorable to the view that this verb, "tented," was chosen with reference to the brevity of Christ's sojourn upon earth. The pronoun **us** means the disciples of Christ, of whom the writer was one. The last words of the verse, **full of grace and truth**, are descriptive of the Word as he dwelt among his people. Redemption was in him, and was revealed by him. What he was he manifested, and he was the Saviour of sinners. The word **grace** answers to the word **life** above, and the word **truth** to the word **light.** Life and light are equivalent to grace and truth. Several excellent expositors (Meyer, Lange, Alford, Schaff) regard these words—**full of grace and truth**—as a final exclamation, not referable to the second clause, or as belonging, by an irregular construction, with **his** (αὐτοῦ) of the next preceding clause. But it is safer to connect them with the **Word**, the subject of the verb **dwelt.** We now return to the intervening clause, which may be literally rendered: **And we beheld his glory,** *a glory as of an only begotten from with the Father.* The word **beheld** means to look at, or contemplate with admiration. "It needed belief to see the Son of God in Jesus, but that belief could see even in the incarnate One the fullness of the divine glory" (Luthardt, freely). This glory was revealed to believers by the whole life, bearing, teaching, work, of the incarnate Word. And it was such a glory as answered to the true idea of an Only Begotten from the Father. The preposition (παρά) before Father means "from with," or "from the presence of," and it is plain that the peculiarity of Christ's Sonship depends on the divine nature of the Word, since he could be "from with God" by virtue of his higher nature only. But it may be doubted whether this language proves the eternal Sonship of the Word; though it clearly proves that the Sonship of Christ was, in a true sense, natural as well as unique. A different preposition would probably have been selected by John, if he had intended to speak of the pre-incarnate Word as the Son of the Father. Whether then the doctrine of the eternal generation of the Word from the Father is Biblical or not, it is not directly taught in this passage. Only this is said, that the glory of Jesus was such as could belong to none but an only begotten Son, who, as to his

CH. I.] JOHN. 67

15 a John bare witness of him, and cried, saying, This was he of whom I spake, b He that cometh after me is preferred before me; c for he was before me.

15 full of grace and truth. John beareth witness of him, and crieth, saying, 1 This was he of whom I said, He that cometh after me is become before me:

a ver. 32; ch. 3: 32; 5: 33....b Matt. 3: 11; Mark 1: 7; Luke 3: 16; ver. 27: 30; ch. 3: 31.....c ch. 3: 58; Col. 1: 17——1 Some ancient authorities read (this was he that said).

higher nature, had come from with the Father. That Christ was this gracious and glorious Being is now re-asserted, by appealing to the testimony of John the Baptist, and to the grace which the first disciples had received from him.

15. **John bare witness of him, and cried, saying** (Literally: *John beareth witness of him, and hath cried, saying*). The tense of the former verb (*beareth*) may be explained by supposing that the Evangelist merely thought of John's testimony as always pertinent, valid, and decisive, or by supposing that it was vividly present to him, and sounding as it were in his ears. The latter hypothesis is perhaps preferable to the former; for the testimony of the Baptist, received in faith, had proved the turning point in the writer's life, and would therefore be likely to remain in his soul as fresh and powerful as when it was first heard. If the former explanation of this verb were adopted, it would still be necessary to suppose the writer a disciple of John, as well as of Christ, in order to account for the graphic description and singular prominence which he has given to the testimony of the Baptist. An unknown Christian of the second century could not have written the remainder of this chapter.—The verb translated **cried,** or *hath cried,* is in the perfect tense, and represents the act as sounding over from the past into the present. Meyer says that the perfect is here used as a present, but it is not really necessary to assume this; for from the testifying, as a present reality, the mind of the Evangelist might easily pass to the vocal utterance as bringing that testimony from the past to the present, and continuing it still.—**This was he of whom I spake, He that cometh after me is preferred** (*has come to be*) **before me; for he was before me.** The tense of the verb **was,** in the first clause, may be accounted for by supposing that John refers to Jesus on some other past occasion, *e. g.,* "The teacher, whom I saw again yesterday, **was he of whom I spake,**" etc. Weiss thinks that John the Baptist is conceived of by the Evangelist as still bearing witness, and therefore as now saying, **This was he of whom I spake.** His view is possibly correct; for the perfect, *hath cried,* includes the present as well as the past. Weiss holds that this is an instance, though the only one in the New Testament, of a perfect tense used for a present; but we do not see any solid ground for such an opinion.1 The clause, *has come to be before me,* may refer either to time or to rank. If it refers to time, the Baptist meant to say that the coming of Jesus into the world preceded his own; or, in other words, that Jesus was the One who had appeared to the fathers as the Angel of Jehovah, the Angel of the Covenant, etc. But by the tense of the verb employed, *has come to be* (γέγονεν), the coming of Jesus in flesh would, in that case, be represented as a continuance of his coming in a very different way, which is scarcely natural. The view that this clause refers to the superior dignity or rank obtained by Christ, is therefore better. "He that is coming after me has taken his place before me, *i. e.,* in authority and rank—a position to which he is entitled, because he was before me, or *first* in relation to me." This precedence in existence (last clause) might surely be appealed to as a sufficient ground for precedence in dignity, for it implied the superhuman nature of Christ. (Notice, too, that the verb here is in the im-

1 ["This was he of whom I said" (ὃν εἶπον), is supported by all known documents except ℵ (first corrector) B C, which read. "This was he who said" (ὁ εἰπών); and the original scribe of ℵ gave, "This was he that cometh after me, who is become before me," showing confusion and uncertainty as to the text. Now any reader will notice that John the Baptist has not been recorded as previously saying what in the common text he here declares himself to have said. Hence an apparent difficulty, which the reading of ℵ B C tends to remove. If only ℵ and C had given this, Westcott and Hort would have promptly called it an "Alexandrian" correction, a well meant attempt to remove a difficulty. Their general position that B added to other early authorities gives a "neutral" form of text, free from "Alexandrian" and "Western" corrections, cannot, in our opinion, be maintained without allowing somewhat numerous exceptions. Compare on 3: 13; 7: 8, 39; 18: 1. There can be little hesitation in here rejecting the reading ὁ εἰπών as a correction. B.]

16 And of his *fulness have all we received, and grace for grace.
17 For *the law was given by Moses, but *grace and *truth came by Jesus Christ.

16 for he was ¹before me. For of his fulness we all 17 received, and grace for grace. For the law was given through Moses; grace and truth came

a ch. 3:34; Eph. 1:6, 7, 8; Col. 1:19; 2:9, 10....b Ex. 20:1, etc.; Deut. 4:44; ¹:1; 33:4....c Rom. 3:24; 5:21; 6:14....d ch. 8:32; 14:6.—1 Gr. *first in regard to me.*

perfect tense, ἦν.) Moreover, when this proclamation was made by the Baptist (see ver. 30), Jesus had already begun to take his true position as compared with John. The tense of the verb (γέγονεν), in the second clause of John's testimony, is therefore fully accounted for by this interpretation.

16. And of his fulness have all we received, and grace for grace. Yielding to the force of authority,¹ we must substitute *for*, in place of **and**, at the beginning of this verse. Yet we cannot attribute these words to John the Baptist. Like the words **we beheld**, etc., of verse 14, they evidently belong to the Evangelist, and the **all we** refers to himself and the whole body of primitive disciples. The time indicated by the verb (lit., *received*) is that in which they first believed in Jesus. And the expression, **his fulness,** shows that this verse was meant to be a confirmation of the last statement in verse fourteenth. Whether it is to be directly connected with that verse, however, or with the fifteenth, is doubtful. If, with the latter, the course of thought is somewhat obscure, but as follows: "We beheld him dwelling among us, *full of grace and truth.*" For the witness of John the Baptist is to this effect, that Jesus had justly taken precedence of himself, because he was in existence first, even in eternity. And that he was thus preexistent and superior to John, and therefore full of grace and truth, is also certain, "because we all received grace out of his fullness at the time of our espousals to him." The

¹[This verse ought to begin with ὅτι, "because" or "for," which is supported by א B C (first hand) D L X, 33, some copies of the Old Latin, the Memphitic, Armenian, and Æthiopic, and numerous patristic quotations. Notice that the uncials include three groups, א B, C L, D. We can see how this reading may have been changed to καί, "and" (which has inferior outward evidence), by persons who could not see any such relation as "because" between verse 15 and verse 16, and who did not perceive that verse 15 is parenthetical or digressive, and in verse 16 the Evangelist gives the "because" for verse 14. There is even a verbal connection, "full . . . fulness," "grace . . . grace." B.]

word *received* has no expressed object, but its implied object is a portion of that with which Christ was filled, namely, "grace and truth." The manner in which this was received is described by the words **and grace for grace.** That is, "new grace constantly took the place of that which had been received before." —*Meyer.* "A grace received becomes our title to receive a new grace."—*Godet.* "Every new wave taking the place of, and overwhelming, though not superseding or destroying, the other."—*Schaff.* Not only the freeness of divine grace is suggested by this expression, but also its adaptation to every state and want of the renewed man, as he passes on from childhood to maturity in the divine life. It will be observed that these additional words, **and grace for grace,** appear to glance at the whole course of Christian life, while the verb *received* fixes the mind on a particular time or act.

17. For the law was given by Moses, but grace and truth came by Jesus Christ. This verse assigns a reason (**For**) why Christians could and did receive from his fullness grace for grace, namely, because through him *the grace* and *the truth* of salvation, or grace and truth in their ideal sense, were brought into existence (ἐγένετο); and while assigning this reason, it magnifies his work by contrasting it with that of Moses. **The law** was, at best, only the shadow of good things to come. It manifested the justice of God and the sinfulness of man with great clearness, but it only intimated, through types, the reality and the method of divine forgiveness. These were disclosed by the mediation of Christ, even as they depended on that mediation. Hence, it is said that grace and truth **came,** *i. e.*, came into being, or view, through Jesus Christ. The law was only **given** (ἐδόθη) or transmitted through Moses; for it was in substance the eternal rule of right, existing in the mind of God; but saving grace and truth were brought into being by the work of Christ. He himself was the perfect revelation of the Divine Will. In him was "the redemption," and

18 a No man hath seen God at any time; b the only begotten Son, which is in the bosom of the Father, he hath declared him.

18 through Jesus Christ. No man hath seen God at any time; b the only begotten Son, who is in the bosom of the Father, he hath declared him.

a Ex. 33: 20; Deut. 4: 12; Matt. 11: 27; Luke 10: 22; ch. 6: 46; 1 Tim. 1: 17; 6: 16; 1 John 4: 12, 20....b ver. 14; ch. 3: 16, 18; 1 John 4: 9.—1 Many very ancient authorities read, God only begotten.

by him was it made known to men. Here, first in the prologue, do we meet the full name of the Saviour, who has been designated hitherto as the Word, the Light, and, by implication, the Only Begotten from with the Father.

18. No man hath seen God at any time; the only begotten Son, which is in the bosom of the Father—he hath declared him. By its position in the original—*God—hath no man ever seen*—the word God is made emphatic; and, according to this last and crowning declaration of the prologue, God the Father has never been seen by mortal eye, but was made known by Jesus Christ, the only begotten Son, who enjoys perfect and uninterrupted communion with him. Jesus Christ, in the days of his flesh, interpreted and revealed the Father to men; this he was able to do, because he is the only begotten Son, having the same nature with the Father, and because he is ever at home in the bosom of the Father, loving him and knowing all his heart.¹

Meyer supposes that the expression **which is in the bosom of the Father,** refers to Jesus Christ after his glorification, but does not cover the period of his humiliation on earth. But, if that were the case, I cannot see why the clause was inserted here. It would have seemed far more natural to have referred to his pre-incarnate fellowship with the Father, but most natural of all to have referred to his intimacy with the Father while he was declaring him. The participle (ὤν) translated **is**, seems to be used to express what is permanently true of Christ, and true in such a sense as to make his account of the Father worthy of all acceptation. Lücke says that the "timeless present participle is here used, like the finite present in 1 John 3: 3, 7, to express an inherent, permanent relation of the only begotten Son to the Father" (I. 363). It may also be remarked that there is no expressed object of the word "**declared**" (ἐξηγήσατο), *he expounded, explained, taught* (i. e., *ea, quæ ad deum spectant*); or, what he knew by being in the

¹ [It is quite difficult to decide whether the true reading here is (1) ὁ μονογενὴς υἱός, "the only-begotten Son," or (2) μονογενὴς Θεός (without article) "one who is only-begotten God." The evidence of manuscripts, versions, and Fathers, is very strong on both sides; and that of the Fathers is curiously complicated with questions as to the early creeds, and the current phraseology of the early centuries. Each reading may claim some transcriptional, and some intrinsic probability. The question does not materially affect the general teaching of the New Testament as to the Son of God, and so we can hardly suppose changes on that account. Athanasius seems to have had only the former reading, while Arius, and some of his followers, quote the latter, explaining it in accordance with their theory.

(1) ὁ μονογενὴς υἱός is supported by A C (third hand) X T Δ Λ Π, nine other uncials, nearly all cursives, old Latin, Vulgate, old Syriac (Curetonian), Harklean (text) and Jerusalem Syriac, Armenian, and some manuscripts of the Æthiopic. It is found in Irenæus (Latin translation), Hippolytus; Eusebius several times (once giving the alternative reading "the only-begotten Son, or (one who is) only-begotten God," as either sufficed for his argument); Athanasius repeatedly; and often in Basil, Chrysostom, and many other Greek Fathers; also in Tertullian, Hilary, often (in a work on the Trinity), and other Latin Fathers.

(2) μονογενὴς Θεός is supported by ℵ B C (first hand) L, 33 (which very often concurs with this group of uncials), Memphitic, Peshito, and margin of Harklean Syriac, Æthiopic (some Mss.). It is found in Irenæus (Latin translation, next page to the quotation of the other reading), is said to have been used by the Valentinian Gnostics, is given once in Clement of Alex., and several times in Origen, repeatedly in Didymus (on the Trinity), and Gregory of Nyssa, and Epiphanius and Cyril of Alex. (in commentary on John), and in various other Greek Fathers.

Carefully to be distinguished from *quotations of this passage* is the frequent use of the *expression* μονογενὴς Θεός without any apparent reference to this connection by many Fathers, including Athanasius (who *quotes* only the other text), Basil, Gregory of Nyssa, and Gregory Nazianzen, Cyril of Alex., and the Latin Fathers Hilary (who quotes only the other) and Fulgentius; also by Arius (in Epiphanius) and some obscure Latin Arian writers. This same expression is found in certain early creeds (see Hort, "Two Dissertations," Cambridge, 1877).

Internal evidence as to this passage is not decisive, but seems somewhat more favorable to Θεός. The unique and strange-looking μονογενὴς Θεός would

70   JOHN.   [Ch. I.

19 And this is "the record of John, when the Jews sent priests and Levites from Jerusalem to ask him, Who art thou?

19 And this is the witness of John, when the Jews sent unto him from Jerusalem priests and Levites

a ch. 5: 33.

bosom of the Father; or, perhaps, the Father, as he could do this by being in the Father's bosom.

19-28. John's Testimony to the Deputation from Jerusalem.

Having prepared the minds of his readers by this marvelous introduction to appreciate the events and discourses which he is about to relate, the Evangelist, whose object did not require him to rehearse again the well-known story of the birth, the early history, and the opening ministry of John the Baptist, or of Jesus, the son of Mary, begins his narrative by describing an interview between the Baptist, and a deputation of priests and Levites from Jerusalem. This interview took place on the east side of the Jordan, in Bethabara (see ver. 28), more than forty days after the baptism of Christ. Hence, according to the best conjecture, John had been preaching and baptizing between seven and eight months, and many of the people were beginning to speak of him as in all probability, the expected Messiah. It was time, therefore, for the rulers to ascertain his claims, and prepare themselves to oppose or to support them.

19. And this is the record (better, *witness*) **of John.** A slight but natural emphasis is thrown upon the predicate **this** by giving it the first place in the sentence. The writer calls attention thereby to the character of the testimony which is to be recited. "The witness which John bore on a particular occasion is *this* (observe its character) which I now repeat, and it was given": **When the Jews sent priests and Levites from Jerusalem.** By **the Jews** must be understood in this place, the Jewish authorities, probably the members of the Sanhedrin. This was a formal deputation, and was naturally composed of priests and Levites, as men who were occupied with religious services, and familiar with the prophetic Scriptures. They were sent from **Jerusalem**, the capital of the nation, by the chiefs of the Jewish people, to ascertain the precise claims of the Baptist, as appears from the next clause; for they were sent, it is said, **to ask him, Who art thou?** (For the use of ἵνα, and the subjunctive in the sense of the infinitive, see Winer ¿ 45, 9, and Buttmann ¿ 139, 4.) The question thus proposed was perfectly general, but in view of the circumstances, was equivalent to the definite inquiry, Art thou the Messiah? And

more readily be changed into the familiar ὁ μονογενὴς υἱός of 3: 16, 18; 1 John 4: 9. Still it may be answered that the *expression* μονογενὴς θεός was familiar in various quarters. It is more likely that the creeds and theologians borrowed this expression from the Gospel, than that it crept into the Gospel from their usage. Dr. E. Abbot replies (Bibliotheca Sacra, 1861, and Unitarian Review, 1875), that the favorite phrase θεὸς λόγος was not borrowed from Scripture, but made by combining two words in John 1: 1; and so μονογενὴς θεός might have been made by combination from 1: 1 and 14. But the two cases present the important difference that θεὸς λόγος has not crept into the text. And Dr. Hort points out that if the use of μονογενὴς θεός in the theologians and creeds brought it into our passage, then there must have been such use early in the second century, to account for its appearance in the various documents which contain it. The possibility that θεός may have been changed to υἱός because of the closely following πατρός, is met by the possibility that a scribe retained the impression of the foregoing θεόν, and thus unconsciously mistook the contracted form of υἱός for the other. Many have argued that "only

begotten God" is intrinsically improbable, because unique and foreign to New Testament phraseology. But Hort justly replies, ("Two Dissertations,") that the entire prologue to John (1: 1-18) is thoroughly unique, and he shows that "only begotten God" at the close, would well sum up the the thought of the whole passage. Thus, transcriptional probability is rather in favor of μονογενὴς θεός, and intrinsic probability is not clearly opposed to it. And as the remarkable group of documents which contain it, are so commonly shown by clear, internal evidence to contain the true text, it seems right to regard μονογενὴς θεός as more probably the correct reading. There is, of late years, as critics become used to the strange expression, an increasing readiness to accept this probable conclusion. But the complex difficulties of the problem are very serious, and one can hardly speak with great confidence. In text-criticism, as in exegesis, we must not be surprised if some questions remain unsettled. It should be carefully observed that "only-begotten" is here without an article, as in ver. 14. Even "God only-begotten" (*margin* of Revised Version) is too definite an expression.   B.]

20 And *he confessed, and denied not; but confessed, I am not the Christ.
21 And they asked him, What then? Art thou *b* Elias? And he saith, I am not. Art thou *c* that Prophet? And he answered, No.
22 Then said they unto him, Who art thou? that we may give an answer to them that sent us. What sayest thou of thyself?
23 *d* He said, I *am* the voice of one crying in the wilderness, Make straight the way of the Lord, as *e* said the prophet Esaias.

20 to ask him, Who art thou? And he confessed, and denied not; and he confessed, I am not the Christ.
21 And they asked him, What then? Art thou Elijah? And he saith, I am not. Art thou the prophet?
22 And he answered, No. They said therefore unto him, Who art thou? that we may give an answer to them that sent us. What sayest thou of thyself?
23 He said, I am the voice of one crying in the wilderness, Make straight the way of the Lord, as said

a Luke 3: 15; ch. 3: 28; Acts 13: 25....*b* Mal. 4: 5; Matt. 17: 10....*c* Deut. 18: 15, 18....*d* Matt. 3: 3; Mark 1: 3; Luke 3: 4; ch. 3: 28.... *e* Isa. 40: 3.

the Baptist responded to its import, rather than to its form. Meyer supposes that this import is slightly indicated by the emphatic position of the pronoun **thou** (σὺ τίς εἶ); but this is perhaps doubtful.

20. And he confessed, and denied not; but (rather, *and he*) **confessed, I am not the Christ.** Two points deserve special attention. 1. The manner in which the Evangelist introduces this testimony of the Baptist. For by his double statement, positive and negative, and by his deliberate repetition of the positive statement, **he confessed,** he clearly reveals the extraordinary impression which this answer and testimony had made on his own mind. The language is evidently that of a hearer and believer; perhaps, too, of one who was at the time half expecting a different answer from the Baptist. 2. The position of the pronoun **I** in the answer of the Baptist renders it emphatic, and gives to that answer the meaning, "I myself am not the Christ" (thus suggesting that there was another among them who was the Christ). This meaning arises chiefly from the order of words established by the highest authorities, and adopted by Lachmann, Tischendorf, and Tregelles, though the use of the pronoun at all, renders it somewhat emphatic.

21. But the deputation was not satisfied; it would have a more definite answer from John. Hence the next question: **What then? Art thou Elias?** For it was expected, according to Mal. 4: 5, that Elijah would reappear on earth and introduce the Messiah; while it is evident that the deputation supposed the mission of the Baptist to be connected in some way with the Messiah. Hence they say: "If this is so, if thou art not the Christ, how does the case stand? Art thou Elijah?" They probably suppose that he will claim to be at least Elijah. But no.—**He saith, I am not.** Meaning, I am not Elijah the Tishbite, to whom you refer. This answer of the Baptist need not be pronounced inconsistent with the words of the angel to Zachariah his father (Luke 1: 17), or with those of Christ (Matt. 11: 11; 17: 11, 12); for it was doubtless a true answer to the precise thought as well as language of his interrogators. For some reason he deemed it unnecessary to interpret the words of Malachi, which signified that he was an Elijah in "spirit and power," though not identical with him in person. The deputies, therefore, continue their scrutiny: **Art thou that prophet?** (Literally, *The prophet, art thou?*) **And he answered, No.** It is presumable that the questioners meant by *the prophet,* the unnamed prophet foretold by Moses in Deut. 18: 15, whom they did not identify with the promised Messiah, while John briefly answered, No, because he knew that the prediction of Moses referred to the Messiah, or at least did not refer to himself. Observe the life-like style of the dialogue, and the curt, decisive manner of the Baptist. It was a dialogue well-remembered by the writer—not a colloquy invented by a literary forger of the second century.

22. Then said they unto him, Who art thou? that we may give an answer to them that sent us. This question could not be answered by a single negative, and therefore John gives an account of himself in the language of Scripture, but in such a way as to keep his own personality in the background while he exalted Christ. "Notice—they ever ask him about his *person;* he ever refers them to his *office.* He is no one—a *voice* merely; it is the work of God, the testimony of Christ, which is everything. So the formalist ever in the church asks, *Who* is he? while the witness for Christ only exalts, only cares, for Christ's work."—*Alford.*

23. He said, I am the (rather *a*) **voice of one crying in the wilderness, Make straight the way of the Lord, as said the**

24 And they which were sent were of the Pharisees.
25 And they asked him and said unto him Why baptizest thou then, if thou be not that Christ, nor Elias, neither that Prophet?
26 John answered them, saying, ᵃI baptize with water: ᵇbut there standeth one among you, whom ye know not;
27 ᶜHe it is, who coming after me is preferred before me, whose shoe's latchet I am not worthy to unloose.

24 Isaiah the prophet. ¹And they had been sent from
25 the Pharisees. And they asked him, and said unto him, Why then baptizest thou, if thou art not the
26 Christ, neither Elijah, neither the prophet? John answered them, saying, I baptize ²in water: in the
27 midst of you standeth one whom ye know not, *even* he that cometh after me, the latchet of whose shoe

a Matt. 3:11.. .b Mal. 3:1....c ver. 15, 30; Acts 19:4.—1 Or. *And certain had been sent from among the Pharisees*....2 Or. *with*.

prophet Esaias. The second clause of the quotation from Isa. 40:3 is not literal, but it gives the substance of two sentences of the original, which reads: "Prepare ye the way of the Lord, make straight in the desert a highway for our God." Matthew (3:3) applies the same passage to John the Baptist. This answer to the deputation is in perfect keeping with the Evangelist's own language in verses 7 and 8, above. The greatness of John was in his being a voice, a herald, a witness, announcing Christ and directing men to him. He was less than his office, while Jesus was greater than his office; he was great because of his office, while the office of Christ was supremely great because it was filled by him.

24. And they which were sent were of the Pharisees. The Revised Version, following the oldest reading, translates: *And they had been sent from the Pharisees.* This remark is inserted to prepare the way for what follows; for the Pharisees, who attached the highest importance to all ceremonial observances, were just the people to call in question the authority of one who should introduce a new religious rite. And this John had done.

25. And they asked him, and said unto him, Why baptizest thou then, if thou be not that (*the*) Christ, nor Elias, neither that (*the*) prophet? It appears from this, that the Pharisees looked upon baptism as a rite which appertained to the Messiah's reign, and which could only be introduced by the Messiah himself, by Elijah his forerunner, or by the prophet like unto Moses. But they did not interpret Isa. 40:3 as referring to any one of these. Hence, they called in question the right of John to baptize; and he, taking little pains to vindicate his right, pointed them to his Master.

26, 27. I baptize with (*in*) water, etc. The Revised Version reads: *In the midst of you standeth one whom ye know not, even he that cometh after me, the latchet of whose shoe I am not worthy to unloose.* This, according to the best editors, Lachmann, Tischendorf, Tregelles, Westcott and Hort, is the true text of the verse. And if so, the response of John to his inquisitors was brief, even to obscurity; yet it was probably understood by the deputation. Their question assumed that none but the Messiah, or one closely and officially connected with him—as Elijah or "the prophet"—could have authority to baptize; and the answer of John, though obscure, is exactly to the point, and may be paraphrased thus: "I myself do indeed baptize in water: I myself am administering this new and significant rite by which those who are entering upon a new religious life solemnly testify their repentance and readiness to welcome the Coming One; and my authority for doing this is the fact that he who cometh after me, whose way I am calling on the people to prepare, but whom you yourselves do not know or recognize, is even now standing among you; and so great and wonderful is he, that I, though sent to announce him and to prepare the people for him by this divinely appointed and significant rite, feel myself unworthy to render him the humblest service."
Meyer says that, after I in the first clause, the emphasis falls on **in water;** but there is nothing in the Greek text to warrant this. For the order of the words is the natural and logical order, and the only emphatic part is the pronoun I. Perhaps there is a definite feeling of rightful authority implied in the accentuated pronoun: "This is *my* mission, *my* work as the herald of the far greater One who is even now standing among you"; yet the pronoun may be expressed for the sake only of a more marked antithesis between the speaker and the One described as *he that cometh after me.* When speaking to the more docile, but less instructed people, John had expressly contrasted the baptism in water, which he administered, with the baptism in the Holy Spirit, which the One coming after

28 These things were done *a* in Bethabara beyond Jordan, where John was baptizing.

28 I am not worthy to unloose. These things were done in 'Bethany beyond Jordan, where John was baptizing.

a Judges 7 : 24 ; ch. 10 : 40. —1 Many ancient authorities read, *Bethabarah*, some *Betharabah*.

him would administer; (See Matt. 3: 11; Mark 1: 7, 8; Luke 3: 16); but in responding to the more learned and captious Pharisees from Jerusalem, a briefer statement was enough.

28. These things were done in Bethabara (or *Bethany*) beyond Jordan, where John was baptizing. The importance which the Evangelist attaches to this interview, on account of the testimony which the Baptist gave in it respecting the Christ, leads him to mention the place where the deputation examined the prophet and harbinger of the Lord. Bethany, instead of Bethabara, is the reading of the oldest manuscripts (*e. g.*, א A B C), and is adopted by the critical editors. Origen says: "We are not ignorant that almost all the copies have, *These things took place in Bethany;* and this, it seems, also formerly to have been; therefore we have read Bethany in Heraklcon. But we were persuaded that it is not necessary to read Bethany, but Bethabara, when we were in those places for the purpose of tracing by sight the footsteps of Jesus, and of his disciples, and of the prophets. For Bethany, as the Evangelist himself says, the native place of Lazarus and Martha, and Mary, was fifteen furlongs distant from Jerusalem, while the river Jordan is one hundred and eighty furlongs beyond this. Neither is there a place of the same name as Bethany about the Jordan. But *they say* that there is pointed out on the bank of the Jordan the Bethabara, where they relate that John baptized" (VI. 24). It seems necessary in accordance with the testimony, though against the opinion of Origen, to follow the best authorized reading, and to suppose that the place over the Jordan called Bethany had disappeared, or changed its name before the time of Origen. Somewhere in the neighborhood of the Jabbok, as it enters the Jordan, there was a Bethabara in the days of Gideon (Judg. 7:24), and at that place, as well as at Bethany, John may have baptized. This would account for the tradition which Origen found. Caspari argues ingeniously that Bethany is represented by Tell Anihje, on the east side of the Jordan,

a few miles north of Lake Gennesareth; for, as he maintains that the word Tell has taken the place of Beth as a prefix to many names of places in Palestine, he considers Tell Anihje equivalent to Beth Anihje, that is, Bethany. (See "Chronological and Geographical Intro. to the Life of Christ," pp. 92, 93). Von Raumer also argues that there was a Judah beyond Jordan, northeast of the Sea of Galilee, called Golan, Jaulan, or Gaulonitis. If so, a comparison of Matt. 19: 1 with John 10: 40, might lead to the conclusion that Bethany was in that province. Yet it is by no means certain that John first baptized in Bethany beyond the Jordan, and it seems quite improbable that Matt. 3: 5, 6, and Mark 1: 6, refer to any place north of the Sea of Galilee. Some members of the English Company sent out to explore the Holy Land, locate Bethany on the east of the Jordan, not far south of the Sea of Galilee. But its exact topography is still unknown. Mr. Condor, of the Royal Engineers, speaks of a ford of the Jordan named 'Abârah, "just above the place where the Jalûd River, flowing down the valley Jezreel by Beisân, debouches into Jordan. . . . We have collected the names of over forty fords, and no other is called 'Abârah; nor does the word occur again in all the 9,000 names collected by the survey party. . . . The ford 'Abârah is about twenty-two miles from Kefr Kenna, and no place can be found, on the Jordan, much nearer or more easily accessible to the neighborhood of Cana. . . . Bathania, meaning 'soft soil,' was the well-known form used in the time of Christ, of the old name Bashan, which district was in Perœa, or the country beyond Jordan. . . . If Bethabara be a true reading, the place should thus, most probably, be sought in Bathania, and the ford should, therefore, lead over to Bashan. This, again, strengthens the case for the 'Abârah ford, which is near the hills of Bashan, whereas the Jericho fords are far away, leading over towards Gilead and Moab" (Vol. II. pp. 64 sq.).

29–34. JOHN'S TESTIMONY TO HIS OWN DISCIPLES THE NEXT DAY.

29 The next day John seeth Jesus coming unto him, and saith, Behold *the Lamb of God, which *taketh away the sin of the world!

29 On the morrow he seeth Jesus coming unto him, and saith, Behold, the Lamb of God, that *taketh

a Ex. 12:3; Isa. 53:7; ver. 36; Acts 8:32; 1 Pet. 1:19; Rev. 5. 6. etc....*b* Isa. 53:11; 1 Cor. 15:3; Gal. 1:4; Heb. 1:3; 2:17; 9:28; 1 Pet. 2:24; 3:18; 1 John 2:2; 3:5; 4:10; Rev. 1:5.—1 Or. *beareth the sin.*

29. The next day John (or *he*, meaning John), **seeth Jesus coming unto him.** Jesus now appears for the first time in the proper narrative of the Evangelist. All the interesting circumstances of his birth, his infancy, his childhood, his visit to the Temple at the age of twelve, his baptism, and his temptation in the wilderness, are passed by in silence, and he is brought forward at the very time when, probably, the writer first saw him, and began to think of him as the hope of Israel. The purpose for which Jesus was coming to John is not named, and it can only be conjectured from what follows. He was about to enter upon his public ministry, to call about him disciples, and to prepare a select company of them to be witnesses of his miracles and resurrection: where could he expect to find men so well prepared to receive him as were some of those who had been taught by John the Baptist? by one who was "more than a prophet," because he was a messenger sent to prepare the way of the Lord?

When now the Baptist saw Jesus approaching, he said to the group of serious men about him: **Behold the Lamb of God, which taketh away the sin of the world!** For he recognized Jesus, and knew that he was the Son of God (ver. 32-34). But why did he call Jesus **the Lamb of God?** Without doubt because he saw in him "the servant of Jehovah," described in the fifty-third chapter of Isaiah, who was "led as a lamb to the slaughter." The best interpreters unite in this answer—*e. g.*, Lücke, Meyer, Godet, Lange, Alford, and many others. The principal reasons for this answer are found in the use of the definite article before the word lamb (ὁ ἀμνός), and in the meaning of the next clause. It is indeed possible that, by directing attention to Jesus as **the Lamb of God,** John meant to affirm that in him was to be fulfilled, in a perfect manner, the whole idea and office of sacrifice by blood. Yet, if this was his meaning, it is not very obvious why he made choice of "the lamb" to represent all the animals that were offered in sacrifice; for some of the most important sacrifices of the Mosaic Economy were made with other animals. But in the fifty-third of Isaiah, "the servant of Jehovah" is represented as "a lamb," and was believed by many, if not by all of the pious Israelites of that time, to be the Messiah. That the Messiah is there depicted as one who "is brought as a lamb to the slaughter," as one who bore up the sins of many upon the altar of sacrifice, as one who "was wounded for our transgressions," and "bruised for our iniquities," is reason enough why the Baptist should point him out as the Lamb of God. The next clause also favors this interpretation, though it is properly translated, **which taketh away the sin of the world.** For it has been well said: "How does Christ take away sin? Not, as we are often told, by simply removing it from the offender, and putting it out of sight. . . . A careful examination of the word (αἴρω), meaning, *to take away*, will show that it permits one to take an object away only by taking it upon himself. . . . Christ took away our sins, therefore, by taking them upon himself. . . . We may then say, that while we are to translate by "take away," and while the idea of deportation is in the foreground of the picture, there is in the background the idea of taking up sin as a load and bearing it to sacrifice." (Bib. Sac., Vol. xxxii., pp. 48, 49). Some interpreters have thought it improbable that John the Baptist knew as much respecting the work of Christ as this language suggests, and have, therefore, called in question the accuracy of the Evangelist's report. But, in reply to this, it may be remarked, that the Baptist was not as a prophet inferior to Isaiah, that he had the predictions of Isaiah in his hands, that he was the harbinger of Christ, enlightened beyond others in respect to him, and that he may have seen in the baptism of Jesus a type of his death for sinners. There is, therefore, no good reason for supposing that he could not have uttered the words here attributed to him, meaning by them all that has been explained above.

30 *This is he of whom I said, After me cometh a man which is preferred before me; for he was before me.
31 And I knew him not: but that he should be made manifest to Israel, *therefore am I come baptizing with water.
32 *And John bare record, saying, I saw the Spirit

30 away the sin of the world! This is he of whom I said, After me cometh a man who is become before me: for he was *before me. And I knew him not; but that he should be made manifest to Israel, for 32 this cause came I baptizing *in water. And John bare witness, saying, I have beheld the Spirit descending as a dove out of heaven; and it abode

a ver. 15: 27....*b* Mal. 3: 1; Matt. 3: 6; Luke 1: 17, 76, 77; 3: 3, 4....*c* Matt. 3: 16; Mark 1: 10; Luke 3: 22; ch. 5: 32.—1 Gr. *first in regard of me*....2 Or, *with*.

30. This is he of whom I said, After me cometh a man which is preferred before me; for he was before me. The interpretation of this language, which was given at verse 15, need not be repeated. But it is worthy of notice that the first clause there had **was**, while the first clause here has **is**. We are unable to account for this variation, if both passages refer to the same occasion and testimony, (unless we adopt Weiss's explanation of **was,** in ver. 15). But there is no necessity for supposing this. In the case here related, John may have been speaking of Jesus with reference to his present movements, while in that, he may have been speaking of him with reference to some past action in which he had been concerned. The probability of this explanation is increased, if Lachmann, Tischendorf, and Tregelles, are correct in substituting *for*—*in behalf of*—(ὑπέρ) for *of*, *concerning*, (περί), before the pronoun **whom**, thus: **This is he** *in behalf of* **whom I said**. The manuscript evidence for the two prepositions is about equal, but a change from *of* (περί) to *for* (ὑπέρ) would be less likely to occur, than a change from *for* to *of*. The more difficult reading is therefore likely to be correct; and John must be supposed to have referred, in this instance, to his testimony as giver in behalf of Christ.

31. And I knew him not. Some expositors find evidence in this statement that the Evangelist was ignorant of the facts recorded by Luke and Matthew in respect to the kinship and acquaintance of Elisabeth and Mary (Luke 1), and also of the reluctance of John to baptize Jesus (Matt. 3: 14). But a *falsarius* of the second century would have been likely to know the contents of the first and third Gospels, and *not* likely to write anything palpably inconsistent with their accounts. There is, however, no sufficient ground for the assertion, that Jesus and John must have been personally acquainted. For, from his childhood, John had lived a Nazarite, mostly in the desert, while Jesus had lived, with his mother and her other children, in Nazareth. Still further, the knowledge here disclaimed by John may have been the certain knowledge that Jesus was the Messiah, which was to be given by a sign from heaven; and if so, he may have been acquainted with Jesus, and may have expected that he might prove to be the Messiah. This expectation would also account for his language to Jesus, when the latter applied to him for baptism. Besides, John required of those whom he baptized a confession of sin, and the unrecorded response of Jesus to such a requirement may have led, by its profound and holy character, to the Baptist's exclamation: "I have need to be baptized of thee: and comest thou to me?" (Matt. 3: 14).—**But that he should be made manifest to Israel, therefore am I come baptizing with** (*in*) **water.** While John did not know Jesus as the Messiah until the hour of his baptism, he did know that his own work of baptizing in water was ordained for the purpose, among others, of manifesting the Messiah to Israel. It was deemed proper, by the wisdom of God, that Jesus be announced to the people, and identified as the Christ, by a great prophet, entrusted with the function of introducing a new religious ordinance and era. The order of the words in the last clause makes *in water* emphatic, and suggests that John had in mind, as a contrast, Christ's baptizing in the Holy Spirit. Observe, also, that the order of the last two clauses gives special prominence to the manifestation of Christ to the people as a leading object of John's baptism. We have omitted the article before **water** in agreement with a majority of the early copies, though there is considerable force in Meyer's argument that a transcriber, with verses 26 and 33, where the article is not used before him, would be more likely to omit it here if it was in the original text, than to insert it if it was not in the text. Lachmann, Tischendorf, Tregelles, with Westcott and Hort, unite in omitting it.

32. And John bare record (or *witness*)

76 JOHN. [CH. I.

descending from heaven like a dove, and it abode upon him. 33 And I knew him not: but he that sent me to baptize with water, the same said unto me, Upon whom thou shalt see the Spirit descending, and remaining on him, *the same is he which baptizeth with the Holy Ghost.

33 upon him. And I knew him not; but he that sent me to baptize ¹in water, he said unto me, Upon whomsoever thou shalt see the Spirit descending, and abiding upon him, the same is he that baptizeth with the Holy Ghost.

a Matt. 3: 11; Acts 1: 5; 2: 4; 10: 44; 19: 6.—1 Or, *with*.

saying, I saw (rather, *I have beheld*) the Spirit descending from heaven like a dove, and it abode upon him. By saying, "*I have beheld*," instead of "I beheld," John affirms that he is still vividly conscious of the sight. The vision was not transitory in its effect upon his soul. What he saw as a symbol of the Spirit had a dove-like shape, though the significance of this is nowhere explained. In view of it Alford says, that "the Spirit manifested in our Lord was *gentle* and *benign*." Lange remarks that "no one virtue of the dove" is meant; "but her virtues; . . . hence purity, loveliness, gentleness, friendliness to men, and vital warmth." But most expositors, influenced by the words of Christ, recorded in Matt. 10: 16, suppose that the dove is a symbol of purity and innocence. The precise meaning of the last clause is not easily given by a translation. For (*ἐπί*) **upon,** followed by the accusative, signifies motion towards, or down upon; and the symbol which John saw, represented the Holy Spirit as having floated swiftly down from the opened heaven, and as about to rest, or, perhaps, as already resting, on the head of Jesus.

33. And I (or *I myself*) **knew him not; but he that sent me to baptize with** (or *in*) **water, the same** (or *he*) **said unto me: Upon whom thou shalt see the Spirit descending, and remaining on him, the same is he which baptizeth with** (*in*) **the Holy Ghost.** The note of Godet on this passage is very satisfactory. "Not only has a sign been announced to him (ver. 31), and he had seen a sign (ver. 32), but that sign was precisely the one announced. Everything like human caprice is, therefore, excluded from the interpretation of the sign which he gives. . . The expression, *he that sent me*, has in it something solemn and mysterious; it evidently means God himself, who spoke to him in the wilderness, and gave him his commission. . . The act of baptizing with the Holy Spirit, is named as the essential characteristic of the Messiah."

But what is meant by **baptizeth with** (*in*) the **Holy Spirit?** In answering this question we must consider the special connection of this baptism with Christ, the natural import of the expression, the instances of this baptism mentioned in the New Testament, and the references to the same thing in other language.

It is plain that John thought of baptism in the Holy Spirit as a very important and characteristic part of Christ's work. Perhaps he referred to it all the more frequently because of the resemblance which he perceived between his own work and this part of the Messiah's work. Christ alone was to introduce and give this baptism. It must therefore have been regarded as something different in kind or degree from any blessing conferred on saints under the Mosaic Economy.

But the expression, to baptize in the Holy Spirit, points to a difference in degree, rather than in kind, between this blessing and any that had been given before. Moses and Samuel, David and Isaiah, were not strangers to the illuminating and sanctifying work of the Spirit. All good men from the beginning had felt his gracious influence. But this influence was not so all-embracing and overflowing as immersion in the Spirit. It did not flood their souls with such light and power as came on the early disciples. This general difference between the presence of the Holy Spirit before, and his presence after the Day of Pentecost, is obvious to every student of the Scriptures.

But in describing the fulfillment of this prediction of the Baptist, the sacred record does not affirm that all Christians, from the Day of Pentecost onward, were baptized in the Spirit. In two instances it represents the prediction as fulfilled, that is, on the Day of Pentecost and before the baptism of Cornelius (Acts 1: 5. 8; 2: 1 sq.; 10: 44–49; 11: 15, 16), and in both these instances some of the results were extraordinary. Great power, as well as great grace, was imparted to those who were immersed in the Spirit; for they spoke with tongues and prophesied.

34 And I saw, and bare record that this is the Son of God.
35 Again the next day after, John stood, and two of his disciples;
36 And looking upon Jesus as he walked, he saith, *Behold the Lamb of God!
37 And the two disciples heard him speak, and they followed Jesus.

34 tizeth ¹in the Holy Spirit. And I have seen, and have borne witness that this is the Son of God.
35 Again on the morrow John was standing, and 36 two of his disciples; and he looked upon Jesus as he walked, and saith, Behold, the Lamb of God!
37 And the two disciples heard him speak, and they

a ver. 20.——1 Or, *with*.

But the fulfillment of the promise was not limited to those instances, any more than was the promise itself to the form which it took on the lips of John the Baptist. The same promise was uttered by Joel, in other terms, and the same promise was fulfilled when other terms were used to describe the event. Yet there is some reason to believe that, as it was understood by the apostles, its fulfillment included in every instance one or more of the special gifts which distinguished the first age of the church (Joel 2: 28 sq.; Isa. 44: 3; John 16: 12-15; 20: 22, 23; Acts 1: 8; 2: 16 sq.; 6: 3, 5, 8; 8: 6, 7, 16, 17; 19: 6). Not that these gifts were deemed more precious than faith, hope, and love, but that the former as well as the latter are fruits of the Spirit, and were embraced in that wonderful work which was foretold by Joel, by John, and by Christ.

If this be correct, it can hardly be said that baptism in the Spirit is equally the privilege of all Christians. Yet it may be said that the presence of the Spirit is with every Christian, doing for him, in the way of sanctification and support, all that he needs or accepts. This gracious presence of the Spirit is the spring of holy peace, and joy, and strength in the soul. Whether anything like miraculous endowment would be of real service to Christians in the present age, may be doubtful; but if it is needed now, or should be needed hereafter, it will surely be given; for he who **baptizeth in the Holy Spirit** sits upon the throne.

34. And I saw, etc. The Revised Version of this verse is correct: *And I have seen, and have borne witness that this is the Son of God.* Thus the Baptist repeats the two great facts of his work as the harbinger of Christ, viz., that he himself has witnessed the divinely appointed sign of the Messiah, and has borne witness of Jesus, when he had been thus pointed out by a sign from heaven, as the Son of God. And this expression, **the Son of God,** simply echoes the voice from heaven, which accompanied the descent of the Spirit, and was heard by Jesus and by John (Matt. 3: 17; Luke 3: 22). To explain the importance which the Evangelist attaches to this testimony of the Baptist, it is only necessary to suppose that he was a disciple of the Baptist and heard it from his lips; and to explain the importance which the Baptist attached to it, it is only necessary to suppose that he had received from God the communication described in this verse, before he witnessed the descent of the Spirit and the voice from heaven. Besides, it is possible that Jesus and John were alone at the baptism, or that the vision and voice were a subjective revelation to them, or that, though perceived by the people, they were not understood. (See John 12: 28, 29.) If either of these suppositions is correct, the testimony of John would seem to be more isolated and important still.

35-42. THE FIRST DISCIPLES OF JESUS.

35. Again, the next day after, John stood (or, *was standing*), **and two of his disciples.** It is not surprising that the writer, if he was himself one of these two disciples, should have been thus particular in his notices of time. These were days never to be forgotten, and these were testimonies that led him to the Lord.

36. And looking upon Jesus as he walked, etc. The participle translated *looking upon* seems to denote an earnest and perhaps fixed gaze (compare John 1: 42; Mark 10: 21, 27; 14: 67; Luke 20: 17; 22: 61); and the brief expression uttered by the Baptist was full of meaning, and recalled all his testimony of the day before.

37. And the two disciples heard him speak (or, *speaking*). Evidently his exclamation was not addressed particularly to them; perhaps it was merely the cry of his heart that must needs utter itself. Some of the greatest and best results are brought to pass by almost aimless acts of a holy soul. In this case, the words, though addressed to no one in particular, fell upon prepared

38 Then Jesus turned, and saw them following, and saith unto them, What seek ye? They said unto him, Rabbi, (which is to say, being interpreted, Master,) where dwellest thou?
39 He saith unto them, Come and see. They came and saw where he dwelt, and abode with him that day: for it was about the tenth hour.
40 One of the two which heard John speak, and followed him, was a Andrew, Simon Peter's brother.

38 followed Jesus. And Jesus turned, and beheld them following, and saith unto them, What seek ye? And they said unto him, Rabbi (which is to say, being interpreted, ¹Master), where abidest
39 thou? He saith unto them, Come, and ye shall see. They came therefore and saw where he abode; and they abode with him that day: it was about 40 the tenth hour. One of the two that heard John speak, and followed him, was Andrew, Simon

a Matt. 4:18.—1 Or. *Teacher.*

hearts, and bore fruit in action.—**And they followed Jesus.** That is, they went after him, as he walked away, for the purpose of learning more about him from his own lips, and expecting, no doubt, to find in him the Messiah. But their steps were heard by the Saviour.

38. Then (better, *And*) **Jesus turned, and saw** (*beheld*) **them following, and saith unto them, What seek ye?** This question was perfectly natural, whether it was asked for the purpose of ascertaining why they followed his steps, or whether it was intended, as we rather believe, to open the way for them to express what he saw already was in their hearts.—**Rabbi (which is to say, being interpreted, Master), where dwellest** (*i. e., abidest*) **thou?** By this response they recognize him as a Teacher, and intimate their desire to speak with him at some convenient time in private. His answer to their suggestion is prompt and cordial, for

39. He saith unto them, Come and see: or, *Come, and ye shall see* (Rev. Ver.). This was an invitation to come at once. Let Christian teachers imitate their Master. Now is the convenient time for one who is eager to do good. As to the text, the evidence for the reading *ye shall see*, outweighs that for *see*.—**They came** (*therefore*) **and saw where he dwelt** (or, *abode*); literally, *where he abides;* a reminiscence of the form of their question, verse 38. *Therefore* makes their coming a consequence of his invitation.—**And they abode** (*remained*) **with him that day: for it was about the tenth hour.** *For* should be omitted as an interpolation. "The great importance of this hour for John himself (*it was the first of his Christian life*) made it forever memorable to him, and led him to mention it expressly in this place."—*Meyer.* According to Jewish reckoning, the tenth hour of the day was four o'clock in the afternoon; but there is

reason to believe that John did not follow this method of reckoning the hours of the day, but reckoned from midnight to noonday, and from noonday to midnight. (Compare 4:6, 52; 19:14.) From ten in the morning until the evening was, doubtless, the period which is here called **that day,** *i. e.,* the rest of that day. With this view the language of the Evangelist is certainly more expressive, if not more natural, than it would be if the other mode of reckoning had been followed, so that this would have been four o'clock p. m. See notes under 4:6, 52, and 19:14; also Edersheim, "The Life and Times of Jesus the Messiah" on these passages.

40. One of the two which heard John speak, and followed him, was Andrew, Simon Peter's brother. According to certain modern critics of the Fourth Gospel, its author sought to diminish the influence of the Petrine party in his own day, by giving to Peter a lower place among the apostles than had been assigned to him by Synoptical tradition. But we discover no evidence of such a purpose in the Gospel. On the contrary, the same leading position is given to him in this Gospel as in the others. Andrew is introduced as **Simon Peter's brother,** while the character of Peter is perceived by the Lord at once, and recognized by the gift of a new name (ver. 42.).

But who was the unnamed companion of Andrew? Probably the Evangelist himself. For (1) the narrative in this place is very particular and graphic, making it probable that the writer was an eye-witness. (2) The writer of such a narrative would have been sure to mention the name of the other disciple as well as that of Andrew, unless there had been some reason for withholding it. (3) The writer of this Gospel never refers to himself elsewhere by name, and the same feeling which led him to withhold his name elsewhere accounts for his withholding it here.

41 He first findeth his own brother Simon, and saith unto him, We have found the Messias, which is, being interpreted, the Christ.
42 And he brought him to Jesus. And when Jesus beheld him, he said, Thou art Simon the son of Jona: thou shalt be called Cephas, which is by interpretation, A stone.
43 The day following Jesus would go forth into Galilee, and findeth Philip, and saith unto him, Follow me.

41 Peter's brother. He findeth first his own brother Simon, and saith unto him, We have found the Messiah) which is, being interpreted, Christ). He brought him unto Jesus. Jesus looked upon him, and said, Thou art Simon the son of ³John: thou shalt be called Cephas (which is by interpretation, ⁴Peter).
43 On the morrow he was minded to go forth into Galilee, and he findeth Philip; and Jesus saith

a Matt. 26: 18.——1 That is, Anointed....2 Gr., Joanes: called in Matt. xvi. 17, Jonah....3 That is, Rock or Stone.

41. He first findeth his own brother Simon, and saith unto him, We have found the Messias, which is, being interpreted, the Christ. The word **first** is probably an adjective agreeing with he, or *this one;* and, if so, it suggests that there was another, a second, viz., the Evangelist, who also went after his own brother, but did not find him as soon as Andrew found Peter. But each went after his own brother, and was successful in finding and bringing him to Jesus. A good example! It is then a reasonable conjecture that Andrew and Peter, John and James were at Bethany, beyond the Jordan, attending on the ministry of John the Baptist, when Jesus returned from his trial in the wilderness, that all were made acquainted with Jesus the same day, and that, after the Baptist, these four men were the first to acknowledge Jesus as the Messiah. And it is worthy of notice that Andrew says, "We have found the Messias," as if they had been seeking him. Hence they were truly devout men, "waiting for the consolation of Israel." They were prepared to follow the Messiah as soon as he was known to them. They were already renewed in heart, and therefore eager to discover the promised Christ. No wonder then that they felt, from the first moment, the attractive power of his presence, the divine purity and sweetness of his spirit. The ministry of John had borne fruit, and the way of the Lord was prepared in these hearts. The parenthesis, which simply translates the Hebrew term Messiah into Greek, shows that the Evangelist was writing for persons, some of whom were not supposed to know the Hebrew language. Both terms signify *anointed*. Prophets, priests, and kings were anointed, in token of their having the Holy Spirit to qualify them for their respective offices. In the person of Jesus of Nazareth were united the offices of prophet, priest, and king, and to him the Spirit was given without measure. He was therefore pre-eminently the Anointed.

If now it be asked: What did the Holy Spirit do for the Lord Jesus? this answer may be suggested: Just what the relation of the Spirit's work in the soul of Christ may have been to that of his higher nature, the Word, is unrevealed; but from the office of the Spirit in the economy of salvation, *i. e.*, to renew, sanctify, and prepare men for the reception of truth, it may be inferred that the human soul of Jesus was moved by the Spirit to desire and seek the very things which the incarnate Word desired and sought, thus contributing to the perfect unity of aim and spirit which distinguished Christ from all other men.

42. For a literal translation of this verse, see Revised Version above. It was probably a very easy task which Andrew performed in leading his brother to Jesus. As they drew near, Jesus fixed his eyes upon Simon with a gaze that pierced even the depths of his soul. Perceiving the strength of his character, he at once bestowed on him a name expressive of that strength; he declared that he should be called Cephas, that is, Peter, that is, Rock. Surely the writer who mentions this early recognition of Peter's greatness by his Lord did not seek to diminish the influence of this prompt and noble servant of Christ. It will be noticed that the Revised Version omits the conjunction **and** (καί) before **brought**, with Tischendorf, Tregelles, Westcott and Hort; also **and** (δέ) before **beheld**, or *looked* (ἐμβλέψας), with Tisch., Treg., W. and H.; and substitutes *John* for **Jona**, as the name of Peter's father, with Lachmann, Tisch., Treg., W. and H.

43-51. ANOTHER GROUP OF DISCIPLES CALLED.

43. The day following, etc., better as in Revised Version: *On the morrow he was minded to go forth into Galilee, and he findeth Philip: and Jesus saith unto him,* Follow me. This was probably the fourth day from the visit of the deputation (v. 19, sq.), and the finding of Philip seems to

80 JOHN. [Ch. I.

44 Now *Philip was of Bethsaida, the city of Andrew and Peter.
45 Philip findeth *Nathanael, and saith unto him, We have found him, of whom *Moses in the law, and the *prophets, did write, Jesus* of Nazareth, the son of Joseph.
46 And Nathanael said unto him, *Can there any good thing come out of Nazareth? Philip saith unto him, Come and see.
47 Jesus saw Nathanael coming to him, and saith of him, Behold *an Israelite indeed, in whom is no guile!

44 unto him, Follow me. Now Philip was from Bethsaida, of the city of Andrew and Peter. Philip findeth Nathanael, and saith unto him, We have found him, of whom Moses in the law, and the prophets, did write, Jesus of Nazareth, the son of Joseph. And Nathanael said unto him, Can any good thing come out of Nazareth? Philip saith
47 unto him, Come and see. Jesus saw Nathanael coming to him, and saith of him, Behold, an Israel-

a ch. 12: 21...*b* ch. 21: 2....*c* Gen. 3: 15; 49: 10; Deut. 18: 18. See on Luke 21: 27.....*d* Isa. 4: 2; 7: 14; 9: 6; 53: 2; Mic. 5: 2; Zech. 6: 12; 9: 9. See more on Luke 21: 27.....*e* Matt. 2: 23; Luke 2: 4...,*f* ch. 7: 41, 42, 52.....*g* Ps. 32: 2; 73: 1; ch. 8: 30; Rom. 2: 28, 29; 9: 6.

have occurred when Jesus was about leaving his temporary abode in the trans-Jordanic Bethany. See the note of Meyer on this passage, and the remarks of Luthardt on the frequent co-ordination of one clause with another in the New Testament, and especially in the writings of John, when in classic Greek one of them would have been subordinated to the other. Thus: "As he was minded to go forth into Galilee, he findeth Philip," would have been more classical than the text.

Was Jesus seeking for Philip? Or did he meet him casually? The import of **findeth** would, perhaps, be satisfied by merely assuming that Jesus was already intent upon winning disciples, so that the apparently casual meeting with Philip led at once to a call which expressed the feeling of a person who was seeking him. The words, **follow me,** were surely a call to accept Christ as a spiritual guide and teacher, and not merely to accompany him into Galilee. They were not, however, a definite call to the Apostleship. According to the best authorities, the word **Jesus** should be omitted in the first clause of the common text, and inserted in the third.

44. Now Philip was of Bethsaida, the city of Andrew and Peter. The exact position of Bethsaida is unknown, but it appears to have been situated near the Sea of Galilee, on the northwest side. Dr. Thompson supposes that it was situated east of the entrance of the Jordan into the Sea of Galilee; but Major Wilson identifies it with Khan Minyeh, further south. ("Sea of Galilee," in Warren's "Recovery of Jerusalem," pp. 342, 387.) Philip is mentioned several times in this Gospel (*e. g.,* 6: 5, 7; 12: 21, 22; 14: 8).

45. We have found him, of whom Moses in the law, and the prophets, did write, Jesus of Nazareth, the son of Joseph. Philip was acquainted with Nathanael (Theodore, Gift-of-God), and knew him to be a devout soul, waiting for the Messiah. He, therefore, at once sought and found him. And from his language to Nathanael, **We have found,** it may be inferred that Philip was also seeking in spirit for the Christ when Jesus found him. It seems probable, therefore, that all these, Andrew and Peter, James and John, Philp and Nathanael (called, also, Bartholomew), were disciples of John, from the same part of Galilee, and so were acquainted with one another; also, that they were all at Bethany, and accompanied Jesus to Galilee. Philip was not mistaken when he said that Moses and the prophets wrote of Christ; for the Lord himself afterwards asserted the same (5: 39, 46; Luke 24: 44). At this time Philip did not know the particulars of Jesus' birth, and therefore described him as the son of Joseph, his reputed father.

46. Can there any good thing come out of Nazareth? What may be inferred from the question of Nathanael as to Nazareth? Was it simply an insignificant town? Or was it a place of ill repute also? Since Nathanael was from Cana of Galilee, a village not far from Nazareth, and in the same province, it is presumable that he would not speak thus of the latter place simply because it was situated in Galilee, or because it was an inconsiderable village. Nazareth must have been in ill repute for morality. And this circumstance may afford a clue to the interpretation of Matt. 2: 23, if the phrase, "He shall be called a Nazarene," is regarded as an epitome of the predictions which speak of him as "despised and rejected of men." On Philip's brief response, **Come and see,** Bengel remarks: "The best remedy for preconceived opinions!" and Lange: "A watchword of the Christian faith!"

47. Behold an Israelite indeed, in whom is no guile! The Evangelist, doubtless, means to suggest that Jesus looked into the soul of Nathanael and perceived him to be a genuine servant of God, sincere,

[Cн. I.]   JOHN.   81

48 Nathanael saith unto him, Whence knowest thou me? Jesus answered and said unto him, Before that Philip called thee, when thou wast under the fig tree, I saw thee.
49 Nathanael answered and saith unto him, Rabbi, *thou art the Son of God; thou art [b] the King of Israel.
50 Jesus answered and said unto him, Because I said unto thee, I saw thee under the fig tree, believest thou? thou shalt see greater things than these.
51 And he saith unto him, Verily, verily, I say unto you, [c] Hereafter ye shall see heaven open, and the angels of God ascending and descending upon the Son of man.

48 ite indeed, in whom is no guile! Nathanael saith unto him, Whence knowest thou me? Jesus answered and said unto him, Before Philip called thee, when thou wast under the fig tree, I saw thee.
49 Nathanael answered him, Rabbi, thou art the Son 50 of God; thou art King of Israel. Jesus answered and said unto him, Because I said unto thee, I saw thee underneath the fig tree, believest thou? thou 51 shalt see greater things than these. And he saith unto him, Verily, verily, I say unto you, Ye shall see the heaven opened, and the angels of God ascending and descending upon the Son of man.

a Matt. 14: 33....b Matt. 21: 5; 27: 11, 42; ch. 18: 37; 19: 3....c Gen. 28: 12; Matt. 4: 11; Luke 2: 9, 13; 22: 43; 24: 4; Acts 1: 10.

truthful, open-hearted. His remark was not addressed to Nathanael, but was heard by him as he drew near. Hence, the next verse.

48. Before that Philip called thee, when thou wast under the fig tree, I saw thee. By this answer to Nathanael's question, **Whence knowest thou me?** Jesus evidently intended to claim supernatural knowledge. The fig tree in question must therefore have been *out of sight* from any and every place where Jesus might have been at the time. Otherwise, his answer would not have made such an impression on the mind of Nathanael as it did make, and as he surely intended to have it make. But if Jesus had seen Nathanael when and where it was impossible to do this by any natural power of vision, he might well be supposed to look into the soul itself, and discover its true character. By this reference to an event which Nathanael recognized, he proved that he had supernatural knowledge in the world of sense, and plainly intimated that he had similar access to the soul of man, and had learned the character of Nathanael by direct intuition. Hence, the conviction uttered by Nathanael in response to this revelation. Whether there was anything in the purpose for which Nathanael had resorted to the fig tree, or in his action while under it, which added force to the Saviour's remark, we are unable to say; but it is very natural to imagine that he was there for a religious purpose—for solitary communion with God; and it is quite possible that his spirit had been deeply moved at that time by the Spirit of God with reference to the Messiah, if not with reference to Jesus as the Messiah. If this was so, the statement of Jesus must have been all the more impressive and convincing.

49. Rabbi, thou art the Son of God; thou art the King of Israel. If Nathanael was present when John the Baptist uttered the words recorded in verse 34 above, and knew that they referred to Jesus, or, at least, to the Messiah, it is not in the least surprising that he now expressed his faith in Jesus by the same words, **Thou art the Son of God.** Especially natural would this have been, if he had gone to the fig tree with this remarkable testimony of the Baptist in his mind, and had there in solitary communion with God been prepared for the message brought by Philip. Yet, it is not to be forgotten that the Messiah is represented as the Son of God in the Second Psalm. Very excellent are the comments of Godet on this verse: "The two titles complete one another: *Son of God*, bears on the relation of Jesus to God; *King of Israel*, on his relation to the chosen people. The second title is the logical consequence of the first. The personage who lives in so intimate a relation to God, can only be, as is alleged, the King of Israel, the Messiah. This second title corresponds to the *Israelite indeed*, with which Jesus has saluted Nathanael. The faithful subject has recognized and salutes his king." Lücke remarks, "that the order of these two designations may be due to the immediate impression of the divine in Jesus, from which the utterance of Nathanael flowed."

50. Because I said unto thee, I saw thee under the fig tree, believest thou? Thou shalt see greater things than these. The words translated, **believest thou?** might be translated *thou believest;* but the meaning would remain essentially the same. Jesus accepts the utterance of Nathanael as a sincere expression of faith, and assures him that the evidence on which that faith rests will be greatly surpassed by other evidence to be given by the Messiah.

**51. Verily, verily, I say unto you, Hereafter ye shall see heaven open, and the angels of God ascending and de-

F

CHAPTER II.

AND the third day there was a marriage in ªCana of Galilee; and the mother of Jesus was there:

1 AND the third day there was a marriage in Cana of Galilee; and the mother of Jesus was there; and

---

a See Josh. 19: 28.

---

scending upon the Son of man. Though the Evangelist represents Christ as speaking these words to Nathanael, they were meant without doubt for the others also, as the plural ye intimates. The double **verily**, or *amen*, which this Evangelist attributes to Jesus twenty-five times (Meyer), is never attributed to him by the other Evangelists, is never used for himself by the writer of the Fourth Gospel, and is never attributed by him to any one save Christ. These facts are unaccountable, if this Gospel was written by a forger of the second century; they can only be explained, if it was written by a disciple of Jesus whose spirit had been deeply moved by this form of expression. The words that follow seem to be taken, in part, from the language used in describing Jacob's vision at Bethel (Gen. 28: 12). But to what do they refer? If we draw an answer to this question from the probable import of that vision, it will be to this effect: "You will have the clearest evidence that heaven is near, and open to the Son of man, and that the angels of God are ever ready to do his will." We do not mean to say that a frequent *appearance* of angels was predicted by Christ in connection with his ministry, but rather that the powers of heaven were to be with him, and to befriend him.—If we adhere to the common text, the word **hereafter** (ἀπ' ἄρτι), meaning "from this time forward," shows that no special reference is here made to the Transfiguration, or to the Agony in the Garden; and without doubt the phrase (ἀπ' ἄρτι) would be more naturally omitted, from an idea that Christ referred to those particular events, than inserted, when there seems to be no reason whatever for the insertion. Yet some of the best manuscripts (א B L) and early Versions, with Origen, Epiphanius, and Cyril, omit these words, meaning **hereafter**, or *henceforth;* and are followed in this by Lachmann, Tregelles, Tischendorf, Westcott and Hort, the Revised Version, and many able scholars. We cannot, therefore, feel at all confident that they belong to the original text, though the improbability of their insertion by a transcriber appears to us very great.

Jesus here refers to himself as the Son of man, and there is no record of his appropriating the title before. What then did it signify in his lips? And why did he apply it so often to himself? Some have answered these questions by referring to Daniel (7: 13): "I saw in the night visions, and behold one like the Son of man came with the clouds of heaven; and he came to the Ancient of Days," etc. But this prophecy merely describes the Messiah as "like unto a Son of man" (see Rev. Ver. of Old Test.). It does not call him *"the* Son of man." It may, however, be said to describe him as one who was to be connected by nature with mankind in general, rather than with the chosen people, or with the house of David in particular. And this bearing of the expression was intended, as the context proves, just as the effect of calling himself **the Son of man** was intended by Christ, to wit, that his connection with the whole human race should be emphasized. The title must therefore, in the last resort, be appealed to as self-interpreting. And looking at the expression as used by Jesus, it may be said to imply three things, viz.: (1) That he was born of man; (2) that he was a veritable man; and (3) that he was the perfect man, or the one member of the human race in whom the idea of man was realized. He was a son of man, and therefore man; he was *the* Son of man, and therefore the perfect or ideal man. He was neither Jew nor Greek in character or sympathy, but the representative man, the head of renewed humanity. All this is expressed by the designation which he here appropriates to himself—**the Son of man.**

Ch. 2: 1-11. MARRIAGE AND MIRACLE IN CANA OF GALILEE.

1. And the third day there was a marriage in Cana of Galilee. The Evangelist passes at once from the neighborhood of Bethany beyond the Jordan, to Cana of Galilee, a village situated, according to Dr. Robinson's identification, about nine miles north of Nazareth, on the southern declivity of a hill,

2 And both Jesus was called, and his disciples, to the marriage.
3 And when they wanted wine, the mother of Jesus saith unto him, They have no wine.

2 Jesus also was bidden, and his disciples, to the marriage. And when the wine failed, the mother of

and overlooking a broad and fruitful plain. This village is now called Khurbet-Cana, which is said to have retained the name Kana el-Jelil (see Robinson's "Biblical Researches," etc., II. 346-449). Others have insisted that the site was at Kefr Kenna, less than four miles to the northeast of Nazareth. This, we observe, is the view of Professor Stevens, of Rochester, in a recent article describing a journey from Nazareth to Capernaum. (See the "Sunday School Times," for Feb. 7, 1885, entitled, "From Nazareth to Capernaum.") Kefr Kenna lies on the side of a hill sloping towards the north or northwest. The valley towards the west is well-watered and fertile; but the prospect from the village is not very extensive. If Bethany was east of the southern part of the Jordan, the journey from that place to Cana may have occupied between two and three days; for the distance was about sixty miles, and the marriage and miracle here described, belong to the third day after the one last named (1:43). But if the Bethany referred to was at or near the ford Abârah, discovered by Conder (see note on 1:28), it was only about twenty-two miles from Cana; and Jesus may have rested a day at Nazareth on his way to the more northern village. **And the mother of Jesus was there.** From the solicitude which the mother of Jesus felt in respect to the entertainment, and from the authority which she used in speaking to the servants (ver. 5), it has been conjectured that the wedding was in the family of a relative. Dr. Hanna remarks: "If Simon, called the Canaanite, was called so because of his connection with the village of Cana, his father Alphæus, or Clophas, who was married to a sister of Christ's mother, may have resided there; and it may have been in his family that this marriage occurred. . . . . At any rate, we may assume that it was [in] a family connected by some close ties, whether of acquaintance or of relationship with that of Jesus, that the marriage feast was kept." The Evangelist, however, simply states that "the mother of Jesus was there," without intimating the reason why she was there. Everything beyond this is conjecture, though there may be considerable ground for the conjecture.

2. And both Jesus was called, and his disciples, to the marriage. The invitation of the disciples was, probably, due to their connection with Jesus; and the invitation of Jesus was probably given after his return to Galilee, though it is possible that his wish to return into Galilee, mentioned above (1:43), was occasioned by his knowledge of this wedding. We know that he was pleased to honor this marriage festival with his presence, and we may conjecture that, if he was on the lower Jordan, he desired to leave his place just three days before, because it was necessary for him to do so, in order to reach Cana in time for the marriage. But there seem to be strong reasons for doubting whether he was south of the Jabbok, and not rather north of that stream, and so within twenty or thirty miles of Cana. Here, first, are "the disciples," mentioned as a group of followers, who accompany the Lord in his journeys from place to place. A more exact rendering of the original would be: *And Jesus also was bidden, and his disciples, to the marriage.*

3. And when they wanted wine. More precisely: *And when the wine failed.* Whether this failure of wine was due to the presence of more guests than had been expected, or to some other cause, will never be known; and how long the marriage had been in progress, must also be a matter for conjecture. But for some reason, perhaps from an unexpected accession of guests coming with Jesus, there was now a lack of wine, and this lack was known to the mother of Jesus. Relying on the ability of her son, she informed him of the want that would soon be felt; but with something in her look or tone which indicated an expectation of timely help.—**They have no wine.** To state the want is, in such a case, to make request for relief. Whether she anticipated anything miraculous may be doubtful; but it is plain that she looked for assistance in some way. This might come by natural means, and she may have thought of nothing else; yet the circumstance that Jesus had returned to Galilee with a band of disciples, may have led her to

4 Jesus saith unto her, *Woman, *what have I to do with thee? *mine hour is not yet come.
5 His mother saith unto the servants, Whatsoever he saith unto you, do *it*.
6 And there were set there six waterpots of stone, *after the manner of the purifying of the Jews, containing two or three firkins apiece.

4 Jesus saith unto him, They have no wine. And Jesus saith unto her, Woman, what have I to do 5 with thee? mine hour is not yet come. His mother saith unto the servants, Whatsoever he saith unto 6 you, do it. Now there were six waterpots of stone set there after the Jews' manner of purifying, containing

a ch. 19: 26....*b* So 2 Sam. 16: 10; 19: 22....*c* ch. 7: 6....*d* Mark 7: 3.

anticipate some sign or proof of his Messianic power.[1]

4. Jesus saith unto her. The best text has a connective, thus: *And* **Jesus saith unto her, Woman, what have I to do with thee ?** It may be confidently affirmed that there is nothing disrespectful in the address, **woman** (comp. 19: 26; 20: 13, 15; 4: 21), but it must at the same time be conceded that it fails to give any definite expression to filial sentiment or obedience. It could not have meant to recognize and honor the dearest human relationship. And in this respect it was suitable; for it was associated with words that denied to his mother any share in marking out his course, any part in the work he was sent to do (see 2 Sam. 16: 10; 1 Kings 17: 18; 2 Chron. 35: 21; Matt. 8: 29). As the Messiah, he must act in sole subordination to his Father's will. Every thing must be done at the exact time and in the precise manner prescribed by divine wisdom. Yet he did not, in this case, refuse to do what his mother had virtually requested; he rather intimated by the saying, **mine hour is not yet come,** that he would, in his own time, fulfill her desire. Perhaps there was enough in the tone of his emphatic **not yet,** to assure Mary that her request was granted. "There is no inconsistency between this declaration of Christ that his 'hour was not yet come,' and the fulfillment of the prayer which followed immediately. A change of moral and spiritual conditions is not measured by length of time."—(*Westcott.*)

5. Whatsoever he saith unto you, do it. The **it** which is added by the translators, is unnecessary. The mother of Jesus appears to have had authority over the servants who waited on the guests, and she appears, also, to have expected that Jesus would, in some way, provide the wine that was needed. *How* it was to be procured, she had, as yet, no means of knowing; but anything which her Son might direct, she was sure would be wise. Thus she left all to Jesus.

6. And there were set there six waterpots of stone. More exactly: *Now there were six waterpots of stone set there after the manner of the purifying of the Jews.* The place in the house where these waterpots stood is not mentioned, but the exact number of them is stated, as well as the purpose which they were intended to serve. Some of the Jews carefully observed rites of purification not prescribed by the Mosaic law. They were accustomed to wash their feet after walking in the highway (John 13: 4-10), and their hands before eating (Mark 7: 3). They also kept a tradition which required sundry immersions of cups and pots, and vessels of brass, if not of couches (Ibid). To hold the water needed for such rites of purification, these six waterpots had been provided, and they were now at hand for another use. As everything touching the substance of this miracle was deemed important by the Evangelist, he mentions the size, as well as the number, of the waterpots: **containing two or three firkins apiece.** A firkin was a little less than nine gallons. If, then, we suppose that they held two and a half firkins apiece, on an average, or fifteen firkins in all, it would take about 133 gallons of water to fill them—certainly a moderate provision for the purifications that might be needed at such a feast, even though they were occasionally replenished, and though the company was not very large. . . . "Walking among these ruins [at Cana] we saw large, massive stone waterpots . . . not preserved nor exhibited as reliques, but lying about, disregarded by the present inhabitants. . . . From their appearance and the number of them, it was quite evident that a practice of keeping water in large stone pots, each hold-

[1] According to a reading which Tischendorf adopts, this verse should be translated: "And they had no wine, because the wine of the marriage feast had failed." In support of this text, he appeals to ℵ with a b ff² e l, five Latin MSS. (iv.-vii cent.), Gaudentius, Syr. (White) margin, and AEth., while the common text is sustained by ℵᵃ A B L X T Δ Λ Π etc., also c f q, Vulg. Cop. Syr. (three editions). Epiph. Chrys. Cyr. Plainly the ordinary text must stand.

7 Jesus saith unto them, Fill the waterpots with water. And they filled them up to the brim.
8 And he saith unto them, Draw out now, and bear unto the governor of the feast. And they bare *it*.
9 When the ruler of the feast had tasted ᵃthe water

7 taining two or three firkins apiece. Jesus saith unto them, Fill the waterpots with water. And
8 they filled them up to the brim. And he saith unto them, Draw out now, and bear unto the ¹ruler of
9 the feast. And they bare it. And when the ruler

a ch. 4: 46.——1 Or, *steward*.

ing from eighteen to twenty-seven gallons, was once common in the country" (E. D. Clarke, "Travels," II. p. 445; Van Lennep, "Bible Customs," p. 45, note).

7. Fill the waterpots with water, etc. The persons addressed by Jesus were servants, and what they put into the vessels was water. **—And they filled them up to the brim.** A significant statement. The Evangelist himself was doubtless a witness of this whole transaction, and therefore was aware of the minute particulars, and knew that there was no collusion. But if he did not hear the words of Jesus and of his mother, or see what the servants did in obedience to the words of Mary and of Christ, he was of all the disciples just the one who would in all probability have heard a minute account of this miracle from the lips of Mary; for he it was to whom the Lord committed his mother from the cross, and who from that hour took her to his own home (See 19: 26, 27).

8. . . . Draw out now, or, *Draw now,* **and bear unto the governor of the feast.** Between the filling of the waterpots and this drawing of a portion for the ruler of the feast, the miracle seems to have been wrought. This is the most natural hypothesis, though it is certainly possible that the water was changed to wine after it was drawn and while it was being carried to the ruler of the feast. Westcott, however, questions this view, as follows: "There is nothing in the text which definitely points to such an interpretation; and the original word is applied most naturally to drawing water from the well (4: 7-15), and not from a vessel like the waterpot. Moreover, the emphatic addition of now seems to mark the continuance of the same action of drawing as before, but with a different end. Hitherto they had drawn to fill the vessels of purification; they were charged *now* to 'draw and bear to the governor of the feast.' It seems most unlikely that water taken from vessels of purification could have been employed for the purpose of the miracle. On the other hand, the significance of the miracle comes out with infinitely greater force, if the change is wrought through the destination of the element. That which remained water when kept for a ceremonial use, became wine when borne in faith to minister to the needs, even to the superfluous requirements, of life. This view, that the change in the water was determined by its destination for use at the feast, can be held equally if the water so used and limited to that which was used were 'drawn' from the vessels, and not from the well." I cannot see that there is much force in any one of these reasons. The verb may be used as naturally of drawing water from a deep jar as from a well. (See Liddell & Scott on the word). The word **now** is as appropriate if the servants drew from a waterpot to carry to the ruler of the feast, as if they drew from a well. It naturally points to some change in the action of the servants. No reason is obvious why water from the stone jars might not be changed into wine as fitly as water from a well. And how the change could be wrought "through the destination of the element" does not appear. That it was wrought in *view of* the destination of the element, is supposed by the common interpretation as well as by the one suggested by Westcott. Moreover, why were the waterpots mentioned at all, if the filling of them had nothing to do with the miracle? Manifestly, the Evangelist would have his readers understand that the water in the six stone vessels was changed into wine. If not, why did he state the number and the capacity of these vessels? His doing this would surely mislead his readers; for they would be certain to conclude that the exact account of the waterpots and the record that they were filled to the brim, had something to do with the miracle. This Evangelist never mentions circumstances without a reason for doing it. On the whole, then, though it is possible that the change occurred after the water was drawn from the vessel, it is much more probable that the water was changed to wine in the jars.

9, 10. And when the ruler, etc. The

that was made wine, and knew not whence it was, (but the servants which drew the water knew,) the governor of the feast called the bridegroom,

10 And saith unto him, Every man at the beginning doth set forth good wine; and when men have well drunk, then that which is worse; *but* thou hast kept the good wine until now.

11 This beginning of miracles did Jesus in Cana of Galilee, *a* and manifested forth his glory; and his disciples believed on him.

of the feast tasted the water ¹ now become wine, and knew not whence it was (but the servants who had drawn the water knew), the ruler of the feast calleth 10 the bridegroom, and saith unto him, Every man setteth on first the good wine, and when *men* have drunk freely, *then* that which is worse: thou hast 11 kept the good wine until now. This beginning of his signs did Jesus in Cana of Galilee, and manifested his glory; and his disciples believed on him.

a ch. 1: 14.——¹ *Or, that it had become.*

Revised Version reads as follows: *And when the ruler of the feast tasted the water now become wine, and knew not whence it was (but the servants who had drawn the water knew), the ruler of the feast calleth the bridegroom, and saith unto him, Every man setteth on first the good wine; and when (men) have drunk freely, (then) that which is worse: thou hast kept the good wine until now.* The word translated **ruler of the feast** signifies, according to Grimm, "One whose office it was to spread the tables and couches, to arrange the courses of the feast, and to taste before others the dishes and wines." To him, therefore, the servants were properly directed to bear the first cup of water now become wine; and for him it was specially natural and suitable to commend the unusual excellence of the wine. This he did, without knowing by whom it was provided; and therefore his testimony was regarded by the Evangelist as conclusive. The expression, *when men have drunk freely*, is part of the ruler's description of a common custom which rested, perhaps, on the idea that men somewhat affected by the wine they have drunken are less particular, than at first, about the quality of what they drink. The ruler's remark has no reference to the actual state of the guests before him; it only expresses his surprise and pleasure that the good wine had been brought in at so late an hour of the feast.

11. This beginning of miracles did Jesus, etc. Better, *This beginning of the signs did Jesus,* etc. The miracles of Christ are designated by four different terms in the Gospels, viz.: (1) *Works*, (ἔργα), because they were wrought by Jesus as a part of his Messianic service (comp. Matt. 41: 1; John 5: 20, 36; 7: 3; 10: 38; 14: 11 sq.; 15: 24). (2) *Powers*, or *effects of power* (δυνάμεις), because they were wrought by divine power (comp. Matt. 11: 20, 23; Mark 6: 2, 5; 9: 39; Luke 10: 13; 19: 37). (3) *Miracles* (τέρατα, *miracula*), because they were events fitted to excite the wonder of beholders (comp. Matt. 24: 24; Mark 13: 22; John 4: 48). (4) *Signs*, (σημεῖα), because they were indications of God's will, "revelations of truth through the symbolism of outward acts" (comp. Matt. 12: 38 sq.; 16: 1, 4; Mark 8: 11 sq.; 16: 17, 20; Luke 11: 16, 29; 23: 8; John 2: 18, 23; 3: 2; 4: 54; 6: 2, 14, and often). The word *signs* is, therefore, in some respects, the most important name given to these extraordinary deeds of Christ. And the changing of water into wine was the beginning of the signs which Jesus wrought in revealing his divine power and mission. It was one which manifested his glory, and increased his disciples' faith in him as the Son of God and the King of Israel. The evidence for this marvelous sign is thus characterized by Kitto: "First, the vessels used were such as were standing by for ordinary purposes, precluding any idea of collusion; then they were not wine-vessels, but waterpots, so that it could not be suggested that there was some sediment of wine remaining in them, which gave a flavor to the water poured in; . . . then there is the intervention of the servants in filling the vessels; but for which it might have appeared . . . that the wine had come from some unexpected quarter; lastly, there is the evidence of the . . . 'ruler of the feast,' who, knowing nothing of the history of this wine, pronounced upon it that it is not only real wine, but good wine—better than had yet been produced in the feast. Nothing can be more complete than this evidence."

Again, this first miracle of Jesus showed his sympathy with mankind, and his purpose to honor and ennoble all the relations and enjoyments of life. Had he been a teacher of asceticism, this miracle would have been incongruous; but not so when we understand the whole purpose of his mission. He came to quicken, to exalt, to spiritualize all things,

12 After this he went down to Capernaum, he, and his mother, and *his brethren, and his disciples; and they continued there not many days.

12 After this he went down to Capernaum, he, and his mother, and *his* brethren, and his disciples: and there they abode not many days.

a Matt. 12: 46.

and this miracle was a symbol of his work. Two things are worthy of special notice: *First*, that Jesus by this sign honored marriage and all the relations of domestic life; and, *second*, that he recognized the propriety of doing something for enjoyment as well as for sustenance. Hence, a Christian father is warranted in seeking for his family more than the necessaries of life; some of its luxuries may at times be enjoyed.

It may also be remarked, that this miracle lays no foundation for the papal doctrine of transubstantiation. For, according to John, the new substance was recognized and identified by the senses of men, while, according to the papal doctrine, the new substance in the eucharist, the real presence, cannot be thus known. In the one case, properties and substance answer to each other after, as well as before, the miracle; in the other they do not. In the one case, appearance corresponds with reality; in the other case, it does not, but is illusory. The Christian fact is, therefore, no argument for the papal theory.

12. VISIT TO CAPERNAUM.

12. After this, etc. The first note of time here employed is general, but it suggests a comparatively brief interval between the wedding and the going **down to Capernaum.** A few days at most were probably spent in a visit to the home in Nazareth; and then the Saviour, at the head of his little company of kindred and disciples, went down to Capernaum, with a view to joining a larger company, and going up to the passover in Jerusalem. He is said to have gone **down** to Capernaum; and the expression is exact, whether his journey was from Nazareth, or from Cana of Galilee. The distance from Nazareth to the place of destination could not have been less than sixteen miles, while the distance from Cana may have been somewhat less.

The site of Capernaum has not been satisfactorily ascertained; but it was certainly on the western side of Lake Gennesaret, and as far north as the northern side of the plain from which the lake took its name. Dr.

SUPPOSED SITE OF CAPERNAUM.

13 aAnd the Jews' passover was at hand, and Jesus went up to Jerusalem,

13 And the passover of the Jews was at hand, and

a Ex. 12: 14; Deut. 16: 1, 16; ver. 23; ch. 5: 1; 11: 55.

Robinson supposed that it was situated at Khan Minyeh, near the lake, and just on the northern border of the plain of Gennesaret, while Dr. Thompson believes that it was situated at Tell Hûm, about three miles north of Khan Minyeh (comp. Robinson, "Biblical Researches" etc., II. 403 sq. 406 sq.; Merrill. "East of the Jordan," p. 457; Thompson, "The Land and the Book," I., pp. 542-548; Warren, "Recovery of Jerusalem," pp. 342 sq.; Tristram, "Land of Israel," pp. 428 sq., ed. 3).

In respect to the **brethren,** or *brothers,* of Jesus, it has been conjectured (1) that they were in reality his cousins, the children of a sister of Mary, his mother, or of a brother of Joseph, his reputed father—an interpretation which was first proposed by Jerome, in the interest, probably, of the perpetual virginity of Mary. (2) That they were children of Joseph by a former marriage, and therefore, nominally, half brothers of Jesus; an interpretation which was proposed by Epiphanius, also designed to save the perpetual virginity of Mary. (3) That they were children of Joseph and Mary, younger than Jesus, and therefore his brothers, as born of the same mother. The question of their relationship to Jesus is a difficult one to answer; but the reasons for taking the word *brothers* in its most natural sense, as denoting sons of Joseph and Mary, seem to outweigh those for any other view. This we say: (1) Because the word *nephews* or *kindred* is never used by the sacred writers instead of *brothers,* to denote the persons referred to, viz.: James, and Joseph, and Simon, and Judas (Matt. 13: 55); also because sisters are mentioned, without any hint that they were more distant relatives. (2) Because Luke (2: 7) says of Mary, that "she brought forth her first-born son," when she gave birth to Jesus; and this language implies that she had other sons, born after the birth of Jesus. His brothers seem to have gone no farther than Capernaum with Jesus.

The Evangelist gives no account of what Jesus did in the **not many days** of his present sojourn in Capernaum. This silence may be accounted for, if needful, by assuming that John took the opportunity of spending a few days at his own home, and so was not an eye-witness of the Saviour's ministry. But the works of Jesus at this time were probably referred to by himself, when he addressed the people of Nazareth, on his next visit to that place: "Ye will surely say unto me this proverb, Physician, heal thyself; whatsoever we have heard done in Capernaum, do also here in thy country," (Luke 4: 23).

13-25. JOURNEY TO JERUSALEM, AND PURIFICATION OF THE TEMPLE. *First Passover in Christ's ministry,* April 11, A. D. 27.

13. **And the Jews' passover was at hand.** For an account of the Jewish passover, see Ex. 12: 1-49; Deut. 16: 1-8. That it is called **the Jews' passover** has been supposed to imply the existence of a recognized "Christian Passover" at the time when the Gospel was written (Westcott). But is not the expression fairly explained by the circumstance that the writer had in mind Gentile readers? Or by the fact that he had lived so long out of Palestine, and with Gentile Christians, as to have appropriated their manner of referring to the chosen people?—**And Jesus went up to Jerusalem.** The site of Jerusalem was elevated above that of most places in Palestine, and therefore it was natural to speak of going up to it (comp. 5: 1; 7: 8, 10; 11: 55; 12: 20; Luke 2: 42, sq.). Whether the political and religious eminence of the city contributed any influence in favor of this phraseology, is uncertain. The road by which Jesus in all probability went to the holy city, is thus described by Merrill: "This road crossed the Jordan immediately below the Lake of Tiberias, and followed down the east side until just below the Jabbok, where it recrossed and followed down the west side to Jericho. There are, just below the mouth of the Jabbok, the remains of an ancient bridge which there is reason to believe existed in Christ's time. Along this road the Christians fled to Pella, their place of refuge during the destruction of Jerusalem; and along this road, also, a portion of the army of Titus marched, on its way to besiege the holy city. So little has been known of this region, that the Christian has, no doubt, thought of Christ as passing along a lonely

14 "And found in the temple those that sold oxen and sheep and doves, and the changers of money sitting:

14 Jesus went up to Jerusalem. And he found in the temple those that sold oxen and sheep and doves,

a Matt. 21: 12; Mark 11: 15; Luke 19. 45.

road when he went from Galilee to Jerusalem by this valley route; but there could be no greater mistake. In some of the towns that I have indicated as existing here, our Saviour would pass the night; and as Pella was one of them, it is pleasant to reflect that the good seed sown by him in person, took root and brought forth such abundant fruit, that when, thirty or more years after his death, the storm of war swept over the land, his followers and disciples found an asylum in this very city." From Jericho the road passes by a steep and wild ascent up to Jerusalem. Of the region through which it winds upward, Hackett says: "Hardly a season passes in which some luckless wayfarer is not killed or robbed in 'going down from Jerusalem to Jericho.' The place derives its hostile character from its terrible wildness and desolation. If we might conceive of the ocean as being suddenly congealed and petrified when its waves are tossed mountain high, and dash-

ROAD FROM JERICHO TO JERUSALEM.

ing in wild confusion against each other, we should then have some idea of the aspect of the desert in which the Saviour has placed so truthfully the parable of the Good Samaritan. The ravines, the almost inaccessible cliffs, the caverns, furnish admirable lurking places for robbers; they can rush forth unexpectedly upon their victims, and escape as soon almost beyond the possibility of pursuit" ("Illustrations of Scripture," p. 207).

14. And found in the temple, etc. The word translated **temple** (*ἱερόν*) signifies not

15 And when he had made a scourge of small cords, he drove them all out of the temple, and the sheep, and the oxen; and poured out the changers' money, and overthrew the tables;
16 And said unto them that sold doves, Take these things hence; make not *my Father's house a house of merchandise.
17 And his disciples remembered that it was written, ᵇThe zeal of thine house hath eaten me up.

15 and the changers of money sitting; and he made a scourge of cords, and cast all out of the temple, both the sheep and the oxen; and he poured out the changers' money, and overthrew their tables; and
16 to them that sold the doves he said, Take these things hence; make not my Father's house a house
17 of merchandise. His disciples remembered that it was written, Zeal for thy house shall eat me up.

a Luke 2: 49....*b* Ps. 69: 9.

merely the central edifice, wherein were the holy place and the holy of holies, but that edifice with all its surrounding courts, including the Court of the Gentiles, in which the noisy and irreverent traders were now busy. Yet it has been well said by Schaff (in Lange) that the traffic here described "was no doubt justified or excused, as a convenience to foreign Jews for the purchase of sacrificial beasts, incense, oil, and the sacred shekel or double drachma, in which the temple-tax had to be paid" (Ex. 30: 13). Men who desecrate holy things are commonly able to offer some plausible reason for their course.

15. And when he had made a scourge of small cords, etc. It need not be supposed that Jesus used the scourge upon any of the men, even if he did upon the animals which they had brought into the sacred enclosure. But there is, strictly speaking, no evidence that he used it on the latter. The scourge may have been only a sign of the indignation which glowed with holy fervor in the soul of Jesus, and of the punishment which was justly deserved by men thus desecrating the temple; while it was the divine authority, revealed by his look and bearing, which overawed the traders, and the dumb beasts as well. For once the second Adam took the place of authority over sheep and cattle that was given to the first Adam before the fall. Instead of **and** read (as in Rev. Ver.) *both* **the sheep and the oxen. And poured out,** etc. This, too, must have been done under the impulse of a commanding indignation, more divine than human; otherwise the strange intruder would surely have been interrupted in his work. With what surprise and awe must the disciples have watched the movements of their Master!

16. And said unto them that sold doves. Literally, *that sold the doves*—namely, the doves that were referred to in the preceding verse. **Take these things hence:** because they were such as could not be driven out of

the sacred precincts, but must be carried thence. The doves were doubtless kept in baskets or cages; and at the command of Jesus, their owners bore them reluctantly away. Then the Son stood in the court of his Father's house, which had been reclaimed, for the time, from the desecrations of avarice, and hushed to silence, as became the place of prayer.

The Synoptical Gospels describe a very similar expulsion of traders from the temple by Jesus a few days before his crucifixion (Matt. 21: 12, 13; Mark 11: 15-17; Luke 19: 45-47). Some therefore insist that there was but one expulsion, either John or the Synoptists being in error as to the time when it occurred. Against this view it may, however, be remarked: (1) That the act was one that might properly be repeated; (2) That the particulars differ as much as could be expected if a second expulsion took place; (3) That the language of Jesus is naturally much severer in the second instance than in the first, for "a den of thieves" is a worse place than a **house of merchandise;** and (4) That the date of each expulsion is virtually given, separating them from each other by almost the whole public ministry of Christ. There can be no reasonable doubt of the repetition of the great lesson taught by Christ so near the beginning of his ministry.

17. And his disciples remembered. And does not belong to the true text, according to Tisch, Treg, Westcott and Hort, (with ℵ B L Tᵇ X etc.). **The zeal of thine house hath eaten me up.** The evidence of early manuscripts (ℵ A B L P Tᵇ X Γ Δ Λ Π) shows that the verb should be in the future tense, and the Revised Version expresses therefore the sense of the original: *The zeal of thy house shall eat me up.* This passage of the Psalms (69:9) came into the minds of the disciples as they gazed with astonishment upon Jesus during this remarkable scene. The only deviation from the sense of

18 Then answered the Jews and said unto him, What sign shewest thou unto us, seeing that thou doest these things?
19 Jesus answered and said unto them, *Destroy this temple, and in three days I will raise it up.
20 Then said the Jews, Forty and six years was this temple in building, and wilt thou rear it up in three days?

18 The Jews therefore answered and said unto him, What sign shewest thou unto us, seeing that thou doest these things? Jesus answered and said unto them, Destroy this temple, and in three days I will
20 raise it up. The Jews therefore said, Forty and s.x years was this ¹temple in building, and wilt thou

a Matt. 12: 38; ch. 6: 30....*b* Matt. 26: 61; 27: 40; Mark 11: 58; 15: 29.——1 Or, *sanctuary.*

the Hebrew passage, is in the sense of the verb. Perrowne translates the passage thus: "Zeal for thine house hath consumed me"; while the Evangelist, regarding the sufferer of the Psalm as a type of Christ, and his language as really prophetic, may have used the future tense as expressive of its deepest meaning. Says Perowne: "Similar expressions concerning the prophets will be found, Jer. 6: 11; 15: 17; 20: 9; 23: 9; Ezek 3: 14. This which was true in various imperfect degrees of these servants of God, was, in a far higher sense, true of the only-begotten Son, who could say: 'I seek not mine own glory.' Hence, when he purged the temple, the disciples could not help thinking of these words of the Psalm as finding their best application in him." Lange supposed that "here for the first time met and struck them the conflict of the Spirit of Christ with the spirit of the people, the terrible, life-staking earnestness in the appearance of Christ, which threatened to bring incalculable dangers after it"; while Alford says that the eating up (καταφάγειν) "spoken of in that passion Psalm, while the marring and wasting of the Saviour's frame, by his zeal for God and God's church, which resulted in the buffeting, the scourging, the cross." It is quite possible that the zeal spoken of both consumed and imperiled the life of its possessor; both devoured his strength by its own fervor, and provoked the wrath of his enemies.

18. **Then answered the Jews,** etc. Better: *The Jews answered therefore,* etc. By **the Jews** must be understood some of the leaders or rulers of the people in religious affairs. They were probably displeased by his claim of special Sonship to God, involved in the words, **Make not my Father's house a house of merchandise;** and they plainly intimated that his conduct could only be justified to their minds by a sign from heaven. Moreover, such was their character, that their language was a natural result of his act and word; hence the connective *therefore.* The

word answered is sometimes used by the Evangelists, when the saying that follows has reference to something done, or to something in the mind of the person addressed (*e. g.*, Matt. 11: 25; 17: 4; 28: 5; Mark 10: 51; 12: 35; Luke 1: 60; 13: 14).

19. . . . **Destroy this temple.** Here the word translated **temple** (ναός, not ἱερόν), refers to the central building, exclusive of the surrounding courts. The **destroy** (λύσατε) is neither permissive nor provocative, but either prophetic, *destroy* (as you will), or subjunctive, *if you destroy.* I prefer the latter (comp. Winer ?. 44, 2; Buttman ?. 139, p. 227). **In three days** means within that period of time. The expression, perhaps because of its enigmatical character, was remembered by the Jews, and, by a malignant perversion, introduced as testimony against Jesus: "This fellow said, I am able to destroy the temple of God, and build it in three days." (Matt. 26: 61; Mark 11. 58). For the interpretation, see verse 21, below. It is, however, noteworthy that the resurrection is here represented by Christ as his own work.

20. **Forty and six years,** etc. A more exact rendering would read: *In forty and six years was this temple built; and wilt thou in three days raise it up?* The emphatic words of the first clause are, **forty and six years;** those of the second, **thou** (uttered with a tone of incredulity and perhaps mockery) and **three days.** Thus: In *forty and six years* was this temple built; and wilt *thou, in three days,* raise it up? The order of the Greek words is very significant.

"There can be no doubt that this refers to the rebuilding of the temple by Herod; it cannot mean the second temple, built after the captivity; for this was finished in twenty years (B. C. 535 to B. C. 515). Herod, in the eighteenth year of his reign (Joseph. "Ant." XV. 11. 1), began to reconstruct the temple on a larger and more splendid scale (A. U. C. 734). The work was not finished till long after his death, till A. U. C. 818. It is in-

21 But he spake *of the temple of his body. 22 When therefore he was risen from the dead, ᵇhis disciples remembered that he had said this unto them; and they believed the Scripture, and the word which Jesus had said.

21 raise it up in three days? But he spake of the 22 ¹ temple of his body. When therefore he was raised from the dead, his disciples remembered that he spake this; and they believed the scripture, and the word which Jesus had said.

a Col. 2:9; Heb. 8:2; So 1 Cor. 3:16; 6:19; 2 Cor. 6:16....*b* Luke 24:8.—¹ Or, *sanctuary.*

ferred from Josephus ("Ant" XV. 11. 5-6) that it was begun in the month Chisleu, A. U. C. 734. And if the passover at which this remark was made was that of A. U. C. 780, then forty-five years and some months have elapsed, which, according to the Jewish mode of reckoning (p. 1381), would be spoken of as 'forty and six years.'" (Smith's Dict. of the Bible, *Jesus Christ,* p. 1383).

21. But he spake of the temple of his body. As might have been expected, this interpretation of Christ's words is pronounced erroneous by many liberal expositors. Even Lücke, who holds the writer of this Gospel to have been the Apostle John, and who appreciates very highly his work, rejects this statement as incorrect; for he is unable to believe that Jesus referred to his own death at so early a day, and in terms so enigmatical. But we have already seen, in the cases of Peter and Nathanael (1:42, 47), that Jesus could read the hearts of men with marvelous accuracy, and, therefore, it is vain to say that he could not have detected in these Jews the germs of deadly hatred. Indeed, there may have been something in their look and tone which foreboded evil, which reminded him of the hour when he would be "led as a lamb to the slaughter," and which occasioned his profound but enigmatical response. They belonged to a class of men to whom no sign was to be given, save the sign of the prophet Jonah (Matt. 12:39, 40).

Yet the answer of Christ must have arrested their attention by its very strangeness and apparent extravagance; for nothing could have seemed to them more absurd than the hypothesis of *their* destroying the temple, u :less it were the assumption of Jesus that *he* would raise it up *in three days.* It was an answer therefore which would stick in their memory; and if it had any occult sense, to be revealed by later events, that sense might at last be perceived by them and recognized by them as a sign from heaven.

Such a sense it had, and such a prophecy it was. For as the temple was God's house, in which he dwelt among the people and manifested his glory, so was the body of Christ God's house, in which he dwelt and manifested his glory. The temple on Moriah was, in fact, but a symbol or shadow of the true temple. For Christ could say, "I am in the Father and the Father in me" (10:38; 14:11), and "he that hath seen me hath seen the Father" (14:9). "In him dwelleth all the fulness of the Godhead bodily" (Col 2:9). His reference, therefore, was to the substance *by means of the shadow.* He knew that, by and by, they would destroy the substance, and thereby bring to an end the shadow also; and he purposed to raise up the true temple in less than three days from the time of its dissolution.

If it be urged against this interpretation that, not Jesus himself, but the Father, raised the body of our Lord from the dead, it may be answered that we need not suppose that Christ intended by this expression to separate his own action from the Father's (comp. 5:19 sq.). The Father as well as the Spirit may properly be regarded as acting wit ι the Son and in behalf of the Son. Their action is inseparable (see 10:18).

It may be added that the pronoun **he** (ἐκεῖνος) is one that tends to separate Jesus from the writer, or from some other party. In this case, the separation was due to the fact that neither John nor the Jews shared with Jesus this knowledge of the reference of his words. "St. John seems to look back again upon the far distant scene, as interpreted by his later knowledge, and to realize how the Master foresaw that which was wholly hidden from the disciples."—(*Westcott*).

22. When therefore he was risen from the dead, etc. The deep and prophetic import of this saying was not understood by the disciples of Christ at the time. They did not reflect much upon it, or question their Lord as to its meaning. But after his resurrection, it was remembered by them, and interpret d as John interprets it. Then, too, it increased their faith, even as it was recalled in faith. A great light was reflected upon it from his

23 Now when he was in Jerusalem at the passover, in the feast-*day*, many believed in his name, when they saw the miracles which he did.
24 But Jesus did not commit himself unto them, because he knew all *men*,
25 And needed not that any should testify of man; for ᵃ he knew what was in man.

23 Now when he was in Jerusalem at the passover, during the feast, many believed on his name, beholding his signs which he did. But Jesus did not trust himself unto them, for that he knew all men, and because he needed not that any should bear witness concerning ¹man; for he himself knew what was in man.

a 1 Sam. 16: 7; 1 Chron. 28: 9; Matt. 9: 4; Mark 2: 8; ch. 6: 61; 16: 30; Acts 1: 24; Rev. 2: 23.—1 Or, *a man; for . . . the man.*

raised body, as he communed with them during forty days. Then also, as never before, they believed **the Scripture.**

But what is meant by **the Scripture?** Either some part or passage of the Old Testament which foreshadowed the death and resurrection of the Messiah (Ps. 16: 10), or the entire Old Testament, regarded as a connected whole, which was proved to be true by the fulfillment of an important part of it. The latter is, probably, the Evangelist's thought.

While Christ was with his disciples in the flesh, the latter appear to have been singularly dull or incredulous when he referred to his approaching death and resurrection. For many reasons the meaning of the Scripture, when it foretold the sufferings of Christ and the glory that should follow, was hidden from their sight. But when Jesus had been crucified and raised from the dead, the meaning of the Scripture flashed upon their souls with surprising clearness. They saw at once that the language of Isaiah (ch. 53), and of many other prophets, had described both the suffering and the triumph of the Messiah— the latter being indeed a consequence of the former. But they saw the fulfillment of Scripture in the former, as well as in the latter respect, yet they saw it in neither till they saw it in both. Not till Christ had risen from the dead, were they able to perceive the necessity of his dying at all. And when he had risen from the dead, they perceived that his resurrection and eternal glory were as fully implied in the Old Testament, as were his sufferings and death. **His disciples,** etc. According to the best editors and manuscripts, the second clause should read: his **disciples remembered that he** *spake this—* unto them being no part of the original text. The tense also of the Greek verb (ἔλεγεν) suggests a repetition or dwelling upon the words (comp. 5: 18; 6: 6, 65; 8: 27, 31; 12 33), which John distinctly recalls in giving his account of the scene.

23-25. Christ's Mighty Works in Jerusalem, and their Effect on Many of the People.

23. Now when he was in Jerusalem, etc. Meyer holds that the words **in Jerusalem** denote place, **at the passover,** time, and **in the feast,** occupation. Though Jesus declined to do any miracle as a sign to the Jews who questioned him as to his authority, it appears from this verse that he wrought several miracles during this passover, in Jerusalem. We say "several," *first,* because the plural *miracles,* (or *signs*) is used, and, *secondly,* because the imperfect tense (not **did** but *was doing,* ἐποίει) suggests continued action of that kind. These signs led many to believe that Jesus was the promised Christ. But their faith was mere belief on the ground of evidence, implying no radical change of character. It might lead to further inquiry, as in the case of Nicodemus, but it was not in itself a proof of willingness to serve God by forsaking all to follow Jesus. To believe on one's name is to believe on what that name represents, whether of character or of office.

24, 25. But Jesus did not commit himself unto them. The contrast is stronger in the original: *But Jesus himself;* i. e., *Jesus on his part.* The verb which, with the negative particle, is translated **did not commit,** i. e., *trust,* is in the imperfect tense, and, therefore, denotes continued action. The same is true of the verb **knew** in verse 25. And these verses afford proof, *first,* that the Evangelist did not mean to ascribe saving faith to the **many** spoken of in verse 23; and, *secondly,* that Christ knew both men and man, both the hearts of all men, and the inmost nature of man. His knowledge was perfect, independent, and, therefore, divine (comp. John 1: 48 sq.; 4: 19, 29; 6: 61, 64; 11: 4, 15; 13: 11; 16, 19; 21: 17); for such knowledge points to a divine nature (Ps. 7: 9; 139: 2; Acts 15: 8). See also "Bib. Sac." 1882, p. 182. It is however possible that the expression **all** (πάντας) means, in this connection, all

CHAPTER III.

1 THERE was a man of the Pharisees, named Nicodemus, a ruler of the Jews:
2 The same came to Jesus by night, and said unto him, Rabbi, we know that thou art a teacher come from God: for *no man can do these miracles that thou doest, except God be with him.

1 Now there was a man of the Pharisees, named
2 Nicodemus, a ruler of the Jews: the same came unto him by night, and said to him, Rabbi, we know that thou art a teacher come from God; for no man can do these signs that thou doest, except

a ch. 7: 50; 19: 39....*b* ch. 9: 16, 33; Acts 2: 22....*c* Acts 10: 38.

with whom the Lord had to do—all whom he met or attempted to influence.

The expression, **did not commit** (or *trust*) **himself unto them,** has been supposed to mean that he did not associate with them confidentially, as he did with his disciples (Meyer); or that he did not frankly announce himself to them as the Messiah (Lange); or, simply, that he did not hold them to be his true disciples, because he knew the weakness of their faith (Lücke). Does it not rather mean that he did not give them his confidence as genuine disciples, but kept himself aloof from them as persons who could not yet be fully trusted in that way, as men who, though professing to be friends and believers, might, at any moment, become foes?

Ch. 3: 1-21. CHRIST'S CONVERSATION WITH NICODEMUS.

1. There was a man of the Pharisees, named Nicodemus, a ruler of the Jews. The Evangelist now describes a remarkable interview which Jesus had with a believer of the class just mentioned (2:23). This believer was a Pharisee, and the Pharisees were distinguished for their orthodox creed and punctilious observance of the Jewish ritual. Paul speaks of them as "the straitest sect of our religion" (Acts 26: 5, Rev. Ver.), and Christ frequently denounces their sanctimonious hypocrisy. Yet many of them were, no doubt, earnest and sincere, as well as scrupulous. Saul of Tarsus was such a man before his conversion. And Nicodemus, though timid, was probably another.

He was, moreover, **a ruler of the Jews,** and "the teacher of Israel" (ver. 10. Rev. Ver.); and, as the former title "is given in some passages (John 7: 26; Acts 3: 17, etc.), to members of the Sanhedrin, it has been inferred that he was a member of that body. He was, probably, also a scribe or teacher of the law (John 3: 10); and hence belonged to that branch of the council which represented the learned class of the nation" (Hackett). The name Nicodemus was current among the Greeks, as well as among the Jews.

Meyer remarks very justly, that there is no objection to supposing that the disciples, and especially John, were present at this conversation. For it was not from fear of the disciples, but from fear of *the Jews,* that he came to Jesus by night; and the vivid and consistent characterization of the interview favors the idea that the Evangelist was present. If not, he probably received an account of it from the Lord.

2. The same came to Jesus (rather, *unto him*) **by night.** Various conjectures have been offered as to the reason which led Nicodemus to visit Jesus by night, rather than by day. His engagements during the day may have left him no time for such a visit, so that he must make it by night, or not at all. The nature of Christ's ministry at this time may have rendered a quiet conversation, such as Nicodemus sought, impossible by day, and, therefore, he was constrained to come at night. But when we bear in mind the connection of Nicodemus with the chief council of the Jews, the spirit which animated that council in its subsequent dealings with Christ and his disciples, and the caution which appears in the later acts of Nicodemus, it seems just to suppose that he was influenced by fear of the Jews, to select the night for his interview with Christ (see Edersheim I. p. 381 sq.; Weiss "Leben Jesu," I. 400 sq). Convinced that Jesus was at least a prophet, and suspecting that he might be the Messiah, he had not "the courage of his convictions," but was influenced by fear of God and fear of man at the same time—a not unfrequent state of mind. For many persons strive to serve both God and self in the same act. Yet, in reality, they consent to serve God only so far as may be consistent, in their view, with a supreme regard to self. **Rabbi, we know that thou art a teacher come from God: for no**

JOHN.

3 Jesus answered and said unto him, Verily, verily, I say unto thee, *Except a man be born again, he cannot see the kingdom of God.
4 Nicodemus saith unto him, How can a man be born when he is old? can he enter the second time into his mother's womb, and be born?

3 God be with him. Jesus answered and said unto him, Verily, verily, I say unto thee, Except a man be born ¹anew, he cannot see the kingdom of God.
4 Nicodemus saith unto him, How can a man be born when he is old? can he enter a second time into his

a ch. 1: 13; Gal. 6: 15; Tit. 3: 5; James 1: 18; 1 Pet. 1: 23; 1 John 3: 9.—1 Or. *from above.*

man can do these miracles (*signs*) that thou doest, except God be with him. This language of Nicodemus appears to express very exactly the extent of his faith in Jesus. For (1) he addresses Jesus as **Rabbi**, and this, in the circumstances, was a recognition of his right to be heard as a religious teacher; (2) joining others with himself, he declares that they knew Jesus to be One who had **come from God** as a teacher; and (3) he specifies the source of their knowledge on this point, viz., *the signs* which Jesus was working; for these signs were such as showed the presence of God with him who wrought them. It will be observed that he emphasizes the divine mission of Jesus, that he was certainly a prophet; for this is the force of the Greek words in their order: "*from God*, hast thou come, a teacher."

3. . . . **Verily, verily, I say unto thee, Except a man be born again, he cannot see the kingdom of God.** This answer seems abrupt, but it is unnecessary to suppose the omission of any connecting thought. For Jesus, being recognized as a teacher from God, and reading for himself at a glance the character of Nicodemus, as well as the question that was in his heart, viz.: "What must a man do in order to enter the Messiah's kingdom?" (Meyer), does not wait for this question to be put in words, but declares at once that a new birth, a new life, is indispensable, in order to any real knowledge of the kingdom of God. "No one," he says, "whether Jew or Gentile, can grow up, or glide over, from nature into grace; every one must begin his life altogether anew, in order to share in my kingdom."

Many interpreters insist on the primary sense of the word translated **again** (ἄνωθεν). That sense is local, "from above," and is the prevailing meaning of the word. (See John 3: 31; 19: 11; James 1: 17; 3: 15). It also agrees with the teaching of this Evangelist (John 1: 13; 1 John 2: 29; 3: 9, 4: 7; 5: 1; 4, 18). But the word has also a temporal sense, "from the first" (Luke 1: 3; Acts 26: 5). And, derived from this, it has a meaning suggested by the answer of Nicodemus, viz., "anew," or "afresh." (See Gal. 4: 9; Wisdom of Sirach 19: 6). Against the first sense, "from above," Godet remarks: If it (ἄνωθεν) "had this signification, the emphasis would certainly fall on this word, since Jesus would have in view the antithesis between terrestrial birth and birth from above. And, in this case, the adverb would have preceded the verb. Placed after the verb, it merely reinforces the idea of birth; and with this agrees the meaning "anew." In Gal. 4: 9 this word, with the addition of "again" (πάλιν), is taken in the same sense. The bondage into which the Galatians replunge themselves, is described by the word "again," as the *second* (numerically), and by "anew" or "afresh," as the moral reproduction of the "first."

By the **kingdom of God** is meant the kingdom of Christ, which embraces all who truly believe in him, and are therefore obedient to his commands. And the commands of Christ have respect, *first*, to the inward life of faith, love, joy, hope; and, *secondly*, to the outward life, which manifests and strengthens the inward. The reign of Christ begins, no doubt, in the soul; but by his command it passes at once into ritual and practical expression, and the blessed order of church life. It is first invisible, personal, and then social, corporate. The ritual and order of his kingdom were not fully declared in his early ministry; but they were to be observed as soon as they were made known.

To **see the kingdom of God** (comp. Mark 9: 1; Luke 2: 26, 30), is to perceive and appreciate its character; and to appreciate its character, one needs to *enter into* it with the whole heart (ver. 5). We do not therefore find any important difference between the two expressions used by Christ.

4. . . . **How can a man be born when he is old?** etc. The precise meaning of this reply is doubtful. It may be that Nicodemus understood the words of Jesus correctly (comp. Jer. 31: 33; Ezek. 11: 19, 20; 36: 26);

5 Jesus answered, Verily, verily, I say unto thee, *Except a man be born of water and *of* the Spirit, he cannot enter into the kingdom of God.

a Mark 16: 16; Acts 2: 38.

for the metaphor of a new birth appears to have been used by the Rabbins to describe the religious change in a Gentile who became a proselyte to the Jewish faith; and the import of baptism, as administered by John, implied the same view of repentance, namely, that it was a burial of the old life, and entrance upon a new life. But, if he understood these words, he doubtless felt them to be "a hard saying" when applied to orthodox Jews, and especially when applied to good men of advanced age, whose habits of thinking, of feeling, and of action have been long fixed. So radical a change, so utter a renunciation of the old and appropriation of the new in religious life, may have seemed to him as difficult a matter as for one to enter a second time into his mother's womb and be born. Yet there is perhaps a touch of irony and exaggeration in the latter question, which was certainly meant to suggest the impossibility of the change demanded by Christ. But whether we can ascertain the precise thought of Nicodemus in this response or not is of comparatively little consequence, since it is not noticed in the further teaching of Jesus, and therefore our interpretation of the Saviour's language does not depend upon our knowing the purport of the Pharisee's reply to his first declaration.

5. . . . Verily, verily, I say unto thee, Except a man be born of water and of the Spirit, he cannot enter into the kingdom of God. Jesus makes no reply to the words of Nicodemus, unless it be by re-asserting, in the most impressive language, the necessity of another birth or generation for every man who would enter the kingdom of God, and by describing this new birth as one that is **of water, and of the Spirit.** But this description, though brief, includes a peculiar expression. Had it simply characterized the new birth as one **of** (or *from*) the **Spirit,** the interpretation would have been comparatively obvious; the reference to a change of character, purpose, and life, effected by the Spirit of God working in the soul, would have been clear and forcible. But it characterizes the new birth as one *from water* and *Spirit,* as if it had both a ritual origin and a spiritual, an outward side and an inward, a visible expression and an invisible reality. This at least is one explanation of the words.

According to this view, Nicodemus probably came to Jesus by night, because he was subject to the fear of man. Half-persuaded that Jesus was the promised Messiah, and half-inclined to become his disciple, the fear of man made him seek to be so in secret. With the Pharisees generally (see Luke 7: 30) he had rejected the baptism of John, who did no miracle (John 10: 41); and now, though looking wistfully toward Jesus, who was working miracles that must be ascribed to the presence and power of God, he was inwardly resolved not to break with the Pharisees by submitting to baptism, and thus openly professing his allegiance to Christ. With this view of his character and state of mind, Jesus might tell the prudent Pharisee now before him, that no one could be a member of the Messiah's kingdom without entering it in the prescribed way, without submitting to the rite which had been appointed to symbolize and declare the spiritual change involved in becoming a Christian. And surely it would be natural for Jesus, when speaking of birth from Spirit, to call the rite, which symbolizes this, birth from water. One stands at the beginning of the inward life, and the other at the beginning of the corresponding outward life. And therefore Jesus could say, with the utmost propriety: "You must confess me openly in the prescribed way—which you are unwilling to do—and you must also be the subject of a great spiritual change, which is represented by that confession, or you cannot enter my kingdom." For the order of expression, which is rhetorical rather than logical, compare Rom. 10: 9: "If thou shalt confess with thy mouth the Lord Jesus, and shalt believe in thy heart that God raised him from the dead, thou shalt be saved."

But another interpretation is sometimes given to the words *from water* (ἐξ ὕδατος), viz., that they denote "a pure source of a new spiritual life in man," while the next words,

6 That which is born of the flesh is flesh; and that which is born of the Spirit is spirit.
7 Marvel not that I said unto thee, Ye must be born again.
8 ᵃThe wind bloweth where it listeth, and thou hearest the sound thereof, but canst not tell whence it cometh, and whither it goeth; so is every one that is born of the Spirit.

6 the kingdom of God. That which is born of the flesh is flesh; and that which is born of the Spirit is spirit. Marvel not that I said unto thee, Ye must be
7 spirit.
8 born ¹anew. ²The wind bloweth where it listeth, and thou hearest the voice thereof, but knowest not whence it cometh, and whither it goeth: so is every

a Eccl. 11 : 5; 1 Cor. 2 : 11.——1 *Or. from above....*2 *Or. The Spirit breatheth.*

from Spirit (ἐ . . . πνεύματος), "mention in plain language the author of this new birth." —(Ripley.) In other words, "water is a figurative term for the purifying power of the Spirit" (comp. 1 : 13). But this interpretation was probably suggested by a strong re-action of the mind against the error of baptismal regeneration, and it seems to have much less in its favor than the one first given. Yet it must be conceded that the use of the words *from water*, instead of *from baptism*, renders this a possible interpretation.

The word **spirit** should perhaps be written without the article in English as well as in Greek, in order that it may denote in the simplest way the *kind* of source from which the new birth springs, though it is perfectly evident that no spirit save the divine could be thought of as that source. (See ver. 6-8) Weiss holds that "the omission of the article before 'water' and 'spirit' shows that water and spirit are contemplated generically; . . . that the two factors are simply co-ordinated, the water being thought of as, by its nature, a purifying factor, and the spirit as an efficient principle of new life; while the essential doctrine is that, without a putting off of the old, sinful nature, and the generation of a wholly new nature from a powerful new principle, the birth intended in verse 3 is not realized." For a further discussion of this passage, and of others that are sometimes supposed to teach the doctrine of baptismal regeneration, see Appendix.

6. **That which is** (or, *has been*) **born of the flesh is flesh, and that which is** (*has been*) **born of the Spirit is spirit.** In these words Jesus assumes that the kingdom of God is primarily spiritual, consisting of "righteousness, and peace, and joy in the Holy Ghost" (Rom. 14: 17). Hence, that which is carnal cannot enter it. But those who have been begotten and born of sinful men, resemble their parents in character—they are carnal, sinful. Natural birth does not qualify one to be a member of a spiritual kingdom.

Accordingly, the word **flesh** seems to be used here in the same sense as in Gen. 6: 3, and in many passages of Paul; and, if so, the new birth is here represented as being, at once, a cleansing and a creation. It raises one from a life of unbelief and condemnation, into a life of faith and justification. It translates one from a kingdom of darkness into a kingdom of light. It makes one who is an enemy of God his friend and his child. And this change is wrought by the Holy Spirit. This delight in God and communion with him, which may be called the only true life of the soul, must be ascribed to the grace of God as its fountain. For this reason the change is wonderful, and, at the same time, credible; a change beyond the power of man, and worthy of the nature of God.

7. **Marvel not that I said unto thee, Ye must be born again.** The pronoun ye is emphatic; and the reference of the assertion to Nicodemus and his friends is, thereby, strongly affirmed, while its application to Jesus is, perhaps, virtually denied. In truth, he alone of all the sons of men, was holy and well pleasing to God, from the first moment of his earthly existence to the last. And his generation was supernatural. "The Holy Spirit shall come upon thee, and the power of the Highest shall overshadow thee! Therefore, also, that holy thing (child) which shall be born of thee, shall be called the Son of God" (Luke 1: 35).

8. **The wind bloweth where it listeth** (or, *will*), etc. The independence, the mysteriousness, and the power of the wind, are here used by the Saviour to illustrate the secret and mighty agency of the Holy Spirit in regeneration. But the carrying out of the simile in the last clause is disappointing. For the reader naturally expects the comparison to be finished by a direct reference to the Spirit. As the wind acts, the Spirit acts— secretly, mightily, unaccountably; in the one case apparently, and in the other case really, self-moved. Instead of this expected appli-

9 Nicodemus answered and said unto him, *How can these things be?
10 Jesus answered and said unto him, Art thou a master of Israel, and knowest not these things?
11 *Verily, verily, I say unto thee, We speak that we do know, and testify that we have seen; and *ye receive not our witness.

9 one that is born of the Spirit. Nicodemus answered
10 and said unto him, How can these things be? Jesus answered and said unto him, Art thou the teacher of Israel, and understandest not these things?
11 Verily, verily, I say unto thee, We speak that we do know, and bear witness of that we have seen; and

a ch. 6: 52, 60....*b* Matt. 11: 27; ch. 1: 18; 7: 16; 8: 28; 12: 49; 14: 24....*c* ver. 32.

cation of the figure, we have a reference to him who experiences this mysterious influence of the Spirit. But the difficulty is merely formal. For, either the second member of the comparison is a popular, but slightly ungrammatical substitute for the expression: "So is it with every one that has been born of the Spirit"; or else the experience of one who perceives the effect of the wind in nature, is compared with the experience of one who feels the effect of the Spirit acting on his soul, thus: "As thou hearest the sound of the free, mysterious wind, knowing only its effect and not its source or end, so is every one that has been born of the Spirit, conscious of the Spirit's action by its effects, though the Spirit comes and goes mysteriously, and as he will." "The night is quiet around you, not a sound of bending branch or rustling leaf comes from the neighboring wood; but now the air is stirred as by an invisible hand; the sigh of the night-breeze comes through the bending branches and nestling leaves; you hear the sound; but who can take you to that breeze's birth-place, and show you where and how it was begotten; who can carry you to its place of sepulchre, and show you where and how it died?"—(Hanna.) Chadwick supposes that the action of the new-born soul is here compared with that of the wind. "The mysterious movements of the wind, heard but not comprehended, are like the man born of the Spirit, who is, therefore, not indeed lawless, but obedient to finer and more subtle laws, which a natural man cannot understand, even when their effects are palpable." But this view is foreign to the context, and must therefore be rejected.

10. . . . **Art thou a master** (rather, *the teacher*) **of Israel, and knowest not these things?** Namely, that these things are so, are realities in the moral government of God? There was much in the Old Testament which ought to have led a true Israelite to believe in the power of God's Spirit to renew the hearts of men, and much which ought to have led a teacher of religion to expect a wonderful increase of spiritual power at the coming of Christ. The definite article before *teacher* has perplexed many interpreters, since there is no evidence that Nicodemus was pre-eminently *the* teacher of Israel at this time. But he was probably a learned and prudent man, well known as a teacher of the law; and Winer is, perhaps, correct in supposing that the article is here employed in a rhetorical way, to contrast the teacher with the doubter, the instructor of God's people with the man who knows nothing of the new birth and of the life in God. Compare such an expression as this: "Are you the theological professor, and cannot understand this passage?" Also Luke 18: 13.

11. Verily, verily, I say unto thee, We speak that we do know, and testify that we have seen. By these words Jesus assures Nicodemus, in the most solemn manner, that his knowledge of what he is teaching is certain and direct, that his word is equivalent to that of an eye-witness, and can only be doubted by doubting his integrity. At the same time he charges the Pharisee before him, and, without doubt, the large body of men with which Nicodemus was associated, with not receiving his testimony.

But what distinguished this part of Christ's answer from that which follows, and from his well-nigh uniform manner, is the use of the pronoun **we**, instead of "I." Is it possible to account for this deviation from his usual style? Some believe that he associates with himself, by means of this exceptional **we**, John the Baptist, who is represented in this Gospel as distinctively a "witness of the light" (1:7), both because he was divinely inspired to announce the great characteristic of the Messiah's reign, to wit, baptism in the Spirit, which presupposes regeneration, and because he saw the descending dove, and heard the voice from heaven by which the Messiah was pointed out to him. For thus

12 If I have told you earthly things, and ye believe not, how shall ye believe, if I tell you *of* heavenly things?

13 And ᵃ no man hath ascended up to heaven, but he that came down from heaven, even the Son of man which is in heaven.

12 ye receive not our witness. If I told you earthly things, and ye believe not, how shall ye believe, if I
13 tell you heavenly things? And no man hath ascended into heaven, but he that descended out of heaven, even the Son of man ¹ who is in heaven.

a Prov. 30:4; ch. 6:33, 38, 51, 62; 16:28; Acts 2:34; 1 Cor. 15:47; Eph. 4:9, 10.—¹ Many ancient authorities omit, *who is in heaven*.

far, it is said, Jesus has been speaking with Nicodemus of the work of the Spirit, having made, at most, but a single reference to baptism, which is a rite associated with, and representative of, the work of the Spirit in regeneration. This view would seem to be very reasonable, if we knew that Nicodemus himself had rejected the baptism and testimony of John—which is certainly probable—and if we knew that Jesus had referred (however indicated) to this fact in speaking of the necessity of birth from water and Spirit (ver. 5.)

Weiss remarks that "Jesus joins himself with those sent from God . . . whose word must be received in faith, if any would come to the same experience; but, in the historical situation, the only one besides himself, was John the Baptist; who, by his preaching of the baptism of water, and of the baptism of the Spirit through the Messiah (1:33), had already pointed men to the necessity of a new birth from water and Spirit, even as he himself was doing.

But if this explanation is rejected, Christ's use of the plural must be understood as either rhetorical (Meyer), or proverbial (Alford), the reference being strictly and only to himself; for it can hardly be supposed that any of his attendant disciples were already associated with him as able to testify of the things to which he refers. But the former view, viz., that in this instance he associates the testimony of John the Baptist with his own: We, (*i. e.*, I myself and John the Baptist whom you have rejected), **speak that we do know, and testify that we have seen,** need not be rejected. The pronoun ye in the last clause, refers to Nicodemus and those whom he represented. Neither he nor they would give full credence to the words of Jesus or of his harbinger; for these words were inconsistent with their deeply-rooted prejudices.

12. If I have told you (*the*) earthly things and ye believe not, how shall ye believe if I tell you of (*the*) heavenly things? By the earthly things Jesus means the things of which he has been speaking, and, especially, the regenerating work of the Spirit; for this, however secret and powerful, is experienced by men here on earth, and may be known in its effects with a reasonable degree of certainty. There were many in Israel who had already entered upon the new life of repentance toward God, and faith in the Lord Jesus, and who could testify of a new peace and joy mysteriously originated in their souls. On the other hand, by *the* **heavenly things,** he means those which they could only know by his testimony—the counsels of eternal love which were finding their accomplishment in the incarnation of the Son of God, in his atoning death, and in the glory of his spiritual reign. Of these, he proceeds to speak in the remainder of his conversation with Nicodemus. The article before **earthly things** and also before **heavenly things,** limits the things in question to those of the Messiah's kingdom.

13. And no man hath ascended up to heaven, but he that came down from heaven, even the Son of man which is in heaven. If this difficult verse be interpreted strictly according to the context, Jesus appears to teach: 1. That no person on earth has ascended into heaven and had direct knowledge of the mind and action of God, to whom "the heavenly things" just mentioned belong as their first cause. But this denial has no respect to the state of departed spirits, who have gone from this life not to return. 2. That he himself who came down from heaven at his incarnation, has thus ascended into heaven, and can therefore testify of "the heavenly things," the counsels of the Father as to the redemption of men. Even since the incarnation, his intercourse with the Father has been direct, his access to heaven unimpeded (comp. notes on 1:5; 5:19 sq.). 3. That the Son of man, though now on earth, is at the same time in heaven—an assertion which implies, without doubt, the ubiquity of the Incarnate Word, and refutes the opinion of those who insist that he did not have the use of his divine attributes, while he was in the flesh.

To this natural interpretation of his lan-

14 *And as Moses lifted up the serpent in the wilderness, even so ^bmust the Son of man be lifted up; 15 That whosoever believeth in him should not perish, but ^chave eternal life.

14 And as Moses lifted up the serpent in the wilderness, even so must the Son of man be lifted up: that whosoever ¹believeth may in him have eternal life.

a Num. 21: 9....*b* ch. 8: 28; 12: 32....*c* ver. 36; ch. 6: 47.—¹ Or, *believeth in him may have*.

guage, there seems to be no conclusive objection. Thus understood, it was, indeed, wonderful language to be uttered to a cautious Pharisee; but it may have been adapted to fill his mind with wholesome awe as, in the night, he listened to it, falling with a mysterious solemnity from the lips of Jesus. Who knows the character and feeling of Nicodemus at this time well enough to say that such discourse would have been less impressive or less useful than any other?

The only interpretation, besides the above, which deserves attention is this: that Jesus, instead of saying, *No one hath been in heaven*, etc., says, *No one hath ascended up to heaven*, etc., because in case of every other person but himself, *being* in heaven must depend on *ascending* into heaven. Hence, the word save or "except" (εἰ μή), refers to the idea of being in heaven, as implied in that of ascending into heaven. This is Meyer's view.¹

14, 15. And as Moses lifted up the serpent in the wilderness, etc. According to Num. 21: 6-8, when many of the Israelites had been bitten by venomous serpents, Moses, at the command of God, made a serpent of brass, and put it on a pole, that any one who had been bitten might look upon the serpent and live. In no other way could the deadly operation of the poison be overcome and life be saved. Jesus now uses this remarkable narrative to illustrate the necessity of his own death, and the certainty of eternal life to those who should believe. He affirms that, according to the merciful plan of God, he himself, the Son of man, must be lifted up on the cross for the salvation of all who will trust in him. It is perfectly evident that he now refers to his death for sinners; and hence that, in the beginning of his ministry, the mystery of his sacrificial death was distinctly present to his mind. He felt himself to be the Lamb of God, and foresaw his pathway through suffering to glory. And surely he who was at home in the plans of heaven might be expected to speak, with even greater clearness than John the Baptist, of his atoning death; and it is evident that in this quiet hour he did thus speak to the "ruler of the Jews," who came to him for light. The words of the common text, **should not perish, but,** should be omitted, because they are probably an interpolation, which was first made accidentally by some copyist whose eye fell on the next verse. The highest authorities omit. It will be observed that, besides omitting the words, **should not perish,** in verse 15, the Rev. Ver. connects **in him** with *may have eternal life*, rather than with **believeth**. The Greek admits of either construction. When the text is carefully studied, the construction of the revisers appears preferable to the other.

According to Erasmus, and many interpreters since his day (*e. g.*, Westcott, Milligan and Moulton in Schaff's "Popular Commentary," etc.), the conversation of Jesus with

---

¹ The closing words, **which is in heaven,** are omitted by א B L T^b, 33, Memphitic (best codices, according to Hort), Æthiopic. There is no known patristic quotation of ver. 13 and 14 together. Several Fathers, Cyril of Alexandria many times, quote ver. 13 without including these closing words; but we cannot be sure they did not have them in their copies. There is a superficial appearance of contradiction between the clauses **he that came down from heaven** and **he which is in heaven.** That this was felt is shown by the fact that it omits **he which is,** leaving simply, **the Son of man in heaven,** and two cursives make it, "he that is from heaven," answering to **he that came down from heaven.** Now this superficial difficulty will account for the *omission* of the words in the above-mentioned MSS. and versions, *and also* for their omission by certain Fathers in citing the passages. Chap. 1: 18 has a somewhat similar expression, but not presenting the same difficulty. On the other hand, no reason occurs to the mind for the *insertion* of the words in nearly all the early versions, as well as in most MSS. and many Fathers, if they were not originally present. Hort thinks "they may have been inserted to correct any misunderstanding arising out of the position of 'has ascended,' as coming before 'descended;'" but this would be correcting a slight difficulty by introducing one apparently more serious. The words may therefore be confidently retained, and they occasion no real difficulty to one who takes thoughtful and Scriptural views of the Incarnation and of heaven. If attested only by א L, Memphitic, Æthiopic, the omission would be readily regarded by Hort as an "Alexandrian" correction.—B.

16 a For God so loved the world, that he gave his only begotten Son, that whosoever believeth in him should not perish, but have everlasting life.
17 b For God sent not his Son into the world to

16 For God so loved the world, that he gave his only begotten Son, that whosoever believeth on him
17 should not perish, but have eternal life. For God sent not the Son into the world to judge the world;

a Rom. 5:8; 1 John 4:9....b Luke 9:56; ch. 5. 45; 8:15; 12:47; 1 John 4:14.

Nicodemus ends with the fifteenth verse, and the words that follow, to the twenty-first verse, belong to the Evangelist only. In favor of this view it is urged (1) that the word translated **only begotten** is never elsewhere applied by Christ to himself as the Son of God, while it is a characteristic expression of John. There is considerable weight in this argument, especially when we bear in mind how early in Christ's ministry this interview with Nicodemus took place, and how habitually Jesus called himself *the Son of man*, avoiding in the first months of his ministry any direct assertion of his Sonship to God. But, on the other hand, it may be said that, apart from these verses (16-21), the authorship of which is in question, John applies this epithet to Christ only three times (1:14-18; 1 John 4:9), and it may be asked: May not Jesus have used it twice and John thrice, rather than John five times? Is it not more reasonable to suppose that John borrowed this word from the lips of Jesus, than to suppose that he first applied it to the Son of God? (2) That there is no reference in what follows to Nicodemus. But may it not be fairly assumed that Nicodemus was now a deeply interested listener, while Jesus continued for a short time to lay before his mind, in words of heavenly wisdom, the origin and nature of his kingdom? Other arguments for the Erasmian theory are, that *believed in the name of* (v. 18) is an expression used by the Evangelist (e. g., 1:12; 2:23; 1 John 5:13), but not elsewhere by Jesus; that such an addition finds a parallel in 1:16-18, and probably in 3:31-36, and almost certainly in 12:37-41; and that the past tense of the verbs in verse 19 agree with those in 1:11, 12, and with the position of the Evangelist better than with that of Jesus when conversing with Nicodemus. It must be granted, we think, that these arguments are weighty, though they do not seem to be wholly decisive.

In favor of regarding the following to verse 21 as the words of Jesus, may be urged two circumstances: (1) That the Evangelist has given the reader no hint of passing from the words of Jesus to his own words at this point; and (2) that he has made no reference in this place to a close of the Lord's interview with Nicodemus, while he has used in verse 22 an expression which implies that close. Yet, on the whole, the more one studies the Fourth Gospel the more probable will it seem to him that these five verses (16-21) give the testimony of John, rather than the very words of Christ.

16. For God so loved the world, etc. This verse has been called an epitome of the whole gospel, and no single statement of the New Testament is better entitled, to this designation. (1) It goes back of the whole work of redemption, and reveals the motive in which that work had its origin. (2) It describes that motive as love or good-will, not merely to the chosen people, or to the elect from every nation, but to all mankind; for this is the only tenable meaning of **the world,** as here used. (3) It pronounces the gift of Christ, with the work implied in that gift, a sufficient reason for the salvation of every man who will believe in him. And (4) it presents that salvation to the mind as **eternal life,** or, in other words, a blessed state of being begun on earth and continued forever. On the other hand, it may be said to imply (a) that, without the work of Christ, men could not have had eternal life, and (b) that, without faith in him, they cannot now have eternal life, although he has been lifted up on the cross. The adverb **so** means, with so great a love, and the verb **gave** has respect to all the humiliation and suffering which he endured for men, and which culminated on Calvary. (See Rom. 8:32.)

17. For God sent not his Son into the world to condemn the world, etc. The word translated **condemn,** literally signifies *to judge;* but generally, in this Gospel, with an implication that the decision is unfavorable. Hence it is not improperly rendered **condemn.** The Jews are said to have expected a Messiah who should judge and punish the Gentile world, and the language here used may be directed against this error. But it can hardly be supposed that this was the

condemn the world; but that the world through him might be saved.
18 *He that believeth on him is not condemned: but he that believeth not is condemned already, because he hath not believed in the name of the only begotten Son of God.
19 And this is the condemnation, *that light is come into the world, and men loved darkness rather than light, because their deeds were evil.
20 For *every one that doeth evil hateth the light, neither cometh to the light, lest his deeds should be reproved.

but that the world should be saved through him.
18 He that believeth on him is not judged; he that believeth not hath been judged already, because he hath not believed on the name of the only begotten
19 Son of God. And this is the judgment, that the light is come into the world, and men loved the darkness rather than the light; for their works
20 were evil. For every one that ¹doeth evil hateth the light, and cometh not to the light, lest his works

a ch. 5:24; 6:40, 47; 20:31....b ch. 1:4, 9, 10, 11; 8:12....c Job 24:13, 17; Eph. 5:13.—1 Or. practiseth.

principal reason for these words. They have a larger scope. They apply to all men—Jews as well as Gentiles. In so far as men are concerned, the object of the Father in sending the Son was to furnish them the means of salvation. They were already judged and condemned as sinners; but the Father had purposes of mercy, and sent his Son to open a way of escape to those under condemnation. Yet it was a provision which recognized the moral agency of man. The sending of the Son did not, in and of itself, save the world; but it was necessary, in order that the world might be saved, if it would. These two verses (16 and 17) give the motive and purpose of the incarnation. The result of it is next pointed out.

18. He that believeth on him is not condemned: but he that believeth not is condemned already, because he hath not believed in the name of the only begotten Son of God. No reader can fail to see the harmony of this saying with the gospel as preached by the Apostle Paul. He who is a believer in Christ as the Son of God and Saviour of men, is no longer under law, but is under grace. He is no longer "being judged" (κρίνεται), but is forgiven, and recognized as an heir of life eternal. On the other hand, he who does not believe, has been already judged (i. e., condemned. See above for the meaning of the word in this connection), because he has not believed—the judgment or condemnation covering the same period as the want of faith, and indeed depending on that want of faith. Observe the tense of the verbs, literally *hath been condemned* (κέκριται), and **hath** (*not*) **believed** (πεπίστευκεν). The doctrine here taught is not that unbelief is the only sin for which man is accountable, but that it is a rejection of pardon through Christ, a rejection of Christ, the Bringer of life; and is therefore the reason why, as a matter of fact, he is still condemned for sin of whatever kind. "God has provided a remedy for the deadly bite of sin; this remedy the man has not accepted, not *taken:* he must then perish in his sins; he is already judged and sentenced."—(Alford.) Notice that, in speaking of the actual relation of men to Christ and eternal life, "every one" is referred to as believing for himself. It is not the family, the nation, or the world, but every one who is represented as either believing or not believing in him.

19. And this is the condemnation (or *judgment*), etc. The nature and reasonableness of the judgment in question are set forth by these words. Jesus is declared to be the Light of men, the clearest revelation of God's holiness and love. In rejecting him, therefore, they reject the true Light; and they do this because they prefer the darkness of sin to the light of God; and this preference has its source in their sinful conduct, their practical evil. Reversing the order, and proceeding from cause to effect, we have (1) personal sinning; (2) preference or love of moral darkness and evil, rather than of "light and truth" as revealed in Christ; and (3) condemnation unremoved.

20. For every one that doeth evil hateth the light, etc. Not only may the evil doer be said to love the darkness of sin rather than the light of God, he may also be truly said to hate the light, and to refuse to approach the highest source of blessing to his soul. For he is conscious of personal sin, and is unwilling to see it in the light of infinite purity; he is conscious of finding pleasure in moral evil, and is opposed to everything which tends to reveal its true nature and subdue the heart to penitence. The word here translated "evil" (φαῦλα) represents bad deeds as those out of which no real gain can ever come. Sin is profitless as well as wrong.

CH. III.] JOHN. 103

21 But he that doeth truth cometh to the light, that his deeds may be made manifest, that they are wrought in God.
22 After these things came Jesus and his disciples into the land of Judea; and there he tarried with them, ^a and baptized.

21 should be ¹ reproved. But he that doeth the truth cometh to the light, that his works may be made manifest, ² that they have been wrought in God.
22 After these things came Jesus and his disciples into the land of Judæa; and there he tarried with

a ch. 4: 2.——1 Or, *convicted*....2 Or, *because*.

21. But he that doeth truth cometh to the light, etc. Here are described a character and life just the opposite of those described in the twentieth verse. For **he that doeth truth,** is one who is habitually doing what the truth requires, even as a doer of the law is one who constantly does what the law requires. But **the truth** comprehends more than "the law;" for "the law" was given by Moses, while **truth** came by Jesus Christ (1:17). It has special reference, therefore, to the gospel of the grace of God; and whoever **doeth truth** accepts that grace, or, in other words, comes to the light. Indeed, the two things are inseparable, being different phases of the same life. Moreover, this response to the grace of God in Christ, which is here called doing the truth, will be open and manly, involving a frank confession of sinfulness and a loyal adhesion to Christ, together with a desire to have all men know that even repentance and faith have their source in God. Not in a spirit of self-righteousness, but in one of gratitude and love, will the grace of God through Christ be openly acknowledged, and this acknowledgment itself will be ascribed to the Spirit of God breathing upon the soul.

If Jesus uttered all these words to Nicodemus, we may say that "it speaks for the simplicity and historic truthfulness of our Evangelist, that he adds nothing more, and even leaves untold the immediate result which the discourse had" (Baumgarten-Crusius, in Alford). But if the last five verses are merely the words of the Evangelist, it is still true that the record bears every mark of simplicity and genuineness, that the teaching of Jesus was adapted to the spiritual state of the inquirer, and that it proved in the end to be good seed cast into good soil (see 7: 50; 19: 39).

22-24. CONTEMPORANEOUS MINISTRY OF JESUS AND OF JOHN.

22. After these things. Namely, the events which have been narrated as taking place in Jerusalem, *i. e.*, the cleansing of the temple, the signs wrought by Jesus, and the conversation with Nicodemus; but how long after these events the Evangelist does not mention. It is, however, commonly supposed, that Jesus left the city soon after the close of the passover, or about the end of April, A. D. 27. **Came Jesus and his disciples.** By his disciples may be understood Andrew and Peter, James and John, Philip and Nathanael, the six who had followed him from the Jordan to Cana of Galilee, and perhaps from Cana of Galilee to Jerusalem. We cannot, indeed, be perfectly certain that all these were with him, or that others were not now called disciples; but the narrative of John leads us to think especially of these, and we may be reasonably certain that John was one of those who attended Jesus at this time. Perhaps Andrew and Simon Peter had returned to Galilee. **Into the land of Judea.** That is, into the province or country of Judea, as distinguished from Jerusalem. But the Evangelist does not specify any particular part of the province, probably because Jesus went from place to place, visiting many villages of Judea. **And there he tarried with them and baptized.** As both verbs are in the imperfect tense, which denotes continuous action, this clause may be translated, *And there he was remaining with them and baptizing.* (1) This Judean ministry occupied, it is thought, about seven months, from the first of May to the first of December (see note on 4: 35). (2) It is not mentioned by the other Evangelists, who limit their narratives of the ministry of Christ before his last passover, to what he did in Galilee. (3) Yet it serves to account for several facts mentioned by the other Evangelists (see Matt. 26: 6-13; Mark 14: 3-7; Matt. 23: 37-39; Luke 13: 34, 35). (4) It brings the ministry of Christ himself into accord with that of his servants, inasmuch as the gospel is first offered to those who are pre-eminently "the Jews," the chosen people of God. (5) Jesus himself acted as a teacher. He also administered baptism, but only by the hands of his disciples (see 4: 2). This baptism could

23 And John also was baptizing in Enon near to *Salim, because there was much water there; *and they came, and were baptized.

23 them and baptized. And John also was baptizing in Ænon near to Salim, because there ¹ was much

a 1 Sam. 9:4....*b* Matt. 3:5, 6.—1 Gr. *were many waters.*

not have differed essentially from that of John. It must have been a sign of true repentance and faith in Jesus as the promised Messiah. It must have been a symbol of entrance upon a new life of service to God and his Christ. Compare Edersheim ("The Life and Times of Jesus the Messiah," I., p. 393). "It was only on this occasion that the rite was administered under his sanction. But the circumstances were exceptional. It was John's last testimony to Jesus, and it was preceded by the testimony of Jesus to John. For divergent, almost opposite, as from the first their paths had been, this practical sanction on the part of Jesus of John's baptism, when the Baptist was about to be forsaken, betrayed, and murdered, was Christ's highest testimony to him. Jesus adopted his baptism, ere its waters forever ceased to flow, and thus he blessed and consecrated them. He took up the work of his forerunner, and continued it. The baptismal rite of John administered with the sanction of Jesus, was the highest witness that could be borne to it." But had not Jesus sanctioned the baptism of John by submitting to it himself? Or, is it reasonable to suppose that he would have caused his own disciples to be baptized simply to endorse the baptism of John? Weiss ("Leben Jesu," I. S. 406 sq.) observes that "the people, especially the inhabitants of the capital and southern province, were not yet ripe for his properly Messianic activity. Jesus must become his own harbinger. In these experiences [with Nicodemus, etc.], he saw an intimation of his God, that he should now turn back to a more preparatory work. What other form could this take than that which had been assigned by God himself to his forerunner?"

23. And John also was baptizing. Surprise has been expressed at the separate ministry of John after he knew that Jesus was the Christ, and had entered on his work. But there is no occasion for surprise, any more than there was when Jesus afterwards sent out the twelve, or the seventy. For the office of John was still the same—to prepare men for the reception of Christ; not to follow in the footsteps of Christ, but to go before and make ready a people for the Lord. In reply to Bruno Bauer's question: "Why did not the Baptist lay down his herald's office after so distinctly recognizing the *pre-eminence* of Christ?" Ebrard says: "Because the teachers in a gymnasium do not lay down their office as soon as a new university is founded." **In Enon near to Salim.** The site of Salim has not been identified in a manner wholly satisfactory to scholars. It seems to have been west of the Jordan (ver. 26). Jerome testifies that it was shown in his day eight miles south of Scythopolis, the ancient Bethshean and modern Beisan. Dr. Thomson says that the Jordan Valley, south of Beisau, "once teemed with inhabitants, as is evident from ruined sites, and tells too old for ruins, which are scattered over the plain. Of Salim and Enon, which must have been in the Ghor, at no great distance, I could hear nothing." This plain he represents as "watered in every part by fertilizing streams." In such a plain there may have been a place answering to the description of "Enon, near to Salim." Dr. Barclay believes that he has discovered the site of Enon at Wady Farah, a valley about five miles northeast of Jerusalem. This Wady abounds with very copious springs and large pools, while another Wady, quite near, is called Selam, or Seleim. ("City of the Great King," pp. 558–570.) This identification has not been accepted by Biblical scholars, though it has several points in its favor. There is nothing in the narrative of John that requires one to place Enon in the neighborhood of the Jordan, and the testimony of Jerome is too remote from the time of Christ to be at all decisive.

Yet another site has been proposed. In his "Biblical Researches" (III., p. 333) Dr. Robinson remarks "that so far as the language of Scripture is concerned, the place near which John was baptizing may just as well have been the Sâlim over against Nâbulus; where, as we have seen, there are two large fountains." C. R. Conder, author of "Tent Work in Palestine" (I., p. 91 sq.), remarks that the Shalem near Shechem "possesses a yet higher interest as the probable site of the *Enon near to Salim*, where John was baptizing, *because there was much water there*. The head springs are found in an open valley, surrounded by desolate and shapeless hills. The water gushes out over a stony bed, and flows rapidly down in a fine stream surrounded by bushes of oleander. The supply is perennial, and a continual succession of little springs occurs along the bed of the valley, so that the current becomes the principal western affluent of Jordan, south of the Vale of Jezreel. The valley is open in most parts of its course, and we find the two requisites for the scene of baptism of a huge multitude—an open space, and abundance of water. Not only does the name Salem occur in the village three miles south of the valley, but the name Ænon, signifying 'springs,' is recognizable at the village of 'Ainûn, four miles north of the stream. There is one other place of the latter name in Palestine, Beit 'Ainûn near Hebron, but this is a place which has no very fine supply of water, and no Salem near it. On the other hand, there are many other Salems all over Palestine, but none of them have an Ænon near them." The place where John is said to have been baptizing, "because there was much water there," is so wild and inaccessible, and so off the usual lines of travel, that comparatively few tourists attempt to visit it. Prof. McGarvey thus tells the story of his visit:

"Salim, near to which Enon was located (John 3: 23), is a village on the slope of the hills east of the plain of Moreh, and nearly opposite to Jacob's well. Our nearest route would have been to pass by it; but we preferred tracing the waters from near their fountain head; so we turned to the left near Joseph's tomb, and went northward a few miles along the Damascus road.

"This brought us to the head waters of Wady Bedan, a tributary of the Wady on which Enon is located, called Wady Farra. We struck Wady Bedan at a point where four mills, propelled by its water, are situated in sight of one another. We followed its course to its junction with Wady Farra, and in doing so passed twelve mills, the last situated in the fork of the two streams, and propelled by water drawn from Wady Farra. The rapid descent of the principal stream makes it practicable to draw off these side channels at short intervals, and to build the mills close together. In some instances the mill-race is so high above the principal stream that it runs through and propels two mills in making its way down. From the junction of the two streams we continued down Wady Farra in search of a place answering to Enon. The 'much water' we found all the way; and, although the season was exceptionally dry, pools well suited for baptizing were abundant. We rode into a number of these to try their depth. But we wanted to find, in addition to the 'much water,' an open space on the bank of the stream suitable for the assembling of the great multitudes who flocked to John's place of baptizing; and for several miles we found no such place. We pursued our pathless way on the slopes of a narrow ravine, with high and precipitous hills on each side. We had to ford the stream frequently, and its banks were everywhere so thickly crowded with a jungle of oleanders in full bloom that we could not always pass where we would. Never, in a single day, have I seen so many oleanders. For as many as five miles their line of mingled pink and green was as continuous as the current of the stream which nourished them. *Finally, after a fatiguing ride, during which both our dragomen and our escort became discouraged and fell behind, there suddenly opened before us a beautiful valley among the mountains, about one mile wide and three miles long. Bedouin tents were pitched in groups here and there; herds of camels, to the number of three or four hundred, were grazing, or drinking, or moving about; and swarms of brown-skinned boys, both large and small, were bathing at different places in the stream. Here, then, was the open space required, and a more suitable place for the gathering of a multitude could not be found on the banks of any stream in Palestine.*"—(Quoted by the "Journal and Messenger," Sept. 10. 1879.) **Because there was much water there.** The expression, translated **much water** (ὕδατα πολλά), is plural, and is somtimes rendered "many waters.' But by use it seems to denote a large body, or large bodies of water, rather than numerous small streams. Dr. Hackett understands it to signify "deep waters." (Smith's

24 For *John was not yet cast into prison.
25 Then there arose a question between *some of* John's disciples and the Jews about purifying.
26 And they came unto John, and said unto him, Rabbi, he that was with thee beyond Jordan, *to whom thou barest witness, behold, the same baptizeth, and all *men* come to him.
27 John answered and said, *A man can receive nothing, except it be given him from heaven.

24 water there: and they came and were baptized. For
25 John was not yet cast into prison. There arose therefore a questioning on the part of John's disciples with a Jew about purifying. And they came
26 unto John, and said to him, Rabbi, he that was with thee beyond Jordan, to whom thou hast borne witness, behold, the same baptizeth, and all men come
27 to him. John answered and said, A man can receive nothing, except it have been given him from

a Matt. 14:3....*b* ch. 1:7, 15, 27, 34.....*c* 1 Cor. 4:7; Heb. 5:4; James 1:17.

Dict. of the Bible, s. v. Ænon.) The only other places where the words occur in the New Testament are Rev. 1:15; 14:2; 17:1; and 19:6. The corresponding Hebrew expression is found in the following passages: Num. 20:11; 24:7; 2 Sam. 22:17; 2 Chron. 32:4; Ps. 18:16; 29:3; 32:6; 77:19; 93:4; 107:23; 144:7; Isa. 17:13; 23:3; Jer. 51:13, 55; Ezek. 1:24; 17:5, 8; 19:10; 26:19; 27:26; 31:5, 7, 15; 32:13; 43:2; Hab. 3:15. **And they came, and were baptized,** that is, *were immersed;* for that is the meaning of the word. A literal translation of the verse renders its meaning perfectly plain: "And John also was immersing in Ænon near Salim, because there was much water there; and they were coming, and being immersed." The process was continuous; hence the imperfect tense of the verbs. This passage virtually affirms that baptism could not be conveniently administered without a considerable body of water. The plea that the water was needed for other purposes than baptizing is set aside by the language of the sacred writer. For the reason why John was *baptizing* there (not why he was *preaching* there), was because there was much water in the place.

24. For John was not yet cast into prison. A seemingly incidental remark, occasioned perhaps by the circumstance that the first three Evangelists had given no account of the contemporaneous ministry of Jesus and of John. The definite article might be inserted before **prison,** making the form of the translation agree with the original; for the reference is to the well-known prison or imprisonment of John.

25, 26. OCCASION OF JOHN'S FURTHER TESTIMONY FOR JESUS. The account just given was probably inserted with a view to what now follows.

25. Then there arose. (Better, as in Rev. Ver., *there arose therefore a questioning on the part of John's disciples with a Jew about*

purifying). "Therefore" (δὺν) represents this dispute as a consequence of the administration of baptism by Jesus and by John at the same time; and the words of the Evangelist seem to indicate that it was begun by the disciples of John. The Jew, whether a friend or an enemy of Jesus, had doubtless reported that multitudes were receiving baptism from the Lord; and this report led to a discussion on the origin and meaning of the rite as a symbol of purification. Had Jesus as well as John a right to administer it? If so, was its meaning the same when administered by John and by Jesus? Or, was its value greater in the latter case than in the former? Were the ministry and baptism of John to be superseded by those of Jesus? Such may have been the questions discussed, as we infer from the terms of this verse and of those that follow.

26. Rabbi, he that was with thee beyond (*the*) **Jordan, to whom thou barest** (*hast borne*) **witness, behold, the same baptizeth, and all men come to him.** Wisely do the followers of John repair to him for instruction. But their language betrays a feeling of jealousy for the honor of their Master, a fear lest the growing influence of Christ should weaken that of John. Yet they do not go so far as to criticise the ministry of Jesus; they merely suggest their perplexity and their feeling, by a brief statement of the case. It is probable that, with their jealousy for the honor of John, there was mingled a desire to know more exactly his relation, and their own, likewise, to Jesus. They were not left in doubt, as the narrative of the Evangelist shows.

27-30. LAST RECORDED TESTIMONY OF JOHN THE BAPTIST.

27. A man can receive nothing, except it be (or, *have been*) **given him from heaven.** A universal truth which John enunciates with reference either to himself, or to Jesus, or to both. No man has any claim to office, honor,

28 Ye yourselves bear me witness, that I said, *a* I am not the Christ, but *b* that I am sent before him.
29 *c* He that hath the bride is the bridegroom: but *d* the friend of the bridegroom, which standeth and heareth him, rejoiceth greatly because of the bridegroom's voice: this my joy therefore is fulfilled.

28 heaven. Ye yourselves bear me witness, that I said, I am not the Christ, but that I am sent before 29 him. He that hath the bride is the bridegroom: but the friend of the bridegroom, who standeth and heareth him, rejoiceth greatly because of the bridegroom's voice: this my joy therefore is made full.

a ch. 1: 20, 27.....*b* Mal. 3: 1; Mark 1: 2; Luke 1: 17.....*c* Matt. 22: 2; 2 Cor. 11: 2; Eph. 5: 25, 27; Rev. 21: 9.....*d* Cant. 5: 1.

or success. These are all gifts from God, and may be increased or diminished as he pleases. The principle is applied to the priestly office in Heb. 5: 4. Forgetfulness of it has filled many a heart with pain; remembrance of it has filled many a heart with peace. It is, however, impossible to determine whether John announced this principle because it was applicable to himself, or because it was applicable to Jesus, or because it was applicable to both. But, in view of the whole context, we believe it safe to adopt the last hypothesis. The change which was taking place in public sentiment, by which Jesus was increasing and John decreasing in importance, had its source in the counsels of heaven.

28. Ye yourselves bear me witness. The very men who were now troubled at the waning influence of John, and the growing influence of Jesus, ought to have anticipated this; for they themselves had heard from the lips of their powerful teacher words which foreshadowed what was now coming to pass. He had done what he could to prepare them for it. That I said, I (*myself*) am not the Christ, but that I am (or, *have been*) sent before him. Referring probably to his answer to the deputation from the Pharisees (1: 19-28). An answer the substance of which had been repeated more than once. It appears therefore that some of those who came to John from the dispute with a Jew had been his disciples for a considerable time; yet it is by no means certain that they were present when he cried: "Behold, the Lamb of God, that taketh away the sin of the world!"

But why had not John sent his disciples to Jesus from the hour when he knew him to be the Christ? Or why had he baptized men who were not yet ready to follow Jesus? Doubtless because this was his mission; because he was sent to lead men to repentance as the best preparation for the Messiah, rather than to convince them that Jesus was the Messiah. Christ himself proposed to furnish the evidence of his Messiahship, and it was to

be better evidence than even John could give (5: 36, 37). It is not therefore surprising that John's ministry continued essentially unchanged to the last, whether he taught that the Christ was now coming, or that he had already appeared.

The pronoun "him" (ἐκείνου) is supposed to refer, not to **the Christ** of the preceding clause, but to Jesus, as described in verse 26. It means "that one" of whom you have spoken. (So Bengel, Lücke, De Wette, Meyer, Lange, Alford.)

29. He that hath the bride is the bridegroom. By **the bride** is here meant the true people of God; and the language of John is to this effect: From the fact that multitudes are flocking to Jesus, and becoming his disciples, you ought to infer that he is their Lord; for he who has the bride is the bridegroom. There is no article before bridegroom in the Greek original; it is therefore the predicate, and the interpretation now given is required by the language. **But the friend of the bridegroom, which** (or, *who*) **standeth and heareth him, rejoiceth greatly** (or, *with joy*) **because of the bridegroom's voice.** According to Jewish custom, the business of negotiating and completing a marriage was entrusted to a friend of the bridegroom; and therefore, when at the wedding he heard the voice of the bridegroom conversing with the bride, he rejoiced at the successful accomplishment of the task committed to him. "To rejoice with joy is to rejoice greatly, with joy, and joy only."—(Schaff.) The beautiful figure which John here uses to set forth the relation of Christ to his people is found in the Old Testament as well as in the New (Isa. 54: 5; Hos. 2: 19, 20; Ps. 45; Eph. 5: 32; Rev. 19: 7; 21: 2, 9); but, in using this figure, he alone assigns a place to **the friend of the bridegroom.** Yet the place which he assigns to himself, as "the friend of the bridegroom," is one that he nobly and truly filled; and the addition of this feature to the comparison does not mar in the least its dignity or beauty. **This my**

108 JOHN. [CH. III.

30 He must increase, but I must decrease.
31 *He that cometh from above* is above all; *he that is of the earth is earthly, and speaketh of the earth: *he that cometh from heaven is above all.
32 And *what he hath seen and heard, that he testifieth; and no man receiveth his testimony.

30 He must increase, but I must decrease.
31 He that cometh from above is above all: he that is of the earth is of the earth, and of the earth he speaketh: ¹ he that cometh from heaven is above all. What he hath seen and heard, of that he beareth witness; and no man receiveth his witness.

a ver. 13; ch. 8: 23....*b* Matt. 2ᵈ: 18; ch. 1: 15, 27; Rom. 9: 5....*c* 1 Cor. 15: 47.....*d* ch. 6: 33; 1 Cor. 15: 47; Eph. 1: 21; Phil 2: 9....*e* ver. 11; ch. 8: 26; 15: 15.——¹ Some ancient authorities read, *he that cometh from heaven beareth witness of what he hath seen and heard.*

joy therefore is fulfilled. Or, to copy more closely the form of the Greek expression: *This joy which is mine has therefore been made full*, i. e., complete. Not a ripple of envy passes over the mighty prophet's soul; but he is glad, with a pure and perfect gladness, that the eyes of the people are turning to the King in his beauty. He is satisfied with the joy which belongs to himself, as the friend of the bridegroom.

30. He must increase, but I must decrease. By a holy necessity, grounded in the purpose of God, in the nature of the Messiah, and in the work which he does for the world (1:29), must the power, the influence, and the glory of Jesus become greater and greater forever. "Of the increase of his government and peace there shall be no end" (Isa. 9:7). But by a divine necessity, no less profound and reasonable, the importance of John's work will decrease, and the end of his mission soon come.

Are the remaining words of this chapter (ver. 31-36) those of John the Baptist, or those of the Evangelist? Many affirm that neither the sentiment nor the style belongs to the Baptist, while both direct us to the Evangelist. Says Westcott: "The verses 27-30 are in form clear and sharp, with echoes of the abrupt prophetic speech. These (31-36) have a subtle undertone of thought, which binds them together closely, and carries them forward to the climax in ver. 36." He also insists that ver. 31 and 32 refer to words of the Lord in ver. 11 ff., and ver. 35 to 10: 28, 29; a reference which would have been obvious in case of the Evangelist, but impossible in case of the Baptist; moreover, that it would have been unnatural for the Baptist to have used the words of ver. 29 in connection with the report made to him in ver. 26, and his own language in ver. 27-30; still further, that "the use of the title 'Son' absolutely (ver. 35, 36) appears to be alien from the position of the Baptist"; and finally, that "the aorists in ver. 33 describe the later experience of Christian life (cf. 1: 16)." These reasons are sufficient to overcome the improbability that the Evangelist would have passed without notice from the record of the Baptist's words to his own testimony concerning Jesus. Indeed, the words of the Baptist were a text which might easily suggest to him his own brief, but profound discourse.

31. He that cometh from above, is above all. This language describes Jesus as one who, from the heavenly world where he was from eternity, comes down and draws near to men in his ever-present and continuous work. The word **all** in the expression **is above all**, though probably masculine, does not refer, as has been supposed, to a single class of men, viz., the authorized interpreters of God's will, but to all men without exception. **He that is of the earth is earthly, and speaketh of the earth** (better, *is of the earth, and of the earth he speaketh*, Rev. Ver.) **Of,** or *from*, **the earth,** is emphatic in the second and third clauses. **He that is of the earth**—let it be remembered—*of the earth is he*, and therefore *from the earth he speaks, i. e.*, from an earthly stand-point and experience. Such a man cannot speak as one from heaven; for he has never been there, and is a stranger to the experience of that higher world. The Evangelist does not here deny his own inspiration, or affirm that his teaching is confined to earthly things; but he confesses that he cannot bear witness of heavenly things, or teach more than is given him by another. **He that cometh from heaven is above all.** An emphatic repetition to prepare the minds of his hearers for the next statement.

32. And what he hath seen and heard, *i. e.*, in heaven, before his appearance among men. This interpretation is required by the context. By the use of the perfect tense, "hath seen and heard," the past is closely connected with the present. **That he testifieth.** For one who has seen and heard, is competent to bear witness. His knowledge is

33 He that hath received his testimony *hath set to his seal that God is true.
34 *For he whom God hath sent speaketh the words of God: for God giveth not the Spirit ᶜby measure unto him.
35 ᵈThe Father loveth the Son, and hath given all things into his hand.
36 ᵉHe that believeth on the Son hath everlasting life: and he that believeth not the Son shall not see life; but the wrath of God abideth on him.

33 He that hath received his witness hath set his seal
34 to *this*, that God is true. For he whom God hath sent speaketh the words of God: for he giveth not
35 the Spirit by measure. The Father loveth the Son,
36 and hath given all things into his hand. He that believeth on the Son hath eternal life; but he that ¹obeyeth not the Son shall not see life, but the wrath of God abideth on him.

a Rom. 3:4; 1 John 5:10....*b* ch. 7:16....*c* ch. 1:16....*d* Matt. 11:27; 28:18; Luke 10:2 ; ch. 5:20,22; 13:3; 17:2; Heb. 2:8....
e Hab. 2:4; ch. 1:12; 6:47; ver. 15,16; Rom. 1:17; 1 John 5:10.—¹ Or, *believeth not*.

original and positive. And no man receiveth his testimony. A hyperbole, revealing deep sadness on the part of the Evangelist because so few had received the Lord in faith. "The close of the apostolic age, was a period of singular darkness and hopelessness."—Westcott. So few, as compared with the world of mankind, had accepted the gospel, that it seemed as if no one was willing to believe.

33. He that hath received his testimony. By this expression the Evangelist qualifies the exaggeration of his previous statement. There were indeed some, yet very few in comparison with the whole world, who had welcomed Jesus as the Messiah, and had accepted his word as divine. **Hath set to his seal that God is true** (better, *hath set his seal to this, that God is true*). "To set a seal," or "to seal," is here used in a figurative sense, and means to ratify, confirm, or solemnly declare. The substance of what is ratified or declared is this: **that God is true.** (See John 6:27; Rom. 4:11; 15:28; 1 Cor. 9:2; 2 Cor. 1:22; Eph.1:13.)

34. For he whom God hath sent (rather, *sent*) **speaketh the words of God.** Since Jesus is the interpreter of God to men, to receive his testimony as true, is to acknowledge the supreme veracity of God. **For God giveth not the Spirit by measure.** This statement assigns a reason for the preceding one. It must therefore show why the Sent of God is to be regarded as speaking the words of God. Hence the giving of the Spirit here mentioned must be a giving of the Spirit to Jesus, the Sent of God. Even the Baptist had witnessed the descent of the Spirit, in the form of a dove, *to remain* upon Christ. (See note on 1:34.) Meyer holds that this is a general proposition, meaning that God does not give his Spirit in the same measure to all, but rather to one more of the Spirit, and to another less, as he pleased (1 Cor. 12:7 sq.).

But Jesus, in view of his origin and work, must have received the fullness of the Spirit.

35. The Father loveth the Son. Even John the Baptist had heard the voice from heaven: "This is my beloved Son, in whom I am well pleased" (Matt. 3:17). But it would perhaps have been more natural for him to say, loveth his Son, than to say, loveth the Son. **And hath given all things into his hand.** "We need not be surprised," says Tholuck, "that, with the absolute love of the Father to the Son, he imparts to him, not only the Spirit, but absolutely all things." This statement, if made by the Evangelist, was probably founded on the words of Jesus himself (Matt. 11:27; 28:18; John 13:3; 17:1,2).

36. He that believeth on the Son hath everlasting (or, *eternal*) **life.** Observe, then, that eternal life begins here, and is conditioned on faith in the Son of God. It is therefore something above and beyond mere conscious existence; it is a normal and blessed fellowship with God, as well as with men. **And he that believeth not the Son.** It has been asserted that the word translated, **believeth not** (ἀπειθῶν), should be rendered "disobeyeth," or "disbelieveth," on the ground that a more hostile attitude to Christ than one of mere unbelief is referred to. But unbelief implies disobedience as certainly as disbelief. To neglect the Saviour is to reject him. For it is the duty of men to believe in him. **Shall not see life.** Either here or hereafter. Men who flatter themselves that the world to come will bring some kind of change in this respect, so that sin will be consistent with true peace, disregard the plain language of Scripture. **But the wrath of God abideth on him.** He has been already judged (ver. 18, *supra*), and the displeasure of God is even now coming down and resting upon him. Thus we are plainly taught the necessity of believing in Christ. Faith in him is the only means of deliverance from

CHAPTER IV.

WHEN therefore the Lord knew how the Pharisees had heard that Jesus made and a baptized more disciples than John,
2 (Though Jesus himself baptized not, but his disciples,)

1 WHEN therefore the Lord knew how that the Pharisees had heard that Jesus was making and
2 baptizing more disciples than John (although Jesus

a ch. 3: 22, 26.

the "wrath of God," that arises from his steadfast and holy opposition to sin, revealed in the moral nature of man, and in the uniform testimony of Scripture.

Ch. IV. 1-4. JESUS RETURNS THROUGH SAMARIA INTO GALILEE, Dec., A. D. 27.

1. When therefore the Lord knew how (or, *that*) **the Pharisees had heard.** How the Lord came to know this, whether by supernatural or by natural means, the Evangelist does not state. But the word **therefore** implies that there was a connection between something already referred to, and this knowledge of Jesus. That something may have been no more than the facts recorded in 3: 22, 23; for on these facts depended the report which the Pharisees had heard, and the Saviour's knowledge that they had heard it. If this is all to which the **therefore** points back, the knowledge of Jesus may have been strictly supernatural in origin. But the something referred to may embrace all the facts of the narrative from 3: 22 to 3: 30, or to the end of the chapter. And if so, as seems quite probable, the *Jew* spoken of (3: 25) may have been a Pharisee, and his words may have revealed to the disciples of John what the Pharisees had heard, and with what feelings they had heard it; while some of these disciples of John, moved by the last great testimony of their master, may have repaired to Jesus and reported all they had learned. In this case the knowledge of Jesus would have been natural in its origin. By the word **Pharisees,** in this verse, must be meant the leaders of that sect in Jerusalem; for no doubt some of the Pharisees resided in the country, and were direct witnesses of the success of Jesus. Several of the early manuscripts, versions, and Fathers, have "Jesus," instead of **the Lord,** in the first clause of this verse; but a preponderance of evidence favors the common reading. **That Jesus made and baptized more disciples than John** (more exactly, *was making and*

baptizing). It will be observed that *making disciples* is here distinguished from *baptizing* them—a distinction which would be unnecessary and unnatural if they were made disciples by means of baptism. Hence this language does not agree with the doctrine of baptismal regeneration. Notice, also, the present tense of the Greek verbs, reproducing the report as it came to the Pharisees.[1]

2. Though Jesus himself baptized not, but his disciples. This is not, strictly speaking, a correction of the report heard by the Pharisees, for it is a maxim that "what one does by another, he does himself"; but it is rather an explanation of the manner in which Jesus baptized (cf. 3: 22). But why is this explanation made? Doubtless because Jesus refrained *on principle* from baptizing with his own hands; either (1) because baptizing in water is a ministerial act, as compared with baptizing in the Spirit, and should therefore be performed by the servants, rather

---

[1] [A singular various reading here occurs. The word "than" (ἤ), is omitted by A B (first hand) L G Γ, a few cursives, once by Origen, and by Epiphanius. The Greek could then only mean "heard that Jesus was making quite a number of disciples, and John was baptizing them." This would seem intrinsically inadmissible, as stating what cannot possibly be true, especially as it would make ver. 2 utterly meaningless. Yet let it be remembered that intrinsic probabilities must always be cautiously handled, for an idea at first very startling might nevertheless be true, and might, by degrees, come to appear quite possible, and even probable. It is easy to account, on transcriptional grounds, for the insertion of "than" (ἤ). On the other hand, how can we account for its omission? Hort thinks of nothing but a slip in copying, from the similarity of the Greek particle to the closing sound of the foregoing word, and justly reckons it strange that such a sl:p should pass into so many good documents. But in Mark 4: 21, an evident error in copying, "under the stand" (a " mechanical repetition" of the "under," which twice occurs just before), is found in ℵ B (first hand) in the old uncial represented by 13, 69, and 346, in 33, and, we may now add, in the newly discovered ∑—the Codex Rossanensis—making a case nearly as remarkable as that before us. One cannot here feel quite satisfied, but we seem compelled to retain "than."—B.]

3 He left Judea, and departed again into Galilee.
4 And he must needs go through Samaria.
5 Then cometh he to a city of Samaria, which is called Sychar, near to the parcel of ground ᵃ that Jacob gave to his son Joseph.

3 himself baptized not, but his disciples), he left Judæa, and departed again into Galilee. And he 5 must needs pass through Samaria. So he cometh to a city of Samaria, called Sychar, near to the parcel of ground that Jacob gave to his son Joseph; and

ᵃ Gen. 33:19; 48:22; Josh. 24:32.

than by the Lord, or (2) because any persons baptized by the hands of Jesus would have been in danger of attaching undue importance to that circumstance, and of falling thereby into the sin of spiritual pride. The former reason commends itself to Bengel, Meyer, Lange, Godet, and others; but the latter is more likely to have influenced the Saviour. For to him decorum was less than the spiritual safety and brotherly love of his disciples. Weiss supposes that he could not himself baptize with water without appearing to renounce any claim to being the Greater One, who was to baptize in the Spirit. Doubtful.

3. He left Judea, and departed again into Galilee. The occasion for his departure is given in the first verse. And from the fact that the Lord left Judea because the Pharisees had heard, as he knew, of his success in making disciples, it may be certainly inferred that he saw in their hearts or conduct signs of hostility to himself. The centre of their power was at Jerusalem, and the territory in which their influence was controlling was Judea. Inasmuch therefore as the hour of his death was still distant, he withdrew for a time from this part of the land. It has been conjectured that he also discontinued the practice of baptizing his disciples—either through fear of arousing opposition, or from some other cause. But there is no evidence of the fact, and therefore no reason to seek for a cause. "That he *gave up baptizing* when he left Judea, because the imprisonment of John had brought a ban of uncleanness upon Israel" (Lange), is a capricious fancy. "That those who were converted (as ver. 53) should be baptized, was a matter of course (comp. 3: 5)."—(Meyer.) Yet, if the disciples of Jesus continued until the end of his ministry the practice of baptizing those who professed to receive him as the Messiah, it is surprising that the Evangelists nowhere allude to this fact. It is therefore probable that for some reason the practice was interrupted for a time, to be resumed after the Lord's death and resurrection, when its full significance could be more readily perceived. Whether the imprisonment of John, which seems to have taken place about this time (Matt. 4:12; Mark 1:14; Luke 4:14), had anything to do with the Saviour's departure into Galilee, is uncertain.

4. And he must needs go through Samaria. Was this necessity geographical or moral? If geographical, as interpreters generally assume, Jesus could not have been near the Jordan when he started on his way to Galilee, but must have been in the central, southern, or western part of Judea. And there is no reason to deny that he was thus remote from the Jordan, so that the nearest way to Galilee was through Samaria. But there is, on the other hand, no special indication of haste in his journey (see ver. 40), while the result of his labors in Sychar was such as to justify the belief that a divine necessity led him to select that way, that the plan and purpose of his ministry moved him to go through Samaria to Galilee. It was probably safer, or, at least, less annoying to go from Judea, through Samaria, to Galilee, than to go from Galilee through Samaria, to the temple in Jerusalem (Luke 9:52). For a bitter hostility, springing from differences of religious belief and worship, separated the Jews from the Samaritans; and the latter would be more likely to manifest their hostility when they encountered the former going up to the temple, than when they saw them going northward to Galilee.

5-26. CONVERSATION WITH A SAMARITAN WOMAN AT JACOB'S WELL.

5. Then (*so*, or *therefore*) **cometh he to a city of Samaria, which is called Sychar.** Many Biblical scholars, including Dr. Edward Robinson, believe that Sychar was, in the time of Christ, the name of the ancient Shechem; and they generally propose to account for the change of name by assuming (1) that Sychar was "a provincial mispronunciation of Shechem," or, (2) that it was "a term of reproach," meaning "a lie," with reference to the Samaritan faith. Others, with greater reason, hold that it was a small

6 Now Jacob's well was there. Jesus therefore, being wearied with *his* journey, sat thus on the well; *and* it was about the sixth hour.
7 There cometh a woman of Samaria to draw water: Jesus saith unto her, Give me to drink.

6 Jacob's ¹ well was there. Jesus therefore, being wearied with his journey, sat ²thus by the ¹well.
7 It was about the sixth hour. There cometh a woman of Samaria to draw water: Jesus saith unto

1 Gr. *spring:* and so in ver. 14; but not in ver. 11, 12.....2 Or. *as he was.*

city situated farther east than Shechem, and nearer to Jacob's well. For beautiful descriptions of Shechem and its environs, the reader is referred to Hackett's "Illustrations of Scripture," p. 192 sq., and "Smith's Dictionary of the Bible," under "Shechem." **Near to the parcel of ground that Jacob gave to his son Joseph.** With this statement may be compared Gen. 33:19; and Josh. 24:32. From the former, it appears, that Jacob bought a parcel of ground near Shechem for a hundred pieces of silver; and from the latter, that the bones of Joseph, when brought up from Egypt, were buried in that piece of ground, which had become the possession of the children of Joseph. These two facts agree with the tradition that Joseph received this land by gift from his father.
6. Now Jacob's well (or *spring*) **was there.** Says Dr. Hackett: "The well is near the western edge of the plain, just in front of the opening between the hills where Nablous, the site of Shechem, is situated. Before me, therefore, as I sat there, was the town from which the people came forth, on the report of the woman, to see and hear the prophet for themselves. Behind me were the fields, then waving with grain; but at the earlier season of the year, when Christ was there, recently ploughed and sowed. There is Gerizim just at hand, at which the woman pointed at the moment, or glanced with the eye, as she uttered these words: 'In this mountain our fathers worshiped.' In short, John's narrative of the occurrence at the well forms a picture, for which one sees that the perfect frame-work is provided, as he looks around him, in front of the hills which enclose the modern Nablous. . . . The original mouth of the well is no longer visible on the outside; a vaulted roof having been built over it, through which it is necessary to descend, in order to reach the proper entrance of the excavation. The aperture is barely large enough to allow a person to crowd his body through. I have no doubt whatever of the identification of this well; the various local proofs which point to that spot, and the uni- formity of the tradition, furnish an amount of testimony respecting the question, too strong to be set aside." (Ill. of Scrip., p. 199 sq.) "The well," remarks Porter, "is deep—seventy-five feet when last measured—and there was, probably, a considerable accumulation of rubbish at the bottom. It is entirely excavated in the solid rock, perfectly round, nine feet in diameter, with the sides hewn smooth and regular. Sometimes it contains a few feet of water but at others, it is quite dry." (Handbook, p. 340.) But this statement as to the "solid rock" is controverted. "Lieut. Anderson, who descended to the bottom in May, 1866, found it then seventy-five feet deep, and quite dry. 'It is,' he says, 'lined throughout with rough masonry, as it is dug in alluvial soil.'" (Warren's "Recovery of Jerusalem," pp. 464 sq.) **Jesus therefore, being wearied with his** (or *the*) **journey, sat thus on the well.** He had become very weary by the toilsome way, and was now, as the perfect participle (κεκοπιακὼς) indicates, feeling the effect of his long-continued exertion. His weariness is also brought to mind again by the adverb **thus. It was about the sixth hour.** That is, probably, about 6 P. M.; a note of time, which is partly due to the interest which the Evangelist felt in the events of that day; and perhaps still more, to his recollection of the physical exhaustion of Christ, occasioned by a long journey from morning till near evening. How clearly is the human nature of the Lord revealed by his weariness! For some reason the disciples appear to have been less exhausted than their Lord.
7. There cometh a woman of Samaria to draw water. By a woman of Samaria is meant a native of the province, not of the city of that name. Where this woman resided, whether in Sychar itself, or in some hamlet near the well, is not known. Nablous is said to be about a mile and a half from Jacob's well; and if it occupies the site of Sychar, no one, except for a special reason, would come so far to obtain water. Porter says, however: "The mere fact of the well

8 (For his disciples were gone away unto the city to buy meat.)
9 Then saith the woman of Samaria unto him, How is it that thou, being a Jew, askest drink of me, which am a woman of Samaria? *a* for the Jews have no dealings with the Samaritans.
10 Jesus answered and said unto her, If thou knewest the gift of God, and who it is that saith to thee, Give me to drink; thou wouldest have asked of him, and he would have given thee *b* living water.

8 her, Give me to drink. For his disciples were gone
9 away into the city to buy food. The Samaritan woman therefore saith unto him, How is it that thou, being a Jew, askest drink of me, who am a Samaritan woman? (¹ For Jews have no dealings
10 with Samaritans). Jesus answered and said unto her, If thou knewest the gift of God, and who it is that saith to thee, Give me to drink; thou wouldest have asked of him, and he would have given thee living water.

a 2 Kings 17:24; Luke 9:52, 53; Acts 10:28....*b* Isa. 12:3; 44:3; Jer. 2:13; Zech. 13:1; 14:8.—¹ Some ancient authorities omit, *For Jews have no dealings with Samaritans.*

having been Jacob's, would have brought numbers to it, had the distance been twice as great. And even independent of its history, some little superiority in the quality of the water, such as we might expect in a deep well, would have attracted the Orientals, who are, and have always been, epicures in this element." But it does not appear that many resorted to this well; and it is unnecessary to assume that the woman, though acquainted with some of the people of Sychar, had her residence in that city; much less is it necessary to identify Sychar with Shechem. It was a nearer village. **Jesus saith unto her: Give me to drink.** A request occasioned partly by physical thirst, and partly, we may believe, by an ever-present desire to communicate spiritual good. It illustrates the Saviour's wisdom in making even the wants of his own humanity a means of approach to the souls of men (comp. Mark 11:12-14). To ask of one a small favor, in fitting circumstances, is at least to express confidence in his kindness, and thus to open the way for friendly intercourse. For no man wishes any expression of goodness from a person whom he is resolved to treat as an enemy; much less does any one wish to be under obligation to a person whom he hates.

8. For his disciples were gone away into the city to buy meat (or, *food*). The absence of his disciples is here assigned as a reason (for γὰρ) why Christ made the request of the preceding verse; possibly because they had taken with them some apparatus of their own for drawing water. This reason does not, however, exclude the deeper ones mentioned under verse 7. It appears, from the words of the Evangelist, that, notwithstanding their enmity, Jews and Samaritans were accustomed to trade with one another for the necessaries of life, and that even the former would eat that which was purchased from the latter.

9. How is it that thou, being a Jew, askest drink of me, which am a woman of Samaria? (Lit., *Who am a Samaritan woman?*) The woman inferred, probably from his dialect, that Jesus was a Jew; and Alford thinks there is a sort of playful triumph in her question, as if she had said: "Even a Jew, when weary and athirst, can humble himself to ask drink of a Samaritan woman." In like manner Meyer detects a vein of *badinage* in her question. Perhaps it was rather a question of serious surprise at the kind and respectful tone with which the Saviour preferred his request to a Samaritan woman. With this view the answer of Jesus well agrees. **For the Jews have no dealings with the Samaritans.** Many expositors consider this to be a remark of the Evangelist, accounting for the woman's answer, and inserted for the benefit of persons not familiar with Jewish history. It may be so, yet there is no conclusive reason for thinking that the woman herself might not have uttered these words. Would it have been unnatural for her, in the circumstances, to trace the non-intercourse to the Jews rather than to the Samaritans, since she was expressing her surprise that a Jew had forgotten it? On the other hand, the explanation is one that the Evangelist himself might naturally make —perhaps, a little more naturally than the woman. It is omitted by Tischendorf (8th Ed.), and may, possibly, be an interpolation; but the weight of evidence is strongly in its favor.

10. If thou knewest (or, *hadst known*), *i. e.*, when I was asking you, a moment ago, for water. The common translation, "if thou knewest," though formally correct, is liable to be misunderstood, as if it referred to the present, the moment when Jesus made the response. **The gift of God.** This is called in the last clause of the verse **living water**, and is described by Calvin as *tota*

H

11 The woman saith unto him, Sir, thou hast nothing to draw with, and the well is deep: from whence then hast thou that living water?
12 Art thou greater than our father Jacob, which gave us the well, and drank thereof himself, and his children, and his cattle?

11 living water. The woman saith unto him, [1]Sir, thou hast nothing to draw with, and the well is deep: from whence then hast thou that living water? Art thou greater than our father Jacob, who gave us the well, and drank thereof himself,

[1] Or, *Lord.*

renovationis gratia, or, "the whole blessing of renewing grace." **And who it is that saith to thee, Give me to drink,** that is, One by whom the grace of God is revealed and imparted to men. **Thou** (*thyself,* for the pronoun is emphatic) **wouldest have asked of him.** In other words, not he, but thou wouldest have been the petitioner. Notice the insertion of the pronoun **thou** (σύ) in the Greek, which does not, in such a case, require the pronoun, except for emphasis. **And he would have given thee living water.** By living water is here meant the grace of God in Christ, which is renewing, sanctifying, peace-giving, unfailing. "By the gift he means the *life,* emanating from him; and the point of comparison is its freshness and perennial character."— (Tholuck.) Living water is rather a figurative designation of the source of that life, and is therefore very nearly equivalent to "grace and truth," by the united influence of which the spiritual life is originated and sustained.

11. Sir, thou hast nothing to draw with, and the well is deep. Not perceiving the spiritual sense of Christ's language, the woman takes him to mean by living water, water welling up from its source in the heart of the earth—fresh, sweet, spring water. Such water might be found at the very bottom of Jacob's Well; for this was not a cistern, a reservoir, fed by water from the surface of the ground, but a true fountain (πηγή, ver. 6), fed by water from the depths of the earth, which had been reached by sinking the shaft (ὄρεαρ) nearly, or quite, a hundred feet. In Maundrell's time (March, 1697) it was one hundred and five feet deep, and had fifteen feet of water in it. Dr. Tristram ("Land of Israel," p 143, Ed. 3), found in it only "wet mud" in December, but towards the end of February it was "full of water." (*Ibid,* p. 401.) From this source she sees that Jesus cannot draw, for want of the necessary apparatus, and therefore, reminding him of this, she asks: **From**

whence then hast thou that (or, *the*) **living water?** "If thou canst not draw it from the bottom of the well below, from what source canst thou obtain it?" A pretty distinct intimation of her want of confidence in the stranger's power to do what he said, or at least of her feeling that his words had been somewhat extravagant.

12. Art thou greater than our father Jacob? That is, greater in power, so that, without drawing it from the well, thou canst furnish "living water"—perhaps by miracle, as Moses did from the rock. Notice the emphatic **thou,** (σύ), and the interrogative particle (μή), which assumes that the answer should be in the negative. The woman says, **our father Jacob,** because the Samaritans claimed to be descendants of Jacob, through Joseph. (Josephus "Ant.," VII. 7, 8; VIII. 4, 3; IX. 8, 6.) **Which** (or, *who*) **gave us the well, and drank thereof himself, and his children** (or, *sons*)**, and his cattle?** The pith of these clauses is contained in the statement that Jacob drank from the well, and not at all in the circumstance that he gave it to the Samaritans. Deep as it is, Jacob drank from this well, but only by drawing water therefrom; thou canst not then pretend to have "living water" without the labor of drawing it, unless thou art greater than our father Jacob. It is, however, a touch of nature, that the woman dwells on the use which Jacob made of the well, by mentioning his sons, with his flocks and herds, and especially that she recalls the (traditional) gift of the well to the Samaritans; for she was herself a Samaritan by birth, sympathy, and prejudice.

Many interpreters suppose that, after uttering the words: "Whence then hast thou that living water?" the woman's mind turned rather to the idea of some better kind of water, and that she intended to say: "If thou canst give better water than this, thou must be greater than Jacob our father. This was good enough for him; and thou canst not pretend to be of greater dignity or worth

13 Jesus answered and said unto her, Whosoever drinketh of this water shall thirst again:
14 But *a* whosoever drinketh of the water that I shall give him shall never thirst ; but the water that I shall give him *b* shall be in him a well of water springing up into everlasting life.
15 *c* The woman ;saith unto him, Sir, give me this water, that I thirst not, neither come hither to draw.

13 and his sons, and his cattle? Jesus answered and said unto her, Every one that drinketh of this water 14 shall thirst again: but whosoever drinketh of the water that I shall give him shall never thirst; but the water that I shall give him shall become in him 15 a well of water springing up unto eternal life. The woman saith unto him, ¹Sir, give me this water, that I thirst not, neither come all the way hither to

a ch. 6: 35, 58....*b* ch. 7: 38....*c* See ch. 6: 34 ; 17: 2, 3 ; Rom. 6: 23; 1 John 5: 20.—1 Or, *Lord.*

than he." But this reference to the quality of the water does not spring so naturally out of the preceding question as does the view given above.

13. Whosoever (or, *every one who*) **drinketh of this water shall thirst again.** Jesus does not suffer himself to be drawn into a discussion of his own greatness or power as compared with that of Jacob. No side issue diverts him from the end sought by this conversation. He fixes the woman's mind on a single point—the difference between the water of the well, and the water which he is ready to give—with the evident purpose of leading her from the transient good to the permanent, from the natural to the spiritual. This water, referring to the well, brings temporary but not lasting relief from thirst. Its effect soon passes away, and leaves him who drinks of it in the same state as before. Ever returning thirst, with no progress towards a condition without thirst!—this must be expected, though you drink of this well.

14. But whosoever drinketh of the water that I shall give him shall never thirst. The effect of my grace is enduring. It does not pass away, and leave him who receives it in the same condition as before. The old thirst of the soul, raging and painful, will not return. Faintness of spirit, in view of sins unforgiven, will no more be felt. The desire for peace, which only God can satisfy, will no longer rage unsatisfied as before. "God entered into my mind," says Augustine, "sweeter than all pleasure, brighter than all light, higher than all honor." "Certainly," remarks Bengel, "that water, so far as its own nature is concerned, has perennial virtue; and whenever thirst returns, it is from a defect in the man, not in the water." "It is no common water; but water of which a man should constantly be drinking; and if he did so, would constantly be satisfied, so that there would be no recurring intervals of desire and gratification "—(Hanna.) "The Christian must continue to drink of the water

of life to the end "—(Schaff). It is, however, to be remarked that, according to the received text, the word **drinketh**, in this clause, represents a Greek verb in the aorist subjunctive, and therefore denotes a completed, not a continuous act. And there is a sense in which a man receives Christ, or his grace, once for all. His condition is thereby permanently changed, and his thirst will thenceforth be different from what it was before. (Compare Isa. 12: 3; Rev. 7: 16, 17; 21. 6; 22: 1, 2.) **But the water that I shall give him will be** (or, *become*) **in him a well** (*i. e., fountain*) **of water, springing up into eternal life.** The true believer need not look abroad for the fountain of God's grace; it has been opened in his own heart, fresh and pure and sweet. In other words, the Spirit and the truth of God have entered into the life of his soul, and are felt to be an abiding, indwelling, unfailing source of spiritual peace, strength, and hope. He can drink from a fountain which Christ has opened within, the refreshing waters of which he will never be able to exhaust in time or in eternity. From the grace and truth of Christ, which he has already experienced, he will derive joy forevermore. The blessed life now begun will rise into life eternal.

15. Sir, give me this water, that I thirst not (or, *may not thirst*), **neither come hither** (or, *all the way hither*) **to draw.** From the last part of this verse it appears that the woman did not yet perceive the meaning of Christ. She knew too little of spiritual good to discover it at once under images of natural good. But she was moved by the strange and serious language of Christ; she was convinced that he had a great blessing to impart; and, conscious of her toil in bearing water from the well, she asked for that which seemed to promise relief from this toil. There is no indication of levity or irony in her words. On the other hand, she was so far convinced of the greatness and goodness of Christ, as to be prepared for a

16 Jesus saith unto her, Go, call thy husband, and come hither.
17 The woman answered and said, I have no husband. Jesus said unto her, Thou hast well said, I have no husband;
18 For thou hast had five husbands; and he whom thou now hast is not thy husband: in that saidst thou truly.
19 The woman saith unto him, Sir, ᵃ I perceive that thou art a prophet.

16 draw. Jesus saith unto her, Go, call thy husband, 17 and come hither. The woman answered and said unto him, I have no husband. Jesus saith unto 18 her. Thou saidst well, I have no husband: for thou hast had five husbands; and he whom thou now hast is not thy husband: this hast thou said truly.
19 The woman saith unto him, ¹Sir, I perceive that

a Luke 7: 16; 24: 19; ch. 6: 14; 7: 40.——1 Or, *Lord*.

clear exposure of her sin, and a distinct assertion of his Messiahship. Christ therefore gives to the conversation a more searching and plainly religious turn.

16. Go, call thy husband, and come hither. It is evident, from what follows, that Jesus knew her manner of life from her youth up; why then did he say this? Probably to awaken in her a sense of sin, and to give her an opportunity of confessing it. "The first work of the Spirit of God, and of him who here spoke in the fullness of that Spirit, is, to *convince of sin*."—(Alford). It is unnecessary to seek for any further reason for the Lord's word.

17. I have no husband. The tone of voice with which these words were uttered may have been such as to betray a desire to expose a mistake in the Saviour's language, or it may have been such as to reveal a sense of sin and shame. The latter is perhaps more likely to have been its character than the former. At any rate, what she said was true, though it was not the whole truth. **Thou hast well said, I have no husband.** By the emphasis which Jesus gave to the word husband (notice the change in the order of the Greek words: "*Husband* I have not, instead of, *I have not a husband*), he prepared the woman for his statement of her relation to the man with whom she was living. The whole truth must be uttered, if not in humble sorrow by the woman herself, then in tender severity by the Lord, to produce repentance.

18. For thou hast had five husbands. These five were lawful husbands, and, whatever may be conjectured, there is certainly nothing in the words of Jesus to show that she had been unfaithful to any of them, or had been divorced from any of them. **And he whom thou now hast is not thy husband.** Godet remarks that the position of the pronoun **thy** (σου) before **husband** (ἀνήρ) seems to imply an antithesis not expressed:

"not thine, *but another's husband.*" Yet he adds very justly, as we think, that "it is not necessary thus to press the sense of the pronoun." All that can be certainly known, is, that she had been married five times, and was now living in open vice. **In that saidst thou truly.** Better, *This hast thou said truly.* (Rev. Ver.) A recognition of the literal truth of her words, but not of their moral sufficiency. Yet no such woman would have been likely to say more on that point until she had been brought to genuine repentance before God. For her to have said: "The man with whom I am now living is not my husband," would have been out of harmony with the preceding conversation; but what she does say is extremely natural. The picture is life-like, and therefore credible. Meyer is also justified in affirming that "the knowledge of Jesus, in respect to the woman's relations, is *immediate* and *supernatural*. To assume that he had learned the events of her life from others, is contrary to the view of the Evangelist; and there is no psychological foundation for the opinion that his disciples introduced into the conversation what they afterwards learned, when once we are unable to confine the knowledge of Jesus concerning the moral state of others within ordinary human limits. Strangely and needlessly does Lange imagine that the psychical influence of the five men upon the woman had left on her countenance traces which Jesus perceived."

19. Sir, I perceive that thou art a prophet. By this response the woman admits the perfect truth of his statement, inasmuch as she virtually traces it back to God as its author; for a prophet was one who spoke for God, delivering to men truth received from him. The woman, therefore, perceiving that Jesus had superhuman knowledge, ascribes that knowledge to God, and calls him a prophet.

JOHN. [CH. IV.] 117

20 Our fathers worshipped in *this mountain; and ye say, that in *Jerusalem is the place where men ought to worship.
21 Jesus saith unto her, Woman, believe me, the hour cometh, *when ye shall neither in this mountain, nor yet at Jerusalem, worship the Father.
22 Ye worship *ye know not what: we know what we worship; for *salvation is of the Jews.

20 thou art a prophet. Our fathers worshipped in this mountain; and ye say, that in Jerusalem is the place where men ought to worship. Jesus saith unto her, Woman, believe me, the hour cometh, when neither in this mountain, nor in Jerusalem,
22 shall ye worship the Father. Ye worship that which ye know not: we worship that which we

a Judges 9:7....*b* Deut. 12:5, 11; 1 Kings 9:3; 2 Chron. 7:12....*c* Mal. 1:11; 1 Tim. 2:8....*d* 2 Kings 17:29....*e* Isa. 2:3; Luke 24:47; Rom. 9:4, 5.

20. Our fathers worshipped in this mountain. Subtle and often inexplicable are the movements of the human spirit. But it is not surprising that the woman should wish to introduce a topic less personal and painful, for she was not so hardened as to glory in her shame. Nor is it surprising that she should select a religious topic, for her heart was yet open to religious influences, and she felt herself to be in conversation with one who was a true prophet. Moreover, it was extremely natural for her to refer to the controversy between her own people and the Jews concerning the holiest place for worship, for Jacob's Well was at the foot of Gerizim, and her eyes were probably often directed to **this mountain.** It may be also that a certain indescribable candor, purity, and graciousness in the Saviour's countenance and tones of voice made her desire his opinion on the question so long debated between the two peoples. On the whole, it is difficult to imagine anything more natural in conversation than the introduction of precisely this topic, at this point, by the Samaritan woman. By **our fathers** she probably meant, not Jacob and his sons, but the ancestors of the Samaritans of her own day. Though the temple built by Sanballat on Gerizim, in the time of Nehemiah (Josephus, "Ant.," XI. 8, 2-4), had been destroyed, two hundred years after, by John Hyrcanus (Josephus "Ant.," XIII. 9, 1), the Samaritans still resorted to the place where it stood for prayer and sacrifice. The few who still live in Nablous turn their faces to this mount in prayer, and kill the passover on it once a year. **And ye say, that in Jerusalem is the place where men ought to worship.** The question which seems to have been in the woman's mind is rather suggested than proposed. The answer, however, came as promptly as if she had solicited it by a formal question.

21. Woman, believe me, the (or, *an*) hour cometh, when ye shall neither in this mountain, nor yet at Jerusalem, worship the Father. Notice the introductory words, calling attention to that which was to follow. They may may be compared to the "verily, verily," with which, according to this Evangelist, Jesus sometimes called upon his hearers to believe an important truth. Observe, also, that he lifts the woman's thoughts above the controversy in respect to Moriah and Gerizim, by reminding her, with the authority of a prophet, that a time was at hand when neither of these would have any claim to exclusive, or even special consideration, as a place of worship. If the pronoun **ye** refers particularly to the Samaritans, as the same pronoun in the preceding verse refers to the Jews, the words of Christ predict the conversion of the Samaritans—a conversion which would lead them to abandon their worship on Gerizim, without leading them to resort to Jerusalem. "The divine order of the temple worship is *pedagogical.* Christ is its object and end, its fulfilling; the modern doctrine of the restoration of the glory of Jerusalem is a Chiliastic dream."—(Meyer). By the word **Father,** says Grotius, "he tacitly hints the sweetness of the new covenant. (*Tacita novi fœderis suavitatem innuit*)."

22. Ye worship ye know not what. (Better, *Ye worship that which ye know not.*—Rev. Ver.) This language is meant to affirm not absolute, but comparative ignorance on the part of the Samaritans as to the object of their worship. They accepted the Pentateuch, but rejected all the rest of the Old Testament. Hence they knew much less in respect to Jehovah and his purpose of mercy, than had been revealed to the devout Israelites. By rejecting a large part of the truth which God had made known by sacred history and holy song and manifold prediction, they had put themselves in the condition of those who worship an unknown God.

118   JOHN.   [CH. IV.

23 But the hour cometh, and now is, when the true worshippers shall worship the Father in *a* spirit *b* and in truth; for the Father seeketh such to worship him. 24 *c* God *is* a Spirit: and they that worship him must worship *him* in spirit and in truth.

23 know: for salvation is from the Jews. But the hour cometh, and now is, when the true worshippers shall worship the Father in spirit and in truth: *1* for such doth the Father seek to be his worshippers. 24 pers. *2* God is a spirit: and they that worship him

a Phil. 3 : 3....*b* ch. 1 : 17....*c* 2 Cor. 3 : 17.——*1* Or, *for such the Father also seeketh*....*2 Or, God is spirit*.

—**We know what** (or, *that which*) **we worship.** Jesus was addressed by the woman as a Jew, and in accommodation to her use of language, he associates himself with the Jews, and says: "*We* know that which we worship." Hence it is comparative, rather than absolute knowledge, which Christ here claims. Speaking not for himself, but for the Jews as a people, he could only mean to say, We have a knowledge of God which is worthy to be called knowledge, when contrasted with the light possessed by the Samaritans. Farther than this his words do not go.—**For salvation is of** (or, *from*) **the Jews.** It was God's plan to have the salvation which he had provided for mankind come to them from the Jews. Not only were his clearest revelations made first to the chosen people, but the Messiah himself was to be of the seed of David according to the flesh. And if the Messiah was to be from the Jews, God would not leave them without a knowledge of himself.

23. But the (or, *an*) **hour cometh, and now is.** In other words, the period referred to is mainly future, yet it is already begun. **When the true worshippers**—to wit, those whose worship, being at once sincere and intelligent, realizes the proper idea of worship—**shall worship the Father in spirit and in truth.** The preposition **in** before **truth**, should be omitted. The statement is both a prediction and a description of true worship. For, to worship the Father **in spirit**, is to worship him in the innermost soul, to pay unto him the homage of reverent thought and feeling, of filial trust and love. And this spiritual worship is better than any formal service, depending on place and ritual; for it is inspired by the Spirit of God, dwelling in a human spirit, and sanctifying its service. Not a worship in flesh, sensuous, ritual, confined to particular places, seasons, forms, but a worship in spirit, offered wherever there is a human soul quickened by the Spirit of the Most High, is henceforth to prevail among men. This rational worship will not indeed reject outward rites, but it will use them only as helps and expressions of spiritual service (Rom. 1 : 9; 12 : 1). To worship the Father **in truth,** is to worship him within the sphere of truth, or in fellowship and conformity with truth. It is to render him the honor and service which his own nature, or the truth which reveals that nature, prescribes. "Otherwise," as Meyer says, "the worship belongs in the sphere of conscious or unconscious falsehood." The Samaritans were to welcome the full and final revelation of God in the person of his Son, and to serve him in the light of that revelation. Superstition, however sincere and devout, is not acceptable worship. **For the Father seeketh such to worship him.** The Revised Version is preferable: *For such doth the Father seek to be his worshippers.* Not only are the genuine worshipers of God about to render him intelligent homage in the sanctuary of their spirit, without feeling it necessary to appear in Jerusalem or in Gerizim; but the Father is even now seeking to have those who worship him be such as do this. This more spiritual economy springs from the heart, plan, and action of Jehovah himself, who will be a Father to all who thus honor him.

24. God is a Spirit (or, *God is spirit*), *i. e.,* in *essence;* and therefore confined to no mountain-tops, inclosed by no temple-walls. Immaterial, imperceptible to sense, he is everywhere in the fullness of his being; and that being is personal, knowing, feeling, and willing, with a knowledge that is infinite, a love that is perfect, and a power that is boundless. Hence the Psalmist cries: "Whither shall I go from thy Spirit, or whither shall I flee from thy presence? If I ascend into heaven, thou art there; if I make my bed in hell (or, *make Sheol my bed*), behold thou art there. If I take the wings of the morning and dwell in the uttermost parts of the sea, even there shall thy hand lead me, and thy right hand shall hold me" (Ps. 139 : 7-12). The translation, *God is spirit,*

Ch. IV.] JOHN. 119

25 The woman saith unto him, I know that Messias cometh, which is called Christ: when he is come, *he will tell us all things.
26 Jesus saith unto her, *I that speak unto thee am he.
27 And upon this came his disciples, and marvelled that he talked with the woman: yet no man said, What seekest thou? or, Why talkest thou with her?

25 must worship him in spirit and truth. The woman saith unto him, I know that Messiah cometh (who is called Christ): when he is come, he will declare unto us all things. Jesus saith unto her, I that speak unto thee am he.
27 And upon this came his disciples; and they marvelled that he was speaking with a woman; yet no man said, What seekest thou? or, Why speakest

a ver. 29: 39....b Matt. 26: 63. 64; Mark 14: 61. 62; ch. 9: 37.

appears to be the only correct one; for there is no more reason for inserting the indefinite article before the word **spirit,** in this place, than there is for inserting it before the word "light," in the sentence, "God is light" (1 John 1: 5). **And they that worship him must worship him in spirit and in truth.** Only such worship corresponds with his nature. As he is present, though unseen, in every place, and even in the innermost spirit of man, nothing save the filial homage of that spirit, illumined by truth, can be acceptable worship in his sight. Two other interpretations of the expression, "in spirit and truth," ought perhaps to be mentioned. According to one of them, the word "spirit" here means God's Spirit, as gracious influence, which, in union with his truth, is represented as the atmosphere or element of all true worship. Worship that lives and moves, and has its being in the grace and truth of God, is the worship which he requires. It may, however, be questioned whether this interpretation of the word "spirit" is not imported into the text rather than suggested by it, while the doctrine which it finds is really implied in the view given above. According to the other interpretation, the word "spirit" is here used as the opposite of "form," and the word "truth" as the opposite of "pretense"—Jesus teaching merely that worship must be hereafter informal and sincere. This is too superficial.

25. I know that Messias cometh, which is called Christ. Although the Samaritans did not receive the later books of the Old Testament as having divine authority, they did expect a Messiah, and probably connected the language of Deut. 18: 18, with him. The woman uses Messiah as a proper name, without the article, doubtless because it was a designation current in Samaria, as well as in Judea, and because she was conversing with a Jew. The explanation, **which is called Christ,** may be ascribed either to the Evangelist or to the woman. The latter appears to have employed the Greek name in speaking to the men of Sychar (ver. 29). **When he is come, he will tell us** (or, *announce to us*) **all things.** These words may have been due to a feeling that she did not understand the wonderful language of Jesus, and must therefore wait for instruction, which could only be given by the Christ; or they may have been due to a suspicion that Christ was perhaps now conversing with her. Trench sees in these words of the woman a cry of helplessness, connected with a timid presentiment, such as she hardly dares own, much less ventures to utter: "Thou perhaps art he whom we look for."—(Schaff.) The latter account of her language is probably correct; though it is also reasonable to presume that she was conscious of something in his words that she did not fully comprehend.

26. I that speak unto thee am he. (Or, *I that talk to thee; ὁ λαλῶν, of familiar conversation*). Why did Jesus, speaking with this woman, declare himself to be the Messiah, while he avoided making this declaration among the Jews? Several reasons may be suggested, e. g., (1) he may have discerned in the woman's heart a desire to know the truth; (2) he doubtless foresaw that he should remain but a short time in the place; and (3) he knew that an avowal of his Messiahship in that place would lead to no political excitement. "The Jews looked upon the Messiah as the *king* of Israel, and expected from him, first of all, political changes (comp. John 6: 15); while the Samaritans, deriving their Messianic expectations chiefly from Deut. 18: 15-19, regarded him simply as a *prophet* or *teacher*, and were less liable to abuse this revelation for disturbing political purposes." (*Schaff.*)

27. And upon this came his disciples; *i. e.*, as Jesus was making this last remark to the woman, his disciples arrived at the well, on their return from the city. **And they marvelled** (or, *were wondering; ἐθαύμαζον* is substituted for *ἐθαύμασαν* by Lach., Tisch.,

28 The woman then left her waterpot, and went her way into the city, and saith to the men,
29 Come, see a man, *which told me all things that ever I did: is not this the Christ?

28 thou with her? So the woman left her waterpot, and went away into the city, and saith to the men,
29 Come, see a man, who told me all things that *ever I*

a ver. 25.

Treg., and West. and Hort, according to the best evidence). While they were drawing near to the well, from some distance, they were observing and wondering that **he talked with the woman** (or, rather, *was talking with a woman*.) The tense of these verbs is one that represents action in progress, action which is continuous rather than momentary. The wonder of the disciples was not occasioned by anything which they knew of this particular woman, but by the simple circumstance that he was talking with a *woman*. They now saw, perhaps for the first time, how far the holy independence and divine compassion of Jesus lifted him above the Oriental and Rabbinic contempt for woman, in which they had been educated. (See Lightfoot, Tholuck). For it was said by some of the Jewish doctors that "a man should not salute a woman in a public place, not even his own wife," and that it was "better that the words of the law should be burnt than delivered to women." Yet **no man said: What seekest thou? or, Why talkest thou with her?** They did not presume to call in question his action, by asking what he desired from the woman, or why he conversed with her. A feeling of awe restrained them. Is it not probable that the face of Jesus was lighted up at the moment with divine joy, because he saw that a lost soul was beginning to drink of the water of life? They wondered in silence. Would that some others were as reverent as they! Criticism is often foolish, though it is sharp; and silence is often wise, because it is humble and trustful.

28. Then=*therefore*—either because the arrival of the disciples interrupted the conversation, or because the final declaration of Jesus made so deep an impression upon her mind: the latter is to be preferred — **the woman left her waterpot** — forgetful, it may be, of the object for which she had come to the well, or else purposing to return at once, after reporting to others what she had learned—**and went her way** (or, *away*) **into the city**—which was a mile and a half from the well, if Sychar was not nearer than the modern Nablous. We assume, however, that it was much nearer. Yet this walk would furnish time for reflection on the words of Jesus, and for resolving what she would say to the people. **And saith to the men:** whom she met as she entered the city; for she appears to have told her wonderful story to the people whom she first saw.

29. Come, see a man which told me all things that ever I did. An invitation, and a reason for complying with it. Nothing which Jesus said made a deeper impression on the woman than his exact account of her past life. It seemed to her as if he had told the whole sad story of it, though his words were few; and she was so moved, that no feeling of personal shame prevented her from appealing to this proof of the stranger's knowledge. And of all that Jesus had said to her, this was probably just the part which was most likely to arrest the attention, and secure beforehand the confidence of the people. It was something which they could appreciate without difficulty, and which gave evidence of prophetic, if not of Messianic power. **Is not this the Christ?** The Common Version, by introducing **not,** supposes that the woman intimated that she regarded an affirmative answer as correct. But the form of her question, as recorded by John: *Can this be the Christ?* intimates just the opposite—that she wished to be regarded as inclining to a negative answer. Thus: "This cannot be the Christ, I suppose; do you think he can?" Is there not in this form of the question a trait of originality and reality too delicate for any *falsarius* of the second century? The woman, according to the narrative, believed that Jesus was the Christ; would not a writer of fiction have suffered her to intimate this in her question? But in fact she did not. For some reason she saw fit to speak as if she were in doubt herself, and a little inclined to think that Jesus could not be the Christ, though she was anxious to have the judgment of men on that point; and so the Evangelist records her question as she

CH. IV.]   JOHN.   121

30 Then they went out of the city, and came unto him.
31 In the mean while his disciples prayed him, saying, Master, eat.
32 But he said unto them, I have meat to eat that ye know not of.
33 Therefore said the disciples one to another, Hath any man brought him aught to eat?
34 Jesus saith unto them, ᵃMy meat is to do the will of him that sent me, and to finish his work.
35 Say not ye, There are yet four months, and then cometh harvest? behold, I say unto you, Lift up your eyes, and look on the fields; ᵇfor they are white already to harvest.

30 did: can this be the Christ? They went out of the city, and were coming to him. In the mean while
32 the disciples prayed him, saying, Rabbi, eat. But he said unto them, I have meat to eat that ye know
33 not. The disciples therefore said one to another,
34 Hath any man brought him *aught* to eat? Jesus saith unto them, My meat is to do the will of him
35 that sent me, and to accomplish his work. Say not ye, There are yet four months, and *then* cometh the harvest? behold, I say unto you, Lift up your eyes, and look on the fields, that they are ¹ white already

a Job 23: 12; ch. 6: 38; 17: 4; 19: 30.... *b* Matt. 9: 37; Luke 10: 2.——1 Or. *white unto harvest.   Already he that reapeth. etc.*

uttered it. "She believes more than she says; but she does not venture to assume, even as probable, so great news. Nothing could be more natural than this little trait."—(*Godet.*)

30. Then they went out of the city, and came (or, *were coming*) **to him.** The oldest manuscripts and latest editors omit **Then.** The tense of the last verb, *were coming* (ἤρχοντο), represents action in progress, and thus prepares the mind of the reader for a narrative of what took place at the well while the people were coming.

31. In the mean while, *i. e.,* in the time which passed between the departure of the woman for the city and the arrival of the people from the city, **his** (rather, *the*) **disciples prayed** (or, *asked*) **him, saying, Master, eat.** They had left him weary and faint, and they naturally imagined that he must be so still. How great then must have been their surprise at his answer:

32. I have meat (*food*) **to eat that ye know not of.** As Jesus had spoken to the woman of spiritual refreshment under the figure of "living water," so now he testifies of spiritual nourishment under the figure of *food.* The aptness of his emblems is only rivaled by their obviousness. He is at home in the realm of nature, and his use of figurative speech is perfect. Yet his words are not, in this case, altogether figurative. For soul and body are mysteriously united, and the joyful activity of the former is often a literal refreshment to the latter. Spiritual satisfaction seems to nullify bodily want. Hunger ceases when the soul exults. It was after forty days that Christ hungered (Matt. 4: 2). Observe the contrast between the pronouns **I** and **ye**; for the fact that these pronouns are expressed in the Greek makes them in some degree emphatic. Jesus knew, as the disciples did not, the refreshing influence of spiritual service on the whole being, especially when that service springs from holy love, and bears fruit to the glory of God.

33. Therefore said (or, *were saying*) **the disciples one to another.** The Evangelist recollects how this question was passing from one to another: **Hath any man brought him aught to eat?** The form of the question (μή τις) anticipates a negative answer: but the fact that it passed from one to another shows that the disciples did not comprehend his deep and spiritual saying. In this respect they were like the Samaritan woman. Yet how frankly the Evangelist records their dullness, even as if he were not one of them himself. And how promptly Jesus proceeds to express his meaning in words that the dullest must understand.

34. My meat (*food*) **is to do** (or, *that I may do*) **the will of him that sent me, and to finish his work.** Thus Jesus solemnly affirms that the privilege of doing the will of his Father, and of completing at last his Father's work on earth, is his highest satisfaction and refreshment. 'To carry on that work, step by step, according to the Father's will, and to have in prospect its completion on the cross, is my food; and by this I have been nourished and quickened while you were gone to the city.' The original expression here translated, **to do . . . and to finish** (ἵνα ποιῶ), "emphasizes the *end* and not the *process,* not *the doing . . .* and *finishing,* but *that I may do . . . and finish.* (Compare 6: 29; 15: 8; 17: 3; 1 John 3: 11; 5: 3.)"—(Westcott.) We are not sure of this distinction. The Greek expression seems to be fairly represented in English by the infinitive.

35. Say not ye, There are yet four months, and then cometh (*the*) **harves**t**?** This question may be relied upon with rea-

36 a And he that reapeth receiveth wages, and gathereth fruit unto life eternal; that both he that soweth and he that reapeth may rejoice together.

36 unto harvest. He that reapeth receiveth wages, and gathereth fruit unto life eternal; that he that soweth and he that reapeth may rejoice together.

a Dan. 12:3.

sonable confidence as indicating the season of the year when Jesus passed through Samaria, and sat by Jacob's Well. It was about four months previous to the beginning of harvest. And as harvest began about the middle of Nisan (April), at Easter, and lasted till Pentecost, by counting back four months, December is reached. Seed-time was about the first of November, and therefore the fields were now, it is probable, green with the springing grain. Says Dr. Hackett: "Of course there is some doubt whether, in speaking of the interval between sowing and reaping as 'four months,' he employed the language of a proverb merely, or meant that this was the actual time to elapse before the fields around them just sown would yield a harvest. Even if such a proverb was in use (which has not been shown), his availing himself of it would be more significant if the four months of the proverb happened on this occasion to coincide with the season of the year." (Smith's "Dict. of the Bible," Am. Ed., p. 1,361.) This is certainly a very moderate estimate of the probability that Christ's question determines the season of the year when it was asked. Four points may be made against the idea that this is a proverb. (1) That no starting point for the period is given; (2) that the adverb *yet* is inserted; (3) that the pronoun *ye* is emphatic; and (4) that there is no other trace of the existence of such a proverb. **Behold, I say unto you, Lift up your eyes, and look on the fields; for they are white already to harvest.** The conjunction translated **for** should here be rendered *that*, as in the Rev. Ver. The people from the city, it may be presumed, were now visible at no great distance, hastening through the fields towards the well; and by turning his eye upon them, or stretching forth his hand towards them, Jesus interpreted his words to his disciples. More precious than the waving harvests of Mukhna—a valley or plain unsurpassed in point of fertility by any other region of Palestine (Hackett), were these approaching Samaritans, who could now be gathered into the garner of the Lord. These were to be the first-fruits of the Gentiles, brought in by the labor of Christ himself, assisted, it may be, in some way by the presence of his disciples. For the Samaritans, who appear to have expected the Christ as a teacher, rather than as a king, received the truth at this time with great readiness of mind. The Pharisees, with more light, rejected Jesus; the Samaritans, with less self-sufficiency, welcomed him. "Blessed are the poor in spirit" It seems probable that the word **already** belongs to the next verse, rather than to the clause before us. This change is required by some of the early manuscripts, and is approved by Westcott, Schaff, Tischendorf, and others.

36. And (*already*) **he that reapeth receiveth wages, and gathereth fruit unto life eternal.** This language announces both a reward and a result of labor for the salvation of men. Several interpreters, however, suppose that the reward is found in the result, "in having gathered many into eternal life." —(Alford). But it is better to regard the two as, in some measure, distinct; and, if both may be thought of as reward, to look upon that reward as twofold, present and future, involved in the very nature of the service, as well as in its result. The language of Jesus also implies that the reaper, if not the sower, is a servant, and, therefore, reminds one of the saying recorded by Matthew: "The harvest truly is great, but the laborers are few; pray ye therefore the Lord of the harvest, that he will send forth laborers into his harvest" (9:37,38). (*In order*) **that both he that soweth and he that reapeth may rejoice together.** It seems on the whole probable that Jesus means by **he that soweth**, himself, or himself principally. "He that soweth the good seed is the Son of man" (Matt. 13:37); and in the present instance, the gospel comes first to the Samaritans from the lips of Jesus. Afterwards, when Philip went down to Samaria, there was a great ingathering; and, if it was in Sychar, it may be presumed that the sowing of Jesus at this time prepared the way for the reaping by Philip a few years later. At any

37 And herein is that saying true, One soweth, and another reapeth.
38 I sent you to reap that whereon ye bestowed no labour: other men laboured, and ye are entered into their labours.
39 And many of the Samaritans of that city believed on him *for the saying of the woman, which testified, He told me all that ever I did.

37 For herein is the saying true, One soweth, and another reapeth. 1 sent you to reap that whereon ye have not laboured: others have laboured, and ye are entered into their labour.
39 And from that city many of the Samaritans believed on him because of the word of the woman, who testified, He told me all things that ever I did.

a ver. 29.

rate, the sower and the reaper will rejoice together hereafter, when the result of both sowing and reaping is fully revealed. The work of Jesus resembled that of a sower much more than it did that of a reaper.

37. And herein is that saying true: One soweth and another reapeth. As to the purpose of this language, nearly all interpreters are agreed. Christ intends to affirm that in the work of saving men through the gospel, the idea which is expressed by the proverb: **One soweth and another reapeth,** is fully realized. But there is some difference of judgment in respect to the proper rendering and construction of the first clause. It might be rendered very literally: *For herein the saying is the true* [one]: *One is he that soweth, and another he that reapeth.* This translation follows the order of the Greek words, and accords with the interpretation of Lücke and Meyer. "In this case (in this our common work) the proverb: *One soweth and another reapeth,* finds its full application."— (Lücke). The Bible Union translates: "For herein is the true saying," etc.; and Alford: "For herein is [fulfilled] that true saying," etc. I prefer the translation first given, and the interpretation defended by Lücke, Meyer, and others. The article before **true** is doubtful.

38. I sent you to reap that whereon ye bestowed no labor (or, *whereon ye have not labored*); **other men** (*have*) **labored, and ye are** (or, *have*) **entered into their labors.** These words were intended to encourage the disciples by a view of the work to which they had been virtually appointed. The possibility, the success, and the joy of that work had been secured by wearisome toil on the part of some who had gone before. But two difficulties present themselves to an interpreter, (a) in the use of past tenses, while, so far at least as the disciples were concerned, the reference must be mainly to the future; and, (b) in the use of the plural **others** (ἄλλοι), while the reference must be chiefly to Christ himself. In respect to the former, Alford remarks that "here, as often, our Lord speaks of the office and its work as *accomplished,* which is but beginning"; and Meyer, that "the sending of the disciples and the fulfillment of their mission, were essentially involved in their being received into the apostleship." It may as well be said, that, to the eye of Jesus, the future seems to have been already present, and the work of his disciples already past. Not only could he foresee the oak in the acorn, the fruit in the germ, the future in the present, but, if we may judge by his own words, his point of observation was divine as well as human, and he could survey that which was to be, as if it had already been. In respect to the latter difficulty, it is not unreasonable to suppose that Jesus used the word **others** (ἄλλοι), because he wished to associate with himself John the Baptist; for he was addressing a band of men who had been, most of them at least, recently disciples of John. Meyer supposes that it is a plural of category, and Alford, that it is purely rhetorical, to correspond with the plural **ye.** Godet imagines that Christ has in mind the Samaritan woman also, who had gone into the city to speak of him. "In respect to the whole extent of the apostolic work, he thinks, no doubt, of his precursor and of himself. But, with reference to the case before him, he thinks assuredly of himself and of his agile messenger. For he is pleased to recognize the co-operation of the feeblest agent who consents to be associated with him" (3:11). It is, however, exceedingly improbable that he thought of the Samaritan woman in this expression. Her relation to the work was wholly different from that of Christ, of John the Baptist, or of the apostles. The aorist tense of the first verb "sent," is better supported than the perfect.

39-42. MANY SAMARITANS BELIEVE IN JESUS.

39. From this verse it appears that many

124 JOHN. [Ch. IV.

40 So when the Samaritans were come unto him, they besought him that he would tarry with them: and he abode there two days.
41 And many more believed because of his own word;
42 And said unto the woman, Now we believe, not because of thy saying: for *a* we have heard *him* ourselves, and know that this is indeed the Christ, the Saviour of the world.
43 Now after two days he departed thence, and went into Galilee.
44 For *b* Jesus himself testified, that a prophet hath no honour in his own country.

40 So when the Samaritans came unto him, they besought him to abide with them: and he abode there 41 two days. And many more believed because of 42 word: and they said to the woman, Now we believe, not because of thy speaking: for we have heard for ourselves, and know that this is indeed the Saviour of the world.
43 And after the two days, he went forth from 44 thence into Galilee. For Jesus himself testified, that a prophet hath no honour in his own country.

a ch. 17: 8; 1 John 4: 14....*b* Matt. 13: 57; Mark 6: 4; Luke 4: 24.

of the people belonging to Sychar gave full credit to the word of the woman, and, therefore, without asking for any miracle, believed in Jesus as the Messiah. "Whenever Jesus found his word sufficient, he omitted, on principle, the working of miracles."— (*Meyer*.)[1]

40. A wise request and a gracious answer. This simple incident may be studied as an illustration of the nature of true prayer, and of the readiness of God to bestow on his people the greatest conceivable good—his own presence; his own presence, not merely for two days, but for all time and all eternity!

41. The sowing of Jesus was sometimes reaping. In the present instance, more were led to faith in him by his own word, than by that of the woman. What holy and quickening truths fell from his lips during these two December days in the heart of Samaria! Plainly enough, the Evangelist could not put on record all that he said (21: 25).

42. And said (or, *were saying*) **unto the woman.** The remark was often made during those days of profound excitement and joy; but not, we may be certain, with any feeling of contempt for the woman's testimony. She had been too highly honored by Jesus for them to despise her at that time. Some, indeed, suppose that the word translated **saying** (λαλιά), is here used by the Samaritans in its classical sense of "mere talk" —*i. e.*, as compared with the powerful and convincing discourse of Jesus; but against this it may be objected, (1) that the word has this meaning nowhere else in the New Testament; (2) that Christ applies it to his own teaching: "Why do ye not understand my speech?" (John 8: 43); (3) that the corresponding verb is nowhere in the New Testament used of mere talk; (4) that the Samaritans in this very sentence admit that her words had produced in them a belief in Jesus: "Now we believe, not because of thy saying"; and (5) that the circumstances do not render a contemptuous reference to her words probable. It is noteworthy that they use very strong language in expressing their present faith, viz., **we know,** (οἴδαμεν) and that they recognize in Jesus **the Saviour of the world.** Having accepted him as the Messiah, they were prepared to learn that his mission was to **the world,** rather than to the chosen people only. In this respect they were more docile than the Jews, and, though Jesus tarried with them but two days, he was able to convince them that he was the Son of man appearing in the world for the salvation of mankind. Nothing is more remarkable in the ministry of the Lord than his wisdom in adapting his instruction to the spiritual state of those whom he taught.

43–45. Departure into Galilee— Reason for It—Reception There.

43. After (*the*) **two days**—namely, the two days mentioned in verse 40. **Galilee**—*i. e.*, the province of that name. This is the most obvious meaning of the word, and, if it is used in any restricted sense, the fact must be learned from the context.

44. Taken in its only natural sense, this verse assigns a reason for the Lord's going into Galilee at this time, namely, that he knew (for he bore witness to the fact) that a prophet is not likely to be honored in his own country. "Familiarity breeds contempt." But why was this a reason for his going into Galilee? Various answers have been given

---

[1] On the position of the word "Samaritans," in the original, see the remark of Buttmann ("Grammar of the N. T. Greek," p. 387): "In Greek as in Latin, there is a predilection for separating the *Partitive Genitive* in this way from its governing word, sometimes to such an extent, that the two words belonging together occupy the first place in the clause and the last."

45 Then when he was come into Galilee, the Galileans received him, *a* having seen all the things that he did at Jerusalem at the feast: *b* for they also went unto the feast.
46 So Jesus came again into Cana of Galilee, *c* where he made the water wine. And there was a certain nobleman, whose son was sick at Capernaum.

45 So when he came into Galilee, the Galilæans received him, having seen all the things that he did in Jerusalem at the feast: for they also went unto the feast.
46 He came therefore again unto Cana of Galilee, where he made the water wine. And there was a certain 1 nobleman, whose son was sick at Caper-

a ch. 2: 23; 3: 2....*b* Deut. 16: 16....*c* ch. 2: 1, 11.—1 Or, *king's officer.*

to this question. Thus (1) Alford says that he wished to avoid fame at this time. What he desired was quiet and comparative seclusion; and these he would be most likely to find in the region where he had been known from childhood. But this interpretation hardly accords with the result, or with the **so**—or, *therefore* (οὖν)—in verse 46. (2) Bückner thinks that he anticipated special opposition in Galilee, and therefore resolved to meet it promptly. But this view does not agree with the sequel. From this time onward his reception in Galilee was more favorable than his reception in Judea. (3) Wieseler supposes that by **his own country** Judea was meant as the place of his birth. But in the sense of the proverb, Galilee, rather than Judea, was **his own country.** For he was brought up in Nazareth, and was considered a Nazarene. Besides, he had on the whole been well received in Judea. (4) Hengstenberg believes that Nazareth is meant by **his own country** (comp. Luke 4: 24), while Lange believes that *Lower Galilee,* including Nazareth, must be meant. But the word Galilee seems to be used in distinction from Judea and Samaria, and not in distinction from the lower part of the province. (5) Meyer thinks that Galilee is referred to as **his own country,** and that the reason for his return is rather suggested than expressed by this designation. "If a prophet, as Jesus himself testified, is without honor in his own country, he must earn it in another. And this Jesus had done in Jerusalem. He now brought with him the honor of a prophet from a distance. Hence too he found acceptance with the Galileans, because they had seen his miracles in Jerusalem (3: 23)." This last view may be accepted as the best yet proposed. But the connection of thought in the passage is obscure; though the obscurity is not such as to shake in any degree our confidence in the narrative.

45. Acting as the general law of society recognized by his testimony required, Jesus went into Galilee, and was received favorably by the Galileans, because they had seen all things that he did in the feast at Jerusalem. Observe that it was what he *did,* and not what he said—his mighty works, and not his gracious words—which won their respect. How unlike the Samaritans! And it was also what he did in *Jerusalem,* rather than what he did in Cana or in Capernaum, which made him now welcome as a prophet in his own country. From the circumstance that the Evangelist refers to **the feast** simply, it is unsafe to infer with Westcott that no "great feast" had occurred since the one here referred to. John probably calls it simply **the feast** because it is the only one that he had yet mentioned, the one at which Jesus had wrought the signs here meant by **the things that he did.** At this point may be placed the work of Jesus described in general terms in Matt. 4: 17; Mark 1: 14, 15; and Luke 4: 14, 15.

46-54. HEALING OF THE NOBLEMAN'S SON.

46. For some reason Jesus appears to have passed by Nazareth, going at once to Cana in Galilee. He may have done this, because he wished to abide for a few days with Nathanael, one of his disciples (21: 2), or with the family in which the marriage, previously described, took place. Or he may have repaired to this town, because he knew that the inhabitants of it had been more deeply impressed than others by his miracles in Jerusalem—with which some of them may have associated the wonderful supply of wine at the wedding a short time before. At all events, whether for one reason or for many, the Saviour returned to Cana, the scene of his first miracle. **Jesus came.** The word **Jesus** does not belong to the text, according to L. T. Tisch., W. and H. It should read, *he came.* **And there was at (or,** *in*) **Capernaum.** Capernaum is connected by the preposition *in,* with the principal verb **was,** though it stands in the Greek original at the close of the verse. **A certain nobleman.** The word

47 When he heard that Jesus was come out of Judea into Galilee, he went unto him, and besought him that he would come down, and heal his son: for he was at the point of death.
48 Then said Jesus unto him, *Except ye see signs and wonders, ye will not believe.
49 The nobleman saith unto him, Sir, come down ere my child die.
50 Jesus saith unto him, Go thy way; thy son liveth. And the man believed the word that Jesus had spoken unto him, and he went his way.

47 naum. When he heard that Jesus was come out of Judæa into Galilee, he went unto him, and besought *him* that he would come down, and heal his son; for he was at the point of death. Jesus therefore said unto him, Except ye see signs and wonders, ye will in no wise believe. The ¹ nobleman saith unto him, ² Sir, come down ere my child die.
50 Jesus saith unto him, Go thy way; thy son liveth. The man believed the word that Jesus spake unto

---

a 1 Cor. 1: 22.——1 Or, *king's officer*....2 Or, *Lord.*

(Βασιλικός), translated **nobleman**, is used by Josephus to denote a royal officer or servant, whether civil, military, or domestic. This nobleman is generally supposed to have been an officer in the court or household of Herod Antipas—possibly Chusa his steward (Luke 8: 3), though of this there is no evidence. **Whose son was sick.** Literally, *the son of whom.* And Meyer suggests that the article may be used because he was an *only* son. On **Capernaum,** see note at 2: 12.

47. That Jesus was (or, *is*) **come,** etc. What the nobleman heard is repeated in the very form in which he heard it; for the report, as it passed from lip to lip, was this: *Jesus is come from Judea into Galilee.* Hearing this, and learning where he was, the nobleman **went** (*away*), *i. e.,* from Capernaum, **unto him,** in Cana of Galilee. **And besought** (or, *asked*) **him**—the word *ask* (ἐρωτάω) is here as often used in the sense of *request*—**that he would come down and heal his son.** The tense of these verbs calls for action prompt and complete. The father wished to have it done at once; he asked for a miraculous cure.¹ **For he was at the point of death.** As his son was at the point of death, he felt that help must come very soon, or it would be too late. How brief, yet distinct and graphic is this account!

48. Then (or, *therefore*) **said Jesus unto him.** The conjunction *therefore* (οὖν), employed by John, proves that the saying of Jesus was occasioned by the nobleman's request, and the words **unto him** prove that it was addressed to the nobleman. It will not then do to affirm that this saying refers to others only, and implies no criticism on the nobleman's attitude of mind towards the Lord Jesus. It reads thus: **Except ye see**

¹ ἵνα instead of ὅτι, because the reason why the request was made, or the end of making it, was identical with the thing requested.—(*Meyer.*)

signs and wonders, ye will not believe. At first sight this response appears to be unnatural and severe. But it should be borne in mind (1) that the nobleman may not have come to Jesus because he had full confidence in his power to heal the sick, but simply as a last resort, to see if peradventure this reputed wonder-worker might not save the life of his dear child; (2) that Jesus, reading his heart, may have perceived that he would reject his claim to be the Messiah, unless it was supported by evident miracles; and (3) that he had no deep sense of spiritual need, preparing him to appreciate, in ordinary circumstances, Jesus as a holy teacher and representative of God. If so, this royal officer was but a fair specimen of Galileans in general, so far as belief in Christ was concerned, though despair of help from any other source impelled him to make trial of the Saviour's power and grace. This view of his state of mind and character accounts for the response of Jesus. He was like the people, and the people like him; and Jesus felt the difference between the Galileans and the Samaritans. Yet the answer of Christ was not a refusal to do what the father asked. Nay, it was adapted to strengthen his hope that Jesus could save the life of his boy. Hence the urgency of his position.

49. Sir, come down ere my child die. *My little child* would be a more exact rendering of the Greek words here used by the father. He does not seem to have thought it possible for Jesus to heal his child without going down to Capernaum. But the urgency and tenderness of his appeal show that his confidence in the power of Jesus was increased. A father's heart cries out for help without delay.

50. Go thy way; thy son liveth. These words must have been spoken with divine authority; for **the man believed the word that Jesus had spoken unto him, and he**

51 And as he was now going down, his servants met him, and told him, saying, Thy son liveth.
52 Then inquired he of them the hour when he began to amend. And they said unto him, Yesterday at the seventh hour the fever left him.
53 So the father knew that it was at the same hour, in the which Jesus said unto him, Thy son liveth: and himself believed, and his whole house.
54 This is again the second miracle that Jesus did, when he was come out of Judea into Galilee.

1 Or, *bond-servants.*

went his way. Hence the remark of Alford: "The bringing out and strengthening of the man's faith by these words was almost as great a spiritual miracle as the material one which they indicated." The healing was wrought by the will of Christ acting directly, without the intervention of any angelic or magnetic influence. This certainly was the view of the Evangelist.

51. **And as he was now going down—**probably near the end of the way, but before he entered Capernaum—**his servants met him, and told him, saying, Thy son liveth.** The true reading may be rendered, literally, *saying, that his boy liveth.* Doubtless, they had been sent with the glad news to cheer the father's heart, and to inform him that the presence of Jesus was no longer needed. For the word **liveth** evidently signifies "is alive, and likely to live"; is convalescent and out of danger.

52. **Then inquired he of them the hour when he began to amend.** For he now wished to trace the recovery of his son to the word of Jesus on which he had believed. True gratitude longs to know the giver of its blessings, while an unthankful heart is willing to be ignorant of its benefactor. **Yesterday at the seventh hour the fever left him.** *During the seventh hour,* would better represent the meaning of the Greek original. At some time during that hour, or gradually, as that hour was passing, the fever subsided and disappeared. According to Jewish reckoning, the seventh hour was one o'clock P. M., and the period here referred to from twelve to one. But according to the reckoning of Asia Minor and Rome, which was probably followed by John, it was seven o'clock A. M., or P. M., and doubtless the latter. (Compare Edersheim, the "Life and Times of the Messiah," Vol. I., p. 428, 429.) At the present time, as well as in the time of Christ, the inhabitants of the Jordan Valley are exposed to severe attacks of fever.

53. **So the father knew that it was at the same hour, in the which Jesus said unto him, Thy son liveth.** If we assume that the Evangelist follows the Hebrew mode of denoting the hours of the day, it is necessary to account for the length of time consumed by the nobleman in returning to Capernaum. The distance between the two places could not have been more than about fifteen miles; and at a very moderate pace the nobleman could have reached home before sunset—*i. e.*, by a journey of four or five hours. But his servants met him on his way homeward, and reported that the change in the condition of his child had occurred the day before. Would this language have been natural if used in the early evening of what had taken place in the previous afternoon? We cannot pronounce it impossible; nor can we be absolutely sure that the nobleman was not detained by some unknown circumstance on his way homeward, so that he failed to reach Capernaum that evening. But the narrative suggests no delay; and, on the whole, it seems improbable that he left Cana at one o'clock P. M., and did not meet his servants until the next day. But if John, as we believe, follows the other mode of reckoning the hours of the day, this difficulty at once vanishes away. For, starting from Cana of Galilee at seven o'clock P. M., the father would be unable, even if he picked his way slowly downward through the darkness of the night, to arrive in the vicinity of Capernaum before the midnight hour had passed, and another day begun. **And himself believed**—*i. e.*, in Jesus as the Messiah; became a true disciple of Christ. **And his whole house.** This perhaps was the first instance of household conversion, and possibly of household baptism. See notes on verse 3.

54. **This is again the second miracle** (or *sign*) **that Jesus did when he was come out of Judea into Galilee.** That is, when Jesus had come from Judea into

CHAPTER V.

AFTER ªthis there was a feast of the Jews; and Jesus went up to Jerusalem.

AFTER these things there was ¹ a feast of the Jews; and Jesus went up to Jerusalem.

a Lev. 23: 2; Deut. 16: 1; ch. 2: 13.——1 Many ancient authorities read, *the feast*.

Galilee, he again wrought a sign—a second one for that region. Many had been wrought by him in Jerusalem, but this was the second one performed in Galilee. Notice the style of this narrative; for it bears all the marks of truth. It is simple, minute, graphic, objective. It says nothing of the motives of Christ, or of the nobleman; it eulogizes neither, criticises neither; it confines itself to a bare recital of events as they occurred. We are unable to detect the slightest effort to do more than this or less than this.

The healing of the nobleman's son is not to be confounded with the healing of the centurion's servant (Matt. 8: 5-13; Luke 7: 1-10). For, while there are but two points of coincidence, namely, that in both instances the person cured was in Capernaum, and the miracle described was wrought from a distance, there are many points of difference—*e. g.*, in this, Christ is said to have been at Cana, in that, at Capernaum; in this, he is said to have wrought the miracle just after his return to Galilee through Samaria, in that, just after his coming down from the place of his Sermon on the Mount; in this, the person healed is called a son of the petitioner, in that, a servant of the petitioner; in this, the petitioner is called a king's servant (Βασιλικός), in that, he is called a centurion; in this, he appears to be a Jew, in that, he is a Gentile; in this, he is represented as a man of *weak faith*, in that, as a man of *great faith*; in this, Christ virtually refuses to go with him to his home, in that he offers to go thither with him. These differences are so many and important, that the miracles cannot be regarded as one and the same.

Ch. 5: 1-9. CURE OF AN INFIRM MAN ON THE SABBATH. SECOND PASSOVER, March 30, A. D 28, or Pentecost, May 19, A. D. 28.

1. After this. How long after, the phrase does not determine. But there is reason to believe that, after healing the nobleman's son (John 4: 46-54), he tarried a little while in that neighborhood, visiting together with other places Nazareth, where, in the synagogue, he expounded the Scripture in relation to himself, and was rejected with wrath by the people (Luke 4: 16-30); that thus rejected he went down again to Capernaum (see John 2: 12, and Luke 4: 31), and made it his residence, finding there Andrew and Peter, James and John, who had returned to their employment, and whom he called to be his regular attendants and pupils (Matt. 4: 18-22; Luke 5: 1-11). There, also, he healed a demoniac in the synagogue (Mark 1: 21-28; Luke 4: 31-37), and Peter's wife's mother who was sick of a fever (Matt. 8: 14-17; Luke 1: 38, 39), and wrought other cures. Moreover, he preached throughout Galilee, healing many, and especially a leper (Mark 1: 35-45; Luke 4: 42-64; 5: 12-15), after which circuit he healed a paralytic in Capernaum (Mark 2: 1-12; Luke 5: 17-26), called Levi (or Matthew) to discipleship, and attended a feast in his house (Mark 2: 13-17; Luke 5: 27-32), and probably gave instruction in respect to fasting (Mark 2: 16-20). All this, at least, occurred between what is recorded by John in the preceding chapter, and the visit to Jerusalem here described. **There was a feast of the Jews.** What feast of the Jews is here meant, has long been a matter of doubt. (a) Westcott supposes that it may have been the Feast of Trumpets or Trumpet-blowing at the beginning of the seventh month (September-October), the first month of the civil year (see Lev. 23: 24; Numb. 29: 1-6). But this is forbidden by a correct interpretation of 4: 35—an interpretation which he admits to be more natural than any other, and which proves that it was already as late as December when Jesus came through Samaria to Galilee. (b) Meyer supposes that it must be the Feast of Purim, which occurred about the middle of March, and which might have been called simply "a feast of the Jews," because it was one of minor importance. But there are objections of some weight to this reference. (1) The feast seems to be mentioned for no reason but that of accounting for Christ's going up to Jerusalem, while Purim was not a feast at which the Galileans were accustomed to visit

Ch. V.] JOHN. 129

2 Now there is at Jerusalem a by the sheep *market* a pool, which is called in the Hebrew tongue Bethesda, having five porches. | 2 Now there is in Jerusalem by the sheep *gate* a pool, which is called in Hebrew [1] Bethesda, having

a Neh. 3:1; 12:39.——1 Some ancient authorities read, *Bethsaida* ; others, *Bethzatha.*

the holy city. (2) The usages connected with it were such as the Lord would not have been likely to honor by his presence. (3) The theory that this feast was Purim, and that the feast mentioned in 6:4 was the Passover, occurring one month later, limits the ministry of Christ to about two and a quarter years, instead of about three and a quarter years, which latter appears to us its probable duration. (4) It crowds too many events into the three weeks that may be assigned to Galilee between Purim and the Passover. (5) It does not account so well for the early textual variation (*the* feast for *a* feast) as does the view that it was the Passover, or some important religious festival; for that variant reading shows at least an early interpretation. (c) Robinson supposes that it was the Passover. In favor of this view it has been urged (1) that, unless something prevented, Jesus would be very likely to visit Jerusalem at this great festival. (2) That, if this feast was the Passover, an early tradition to this effect might account for the insertion of the article in some ancient manuscripts before the word "feast." (3) That it leads us to believe that the ministry of Jesus continued more than three years, giving suitable time for his manifold works; for the instruction of the eleven, and for the gathering storm of opposition to reach its height. But against it has been pressed the fact that John elsewhere gives the name of this feast, as well as of other important feasts (see 2:13, 23; 6:4; 11:55; 12:1; 13:1; 18:28, 39; 19:14). (d) McClellan believes that it was the Pentecost following the second Passover of Christ's ministry. And it may be more probable that John would refer to the Pentecost—a kind of appendix to the Passover—as a feast of the Jews, without naming it, than that he would thus refer to the Passover. On the whole we see less objection to this view than to any other, but hesitate between it and the Passover. **And Jesus went up to Jerusalem.** Doubtless attended by his disciples, now including Matthew, or at least by some of them. For, during the four, or five and a half, months which Jesus had spent in Galilee, since his return from Judea through Samaria, must have occurred his rejection at Nazareth (Luke 4:16-30), his selection of Capernaum as an abode (Luke 4:31; Matt. 4:13-16), the call of Peter and Andrew, James and John, to special discipleship (Luke 5:1-11; Matt. 4:18-22; Mark 1:16-20), with the miraculous draught of fishes, the healing of a demoniac in the synagogue (Mark 1:21-28; Luke 4:31-37), the cure of Peter's wife's mother and many others (Matt. 8:14-17; Mark 1:29-34; Luke 4:38-41), a circuit of Jesus throughout Galilee (Mark 1:35-39; Luke 4:42-44; Matt. 4:23-25), the healing of a leper (Matt. 8:2-4; Mark 1:40-45; Luke 5:12-16), the healing of a paralytic (Mark 2:1-12; Luke 5:17-26; Matt. 9:2-8), and the call of Matthew (Matt. 9:9; Mark 2:13, 14; Luke 5:27, 28).

2. Now there is at Jerusalem. The expression **there is**, has been supposed to prove that this Gospel was written by one not familiar with the history of Jerusalem. But the evidence which it gives is of little value; for, not to insist that some remains of the pool probably existed after the overthrow of the city, the present tense of the verb may be explained as due to the writer's vivid recollection.—**By the sheep-market a pool.** The Greek word translated **sheep-market**, is simply an adjective, meaning, "belonging to sheep" (προβατικῇ), and if any noun is supplied after it, that noun should be "gate" rather than "market." For there appears to have been a sheep-gate (Neh. 3:1, 32; 12:39) in the wall of the city, not far from the temple. But Meyer, Weiss, Milligan and Moulton, and others, suppose that the word for **pool** (κόλυμβήθρα) was originally in the dative case (κολυμβήθρᾳ), so that John wrote, *There is in Jerusalem, near the sheep-pool, the* (one) *named* (or *surnamed*) *Bethesda.* Weiss supposes the surname *Bethesda*, "house of mercy," was applied to the porches and building, rather than to the pool with which they were connected. Thus understood, the language of John may be rendered: *There is in Jerusalem, by the sheep-pool, the* house *surnamed House of Mercy.* "Early writers also (Eusebius and Jerome) do actually speak of a sheep-pool in Jerusalem in connection with this passage. Ammonius tells us that

I

3 In these lay a great multitude of impotent folk, of blind, halt, withered, waiting for the moving of the water.
4 For an angel went down at a certain season into the pool, and troubled the water: whosoever then first after the troubling of the water stepped in was made whole of whatsoever disease he had.

3 five porches. In these lay a multitude of them that

the pool was so called from the habit of gathering together there the sheep that were to be sacrificed for the feast; similarly Theodore of Mopsuestia."—(Milligan and Moulton.) These expositors suppose that there are two pools referred to, the location of the one being described by its nearness to the other, which may have been larger and better known. But Weiss appears to think there may have been only one pool, with a kind of infirmary attached. **Having five porches—** i. e., small buildings or porticos, for the convenience of the sick who waited for the moving of the water.

The site of Bethesda has not been satisfactorily identified. The Birket Israel, north of the temple area, the Fountain of the Virgin, and the Pool of Siloam, have been suggested by different scholars as the scene of the following miracle. For arguments supposed to favor the Fountain of the Virgin, see Robinson's " Biblical Researches," etc., Vol. I., pp. 337 sq., (Am. Ed.); and for those which are brought for the Pool of Siloam, see note at the close of Alford's Greek Testament, Vol. I.

3. In these lay a great multitude. The word **great** before **multitude** is rejected from the common text by the best editors and scholars. **Of impotent folk, of blind, halt, withered.** The last three words are probably specifications of the classes of sick folk that resorted to the "House of Mercy." They seem to have been, for the most part, those who were afflicted beyond the reach of medicine as administered by physicians.[1]

5. Which had an infirmity thirty and

[1] The words, "waiting for the moving of the water" in ver. 3, and the whole of ver. 4, must, beyond question, be omitted from the text. The clause of ver. 3 is wanting in ℵ A (first hand) B C (first hand) L, 18, 157, 314, one copy of the Old Latin, the Old Syriac (Curetonian), Memphitic (in at least fifteen of the best codices, according to Bishop Lightfoot), Thebaic. The whole of ver. 4 is wanting in ℵ B C (first hand) D, 33, 157, 314, two or three copies of the Old Latin, several copies of the Latin Vulgate, the Old Syriac, Memphitic, (nearly as above), Thebaic, many codices of the Armenian. Chrysostom is the first Greek Father giving either passage. Here the internal evidence (transcriptional) is clear and conclusive. Ver. 7 shows that at intervals the water was "troubled," and that people believed that the first infirm person who then entered the pool received the only, or by far the principal benefit. The Evangelist does not say that this was true. But it was a notion highly acceptable to many minds among the early Christians, who would easily ascribe this beneficent troubling of the pool to an angel. Accordingly, Tertullian, in his treatise on Baptism (written about A. D. 200), says that an angel used to come and disturb the Pool of Bethsaida (so B, and many versions), etc. It has not been pointed out, but this seems to be Tertullian's own explanation of John 5 : 7, even as he speaks elsewhere in the same treatise of an angel superintending baptism, and in other treatises of an angel of prayer, an angel of marriage, etc. He says: "An angel used to interfere and trouble the water of Bethsaida; it was observed by those who complained of ill-health: *for* whoever was first to descend thither, ceased after the bath to complain." The clause beginning with "for" is drawn from ver. 7; and the rest he seems to be inferring from this fact, and establishing by it. Similar statements are made by the Greek Fathers Didymus (fourth cent.), and Cyril of Alexandria (fifth cent.). This notion, grown into a tradition, would very naturally be put by some persons on the margin of the Gospel, to account for ver. 7, and being supposed by later copyists to be a part of the text accidentally omitted, would be introduced after ver. 3, seeming to fit exactly. Even without the tradition the mere contemplation of ver. 7 might lead some one to make the other explanatory marginal note, "waiting for the moving of the water," which would then creep into the text. So we notice that D has this clause, but has not ver. 4; while A has ver. 4, but not the preceding clause. The tradition would naturally be written on the margin by different persons in different terms, and accordingly we find much variety of expression in the documents which give ver. 4. Thus the entrance of these two clauses into the text of many documents is readily accounted for, and all the minor differences explained. On the other hand, we cannot in any wise account for the omission of these statements, if originally present in the text. They agree with ver. 7, and with the whole connection. Some devout persons of the present day might prefer to be rid of the miraculous healing and the angel; but there was no such feeling in the early centuries. Since then the two passages are wanting in so many of the earliest and best documents, and their subsequent insertion can be very easily explained, while their omission would be unaccountable, there can be no question that they are spurious; and they are so regarded by nearly all recent critics, even of the more conservative school.—B.

CH. V.]   JOHN.   131

5 And a certain man was there, which had an infirmity thirty and eight years.
6 When Jesus saw him lie, and knew that he had been now a long time *in that case*, he saith unto him, Wilt thou be made whole?
7 The impotent man answered him, Sir, I have no man, when the water is troubled, to put me into the pool; but while I am coming, another steppeth down before me.
8 Jesus saith unto him, *a* Rise, take up thy bed, and walk.

5 were sick, blind, halt, withered.¹ And a certain man was there, who had been thirty and eight years
6 in his infirmity. When Jesus saw him lying, and knew that he had been now a long time *in that case*, he saith unto him, Wouldest thou be made whole?
7 The sick man answered him, ² Sir, I have no man, when the water is troubled, to put me into the pool; but while I am coming, another steppeth down before me.
8 Jesus saith unto him, Arise, take up thy

a Matt. 9: 6; Mark 2: 11; Luke 5: 24.—¹ Many ancient authorities insert, wholly or in part. *waiting for the moving of the water:* **4** *for an angel of the Lord went down at certain seasons into the pool, and troubled the water: whosoever then first after the troubling of the water stepped in was made whole, with whatsoever disease he was holden*.... ² Or. *Lord*.

eight years. It is to be observed that the text does not mention the time which had been spent by this man at the pool, whether a week, a month, or a year, but it does refer to the duration of his infirmity—he had been an invalid thirty-eight years, and, therefore, recovery by any ordinary means was hopeless. Perhaps he made his way to the pool day by day with much effort.

6. And knew that he had been now a long time. The knowledge of Jesus was evidently superhuman, as in the case of the woman of Samaria (4: 17-19), of those who believed in Jerusalem (2: 23-25), and of Nathanael (1: 48). To suppose that he had obtained a knowledge of this cripple by natural means, is inconsistent with the manifest tenor of this narrative, and of the whole Gospel. The **long time** here noted appears to refer to the thirty-eight years of infirmity, and not to the lying in one of the porches at the pool. **Wilt thou** (or, *dost thou wish to*) **be made whole?** An absurd or impertinent question, unless it were meant to intimate a power and disposition on the part of Jesus to heal the sufferer. For why was he there, if not to be healed?

7. I have no man, etc. The impotent man failed to catch the meaning of our Saviour's question, and to feel the power of his presence. He may have been penitent; but he was losing all hope. Neglected, and perhaps despised by men, his quickness of observation had suffered with his body. His thoughts flowed on in their wonted course; to enter the pool at the proper moment was his last hope; but he was poor and friendless, unable to move quickly without help, and yet looking in vain for help. His infirmity was, doubtless, the fruit of sinful indulgence (ver. 14), and his character had, probably, been lost with his health. **When the water is troubled.** This expression implies a move-

ment of the water at irregular times. And there may have been such a movement, without any miracle. For it is well-known that certain intermittent springs flow at irregular intervals, and that the water of others is increased in the same way. This is said to be true of the Fountain of the Virgin, east of Jerusalem. But a sudden commotion and increase of the waters, taking place after unequal intervals, would be very naturally ascribed to divine interposition. **But while I am coming, another steppeth down before me.** Hence it appears that the troubling of the water was of short duration, and confined to only a small part of the pool, so that but one could test its healing virtue on a single occasion. These circumstances fully account for the marginal gloss which has found its way into the text in ver. 4, and a part of ver. 3.

8. Rise, take up thy bed, and walk. Meyer says: "The command presupposes that the man had faith, which was recognized by Christ." But the narrative affords no trace of this faith prior to the word of command. If one is guided, not by theory, but by the language of John, he will conclude that faith was born in the poor man's heart when the triple command, uttered with divine authority, and accompanied with healing energy, fell upon his ear—and not a moment before. The grace of Christ was in this case prevenient. The Greek student will notice the difference between the tense of the verb translated **take up,** and that of the verb translated **walk**—the former denoting an act completed, and the latter picturing an act in progress. He will also observe that the word rendered **bed** (κράββατος or κράβαττος), means a small couch, mattress, or pallet, which the cripple could easily bear away. It may indeed be presumed that he himself, though slowly and painfully, had brought this bed

132 JOHN. [CH. V.

9 And immediately the man was made whole, and took up his bed, and walked: and ᵃon the same day was the sabbath.
10 The Jews therefore said unto him that was cured, It is the sabbath day: ᵇit is not lawful for thee to carry *thy* bed.
11 He answered them, He that made me whole, the same said unto me, Take up thy bed, and walk.
12 Then asked they him, What man is that which said unto thee, Take up thy bed, and walk?

9 ¹ bed, and walk. And straightway the man was made whole, and took up his ¹ bed and walked.
10 Now it was the sabbath on that day. So the Jews said unto him that was cured, It is the sabbath, and it is not lawful for thee to take up thy ¹ bed.
11 But he answered them, He that made me whole, the same said unto me, Take up thy ¹ bed, and walk.
12 They asked him, Who is the man that said unto

a ch. 9:11,....*b* Ex. 20:10; Neh. 13:19; Jer. 17:21, etc.; Matt. 12:2; Mark 2:24; 3:4; Luke 6:2; 13:14.——1 *Or, pallet.*

to the House of Mercy. With what ease he now bore it away!

9. Immediately the man was made whole. The cure was instantaneous and perfect, preceding the act of obedience. **Took up his bed**—aorist of completed action—**and walked**, or, *began walking*; imperfect tense, used of incomplete action. Feeling his strength restored, the man yielded to the command of Jesus; but apparently without exultation, and certainly without asking the name of his benefactor (comp. Acts 3:8). He appears to have been in this respect like the nine lepers who did not return to give thanks to Jesus (Luke 17:17).

9-16. THE JEWS OFFENDED BECAUSE THIS WAS DONE ON THE SABBATH.

And on the same day,—more correctly, as in Rev. Ver..—*Now it was the Sabbath on that day.* A circumstance mentioned by the Evangelist to prepare the mind of the reader for what is now to be related.

10. The Jews therefore. Not the common people, but those in authority. Meyer limits the reference to members of the Sanhedrin; but there seems to be no sufficient reason for supposing that leading scribes and priests, not belonging to the Sanhedrin, were not included. **Said unto him that was cured. Said** = *were saying*—because the reproof was repeated by one and another as the man bore along his couch. **It is the sabbath-day; it is not lawful for thee to carry thy bed**—or, *the bed*, which they saw him bearing. Godet remarks that "the Rabbins distinguished thirty kinds of labor as prohibited by the Fourth Commandment. The act of bearing a couch, and that of healing, are expressly forbidden by their tradition. Hence the reproach addressed to this man by the Jews, who identified the Rabbinic explanation of the command with its real meaning." Alford alleges Neh. 13: 15-19; Ex. 31: 13-17; Jer. 17:21, 22, as proof

that the bearing of such a burden "was forbidden by the law itself." But the passages are scarcely definite enough to prove the statement. Yet Schaff agrees with Alford in maintaining that this act of the restored man was, in itself, a transgression of the Mosaic law.

11. This response was both natural and sufficient. Whatever might be the import of the Fourth Commandment, the man who had been healed felt that the authority of One, at whose word so great a cure had been wrought, must be divine. This is evident from his use of the pronoun translated **the same** (ἐκεῖνος); for this pronoun would have been superfluous, had he not wished to emphasize the identity of the one by whose direction he was bearing his couch with the one who had made him whole. "The person who made me whole, that one, and no other, said unto me: Take up thy bed, and walk." On the least favorable hypothesis of the infirm man's character, he urges this as a good excuse for bearing his couch on the Sabbath.

12. The restored cripple may have laid down his bed at their reproof, so that they had no occasion to remonstrate further with him; or the mention of one who had made him whole, and commanded him to bear his couch, may have turned away their thoughts from the healed to the healer, or, as they looked at the matter, from the secondary transgressor to the primary. For they do not ask: "Who is the man that made thee whole?" but: **What man is that,** etc. Better, *Who is the man that said unto thee: Take up thy bed and walk?* Plainly they were in a critical mood. The law of the Sabbath, as they interpreted it, had been broken, and they wished to get at the principal offender. Some of them probably recollected the signs wrought by Jesus at the preceding passover, the success which he had had in the province of Judea for months after, and perhaps the

13 And he that was healed wist not who it was: for Jesus had conveyed himself away, a multitude being in *that* place.
14 Afterward Jesus findeth him in the temple, and said unto him, Behold, thou art made whole; "sin no more, lest a worse thing come unto thee.
15 The man departed, and told the Jews that it was Jesus, which had made him whole
16 And therefore did the Jews persecute Jesus, and sought to slay him, because he had done these things on the sabbath day.

13 thee, Take up *thy* ¹*bed*, and walk? But he that was healed knew not who it was: for Jesus had conveyed himself away, a multitude being in the place.
14 Afterward Jesus findeth him in the temple, and said unto him, Behold, thou art made whole: sin no more, lest a worse thing befall thee. The man went away, and told the Jews that it was Jesus who had made him whole. And for this cause did the Jews persecute Jesus, because he did these things on the

a Matt, 12: 45; ch. 8: 11.——1 Or, *pallet.*

---

reports which had reached them of his work in Galilee. If so, they must have suspected that the same Jesus had returned to Jerusalem again. Meyer thinks that their reference to him as *the man* was slightly contemptuous, and the same view may be taken of their abbreviated repetition of his command to the cripple; for, according to the best authorities, they made it as curt as possible: *Take up, and walk;* instead of: **Take up thy bed and walk.**

13. But the man who had been healed knew not his benefactor; for Jesus had quietly withdrawn. "He spoke the healing word, and passed on unobserved"—(Schaff.) **A multitude being in that place.** This clause may have been added to explain why Jesus *wished* to withdraw unrecognized, or why he was *able* to do so. The former is probably the reason in the mind of the Evangelist. He knew that Jesus did not wish to attract the attention of the people to him as a miracle-worker at that time and place. Doubtless, there were many sick persons there; but the Saviour saw no sufficient reason for restoring others to health by a word. This, then, may be regarded as an instance of *personal* election, not arbitrary, but for reasons unrevealed.

14. Though the infirm man had been afflicted thirty-eight years, Jesus seems to have known his past life as perfectly as he knew that of the Samaritan woman; and so, finding him soon after in the sacred enclosure, he said to him: **Behold thou art** (*hast been*) **made whole: sin no more, lest a worse thing come unto thee.** This admonition implies that his thirty-eight years of suffering were the result of some particular kind of sin (Chrys., Mey., Lange, Alf., and others). But "neither the special sin nor the special disease is known."—(Lange.) The "something worse" (χεῖρόν τι), says Trench,

"gives us an awful glimpse of the severity of God's judgments."

15. Various motives for this act have been conjectured—*e. g.*, (1) gratitude to Christ, whom he would have the rulers know and honor; (2) desire to assert the authority under which he had acted in bearing his couch on the Sabbath; (3) deference to the rulers who had asked him to point out *the man* who told him to bear his couch; (4) fear of the rulers, whose malice against Jesus he was too dull to perceive. It seems to us that both his quickness of perception and manliness of character had suffered with his body. He reminds us of "Mr. Feeblemind," in the allegory of Bunyan. When told that it was unlawful for him to carry his bed on the Sabbath, he put the responsibility of the act on his restorer, but without distinctly saying that one who could thus heal must be from God. When the Jews wished to know who had said to him, *Take up and walk*, he but half perceived their malice; and when he had learned the name of his benefactor, reported it forthwith to them. Not a word of faith or courage falls from his lips. Thus a singular self-consistency characterizes the bearing of the infirm man throughout; a self-consistency so unobtrusive in its character, and simple in its manifestation as to prove it undesigned, and the narrative itself truthful.

16. **And therefore did the Jews persecute Jesus, and sought to slay him.** The latter clause of the received text is rejected by the best editors. According to John, they persecuted **Jesus, because he had done these things on the sabbath. By the Jews** must be understood the leaders of the nation, and especially the members of the Sanhedrin (see ver. 10), and by the expression, **did persecute** (lit., *were persecuting*, ἐδίωκον), their persistent effort to malign his character, destroy his influence, and imperil his life.

17 But Jesus answered them, *My Father worketh hitherto, and I work.
18 Therefore the Jews *b* sought the more to kill him, because he not only had broken the sabbath, but said also that God was his Father, *c* making himself equal with God.

17 sabbath. But Jesus answered them, My Father 18 worketh even until now, and I work. For this cause therefore the Jews sought the more to kill him, because he not only brake the sabbath, but also called God his own Father, making himself equal with God.

a ch. 9:4; 14:10.... *b* ch. 7:19.... *c* ch. 10:30, 33; Phil. 2:6.

Whether this was done by a form of legal prosecution; whether Jesus was brought before the Sanhedrin, or any smaller court, and required to answer to the charge of Sabbath-breaking, does not appear. But the original word is not often used in the New Testament of a legal prosecution. It is almost always fairly represented by the word *persecuted*.

The last clause seems to describe the action of Jesus as it was represented by his persecutors. His healing the infirm man, and commanding him to bear his couch, are made separate offences (**these things**), and what he had done in a single instance is represented as going on still, as if it were habitual—(**had done** = "was doing"). Less probable is the assumption that the miracle related was one of a series, the rest of which are not distinctly mentioned. (See the following verse.)

17, 18. JESUS JUSTIFIES HIS ACTION, AND PROVOKES THE JEWS BY CLAIMING TO BE THE SON OF GOD.

17. **But Jesus answered them.** The word **answered** is best accounted for in this case by supposing that the last clause of ver. 16 represents the accusation of "the Jews." To this accusation, which charged him with breaking the Sabbath on principle, he replies: **My Father worketh hitherto** (=*until now*), **and I work.** By this remarkable language Jesus represents, or implies, (1) that God is his Father, in a true and real sense of the expression; (2) that his Father is distinguishable, in a personal respect, from himself; (3) that his Father, though resting from creation, has been working in that rest until now; (4) that he, as Son, is working in the same way, and to the same end, on a human Sabbath, which is but a shadow of the Sabbath-rest of God; and (5) that his Father's action is therefore the model and justification of his own action. This saying of Jesus appears to assume that the seventh day, or God's rest (Gen. 2:2, 3), is the period which succeeded the creation of the heavens and the earth, and which is not yet completed. Whether this assumption of Christ has any bearing upon the length of the six days of creation, need not be discussed; it certainly has some bearing upon the manner in which the Sabbath ought to have been kept by the Jews; it proves that the rest of the Sabbath was not intended to be inaction—was not meant to interfere with moral and religious effort, or with works of mercy.

18. This answer of Jesus increased the enmity of "the Jews," so that the Evangelist could say of them, that they sought or (*were seeking*) **the more to kill him.** And it is noticeable that this statement assumes the deadly aim of the persecution mentioned in ver. 16, though greater bitterness and, perhaps, openness (Lange) were put into it in consequence of the answer preserved in ver. 17. For they interpreted that answer as an assertion by Jesus that **God was his** (*own*) **Father.** Nor is there any reason to suppose that they misunderstood or perverted his meaning. Says John Owen: "There is not the shadow of a doubt that Jesus did here claim, and intended to claim, absolute equality with the Father." Alford remarks: "The Jews understood his words to mean nothing short of a *peculiar personal Sonship*, and thus equality of nature with God. And that their understanding was *the right one*, the discourse testifies." The same is Meyer's view: "They interpreted the expression, 'my Father,' correctly, of a *peculiar* Fatherhood not true of God in relation to others." The last clause: **making himself equal with God,** has been interpreted in three ways, as though it were (*a*) inferential, (*b*) causal, (*c*) co-ordinate. (*a*) It is said to be an inference of the Jews from the claim of proper Sonship to the claim of equality in nature. "Since this Jesus claims to be *the own Son of God*, he claims *to be equal in nature* with God; which is blasphemy." (*b*) It is said to be a justification of their view of his words, **my Father,** as being an assertion that God was his own Father. By saying, "my Father," he must have meant that God was *his own* Father (πατέρα ἴδιον), for he made himself equal

19 Then answered Jesus and said unto them, Verily, verily, I say unto you, *The Son can do nothing of himself, but what he seeth the Father do: for what things soever he doeth, these also doeth the Son likewise.
20 For *the Father loveth the Son, and sheweth him all things that himself doeth: and he will shew him greater works than these, that ye may marvel.

19 Jesus therefore answered and said unto them, Verily, verily, I say unto you, The Son can do nothing of himself, but what he seeth the Father doing: for what things soever he doeth, these the
20 Son also doeth in like manner. For the Father loveth the Son, and sheweth him all things that himself doeth: and greater works than these will he

a ver. 30; ch. 8: 28; 9: 4; 12: 40; 14: 10.....b Matt. 3: 17; ch. 3: 35; 2 Pet. 1: 17.

with God when he added: "and I work." (c) It is said to be co-ordinate with what is before affirmed of the Fatherhood of God. "Along with that which Jesus says of *God's* relation to him, is stated also what he *makes out of himself* in *his* relation to *God.*" This is Meyer's view; and he would translate the clause: *While he places himself on the same level with God*—i. e., as to freedom of action. The first of these interpretations appears to be correct. It is certainly more obvious than either of the others, and therefore more likely to be correct, unless there is something in the context, or in the thought, which forbids us to adopt it.

19-30. OFFICE, OR WORK OF THE SON.

19. In consequence (οὖν) of this accusation, which was their pretext for seeking his life, Jesus answers for himself (ἀπεκρίνατο, middle voice), in a discourse of extraordinary depth and power. His prime object is to convince his foes, if they will suffer themselves to be convinced, that his action has been in harmony with the will of God. In doing this, he is not called upon to emphasize his personal distinction from the Father (for that was admitted by his accusers), or to insist directly on his equality with the Father (for to do that would be to confirm their impression that he was a blasphemer), but rather, without denying either of these, to convince them, if possible, of his absolute unity with the Father in action. Hence he begins by saying: **The Son can do nothing of himself.** Such is the union between the Father and the Son that it is impossible for any act of the Son to spring from self, from his own will, irrespective of the Father's will. But this inability was a glory and perfection, and the Jews must have felt that Jesus could not have affirmed in stronger language his union with the Father, or the Father's approbation of what he had done. Yet he does not deny that this act of healing the impotent man was performed by himself; he does not say that no act can spring from the Son's will as the immediate

and efficient cause, but only that the Son can do nothing from self as the spring and motive of action—nothing but what he seeth the Father do. Meyer says: "*But what* (ἐὰν μή τι) refers to *do nothing* (ποιεῖν οὐδέν) merely, and not also to *from himself* (ἀφ' ἑαυτοῦ)," appealing to Matt. 12: 4 and Gal. 2: 16. Our interpretation agrees with his. But these passages only show that his interpretation is possible; they do not establish it. If anything does that, it must be the connection of thought here, and the exact sense of the words *from himself* (ἀφ' ἑαυτοῦ). We understand Christ to affirm that (see 14) only what is divine can be done by himself. The Son of God can perform no act which differs in character from the action of the Father. If he performs works of mercy on the Sabbath, it is only what he sees the Father doing on that day. God's action is the pattern for his action. This is now positively affirmed. **For what things soever he doeth, these also doeth the Son likewise** (*in like manner*). Alford remarks: "*For* it is the very nature of the Son to do whatever the Father doeth. Also, to do these works after the same plan and proceeding (ὁμοίως), so that there can be no discord, but unity." And Schaff says that this " points to the equality of the Son with the Father. The Son does the same things with the same power and in the same manner." "In this word," writes Godet, "one knows not which is more astounding, the naïveté of the form or the sublimity of the idea. Jesus speaks of this intimate relation with the Being of beings, as if he were treating of the simplest thing in the world. It is the word of the child of twelve years: 'Wot ye not that I must be about my Father's business?' raised to the highest power."

20. Two facts have been stated: *first*, that in a true and deep sense the Son is unable to do anything save what he sees the Father doing, and *second*, that he does whatever the Father does. But the latter statement supposes that he sees all that the Father is

21 For as the Father raiseth up the dead, and quickeneth *them*; *a* even so the Son quickeneth whom he will.

21 shew him, that ye may marvel. For as the Father raiseth the dead and quickeneth them, even so the

a Luke 7: 14; 8: 54; ch. 11: 25, 43.

doing, and this statement he now explains and justifies. **For the Father loveth the Son.** The word here translated *loveth* (φιλεῖ) denotes tender, personal affection. **And sheweth him all things that himself doeth.** While these words presuppose a personal distinction between the Father and the Son, and assign a logical precedence to the action of the Father, they claim for the Son a perfect "knowledge" of the Father's action. And by **the Son,** Jesus Christ must have meant himself, the Incarnate Word. (See 1: 18, 51; 3: 13; 5: 27). This interpretation may require us to restrict the expression **all things** to such as were connected with the work of redemption, because the human faculties of Christ put limits to his strictly *theanthropic* knowledge, though not perhaps to the knowledge which he was conscious of having in the faculties of his divine nature, and certainly not to that which was needed at any moment for the Messianic work committed to him. **And he will shew him greater works than these.** Does this mean that the Father will shew greater works to the Son by doing them first himself, that the Son may do them afterward? Or is the doing of them by the Father subjective and synonymous with willing? So that the works are to be performed by the Son according to the will of the Father? (See ver. 20, 26). The latter view agrees with the various representations of the Bible concerning the creation—(compare John 1: 3; Heb. 1: 2; Col. 1: 16 sq. with 1 Cor 8: 6; Heb. 2: 10; Acts 4: 24). "With the Father," says Alford, "*doing* is *willing;* it is *only the Son who acts in time.*" Jesus here represents the Father as taking the initiative in the works performed by the Son, but it is not probable that this precedence implies any separate doing of the works, so that they are twice performed (comp. John 14: 9-11). **That ye may marvel.** In the original, the pronoun ye is expressed, and therefore slightly emphatic, and the end contemplated by God in these greater works is not faith, but *wonder*, on the part of those addressed. What a portentous warning is contained in this saying, if it implies that merely wonder, and nothing more, was contemplated as the fruit of such signs in their case! But it is possible that Jesus thought of wonder as a natural preliminary to faith, though it might not reach this end in their case; as if he had begun to say, *that ye may wonder and believe*, but was constrained to pause with the first effect, because it was all that he foresaw would be produced in the minds of his hearers, and all that was necessary to condemn their course and to justify the **greater works.** But Jesus does not say that their wonder is the *only* or the *principal* end that God would reach by the **greater works** predicted. If these works are described in the following verses, another reason for their performance is the honor which they bring to Christ, and the blessedness of those saved by him. Buttmann ("Gr of N. T. Greek," p. 239) supposes that the word translated **that** should be translated in this place "*so that.*"

In the next verses (21-29), Jesus illustrates and confirms the statement just made, by declaring that the work of spiritual and corporeal resurrection is committed to the Son.

21. For as the Father raiseth up the dead and quickeneth them (or, *maketh them alive*). This statement may naturally be understood to embrace a revivifying of both soul and body; the present tense being used because it is the Father's work to do this. (Deut. 32: 39; 1 Sam. 2: 6, Rom. 4: 17; 8: 11). According to Tholuck, the word **raiseth** (ἐγείρει) points to the negative, and *maketh alive* (ζωοποιεῖ) to the positive side of the same act. According to Meyer, the "making alive" is the principal thing, and is represented, in a popular way, as beginning with the raising up. Perhaps the thought is this: "As the Father raiseth the dead, and by so doing gives them life." **Even so the Son quickeneth whom he will.** Alford appears to be correct in saying that the words **whom he will** mean "that in every instance where *his will is to vivify*, the result invariably follows." And what greater power, what power more strictly divine, could Jesus have claimed for himself? The expression **quickeneth,** or, *maketh alive*, embraces in this clause also, (against Meyer),

Cɪɪ. V.] JOHN. 137

22 For the Father judgeth no man, but ᵃ hath committed all judgment unto the Son:
23 That all men should honour the Son, even as they honour the Father. ᵇ He that honoureth not the Son honoureth not the Father which hath sent him.
24 Verily, verily, I say unto you, ᶜ He that heareth my word, and believeth on him that sent me, hath everlasting life, and shall not come into condemnation; ᵈ but is passed from death unto life.

22 Son also quickeneth whom he will. For neither doth the Father judge any man, but he hath given 23 all judgment unto the Son; that all may honour the Son, even as they honour the Father. He that honoureth not the Son honoureth not the Father 24 that sent him. Verily, verily, I say unto you, He that heareth my word, and believeth him that sent me, hath eternal life, and cometh not into judgment

a Matt. 11: 27; 28: 18; ver. 27; ch. 3: 35; 17: 2; Acts 17: 31; 1 Pet. 4: 5....*b* 1 John 2: 23....*c* ch. 3: 16, 18; 6: 40, 47; 8: 5) ᵃ 20: 31.
d 1 John 3: 14.

both spiritual and corporeal quickening, or resurrection.

22. For the Father judgeth no man. (Better: *For not even the Father judgeth any man*). The conjunction **for** (γάρ) introduces this statement as a reason for the foregoing, viz., "quickeneth whom he will"; and the adverb "neither," or, "not even" (οὐδέ), intimates that the work of judging, which is higher than that of quickening, is not to be performed, *even by the Father*, apart from the Son. All is to be done through the Son. "When it is denied that the Father judges, it is done in the same way in which (5: 19; 8: 28) it is denied that the Son can do anything of himself—to wit: in isolation from the Father."—(Tholuck). **But hath committed** (*given*) **all** (*the*) **judgment unto the Son.** The entire work of judging mankind is committed to the Son, that is, to Jesus Christ, the divine-human Mediator. (Compare Acts 17: 31; 2 Cor. 5: 10; 2 Tim. 4: 1; Matt. 25: 31–46).

23. (*In order*) **that all men should honour the Son, even as they honour the Father.** For what end does the Father give to Jesus the two supreme attributes of Deity, *vivifying* and *judging?* He desires to have the adoration which humanity pays to himself rendered also to the Son. *The Father loveth the Son* (3: 35), and therefore wishes to see the world at the feet of the Son, as at his own feet. The word **honour** (τιμῶν) does not, indeed, directly express the act of worship (προσκυνεῖν). But in the context it evidently expresses that feeling of religious veneration of which worship is the expression. And by boldly claiming for his own person this feeling, in the same sense in which it is due to the Father (καθώς), Jesus certainly authorizes men to render to him worship properly so called. Compare 20: 28; Phil. 2: 10—(Godet). **He that honoureth not the Son, honoureth not the Father which hath sent him.** Significant words, as addressed to men who were seeking the life of Jesus! It would have been much to say, that persecution of the Son must be displeasing to the Father who had sent him (Matt. 21: 37 sq.); but it was more to say to men who prided themselves on being special asserters of God's honor, that they could not honor the Father unless they honored the Son who was now addressing them, and, indeed (see the previous clause), unless they honored him even as they honored the Father. For it must be borne in mind that Jesus was really speaking of himself, the God-man, and saying, "The Son represents and reveals the Father; therefore, to withhold divine honor from him is to withhold it from the Father." "As Christ claims precisely the same honor as is due to the Father (καθώς), he puts himself on such a footing of equality with him as implies unity of essence; since Monotheism is very jealous of the honor of Jehovah, as the only being entitled to the worship of the creature. There can be no two rival Gods."—(Schaff). (On the negative particles in this verse, compare Winer § 59, 1.)

24. He that heareth my word, and believeth on him that sent me. The word **heareth,** in the first clause, may, perhaps, as Meyer says, have its simplest meaning, that of mere hearing; while the next clause reveals the action consequent upon this hearing. But it is more natural to understand the word, as it is often used, in the deeper sense of *hearkening to,* by which the mind is prepared for the next term, *believing on.* And the belief which is here described is belief in God *as the One who sent Jesus Christ, his Son,* into the world. The verb to believe (πιστεύειν), with the following dative, expresses the "belief in the *testimony* of God, that he hath sent his Son, which is dwelt on so much. (1 John 5: 9-12)."—(Alford). See Buttman's "Grammar of the N. T. Greek," p. 173 sq. **Hath everlasting life.** Faith is at once the condition and the beginning of eternal life. By it, the soul enjoys that blessed union with God for which it was originally designed. And the possession

25 Verily, verily, I say unto you, The hour is coming, and now is, when *the dead shall hear the voice of the Son of God; and they that hear shall live.
26 For as the Father hath life in himself; so hath he given to the Son to have life in himself;

25 but hath passed out of death into life. Verily, verily, I say unto you, The hour cometh, and now is, when the dead shall hear the voice of the Son of 26 God; and they that hear shall live. For as the Father hath life in himself, even so gave he to the

a ver. 28; Eph. 2: 1, 5; 5: 14; Col. 2: 13.

of that life in its germ is a pledge of its possession forever. **And shall not come into condemnation.** The noun translated **condemnation**, and the verb from which it is formed (κρίσις, κρίνω), have this meaning very often in the writings of John. (See ver. 29, and 3: 17, 18). **But is passed from death unto life.** *Into* life is a more exact rendering of the words. In the believer, this transition has been already effected. He is in the realm and possession of eternal life, instead of being still, as before, in the realm and power of sin and death. A marvelous change! The definite article before the word **life,** in the Greek text, might be represented by the word "this" in English; for it shows that the life referred to is the "everlasting life" just mentioned. Observe how clearly this language proves that life, as this term is used by Christ, is more than conscious existence, and death more than extinction of conscious being.

25. Notice (1) the repeated **verily,** by which the importance of what follows is forcibly expressed (compare also ver. 24). (2) The announcement of a new religious period that had even now begun. **The** (or, *an*) **hour is coming and now is.** Jesus tells "the Jews" very plainly that a revolution has been commenced, and that it will go on. (3) Men, in their natural condition, are, in a most important sense, dead; for they are destitute of the only true and blessed life. (See ver. 21, and Matt. 8: 22). (4) What they are said to hear is, therefore, not the "*word*" (ver. 24) of instruction, but **the voice** of authority, even the voice of him who is here called the **Son of God,** to indicate the *divine* authority and efficiency of his word. (5) The expression, **they that hear** (or, *heard,* οἱ ἀκούσαντες) **shall live,** still retains the figure of a resurrection of the dead, and, therefore, directs attention to the first act of hearing, as that on which the origin and existence of the new life depend. Otherwise, the present participle might have been used in the Greek, and not the aorist. (See 1: 12). (6) Meyer supposes that the word **hear,** in the expression **they that hear,** means "give ear to." All the dead "hear the voice," but all do not "give ear" to it; those who do, will live. There seems to be no sufficient ground for this distinction; and it does not agree very well with the figure of a resurrection of the dead carried through the verse. According to the best authorities, the Greek words translated "shall hear" and "shall live," are in the active voice, and not (as in the textus receptus) in the middle.

26. This verse assigns a reason (γὰρ) for what has just been said, viz.: Those who hear the voice of the Son of God will live, because, in accordance with the Father's will and action, the Son is the Giver of life and the Judge of all. **For as the Father hath life in himself.** To have life in one's self, is to have it as an independent possession, and as a fountain of life for others. The former idea is contained in the expression itself, and the latter is illustrated by the use of the expression by John.—**So hath he given to the Son to have life in himself.** *So gave he, also,* etc., reproduces more exactly the tense of the Greek. According to the best editors of the Greek text, the order of words in this clause renders the expression, **the Son,** emphatic, while, in the nature of the case, the thing predicated, viz.: *having life in himself,* is also emphatic in both clauses. The Son, as well as the Father, has life as an independent possession, from which he can impart life to others. (Compare 11: 25; 14: 6-19). But he has it by gift from the Father. When and how did he receive it? In eternity, and by an eternal act of self-communication to the Word? We think not; but at the time when the Word became flesh (1: 14; Luke 1: 35), and by means of the incarnation. Jesus Christ had life in himself, and was a source of life to men, because he had, in his theanthropic person, "the Word" that "was God," "that eternal Life which was with the Father." (John 1: 1; 1 John 1: 2). For, by the term **Son,** here, as in the previous context, Jesus means himself, as he stands before the wrathful yet over-awed Jews. He is vindicating his own authority and action, by connecting them inseparably with the Father's will and action.

Ch. V.]　　　　　　　　　　JOHN.　　　　　　　　　　139

27 And ^a hath given him authority to execute judgment also, ^b because he is the Son of man.
28 Marvel not at this: for the hour is coming, in the which all that are in the graves shall hear his voice,
29 ^c And shall come forth; ^d they that have done good, unto the resurrection of life; and they that have done evil, unto the resurrection of damnation.
30 ^e I can of mine own self do nothing; as I hear, I judge: and my judgment is just; because ^f I seek not mine own will, but the will of the Father which hath sent me.

27 Son also to have life in himself: and he gave him authority to execute judgment, because he is a son
28 of man. Marvel not at this; for the hour cometh, in which all that are in the tombs shall hear his
29 voice, and shall come forth; they that have done good, unto the resurrection of life; and they that have ¹ done evil, unto the resurrection of judgment.
30 I can of myself do nothing: as I hear, I judge: and my judgment is righteous; because I seek not and my judgment is righteous; because I seek not

a ver. 22; Acts 10: 42; 17: 31....*b* Dan. 7: 13, 14....*c* Isa. 26: 19; 1 Cor. 15: 52; 1 Thess. 4: 16....*d* Dan. 12: 2; Matt. 25: 32, 33, 46....*e* ver. 19..../ Matt. 28: 39; ch. 4: 34; 6: 38.—1 Or. *practised.*

And he was not, as he stood before the Jews, simply the Eternal Word, but, rather, the God-man.

27. And hath given (*gave*) **him authority to execute judgment also, because he is the** (or, *a*) **Son of man.** He who is the Son of God, by virtue of his divine nature, is, at the same time, Son of man, by virtue of his human nature. He is, therefore, qualified to be the one Mediator between God and man (1 Tim. 2: 5), representing both. Hence, the Father performs the whole work of redemption and judgment by him. Hence, too, in a certain sense, humanity judges itself by the condemnation which Jesus pronounces upon the unbelieving. The fact that he is a veritable Son of man, able to share the interests, appreciate the trials, and sympathize with the woes of mankind, is here assigned as a reason why the work of judgment is committed to him. No true man has a tenderer heart than he, and those whom *he* condemns, all good men will condemn likewise, in the light of the final day. (See 1 Cor. 6: 2). Observe that Jesus refers to himself, in this passage, as **Son** of man or *a* Son of man (υἱὸς ἀνθρώπου), and not as *the* Son of man (ὁ υἱὸς τοῦ ἀνθρώπου); for the object of the clause is to assert his true humanity, the fact that he was a born man, and not his Messianic dignity among men. That is asserted in the preceding statement.

28, 29. Marvel not at this, viz.: at what I have said of my work in vivifying and judging mankind; for—the greatest and last stadium of this work is yet in the future—**the** (or, *an*) **hour is coming, in** (omit **the**) **which all that are in the graves shall hear his voice, and shall come forth.** (Compare Acts 24: 15; Dan. 12: 2; 1 Thess. 4: 16; 1 Cor. 15: 52). This language must refer to a bodily rather than to a spiritual resurrection, (1) because those who are to be raised are said to be **in their graves,** a form of statement which is not elsewhere applied to those who are

spiritually dead; (2) because **all** that are in their graves are to be raised, while the good have spiritual life already, and the bad are only raised to be judged; (3) because this resurrection is assigned to the future, with no hint, like that in ver. 25, of its occurrence now. Hence, the language of Jesus agrees with that of Paul in the passages referred to above. **They that have done** (or *those who did the*) **good unto the** (or, *a*) **resurrection of life, and they that have done** (or, *those who wrought the*) **evil unto the** (or, *a*) **resurrection of damnation** (*i. e., condemnation*). The expressions, *did the good,* and *wrought the evil,* point to actions completed in the past, and, doubtless, to what Paul characterizes as "the deeds done in his body." (2 Cor. 5: 10). Hence, they are unfavorable to the notion that the conduct of men after death will determine their relation to Christ and the resurrection. A *resurrection of life* is a resurrection which brings perfect life, or eternal and blessed fellowship with God; while a resurrection of *condemnation* is one which involves final condemnation and woe. Whether the resurrection of the two classes here mentioned will take place at the same time, or at different times, is not made perfectly certain by this language; but if there is nothing elsewhere in the New Testament inconsistent with the view that the resurrection of both will be at the same time, this is, certainly, the most obvious interpretation of the language here used. "The definite article before the words **good** and **evil** gives to these terms, in the original, an absolute sense."—*Godet.*

Jesus has thus asserted most clearly what he *is doing,* and what he *will do.* He now returns to the thought and assertion of his inseparable unity with the Father in all his work.

30. I can of mine own self do nothing. "No act of mine can spring from self. To do anything against or without the Father's

31 a *If I bear witness of myself, my witness is not true.*
32 b *There is another that beareth witness of me; and I know that the witness which he witnesseth of me is true.*
33 *Ye sent unto John, c and he bare witness unto the truth.*
34 *But I receive not testimony from man: but these things I say, that ye might be saved.*

31 mine own will, but the will of him that sent me. If 32 I bear witness of myself, my witness is not true. It is another that beareth witness of me; and I know that the witness which he witnesseth of me is true. 33 Ye have sent unto John, and he hath borne witness 34 unto the truth. But the witness which I receive is not from man: howbeit I say these things, that ye

a See ch. 8: 14; Rev. 3: 14......b Matt. 3: 17; 17: 5; ch. 1: 18; 1 John 5: 6, 7. 9....c ch. 1: 15, 19, 27. 32.

will is contradictory to my very nature. It is the deepest law of my being and the supreme end of my life to reveal the Father and his will." (Comp. ver. 19). **As I hear, I judge.** By this expression Jesus reminds the Jews that he is even now acting as judge, and passing sentence of condemnation on those who reject his word. And this sentence involves and expresses the judgment of another, even God. Observe how the word **hear** in this verse takes the place of "see" in ver. 19; for in this place he is speaking of a sentence pronounced; in that, of miracles wrought; in this, *hearing* represents immediate knowledge of the Father's will; in that, *seeing* represents the same kind of knowledge. Observe also that this expression assumes on the part of Jesus direct and uninterrupted converse with the Father. **And my judgment is just.** The Greek expression translated **my judgment** (ἡ κρίσις ἡ ἐμή), has a certain fullness and force which might naturally strike "the Jews" as a reflection upon their manner of judging. **Because I seek not mine own will.** Nothing is surer to pervert judgment than selfish ends in the judge. When his own will comes in, equity goes out. One reason why God cannot be unjust is because he is self-sufficient and needs the service of no one. Jesus Christ, through his perfect communion with God, was absolutely above the influence of human fear or favor. **But the will of the Father which hath sent me.** "My judgment, because not individual, but divine, *must* be righteous."—(Meyer). To seek what God seeks, to do his will, is always right. The word "Father" is omitted by the best editors.

31-47. CONFIRMATION OF HIS CLAIMS.

31. If I bear witness of myself, my witness is not true. An almost startling concession, which is, however, at the same time the strongest possible implied affirmation of his inseparable unity in action with the Father. For the pronoun **I** (ἐγώ), being emphatic, appears to mean, "I alone," or I in separation from the Father. "If such a separation, and independent testimony, as is here supposed, *could take place*, it would be a falsification of the very conditions of the truth of God as manifested by the Son, who being the Logos speaks, not of himself, but of the Father."—(Alford). Properly understood, therefore, this passage is not inconsistent with John 8: 13-16.

32. There is another that beareth witness of me. The word **another** (ἄλλος) means, without doubt, the Father, and is a clear recognition of personal distinction between the Father and the Son. Indeed, such a distinction is assumed in every part of this wonderful apology, and without it the language of Jesus in this particular verse, as contrasted with the preceding verse, would be, not only inexplicable, but certain to mislead. Some have thought that the word **another** points to John the Baptist; but this is rendered improbable by the whole context, before and after. **And I know that the witness which he witnesseth of me is true.** (Compare 7: 28, 29; 8: 26-55). The reading, "ye know," adopted by Tischendorf, is not as well supported as the common text, nor does it agree as well with the tone of this discourse.

33-34. Ye (*have*) **sent unto John**—as recorded by the Evangelist in 1: 19 sq. **And he bare** (or *hath borne*) **witness to the truth.** Jesus does not undervalue the fidelity of John, or his knowledge of "the truth." **But I receive not testimony from man**—*i. e., the* testimony of which I speak—the testimony of **another. But these things I say that ye might** (or *may*) **be saved.** "Not for *my* benefit, for I do not need this human testimony, having a divine one, which is all sufficient, but for *your* salvation," (Schaff), do I refer to the testimony of John. To you it should be valid, though it be needless to me.

CH. V.] JOHN. 141

35 He was a burning and *a shining light: and *ye were willing for a season to rejoice in his light.
36 But *I have greater witness than *that* of John: for *the works which the Father hath given me to finish, the same works that I do, bear witness of me, that the Father hath sent me.
37 And the Father himself, which hath sent me, *hath borne witness of me. Ye have neither heard his voice at any time, *nor seen his shape.

35 may be saved. He was the lamp that burneth and shineth: and ye were willing to rejoice for a season
36 in his light. But the witness which I have is greater than *that of* John: for the works which the Father hath given me to accomplish, the very works that I do, bear witness of me, that the Father hath sent me.
37 And the Father that sent me, he hath borne witness of me. Ye have neither heard his voice at any time, nor seen his shape.

a 2 Pet. 1: 19.....b See Matt. 13: 20; 21: 26, Mark 6: 20.....c 1 John 5: 9.....d ch. 3: 2; 10; 25; 15: 24.....e Matt. 3: 17; 17: 5; ch. 6: 77; 8: 18.....f Deut. 4: 12; ch. 1: 18; 1 Tim. 1; 17; 1 John 4: 12.

35. He was a burning and a shining light—or, *the lamp that burneth and shineth*. (Rev. Ver.) The article characterizes him as the definite lamp which, according to the Old Testament, was to appear and give a knowledge of salvation to the people (Luke 1: 76 sq.). He is called **the lamp** (ὁ λύχνος) and not *the light* (τὸ φῶς), because, as Schaff remarks, he "was *a* light, but only in a sub-ordinate sense, a derived light, a light *lighted*, not *lighting*; and hence 'in his light' is spoken of in the next clause in the sense of the predicate, not the noun." "He was the lamp that was burning and shining. The English Version here doubly errs both in the way of disparagement and of exaltation. Exaltation, because it elevates to an original light him whom the Saviour designates as only a lamp, shining with borrowed brightness. Of disparagement, in that it omits the emphatically repeated article by which Christ exalts John to a single and sole conspicuousness. He himself was 'the light' (John 1: 4), the fountain of all illumination. John was but a 'lamp,' shining as being shone upon; but still the lamp, that was lighted and shining."—(A. C. Kendrick, D. D.) The verb **was** points to the circumstance that John's ministry was already past; he was either dead, or in prison. **And ye were willing for a season** (literally, *hour*) **to rejoice in his light.** At first and for a time all Jerusalem went after John. Curiosity led even the Scribes and Pharisees to go out into the wilderness to see him. He was the novelty of the hour. But the rulers of the people soon became weary of his earnest calls to repentance, and when they found that he would minister neither to their national pride nor to their personal self-righteousness, they turned away from him, without having received any spiritual benefit.

36. But I have greater witness than that of John. Literally: *But the witness which I have is greater than that of John.* The word **witness** here means "testimony" (μαρτυρίαν), and the whole is a compendious expression for: "But I, on my part, have the witness (referred to, ver. 32) which is greater than that of John." **For the works which the Father hath given me.** These works embrace miracles, but do not exclude other manifestations of his divine or Messianic authority. **To finish** (or, *that I should finish them*). The Greek expression is fairly enough represented by the ordinary English Version, **to finish. The same works** (or, *the works themselves*), etc. Thus Jesus affirms that he is doing the precise works which the Father has sent him to finish, and also that these works are of such a nature as to prove that he has been sent by the Father. **That I do, bear witness of me, that the Father hath sent me.** A full, deliberate, unambiguous, powerful assertion of the divine character of his works.

37. And the Father himself. (Better, as in Revised Version, *And the Father that sent me, he hath borne witness of me*). The word translated *he* (ἐκεῖνος, not αὐτός, according to the best editors), represents **the Father** with a certain dignity and force which belong to no other pronoun, as used by this Evangelist. But to what testimony of the Father does Christ refer? Plainly, not to "the works" spoken of in the preceding verse; for both the change of tense in the verb and the personal emphasis implied in the pronoun point to a distinct testimony. Possibly, he refers to the voice from heaven at his baptism; yet this appears to have been heard by no one save himself and John the Baptist, and it is more likely, on the whole, that he has in mind the witness of prophecy in the Old Testament; for on this he dwells below. **Ye have neither heard his voice at any time, nor seen his shape** (or, *form*). By this language, Jesus reminds "the Jews" that their knowledge of

38 And ye have not his word abiding in you: for whom he hath sent, him ye believe not.
39 *Search the Scriptures; for in them ye think ye have eternal life; and ᵇ they are they which testify of me.
40 ᶜ And ye will not come to me, that ye might have life.

38 nor seen his form. And ye have not his word abiding in you: for whom he sent, him ye believe not.
39 ¹ Ye search the scriptures, because ye think that in them ye have eternal life; and these are they which
40 bear witness of me; and ye will not come to me,

a Isa. 8: 20; 34: 16; Luke 16: 29; ver. 46; Acts 17: 11.... b Deut. 18: 15, 18; Luke 24: 27; ch. 1: 45....c ch. 1: 11; 3: 19.—1 Or, *Search the scriptures.*

God was not direct, like his own. (See ver. 19, 20, 30; and 6: 46). "The true relation of ver. 36-38 is this: In passing from the testimony of *works*, ver. 36, to the *personal* testimony of God, ver. 37, Jesus mentions the two forms which the latter may take: that of a direct appearing, or that of his word in the Old Testament. The first of these was denied them by the nature of things; the second was rendered useless by their own fault."--(Godet.) But it is more natural to suppose that both expressions, "Ye have neither heard his voice nor seen his form," are employed for the same purpose, namely, to emphasize the fact that they had no direct knowledge of God. Their only source of knowledge respecting him was "his word."

38. And ye have not his word abiding in you. "The Jews" might admit their want of the direct knowledge of God, which Jesus claimed to possess, yet they surely considered themselves to be scribes, well instructed in the law. But Jesus denies even this— denies that they have the substantial truth of the Old Testament in their hearts. This truth, he affirms, has no permanent influence on them. It is not the rule of their faith or conduct. What teaching was ever more searching than this? It was like Nathan's word to David: "Thou art the man"! But what reason does the Lord assign for this statement? **For whom he hath sent, him ye believe not.** That they do not receive the Messiah, of whom Moses and the prophets wrote, is brought forward as certain proof that the word of God, in the Old Testament, is not a living power in their souls. Jesus, therefore, assumes that a devout Jew, familiar with the Old Testament, must recognize him as the Sent of God, and Saviour of the world.

39. Search the Scriptures. (Better: *Ye search the Scriptures*)—*i. e.*, after a Rabbinic fashion, with a certain acuteness and diligence, seeking to know the letter of Scripture, ready to multiply external observances, and to bind heavy burdens on the people, willing to pay tithes of mint, anise, and cummin, but forgetting the weightier matters of the law. **For in them ye think ye have eternal life.** They supposed that a knowledge of the Scriptures was enough to ensure their salvation. The Rabbies said: "He who acquires *the words of the law*, acquires for himself eternal life." They were hearers of the law, but not *doers* of it. They gloried in their learning and formal service, but were unspiritual, envious, jealous, and eager to destroy the brightest example of goodness that ever appeared among men. How could they read the law, and still dream of obtaining eternal life by a mere knowledge of the Scriptures? Yet, in another way, as witnesses for Jesus, those Scriptures might have led them to the Source of life everlasting. **And they (or, *those*) are they which testify of me.** It is their very nature and office to bear witness of Jesus. How abundant, then, must be the light which they shed upon his person and work! From this statement alone, it may be inferred that a Messianic element pervades the Old Testament; and Augustine is justified in saying: *Novum Testamentum in Vetere latet. Vetus, Testamentum in Novo patet. The New Testament is hidden in the Old; the Old Testament lies open in the New.*

40. And ye will not come to me, that ye might (or, *may*) **have life.** To come to Jesus is to apply to him for life, to believe in him as the Messiah and Saviour of men. Notice the simplicity, power, and pungency of the Lord's words to these leaders of the Jewish people. "Ye search the Scriptures, because you imagine it possible to obtain through them eternal life, which I alone can give; and those very Scriptures are bearing witness of me, the Giver of spiritual and eternal life; and ye are nevertheless unwilling to come and put your trust in me as the true Messiah, that ye may have life, and may have it even now; for, as I have said, 'the Son maketh alive whom he will.'" (See ver. 21). Well does Schaff remark on this verse: "The

41 a I receive not honour from men.
42 But I know you, that ye have not the love of God in you.
43 I am come in my Father's name, and ye receive me not; if another shall come in his own name, him ye will receive.
44 b How can ye believe, which receive honour one of another, and seek not c the honour that *cometh* from God only?
45 Do not think that I will accuse you to the Father: d there is *one* that accuseth you, *even* Moses, in whom ye trust.

41 that ye may have life. I receive not glory from men.
42 But I know you, that ye have not the love of God in yourselves.
43 I am come in my Father's name, and ye receive me not: if another shall come in his own name, him ye will receive. How can ye believe, who
44 receive glory one of another, and the glory that
45 *cometh* from 1 the only God ye seek not? Think not that I will accuse you to the Father: there is one that accuseth you, *even* Moses, on whom ye have set

a ver. 34; 1 Thess. 7: 6....b ch. 12: 43....c Rom. 2: 29....d Rom 2: 12.—1 Some ancient authorities read, *the only one*.

springs of belief and unbelief are in the heart rather than in the head." Men are sometimes said to be perishing for lack of knowledge: how much oftener do they perish for lack of willingness to use the knowledge within their reach! By a short digression (ver. 41-44) Jesus now points out the reason why "the Jews" would not accept the testimony of the Scriptures, believe in him, and have true life.

41. I receive not honour from men; or, *glory from men I do not receive.* Jesus first repels the reproach which might be rising to the lips of his hearers, that he was himself seeking glory from men by calling upon them to believe in him.

42. But I know (or, *have known*) **you.** The verb is in the perfect tense, signifying a knowledge of them which had come down from the past into the present. **That ye have not the love of God in you.** Says Grotius: "The emphasis falls on the pronoun '*you.*' Such as you suppose me to be, you yourselves really are." And Hengstenberg remarks: "Christ does not utter the charge as a conjecture, but on the ground of clear and certain knowledge; he utters it as the One who knows all men, knows what is in man, and before whom, as before God, the hearts of all men are naked and opened." **The love of God** is the love to God which is required by the law, which is spiritual and supreme, and which is essentially the same in all who possess it. Hence the definite article.

42. I am come in my Father's name, and ye receive me not. Christ was the image of the Father; he came to do the Father's will; he affirmed that he could do nothing apart from the Father; there was no self-seeking in his heart; he valued the favor of God and not human praise; and, therefore, "the Jews" rejected him and sought his life. Just the reverse of this would have been true

had *the love of God* been truly in their hearts. **If another shall come in his own name, him ye will receive.** A piercing glance into the future! "Sixty-four such deceivers have been counted since the time of Christ."—(Schudt in Bengel.) And "the Jews" who were ready to imbrue their hands in the blood of Christ, were just the men to be blinded by the flatteries and taken by the schemes of audacious pretenders to Messianic dignity. For worldly men can enter into the plans of the worldly (compare John 12: 43). This is more distinctly taught in the next verse, or, if not taught, implied.

44. How can ye believe, which receive honour one of another, and seek not the honour that cometh from God only (or, *the only God*). The word which is here translated *honour* is commonly rendered "glory." A selfish spirit, quaffing the cup of human applause and longing for ever deeper draughts, is not likely to bow before Christ and accept of true life from him. "The fear of man bringeth a snare" (Prov. 29:25), and love of human praise does the same. "Not many wise men after the flesh, not many mighty, not many noble are called" (1 Cor. 1:26). "How weighty this declaration is for our time, may be clearly seen. Receiving honor from man has a deep place in our theology. This theology is extremely anxious, not to break with the spirit of the age, but to be in accord with it. This is the worm which is gnawing it, the curse which is resting upon it."—(*Hengstenberg.*)

Resuming his appeal to the witness of God in the Old Testament, Jesus affirms that unbelief in him presupposes unbelief of Moses. (Ver. 45-47).

45. Do not think that I will accuse you to the Father—either now or hereafter; a statement quite in harmony with ver. 22, 23, 30; for the office of a judge is distinct from

46 For had ye believed Moses, ye would have believed me: *for he wrote of me.
47 But if ye believe not his writings, how shall ye believe my words?

46 your hope. For if ye believed Moses, ye would be-
47 lieve me; for he wrote of me. But if ye believe not his writings, how shall ye believe my words?

CHAPTER VI.

AFTER *these things Jesus went over the sea of Galilee, which is *the sea* of Tiberias.

1 AFTER these things Jesus went away to the other side of the sea of Galilee, which is *the sea* of Tiberias.

a Gen. 3: 15; 12: 3; 18: 18; 22: 18; 49: 10; Deut. 18: 15, 18; ch. 1: 45; Acts 26: 22.... *b* Matt. 14: 13; Mark 6: 35; Luke 9: 10, 12.

that of an accuser. **There is one that accuseth you**—constantly; for the present participle used substantively with the article (ὁ κατηγορῶν) signifies one who is doing habitually what the participle expresses. Hence, you have an accuser—**Moses**—the representative of the law (Deut. 31: 26; John 7. 19; Rom. 3: 20; 5: 20; Gal. 3: 19, 21), **in whom ye trust** (or, *have hoped*, or, *set your hope*). (See Rom. 2: 17). Meyer calls attention to the "tragic emphasis" which is given to the pronoun ye (ὑμεῖς) by the Saviour. These Jews had hoped and were still hoping to merit salvation by works of the law.

46. For had ye believed Moses, ye would have believed me. A more exact rendering is given in the Rev. Version. (See above). Notice (1) the conjunction **for,** which shows that this verse confirms the second clause of ver 45. Moses, in the law, is your accuser, because ye do not believe his words, "for had ye believed," etc. Notice (2) that the verbs are both in the imperfect tense, and refer, in a descriptive way, to the near past, or present. The translation of the Rev. Ver. is the best representation of their meaning practicable in our language. (Comp. Kühner, "Gr. Gram.," §350. 2 (2) (*a*); Crosby, "Gr Gram.," §603). **For he wrote of me.** The words of me are rendered emphatic in the original by their position. This is a perfectly clear testimony, on the part of Christ, to a Messianic element in the Pentateuch, as well as to the Mosaic authorship of the same. (Comp. Gen. 12: 3; 22: 18; Num. 21: 9; Deut. 18: 15 sq.; Matt. 5: 17 sq.; Luke 24: 44; Rom. 10: 5).

47. But if ye believe not his writings, how shall ye believe my words? De Wette remarks: "This conclusion assumes that, on account of their reverence for Moses, and their attachment to the written word, the Jews could believe him more easily than they could believe the spoken words of Jesus." The contrast, however, is between **his** and **my,** not between **writings and words.** But this is not all, as Alford and Meyer correctly add: "*Moses leads to Christ:* is one of the witnesses by which the Father hath testified of him."—(Alford). "Belief in Moses is necessary in order to belief in Christ."—(Meyer, substantially). This discourse is truly wonderful for depth, simplicity, and boldness. As uttered by the holy Son, it must have astounded "the Jews," holding them spellbound with awe. It is "so characteristic, grand, pointed, and telling, that the idea of an invention is utterly preposterous."—(Schaff). After quoting the words of Strauss: "If the form of this discourse must be attributed to the Evangelist, it may be that the substance belongs to Jesus," Godet proceeds thus: "If a partial understanding of the discourse has wrested this avowal from such a critic, a fuller understanding of it would give one the right to say: Jesus really spoke in this way. The principal theme is exactly pertinent to the occasion. The secondary ideas subordinate themselves logically to this theme. Not a detail is inconsistent with the whole. And the application is solemn and impressive, as it ought to be, in such a situation. It stamps the whole discourse with the seal of reality."

Ch. 6. According to the interpretation of 5: 1, given above, the Evangelist now passes over in silence one of the longest and busiest periods in the ministry of Christ—a period of either a whole year, or of at least ten months —the events of which are detailed with unusual fullness by the first three Evangelists. These events are set down in the following order by Dr. Robinson: The plucking of ears of grain on the Sabbath (Matt. 12: 1-8), the healing of a withered hand on the Sabbath (Matt. 12: 9-14), Christ's arrival at the Sea of Tiberias followed by multitudes (Matt. 12: 15-21), his withdrawal to a mountain and choice of the Twelve (Mark 3: 13-19), his Sermon on the

2 And a great multitude followed him, because they saw his miracles which he did on them that were diseased.

2 And a great multitude followed him, because they beheld the signs which he did on them that were

Mount (Matt. 5: 1; 8: 1), healing of the centurion's servant (Matt. 8: 5-13), raising to life of the widow's son (Luke 7: 11-17), deputation from the imprisoned Baptist to Jesus (Matt. 11: 2-19), Jesus anointed by a woman who had been a sinner (Luke 7: 36-50), second circuit in Galilee with his disciples (Luke 8: 1-3), healing of a demoniac (Mark 3: 19-30), the Scribes and Pharisees seeking a sign (Matt. 12: 38-45), Christ declaring his disciples to be his nearest kindred (Matt. 12: 46-50), denouncing woes against the Pharisees and others (Luke 11: 37-54), discoursing to his disciples and the multitude (Luke 12: 1-59), slaughter of certain Galileans and parable of the barren fig-tree (Luke 13: 1-9), parable of the sower (Matt. 13: 1-23), parable of the tares, and other parables (Matt. 13: 24-53), stilling the tempest on the lake (Matt. 8: 18-27), the demoniacs of Gadara healed (Matt. 8: 28-34), Levi's feast (Matt. 9: 10-17), raising of Jairus' daughter, etc. (Matt. 9: 18-26), healing of two blind men, etc. (Matt. 9: 27-34), Jesus rejected a second time at Nazareth (Matt. 13: 54-58), third circuit in Galilee, the twelve sent forth (Matt. 9: 35-38), Herod thinks Jesus to be John the Baptist, risen from the dead (Matt. 14: 1, 2, 6-12). A large part, if not all, of these events may be allotted to the ten months or year of Christ's ministry which John has passed in silence.

1–15. FEEDING THE FIVE THOUSAND. (Compare Matt. 14: 13-21; Mark 6: 30-44; Luke 9: 10-17).

1. **After these things.** How long after, the words do not determine. (Comp. 5: 1; 3: 22). The same expression could be used, whether the interval between the events referred to was a week, a month, a year, or even a still longer period; for the Greek phrase (μετὰ ταῦτα) appears to be perfectly represented by the English Version. **Jesus went** (or, *went away*). From what place? from Jerusalem? or from Capernaum? Probably from Capernaum, as indicated by the parallel accounts in the first three Gospels. Besides, the disciples return from the other side to this place (ver. 17), and the multitudes repair to it, as if it were the ordinary home of Jesus (ver. 24). From Matt. 4: 13, we learn that Jesus had left Nazareth, and settled in Capernaum; and from Matt. 9: 1, that it was probably called "his own city." Hence, the Evangelist passes in thought from Jerusalem to Capernaum, and from one feast to the approach of another; but whatever events he describes at all, are described with a distinctness which is admirable. **Over** (or, *beyond*) **the sea of Galilee, which is the sea of Tiberias.** The explanatory words, **which is the sea of Tiberias**, are added because, when this Gospel was written, the Sea of Galilee was, probably, known to the people of Asia Minor, and of the Roman Empire generally, as the Sea of Tiberias. It took this name from a city on its southwestern shore, built by Herod Antipas, and named Tiberias, in honor of the Emperor Tiberius. There is no evidence that Jesus ever visited this city, though his home for some time was within a few miles of it. This Evangelist does not speak of the manner by which Jesus went away to the other side of the sea, unless something on this point is presupposed by "the ship" spoken of in ver. 17. But Matthew says that he went "in a ship," and Mark, that they went "by the ship." The word employed by Luke (ὑπεχώρησε) is quite consistent with these statements.

2. **And a great multitude.** Matthew and Luke omit the adjective, but make the noun plural, "the multitudes." According to paramount critical authority, Mark uses the expression "many" without any noun. **Followed him**—or, *were following him;* for the word pictures the scene, being in the imperfect tense. From the testimony of Matthew and Mark it appears that they were "on foot." While Jesus passed over with his disciples in a small ship to the northeast shore of the lake, the people were hastening on foot around the head of the lake, receiving accessions to their number from the villages near which they passed (Matt. 14: 13; Mark 6: 32). Thus Hanna describes the scene: "The wind blows fresh from the northwest; for shelter they hug the shore. Their departure had been watched by the crowd, and now, when they see how close to the land they keep, and how slow the progress is they make, a great multitude out of all the cities—embracing, in all likelihood, many of those com-

3 And Jesus went up into a mountain, and there he sat with his disciples.
4 ᵃAnd the passover, a feast of the Jews, was nigh.

3 sick. And Jesus went up into the mountain, and 4 there he sat with his disciples. Now the passover,

a Lev. 23:5, 7; Deut. 16:1; ch. 2:13; 5:1.

panies which had gathered to go up to the passover—ran on foot along the shore." **Because they saw**—more exactly—*because they were beholding;* for here also the verb is imperfect, and carries the mind back to the attentive on-looking of the people, as the wonders referred to were performed, one after another. **His miracles which he did on them that were diseased:** or, *the signs which he was working on the sick.* When John the Baptist from his prison sent two of his disciples to Jesus, who was then probably in Capernaum, saying, "Art thou he that should come, or should we look for another?" the answer of Christ was an appeal to his works: "Go and show John those things which ye do hear and see: The blind receive their sight, and the lame walk, the lepers are cleansed, and the deaf hear, the dead are raised, and the poor have the gospel preached to them" (Matt. 11:5). Works of mercy and of power, which were continued in that region for a considerable time.

3. And Jesus went up into a (rather, *the*) **mountain.** The definite article before **mountain** may be due to the circumstance that it was remembered by the Evangelist as the scene of the miracle to be related, or to the circumstance that it was the one nearest "a desert place belonging to Bethsaida." (Comp. Luke 9:10.) This Bethsaida was situated on the east side of the Jordan, a short distance above its entrance into the Sea of Galilee. See Art. Bethsaida in Smith's "Dict. of the Bible." Says Thomson: "This bold headland marks the spot, according to my typography, where the five thousand were fed with five barley loaves and two small fishes. From the four narratives of this stupendous miracle, we gather, 1st, that the place belonged to Bethsaida; 2d, that it was a desert place; 3d, that it was near the shore of the lake, for they came to it by boat; 4th, that there was a mountain close at hand; 5th, that it was a smooth, grassy spot, capable of seating many thousand people. Now all these requisites are found in this exact locality, and nowhere else, so far as I can discover. This Butaiha belonged to Bethsaida. At this extreme southeast corner of it, the mountain shuts down upon the lake bleak and barren. It was, doubtless, desert then as now; for it is not capable of cultivation. In this little cove the ships (boats) were anchored. On this beautiful sward, at the base of the rocky hill, the people were seated to receive from the hands of the Son of God the miraculous bread, emblematic of his body, which is the true bread from heaven."—("The Land and the Book," II. p. 29.) **And there he sat with his disciples.** From the narratives of Mark and Luke it appears that some of the people reached the landing place before the boat itself, and that Jesus, after landing, spent a considerable part of the day in teaching them many things, or in speaking to them of the Kingdom of God, and in healing those that had need of healing. Perhaps he was seated with his disciples, according to Jewish custom, while thus teaching the people. But his teaching was interrupted, ever and anon, by the presence of those who had need of healing; and, as the day wore on, and the disciples mingled with the throngs who showed no signs of departing, they began to feel serious anxiety in respect to food.

4. The passover (the *third in Christ's ministry,* April 18, A. D. 29) is here called **a** (rather, *the*) **feast of the Jews,** showing that it was the most important, in some respects, of their feasts. Others have suggested that this description is added because "the Jews" were now so hostile to Jesus that he could not safely attend the passover in Jerusalem. It was *theirs*, under their control; and thereupon he absented himself from it. But the suggestion is unnecessary and by no means obvious. From the fact that this passover was nigh, may be inferred the season of the year, about the middle of April. It has also been correctly inferred from this statement respecting the passover, that some, at least, of the multitude who followed Jesus were persons on their way to Jerusalem to celebrate this feast. Others have supposed that it had some connection in the Evangelist's mind

JOHN. 147

5 ᵃWhen Jesus then lifted up *his* eyes, and saw a great company come unto him, he saith unto Philip, Whence shall we buy bread, that these may eat?
6 And this he said to prove him: for he himself knew what he would do.

5 the feast of the Jews, was at hand. Jesus therefore lifting up his eyes, and seeing that a great multitude cometh unto him, saith unto Philip, Whence ⁶ are we to buy ¹ bread, that these may eat? And this he said to prove him: for he himself knew

a Matt. 14: 14; Mark 6: 35; Luke 9: 12.——1 Gr., *loaves.*

with Christ's discourse respecting himself as the bread from heaven—which is very doubtful.¹

5. **When Jesus then,** etc. ; or *Jesus therefore lifting up his eyes, and seeing that a great multitude cometh unto him, saith unto Philip: Whence are we to buy bread, that these may eat?* It appears from this that at the time which the Evangelist has in mind, people were still coming to Jesus, though the day was far spent. The word *therefore* may point to a connection between this verse and the preceding. As the passover was near, the multitudes came, and, therefore, Jesus saw them coming. Or, it may point to something in the mind of the Evangelist, and not ex-

¹[Here "the passover," though found in all known manuscripts and versions, is omitted by several important Fathers, and the omission is apparently implied in several other patristic statements and chronological arguments. Dr. Hort (Westcott not concurring) states this adverse evidence at length and with favor, though not venturing to propose excision without any support from manuscripts or versions. It is well known that many early Christians (see list of passages in Hort) regarded "the acceptable year of the Lord" (Luke 4: 19, from Isa. 61: 2) as showing that the ministry of Jesus lasted but one year; and they would suppose this notion to be confirmed by the fact that Matthew, Mark, and Luke mention no passover during his ministry but that of the crucifixion. Now it seems to us that all the patristic arguments and allusions may be accounted for by the hypothesis of an early "Western" omission of "the passover," made in order to bring the Fourth Gospel into harmony with the supposed teaching of the others and with the popular opinion. The direct patristic proofs given by Hort are from Irenæus, who regularly uses a "Western" text; from Origen, who has not a few "Western" readings; from Cyril, who seems in this as in many cases to have closely followed Origen; and from the so-called *Alogi* (replied to by Epiphanius), who may also have used a "Western" text, as we know that Epiphanius himself has many readings of that type. This hypothetical reason for omission will at least counterbalance Dr. Hort's supposition that "the passover" was inserted to suit late chronological theories founded on Phlegon's account of an eclipse; especially as the eclipse was really not three, but four years after the 15th of Tiberius, and would thus have suggested a similar insertion in John 5: 1. The reading of the manuscripts and versions seems therefore to stand quite unshaken.—B.]

pressed. According to the other Evangelists, the disciples first suggested the difficulty about food, and the course of events may be represented as follows: Late in the afternoon, some of the disciples who had been passing among the throngs of people, came to Jesus, saying: "The place is a desert, and it is now late; send the people away, that they may go into the fields and villages round about and buy food for themselves; for they have nothing to eat." (Matt. 14: 15; Mark 6: 35, 36; Luke 9: 12). Jesus *therefore*, without replying at once to this suggestion, lifted up his eyes and thoughtfully surveyed the crowds still pressing towards him. Then turning to Philip, he said: **Whence shall we buy bread that these may eat?**—which was at least an intimation of his desire to feed them rather than to send them away. Why the question was addressed to Philip, and not to all the disciples, can only be conjectured.

6. **And this he said to prove him** (lit., *trying him*)—*i. e.*, testing his faith; for it does not seem to have occurred to the mind of Philip that he who had changed the water into wine might be able to feed the hungry. **For he himself knew what he would** (or, *was about to*) **do.** He needed not to take counsel with Philip, that the latter might assist him in devising means to supply the wants of the people. His purpose was formed, and his question was only asked to test, and, in the end, strengthen, the faith of Philip. Personal questions take hold of men, and are remembered. "I hear you cry, in bewilderment: 'I do not know. I have been to everybody, and I do not know what I shall do.' That is a chronic state with us when we puzzle our own poor brains. Jesus knew what he would do. This is sweet comfort: Jesus knows. He always knows all about it. He knew how many people there were there. He knew how much bread it would take; he knew how many fish he would want, and how he meant to feed the crowd, and send them all away refreshed. He knew all before it happened. He perceived, long before Andrew told him, that there was a lad somewhere in the crowd

148 JOHN. [CH. VI.

7 Philip answered him, *Two hundred pennyworth of bread is not sufficient for them, that every one of them may take a little.
8 One of his disciples, Andrew, Simon Peter's brother, saith unto him,
9 There is a lad here, which hath five barley loaves, and two small fishes: ᵇ but what are they among so many?
10 And Jesus said, Make the men sit down. Now there was much grass in the place. So the men sat down, in number about five thousand.

7 what he would do. Philip answered him, Two hundred ¹ shillings' worth of ² bread is not sufficient for them, that every one may take a little. One of his disciples, Andrew, Simon Peter's brother, saith 9 unto him, There is a lad here, who hath five barley loaves, and two fishes: but what are these among 10 so many? Jesus said, Make the people sit down. Now there was much grass in the place. So the men sat

a See Num. 11:21, 22....b 2 Kings 4:43.—1 See marginal note on Matt. 18:28....2 Gr., *loaves*.

with five barley cakes. When the lad set out in the morning, I cannot make out what made him bring five barley loaves and fishes into that crowd, except the Master had whispered in his heart: 'Young man, take with you a good lunch. Put those barley cakes into the basket, and do not forget the fishes. You do not know how long you may be from home.' Nature bade him provide for contingencies; but, then, nature is God's voice, when he chooses to make it so. . . Where is the man that is to be the universal provider? Where is the chief of the commissariat? It is that youth, and that is the whole of his store-house. . . The Saviour knew that. And he knows exactly, dear friend, where your help is to come from in your hour of trouble."—*Spurgeon.*

7. Two hundred pennyworth of bread is not sufficient for them, that every one (omit of them) may take a little. A penny (or, *denarius*) of the time of Christ was worth about fifteen cents of our money, and is supposed to have been the usual compensation for a day's labor in the field. (Matt. 20:2). The sum mentioned by Philip was, therefore, about thirty dollars, or as much as two hundred men could earn by the labor of a day. At this point may be inserted the words of Jesus preserved by the other Evangelists: "*They need not depart* (Matt.); "*give ye them to eat* (Matt., Mark, Luke); and the response of the disciples: *Shall we go and buy two hundred pennyworth of bread, and give them to eat?* with the Saviour's further remark: "*How many loaves have ye? Go and see.*" And now, either after inquiry, or because he already knew, comes the word of Andrew.

8. One of his disciples, Andrew, Simon Peter's brother. Notice the graphic and personal character of the narrative. Observe, also, the implied concession of Peter's eminence, in a Gospel which has been ascribed to the second century, because it aims to de-

preciate him. But why so full a description of one who made so unimportant a remark? The Evangelist did not look upon Andrew's report as unimportant. It was remembered by him as first directing attention to the little store with which Jesus, the Son of God, had wrought a stupendous miracle; and the disciple who had done this had enjoyed a privilege never to be forgotten—even as it has never ceased to be a privilege to be employed in the humblest way as a friend of Christ. And the greater the work with which one's service is connected, the more delightful a remembrance of it will be. **There is a lad** (or, *little lad*) **here, which hath five barley loaves, and two small fishes.** The expression translated **a lad** (παιδάριον ἕν), may signify a *single lad;* for the numeral *one* (ἕν), though not specially emphatic, may have been chosen by Andrew in order to show that there was but *one* who had any food, and that he was a *small boy,* or servant, who had only a very *small amount* of provisions. Hence, the question, or exclamation : **But what are these among** (or, *for*) **so many?** They were no appreciable relation to the wants of such a multitude. It may, also, be observed that the food was plain, such as was commonly used by the poorer classes, especially the barley bread. Yet suitable; for what the people now required was food, to satisfy hunger; not luxuries, to gratify appetite.

10. Make the men sit down (or, *recline*). **Now there was much grass in the place.** The grass is mentioned because it rendered the reclining posture agreeable. But the notice of it shows the accuracy of the Evangelist in little things ; for just at this season of the year would the grass be green and abundant. **So** (or, *therefore*) **the men sat down, in number about five thousand.** Mark testifies that they "sat down in ranks, by hundreds and by fifties." The number of women and children must have been considerable,

Ca. VI.]   JOHN.   149

11 And Jesus took the loaves; and when he had given thanks, he distributed to the disciples, and the disciples to them that were set down; and likewise of the fishes as much as they would.
12 When they were filled, he said unto his disciples, Gather up the fragments that remain, that nothing be lost.
13 Therefore they gathered *them* together, and filled twelve baskets with the fragments of the five barley loaves, which remained over and above unto them that had eaten.
14 Then those men, when they had seen the miracle that Jesus did, said, This is of a truth ᵃ that Prophet that should come into the world.

11 down, in number about five thousand. Jesus therefore took the loaves; and having given thanks, he distributed to them that were set down; likewise
12 also of the fishes as much as they would. And when they were filled, he saith unto his disciples, Gather up the broken pieces which remain over, that nothing be lost. So they gathered them up, and filled
13 twelve baskets with broken pieces from the five barley loaves, which remained over unto them that had eaten. When therefore the people saw the ¹sign
14 which he did, they said, This is of a truth the prophet that cometh into the world.

a Gen. 49: 10; Deut. 18: 15, 18; Matt. 11: 3; ch. 1: 21; 4: 19, 25; 7: 40.——1 Some ancient authorities read, *signs.*

though they were not counted. "The marshaling of five thousand men, besides women and children, into such an orderly array, must have taken some time. The people, however, quietly consented to be so arranged, and company after company sat down, till the whole were seated in the presence of the Lord, who all the while has stood in silence, watching the operation, with that scanty stock of provisions at hand."—*Hanna.*

11. And Jesus (or, *Jesus therefore*) **took the loaves; and when he had given thanks, he distributed to them that were set down.** This is all that was written by the Evangelist; the words, **the disciples, and the disciples to,** being transferred to this place from Matthew. Yet the distribution was, undoubtedly, made through the disciples, as the Synoptical Gospels relate; and this may, possibly, be intimated by the compound verb employed (διέδωκεν). The other Gospels state, also, that Jesus broke the bread. **And likewise of the fishes, as much as they would.** But when was the miracle wrought? When the food was in the hands of Jesus? or in those of his disciples? or in those of the multitude? Meyer says: "The Lord blessed and gave the loaves and fishes, *as they were,* to the disciples; and then, *during their distribution of them,* the miraculous increase took place, so that they broke and distributed enough for all." We may suppose that Jesus broke the bread partially, and that the disciples carried on the process, as they gave to each one his portion—the bread meanwhile increasing as they continued to break and distribute it.

12. When they were filled, he said unto his disciples, Gather up the fragments that remain, that nothing be lost. The repast was plain, wholesome, bountiful. None went from that supper hungry, unless it was for spiritual food. Indeed, there was more than enough for all. "The command, one end of which was certainly to convince the disciples of the power which had wrought the miracle, is given by our Lord a moral bearing also. They collected the fragments *for their own use* [?], each in his basket (κόφινος), the ordinary furniture of the traveling Jew, to carry his food, lest he should be polluted by that of the people through whose territory he passed."—*Alford.*

13. Of the size of these baskets, nothing very definite is known. They are called by a name (κόφινοι), different from that given to the baskets (σπυρίδες), used when the four thousand were fed. (See Mark 8: 19, 20). According to the Art. in Smith's "Dictionary of the Bible," the former were generally larger than the latter. They must, then, have been of considerable size, for Paul is said to have been let down in one of the latter when he escaped from Damascus. (Acts 9: 25). The "Etymologicum Magnum" defines a *cophinus,* the basket used in this case, as a "deep and hollow vessel." As used by Roman gardeners, it held manure enough to make a hot-bed. (Columella xi. 3). Westcott says: "The stout wicker baskets (κοφίνους), as distinguished from the soft, flexible 'frails' (σπυρίδες)." From the language of this Gospel, it might be inferred that the fragments were those of the barley bread only, while Mark appears to include remnants of the fishes. Perhaps the pieces of fish were a very small part of the whole, and therefore passed without notice, except by Mark.

14, 15. EFFECT OF THE MIRACLE ON THE PEOPLE.

14. Then those men, etc. More exactly: *The men, therefore, when they saw the sign which he did, were saying.* The Evangelist uses the descriptive tense, because the remark

15 When Jesus therefore perceived that they would come and take him by force, to make him a king, he departed again into a mountain himself alone.
16 ᵃAnd when even was *now* come, his disciples went down unto the sea,
17 And entered into a ship, and went over the sea toward Capernaum. And it was now dark, and Jesus was not come to them.

15 Jesus therefore perceiving that they were about to come and take him by force, to make him king, withdrew again into the mountain himself alone.
16 And when evening came, his disciples went down unto the sea; and they entered into a boat, and were
17 going over the sea unto Capernaum. And it was now dark, and Jesus had not yet come to them.

---

a Matt. 14: 23; Mark 6: 47.

---

passed from one to another, and was often repeated. This is of a truth that (rather *the*) Prophet that should come (literally, *that cometh*) into the world. From the next verse it appears that they meant the Messiah. If so, some of the people probably interpreted Deut. 18: 15 of the Messiah to come. Compare 1: 21.

15. When Jesus therefore perceived (or, *knew*, γνούς): not by what he had overheard them saying, nor by his power to look into their hearts and perceive the hopes which his act had kindled, but by his foresight of whatever concerned his own work. That they would (or, *were about to*) come—*i. e.*, unless prevented by himself—and take him by force, to make (or, *that they might make*) him a king. The pronoun him is not expressed in the original. We are astonished that the people, after beholding such a sign of Christ's power with God, should have thought it possible to carry him by force to Jerusalem for such a purpose, or, indeed, for any other. But their enthusiasm was evidently unreasoning—a sudden popular impulse that would soon die out of their hearts. He departed again into a (rather, *the*) mountain himself alone. The word again is probably genuine, and refers to what is said in ver. 3. As the multitude increased, Jesus had come down to the edge of the plain, where he taught and healed the sick, and at last fed the people with the five loaves and two small fishes. Now he withdrew once more into the mountain, not taking even his disciples with him.

16-21. MIRACLE OF WALKING ON THE SEA.
"Omitted by Luke. An important and interesting question arises: *Why* is this miracle here inserted by St. John? That he ever inserts for the mere purpose of narration, I cannot believe. The reason seems to me to be this: to give to the twelve, in the prospect of so apparently strange a discourse respecting his body, a view of the truth respecting that body, that it and the things said of it were not to be understood in a gross, corporeal, but in a supernatural and spiritual, sense."— (Alford.) It is possible, though by no means probable, that this miracle was performed to give to the twelve a view of the truth respecting his body, of which he was about to speak in his discourse at Capernaum, but it is not credible that John inserted this narrative to give them such a view; for they must have been all, or nearly all, dead when he wrote his Gospel. Alford seems to have been influenced by his own view of the nature of Christ's body as related to the holy supper and the salvation of the bodies of believers; but his statement, as it reads, is plainly incorrect.

16. And when evening was (omit now) come. Matthew distinguishes an early evening, before the miracle (14:15), from a later evening, after it (14:23). The evening here referred to is, of course, the later one. His disciples went down unto the sea—literally, *upon the sea*, that is, the sea-shore. And this they were constrained to do, as Matthew (14:22) and Mark (6:45) testify, by Jesus himself, before he sent away the people and retired into the mountain.

17. And (*they*) entered into a ship (or, *boat*), and went (or, *were going*) over the sea toward (*unto*) Capernaum. It is doubtful whether the true text has a ship or *the ship* in this place; but Matthew and Mark have "the ship," and we may, therefore, assume that the disciples entered the same ship, or boat, in which they had come over to the desert place. Notice also the tense of the verb *were going*, not went, for the passage was, for the present, attempted, rather than accomplished. Again, John marks their destination as Capernaum, while Mark gives their direction as "towards Bethsaida." Both may be correct; for in order to reach Capernaum, they might have to go for some time in the direction of the western Bethsaida. Moreover, it is possible that they kept near

18 And the sea arose by reason of a great wind that blew.
19 So when they had rowed about five and twenty or thirty furlongs, they see Jesus walking on the sea, and drawing nigh unto the ship: and they were afraid.
20 But he saith unto them, It is I; be not afraid.

18 And the sea was rising by reason of a great wind that blew. When therefore they had rowed about five and twenty or thirty furlongs, they beheld Jesus walking on the sea, and drawing nigh unto the boat: 20 and they were afraid. But he saith unto them, It

the northern shore, in the hope of receiving Jesus on board. **And it was now dark** (or, *darkness had now come on*), **and Jesus was not** (or, *had not yet*) **come to them.** "It would appear," says Alford, "as if the disciples were lingering along shore with the expectation of taking in Jesus, but night had fallen, and he had not come to them." In some secluded place on the mountain he was engaged in prayer to God (Matt. 14:23). The darkness troubled him not. He had come into the world to dispel a thicker darkness than now covered hill-top or sea; and he saw in the hearts of men a love of that darkness in preference to light. Hence he prayed.

18. And the sea arose (lit., *was rising*) **by reason of a great wind that blew.** In other words, the sea was becoming thoroughly waked up, aroused, agitated, by a strong wind blowing upon it. Matthew says that the ship was "tossed with the waves" (or, *tormented by the waves*), "for the wind was contrary" (14:24); and Mark, that Jesus "saw them toiling (or, *tormented*) in rowing, for the wind was contrary." "Two or three hours' hearty labor at the oar might have carried them over to Capernaum. But the adverse tempest is too strong for them. The whole night long they toil among the waves, against the wind."—(Hanna). "After sunset, I strolled down to the lake, and, seating myself upon a mass of broken wall, enjoyed the freshness of the evening. All the day there had not been a breath of air; the sultry heat had been that of a furnace; but now a cool breeze came off the table-land, and, rushing down the ravines that descend to the lake, began to ruffle its bosom. As it grew darker, the breeze increased to a gale, the lake became a sheet of foam, and the white-headed breakers dashed proudly on the rugged beach; its gentle murmur was now changed into the wild and mournful sound of the whistling wind, and the agitated waters. Afar off, was dimly seen a little barque struggling with the waves, and then lost sight of amidst the misty rack. To have thus seen so striking an exemplification of the Scripture narrative, was as interesting as it was unexpected."—W. H. Bartlett, quoted from Hackett's "Illustrations of Scripture").

19. So when (or, *when, therefore*) **they had** (lit., *have*) **rowed about five and twenty or thirty furlongs.** That is, about three and a half miles, which agrees with the testimony of Matthew and Mark, that the ship was now in the midst of the sea. **They see Jesus walking on the sea, and drawing nigh unto the ship: and they were afraid.** This occurred in the fourth watch of the night (Matt. and Mark), a little before the dawn of day, or in the early morning twilight. Gazing through the dusky atmosphere at the human form, which could be indistinctly seen moving towards them over the agitated sea, they imagined it to be a phantom or spectre, and were terrified. The scene is thus pictured by Hanna: "They were rather more than half across the lake, when, treading on the troubled waves, as on a level, solid pavement, a figure is seen approaching, drawing nearer and nearer to the boat. Their toil is changed to terror—the vigorous hand relaxes its grasp—the oars stand still in the air, or are but feebly plied—the boat rocks heavily —a cry of terror comes from the frightened crew—they think it is a spirit." The word used by the Evangelists Matthew and Mark (φάντασμα) signifies a *phantom*, or *apparition*, **not a spirit.** From the narrative of Mark, it appears that Jesus was pleased to go by them; that is, he did not attempt or desire to enter the ship for his own sake, but only at their request. Yet he was there as a friend, and was prompt in dispelling their illusion and their fear.

20. It is I; be not afraid. There was no mistaking that voice. The form might be spectral, but the voice was their Master's. Matthew and Mark preserve another word: "Have courage; it is I; be not afraid." The Greek expressions are briefer than their English equivalents: "Courage! it is I; fear not"—five strong, clear words, putting heart into the disciples instantly. Matthew adds an incident, showing their wonderful effect upon

21 Then they willingly received him into the ship: and immediately the ship was at the land whither they went.
22 The day following, when the people, which stood on the other side of the sea, saw that there was none other boat there, save that one whereinto his disciples were entered, and that Jesus went not with his disciples into the boat, but *that* his disciples were gone away alone:

21 is I; be not afraid. They were willing therefore to receive him into the boat: and straightway the boat was at the land whither they were going.
22 On the morrow the multitude that stood on the other side of the sea saw that there was none other ¹ boat there, save one, and that Jesus entered not with his disciples into the boat, but *that* his disciples

1 Gr. *little boat.*

Peter, the most impulsive and daring of the twelve. (14: 28-32). The omission of this incident by John accords with the general brevity of his narrative, and does not, therefore, point to any undervaluing of Peter. The incident is not, indeed, as recorded by Matthew, altogether creditable to Peter; for it illustrates the weakness as well as the strength of his faith—the instability as well as the energy of his character.

21. Then they willingly received him into the ship. The Revised Version is better: *They were willing therefore to receive him into the boat.* Willing, because their fear was now gone, since they recognized the One who had come to them in so wonderful a manner as their Lord. Jesus came into the ship, and, according to Matthew, they that were in the ship came and worshiped him, saying: "Of a truth thou art the Son of God." On the other hand, John's language is thought by some to imply that Jesus did not enter the ship: they *wished* to take him into the ship, but did not. This, however, introduces, without any necessity, a contradiction between this Gospel and the first two. Alford's note is correct: "They were afraid:—but being re-assured by his voice, they were willing to take him into the ship; and upon their doing so, the ship, in a comparatively short time, was at the land to which they had been going." Against this interpretation, Godet remarks that the verb "were willing" (ἤθελον), is in the imperfect tense, and denotes an incomplete action." He would explain the words thus: "*At the moment when* they were wishing to receive him, the ship came to land. Jesus indeed entered the barque, but had no time to seat himself there; for, simultaneously with his stepping on board, it reached the shore." But the objection from the imperfect tense is not well taken. No tense could be so suitable to express a feeling which continued from the moment when they heard the voice of Jesus until he was in the boat. With rare and vivid recollection of the scene, John reproduces, as in a picture, the feeling of the disciples, while the impulsive Peter was walking and sinking and being saved, and while their Master was making his way, with Peter, into their storm-tossed boat.

22-24. WHY THE MULTITUDE REMAINED ON THE EASTERN SHORE TILL THE NEXT DAY, AND THEN CAME OVER TO THE WEST SIDE TO CAPERNAUM.

The structure of these verses is involved, and the narrative very compressed, but the meaning of the Evangelist is tolerably evident.

22. The day following—*i. e.*, after the feeding of the five thousand. **When the people, which stood on the other side of the sea.** Omit **when** and substitute *multitude* for **people**, with the Revised Version. **The other side** means the eastern, as contrasted with the western side. **Stood**—*were standing*, or *remaining:* "For this verb often means *to stand*, not as opposed to other attitudes, but to be fixed, stationary, as opposed to the idea of motion."—(Hackett on Acts 9: 7). **Saw that there was none other boat there save one.** For the words *that whereinto his disciples were entered,* are rejected by the best editors. **And that Jesus went not with his disciples into the boat, but that his disciples were gone** (better, *went*) **away alone.** So that Jesus was supposed by them to be still on the eastern side, where he might, perhaps, soon show himself again.

The critical editors (Lach, Tisch, Treg, W. & H.) substitute the verb **saw** (εἶδον) for the participle *having seen* (ἰδών) in the second clause of this verse. But the verbal form may have come from the feeling of a transcriber that the word here must have been exactly repeated in ver. 24. The reference, however, of the verb or participle in this verse, is to the state of affairs at the close of the day of the miracle, and possibly at the beginning of the next day, while the reference of saw in ver. 24, is to the state of affairs farther

23 Howbeit there came other boats from Tiberias nigh unto the place where they did eat bread, after that the Lord had given thanks:
24 When the people therefore saw that Jesus was not there, neither his disciples, they also took shipping, and came to Capernaum, seeking for Jesus.
25 And when they had found him on the other side of the sea, they said unto him, Rabbi, when camest thou hither?
26 Jesus answered them and said, Verily, verily, I say unto you, Ye seek me, not because ye saw the miracles, but because ye did eat of the loaves, and were filled.

23 went away alone (howbeit there came [1] boats from Tiberias nigh unto the place where they ate the 24 bread after the Lord had given thanks): when the multitude therefore saw that Jesus was not there, neither his disciples, they themselves got into the 25 [1] boats, and came to Capernaum, seeking Jesus. And when they found him on the other side of the sea, they said unto him, Rabbi, when camest thou hither? 26 Jesus answered them and said, Verily, verily, I say

[1] Gr. *little boats.*

on in the day following. Hence the participle affords the easier reading, and this may be considered an argument against it. We have supposed the more difficult or verbal form original, but it is a case where certainty is out of the question. And the meaning of the writer must have been essentially the same, whichever form was written by him.

23. **Howbeit there came other boats—** the word *other* should be omitted—**from Tiberias, nigh unto the place where they did eat bread** (or, *where they ate the bread*), **after that the Lord had given thanks.** This parenthetic remark appears to have been inserted to account for the boats which were available for the people who remained on the eastern shore after the disciples had gone away in the only boat which was there on the day of the miracle (see ver. 22). **When the people** (*multitude*) **therefore saw.** That is, on the morrow, (ver. 22:) the mind of the writer going back to the time specified before. **That Jesus was not there, neither his disciples.** For, down to this time they had imagined that Jesus was near them and that his disciples might return for him. **They also,** or, *they themselves,* **took shipping,** (literally, *got into the boats*), namely, those which had come near the place where they were from the southwestern shore at Tiberias. **And came to Capernaum, seeking for Jesus.** It need not be assumed that the number who came by these boats was very great. Many had repaired to their homes, when dismissed by Jesus, the evening before (Matt. 14: 23). That the people directed their way to Capernaum, is evidence that Capernaum was regarded by them as the residence of Jesus—an instance in which the author of this Gospel silently confirms what is related by others. Such incidental harmonies go very far towards establishing the truth of all the Gospels. The people are said to have come over to Capernaum **seeking for Jesus;** but all seeking is not the same: everything in the end depends on the character of the seeking, on the motive which leads to it. There is a seeking of Jesus which is self-seeking only.

25-41. FIRST DIALOGUE. [1]

25. And when they had found him on the other side of the sea. That is, on the western side of the lake, and indeed in the synagogue of Capernaum (ver. 59). Meanwhile, Jesus had not been idle, but had healed many of the sick in "the land of Gennesaret." (Matt. 14: 34-36; Mark 6: 53-56). **Rabbi, when camest thou hither?** "The question in respect to time includes the question in respect to manner."—(Bengel). *When* and *how* hast thou got here? The Greek verb is in the perfect tense. The question may have been one of simple perplexity and surprise. There is no evidence that they were thinking of a miracle in the case.

26. Our attention is arrested, *first,* by the great earnestness of the Lord's reply : **Verily, verily, I say unto you.** This reiterated word reveals the infinite importance of what he is to say. *Secondly,* by the utter want of any appreciation of his spiritual work on the part of those who had found him. They were not awed and elevated and made reverent toward God by the miracles which they had seen. *Thirdly,* by the completely selfish nature of their motives If they longed for the Messiah at all, it was because they expected glory and advantage to themselves from him. The kingdom of God, in their estimation, was "meat and drink," not "righteousness and peace, and joy in the Holy Ghost" (Rom. 14: 17). *Fourthly,* by the perfect knowledge which Jesus had of the hearts of these men. In this

[1] See an interesting and instructive paper on the following discourse in Bib. Sac. for 1854 (vol xi.), p. 693 sq.

154 JOHN. [CH. VI.

27 Labour not for the meat which perisheth, but *a* for that meat which endureth unto everlasting life, which the Son of man shall give unto you: *b* for him hath God the Father sealed.
28 Then said they unto him, What shall we do, that we might work the works of God?
29 Jesus answered and said unto them, *c* This is the work of God, that ye believe on him whom he hath sent.
30 They said therefore unto him, *d* What sign shewest thou then, that we may see, and believe thee? what dost thou work?

unto you, Ye seek me, not because ye saw signs, but 27 because ye ate of the loaves, and were filled. Work not for the meat which perisheth, but for the meat which abideth unto eternal life, which the Son of man shall give unto you: for him the Father, *even* 28 God, hath sealed. They said therefore unto him, What must we do, that we may work the works of 29 God? Jesus answered and said unto them, This is the work of God, that ye believe on him whom] he 30 hath sent. They said therefore unto him, What then doest thou for a sign, that we may see, and believe thee? What dost thou work?

a ver. 54; ch. 4: 14....*b* Matt. 3: 17; 17: 5; Mark 1: 11; 9: 7; Luke 3: 22; 9: 35; ch. 1: 33; 5: 37; 8: 18; Acts 2: 22; 2 Pet. 1: 17.... *c* 1 John 3: 23....*d* Matt. 12: 28; 16: 1; Mark 8: 11; 1 Cor. 1: 22.—1 Or, *he sent.*

instance, as in every other, he appears to be able to look into the souls of those whom he addresses, and speak to every one, with absolute certainty, the appropriate word.

It may also be observed that Jesus refers to the miracles of healing which he had wrought, as well as to the feeding of the multitude, using for this purpose the plural, miracles, or *signs*, not the singular, as would be suitable in referring to one.

27. Labour (lit., *work*) not for the meat (lit., *food*) which perisheth. Many interpreters suppose that rebuke is implied as well as exhortation expressed by the term *work* (ἐργάζεσθε); as if Jesus had said: "You wish to be fed without labor on your part; but I say unto you, Work; obtain food by labor; yet not the food which you desire, food for the body, which satisfies for a time and then perishes, but food for the soul, food that will never lose its power to nourish him who obtains it; food which the Son of man shall (or, *will*) give unto you: for him hath God the Father sealed." This sealing, or acknowledgment of Jesus was made at his baptism, and by every miracle. Alford remarks, that "the future, *will give*, is used because the great sacrifice was not yet offered." But this is scarcely correct; for the benefit of the Saviour's death had been experienced by multitudes before he expired on the cross. The future tense of the verb is more naturally explained by the circumstance that Jesus was thinking of those who had not yet sought the spiritual food in question. To such persons his language was addressed and adapted. And it is to be observed that he distinctly presents himself, the Son of man, as the giver of this spiritual food. This is, perhaps, the most important feature of his reply.

28. What shall (or, *must*) we do, that we might (rather, *may*) work the works of God? The men are Jews, trained to the observance of Rabbinical traditions. By the works of God, they mean works required by God, and, therefore, pleasing to him in particular; those to which they imagine themselves to be summoned by Christ. They perceive that Jesus has in mind a religious or spiritual good, and they conclude that it must be obtained by the performance of certain new but unnamed works of righteousness. These they are willing at least to consider; for they are anxious to stand well in the new kingdom of God. But they quite overlook the most significant part of Christ's response, the declaration that *he* will give them the food which will ensure eternal life. To this point, he therefore directs their attention by words so plain that their meaning cannot be overlooked.

29. This is the work of God—the one new and special thing required by God, on which everything else depends—that ye believe on (or, *in*) him whom he hath sent. The expression *in him*, etc. (εἰς ὅν), represents Jesus as the one towards whom belief must be directed, and in whom it must rest. "As servants of God, they must yield themselves with entire confidence to the messenger of God."—(Schaff). This answer of Jesus has been cited as a brief statement of Paul's great doctrine, that justification depends on faith in Christ, and as a proof that saving faith includes *trust* in Christ. To believe *in* Christ is more than to believe Christ, though the latter should lead to the former. The tense of the verb translated hath sent (lit., *sent*), shows that Christ looked at the act of sending as accomplished.

30. What sign shewest (lit., *doest*) thou then, that we may see, and believe thee? What dost thou work? It seems very surprising that this multitude, some of them fresh from the scene of yesterday's miracle, should now ask for additional evidence of the Messi-

31 a Our fathers did eat manna in the desert: as it is written, b He gave them bread from heaven to eat.
32 Then Jesus said unto them, Verily, verily, I say unto you, Moses gave you not that bread from heaven; but my Father giveth you the true bread from heaven.
33 For the bread of God is he which cometh down from heaven, and giveth life unto the world.
34 c Then said they unto him, Lord, evermore give us this bread.
35 And Jesus said unto them, d I am the bread of life: e he that cometh to me shall never hunger; and he that believeth on me shall never thirst.

31 lieve thee? what workest thou? Our fathers ate the manna in the wilderness; as it is written, He gave them bread out of heaven to eat. Jesus therefore said unto them, Verily, verily, I say unto you, It was not Moses that gave you the bread out of heaven; but my Father giveth you the true bread out of 33 heaven. For the bread of God is that which cometh down out of heaven, and giveth life unto the world.
34 They said therefore unto him, Lord, evermore give 35 us this bread. Jesus said unto them, I am the bread of life: he that cometh to me shall not hunger, and

a Ex. 16:15; Num. 11:7; Neb. 9:15; 1 Cor. 10:3....b Ps. 78: 24, 25....c See ch. 4:15....d ver. 48:58....e ch. 4:14; 7:37.

ahship of Jesus. But it is clear, from the whole narrative, that they were carnal, wonder-loving, and ready to ask for miracle upon miracle. They demand a greater sign before they will believe Jesus (πιστεύσωμέν σοι), to say nothing of believing *in* him.

31. Our fathers did eat (*the*) manna in the desert; as it is written, He gave them bread from heaven to eat. The mention of food that does not perish, but endureth unto eternal life, reminds them of the manna that was given to their fathers, when under the leadership of Moses, and they at once intimate the propriety of a similar blessing from Jesus. If he will give them, by miracle, not barley bread and fishes only, but the food of angels, they may receive him as the Messiah, greater than Moses. (Comp. Ps. 78: 24).

32. With an earnest Verily, verily, showing the importance of his words, Jesus answers: **Moses gave you not that bread from heaven.** Better, Rev. Ver.: *It was not Moses that gave you the bread out of heaven.* As this is a response to the words just used by the people, **the bread from heaven** must refer to the manna. Christ, therefore, says: It is not Moses, as you suppose, who has given to you, the chosen people, the bread from heaven. For, though it was but a type of the true bread from heaven, it was of supernatural origin, and not a gift from Moses. **But my Father giveth (or, *is giving*) you the true bread from heaven.** By **the true bread from heaven**, is meant that which answers perfectly to the idea of bread from heaven.

33. For the bread of God is he (or, *that*) which cometh down from heaven, and giveth life unto the world. In other words, the genuine bread of God, the bread which he gives, is distinguished by these two qualities: (1) it is heaven-descending, coming down from God to men; and (2) it is life-giving, even to every man, whether Jew or Greek, who partakes of it. Hence, **the world of mankind are dead until they receive this food.** The Common Version, **He which cometh down from heaven,** etc., is grammatically possible, and is defended by Godet; but it does not agree with the next verse. The people certainly supposed that Jesus referred to some celestial food, not himself, as giving life to the world; for **then said they unto him:**

34. Lord, evermore give us this bread. This was said, probably, without bitterness or contempt. For the people, doubtless, assumed that bread from heaven must be a good, and, indeed, a miraculous good, though its character was not clearly apprehended by them. Certainly, they supposed it was something distinct from Christ himself.

35. From this point onward Jesus speaks of himself plainly and directly. His language is extremely bold and figurative, but for the most part quite intelligible. **I am the bread of life.** The pronoun I is emphatic; and by **the bread of life** is meant the bread which gives and sustains spiritual life—the life mentioned in ver. 33. For the Greek word meaning **life,** has the definite article before it. **He that cometh to me shall never** (or rather, *not*) **hunger, and he that believeth on me shall never thirst.** (Comp. 5: 40). Coming to Christ is here equivalent to believing in Christ. *He that cometh to me, he that believeth on me—i. e., any person who can be thus characterized,* shall have the satisfaction promised. Yet Schaff attempts to distinguish between the faith by which one comes to Christ, and subsequent faith. "*Coming* to Christ is faith indeed, yet not in repose as mere trust and confidence, or as a state of mind, but in active exercise and motion from the service of sin to the service of Christ. Comp. 37; 44, 45, 65;

36 But I said unto you, that ye also have seen me, and believe not.
37 All that the Father giveth me shall come to me; and him that cometh to me I will in no wise cast out.
38 For I came down from heaven, not to do mine own will, but the will of him that sent me.
39 And this is the Father's will which hath sent me, that of all which he hath given me I should lose nothing, but should raise it up again at the last day.

36 he that believeth on me shall never thirst. But I said unto you, that ye have seen me, and yet believe not.
37 All that the Father giveth me shall come unto me; and him that cometh to me I will in no wise cast out.
38 For I am come down from heaven, not to do mine own will, but the will of him that sent me.
39 And this is the will of him that sent me, that of all that which he hath given me I should lose nothing, but should raise it up at the last day.

a ver. 26, 64....b ver. 45....c Matt. 24: 24; ch. 10: 28, 29; 2 Tim. 2: 19; 1 John 2: 19....d Matt. 26: 39; ch. 5: 30....e ch. 1: 34....f ch. 10: 28; 17: 12; 18: 9.

7: 37, 38." Does not this describe one aspect of faith through all the conflict of this earthly life? Meyer, Godet, and others, agree with the interpretation given above. "Where is there an earthly food which quiets hunger and thirst forever? Only faith in Christ quiets all longings and satifies all real needs in life, in proportion as it increases and becomes pure in the longing, needy soul."—(*Lücke*.)[1]

36. **But I said unto you**—in the words of ver. 26—**that ye also have seen me** (better, *that ye have even seen me*)—*i. e.*, acting as the Messiah, doing wonders of grace, healing the sick, feeding the multitude—**and believe not.** A marvelous contrast! Clear evidence—and no faith! Compare the words of Christ to Thomas, 20: 29.

37. **All that the Father giveth me shall** (or, *will*) **come to me.** While Christ perceives that most of the people who encompass him in the synagogue are earthly, selfish, unbelieving, and ready to reject him as soon as he disappoints their hopes, he is sure that all whom the Father giveth him by the inward working of his grace, will, of their own accord come to him in faith, and receive him as their life. The holy purpose of God will not therefore be defeated by the sinful incredulity of men. **All** whom the Father gives will be the Son's at last. For the word **all** (πᾶν) expresses totality in the strongest manner, viz., as a complete whole, as one body of which no smallest part or most insignificant member will be wanting. Says Bengel of this word: "*Vocabula momentosissima. Words of the greatest importance.* The Father hath given to the Son the whole mass, as it were, that all whom he has given may be a unit; but, in execution of the divine plan, the Son evolves that whole, one by one."

And him that cometh to me I will in no wise cast out—*i. e.*, out of my kingdom, presence, fellowship; for all these are included. "Every one who *comes* is *welcome*." Previous sin does not prevent acceptance. "The negative expression," says Meyer, "is a loving *Litotes;* but I will receive him with a joyful mind, adds Nonnus."

38. By the words of this verse, and the two following, Jesus assigns the reason why he will thus welcome and save every one who believes. His own will is one with the Father's will, and it is the Father's will that he should receive, and keep, and save eternally all that the Father has given him. **For I came** (or, *am come*) **down from heaven, not to do mine own will, but the will of him that sent me.** Compare his very similar words to the Pharisees in Jerusalem (5: 30). Notice, also, how clearly the consciousness of Jesus connects his present with his original life. He is distinctly aware of having come down from (ἀπό) heaven to earth, when he entered into his theanthropic state, and of having a definite purpose to accomplish in doing this. That purpose, whatever else may be said of it, was to do the will of him by whom he was sent. But in what did that will consist? How could the Sent accomplish the will of the Sender? A partial, if not a full, answer to this question is given by the next words of Jesus himself.

39. **And this is the Father's will which hath sent me, that of all which he hath given me I should lose nothing, but should raise it up again at the last day.** The word **Father** is not sufficiently authenticated. We should, therefore, read, as in the Rev. Ver., *the will of him.* Note (1) that the word translated **all** is the same as in ver. 37, and its meaning unchanged. (2) That the verb *hath given* unites the past with the present. The act of giving is conceived of as in progress from eternity, or as abiding in its

---

[1] For the use of the aorist subjunctive with οὐ μή, in a future sense. See Winer § 60. 3. Buttmann's "Gram. of the N. T. Greek," p. 212.

Cʜ. VI.]   JOHN.   157

40 And this is the will of him that sent me, *that every one which seeth the Son, and believeth on him, may have everlasting life: and I will raise him up at the last day.
41 The Jews then murmured at him, because he said, I am the bread which came down from heaven.

40 For this is the will of my Father, that every one that beholdeth the Son, and believeth on him, should have eternal life; and ¹I will raise him up at the last day.
41 The Jews therefore murmured concerning him, because he said, I am the bread that came down out of

a ver. 27, 47, 54; ch. 3: 15, 16; 4: 14.——1 Or, *That I should raise him up.*

force and effect down to the present time. (3) That Jesus makes it the will of the Sender that no part or member of the whole given to him should be lost. Here is the preservation of the saints by the grace of God in Christ. Infinite grace! But he who makes it an excuse for spiritual sloth, has reason to fear that he has no part in Christ. (4) Whoever is kept by the Saviour, will, also, be raised up from the dead by him **at the last day.** There is, then, a last day, when Christ will return in glory to judge the world. Till that day, the bodies of the saints will sleep in the dust of the earth. (Comp. 5: 29). But then they will be raised incorruptible, glorious, and adapted to the wants of the spirit. Christ will thus effect the salvation of the whole man. "Note the recurrence of this blessed refrain in ver. 40, 44, 54, which *Scholten*, in spite of this solemn recurrence, considers a gloss."— *Meyer.*

40. Instead of, **And this is the will of him that sent me,** read, *For this is the will of my Father.* The best editors give the text we have translated, substituting *for* for **and,** and *my Father* for **him that sent me.** Hence, the statement of this verse is co-ordinate with that of ver. 39, showing why Jesus will save those who believe in him, as the preceding statement showed why he would save those given him. In both cases, it is the Father's will which is fulfilled by his action. **That every one which** (*who*) **seeth the Son.** The word rendered **seeth** (θεωρῶν) means *to look at, to behold,* implying a voluntary direction of the eye, or mind (or of both), to the object seen. Earnest consideration precedes faith. **And believeth on him.** Belief includes trust. (See the note on ver. 29). **May** (or, *should*) **have everlasting life.** 'That is, should have it even here, and not merely in some other and future state of being. Eternal life begins with trust in Christ, and culminates in the blessedness of union with him in the life to come. The soul and body will be glorified together, and forever. (Comp. John 17: 3). Notice, also, the refrain of the

last clause. There will be a resurrection of the body, as there is a resurrection of the spirit; the resurrection of the body will be **at the last day;** and this resurrection will be effected by "the Son," Jesus Christ our Lord. Jesus did not leave his hearers in doubt respecting his personal distinction from the Father, his absolute unity of will and action with the Father, or their dependence on himself for true life, here and hereafter. The miracle which he had wrought the day before, and the reference which the people had made to the manna, furnished an occasion for this most wonderful unfolding of his office and work; and he was prompt in making use of the occasion. Yet how few were prepared to welcome the truth! For the effect of his words on a part of his hearers is described in ver. 41, by which the Evangelist passes on to another dialogue.

41-44. Sᴇᴄᴏɴᴅ Dɪᴀʟᴏɢᴜᴇ ɪɴ ᴛʜᴇ Sʏɴᴀɢᴏɢᴜᴇ ᴀᴛ Cᴀᴘᴇʀɴᴀᴜᴍ.

41. The Jews then (or, *therefore*) **murmured at** (or, *concerning*) **him, because he said, I am the bread which came down from heaven.** By the Jews, may be meant the Pharisaic part of the multitude—those who were specially zealous for the law, and suspicious of innovation—people of note and influence, representing the Jewish spirit of the day. For the expression has this meaning in many passages of the Fourth Gospel. These Jews were now speaking with one another in a low voice, without intending their words for the ear of Christ. To bring the scene, as he recalls it, to the mind of his readers, the Evangelist employs the imperfect, or descriptive, tense of the verb. And from what they were saying, rather than from the import of the verb, to murmur, it appears that they were displeased with the utterances of Jesus, and, in particular, with his assertion: **I am the bread which came down from heaven.** For they understood him to claim, by this assertion, an origin different from that of other men.

42 And they said, "Is not this Jesus, the son of Joseph, whose father and mother we know? how is it then that he saith, I came down from heaven?
43 Jesus therefore answered and said unto them, Murmur not among yourselves.
44 ᵇNo man can come to me, except the Father which hath sent me draw him: and I will raise him up at the last day.

42 down out of heaven. And they said, Is not this Jesus, the son of Joseph, whose father and mother we know? how doth he now say, I am come down 43 out of heaven? Jesus answered and said unto them, 44 Murmur not among yourselves. No man can come to me except the Father that sent me draw him:

a Matt. 13:55; Mark 6:3; Luke 4:22....*b* Cant. 1:4; ver. 65.

42. And they said (or, *were saying*)—sotto voce—**Is not this Jesus, the son of Joseph, whose father and mother we know?** This language might have been used honestly by excited and captious men, though their knowledge depended on nothing but common report. They were in a state of mind to put the case strongly, and could not be expected to hesitate in claiming knowledge of that which they wished to believe, and which was affirmed without contradiction by the people of that region. It cannot, therefore, be safely inferred that they were personally acquainted with the reputed parents of Jesus, or that Joseph, as well as Mary, was still alive.—(Meyer). **How is it then that he saith, I came down from heaven?** Important early manuscripts read *now* (νῦν), instead of **then** (οὖν), and still more of them omit the pronoun (οὖτος), which is translated **he,** but should have been translated *this man.* The Revised Version may be followed safely: *How doth he now say, I am come down out of heaven? Now,* that is, after he has been so long known as the son of Joseph and Mary. How can he, at this late hour, make such a claim? The question is expressive of unbelief, rather than of perplexity. In his reply, Jesus recognizes this spirit of unbelief, though he does not refer to the point on which the Jews had fixed their attention. The words **from heaven** are a correct rendering of the Greek expression (ἀπὸ τοῦ οὐρανοῦ) found in ver. 38; but the Greek expression here employed (ἐκ τοῦ οὐρανοῦ) would be represented more exactly by the words *out of heaven.*

43, 44. The MSS. are about equally divided for and against the connective (οὖν) **then** of the Common Version. It should, probably, be omitted. But the meaning is nearly the same, whether the word is retained or rejected. **No man can come to me, except the Father which hath sent me** (rather, *who sent me*) **draw him.** The inability to come to Christ, which is here affirmed of every man, left to himself, is intrinsically moral, and may be identified with unwillingness or disinclination. The sinner cannot, because he will not. The very strength and freedom of his will are his weakness, because they keep him away from Christ. Hence, the Father's drawing is a condition of his willing to come. Says Augustine: "No one comes unless drawn... But some man may say: If one is drawn, he comes unwillingly... (Answer): If he comes unwillingly, he does not believe; and if he does not believe, he does not come. For we approach Christ, not by walking, but by believing; not by motion of body, but by choice of heart.... Do not think that you are drawn against your will; the soul is drawn, and by love." As to the mode of the Father's drawing, Calvin remarks that "it is not a violent drawing, which compels man by an external force, but an efficacious motion of the Holy Spirit, which renders unwilling persons willing." Meyer describes this drawing as "*an inward pressing and guiding to Christ, by the working of God's grace,*" and as "the whole divine influence by which the hearts of men are won to the Son." But he is careful to say that this divine influence "does not destroy human freedom"; while he concedes that "it appears to the consciousness of those who have been won as a *holy necessity,* which they have followed." Schaff seems to distinguish between this drawing of the Father and the work of the Holy Spirit in regeneration; for he says: "No change of mental organization, no new faculty is required, but a radical change of the heart and will. This is effected by the Holy Ghost; but the providential drawing of the Father prepares the way for it." Yet he declares that the latter "expresses the mighty moral power of the infinite love of the Father, who so orders and overrules the affairs of life, and so acts upon our hearts, that we give up at last our natural aversion to holiness, and willingly, cheerfully, and thankfully embrace the Saviour as the gift of gifts for our salvation." When this is done, is not the man already "a new creature," already born of the

45 *a* It is written in the prophets, And they shall be all taught of God. *b* Every man therefore that hath heard, and hath learned of the Father, cometh unto me.
46 *c* Not that any man hath seen the Father, *d* save he which is of God, he hath seen the Father.

45 and I will raise him up in the last day. It is written in the prophets, And they shall all be taught of God. Every one that hath heard from the Father, and hath
46 learned, cometh unto me. Not that any man hath seen the Father, save he that is from God, he hath

a Isa. 54: 13; Jer. 31: 34; Mic. 4: 2; Heb. 8: 10; 10: 16....*b* ver. 37....*c* ch. 1: 18; 5: 37....*d* Matt. 11: 27; Luke 10: 22; ch. 1: 18; 7: 29; 8: 19.

Spirit? It is better, then, to understand the Father's drawing in the most comprehensive sense, as embracing the influence of divine providence, religious truth, and the Holy Spirit, working on the heart; but especially and pre-eminently the influence of the Holy Spirit; for, doubtless, the attractive power of all these precedes and conditions the exercise of true faith. For the use of the word translated **draw** (ἑλκύω) in the New Testament, see John 12: 32; 21: 6, 11; Acts 16: 19; Jas. 2: 6. Notice, also, how Jesus affirms, in the last clause, that he will raise up, at the last day, the man who comes to him through the Father's drawing. The beginning is declared to be the beginning of a glorious end. He that is justified will also be glorified. (Rom. 8: 30). Inference: It is sometimes wise to preach the doctrine of the actual dependence of sinners on the grace of God to those who are still in sin, and especially to those who are conceited and self-sufficient in spiritual things.

45. It is written in the prophets. The perfect tense of the Greek verb is used because, while the act of writing was finished in the past, the result of the act is thought of as present in the written word. And this present result, existing in the sacred record, is doubtless the most prominent fact. Hence the Common Version, **It is written,** may be received as measurably satisfactory. **In the prophets,** probably because the passage is commended to the people as one that may be found in the collection of sacred writings called by them "the prophets" (comp. Matt. 5: 17; Luke 24: 44); yet, possibly because the substance of it may be found in *several* places (Isa. 54: 13; Jer. 31: 33; Joel 3: 1). **And they shall be all taught of God**—or, *And all will be taught of God.* (See Isa. 54: 13.) The original prophecy is descriptive of the true people of God in the Messianic day. It is translated by Alexander: "And all thy children disciples of Jehovah." He observes: "The promise is not one of occasional instruction, but of permanent connection with Jehovah as his followers, and partakers of his constant teaching. That the words are applicable to the highest teaching of which any rational being is susceptible, to wit: that of the Holy Spirit, making known the Father and the Son, we have our Saviour's own authority for stating." The original passage, as well as the present context, limits the word **all** to those who come in fact to Christ and are his genuine disciples. And the word **taught,** which is the principal and emphatic word, is broad enough to comprehend all experience of divine grace, whether that grace is imparted by the direct influence of the Spirit on the soul, or by the operation of divine truth. "The children of the Messianic time are the 'all,' from the fact that an inward, immediate divine illumination gives them faith in the word spoken by Christ."— (Lange). To what extent, if at all, the drawing of the Father, or the teaching of God, may be predicated of those who never come to Christ, cannot be learned from this passage. **Every man** (or, *one*) **that hath heard and hath learned of the Father, cometh unto me.** An expression which seems to prove that Christ has in mind none but his true followers, while, at the same time, it brings to view the reciprocal agency of man. For no one can **hear** and **learn** without action of his own. And the instant any man apprehends divine truth aright, he will believe in Christ, or, in other words, will come to him.

46. Not that any man (or, *one*) **hath seen the Father, save he which is of** (*i. e., from*) **God; he** (or, *this one*) **hath seen the Father.** The object of these words must be sought, not in the general negation, but in the exceptional affirmation. For the Jews were in no danger of supposing that every one who had heard and learned from God had seen the Father, but they were, perhaps, in great danger of imagining that Jesus could add little or nothing to the knowledge of men who had been "taught of God." He, therefore, reminds them of the world-wide distinc-

160 JOHN. [Ch. VI.

47 Verily, verily, I say unto you, *He that believeth on me hath everlasting life.
48 ᵇ I am that bread of life.
49 ᶜ Your fathers did eat manna in the wilderness, and are dead.
50 ᵈ This is the bread which cometh down from heaven, that a man may eat thereof, and not die.
51 I am the living bread ᵉ which came down from heaven: if any man eat of this bread, he shall live for ever: and ᶠ the bread that I will give is my flesh, which I will give for the life of the world.

47 seen the Father. Verily, verily, I say unto you, He that believeth hath eternal life. I am the bread of life. Your fathers did eat the manna in the wilderness, and they died. This is the bread that cometh down out of heaven, that a man may eat thereof, and not die. I am the living bread that came down out of heaven: if any man eat of this bread, he shall live for ever: yea and the bread that I will give is my flesh, for the life of the world.

a ch. 3: 16, 18, 36; ver. 40....*b* ver. 33, 35....*c* ver. 31....*d* ver. 51, 58....*e* ch. 3: 13...*f* Heb. 10: 5, 10.

tion between the knowledge of one who has never seen the Father, and of one who has been with him in the upper-world and has known him by direct and perfect vision. (Comp. 1: 18; 7: 29; Matt. 11: 27). Thus, by way of contrast, he brings back to their minds the amazing fact that he is truly and literally from heaven, *from with* the Father (comp. Note on 1: 14), while at the same time he cautions them against a gross, earthly interpretation of his claim to be "the bread which came down from heaven." (Ver. 42). He is bread to the soul rather than to the body—a source of light and life, of knowledge concerning God and communion with God, rather than of any material blessing. Hence the next verse.

47. Verily, verily, I say unto you: He that believeth on me hath everlasting (or, *eternal*) life. Notice (1) the absolute authority and earnestness given to the principal sentence by the prefatory words; (2) the supreme importance of faith in Christ, and (3) the assertion that the possession of faith presupposes or involves the new life. One does not truly believe in Christ *in order to* regeneration, but in and by regeneration; so that when he believes he has eternal life in possession, and not merely in prospect. As a matter of fact, the supreme drawing of the Father, by the regenerating influence of the Spirit, conditions the exercise of saving faith. (See ver. 44). It must be added, that some critical editors omit the words **on me,** after **believeth.** The words were probably a part of the original text; but if not, they appear to interpret correctly the meaning of Christ; for, according to the context, the faith which he refers to must be a faith looking towards and resting in himself.

48. I am that (or, *the*) **bread of life**—literally, *of the life—i. e.*, the life just named, *eternal life,* which is life in the highest sense —moral, religious, blessed, everlasting. This life, which is one of conscious peace, liberty, love, and fellowship with God, begins with trust in Christ, with a true and hearty reception of him as the Saviour of men. By thus receiving him the soul feeds on bread that is a source of spiritual joy and strength, on bread that gives, nourishes, and sustains, the highest and holiest activity. (Comp. ver. 33, 35). The genitive **of life** (τῆς ζωῆς) is that of attribute or quality.

49. The manna, though a gift from God, was but corruptible food for a corruptible body: your fathers ate of it in the wilderness and died. And this is what you extoll! How different from the bread of which I speak! See the Revised Version above for an exact rendering of this verse.

50. This is the bread which cometh down from heaven, that a man (or, *one*) **may eat thereof and not die.** And, therefore, utterly different in its design and effect from the manna. To eat of it is to be delivered from death; otherwise the very end for which it comes must fail. "This bread from heaven is life-giving and death-destroying"—(Hanna). "To be sure it does not do away with earthly death, but, as it secures *eternal* life, earthly death becomes only a transition to a life without death."—*Lücke*.

51. I am the living bread which came down from heaven. After examination, Lücke concludes that the word "living," in such expressions as "the living Father," "the living water," "the living bread," is meant to signify that which is spiritual, ever-during, imperishable, and heavenly, in contrast with that which is earthly, perishable, and unsubstantial." But we do not think he has touched the precise thought of the Saviour. By liv**ing bread,** the Lord here means bread that has life in itself (comp. 5: 26), and may, therefore, impart life. For only the living can be an original source of life. A being cannot give what it does not possess. It may

52 The Jews therefore strove among themselves, saying, How can this man give us his flesh to eat? 53 Then Jesus said unto them, Verily, verily, I say unto you, Except ye eat the flesh of the Son of man, and drink his blood, ye have no life in you.

52 The Jews therefore strove one with another, saying, How can this man give us his flesh to eat? Jesus therefore said unto them, Verily, verily, I say unto you, Except ye eat the flesh of the Son of man and

a ch. 7: 43; 9: 16; 10: 19....*b* ch. 3: 9....*c* Matt. 26: 26, 28.

also be observed that Jesus refers to his coming down from heaven as a definite event of the past, meaning, no doubt, his incarnation. **If any man (or, one) eat of this bread, he shall live forever.** For the principle of true life is in it, and, therefore, by receiving it, he will pass from a state of spiritual death into a state of spiritual life. And this life-state, or blessed communion with God in Christ, will have no end. "Observe the threefold progress: (1) 'the bread of life'(ver. 48), and the 'living bread' (ver. 51); (2) the general 'is coming down' (ver. 50), and the historical concrete, 'came down' (ver. 51); (3) the negative 'may not die' (ver. 50), and the positive 'shall live forever' (ver. 51)."—(Meyer). **And the bread,** etc. The last part of the verse is given more clearly by the Revised Version: *Yea, and the bread which I will give is my flesh, for the life of the world.* The paragraph beginning with this clause, and ending with ver. 58, is one of the most difficult in the whole Gospel, partly on account of its connection with the foregoing, partly on account of the figurative expression of the thoughts, and partly on account of the relationship of these thoughts to the principal ideas symbolized by the Lord's Supper. What, then, are we to understand by the words **my flesh?** That they might have been used by the Saviour in certain connections to denote his human nature and manifestation, without any reference to his death, is freely conceded. (See 1: 14; 17: 2; Matt. 24: 22; Rom. 1: 3; 9: 5). But there are two insuperable objections to this interpretation of the words here: (1) The distinction which is made between flesh and blood in ver. 53, a distinction which evidently presupposes a separation of the flesh and blood by death; and (2) the connected words **will give—for the life of the world,** for the *usus loquendi* of the writers of the New Testament shows that this phraseology refers to the atoning death of Christ. (See Matt. 20: 28; Luke 22: 19; 1 Cor. 13: 3; Gal. 1: 4; 2: 20; Eph. 5: 2, 25; 1 Tim. 2: 6.) It is, therefore, evident that Jesus speaks of giving up his human

nature to death for the life of the world. (Comp. Eph. 2: 15; Col. 1: 22; Heb. 10: 20; 1 Pet. 2: 24; 4: 1). Hence, the lesson of this clause is, that the true life of man depends on faith in the Saviour *crucified,* on spiritual union with "*the Lamb* of God that taketh away the sin of the world." (1: 29). Such a truth was not likely to be welcomed by the self-righteous hearers of Jesus.[1]

52-59. HENCE, THE THIRD CONVERSATION.

52. The Jews therefore strove among themselves (or, *were debating with one another*), **saying, How can this man give us his** (or, *the*) **flesh to eat?** Namely, *the flesh* which he speaks of—his own flesh? Lücke remarks that the circumstance of the Jews contending with one another how Jesus could give them his flesh to eat, shows that his language was not altogether unintelligible. It doubtless perplexed them by suggesting that his death was in some way indispensable to their highest life; a view utterly foreign to their Messianic aspirations.

53. Except ye eat the flesh of the Son of man, and drink his blood, ye have no life in you. Instead of undertaking to remove their difficulty by explaining the figurative language which he had used, Jesus solemnly repeats it, with a startling addition. Startling, if they understood his language to be literal; but only bold and impressive if they understood it to be figurative. He may have taken this course because he saw that their spirit was not serious but captious, or because he saw that no explanation was really needed. For the added statement, **and drink his blood,** must have strongly tended to convince "the Jews" that his language was figurative. While it presupposes, even more certainly than his previous declaration, that his death was the condition of life to men, it is a warning against a literal

[1] With the critical editors, Lach., Tisch., Treg., Westcott, and Hort., we omit ἣν ἐγὼ δώσω, **which I will give,** after σάρξ μου, **my flesh.**

L

54 ᵃWhoso eateth my flesh, and drinketh my blood, hath eternal life: and I will raise him up at the last day.
55 For my flesh is meat indeed, and my blood is drink indeed.
56 He that eateth my flesh, and drinketh my blood, ᵇdwelleth in me, and I in him.
57 As the living Father hath sent me, and I live by the Father; so he that eateth me, even he shall live by me.

54 drink his blood, ye have not life in yourselves. He that eateth my flesh and drinketh my blood hath
55 eternal life; and I will raise him up at the last day. For my flesh is ¹ meat indeed, and my blood is ² drink
56 indeed. He that eateth my flesh and drinketh my
57 blood abideth in me, and I in him. As the living Father sent me, and I live because of the Father; so he that eateth me, he also shall live because of

a ver. 27, 40, 63; ch. 4: 14....*b* 1 John 3: 24; 4: 13, 16.——Gr. *true meat*....² Gr. *true drink*.

interpretation of the words employed. For the Jews were sometimes required to eat the flesh of animals slain for sacrifice, but they were never allowed to drink their blood. Much less, then, could they imagine that Jesus meant to enjoin a literal eating of his own human flesh, and a literal drinking of his own blood. The very boldness of Christ's language admonished them not to interpret it literally. If eating his flesh would naturally suggest faith in him as one who was to die for the life of the world, still more must drinking his blood suggest the same thing. For the life was conceived to be in the blood, and shed blood was the well-known emblem of life surrendered in death. On the whole, then, it is probable that the Jews were better able to *understand*, than they were to *receive*, the teaching of Jesus.

54. Whoso (or, *he that*) eateth my flesh and drinketh my blood,¹ hath eternal life. Having said in ver. 53 that there is no true life for man without doing this, he now says that eternal life is the present possession of him who does this. No man can be saved in any other way; no man can be lost who takes this way. These statements complement each other and cover the whole ground. And I will raise him up at the last day. The life which begins by a renewal of the spirit shall be perfected by a renewal of the body, so that the whole man will be saved and glorified. (Compare ver. 40, 44).

55. For my flesh is meat indeed (better, *is true food*), and my blood is drink indeed (or, *true drink*).

The reading (ἀληθής) *true*, instead of (ἀληθῶς) *truly* or *indeed*, is given by the best editors, and is doubtless correct. *True food* is food which performs what it promises. It is, according to Meyer, "the opposite of merely seeming or nominal food, hence *real* food." And for this reason (γάρ), he that eats the same, etc., hath eternal life. Of course it is food for the *inner* man, not for the body; the latter will die, but be raised in glory at the last day.

56. He that eateth my flesh and drinketh my blood dwelleth (or, *abideth*) in me, and I in him. Meyer appeals to the language of this verse as proof that "the eating and drinking in question are *uninterrupted*," continuous, and infers from this, "that Jesus could not have had in mind the Holy Supper." The last part of the verse, abideth in me and I in him, manifestly refers to spiritual fellowship or intercommunion (Comp. 15: 4 sq.; 17: 23; 1 John 3: 24; 4: 16), and affords, therefore, clear evidence that the terms eateth and drinketh are used figuratively, to denote the exercise of faith; while the terms flesh and blood, refer to Christ as the "propitiation" (ἱλασμός) for the sins of mankind (1 John 2: 2).

57. As the living Father hath sent me, and I live by (rather, *because of*) the Father; so he that eateth me, even he shall live by (or, *because of*) me. (1) Jesus here speaks of himself as the Son of man, the Messiah, and not as the Word that was with God. (1:1). (2) The life which he ascribes to the Father, to himself, and to the believer, is not mere conscious existence, but life in the very highest sense of the word, the true and blessed life of a moral being. (3) His own life, in this highest sense, is represented as due to perfect fellowship with the Father who sent him, and who shows him all that he himself doeth (5: 19 sq.). "It is because of the holy and ever blessed Father," says Christ, "that I am always joyful in my work, and certain that it cannot fail." (4) A similar life will be the portion of every one who receives Christ into his heart by true faith. According to the measure of his faith, will Christ be to him what the Father is to Christ—a ground of con-

¹ "The tense (ὁ τρώγων) (whoso eateth) or, contrast ver. 45 (ὁ ἀκούσας) (*he that hath heard*), marks an action which must be continuous and not completed once for all."—(*Westcott.*)

JOHN. [Сн. VI.] 163

58 *This is that bread which came down from heaven: not as your fathers did eat manna, and are dead: he that eateth of this bread shall live for ever.
59 These things said he in the synagogue, as he taught in Capernaum.
60 *Many therefore of his disciples, when they had heard *this*, said, This is a hard saying; who can hear it?
61 When Jesus knew in himself that his disciples murmured at it, he said unto them, Doth this offend you?

58 me. This is the bread that came down out of heaven; not as the fathers did eat, and died; he that eateth this bread shall live for ever. These things said he in ¹the synagogue, as he taught in Capernaum.
60 Many therefore of his disciples, when they heard *this*, said, This is a hard saying; who can hear ²it?
61 But Jesus knowing in himself that his disciples murmured at this, said unto them, Doth this cause

a ver. 49, 50, 51....*b* Matt. 11 : 6; ver. 66.——1 Or, *a synagogue*....2 Or, *him*.

fidence, a source of light, a fountain of joy. These are the principal points. But Meyer has two remarks worthy of note: "(*a*) that (ὁ τρώγων με) 'he that eateth me,' expresses a *constant, uninterrupted* relation, not one that comes in from time to time, as at the Lord's Supper"; and (*b*) that, "if Jesus had been thinking of the Holy Supper, he would not have said, '*he that eateth me*,' but, rather, '*he that eateth my flesh and drinketh my blood.*'"

58. Not as your fathers did eat manna, and are dead. This is a final re-affirmation of what Jesus has been saying in all this wonderful conversation, or series of discourses. But, according to the best critics, the words translated **your** (ὑμῶν) and **manna** (τὸ μάννα) do not belong to the original text, which reads: *Not as the Fathers ate and died.* This briefer form is no less pertinent and forcible, as a summary, than the fuller statement of the received text. From the last clause, we learn that the multitude from the other side of the lake found Jesus in a synagogue of Capernaum, and that he said these things while teaching in that place. Some have supposed that, not only the site of Capernaum, at Tell Hum, but even the synagogue where Jesus taught, have been discovered. But the evidence for neither of these identifications is entirely satisfactory.

Had the language of Christ at this time any reference to the Holy Supper which he instituted later? There is no evidence that it had, no hint that he expected to embody this teaching in a sacred rite, no expression at all suggestive of the idea that the eating and drinking here pronounced indispensable to salvation were to be performed sacramentally. Everything shows that his language was simply figurative, requiring an acceptance of himself, or his flesh and blood, in order to eternal life, but saying nothing of an ordinance by which this appropriation was to be accomplished, or, rather, represented. Yet the

Christian truths taught by this discourse, and by the Holy Supper, are essentially the same. In neither case, does Jesus say anything of an appropriation of his glorified body. That will not consist of flesh and blood. In both instances, he refers to his natural humanity subjected to natural death.

60. Many therefore of his disciples, when they (omit **had**) **heard this, said.** The word **disciples** is here applied, not to "the twelve" (ver. 67), but to persons less closely connected with Jesus, though believing him to be the Messiah. Such persons must have been quite numerous at this time in Capernaum, and many of them were, doubtless, in the synagogue. **This is a hard saying; who can hear it?** This word **hard**, or *rough* (σκληρός), is here used in an ethical sense, to denote the disagreeable impression which the last part of Christ's discourse had made on the minds of these disciples. "Who can listen to it?" In other words: "This doctrine is so offensive that no one can be expected to hearken to it or receive it." But in what did the offensiveness of Christ's words consist? Not in this, that it was supposed to require a literal eating of his flesh and drinking of his blood in order to eternal life (an eating and drinking sometimes called Capernaitic, because these disciples were of Capernaum and were thought to have understood Christ's language to be literal), for there is no good reason to charge them with so gross a misconception; but rather in this, that it presupposed the death of Christ, and represented the Messiah as the Lamb of God. This was utterly distasteful to the disciples, as well as to the Jews. (Comp. Matt. 16: 21, sq.: John 12: 34; 1 Cor. 1: 23; Gal. 5; 11). We need not go beyond this for the cause of their dissatisfaction with the saying of Jesus.

61. When Jesus knew in himself— *i. e.*, without hearing the words which these

62 *What* and if ye shall see the Son of man ascend up where he was before?
63 *It* is the Spirit that quickeneth; the flesh profiteth nothing: the words that I speak unto you, *they* are spirit, and *they* are life.

62 you to stumble? *What* then if ye should behold the 63 Son of man ascending where he was before? It is the spirit that quickeneth; the flesh profiteth nothing: the words that I have spoken unto you are

a Mark 16:19; ch. 3:13; Acts 1:9; Eph. 4:8....b 2 Cor. 3:6.

offended disciples were speaking with bated breath, and without being informed by any one of their dissatisfaction. The words indicate perfect, independent, superhuman knowledge. That his **disciples murmured** (or, *were murmuring*) at it (or, *this*), he said unto them: **Doth this offend you?**—*i. e.*, "Is this a rock of offence over which you are beginning to stumble and fall? Do my words disappoint your hopes and shake your confidence in me?"
62. What and if, etc. This may be translated: *If then ye should behold the Son of man ascending up where he was before?* The thought is not fully expressed, and therefore many prefix the word **what.** "What then if ye should behold" this?—*i. e.*, What would be the effect on your minds, if you should see this, and not merely be told of it? The event named was one which would disappoint all their expectations in regard to the Christ and his reign. For they were longing and praying for a Messianic kingdom on the earth, with Jerusalem for its capital, and the children of Israel for its princes and priests. Should Jesus return to heaven, he could not be the king and conqueror whom they looked for as the Messiah.
63. It is the Spirit that quickeneth (or, *maketh alive*); **the flesh profiteth nothing. What is meant by the Spirit?** Certainly not the human spirit of Jesus; for in no other passage is such virtue ascribed to his human spirit; and had this been meant he would doubtless have said, "My spirit." But the expression may refer to spirit in distinction from flesh; that is, it may denote the spirit in a generic sense, wherever it may exist, in connection with flesh. It is that which makes alive, and not the flesh—the implication being that this grand truth is applicable to Christ as the source of eternal life. Yet it is, perhaps, more probable that Jesus means the Holy Spirit, which had been, given him without measure (3:34). For it is this Spirit who is the author of the new and eternal life in man (3:6; Rom. 8:2; 2 Cor. 3:6). Strangely

enough, Alford seems to suppose that the word flesh cannot here refer to the flesh of Christ, on account of ver. 51. But he maintains in his note on that verse, the view, that "in his *resurrection form only* can his flesh be eaten, and be living food for the living man," that "his flesh is the glorified substance of his resurrection body, now at the right hand of God"—a view quite foreign to the obvious meaning of the Saviour's words. **The words that I speak** (or, *have spoken*) **unto you, they are spirit and they are life.** Jesus here affirms that his language has been figurative, since his flesh and his blood—the words which serve as a stumbling block to his disciples—mean spirit and mean life. (Comp. Matt. 26:26, 27; Mark 14:22, 24; 1 Cor. 11:24, 25). To receive his Spirit, and thus to receive spiritual life, is to eat his flesh and drink his blood. For that Spirit is given in consequence of the Saviour's death, and any one who is regenerated by the Spirit accepts the death of Christ as the foundation and reason for all the grace that has been imparted to him. He believes in Christ through the life-giving action of the Spirit in his soul; and he continues a believer because the Spirit abides in him. Says Prof. Stuart ("Bib. Sac." I. p. 113): "When the Son of man has ascended up to heaven, where he was before his incarnation, and his *bodily* presence is wholly withdrawn from you, then it will be very plain, that my words are not to have a literal sense given to them.... When I speak of *eating my flesh and drinking my blood*, I mean that a spiritual communion with me, and a spiritual and life-giving participation of the graces which I bestow, are absolutely necessary to future and eternal happiness."
Many interpreters look upon Jesus as declaring by this clause that his words are to be taken in a spiritual sense. But it is doubtful whether the noun **spirit** is ever used by the sacred writers in that way: and, if it is, how can the words **and are life**, be made to agree with this view? For to say that his words must be understood in a living sense, is

64 But ᵃ there are some of you that believe not. For
ᵇ Jesus knew from the beginning who they were that
believed not, and who should betray him.
65 And he said, Therefore ᶜ said I unto you, that no
man can come unto me, except it were given unto him
of my Father.
66 ᵈ From that *time* many of his disciples went back,
and walked no more with him.
67 Then said Jesus unto the twelve, Will ye also go
away?

64 spirit, and are life. But there are some of you that
believe not. For Jesus knew from the beginning
who they were that believed not, and who it was
65 that should betray him. And he said, For this cause
have I said unto you, that no man can come unto
me, except it be given unto him of the Father.
66 Upon this many of his disciples went back, and
67 walked no more with him. Jesus said therefore

a ver. 36....*b* ch. 2: 24, 25; 13: 11....*c* ver. 44, 45....*d* ver. 60.

scarcely intelligible. Others look upon Christ as affirming "the power of his words to produce life and spirit in man"—(Hengstenberg), or, "to lead man into another world and nature, to give him another heart and mind"—(Luther), or, "to bear and reveal the Divine Spirit which is in him and the Messianic life which is originated by him"—(Meyer). But this view appears to lose sight of the preceding discourse, and especially of the first part of this verse. *Have spoken* is required by the early copies, instead of **speak** in the common text.

64. But there are some of you that believe not. By this remark he reminds his now wavering and dissatisfied followers that, not his teaching, but their own spirit, is wrong. With all their profession of loyalty to him as the Messiah, with all their admiration of his character and wonder at his miracles, they were destitute of true faith in him; were strangers to the self-forgetful devotion and deep religious life which alone could bind them to him when his words crossed their hopes of a temporal kingdom. **For Jesus knew from the beginning who they were that believed not, and who should betray him.** The expression **from the beginning** must always be interpreted in harmony with the context, and generally by the aid of that context. Here it may signify from the commencement of the Lord's ministry (Meyer), or from the time when these professed disciples began to follow him (De Wette). In either case, the Evangelist intends to ascribe to him divine knowledge; in the former case, a knowledge which foresaw the action of his transient followers, even before they met him, or listened to his teachings; and, in the latter, a knowledge which foresaw that action from the hour when they severally met him first. We regard the latter view as preferable to the former.

65. Therefore (or, *for this cause*), viz.: because he knew the unbelief of many whom he was now specially addressing. They were outwardly his disciples, they followed him from place to place, and professed to honor him as the Messiah, but they had never been drawn to him by the Father. **Said I unto you** (see ver. 37, 44), **that no man can come unto me, except it were** (or, *be*) **given unto him of my Father.** These disciples had attached themselves to Jesus without any deep sense of spiritual need. The grace of God had not prepared their hearts to receive his teaching. This is the solemn truth which Jesus now presses upon their attention. And there are times when no other truth is so pertinent as this. There are men, self-righteous and self-confident, who need to be reminded that without the grace of God they will surely perish.

66. From that time (rather, *for this reason*) **many of his disciples**—so called, because they had professed to be such—**went back, and walked no more with him.** (Comp. 1 John 2: 19). They had attended him from time to time, as he went about the country, teaching and preaching and healing the sick; but now they forsook him, and went back each one to his former state and business. He was not the Messiah of their expectations. As the light became clearer, they turned from it, because they loved darkness rather than light.

67. Then said Jesus (better: *Jesus therefore said*) **unto the twelve, Will ye also go away?** By the form of his question, the Saviour intimates his expectation of a negative answer. This fact cannot, however, be represented in the English, though it is fairly suggested by an idiom modeled after the Greek, and uttered as a question, viz.: "*Ye* will not go away"? Observe that the pronoun *ye* is emphatic, in contrast with the disciples who had just forsaken him. Observe, also, that the Evangelist speaks of **the twelve** for the first time in this place, as if they were a well-

68 Then Simon Peter answered him, Lord, to whom shall we go? thou hast *the words of eternal life.
69 ᵇAnd we believe and are sure that thou art that Christ, the Son of the living God.
70 Jesus answered them, ᶜHave not I chosen you twelve, ᵈand one of you is a devil?
71 He spake of Judas Iscariot *the son* of Simon: for he it was that should betray him, being one of the twelve.

68 unto the twelve, Would ye also go away? Simon Peter answered him, Lord, to whom shall we go? 69 thou ¹hast the words of eternal life. And we have believed and know that thou art the Holy One of 70 God. Jesus answered them, Did not I choose you 71 the twelve, and one of you is a devil? Now he spake of Judas, *the son* of Simon Iscariot, for he it was that should betray him, *being* one of the twelve.

---

a Acts 5: 20....*b* Matt. 16: 16; Mark 8: 29; Luke 9: 20; ch. 1: 40; 11: 27....*c* Luke 6: 13....*d* ch. 13: 27.——1 Or, *hast words.*

---

known company of disciples, though he has nowhere referred to their being called. Thus he assumes a knowledge of many things on the part of his readers.

68, 69. Peter, ever prompt and decided, answers for the group: **Lord, to whom shall we go** (*away*)? **Thou hast the words of eternal life.** (There is no article before **words** in the original text.) **And we believe and are sure that thou art that Christ,** etc. (Better: *And we have believed and know that thou art the Holy One of God*). This presents an exact version of Peter's language, according to the earliest copies of the Gospel and the best textual critics. The received text appears to have been conformed to the words of Peter on another occasion. (Matt. 16: 16). Possibly some superstitious transcriber shrank from representing Peter as bearing testimony to Christ in the very words employed by demons. (See Mark 1: 24; Luke 4: 34). The response of Peter distinctly assumes: (1) That the twelve feel their need of a Saviour; (2) that no Saviour but Christ is known to them; and (3) that he is an adequate Saviour, both because his words reveal the way to eternal life, and because he himself is *the Holy One of God.* It may be well to observe once more the leading part which this Evangelist assigns to Peter, agreeing, in this respect, with the earlier Evangelists.

70. Very grateful to the heart of Jesus at that moment must have been the answer of Peter. It was a beam of sunlight breaking through the cloud of unbelief, which seemed to be settling down on the minds of the people. Doubtless, it was welcomed with deep joy. Yet not without pain. For in that favored group there was one whose soul was not represented by the loyal response of Peter. And as the eye of Christ looked into that soul, and perceived its hidden working, his lips uttered the startling sentence: **Have not I chosen you twelve, and one of you is a devil?** In the original, particular stress falls on the pronoun **I,** of the first clause, and on the words **of you,** in the second. **I,** and no one else, selected you, and yet of you, who were thus selected, one is a devil. Jesus did not point out the fiend at this time; it was enough to remind them, by a single terrific word, that they were not, all of them, what they professed to be. Whether Judas had any suspicion that he was intended by the Lord, can only be conjectured.

According to ver. 64, Jesus must have known, when he selected Judas to be one of the twelve, that he was an unbeliever; that he would remain so, in spite of the best influences, and that he would at last deliver up his Master to his foes. But many interpreters feel constrained to reject this view, as incompatible with moral perfection in Christ. (Compare Ullmann's classic work on "The Sinlessness of Jesus," p. 187 sq., and Meyer's 1. Remark on this verse). Yet it is not easy to see how the Saviour's treatment of Judas was either unjust to him or to any other man. If the sight of perfect goodness only served to harden his heart, the same is true of all who reject the gospel. How could it be wrong for Jesus to make use of the voluntary service of a traitor in a sphere of action which gave the traitor every opportunity to repent, even though Christ foresaw that he would not repent?

71. He spake of Judas Iscariot, etc. Better: *Now* (or. *but) he spoke of Judas, the son of Simon Iscariot*—**for he it was that should** (or. *was about to*) **betray him, being one of the twelve.** The critical editors connect the word Iscariot with Simon, and not with Judas. It is probably an adjective, like the word Nazarene, formed from the name of the place to which Judas and his father Simon belonged. The name of the town appears to have been Kerioth. It was probably situated in Juden. (Josh. 15: 25). But Westcott remarks that the common rendering of Josh. 15: 25 ap-

Ch. VII.] JOHN. 167

CHAPTER VII.

AFTER these things Jesus walked in Galilee: for he would not walk in Jewry, *a because the Jews sought to kill him.
2 *b Now the Jews' feast of tabernacles was at hand.

1 AND after these things Jesus walked in Galilee: for he would not walk in Judea, because the Jews sought 2 to kill him. Now the feast of the Jews, the feast of

a ch. 5: 16, 18....*b* Lev. 23: 34.

pears to be incorrect, for Kerioth ought to be joined with Hezron (Kerioth-Hezron); and adds: "May not the town be identified with the Kerioth of Moab, mentioned in Jer. 48: 24?"

Ch. 7 : 1-13. VISIT TO THE FEAST OF TABERNACLES, Oct. 11-18. A. D. 29.
The Evangelist now refers in passing (ver. 1) to a period of about six and a half months, from the Passover (6:4) to the Feast of Tabernacles (7:2), which Jesus spent in Northern Palestine, but without relating any of the events belonging to that period, perhaps because they had been described in the earlier Gospels.

1. And after these things—namely, the things recorded in chapter sixth. **Jesus walked in Galilee.** The word which is translated **walked**, means, literally, *was walking about*, and may have been chosen in preference to any other, because Jesus spent much of his time in itinerant preaching. **In Galilee**, points out the region where most of his time was passed; but we need not infer from it that he did not visit, meanwhile, the coasts of Tyre and Sidon, and the region called Decapolis.

The events which Robinson assigns to this period of Christ's ministry, are these: Christ's reply to the criticisms of the Scribes and Pharisees from Jerusalem on his disciples for eating with unwashen hands (Matt. 15: 1-20; Mark 7: 1-23); his healing the daughter of a Syrophenician woman (Matt. 15: 21-28; Mark 7: 24-30); his healing a deaf and dumb man, with others, (Matt. 15: 29-31; Mark 7: 31-37); his feeding the four thousand (Matt. 15: 32-38; Mark 8: 1-9); his answer to the Pharisees who required a sign (Matt. 16: 1-4; Mark 8: 11, 12); his caution to his disciples to beware of the leaven of the Pharisees, etc. (Matt. 16: 5-12; Mark 8: 14-21); his healing a blind man (Mark 8: 22-26); the confession of Peter and the other disciples, that he was the Christ, the Son of God (Matt. 16: 13-20; Mark 8: 27-30; Luke 9: 18-21) ; his prediction of his own death and resurrection, with the trials of his disciples (Matt. 16: 21-28; Mark 8: 31-38; Luke 9: 22-27); his transfiguration and subsequent discourse with three disciples (Matt. 17: 1-13; Mark 9: 2-13; Luke 9: 28-36); his healing of a lunatic boy (Matt. 17: 14-21; Mark 9: 14-29; Luke 9: 37-43); his renewed prediction of his own death and resurrection (Matt. 17: 22-23; Mark 9: 30-32; Luke 9: 43-45); his provision for the temple tax by miracle (Matt. 17: 24-27; Mark 9: 33); the contention of his disciples as to who should be greatest (Matt. 18: 1-35; Mark 9: 33-50; Luke 9: 46-50); the seventy instructed and sent out (Luke 10: 1-16). But Andrews, in his "Life of Our Lord," assigns the sending out of the seventy to a later period in the ministry of Jesus, and offers strong reasons for this. (See "Life of Our Lord," p. 355 sq.). **For he would not walk in Jewry:** literally, *he did not wish* (or, *will*) *to walk in Judea*, that is, to do the work of his ministry there, by going about from place to place and preaching the gospel. **Because the Jews sought** (or, *were seeking*) **to kill him.** By the Jews are meant the representative men of the nation, especially members of the Sanhedrin. Most of them lived in Judea, and of these a considerable part dwelt in Jerusalem. Their attempt to kill Jesus has been referred to in 5: 18. It was not the effect of sudden and passing hatred, but of deep-seated and enduring hostility, which threatened his life, should he sojourn for any length of time in Judea. So he wisely remained in Galilee, as his earthly ministry was not yet accomplished.

2. Now the Jews' feast of tabernacles was at hand. For an account of this festival, see Lev. 23: 34-36, 39-43; and Deut. 16: 13-15. It was one of the three great festivals at which all the males in Israel were required to appear before God at Jerusalem. (Deut. 16: 16). It began on the fifteenth day of the seventh month, or Tisri, answering to our October, and was celebrated a full week. It was followed, on the eighth day, by a holy convocation. "Ye shall dwell in booths seven days; all that are Israelites born shall dwell in

3 *His brethren therefore said unto him, Depart hence, and go into Judea, that thy disciples also may see the works that thou doest.
4 For *there is* no man *that* doeth any thing in secret, and he himself seeketh to be known openly. If thou do these things, shew thyself to the world.
5 For *b* neither did his brethren believe in him.

3 tabernacles, was at hand. His brethren therefore said unto him. Depart hence, and go into Judæa, that thy disciples also may behold thy works which thou 4 doest. For no man doeth anything in secret, [1] and himself seeketh to be known openly. If thou doest 5 these things, manifest thyself to the world. For

---

a Matt. 12: 46; Mark 3: 31; Acts 1: 14....*b* Mark 3: 21.——1 Some ancient authorities read, *and seeketh it to b known openly.*

---

booths: that your generations may know that I made the children of Israel to dwell in booths, when I brought them out of the land of Egypt." (Lev. 23: 42, 43). It was also called "the feast of ingathering" (Ex. 23: 16); and was a season of joy, commemorating the deliverance of the people from bondage by their journey through the wilderness, and the bringing in of the fruits of the field at the end of the year. Special sacrifices were offered, and parts of the law were publicly read. (Deut. 31: 10 sq.; Neh. 8: 18; Joseph. "Ant." 4, 8, 12). Josephus calls it "a holiest and greatest feast." (8, 4, 1).

3. **His brethren** (*brothers*) **therefore said unto him.** The word *therefore* shows that the proximity of the Feast of Tabernacles was the occasion of his brothers' words. According to the best supported text of Matt. 13: 55, the names of his four brothers were "James and Joseph and Simon and Judas." They were probably either sons of Joseph and Mary, and so younger brothers of Jesus, or sons of Joseph by a former marriage. But the view that they were sons of Joseph and Mary seems to have been the earliest opinion, and to deserve the preference. (See Note on 2: 12). **Depart hence, and go into Judea, that thy disciples also may see the works that thou doest** (or, *may behold thy works which thou doest.*—Rev. Ver.). Nearly all the disciples of Jesus might be expected to visit Jerusalem at this feast. Many of them resided in Judea, and even those of Northern Palestine would be likely to keep the approaching festival in the holy city. Hence, the brothers, who were doubtless expecting that the Messiah would be a great temporal prince, seem to have felt that it was high time for his mighty works to be wrought in the presence of the whole body of his adherents, and for his Messiahship, if genuine, to be proclaimed in the capital of the nation. Their language has sometimes been thought to betoken envy, or ambition—*i. e.*, a wish to have him fall into the hands of his enemies, or a desire to share in his advancement; but neither of these feelings is expressed, or necessarily implied. They evidently desired to have the question as to what he was finally settled; but their words do not reveal the particular motives which led them to speak as they did. Yet it is to be freely admitted that they had failed to appreciate the elevation of his character, and to yield to the evidence of his Messiahship.

4. **For no man doeth** (omit **there is** and **that**) **any thing in secret, and he himself seeketh to be known openly.** Thus the brothers justify their counsel, assuming that Jesus is seeking to be known and received by the whole people, while his conduct is inconsistent with such an aim. The more concealed one's works, the less known will he be; the more public his works, the more known will he himself be. They now proceed to apply this principle to Jesus. **If thou do** (or, *doest*) **these things, shew** (or, *manifest*) **thyself to the world.** By the former clause, the brothers may not have intended to express any actual doubt in respect to his doing the works referred to; they may have used the hypothetical form simply as a premise to the inference expressed in the latter clause. Thus, "the works which thou art doing from time to time, in comparative secrecy, ought to be performed in the most public manner possible, or before the world."

5. **For neither did his brethren believe in him** (or, more exactly, *For even his brothers were not believing in him*). Notice (1) that in this verse the Evangelist represents *the brothers* as being in a state of unbelief. He does not refer to a momentary act, but to a continuous state. (2) That in verse 3, the brothers speak of *thy disciples*, as though they did not regard themselves as belonging to that class of the people. (3) That Jesus plainly separates them from himself in verse 6. Bearing in mind these facts, we cannot suppose that three out of the four were of the twelve. (See 6: 68 sq.). The meaning is, that

6 Then Jesus said unto them, *My time is not yet come: but your time is always ready.
7 ᵇThe world cannot hate you; but me it hateth, ᶜ because I testify of it, that the works thereof are evil.
8 Go ye up unto this feast: I go not up yet unto this feast; ᵈ for my time is not yet full come.

6 even his brethren did not believe on him. Jesus therefore saith unto them, My time is not yet come;
7 but your time is alway ready. The world cannot hate you; but me it hateth, because I testify of it,
8 that its works are evil. Go ye up unto the feast; I go not up¹ unto this feast; because my time is not

a ch. 2:4; 8:20....*b* ch. 15:19....*c* ch. 3:19....*d* ch. 8:20; ver. 6.—1 Many ancient authorities add, *yet.*

---

at this time the brothers of Jesus were without faith in him as the Messiah. They had not, perhaps, definitely rejected his claims; they were *unbelievers*, rather than *disbelievers*. And the Scriptures afford no evidence of a thorough change in their conviction until after his resurrection. To one of them, he appeared in his raised body (1 Cor. 15:7), and it is possible that then, for the first time, he fully believed in Jesus.

6. Then Jesus said unto them. (More exactly, *Jesus therefore saith to them*). The word *therefore* makes the following words a response to what the brothers had said. **My time is not yet come.** That is, "the opportune and appointed moment for me to go up to Jerusalem, for the purpose which you have in mind, has not yet arrived." For Jesus knew that there was more for him to do, especially in teaching and training his twelve disciples, before he should bring on the crisis of his final rejection. **But your time is always ready.** The time of their going up to the feast was a matter of indifference. There was no special reason why they should not freely choose the day and hour for their journey. Ordinary considerations were enough to direct them in ordinary circumstances. As Jews, and nothing more, they could appear in Jerusalem whenever they pleased. It may, perhaps, be inferred from this saying of Christ, that, in the common work of life, God does not reveal to us a definite time for each particular act; that the hour of doing many things is left to the judgment or preference of man; and hence, that we are scarcely to expect, even in answer to prayer, any special intimation of God's will as to our duties, moment by moment—any divine impression that may supersede the use of reason. Inspired illumination is unnecessary to a right performance of ordinary Christian work.

7. The world cannot hate you. By **the world** is here meant the people in general, who were still strangers to the new "kingdom of God" that Christ was establishing. It was morally impossible for this world to hate the brothers of Jesus, because, as the rest of the verse shows, they had taken no stand against the religious belief or conduct of the world. There was no radical opposition between them and the people. Hence this expression proves that none of these brothers belonged to the circle of the twelve whom Christ had selected to be his intimate friends. **But me it hateth—already and bitterly—because I testify of it**—habitually, by word and deed—**that the works thereof are evil;** that is, sinful. Though this language expresses distinctly the estimate which Jesus put on his every day work as a teacher, he may have recalled at this time his words to the Pharisees in Jerusalem (see 5:42, 44, 47); for he had declared with great plainness of speech their profound sinfulness.

8. Go ye up unto this feast: I go not up yet unto this feast; for my time is not yet full come. The word *yet,* in the second clause of the Common Version, should probably be omitted. Westcott and Hort, however, retain it, with some of the best MSS. The words, **I go not** (or, *am not going*) **up unto this feast,** are a pregnant expression, to be interpreted in the light of the demand which had been made. That demand did not have in view a going up to Jerusalem merely to observe the festival, but a going up to the feast for the purpose of manifesting himself to the whole body of his disciples by such mighty works as would settle the question of his Messiahship. Jesus knew that such a course would naturally lead to his death—an event which belonged to a future time and another feast. The interpretation which we have given accords with the style of this Gospel, in which there is a deep, underlying continuity of thought, so that very often single clauses can only be understood by means of the context; and, if it is correct, all appearance of contradiction between this verse and the tenth disappears. Jesus did not mislead his brothers, or change his purpose;

9 When he had said these words unto them, he abode still in Galilee.
10 But when his brethren were gone up, then went he also up unto the feast, not openly, but as it were in secret.
11 Then ᵃ the Jews sought him at the feast, and said, Where is he?

9 yet fulfilled. And having said these things unto them, he abode still in Galilee.
10 But when his brethren were gone up unto the feast, then went he also up, not publicly, but as it were in secret. The Jews therefore sought him at

a ch. 11 : 56.

for he did not go up to this feast in the way, or for the purpose, contemplated by them. "His first public entrance into Jerusalem was the entrance in the procession with palms; by that he showed himself publicly to the world, and by that, also, he brought on his own death"—(Lange). Godet insists that the Greek for "my time is not yet full come," is "too solemn an expression (πεπλήρωται) to be applied to the interval of a few days which separated this response from the sudden appearance of Christ in Jerusalem," and interprets the language of Jesus as we have done above. Westcott remarks: "The Feast of Tabernacles was a festival of peculiar joy for work accomplished. At such a feast Christ had now no place." This able scholar accepts the reading **not yet** (οὔπω), as genuine. The same is true likewise of Dr. Hort. But Weiss strenuously opposes this reading, interpreting Christ's language as "a categorical refusal, equivalent to the words, "I, for my part, go not up to *this* feast, because, not until a later day will the right point of time come, when, with my full self-revelation, the unavoidable decision will take place.'" He also thinks that Jesus was waiting for a divine intimation when to go up, and that this intimation, when it came, "did not direct him to go up to Jerusalem, *in order* to bring on the final decision, but for the purpose of taking up, under the divine protection, once more, and for a considerable time, his work of refutation and instruction in the principal seat of the theocracy." We prefer to say that the divine will was constantly known to Jesus, and that his not going up with his brothers publicly at this time, together with his open refusal to do this, was in its perfect accord with the divine will as his going up at a later day, and in a private manner. He did not wait in darkness for a "wink" that he should go, but he waited in light until the fitting moment came, *knowing* when to remain where he was, and when to visit again the holy city. Every hour had its appropriate work, and that work he recognized and performed.[1]

9. **When he had said** (literally, *saying*) **these words unto them, he abode still in Galilee**. Or, according to another reading of nearly equal authority: "Saying these things, he himself remained in Galilee"; the implication being, that his brothers went up with the rest of the people to the feast.

10. **But when his brethren**—(*brothers*) **were gone up, then went he also up unto the feast.** According to the best editors of the Greek text, the words **unto the feast**, are a part of the first clause, not of the second. Hence it is possible that the Evangelist did not intend to say that Jesus went up to observe the feast, but only that he went up, though for some other purpose. As he appeared in the temple about the middle of the feast (ver. 14), he probably remained in Galilee three or four days after the departure of his brothers. **Not openly, but as it were in secret.** Thus in a very different way from that which his brothers had proposed. Yet the harmonists suppose that he went up with his disciples, that on his way a certain village of Samaria declined to receive him (Luke 9: 51-56), and that he also cleansed ten lepers as he was about to enter another village (Luke 17: 11-19). Other events, as the sending out of the seventy (Luke 10: 1-16), are connected by some with this journey. But he did not go up with the multitude.

11. **Then the Jews**, etc. (Better, *the Jews*

---

[1][Instead of **I go not up yet**, it seems necessary to read *I go not up*, as the American Com. propose in Appendix. The authority for **not** (οὐκ) is ℵ D K M Π, (A is defective here), three cursives, several copies of the Old Latin, the Latin Vulgate (except some codices,) Memphitic, Old Syriac (Curetonian), Armenian, Æthiopic; Jerome mentions that Porphyry accused Jesus of fickleness, in saying he would not go, and then going; Cyril, of Alexandria, Chrysostom, and Ephrahanius speak of the difficulty, and try to explain it. The authority for **not yet** (οὔπω) is B L T and eleven

Ch. VII.]   JOHN.   171

12 And *there was much murmuring among the people concerning him : for *some said, He is a good man : others said, Nay ; but he deceiveth the people.
13 Howbeit no man spake openly of him *for fear of the Jews.
14 Now about the midst of the feast Jesus went up into the temple, and taught.

12 the feast, and said, Where is he? And there was much murmuring among the multitudes concerning him : some said, He is a good man; others said, Not 13 so, but he leadeth the multitude astray. Howbeit no man spake openly of him for fear of the Jews.
14 But when it was now the midst of the feast Jesus

a ch. 9 : 16; 10 : 19....b Matt. 21 ; 46; Luke 7 : 16; ch. 6 : 14; ver. 40....c ch. 9 : 22; 12 : 42; 19 : 38.

therefore) **sought him at the feast, and said, Where is he?** or, *Where is that one?* They **sought,** (or, were *seeking—him* note the imperfect tense). Of course, with hostile intent. Their desire to take his life had not become any weaker. The period, whether of seven months or of eighteen, whether from the Feast of Purim to the Feast of Tabernacles in the same year, or from the festival of the Passover, or of Pentecost, in one year to that of Tabernacles in the next year, had not changed their temper or purpose. Probably they had kept themselves informed of the movements of Jesus during his absence from Jerusalem, and had nursed their enmity by thoughts of their waning influence. For if he should be received as the Messiah, their power would be broken.

12. And there was much murmuring (or, *muttering*) **among the people** (lit., *multitudes*) **concerning him.** For the sense of the word **murmuring,** see Notes on 6 : 41 and 61. Plainly, there was no lack of interest in respect to Jesus ; but the people spoke to one another in low tones of voice, as if a crisis were at hand, **Some said** (or, *were saying*), **He is a good man: others said** (or, *were saying*), **Nay ; but he deceiveth the people** (lit., *multitude*). Thus they were looking at his character ; and this is always a matter of the highest moment. It was not now the miracles or the teaching of Jesus which formed the subject of debate, but himself; whether he was good or bad, truthful or deceptive. And that is, in some sense, the question still. We must now believe that Jesus was the Messiah, the Son of the Holy, or that he was an impostor, deceiving the people. Strange that there should still be doubt in any mind!

13. Howbeit (or, *yet*) **no man spake openly of him, for fear of the Jews.** By **the Jews,** must be meant, in this place, as so often in this Gospel, the chief men of the nation, and especially those belonging to the Sanhedrin. Their judgment had not yet been announced, and therefore the people were afraid to speak out boldly for or against him. It was their judgment which, in all probability, his brothers wished to secure, by advising him to show himself openly to the world. (Ver. 3, 4). But many of the people must have known something of their enmity to Jesus, and therefore those who believed him to be **good** had special reason to fear **the Jews.** This was the state of affairs during the first part of the festival.

14-36. Discussions at the Feast.

14. Now about the midst of the feast Jesus went up into the temple, and taught. Whether Jesus repaired to the tem-

---

other uncials, most cursives (many have not been examined on this passage), three copies of the Old Latin and some of the Vulgate, Thebaic, the Peshito, Harklean and Jerusalem Syriac, the Gothic, and a quotation in Basil. Transcriptional probability is overwhelmingly in favor of **not,** as a very difficult reading, readily changed into **not yet,** which at once removes the difficulty; while we cannot imagine any reason for changing the **not yet** into **not.** And intrinsic probability cannot be arrayed on the other side, except by claiming that the reading **not** is practically impossible, wholly inconsistent with the character of our Lord. But it may be variously explained. (1) As suggested by Chrysostom and Cyril, it may mean that he was not going with the Jews—to share their festivities —or, (Plumptre) in the regular caravan, as a pilgrim (5:1). (2) They urged him to go as Messiah ; but when he did that, it would be the signal for his death : so he is not going up (in that capacity) to *this* feast. (Comp. Godet). The answer was enigmatical, because he could not explain himself to them. (3) It is even possible to say (with Meyer), that Jesus changed his mind (ver. 10), as he did with the Syrophenician mother. Since the difficult reading is intrinsically not at all impossible, the transcriptional probability must carry the day, and the reading **not** must be accepted. Westcott and Hort would, no doubt, say that it is a "Western" reading, being given by ℵ D, Old Latin, and Old Syriac. But apart from the evidence of the Memphitic, and Æthiopic Versions and Greek Fathers, it must be remembered that Westcott and Hort incline strongly to accept various exclusively "Western" readings in the latter part of Luke and Matthew, on internal grounds; and internal evidence is extremely clear and strong in this case; indeed, is overwhelming.—B.]

15 *And the Jews marvelled, saying, How knoweth this man letters, having never learned?
16 Jesus answered them, and said, *My doctrine is not mine, but his that sent me.
17 *If any man will do his will, he shall know of the doctrine, whether it be of God, or *whether I speak of myself.
18 *He that speaketh of himself seeketh his own

15 went up into the temple, and taught. The Jews therefore marvelled, saying, How knoweth this man letters, having never learned? Jesus therefore answered them, and said, My teaching is not mine, but his that sent me. If any man willeth to do his will, he shall know of the teaching, whether it is of God, or *whether I speak from myself. He that speaketh from himself seeketh his own glory; but

a Matt. 13: 54; Mark 6: 2; Luke 4: 22; Acts 2: 7....b ch. 3: 11; 8: 28; 12: 49; 14: 10, 24....c ch. 8: 43....d ch. 5: 41; 8: 50.

ple as soon as he reached the city, is not stated; but it may be presumed that the two events were not far apart. Plainly, however, he did not repair to the holy city, or to the temple, at this time, in order to observe the Feast of Tabernacles in the manner prescribed by the Mosaic law (see on ver. 2), but in order to instruct the people in respect to the things of his kingdom. And, apart from supernatural protection, he could do this most safely when surrounded by multitudes of the common people; for many of these heard him gladly. By using the imperfect tense of the verb, to teach, the Evangelist represents the teaching of Jesus as in progress, or continuous; and, on this account, the translation, "was teaching," would, perhaps, be more exact than the translation, taught.

15-24. WITH "THE JEWS."

15. And the Jews marvelled. By the tense of the verb, we learn that their astonishment, as well as his teaching, was continuous. The language is that of an observer who recalls the scene. Saying, How knoweth this man letters, having never learned? To know letters, means to have literary culture or knowledge—to be trained in the schools and familiar with books. But the learning of the Jews was chiefly religious, founded on the Old Testament Scriptures, or relating to them; and, by the way in which he was now teaching, Jesus proved himself to be a master of language, of interpretation, and, perhaps, of Rabbinic lore. At this, the Jewish leaders were astonished; for they knew that he had been taught by none of their famous masters. Yet it was the form of his teaching, and not its substance, which attracted their attention and excited their wonder. For they were too unspiritual to be moved by its greatest excellence—the sublime and saving truth which it made known.

16. Jesus answered them, and said. The language in which their astonishment found a somewhat incautious expression was not addressed to Jesus, but it was known to him, and was answered in the following words: My doctrine (or, *teaching*) is not mine, but his that sent me. This expression must have recalled to the minds of some what he had said to them during his last previous visit to Jerusalem (see 5: 19-30 sq.), when they accused him of blasphemy, and sought his life. (5: 18). He declares once more his inseparable union with God. His teaching is in no sense or degree from himself, considered apart from the Father. His message, rather, is from God; his learning, the wisdom of God. He is not dependent on human masters for instruction; for he knows intuitively, and reveals perfectly, the mind of the invisible Father.

17. If any man will do his will, he shall know of the doctrine (or, *teaching*), whether it be of God, or whether I speak of myself. The first clause should be translated: *If any man willeth* (or, *is willing*) *to do his will.* These words reveal a great spiritual law, namely, that the moral attitude of a person will affect his view of the character and teaching of Christ. One who is prepared to obey the will of God from the heart, will see the purity of Christ's character, and the divine certainty of what he teaches. But one who is in spirit thoroughly self-seeking, and unprepared to do the will of God, will look upon Christ, the holy, through the atmosphere of his own selfish character, and will therefore hear his teaching without perceiving that it bears the unmistakable impress of heaven. It is the pure in heart who see God; it is the childlike to whom he reveals the things of his kingdom. (Matt. 11: 25). A right will tends to just judgment and knowledge of truth; a perverse will darkens the understanding, and leads to error. Hence, an obedient spirit is indispensable, in order to a proper estimate of the evidence on which divine truth rests, or by which it is commended to rational confidence.

18. He that speaketh of (or, *from*) himself. The emphasis belongs to the words

glory: but he that seeketh his glory that sent him, the same is true, and no unrighteousness is in him.
19 ᵃ Did not Moses give you the law, and *yet* none of you keepeth the law? ᵇ Why go ye about to kill me?
20 The people answered and said, ᶜ Thou hast a devil: who goeth about to kill thee?
21 Jesus answered and said unto them, I have done one work, and ye all marvel.
22 ᵈ Moses therefore gave unto you circumcision; (not because it is of Moses, ᵉ but of the fathers;) and ye on the sabbath day circumcise a man.

he that seeketh the glory of him that sent him, the 19 same is true, and no unrighteousness is in him. Did not Moses give you the law, and *yet* none of you 20 doeth the law? Why seek ye to kill me? The multitude answered, thou hast a demon: who seeketh 21 to kill thee? Jesus answered and said unto them, I did one work, and ye all marvel because thereof. 22 Moses hath given you circumcision (not that it is of Moses, but of the fathers); and on the sabbath ye

ᵃ Ex. 24: 3; Deut. 33: *; ch. 1: 17; Acts 7: 38....ᵇ Matt. 12: 14; Mark 3: 6; ch. 5: 16, 18; 10: 31, 39; 11: 53....ᶜ ch. 8: 48, 52: 10: 20....ᵈ Lev. 12: 3....ᵉ Gen. 17: 10.

from himself, as their position in the original sentence shows. He whose teaching has no other source than himself—the man whose words are prompted by his own wisdom and will, and by nothing else—**seeketh his own glory.** And a self-seeking teacher cannot be trusted; his doctrine is likely to be false. This, manifestly, is the unexpressed thought of Jesus; and it was unexpressed because it was certain to be supplied by the minds of those to whom he was speaking. Moreover, this is one of the sayings of Christ which suggest the doctrine that selfishness is the root of sin. **But he that seeketh his glory that sent him, the same is true, and no unrighteousness is in him.** The last clause might be translated: *"And unrighteousness in him there is not"*—the emphasis being on the words *unrighteousness in him.* Thus Jesus claims to be seeking without selfishness the glory of the Father who sent him, to be absolutely truthful in his teaching, and, indeed, to be without sin. If one of these claims be admitted, all must be admitted. They stand or fall together. He that seeks not his own glory, but that of God only, has no motive to speak anything untrue, or to do anything wrong.

19. Did not Moses give you the law, and yet none of you keepeth the law? Why go ye about (lit., *seek ye*) **to kill me?** These words were evidently addressed to "the Jews," and not to the multitude of common people. "The Jews" had received through Moses the law of God, but they were not obeying it, were unwilling to obey it; and hence, according to verse 17, they could not justly expect to know whether Christ's teaching was, or was not, from God. They were not in sympathy with the law of God given to them by their honored deliverer, Moses; how, then, could they recognize the words of Jesus as divine? The word **law** appears to be used in a general sense of the whole Mosaic code; but one of its precepts they were now planning to break by killing Jesus.

20. The people (lit., *multitude*) **answered and, said, Thou hast a devil** (or, *demon*)**: who goeth about** (or, *seeketh*) **to kill thee?** This multitude was probably composed, for the most part, of people from Galilee, who knew nothing of the deadly purpose of "the Jews" at Jerusalem. They were surprised at the charge which appeared to be made against them. It seemed to them a dark suspicion, like that which was supposed to be injected into the soul by a demon. But those who were specially addressed by Jesus maintained a prudent silence; for they understood very well that the multitude would not tolerate any violence against him.

21. Jesus answered and said unto them. That is, his words were still open, and addressed apparently to all, though they were intended chiefly for "the Jews," who had charged him with breaking the Sabbath by a work of healing. **I have done** (*did*) **one work, and ye all marvel.** The work referred to was the healing of the impotent man. (5: 1-15). Jesus does not hesitate to call it a **work**, though he had done it on the Sabbath. And his language proves that they were still wondering, or pretending to wonder, that he had ventured to do that great and merciful work on the Sabbath. Many interpreters connect with this clause the words **therefore** (*on account of this*, or, *for this cause*, διὰ τοῦτο), which generally stand at the beginning, and rarely, if ever, in John, at the end of a clause. It appears safest, therefore, to connect them with the next verse.

22. The exact meaning of this verse is a matter of doubt, though the general object of it is manifest. If the words translated **therefore,** *for this cause*, are genuine, and do not belong to the preceding sentence, Christ may be understood to teach (1) that one reason for

23 If a man on the sabbath day receive circumcision, that the law of Moses should not be broken; are ye angry at me, because a I have made a man every whit whole on the sabbath day?
24 b Judge not according to the appearance, but judge righteous judgment.

23 circumcise a man. If a man receiveth circumcision on the sabbath, that the law of Moses may not be broken; are ye wroth with me, because I made¹ a 24 man every whit whole on the sabbath? Judge not according to appearance, but judge righteous judgment.

a ch. 5: 8, 9, 16.. .b Deut. 1: 16, 17; Prov. 74: 23; ch. 8: 15; James 2: 1.——1 Gr. a whole man sound.

giving to circumcision the place which it had in the Mosaic economy, as a work that ought to be performed on the eighth day after birth, even if that day should be a Sabbath, was to guard the people against the precise error into which "the Jews" had now fallen. God, in his deep counsel, had warned his people, by the rite of circumcision, against an outward and over-scrupulous observance of the Sabbath. If this be a correct view of the meaning, the idea of Jesus as to the aim of the law may be compared with that of Paul, in 1 Cor. 9: 9; and the verse may be translated thus: *For this cause hath Moses given you circumcision (not that it is from Moses, but from the fathers), and on the Sabbath ye circumcise a man.* The connection of thought is very natural with this interpretation; but it may seem improbable to those who see very little that is deep and spiritual in the ritual of Mosaism. Again, Christ may be understood to teach (2) that the law of circumcision supersedes that of the Jewish Sabbath, because it is more ancient, having been first given to the patriarchs, while that of the Jewish Sabbath was first given to Moses. Underneath this representation may lie the postulate that the religious rites or duties first revealed are the most fundamental and controlling. With this view of the Lord's meaning, his words may be properly translated: *For this cause hath Moses given to you circumcision, not because it is from Moses, but (because it is) from the fathers; and on the Sabbath ye circumcise a man.* In other words: Moses has given you circumcision for this reason, namely, because it is from the fathers. The previous negation, *not because it is from Moses*, is only inserted for the purpose of contrasting the later law with the earlier. This interpretation is sustained by Meyer, and deserves respectful consideration, though we prefer the one first given.

But if Jesus here assumes that the Jewish law of the Sabbath was unknown to the fathers, can we safely teach that the Sabbath was instituted in Eden? (Gen. 2: 2, 3). Not the Sabbath of the Mosaic law, with its rigid cessation from labor, and its immediate penalty for transgression; but a Sabbath, or holy day, consecrated to spiritual service and improvement. It is easy to suppose that Jesus referred exclusively to the post-Mosaic Sabbath of the Jews; for of this, and of this only, would his hearers be likely to think; while the pre-Mosaic Sabbath must be established by other evidence. This expression is, therefore, consistent with the supposition that the seventh day was consecrated and set apart in a general way to religious service from the beginning.

23. **If a man on the Sabbath day receive circumcision, that the law of Moses should not be broken, are ye angry at me, because I made a man every whit whole on the Sabbath day?** In order to a proper observance of the Mosaic law, the prohibition of work on the Sabbath must give way to the requirement of circumcision on the eighth day after birth; much more then must that prohibition give way to the great requirement of love to one's neighbor, fulfilled in restoring a whole man to health. (Compare Mark 2: 27; 3: 4; Luke 6: 9; 13: 15, 16). Where there is an apparent conflict in the precepts of the law, the less important rule must yield to the more important rule. In this way only can the law be obeyed. And one who considers the highest object of the Sabbath to be, not bodily rest, but religious and beneficent service, will not hesitate in deciding which must yield—the requirement of love or the requirement of rest.

24. **Judge not according to the appearance, but judge righteous judgment.** The before **appearance** is without authority, and should be omitted. To judge according to appearance, or according to what is seen, is rarely just. But to go back of the merely external act to the motive which prompts it, and beneath the letter of the law to its aim and spirit, is the judgment which is righteous. Thus Christ said that "on love to God and love to man, hang all the law and the prophets" (Matt. 22: 40), and that "whosoever

25 Then said some of them of Jerusalem, Is not this he, whom they seek to kill?
26 But, lo, he speaketh boldly, and they say nothing unto him. *a* Do the rulers know indeed that this is the very Christ?
27 *b* Howbeit we know this man whence he is: but when Christ cometh, no man knoweth whence he is.
28 Then cried Jesus in the temple as he taught, saying, *c* Ye both know me, and ye know whence I am: and *d* I am not come of myself, but he that sent me *e* is true, *f* whom ye know not.

25 Some therefore of them of Jerusalem said, Is not this he whom they seek to kill? And lo, he speaketh openly, and they say nothing unto him. Can it be that the rulers indeed know that this is the Christ?
27 Howbeit we know this man whence he is: but when the Christ cometh, no one knoweth whence he is.
28 Jesus therefore cried in the temple, teaching and saying, Ye both know me, and know whence I am; and I am not come of myself, but he that sent me

a ver. 48....*b* Matt. 13: 55; Mark 6: 3; Luke 4: 22....*c* See ch. 8: 14....*d* ch. 5: 43; 8: 42....*e* ch. 5: 32; 8: 26; Rom. 3: 4....*f* ch 1: 18; 8: 55.

looketh on a woman, to lust after her, hath committed adultery with her already in his heart" (Matt. 5:28). Moreover, he clearly taught that some matters required by the law were weightier than others (Matt. 23:23). So in the present instance, the act of healing, by which he was charged with breaking the law of Moses, was in harmony with one of its broadest and most spiritual commands. Those who judged otherwise judged according to appearance, and their judgment was really unrighteous.

25-31. SECOND SCENE IN THE TEMPLE.

25. Then said some of them of Jerusalem, Is not this he whom they seek to kill? The people of Jerusalem, in distinction from those of other parts of the land (see note on ver. 20), were aware of the murderous design of "the Jews," or leaders of the nation, and they were, on that account, surprised at the freedom with which Jesus was now speaking in public.

26. But (*and*) **lo, he speaketh boldly, and they say nothing unto him. Do the rulers know indeed** (*in truth*) **that this is the very Christ?** Very before Christ is to be omitted. This question may be ironical; implying that the conduct of "the Jews" was such as would be natural if they had ascertained in truth that Jesus was the Messiah. But the speakers themselves were too well informed to entertain such a belief. Or, noticing the force of the words "in truth" (ἀληθῶς), the question may be understood as suggesting, and at the same time rejecting, what seemed to the speakers the only natural reason for the rulers' course. "The rulers have not at any time come *really* to know that this is the Christ?" *They may suppose* that they have come to know this; but it cannot be that they have *really* ascertained it.

27. Howbeit—whatever they may think—**we know this man whence he is: but**

when (*the*) **Christ cometh, no man knoweth whence he is.** This is their sufficient reason for holding it impossible that Jesus is the Christ. Though it was understood that the Messiah was to be of the seed of David, and from the town of Bethlehem, where David was (ver. 42), it was also believed that his origin and manifestation were to be mysterious and supernatural. Was he not to be Wonderful, Counsellor, Mighty God, Everlasting Father, Prince of Peace? Was he not to come in the clouds of heaven? to come suddenly to his temple? (Isa. 9:6; Dan. 7: 13; Mal. 3: 1). How were these predictions to be reconciled with his being the son of Joseph and Mary, whom they supposed that they knew to be his parents? Could the son of a common carpenter; could a man whose parents and brothers and sisters were well known, be the expected Christ of God? Impossible. The expression "whence he is" does not therefore refer to the birth-place, so much as to the particular family and circumstances of Jesus, or of the Christ.

28. Then cried Jesus (better: *Jesus therefore cried*) **in the temple as he taught, saying.** The word **cried** indicates a force of utterance that was occasioned by strong feeling. (Compare 1: 15; 7: 37; 12: 44; Rom. 9: 27). No wonder that he was moved at the persistence of the people in judging according to appearance. (See on ver. 24). The Evangelist also calls attention to the circumstance that the following words were uttered by Jesus while he was still in the temple teaching; and this particularity is a mark of truth. **Ye both know me, and ye know whence I am.** "We must guard against seeing, with Meyer, a concession in these two propositions. It is true: you know me up to a certain point, but not completely. The tone of the two conjunctions (translated 'both,' 'and') has evidently a touch of irony, and the two proposi-

29 But I know him: for I am from him, and he hath sent me.
30 Then they sought to take him: but no man laid hands on him, because his hour was not yet come.
31 And many of the people believed on him, and said, When Christ cometh, will he do more miracles than these which this man hath done?

29 is true, whom ye know not. I know him; because I am from him, and he sent me. They sought therefore to take him: and no man laid his hand on him, because his hour was not yet come. But of the multitude many believed on him; and they said, When the Christ shall come, will he do more signs

a Matt. 11: 27; ch. 10: 15....b Mark 11: 18; Luke 19: 47; 20: 19; ver. 19; ch. 8: 37.....c ver. 44; ch. 8: 20....d Matt. 12; 23; ch. 3: 2; 8: 30.

tions have therefore an interrogative force."—(Godet). The meaning, however, is almost equally good, if these words be regarded as a concession that his hearers have a certain amount of knowledge as to his human person and history, but a knowledge which is, nevertheless, at best, superficial, not reaching back to his true origin, nor explaining the supernatural character of his ministry. **And I am not come of myself.** Though you infer, from your knowledge of my earthly home and life, that I am a mere man, self-sent, I am not this. You know not "whence I am," for you suppose me to have set myself, unauthorized, to this work. (See on the words "of myself," 5: 19, 30; 7: 17, 18, with Notes). **But he that sent me is true.** On the word translated **true,** which does not mean truthful, but, rather, that which realizes the highest idea of the object in question, see Notes on 1: 9; 4: 23; 6: 32. Whether Jesus means to say that the One by whom he has been sent realizes in himself the true and perfect idea of a Sender (Meyer), or, rather, the true and perfect idea of Being—of the very God—is not material to the course of thought; yet we are inclined to the latter view, because the people must have been already aware of his claim to be the Sent of God, and would therefore be likely to think that the word **true** was used of him in a comprehensive sense. **Whom ye know not**—i. e., in any spiritual sense of the word. They knew about God, but they did not know God. They had no appreciation of his character. How, then, could they know "whence Jesus was"? And if they did not, in the highest respect, know "whence he was," their argument against his being the Christ fell to the ground. Observe, also, that the pronoun **ye** is slightly emphatic, preparing their minds for the next sentence.

29. But I know him, etc. This verse is well translated in the Revised Version: *I know him; because I am from him, and he sent me.* That is: My knowledge of the absolutely real Being is certain, real, immediate; for I am from his immediate presence and fellowship, and he is the One who sent me. (Compare Notes on 1: 1, 14, 19; 6: 46). These words are even more emphatic by reason of the independent position which they hold without the conjunction **but,** which is omitted by the best critical authorities. Thus Jesus declares, in terms of wonderful simplicity and force, his divine knowledge, origin, and mission—in a word, "whence he was."

30. Then they sought (or. *they sought, therefore*) **to take him.** His claim to a strictly divine origin and mission rekindled the deadly animosity of "the Jews," or members of the Sanhedrin, and led to a resumption and continuance of their plotting to take Jesus by violence, that they might put him to death. But (rather, *and*) **no man laid hands** (or, *his hand*) **on him, because his hour was not yet come.** The plots of his enemies were not carried into effect at once, because the time appointed by God for the termination of his ministry was still in the future. The Evangelist looks at the course of events from the highest religious point of view. What is brought about by the agency of second causes he regards as a fulfillment of the will and purpose of the First Cause. The motive which restrained "the Jews" may have been fear of the people, who were friendly to Jesus; but the divine purpose was none the less real and controlling. (Compare 8: 20).

31. And many of the people, etc. See Revised Version: *But of the multitude many believed on him; and they said.* Observe the emphasis which is given to the expression *the multitude* by its position at the beginning of the sentence, and which shows that those referred to in the preceding verse as "seeking to seize Jesus," were not "of the multitude." Observe, also, that the words *believed on him* must, in agreement with what follows, signify, were convinced that Jesus was the Christ. For this is the import of " what they were saying to one another": **When Christ cometh** —an expression not intended to represent their

JOHN.

32 The Pharisees heard that the people murmured such things concerning him: and the Pharisees and the chief priests sent officers to take him.
33 Then said Jesus unto them, *a* Yet a little while am I with you, and *then* I go unto him that sent me.
34 Ye *b* shall seek me, and shall not find me: and where I am, *thither* ye cannot come.

32 than those which this man hath done? The Pharisees heard the multitude murmuring these things concerning him; and the chief priests and the Pharisees sent officers to take him. Jesus therefore said, Yet a little while am I with you, and I go unto him that sent me. Ye shall seek me, and shall not find

a ch. 13: 33; 16: 16....*b* Hos. 5: 6; ch. 8: 21; 13: 33.

own view, but, rather, that of the persons spoken of in ver. 30. It was a timid reply, uttered in low tones of voice, to the enemies of Jesus: You say that this is a blasphemer, and not the Christ; but, if this be so, **when (the) Christ cometh, will he do more miracles** (*signs*) **than these which this man hath done?** that is, here, in Jerusalem (5: 5 sq.), and, more recently, in Galilee. This interpretation agrees with the obvious force of the words **believed on him** much better than the interpretation which supposes that the many here spoken of uttered them doubtingly.—*Lange*. It is also clear from this question of the people, that miracles were looked upon as proper credentials of the Messiah. He was expected to perform them. And it may be added that the form of the question, in the original, is one that anticipates a negative answer. The Christ will not do more signs than this man has done.

32-36. THIRD SCENE IN THE CONTROVERSY.

32. The Pharisees heard that the people murmured, etc. We translate as follows: *The Pharisees heard the multitude murmuring these things concerning him.* Though the multitude, many of them, believed in Jesus as the Christ, their belief did not render them bold and decided in action. Their comments in reply to the enemies of Jesus were made to one another in a low voice, and were not specially intended for the ear of those enemies. Yet they were heard, and were the occasion of an ineffectual attempt to seize Jesus. **And the Pharisees and the chief priests sent officers to take him.** It appears that the Pharisees instigated this attempt to take Jesus, but they easily secured the co-operation of the chief priests, who at that time were, for the most part, Sadducees. Perhaps the Sanhedrin was called together that the officers, or *beadles*, might be clothed with its authority.

33. Then said Jesus. (Better: *Jesus therefore said*). That is, in consequence of

the events related in ver. 32. The first appearance of officers sent to take Jesus was a token of coming events, and led him to speak of these events somewhat plainly. The words **unto them** (αὐτοῖς), are omitted by the best editors. **Yet a little while am I with you, and then I go unto him that sent me.** Omit the word **then** as needless. His mission is not yet accomplished, and therefore he is to remain with them, friend and foe, a while longer. By **you**, he means principally those who are anxious to compass his death. They must wait a little. The time of his departure is near, but it is not fully come. When it comes, he is to go to that most real of all beings, the One who had sent him into the world, but of whom they had no true knowledge.

34. Ye shall seek me, and shall not find. To what does this refer? To the destruction of Jerusalem, according to Meyer. (See Luke 20: 16 sq.; 19: 43.) "Then will the tables be turned. After they have persecuted and killed him when present, they will earnestly but vainly desire to have him with them again, as the miraculous Helper who alone can rescue them from the direst evil." But this interpretation is too narrow. The language of Christ probably denotes that their longing and looking for the Messiah will continue after having rejected him and crucified him. Vainly will they expect the great Prince foretold in their Scriptures, and bitter will be their disappointment, from age to age, because he does not appear. But clinging to their false view of what the Messiah should be, and hardening themselves against the evidence that he has already appeared in the person of Jesus of Nazareth, they will never find the deliverer whom they seek. Though eager to welcome false Christs, they will look in vain for a real Saviour, whether for this life or for the future. **And where I am, thither ye cannot come.** Into the blessed and holy presence of the Father they could never come, while rejecting his Son. Jesus himself was the way, and, disbelieving him,

178 JOHN. [Ch. VII.

35 Then said the Jews among themselves, Whither will he go, that we shall not find him? will he go unto *a* the dispersed among the Gentiles, and teach the Gentiles?
36 What *manner of* saying is this that he said, Ye shall seek me, and shall not find *me:* and where I am, *thither* ye cannot come?
37 *b* In the last day, that great *day* of the feast, Jesus stood and cried, saying, *c* If any man thirst, let him come unto me, and drink.

35 me: and where I am, ye cannot come. The Jews therefore said among themselves, Whither will this man go that we shall not find him? will he go unto the Dispersion *1* among the Greeks, and teach the Greeks? What is this word that he said, Ye shall
36 Greeks? What is this word that he said, Ye shall seek me, and shall not find me: and where I am, ye cannot come?
37 Now on the last day, the great *day* of the feast, Jesus stood and cried, saying, If any man thirst, let

a Isa. 11 : 12; James 1 : 1; 1 Pet. 1: 1....*b* Lev. 23: 36....*c* Isa. 55: 1; ch. 6: 35; Rev. 22 : 17.——1 Gr. *of.*

they would never find the Father, to whom he would have led them gladly. The present, am, is used in vivid delineation for the future, "shall be."

35. Then (*therefore*) said the Jews among themselves: literally, *to themselves.* They did not address their words to Jesus, but to one another, and probably in a mocking tone. Whither will he go, that we shall not find him? will he go unto the dispersed among the Gentiles (*Greeks*), and teach the Gentiles (*Greeks*)? Thus they pay no attention to the saying of Jesus : I go to him that sent me, but in a tone of levity and contempt, not unmingled with perplexity, comment on his other statements. But the form of the question : " Will he go unto the dispersed?" etc., shows that it offered to their own minds no probable explanation of his words; for it is the form which looks to a negative answer. (See on ver. 31.) Yet the apostles of Christ afterwards did just what is here suggested.

36. What manner of saying is this (or, *what is this*) that he said. Notice the use of the verb is, instead of "means," or "signifies," and compare with it the same word in the controverted expression, "This is my body." Ye shall seek me, and shall not find me: and where I am, thither ye cannot come. These words betray anxious perplexity. The language of Jesus has struck into their souls, and awakened a suspicion that it deserves more attention than they are willing to give it. The tone of banter passes into one of sobriety. And with this remark John closes his narrative of Christ's first appearance in the temple, about the middle of the festival.

37-52. Last Day of the Feast.

37. In the last day, that great (day) of the feast. Two or three days must have passed since the events related in ver. 14-36 took place. How Jesus was employed during those days, the Evangelist does not mention.

But it is probable that, wherever he was, the officers of the Sanhedrin were on the watch for a favorable opportunity to seize him and deliver him to their masters. (Ver. 32-15, sq.). Whether this great day was, strictly speaking, the last day of the feast, or the day which followed the feast, but was regarded in some sense as its close, is a question the answer to which is difficult and not very important. (See Lev. 23 : 35-39; Num. 20: 35; Neh. 8: 18; 2 Macc. 10: 6; Josephus' "Ant." 3: 10, 4.) John certainly regarded it as practically the closing day of this feast, which was the last of the three great yearly festivals. It was in character a Sabbath, and was on this account, also, peculiarly sacred. Jesus stood and cried, saying. Thus John recollects the very attitude of his Lord on this occasion, and the special solemnity and force of his utterance. Says Westcott: "The original is singularly vivid : *Jesus was standing*, watching, as it might be, the procession of the people from their booths to the temple, *and* then, moved by some occasion, *he cried.*" If any man thirst—that is, longs for spiritual refreshment—let him come unto me, and drink. (4: 10, 14; 6: 35; Rev. 22: 17). Schaff remarks that "Our Lord certainly seems to allude here to the custom which prevailed during the seven days of the feast, of a priest bringing water in a golden vessel from the Pool of Siloam, with a jubilant procession, to the temple, standing on the altar, and pouring it out there, together with wine, while meantime the Hallel (Ps. cxiii.-cxviii) was sung"; and some reference to this ceremony is assumed by a majority of interpreters. But there is no very obvious connection between that ceremony and the words of Jesus. The water brought from Siloam was poured out on the west side of the altar, while wine was poured out on the east side. There was no *drinking* of either; nor is it certain that the water poured out was regarded as an emblem of water used for

CH. VII.]   JOHN.   179

38 *He that believeth on me, as the Scripture hath said, *out of his belly shall flow rivers of living water.
39 (*But this spake he of the Spirit, which they that believe on him should receive; for the Holy Ghost was not yet given; because that Jesus was not yet *glorified.)

38 him come unto me, and drink. He that believeth on me, as the scripture hath said, ¹ from within him
39 shall flow rivers of living water. But this spake he of the Spirit, which they that believed on him were to receive: ² for the Spirit was not yet given; because

a Deut. 18: 15....b Prov. 18: 4; Isa. 12: 3; 44: 3; ch. 4: 14....c Isa. 44: 3; Joel 2: 28; ch. 16: 7; Acts 2: 17; 33, 38....d ch. 12: 16; 16: 7.——1 Gr. *out of his belly*.....2 Some ancient authorities read, *for the Holy Spirit was not yet given.*

quenching thirst, as, *e. g.*, the water that flowed from the rock smitten by Moses. A strong desire for divine grace, occasioned by a deep sense of sin, is forcibly expressed by the word thirst. "As the hart panteth after the water-brooks, so panteth my soul after thee, O God." (Ps. 42: 1.) "The Lord, Jehovah, is my strength and my song; he also is become my salvation. Therefore with joy shall ye draw water out of the wells of salvation." (Isa. 12: 2, 3.) Hence, there is no particular need of assuming that Jesus referred to the ceremony of pouring out water by the altar—a ceremony which is not known to have been observed on the eighth day. But if he did allude to this practice, it was probably because the water was considered a memorial of the water from the rock in the desert, the real source of which was Christ. (1 Cor. 10: 4.) See, also, 1 Sam. 7: 6, with Note in "The Speaker's Commentary." Accepting this reference as correct, it would have been extremely natural for Jesus to avail himself of the water brought in solemn ceremony from Siloam as a figure of the "living water" which he would give to receptive souls.

38. He that believeth on me. This explains the figurative term "drink." (Ver. 37.) By believing on Christ, one receives him, as it were, with all that he has, into his soul. In other words, he receives the Spirit, who keeps alive in his soul a sense of pardon, peace, hope, joy, and union with Christ; for it is by the Spirit that Christ imparts himself to those who believe.¹ **As the Scripture hath said.** The following words, to which this statement refers, are not found in any one place of the Old Testament; but they represent the thought of several passages. **Out of his belly shall flow rivers of living water.** By this bold figure of speech the Saviour assures his hearers that, believing on him, they will become fountains of spiritual good, sending forth streams of holy influence. The issues of their life will be new and wonderful. By all the

channels of expression; by spiritual utterance, revealing new insight, courage, patience, zeal, and joy; by apologetic wisdom before kings and magistrates; by holy steadfastness in suffering and death; by voice, and hand, and eye, and every outward note of inward life; by prophecy and miracle and tongues—will the new spirit within them be manifested and made a blessing to mankind. Branches of the true Vine, they will bear much fruit. The word **belly**, remarks Lücke, "signifies, in the figurative language of the Hebrew, the *inner* man, and is synonomous with heart. See Prov. 20: 27; Isa. 16: 11; Sirach 51: 21." For Biblical expressions that may have prepared the way for the figure of speech used by Christ, reference may be made to Ex. 17: 6; Num. 20: 11; Ps. 114: 8; Isa. 44: 3; 55: 1; 58: 11; Joel 3: 18; Ezek. 47: 1, 12; Zech. 13: 1; 14: 8.

39. But this spake he of the Spirit, which they that believe on him should receive: for the Holy Ghost (or, *the Spirit*) **was not yet given; because that Jesus was not yet glorified.** This translation, omitting *given* after *yet*, represents probably all that was in the original text. And it means that the Spirit was not yet in the souls of believers after such a manner as to produce the effects suggested by the language of Jesus; for these effects were first to be realized in their fullness after his glorification, on the Day of Pentecost, and thenceforward.¹ Hence

¹ On the grammatical structure of this verse, see Buttman's "Grammar of the N. T. Greek," p. 379 a.

¹ [The reading, *the Spirit was not yet*, has here the great advantage that it accounts for the rise of all the others, as "the Holy Spirit was not yet," "the Holy Spirit was not yet upon them," "the Spirit was not yet given," "the Holy Spirit was not yet given"; while it is difficult to see why any one of these should have been reduced to a simpler form, since they are all perspicuous and unobjectionable. The simple reading would easily suggest such additions as "Holy," "given," by way of supposed explanation. West. and Hort here agree with Tisch. and others, in adopting the simplest form, which is given by ℵ T K Π, Old Syriac, Memphitic, Thebaic (it has a form growing out of this), Armenian, with Origen, Cyril, etc. Observe that D has here a "conflate" reading, "the Holy Spirit was not yet given.—B.]

40 Many of the people therefore, when they heard this saying, said, Of a truth this is *a* the Prophet.
41 Others said, *b* This is the Christ. But some said, Shall Christ come *c* out of Galilee?
42 *d* Hath not the Scripture said, That Christ cometh of the seed of David, and out of the town of Bethlehem, *e* where David was?
43 So *f* there was a division among the people because of him.
44 And *g* some of them would have taken him; but no man laid hands on him.
45 Then came the officers to the chief priests and Pharisees; and they said unto them, Why have ye not brought him?

40 Jesus was not yet glorified. *Some* of the multitude therefore, when they heard these words, said, This 41 is of a truth the prophet. Others said, This is the Christ. But some said, What, doth the Christ come 42 out of Galilee? Hath not the scripture said that the Christ cometh of the seed of David, and from Beth-43 lehem, the village where David was? So there arose 44 a division in the multitude because of him. And some of them would have taken him; but no man laid hands on him.
45 The officers therefore came to the chief priests and Pharisees; and they said unto them, Why did ye not

a Deut. 18: 15, 18; ch. 1: 21; 6: 14....*b* ch. 4: 42; 6: 69....*c* ch. 1: 46; ver. 52....*d* Ps. 132: 11; Jer. 23: 5; Mic. 5: 2; Matt. 2: 5; Luke 2: 4....*e* 1 Sam. 16: 1, 4....*f* ver. 12; ch. 9: 16; 10: 19....*g* ver. 30.

the insertion of the word given is perfectly consistent with the meaning of Jesus. It is to be observed that the word **Spirit** has no article before it in the original, and when it is thus used it generally marks an operation, or gift of the Spirit, rather than the Spirit as a person. (Compare 1: 33; 20: 22; Matt. 1: 18, 20; 3: 11; 12: 28; Luke 1: 15, 35, 41, 67; 2: 25; 4: 1.)

40. **Many of the people therefore.** The Rev. Ver. presents a better text, viz.: *Some of the multitude therefore.* By the order of the words in the original, we perceive that the Evangelist wished to direct attention to the fact that the persons referred to belonged to the common people, *the multitude*, and not to the leaders of the nation, "the Jews," or members of the Sanhedrin. "*Of the multitude, therefore, some,*" is the Greek form, according to the best editors. **When they heard this saying** (lit., *these words*)—just spoken—**said, Of a truth this is the Prophet.** (See Note on 1: 21). That is, the prophet foretold by Moses (Deut. 18: 15, 18), and distinguished by some of the people from the Messiah.

41. **Others said** (or, *were saying*), **This is the Christ. Others said** (or, *were saying*), **Shall (***the***) Christ come out of Galilee?** Their question implies a negative answer. The Christ does not come from Galilee, and therefore this man cannot be the Christ. They are represented as speaking, not according to the knowledge of the Evangelist—for the Evangelist knew that Jesus was born in Bethlehem—but according to common report; for Jesus was generally supposed and reported to be a native of Galilee, born in Nazareth. (See 1: 46.) It is scarcely possible that a writer in the middle of the second century could have been so uniformly true to the circumstances of the case as is this Evangelist.

42. **Hath not the Scripture said, That Christ cometh of the seed of David, and out of the town of Bethlehem, where David was?** Compare Rev. Ver. To this question an affirmative answer is expected; and it is therefore equivalent to an assertion that, according to the Scripture, the Messiah must be from the family and birthplace of David. By a little inquiry, which surely the miracles and teaching of Jesus called upon them to make, they might have learned that he was a native of Bethlehem. But they were not in a mood to investigate the matter fairly.

43. **So there was a division among the people** (*in the multitude*) **because of him.** That is, he was the occasion of a schism in the multitude; it arose because of him.

44. **And some of them would have taken him; but no man laid hands on him.** The class of persons in the multitude that was ready in heart to seize him may be the same as that spoken of in ver. 25-27—citizens of Jerusalem who were under the immediate influence of the hierarchy, though others may have been in accord with them. But it was not the will of God that they should now do what they wished to do. They were in some way restrained—perhaps by the manifest sympathy of a majority of the people with him.

45-53. REPORT OF THE OFFICERS TO THE SANHEDRIN, AND DISCUSSION THEREUPON.

45. **Then came the officers to the chief priests and Pharisees.** (See Note on ver. 32.) **And they**—to whom they came—**said unto them, Why have ye not brought him?** Literally, *Why did ye not bring him?* This calling of their servants to account was

CH. VII.]   JOHN.   181

46 The officers answered, *a* Never man spake like this man.
47 Then answered them the Pharisees, Are ye also deceived?
48 *b* Have any of the rulers or of the Pharisees believed on him?
49 But this people who knoweth not the law are cursed.
50 Nicodemus saith unto them, (*c* he that came to Jesus by night, being one of them,)
51 *d* Doth our law judge any man before it hear him, and know what he doeth?

46 bring him? The officers answered, Never man so spake. The Pharisees therefore answered them, Are
48 ye also led astray? Hath any of the rulers believed
49 on him, or of the Pharisees? But this multitude
50 who knoweth not the law are accursed. Nicodemus saith unto them (he that came to him before, being one
51 of them), Doth our law judge a man, except it first

---

a Matt. 7: 29....*b* ch. 12: 42; Acts 6: 7; 1 Cor. 1: 20, 26; 2: 8....*c* ch. 3: 2....*d* Deut. 1: 17; 17: 8; 19: 15.

---

natural, and it may be assumed that their servants were men not very likely to disregard the will of their superiors, or to be balked in their purpose.

46. The officers answered, Never man spake like this man. Some authorities have the text: *Never man so spake.* Tischendorf gives this reading: "*Never man spake as this man speaks.*" The import of their reply is not affected by these uncertainties as to the text. There was something in the teaching of Jesus which astonished and awed these officers of the Sanhedrin. Augustine is quoted by Lange: *Ejus vita est fulgor, ejus verba tonitrua*—"his life is lightning; his words thunders." Jesus probably said much more than John has recorded.

47. Then answered them the Pharisees—who had instigated this attempt to seize Jesus, and who were chagrined and angered by its failure—**Are ye also deceived?** The emphatic word is ye, and the form of the question assumes that a negative answer must be given. "Ye, the officers of this learned and sacred council, ye certainly have not been deceived?" There is a touch of scorn in the question, and an assumption that all who believed in Jesus were deceived. They do not consider it necessary to hear what Jesus has said, even though it has made such an impression on their servants.

48. Have any of the rulers or of the Pharisees believed on him? The matter is to be settled by authority, and not by looking at the evidence. If no one of the Sanhedrin has believed on him, he must be a deceiver. Perhaps they did not know that one of their own number, a Pharisee, had been convinced that he was a teacher come from God, and had been to see him by night. **Or of the Pharisees?** For their self-conceit must come out. The Pharisees were the orthodox Jews. What they believed, the people might believe; but it was absurd for the people to trust in one whom they rejected. These questions also presuppose a negative answer, and are equivalent to an assertion that no one of the rulers, or of the Pharisees, had believed in Jesus.

49. But this people (lit., *multitude*)—this throng in which you have been—a contemptuous expression—**who** (*that*) **knoweth not the law are cursed.** The expression *that knoweth not the law* implies that, if they knew the law, they would not believe in Christ. By their conduct now, as always, they prove their ignorance of God's law; and those who do not know the law *are accursed.* Bitter, indeed, was this outbreak of religious contempt and wrath. But it does not seem to have been a formal decree or proposition to exclude all adherents of Jesus from the synagogue. (Comp. 9: 22.)

The language of the Pharisees was in accord with their attempt to get Jesus into their hands, that they might kill him. They did not regard his guilt or innocence as an open question. They virtually pronounced a curse on all the people who adhered to him. But there was one of their number who could not keep silence any longer, and would not consent to the condemnation of Jesus without a fair trial, allowing him to be heard for himself.

50. Nicodemus saith unto them—that is, to the Pharisees, but probably in hearing of the whole Sanhedrin. **He that came to Jesus by night** (or, *to him before*)—recalling the narrative of 3: 1-21, and showing that Christ's words at that time had not been altogether fruitless. The words **by night** are not so well supported as *before*, and the rest of the clause; but the whole clause is wanting in a few manuscripts. **Being one of them.** For he was a Pharisee, as well as a ruler of the Jews.

51. Doth our law judge any (lit., *the*)

182 JOHN. [CH. VIII.

52 They answered and said unto him, Art thou also of Galilee? Search, and look: for *out of Galilee ariseth no prophet.

52 hear from himself and know what he doeth? They answered and said unto him, Art thou also of Galilee? Search, and ¹see that out of Galilee ariseth no prophet.

CHAPTER VIII.

53 And every man went unto his own house.
JESUS went unto the mount of Olives.
2 And early in the morning he came again into the temple and all the people came unto him; and he sat down, and taught them.

53 *[And they went every man unto his own house: 1 but Jesus went unto the mount of Olives. And 2 early in the morning he came again into the temple, and all the people came unto him; and he sat down,

a Isa. 9:1, 2 Matt. 4:15; ch. 1:46; ver. 41.——1 Or. *see*: *for out of Galilee, etc.*....2 Most of the ancient authorities omit John 7:53-8: 11. Those which contain it vary much from each other.

man—who in any particular instance is accused—before, etc.—(lit., *except it first hear from him, and know what he doeth ?*) The question assumes that the answer must be negative; and, in favor of such an answer, appeal is made to Deut. 1: 16; 19: 15-19. Modern jurisprudence is recognizing more and more the justice of allowing an accused person to testify in regard to himself. Of course, the fact will not be overlooked that he is an interested witness. In respect to the claims of a religious teacher, there is double reason for letting him speak for himself, namely, because religious prejudice is often strong, and because it is easy to misrepresent another's teaching.

52. Art thou also of (or, *from*) **Galilee?** By this question they assume (1) that no one but a native of Galilee could be expected to suggest that Jesus ought even to be heard in his own defence; and (2) that Nicodemus was not from Galilee, and therefore had spoken very absurdly, unaccountably. **Search, and look** (*see*): **for out of Galilee ariseth no prophet.** And if no prophet ariseth out of Galilee, Jesus cannot be even a prophet; much less can he be the Messiah. It has been thought incredible that the Sanhedrists should have made this statement. But it is not uncommon for persons under the influence of passion to pass beyond the truth. A few only of the prophets, two or three, at most, as Jonah, Hosea, Nahum, had sprung from Galilee; and these were either forgotten or overlooked in their eagerness to make a case against Jesus.

53. This verse, together with the first eleven verses of chapter 8, must be rejected, as forming no part of the original text. But the grounds of this rejection deserve to be stated at some length.¹

Ch. 8. The last verse of chapter 7 belongs with the first eleven verses of chapter 8, and this whole paragraph, containing the account of the Saviour's interview with *the adulteress and her accusers* appears, as we have seen, to have formed no part of the Gospel as it was first written by John. Yet the narrative bears every mark of truthfulness. It is evidently no myth, but the simple story of a real occurrence. "In any case," says Lange, "it is an apostolic relic." And Meyer calls it "a piece of writing from the apostolic age," and "an ancient relic of evangelical history."

7: 53. And every man went unto his own house. More strictly: *And they went every man unto his own house.* If this verse stands in its proper place, and the following narrative describes events which belong to this point of time in the Saviour's ministry, the expression **every man** refers naturally to the members of the Sanhedrin. These had failed in their attempt to seize Jesus, and had learned that one of their number was not his foe. It was time for them to separate; and it may be presumed that many of them repaired to their homes in bitterness of soul, disappointed at their failure, angry with their officers, disturbed by the words of Nicodemus, and eager to devise some new plot by which they might ensnare the prophet of Galilee.

8: 1. Jesus went unto the Mount of Olives. Whether to the house of Mary and Martha and Lazarus, no one can say. Six months later he was accustomed to spend the night in Bethany, or some other place on the Mount of Olives, while he passed the day in Jerusalem. (Luke 21:37.)

2. And early in the morning he came again into the temple. For he was intent upon his ministry, and sure that the hour was

¹[This remarkable passage can no longer be considered a part of the Fourth Gospel, and yet can hardly fail to be reckoned a true story of Jesus. It is wanting in אABCLTXΔ, and at least seventy cursives, and

Ch. VIII.] JOHN. 183

3 And the scribes and Pharisees brought unto him a woman taken in adultery; and when they had set her in the midst,

3 and taught them. And the scribes and the Pharisees bring a woman taken in adultery; and having

not yet come for him to be delivered into the hands of his enemies. **And all the people came** (or, *were coming*) **unto him.** Observe the imperfect tense of the verb, denoting continued action. The rest of this verse: **And he sat down, and taught them,** is not found in the Cambridge manuscript, the oldest authority for this section (Watkins), and should not be considered a part of the text, though it is doubtless true that Jesus was teaching the people as they resorted to him. The Greek word (ὄρθρου), here used to signify **early in**

the morning, is not the one used elsewhere by John.
3. And the scribes and Pharisees brought (rather, *bring*) **unto him a woman taken in adultery, and when they had set her in the midst,** etc. It is natural to conjecture that the woman dwelt in Jerusalem, and that her sin was committed there; but nothing can be certainly known on these points. Nor is the place of her residence or of her sin of the slightest consequence. Sin is the same everywhere. But those who brought

numerous Evangelistaria; and is marked as of doubtful genuineness (with asterisks, or obeli) in many other manuscripts. Also wanting in Old Syriac, Peshito, and Harklean, in some copies of the Old Latin, in Memphitic (best codices), Thebaic, Armenian, and Gothic. Origen, Chrysostom, Cyril, and several other Greek Fathers, in commentaries on John, pass at once from 7: 52 to 8: 12, without allusion to anything be*ween. Tertullian and Cyprian, in copious discussions of the question whether an adulterous person could be restored to fellowship, make no mention of this story. No Greek manuscript earlier than the eighth century contains the passage except D, which has very many unwarranted additions to the text. No Greek patristic writing earlier than the tenth century, except the so-called "Apostolical Constitutions," refers to such a passage. Of eight early Greek commentators on John whose works remain, only Euthymius (twelfth century) mentions the passage, and he says it is wanting, or marked with an obelisk in the accurate copies, and must be an interpolation. Tatian's "Diatessaron" seems not to have included it, to judge from the absence of reference to it in the recently found commentary of Ephrem (Zahn, p. 190). No early version has it but the Æthiopic, the Jerusalem Syriac lesson book, and the Latin Vulgate, with many copies of the Old Latin. Thus the early documentary authority for the passage is almost entirely Latin, including Ambrose, Jerome, and Augustine, with D and the Æthiopic. It is a familiar fact that D, Latin versions and Fathers, and often the Æthiopic, are constantly giving "Western" alterations and interpolations. It must be added that the documents containing this passage exhibit a great number of variations in detail, which is always a suspicious circumstance.

No adequate reason has been suggested for the omission of this passage, if originally present. Augustine, in using the passage as a proof-text in an argument, says that some have removed it from their copies, fearing, he supposes, that it may give their wives impunity. But Hort has pointed out that there is no parallel case of a wide-spread omission of an extended passage, because unacceptable; that while Montanists and Novatians might have found this story a stumbling-block, the early

Christians in general would not at all; and that, if anywhere thus objected to, it would have been in Latin Christendom, while yet the three great Latin Fathers are its chief defenders. Another theory, that it was omitted from lesson books, and then from copies of the Gospel, quite fails to establish itself. (See Hort.) On the other hand, we can easily imagine how so striking and beautiful a story may have been placed on the margin of the Gospel, perhaps (Ewald, Lightfoot) to illustrate our Lord's statement (8: 15); "I judge no man"; and that then it crept into the text of many copies, being usually inserted after 7: 52, but in the cursive 225 after 7: 36. So in the lost uncial, represented by the kindred cursives 13, 69, 124, 346, it is given at the end of Luke, ch. 21, where 21: 37 corresponds to the beginning of the story; and in about a dozen cursives and some codices of the Armenian it is transferred to the *end* of the Fourth Gospel.

The story is eminently characteristic of Jesus, and is not at all likely to have been invented by any of the early Christians; it is, therefore, in all probability, an early account of a real occurrence. The style is so far unlike that of John (though some critics have overstated and misstated the differences), that we cannot suppose it to have come from him, and the narrator cannot be known. Eusebius ("History," 3, 39) tells of Papias, who wrote, about A. D. 130, a work entitled "Expositions of the Lord's Discourses" (or, History), in which he proposed (as Eusebius quotes from his Preface) to put with the Expositions matters derived by him from persons who had conversed with the apostles, thereby confirming his explanations. After quoting from this work certain stories as to the origin of the Gospels of Mark and Matthew, Eusebius says that Papias "has also put forth another story, concerning a woman accused before the Lord touching many sins, which is contained in the Gospel according to the Hebrews." From the collection of Papias, or from the oft mentioned Apocryphal Gospel according to the Hebrews, the story very likely came to the margin of John and of Luke. Various other sayings ascribed to Jesus by D, or by early Fathers, are also, probably real sayings of his, though not a part of the Scriptures.—B.]

184   JOHN.   [Ch. VIII.

4 They say unto him, Master, this woman was taken in adultery, in the very act.
5 ᵃ Now Moses in the law commanded us, that such should be stoned: but what sayest thou?
6 This they said, tempting him, that they might have to accuse him. But Jesus stooped down, and with *his* finger wrote on the ground, *as though he heard them not.*
7 So when they continued asking him, he lifted up himself, and said unto them, ᵇ He that is without sin among you, let him first cast a stone at her.

4 set her in the midst, they say unto him, ¹ Master, this woman hath been taken in adultery, in the very 5 act. Now in the law Moses commanded us to stone 6 such: what then sayest thou of her? And this they said, trying him, that they might have *whereof* to accuse him. But Jesus stooped down, and with his 7 finger wrote on the ground. But when they continued asking him, he lifted up himself, and said unto them, He that is without sin among you, let

a Lev. 20: 10; Deut. 22: 22....*b* Deut. 17: 7; Rom. 2: 1.—¹ Or, *Teacher.*

her to Jesus had, no doubt, some kind of authority in the case. They are called **scribes and Pharisees**—an expression frequently occurring in the first three Gospels, but nowhere else in the Fourth. Instead of it, John employs the expression "the Jews," meaning by it the religious leaders of the people, especially members of the Sanhedrin. Instead of the words **taken in adultery**, the Cambridge manuscript reads "taken in sin." It also omits "unto him" in the first clause, reading thus: *And the Scribes and Pharisees bring a woman taken in sin.*

4. Master, this woman was taken in adultery, in the very act. Meyer remarks that "the adulterer, who was likewise guilty of death (Lev. 20: 10; Deut. 22: 24) *may have escaped.*"

5. Now, Moses in the law commanded us, that such should be stoned. If the passage of the law referred to is Deut. 22: 23, 24, and if the law was strictly applicable to the case in hand, the woman brought before Jesus was betrothed, but not married. Yet her sin was reckoned as great as if she were already married. But if Lev. 20: 10 be compared with Ex. 31: 14 and 35: 2, as interpreted by Num. 15: 32-35, it will seem very probable that stoning was understood to be the way in which adulterers and adulteresses were to be punished with death. **But what sayest thou?** Better: *What sayest thou?* This question was doubtless asked with a bearing and tone of affected candor and respect; but the hearts of the Scribes and Pharisees who proposed it were full of enmity to Jesus.

6. This they said, tempting him, that they might have to accuse him. Their object was to lead him into a snare, as when he was asked whether it was lawful to pay tribute to Cesar, or not. For if, in the present case, he had answered: "Let her be stoned, according to the Mosaic law," it would have been easy to accuse him to Pilate as teaching the Jews to do what was contrary to Roman law; for Roman law did not allow subject peoples to inflict the punishment of death (see 18: 31), nor did it punish with death the crime committed by this woman. Moreover, it is probable that many of the people who loved Jesus for his gentleness and sympathy would have been offended by this answer; for the law of Moses had ceased to be executed upon adulterers by the Jews. But if, on the other hand, he had said, "Let her not be stoned," they would probably have accused him of attempting to make void their law, and subvert their religion, thus increasing the hostility of a certain part of the Jews to himself. The snare was skillfully laid, and it needed superhuman wisdom in Jesus to escape it. Yet he escaped without apparent difficulty. **But Jesus stooped down and with his finger wrote** (or, *was writing*) **on the ground.** Observe the descriptive imperfect. The writer depicts the scene as if he had been an eyewitness. But what did this action of Jesus signify? According to the best light now accessible, it seems to have been a silent but intelligible intimation that he would think of something else rather than their question. Hence that, for some reason, their question was unworthy of attention or response. What he wrote was, therefore, of no consequence; it was the stooping down and writing that was a silent reproof to his questioners, giving them time to reflect and come to a better mind.

7. So (or, *but*) **when they continued asking him**—for they were resolved to accomplish their purpose—**he lifted up himself and said unto them: He that is without sin among you, let him first cast a stone at** (or, *upon*) **her.** These words were so uttered—with such holy insight and authority—that they could not be parried or resisted. They did not condemn the Mosaic law; they rather authorized obedience to it; but on such terms as awakened conscience and prevented any violation of Roman law. He

8 And again he stooped down, and wrote on the ground.
9 And they which heard *it*, ᵃ being convicted by their own conscience, went out one by one, beginning at the eldest, *even* unto the last: and Jesus was left alone, and the woman standing in the midst.
10 When Jesus had lifted up himself, and saw none but the woman, he said unto her, Woman, where are those thine accusers? hath no man condemned thee?
11 She said, No man, Lord. And Jesus said unto her, ᵇ Neither do I condemn thee: go, and ᶜ sin no more.
12 Then spake Jesus again unto them, saying, ᵈ I am the light of the world: he that followeth me shall not walk in darkness, but shall have the light of life.

8 him first cast a stone at her. And again he stooped 9 down, and with his finger wrote on the ground. And they, when they heard it, went out one by one, beginning from the eldest, *even* unto the last: and Jesus was left alone, and the woman, where she was, 10 in the midst. And Jesus lifted up himself, and said unto her, Woman, where are they? did no man con-11 demn thee? And she said, No man, Lord. And Jesus said, Neither do I condemn thee: go thy way; from henceforth sin no more.]
12 Again therefore Jesus spake unto them, saying, I am the light of the world: he that followeth me shall not walk in the darkness, but shall have the light

---

a Rom. 2: 22....*b* Luke 9; 56; 12; 14; ch. 3: 17....*c* ch. 5: 14....*d* ch. 1; 4, 5, 9; 3: 19; 9: 5; 12: 35, 36, 46.

wrought in the domain of spirit, and his only weapon was truth. His foes were discomfited, the spirituality of the divine law was revealed, and mercy was shown to the lost. "The skill of this reply consists in disarming the extemporized judges of this woman, without showing the least disrespect to the ordinance of Moses. The code remains, only there is no one to execute it."—*Godet.* The expression, **without sin,** may have been used by Jesus in an absolute sense; but it is perhaps more natural to suppose a reference to unchastity, though not simply to the outward act. (See Matt. 5: 28.) Desire is sin; and the Saviour may have uttered his words with such a look and tone as led his foes to feel that he was reading the secrets of their spiritual history. At any rate, the effect of his brief response was remarkable.

8. And again he stooped down and wrote (*with his finger*) **on the ground.** Intimating by this act that he had nothing further to say, and had no wish to hear more from them. In so far as they were concerned the case was finished.

9. And they which heard it, etc. *They, when they heard, were convicted by their conscience, and went out one by one, beginning from the older unto the last; and Jesus was left alone, and the woman standing in the midst.* This is a literal rendering of the ordinary text; and it makes a very graphic and life-like picture. The hearing is represented as a completed act, but the being convicted by conscience as a process going on in the minds of the scribes and Pharisees. In the older persons it was more rapid. They saw the position in which they were placed, the unanswerable wisdom of Christ's response, the utter failure of their scheme, and one by one they silently withdrew. The younger men soon followed, and the woman, filled with shame and sorrow, was left alone with the Holy One, in the very place where she had been put by her accusers.

10. When Jesus had lifted up, himself and saw none but the woman, he said unto her, Woman, where are those thine accusers? hath no man condemned thee? The Cambridge manuscript has only the following: "*And when Jesus had lifted himself up, he said unto the woman, Where are they? did no one condemn thee?*" The shorter form implies all that is expressed in the longer form, and is perhaps more likely to be original.

11. And she said, No man, Lord. And Jesus said unto her, Neither do I condemn thee; go and sin no more. The bearing of the woman, so far as it can be inferred from the narrative, and especially from the words of Jesus, render it probable that she was truly penitent. If so, the words, **neither do I condemn thee,** imply forgiveness, and, taken with the words that follow, justify the saying of Augustine that Jesus "forgives the sinner, but condemns the sin." Yet Godet's comment is worthy of consideration: "We need not confound the words of Jesus to this woman with a positive declaration of forgiveness, like that of Luke 7: 48, 50. The woman had not come to Jesus by an impulse of faith, as the woman who was a sinner, but penitent, came. Jesus simply grants her time to repent and believe."

12-19. SUBSEQUENT COLLOQUY WITH THE PHARISEES.

12. Then (or, *therefore*) **spake Jesus again unto them.** If, as we suppose, the paragraph relating to the adulteress did not belong to the original text, this verse followed 7: 52; but in all probability some length of time, a day perhaps, passed between the dialogue ending with that verse, and the dialogue beginning here. The pronoun **them** must be supposed to mean the people generally at

186   JOHN.   [Ch. VIII.

13 The Pharisees therefore said unto him, *a* Thou bearest record of thyself; thy record is not true.
14 Jesus answered and said unto them, Though I bear record of myself, *yet* my record is true; for I know whence I came, and whither I go; but *b* ye cannot tell whence I come, and whither I go.

13 of life. The Pharisees said unto him, Thou bearest witness of thyself; therefore thy witness is not true.
14 Jesus answered and said unto them, Even if I bear witness of myself, my witness is true; for I know whence I came, and whither I go; but ye know not

a ch. 5:31....*b* See ch. 7:28; 9:29.

the feast. The conjunction **then** (or, *therefore*) points to something not mentioned, which was the occasion of the saying of Jesus preserved in this verse. Whatever that occasion may have been, a knowledge of it would not probably add anything to the force of Christ's language as addressed to the readers of the Gospel. **I am the light of the world.** This may have been the basis in John's thought for his declaration in the prologue. (1:4.) Light is the means of seeing, and seeing is knowing. Jesus here claims to be the one medium of divine knowledge—the original light, which is in fact the source of all other light and life which reveal God. By the **world** he evidently means "the world of mankind," as naturally in darkness by reason of sin. (See Maclaren, "Weekday Evening Addresses," for an interesting discourse on this saying of Christ). **He that followeth me**—as a disciple follows his teacher and guide; he who follows me habitually, so that this following is characteristic of him—**shall not walk in darkness** (or, *in the darkness*). The double negative (οὐ μή) may be regarded as emphatic, and might be represented by the phrase *by no means*, which is slightly stronger than the simple **not**. Neither the reality (οὐ) nor the possibility (μή) of walking in darkness is to be feared. The darkness referred to is occasioned by sin, and consists in a want of divine knowledge, that is, of a true knowledge of God. **But shall have the light of** (*the*) **life.** The light which has its source in the true life (1:4). that knowledge of God through Christ, which is the highest blessedness of man. This is one of the clearest and most solemn sayings of Jesus. No mere man, who was not thoroughly insane or inexpressibly arrogant, could have uttered these words. Either Jesus was the Son of God and truly divine, or the Jews were right in rejecting his doctrine and authority. If he was **the light of the world,** he was "in the beginning with God," and "was God"; if he was not the light of the world, he deserved punishment as a blasphemer, or pity as a man bereft of reason. No

middle ground is tenable. And to one who considers the calmness, the moral purity, the deep wisdom, the mighty works, and the imperishable influence of Jesus Christ, the hypothesis of mental or religious insanity is absurd. He was therefore all that his most devout followers have believed—the God-man and only meditator between God and man.

13. The Pharisees therefore said unto him: Thou bearest record of thyself; thy record is not true. That is to say: It was long a principle of law that no one could be allowed to testify in his own behalf; for as he was a party interested, his testimony could not, therefore, be accepted as true. Probably they did not intend to say more than this. But the legal practice of refusing to hear any man's testimony respecting himself, is a human and clumsy expedient to guard against error by rejecting one source of truth. For, in many cases, the testimony of a person concerning himself is the only evidence possible, while in many other cases such testimony is entitled to more confidence than that of witnesses who are supposed to be disinterested. In the last analysis everything depends upon the knowledge and character of the witness.

14. Though (or, *even if*) **I bear record** (or, *witness*) **of** (or, *concerning*) **myself**—as he had just done, and as he was about to do with great positiveness—**my record** (or, *witness*) **is true.** That is to say: Truthful, in harmony with fact, and worthy of all confidence. **For I know whence I came and whither I go; but ye cannot tell** (lit., *know not*) **whence I come, and whither I go.** Thus Jesus overrules the merely formal or technical objection to his testimony by deliberately claiming a knowledge which the Pharisees did not possess. They knew something indeed of his earthly parentage (7:28), and home in Nazareth; but of his heavenly parentage and "glory with the Father before the world was" (17:5) they were entirely ignorant. Of the latter, he only, of all the sons of men, had any direct knowledge; and such were his character (7:16 sq.) and con-

15 a Ye judge after the flesh; b I judge no man.
16 And yet if I judge, my judgment is true: for c I am not alone, but I and the Father that sent me.
17 d It is also written in your law, that the testimony of two men is true.

15 whence I come, or whither I go. Ye judge after the flesh; I judge no man. Yea and if I judge, my judgment is true; for I am not alone, but I and the
17 Father that sent me. Yea and in your law it is writ-

a ch. 7: 24....b ch. 3: 17; 12: 47; 18: 36....c ver. 29; ch. 16: 32....d Deut. 17: 6; 19: 15; Matt. 18: 16; 2 Cor. 13: 1; Heb. 10: 28.

nection with the Father (see ver. 16-18 below), that his testimony ought to be received as perfect and conclusive. The reader will observe that Jesus says: **I know whence I came**, using the past tense because he had in mind his incarnation and ye **cannot tell**, etc. (or, *know not*), using the present tense **come** because he had in mind his present and frequent manifestation of himself to them as the Messiah. They could not be expected to know whence he *came* at his birth; but they might have known that his coming to them, in his public ministry, was with divine power and wisdom, indicative of a heavenly origin.

15. Ye judge after the flesh. Ye is emphatic in contrast with **I** of the next clause. To **judge**, as here used, is to condemn; and this is a very frequent use of the word in the Fourth Gospel. To condemn **after the flesh** is to make the outward appearance, the visible form and state, of any person, the reason for an unfavorable decision respecting him. The Pharisees were doing precisely this. And they were acting as if to judge in such a manner were their business, their office, and the object of their lives. They saw in Jesus a mere man, of humble origin and no visible authority, and therefore they refused to believe that he was the Son of God, the Bread of Life, or the Light of the world. **I judge no man.** This statement is not to be qualified by adding the words, "after the flesh," for such an addition cannot be made to the next clause. The denial of Jesus should rather be traced to his consciousness of having come into the world, not to condemn, but to save. (See 12: 47.) "My true business is not to judge, but to save; and if, by way of *exception*, I judge, it is only those who will not suffer themselves to be saved."—*Meyer.* But Godet insists that the expression *no one* cannot be limited by what follows. It is better, he says, to understand the emphatic pronoun **I**, as equivalent to *I alone*, or "apart from the Father," and meaning the same as 5: 30: "I can of mine own self do nothing," etc. But the interpretation first given is preferable to this.

16. And yet (or, *even*) **if I judge, my judgment is true.** This language concedes that, though judging is not the object of his mission to mankind, he does, nevertheless, at times, judge those with whom he meets, and, indeed, is doing this now; yet it affirms that whenever he judges, his judgment is perfect. It is not "after the flesh," or "according to appearance," but according to truth and righteousness—a divine judgment. This interpretation supposes that John wrote a Greek word (ἀληθινή), which means *true*, as satisfying our conception of what judgment ought to be, and not the word (ἀληθής), which means simply truthful, or veracious. Both of these words, owing to the poverty of our language, must be translated by the term *true*. Lach., Tisch., Treg., West. and Hort unite in the former Greek adjective for this sentence. **For I am not alone, but I and the Father that sent me.** Therefore, my judgment is not merely human, as you suppose, but also divine: it is God's judgment; for such is my relation to the Father that whatever I say, he says, and whatever I do, he does. In judging we are one.

17. It is also written in your law (or, *and even in your law it is written*). Compare 10: 34; 15: 25. Why does Jesus say **your** law? Perhaps because the Pharisees were extreme legalists, joined with the circumstance that they had virtually appealed to the law as a reason for rejecting his testimony. Yet he may mean to suggest that he himself is superior to the technical rules of the Mosaic code, being truly united with God. **That the testimony of two men is true** (Deut. 17: 6; 19: 15). This is a free, rather than a literal quotation, giving the substance, rather than the words of the law. Instead of speaking of the testimony of *two witnesses*, it speaks of the testimony of **two men**, perhaps in order to direct attention to the fact that the law was applicable to ordinary men, rather than to the Messiah. The order of the Greek words favors this view by making the words **two men** emphatic, thus: *that of two men the tes-*

18 I am one that bear witness of myself, and *the Father that sent me beareth witness of me.
19 Then said they unto him, Where is thy Father? Jesus answered, *Ye neither know me, nor my Father: if ye had known me, ye should have known my Father also.
20 These words spake Jesus in *the treasury, as he taught in the temple: and *no man laid hands on him; for *his hour was not yet come.

18 ten, that the witness of two men is true. I am he that beareth witness of myself, and the Father that sent me beareth witness of me. They said therefore unto him, Where is thy Father? Jesus answered, Ye know neither me, nor my Father: if ye knew me, 20 ye would know my Father also. These words spake he in the treasury, as he taught in the temple: and no man took him; because his hour was not yet come.

a ch. 5: 37....b ver. 55; ch. 16: 3....c ch. 14: 7....d Mark 12: 41....e ch. 7: 30....f ch. 7: 8.

timony is true. If not subject to the formal rules of Jewish law, Jesus asserts that his testimony fulfills, in a very real and deep sense, the requirement of that law.

18. I am one (rather, *I am he*) **that bear witness of myself, and the Father that sent me beareth witness of me.** (See 5: 19-30). By this language, Jesus intends to affirm, not that by any act separate from his own the Father bears witness of him, but that his own testimony is the testimony of the Father as well. So profound and complete is the union between them, that the word of the theanthropic Christ is the word of his Father also.

19. Then (or, *therefore*) **said they unto him, Where is thy Father?** Well does Meyer pronounce this question of the Pharisees *"frivolous mockery."* For they could not have been in doubt as to his meaning. They must have been fully convinced that he spoke of God as his Father. But they rejected his claim to be the Son of God, and demanded of him, in derision, where his Father might be. **Ye neither know me, nor my Father.** Ignorance of Christ and ignorance of God go together. Nay, since Christ is the light of the world, to be ignorant of him is to be ignorant of true knowledge—the knowledge of God. **If ye had known me,** etc. The Revised Version is here correct: *If ye knew me, ye would know my Father also.* For the meaning, compare the words of Jesus in 14: 7-9; 16: 3; and Matt. 11: 27. To know Christ is to know God; for at the very root of being they are one. The Father is in the Son, and whatsoever the Father doeth, the Son doeth in like manner. The reverse of this is also true, that whatsoever the Son doeth, the same doth the Father likewise.

20. These words spake Jesus (rather, *he*) **in the treasury, as he taught in the temple.** This exact specification of the place in which Jesus spoke thus to the Pharisees is natural, if the writer was John, and if he was present at the time; but it is by no means natural, if the Fourth Gospel was written, as some aver, by an unknown Christian, living far down in the second century. **The treasury** appears to have been located in the Women's Court. (Compare Mark 12: 41; and Luke 21: 1). According to the Mishna, there were, in the temple, thirteen treasure-chests, for the reception of gifts of money, to be devoted to so many special purposes, designated by the inscriptions upon them. These were called "trumpets," either from their shape, or from the shape of the opening into which the contributions were dropped. They are generally identified with the "treasuries" mentioned by Josephus ("B. J." v. 5, 2), who speaks of the cloisters which surrounded the Court of the Women, on the inside of its wall, as placed before them; and they may, perhaps, have been collectively called "the treasury" in the passages of Mark and Luke above referred to. In John 8: 20, it would seem probable that the Court of the Women is itself called "the treasury," "because it contained these repositories."—*Abbott,* in Smith's "Dict. of the Bible." **And no man laid hands on him** (i. e., *took him*); **for his hour was not yet come.** Doubtless, the Evangelist, who was present, saw many indications of deadly hostility to Jesus on the part of the Jews. They desired to seize him by violence, and put him to death. But the hour which had been fixed in the councils of God for such violence was not yet come. Yet we are not informed of the obstacles which prevented the enemies of Christ from laying hands on him at this time. The Evangelist is satisfied with tracing his escape to the purpose and providence of God. But this is an evidence that the hatred of the Jews seemed to him deadly.

21-30. COLLOQUY RESPECTING HIS DEATH.

Verse 20 suggests that the conversation with the Pharisees ended with the saying of Jesus

CH. VIII.] JOHN. 189

21 Then said Jesus again unto them, I go my way, and ᵃ ye shall seek me, and ᵇ shall die in your sins: whither I go, ye cannot come.
22 Then said the Jews, Will he kill himself? because he saith, Whither I go, ye cannot come.
23 And he said unto them, ᶜ Ye are from beneath; I am from above: ᵈ ye are of this world, I am not of this world.
24 ᵉ I said therefore unto you, that ye shall die in your sins: ᶠ for if ye believe not that I am *he*, ye shall die in your sins.

21 He said therefore again unto them, I go away, and ye shall seek me, and shall die in your sin: whither I go, ye cannot come. The Jews therefore said, Will he kill himself, that he saith, Whither I go, ye
23 cannot come? And he said unto them, Ye are from beneath; I am from above: ye are of this world; I
24 am not of this world. I said therefore unto you, that ye shall die in your sins: for except ye believe

a ch. 7: 34; 13: 33....*b* ver. 24.....*c* ch. 3: 31....*d* ch. 15: 19; 17: 16; 1 John 4: 5....*e* ver. 21..../ Mark 16: 16.

recorded in verse 19. The particular persons who had undertaken to answer him and judge him were silenced, and hence they seem to have passed on their way. But Jesus remained in the Court of the Women, ready to declare the truth to all who would hear.

21. Then said Jesus again unto them. Better: *He said therefore again unto them.* By them must be meant, not the Pharisees spoken of in the foregoing paragraph, but the people who were now in the Court, most of whom were in nearly the same moral state as the Pharisees. **I go my way** (or, *away*). (Compare 7: 33, 34; 13: 33). By these words Jesus predicts his approaching separation from this world, and from those to whom he was speaking. As the end of his earthly life draws near, he often refers to it. **And ye shall** (or, *will*) **seek me.** You will long for deliverance from impending evil; you will wish for the Messiah to rescue you from destruction; but in vain. The evil will come upon you. **And shall** (or, *will*) **die in your sins** (or, *sin*). That is, encompassed by it, oppressed by it, condemned on account of it. You will die unforgiven. The sin here meant is sin in general—all the sin of which the people addressed had been guilty, and not specially the sin of unbelief; though their unbelief in Jesus was certainly the reason why they would find no forgiveness, but die in their sin. **Whither I go, ye cannot come.** The pronouns **I** and **ye** are emphatic. The contrast between the two parties is clear and pronounced. His destination is manifestly assumed to be heaven; but to that blessed place they are unable to come. It is a place without sin, and only those who have been delivered from sin can enter it. The language of Jesus is fearfully direct and positive. But it makes no deep impression on the self-righteous persons addressed.

22. Then said the Jews (or, *therefore, the Jews were saying*). The words passed from one to another, and were uttered with a tone of levity and contempt. **Will he kill himself?** or, "*he will not kill himself, will he?*" As if that were the only way in which he could go to a place, namely, Gehenna, where they could not follow. For suicide was regarded as the greatest sin, dooming one to the lowest hell. "The mockery, which also Hengstenberg denies without reason, is similar to that in 7: 35, but more malignant."—*Meyer.* For the Jewish idea of suicide, see Josephus' "Wars of the Jews," III., viii., 5. No wonder his response was plain, and even severe.

23. Ye are from beneath; I am from above: ye are of (*from*) **this world,** etc. There seems to be no sufficient reason for translating the same preposition **from** in the first two clauses, and **of** in the last two. In both instances it means **from**, pointing to the origin or source. **From beneath** and *from this world* are equivalent expressions, denoting the merely earthly origin of the Jews, while **from above** and *not from* **this world** manifestly point to the heavenly origin of Jesus. (See 3: 31; 1 Cor. 15: 47, 48; 1 John, 4: 5.) That the character of the Jews, and the character of Christ, correspond with their origin respectively, is clearly implied. The stream is like the fountain. That which is born of flesh is flesh, and that which is born of the Spirit is spirit. An evil tree cannot bring forth good fruit, neither can a good tree bring forth evil fruit.

24. I said therefore unto you, that ye shall (*will*) **die in your sins.** Jesus asserts that their origin from a sinful race, with their character agreeing with their origin, renders it certain that, remaining as they are, they will die without being delivered from either the power or the guilt of their sins. For to die in one's sins, is to die unrenewed and unforgiven. By using the plural **sins** instead of the singular *sin* as in (ver. 21), Jesus may have intended to fix special attention on the latter

25 Then said they unto him, Who art thou? And Jesus saith unto them, Even *the same* that I said unto you from the beginning.
26 I have many things to say and to judge of you: but *a* he that sent me is true; and *b* I speak to the world those things which I have heard of him.

25 that I am *he*, ye shall die in your sins. They said therefore unto him, Who art thou? Jesus said unto them, ¹ Even that which I have also spoken unto 26 you from the beginning. I have many things to speak and to judge concerning you: howbeit he that sent me is true; and the things which I heard

a ch. 7: 28....*b* ch. 3: 32; 15: 15.—1 Or, *Altogether that which I also speak unto you.*

fact, that they would die unforgiven; for, while the New Testament often uses the word sin to denote the moral condition of the natural man, it always uses the plural form, sins, when it speaks of forgiveness. **For if ye believe not that I am** (*he*), **ye shall die in your sins.** "There is a possibility of escape, but only through faith in me." The implication being, that they are unprepared to yield this confidence to him, and that they will die under condemnation. We supply the predicate "he," meaning the Messiah, though many excellent interpreters believe that the words **I am** denote the self-existent and divine nature of Jesus. Thus Westcott remarks "that the phrase I am" (ἐγώ εἰμι) occurs three times in this chapter (ver. 24, 28, 58; compare 13: 19), and on each occasion, as it seems, with this pregnant meaning. (Compare Deut. 32: 39; Isa. 43: 10.) But he admits that "elsewhere, in cases where the predicate is directly suggested by the context, this predicate simply is to be supplied: (9: 9; 18: 5; 6: 8; compare 6: 20; Matt. 14: 27; Mark 6: 50; 14: 62; Luke 22: 70). And so it is used of the Messiah: (Mark 13: 6; Luke 21: 8)." Either interpretation is certainly possible, but we believe that the question between Christ and these Jews related to his Messiahship.

25. Who art thou? This question was probably asked in a tone of incredulity and contempt. "Your claim is very extraordinary; who then are you, pray?" Perhaps the verbal indefiniteness of his words recorded in ver. 24—"I am," instead of "I am the Messiah," —led them to ask this question. though they understood well enough what he meant. **Even the same that I said unto you from the beginning.** The meaning of the original sentence is uncommonly obscure. In translating it, the Revised Version, the Revised Bible, the Bible Union Revision, and a number of commentators agree substantially with the Common Version. Yet it is doubtful whether the Greek phrase τὴν ἀρχὴν) translated **from the beginning** ever has that meaning. John expresses that thought by a different phrase (viz: ἀπ' ἀρχῆς or ἐξ ἀρχῆς), and one which is entirely clear. Moreover, the original of the verb translated **said,** is in the present tense, and means, properly, *I speak* or *say*. But the perfect tense would more naturally have been used if the adverbial phrase was understood to signify **from the beginning.** Hence we are not satisfied with this version. But the Revised Bible gives another in the margin, viz.: *Altogether that which I am also telling you.* And it seems to be pretty well established that the expression (τὴν ἀρχὴν) may signify *altogether, wholly*, or *entirely* (= *omnino*). The sentence then means, according to Grimm, Winer and many others, *I am wholly that which I also say to you;* or "not only I am, but I am also saying to you what I am: there is then no reason why you should ask me." There is a touch of displeasure and reproof in his reply, thus interpreted. But there is still more of these according to a third view of his words, namely, that they are to be understood as a question. This view is given in the margin of the Rev. Ver., Eng. Ed.: How is it *that I even speak to you at all?* or, *wherefore do I even speak to you at all?* "Your spirit is such as to render you unworthy of any word from me. It is vain to testify to you the truth concerning myself or my mission." This appears to have been the interpretation given to the sentence by the Greek Fathers, and it is adopted by Meyer, Weiss, Watkins, Milligan and Moulton. Westcott wavers between this and the preceding view. Either of them agrees with the context, but the one last named is more forcible, and besides has in its favor the judgment of those to whom the Greek was their native language.

26. I have many things to say and to judge of you. According to the order of the Greek words, the term signifying **many things** is emphatic, and the same is true in a lower degree of the expression of **you.** Whether these many things of a condemnatory character were actually said by Jesus, or were merely alluded to and passed by in si-

Ch. VIII.] JOHN.

27 They understood not that he spake to them of the Father.
28 Then said Jesus unto them, When ye have *a* lifted up the Son of man, *b* then shall ye know that I am *he*, and *that* I do nothing of myself; but *d* as my Father hath taught me, I speak these things.
29 And *e* he that sent me is with me: *f* the Father hath not left me alone; *g* for I do always those things that please him.

27 from him, these speak I unto the world. They perceived not that he spake to them of the Father.
28 Jesus therefore said, When ye have lifted up the Son of man, then shall ye know that I am *he*, and that I do nothing of myself, but as the Father taught me, I speak these things. And he that sent me is with me; he hath not left me alone; for I do always

a ch. 3: 15; 12: 32....*b* Rom. 1: 4....*c* ch. 5: 19, 30....*d* ch. 3: 11....*e* ch. 14; 10, 11..../ ver. 16....*g* ch. 4; 34; 5: 30; 6; 38.—I Or, *I am he; and I do.*

lence, depends upon the relation of this clause to the following. But he that sent me is true; and I speak to the world those things which I have heard of him (lit., *the things which I heard from him*). The word *but* may indicate that what he speaks is what he heard from the Father, who is true, and that it is something different from the many things which he has it in his power to say of the Jews before him; or it may indicate that these many things are not simply judgments of his own, formed independently of the Father, but, rather, what he had heard from the Source of truth, by whom he was sent into the world. The latter view is preferable to the former.

27. They understood (or, *knew*) **not that he spake to them of the Father.** This statement has been pronounced inconsistent with the context, and therefore incredible. But we are to bear in mind (1) that the multitudes whom Jesus addressed in the temple were, in all probability, constantly changing; (2) that the failure of the Jews whom he was now addressing to perceive that he referred to the Father as the One who had sent him, is mentioned just because it was surprising; (3) that this failure to understand the Lord was, in reality, no more unaccountable than many instances of similar failure on the part of the disciples, when things were said which they did not wish to believe; and (4) that the blinding influence of prejudice and passion is often truly amazing and unaccountable. There is, therefore, no sufficient reason for calling in question this plain assertion of the Evangelist.

28. Omit the words **unto them,** in the first clause; for, according to the best editors, it did not belong to the earliest text. **When ye have lifted up the Son of man.** These words refer to his death on the cross, which was to be effected by the enmity of the Jews, through the agency of Roman soldiers (compare 3: 14; 6: 62). **Then shall ye know that I am [he].** On the question whether

"he" should be supplied after **am,** see Note on verse 21. The crucifixion of Christ was to be the source of his power. By it he was to draw all men to himself. (12: 32.) In consequence of it he was to be glorified with the Father, and to give the Holy Spirit. (Acts 2: 32, sq.; Phil. 2: 9, sq.) **And that I do nothing of** (*from*) **myself.** In other words: "You look upon me as a man, speaking and acting for myself, like other men. But this is not the case. No word or act of mine springs from myself alone, apart from God." **But as my Father hath taught me, I speak these things.** Or, as in the Rev. Ver. : *But as the Father taught me, I speak these things.* The tense of the verb *taught* carries the mind back to the pre-existent state of Jesus, who, in his higher nature, the Word, was with God before the world was. Hence the Saviour claims not only that his teaching is truly divine, but also that it was in the mind of God before the incarnation. And this statement accords with the view that even the details of redemption were all known and fixed in the counsels of heaven from eternity. The pronoun *my*, before Father, in the Common Version, must be considered an addition to the original text.

29. And he that sent me is with me. This clause may be connected with the foregoing statements back to **ye shall know;** thus: "Then shall ye know that I am he, and that I do nothing from myself, but as the Father taught me I speak these things, and that he that sent me is with me." The last assertion is then repeated negatively: *He* (the true reading, instead of **the Father) hath not left me alone**—at any moment or in any act of my career; and for an all-sufficient reason: **because I do always** *the* (not those) **things that please him.** This claim is absolute, unqualified. Jesus declares himself conscious of doing his Father's will always and in all respects. He is certain of being positively holy in conduct; and, according to

30 As he spake these words, *a* many believed on him.
31 Then said Jesus to those Jews which believed on him, If ye continue in my word, then are ye my disciples indeed;
32 And ye shall know the truth, and *b* the truth shall make you free.
33 They answered him, *c* We be Abraham's seed, and were never in bondage to any man: how sayest thou, Ye shall be made free?
34 Jesus answered them, Verily, verily, I say unto you, *d* Whosoever committeth sin is the servant of sin.

30 the things that are pleasing to him. As he spake these things, many believed on him.
31 Jesus therefore said to those Jews who had believed him, If ye abide in my word, then are ye truly
32 my disciples; and ye shall know the truth, and the
33 truth shall make you free. They answered unto him, We are Abraham's seed, and have never yet been in bondage to any man: how sayest thou, Ye
34 shall be made free? Jesus answered them, Verily, verily, I say unto you, Every one that committeth

a ch. 7: 31; 10: 42; 11: 45....*b* Rom. 6: 14, 18, 22; 8: 2; James 1: 25; 2: 12....*c* Lev. 25: 42; Matt. 3: 9; ver. 39....*d* Rom. 6: 16, 20; 2 Pet. 2: 19.

his own view of conduct, this includes all the movements of the heart. (Matt. 5: 28.) Well may Paul say that "he knew no sin." (2 Cor. 5: 21.)

30. As he spake these words, many believed on him. Such dignity and authority were in the look and tone and teaching of Jesus, that many were convinced of his truthfulness, and accepted him in their hearts as the Christ. But, if they are the persons addressed in the next verse, their belief was no more trustworthy than that of the Jews, mentioned in 2: 23 sq. It was a belief to be proved, and not one to be accepted as genuine and sufficient without trial. But it is possible that the **many**, here spoken of, are not identical with "the Jews who had believed," in ver. 31, but were persons who had truly confided in him (εἰς αὐτόν), and patiently waited for a complete revelation of his reign. For the expression here used denotes faith in a person, which is often times a very different thing from mere acceptance of a person's language as true.

31-59. CONVERSATION ON SPIRITUAL FREEDOM AND SONSHIP TO GOD.

31. Then said Jesus, etc.—or better, as in Rev. Ver.: *Jesus therefore said to those Jews who had believed him*, etc. It seems that some of the men who were convinced by his word and led to manifest in some way their belief of it—not their belief *in him*—were persons of influence, perhaps members of the Sanhedrin, certainly adherents of the Jewish view concerning the Messiah. Jesus perceived in them a lack of spiritual trust, and foresaw that they would not, all of them, continue in his word. He therefore proceeded to test their faith by asserting the necessity and the result of continuing in his word. If belief be deep and genuine, it will be permanent; if it be shallow, without root or substance, it will soon vanish away. Its character may therefore be inferred from its endurance and its fruit. **If ye continue,** etc.

32. And ye shall know the truth, and the truth shall make you free. Blessed prospect! By living in the element and atmosphere of Christ's word, they would learn the supreme truth, the secret of peace with God; and this would set them free from bondage and sin. (ver. 34.) But, alas! their minds were intent on earthly things. The Messiah expected by them was one who would make Israel the head of the nations. And therefore, though the tenor of Christ's previous remarks should have led them to think of him as pre-eminently the Revealer of God to men, they missed the sense of his words and were offended. Hence their answer.

33. We be (*are*) **Abraham's seed, and were never in bondage to any man : how sayest thou, Ye shall be made free?** Abraham was to be a father of many nations and a blessing to all the families of mankind, and these Jews consider themselves his offspring, and heirs to his position and destiny. With such a position they deem civil bondage incompatible, and promptly resent the imputation that they have ever been in such bondage, either to the Emperor of Rome or to any one else. Probably, in their zeal, they think only of themselves and their contemporaries, forgetting the captivity in Babylon and the earlier bondage in Egypt. How different were their thoughts from those of Jesus!

34. Whosoever (or, *every one who*) **committeth** (*doeth*) **sin is** *a* (not **the**) **servant of sin.** The expression *who doeth sin* implies a certain continuance in sin on the part of the person thus characterized. But one need not continue long in the practice of sin, in order to find himself in bondage to a hard master. For the worst tyrant a man can serve is his own selfish heart. By rejecting the authority

35 And ᵃ the servant abideth not in the house for ever: but the Son abideth ever.
36 ᵇ If the Son therefore shall make you free, ye shall be free indeed.
37 I know that ye are Abraham's seed; but ᶜ ye seek to kill me, because my word hath no place in you.
38 ᵈ I speak that which I have seen with my Father: and ye do that which ye have seen with your father.

35 sin is the bondservant of sin. And the bondservant abideth not in the house forever; the son abideth 36 for ever. If therefore the Son shall make you free, 37 ye shall be free indeed. I know that ye are Abraham's seed; yet ye seek to kill me, because my 38 word ¹ hath not free course in you. I speak the things which I have seen with ² my Father: and ye also do the things which ye heard from *your* father.

a Gal. 4:30....*b* Rom. 8:2; Gal. 5:1....c ch. 7:19; ver 40....*d* ch. 3:32; 5:19, 30; 14:10, 24.——1 Or. *hath no place in you*....2 Or, *the Father: do ye also therefore the things which ye heard from the Father.*

---

of God in the interest of self-will or supposed freedom, one sinks into the most hopeless slavery. Jesus made no mistake in assuming that the Jews in his presence were slaves of sin, and in need of the true freedom which he alone could give. (See Rom. 6: 17, sq.; 7: 14, sq.)

35. And the servant (or, *bond-servant*) **abideth not in the house for ever: but the Son abideth ever.** A double statement, founded on the customs of civil society. For, according to the law of Moses and the usages of the people, the relation of a bondman to the family was but temporary, while that of a son was permanent. But sonship in the house of God depends, not upon natural, but upon spiritual, descent from Abraham—upon having the faith of Abraham. He, therefore, who is a bond-servant of sin, has not the place and privilege of a son in the house of God. He belongs to the world, and in the world there is no true freedom. Though connected with the theocracy in a temporary and external manner, he is not really at home with the children of God; and when the new and spiritual kingdom is set up, he will be cast out. But it is wholly different with the son—that is, with him who realizes the idea and position of son—he continues in the house forever; it is his home and heritage; all that the father hath is his, and he administers the affairs of the house as heir and ruler. It appears, therefore, that Jesus has in mind himself as the One who is, in a high and full sense, the Son. On this passage Sanday remarks: "The connection between the first two clauses (ver. 34, 35) is distant and subtle. The qualification under which the figure of servitude is introduced is dropped entirely. The servitude (of sin) suggests the idea of servitude in the abstract; and to this the idea of sonship in the abstract is opposed. Then there is a further transition from the abstraction of sonship to the Son in the concrete—the Messiah. And in the inference there is a gap. It is assumed that the Son must communicate his own attributes to those whom he emancipated. The thought is, indeed, throughout, profound and instructive; and to a Jew, always ready to picture to himself the theocracy, or the kingdom of heaven, under the form of a 'household,' it would be easily intelligible." (See Maclaren, Third Series, 2d Sermon, for a different interpretation of this verse.)

36. If the Son therefore shall make you free, ye shall be free indeed (or, *truly free*). Only that freedom which Christ, the Son of God, gives to him who has been in bondage to sin, can make him truly free. (Compare 1 Cor. 3: 22; Rom. 8: 35, sq.; 2 Cor. 6: 4, sq.) A similar thought is expressed in 15: 15: "Henceforth I call you not servants; for the servant knoweth not what his lord doeth; but I have called you friends; for all things that I have heard of my Father I have made known to you."

37. I know that ye are Abraham's seed. Their claim to be the offspring of Abraham by natural descent is thus fully admitted, but only, as it were, in order to exhibit in a more striking manner their moral unlikeness to him. **But ye seek to kill me.** How inconceivable that Abraham should have done this! But why do they engage in so nefarious an attempt? **Because my word hath no place** (better, *maketh no progress*) **in you.** That word had been received by them with a degree of faith (ver. 30), but it was making no advance in their hearts. On the contrary, as it was more clearly explained, it met with more and more opposition, and their momentary good will toward him was changed to deadly antagonism.

38. I speak that which (or, *the things which*) **I have seen with my Father** (or, *with the Father*). The original has *the* Father, instead of **my** Father. And Jesus reaffirms by these words that his knowledge is a result of personal communion with the Father before coming into the world (compare

194   JOHN.   [CH. VIII.

39 They answered and said unto him, *Abraham is our father. Jesus saith unto them, *b If ye were Abraham's children, ye would do the works of Abraham. 40 *But now ye seek to kill me, a man that hath told you the truth, *d which I have heard of God: this did not Abraham. 41 Ye do the deeds of your father. Then said they to him, We be not born of fornication; *e we have one Father, even God.

39 They answered and said unto him, Our father is Abraham. Jesus saith unto them, If ye [1] were Abraham's children, [2] ye would do the works of Abraham. 40 But now ye seek to kill me, a man that hath told you the truth, which I heard from God: 41 this did not Abraham. Ye do the works of your father. They said unto him, We were not born of

a Matt. 3:9; ver. 33....b Rom. 2:28; 9:7; Gal. 3:7, 29....c ver. 37....d ver. 26....e Isa. 63:16; 64:8; Mal. 1:6.—1 Gr. are....
2 Some ancient authorities read, ye do the works of Abraham.

ver. 28). The perfect tense, **have seen,** shows that his present consciousness is linked with the past, his knowledge on earth being a direct fruit of his life in heaven. The next clause is difficult. The Common Version: **And ye do that which ye have seen with your father,** follows a text which is less approved than the one represented by the Revised Version, viz.: *And ye also do the things which ye heard from your father.* But even this does not quite reproduce the original, which may be translated literally, either: *And ye therefore do the things which ye heard from the Father,* or, *and do ye therefore the things which ye heard from the Father.* If the last construction be adopted, Jesus makes another appeal to the Jews to do whatever they had heard from God, whom they esteemed their Father; though he characterized their knowledge as received through others, while his own was due to his immediate vision. This is a possible interpretation, and is, perhaps, slightly favored by the use of the article *the,* instead of the pronoun *your,* before *father.* Had the Greek been *my* Father and *your* father, the contrast would have been more marked. (See ver. 41.) But, on the whole, the sense expressed by the Rev. Ver. is probably correct. The Saviour recognizes the mortal enmity springing up in their hearts, and tells them plainly that they are doing what "the father" has told them to do. Yet he does not name that father, but refers to him, in the first instance, obscurely. We may add, that the varieties of reading in this verse are very numerous, and the difficulty of ascertaining the original text great, if not insuperable. Yet the readings agree to such an extent as to warrant the statement that one of the two interpretations given above must be correct.

39. Abraham is our father (or, more emphatically, *Our father is Abraham.*) There seems to have been enough in the language of Jesus—in the contrast implied by the conjunction "but," of ver. 37, and in the antithetical clauses or tone of ver. 38—to make the Jews understand that he did not have in mind Abraham as their father. Hence they promptly reply: **Abraham is our father.** And therefore he, in turn, justifies their interpretation of his meaning, by saying: **If ye were Abraham's children**—that is, in a moral and religious sense (see Rom 9: 8)—ye **would do the works of Abraham**—or, such works as Abraham did—works of faith. It was the great sin of these Jews that they longed for a visible and earthly kingdom, and because Jesus did not propose to set up such a kingdom, disbelieved, rejected, and opposed him, though they knew the high character of his teaching. Some of the principal editors give *are* (ἐστε), instead of **were** (ἦτε), in the first clause, urging in favor of this change the fact, that an irregular form would be less likely to be changed to a regular form by a transcriber than the reverse. We abide by the Common Text, though the meaning would not be perceptibly changed by accepting the proposed reading.

40. But now ye seek to kill me, a man that hath told you (or, *spoken to you*) **the truth, which I have heard of** (*from*) **God: this did not Abraham.** It will be observed that Jesus here speaks of himself as **a man.** More frequently he calls himself *the Son of man.* He was, indeed, a true man, a man from men, while at the same time, in virtue of his higher nature, he was truly God. But it was as a man, coming to them with messages from God, that they rejected him. Such an act Abraham never performed; he never rejected a well-approved messenger from God, because that messenger spoke the truth.

41. Ye do the deeds (*works*) **of your father.** Thus Jesus affirms that there is one whose character these Jews possess and exhibit—one in whose ways they walk, as a son walks in the ways of his father—one who is the typical enemy of Christ and of truth, and

42 Jesus said unto them, *If God were your Father, ye would love me; b for I proceeded forth and came from God; c neither came I of myself, but he sent me.
43 d Why do ye not understand my speech? *even because ye cannot hear my word.
44 e Ye are of *your* father the devil, and the lusts of your father ye will do: he was a murderer from the beginning, and f abode not in the truth, because there

42 fornication; we have one Father, *even God. Jesus said unto them, If God were your Father, ye would love me: for I came forth and am come from God; for neither have I come of myself, but he sent me.
43 Why do ye not 1 understand my speech? *Even because ye cannot hear my word. Ye are of *your* father the devil, and the lusts of your father it is your will to do. He was a murderer from the be-

a 1 John 5: 1....b ch. 16: 27; 17: 8, 25....c ch. 5: 43; 7: 28, 29....d ch. 7: 17....e Matt. 13: 38; 1 John 3: 8.../ Jude 6.——1 Or, *know*.

of whom all may be called children who reject Christ and his word. Whether these Jews had any suspicion of the exact meaning of Jesus, cannot be known; but they evidently perceived that his words were against them. For they responded: **We be** (rather, *were*) **not born of fornication; we have one Father, even God.** When the children of Israel worshiped idols, they were often represented as committing fornication with the idols. (See Isa. 1: 21; Jer. 2: 20; 3: 8, 9; Ezek. 16: 15, sq.) And these Jews, perceiving that Jesus was not speaking of natural sonship, but rather of spiritual or religious, deny that they have any fellowship in spirit or life with idolaters. They deny that any one could discover in them evidence that they were born of idolaters—that Baal or any other heathen god was their father. "*We*," they proudly say, "have not many fathers, as might be affirmed in a religious sense, if we had been born of Israelites who were given up to idolatry, and were, like them, worshipers of 'gods many'; but we have one Father—God: we are true Israelites, serving Jehovah, and him alone." Thus, as the question before them was in respect to religious paternity and sonship, they claim for themselves the relation of sons.

42. Jesus said unto them. Here, as in the preceding verse, the conjunction "therefore" (οὖν) is omitted by the principal editors, as not belonging to the earliest text. **If God were your Father, ye would love me.** Those who are truly children of God, loving him supremely, must love the Son of God; by him the character of the Father is fully revealed. If what Jesus had so often affirmed in these colloquies was true—if his teaching and his working were also the teaching and the working of the Father—it was, of course, strictly impossible for them to have a filial spirit towards God without loving him who was, in the highest sense, the Son of God—the brightness of the Father's glory, and the ex-

press image of his person. (Heb. 1: 3.) **For I proceeded forth and came from** (or, *out of*, ἐκ) **God.** The pronoun I is emphatic; and the expression **proceeded,** or, *came forth from God,* presupposes an original and perfect union with the Father, while it asserts a voluntary personal entrance into a new condition, effected by the incarnation. The expression here used, says Westcott, "is most remarkable, and occurs only in one other place, 16: 28. . . . The words can only be interpreted of the true divinity of the Son, of which the Father is the source and fountain. The connection described is internal and essential, and not that of presence, or external fellowship." The second verb, **came,** or, *am come,* represents his advent as already accomplished, so that he is now present among men to declare the will of God. **Neither came I of myself, but he sent me.** He has come by the will of the Father, and not by any act of his own will, irrespective of, or separate from, the will of the Father. Father and Son have the same object, the same purpose, the same spirit, the same message. He that loves the Father must needs love the Son also.

43. Why do ye not understand my speech? even because ye cannot hear my word. The term translated **speech** denotes the expression of thought by the voice, and the term translated **word** denotes the thought as expressed. Thus, **speech** refers to the manner, and **word** to the matter of the communication. If their hearts had been prepared to hear and receive the essential truth which he uttered, they would have understood his speech without difficulty. And it is still true that multitudes fail to understand the language of Scripture in many places, because they dislike the substance of what it teaches. An evil heart darkens the understanding. For the use of the word **hear,** see 6: 60.

44. Ye are of your (lit., *the*) **father, the devil.** This is a literal version of the best

is no truth in him. When he speaketh a lie, he speaketh of his own: for he is a liar, and the father of it.

ginning, and standeth not in the truth, because there is no truth in him. ¹ When he speaketh a lie, he speaketh of his own: for he is a liar, and the

---

¹ Or, *When one speaketh a lie, he speaketh of his own: for his father also is a liar.*

---

supported text. *The* **father** means the father spoken of in verses 38 and 41, but now for the first time distinctly named. Jesus declares that by moral resemblance and affinity they are not children of Abraham, or of God, but of the devil, the adversary of all good. **And the lusts of your father ye will do** (lit., *wish to do*). The particular **lusts**, if any, which the Saviour had in mind, are probably indicated by the rest of the verse. It is also worthy of remark that this clause is not strictly predictive, as the Common Version, **ye will do,** may suggest; for the term **will** is not a simple auxiliary, marking the future tense, but an independent verb, signifying *to wish.* The meaning is happily expressed in the Rev. Ver.: *It is your will to do.* **He was a murderer from the beginning.** The spirit of the Jews before him probably led Jesus to characterize Satan in this way. Some have found in the words a special reference to the death of Abel by the hand of Cain; but the use of the expression **from the beginning,** and the prominence assigned to the falsehood of Satan in the rest of the verse, show that Jesus had in mind the temptation by which our first parents were led to apostatize. That was an act which "brought death into the world, and all our woe." It was the murder of mankind. The fratricide that followed was a result of that act, but it is not specially attributed to Satan in the narrative of Moses. **And abode** (rather, *standeth*) **not in the truth.** These words refer to the present and permanent attitude of Satan as a moral being. He is one who lives not in the sphere and element of the truth. He has no fellowship with God. His standing is not in the realm of what is Godlike, but in the realm of what is dark, inane, malignant. **Because there is no truth in him.** When one is in the truth, it is because the truth is in him. He stands and lives, as a moral being, in that which his soul loves—in that which it may be said to inhale as the breath of its inner life. **When he speaketh a** (*the*) **lie, he speaketh of his own.** That is, out of the depths of his own nature, the storehouse of his own being, the lusts or desires which belong to himself. For the word meaning **his own** is plural, and **a** (*the*) **lie** is but one out of many evil things that are his. All his "lusts" are evil. "A good man, out of the good treasure of the heart, bringeth forth good things; and an evil man, out of the evil treasure, bringeth forth evil things." (Matt. 12:35.) *The lie* is generic, and more significant than **a lie. For he is a liar, and the father of it** (or, *thereof*). That is, of the liar. This is regarded as the best interpretation of the somewhat obscure original by Bengel, Meyer, Alford, Godet, Lange, Schaff, Watkins, and others. Whoever, then, is a liar, may justly be called a child of Satan. Weiss, however, adheres to the view which makes the pronoun *it* refer to the lie involved in the idea of the word liar. "While the lie is characterized as proceeding *from his own,* and while a reason for this is to be given, the reference of the pronoun **it** to the object of **when he speaketh** is free from difficulty." Winer and Buttmann favor the same reference. Milligan and Moulton translate as follows: "*Whensoever one speaketh the lie, he speaketh of his own, because his father also is a liar.* Whensoever a man who is a child of the devil uttereth falsehood, he is giving forth what by very nature belongs to him—what is his peculiar property by right of kindred and inheritance—because his father also, the devil, is a liar." But is it Christ's manner to generalize in this way? Is it not more like him to keep close to the persons before him, and point out directly their relation to the evil one? Besides, whence do Milligan and Moulton obtain the indefinite "*one*" which they introduce as the subject of *speaketh ?* Interesting as their interpretation is, we cannot believe it correct. On this passage, Godet remarks that it "contains the most conclusive declaration that fell from the lips of Jesus Christ respecting the existence, the personality, and the activity of Satan. It is impossible to apply here the theory of accommodation, by means of which some have sought to weaken the force of the words of Jesus in his interviews with demoniacs. Of

Ch. VIII.] JOHN.

45 And because I tell *you* the truth, ye believe me not.
46 Which of you convinceth me of sin? And if I say the truth, why do ye not believe me?
47 *a* He that is of God heareth God's words: ye therefore hear *them* not, because ye are not of God.
48 Then answered the Jews, and said unto him, Say we not well that thou art a Samaritan, and *b* hast a devil?
49 Jesus answered, I have not a devil; but I honour my Father, and ye do dishonour me.

45 father thereof. But because I say the truth, ye believe me not. Which of you convicteth me of sin?
47 If I say truth, why do ye not believe me? He that is of God, heareth the words of God: for this cause
48 ye hear *them* not, because ye are not of God. The Jews answered and said unto him, Say we not well that thou art a Samaritan, and hast a demon?
49 Jesus answered, I have not a demon; but I honour

a ch. 10: 26, 27; 1 John 4: 6....*b* ch. 7: 20; 10: 20; ver. 52.

his own accord, and plainly, he gives in this place positive instruction on this mysterious subject."

45. And because I tell you (or, *say*) **the truth, ye believe me not.** According to the nature of things, and the design of God, one should be believed just because he speaks the truth; but here are men so wedded to false views of God and his kingdom, that they reject the teaching of Christ because it is true. In order to be believed by then., you must teach that which is untrue concerning the reign of God through his Anointed. They are at one with Satan; and, therefore, they disbelieve him who has come to destroy the works of Satan.

46. Which of you convinceth (rather, *convicteth*) **me of sin?** Not of *error*, nor of *falsehood*, but of **sin.** "To justify their want of faith in what he said, they must, at least, be able to accuse him of some fault in what he did; for holiness and truth are sisters."—*Godet.* But he challenges them to discover the slightest sin in him; a challenge which is certainly an indirect but decisive claim to holiness. **And if I say the truth** (rather, *truth*), **why do ye not believe me?** No one responded to his challenge. Their silence was, therefore, a tacit admission that his claim could not be refuted by them. But if he was without sin, his teaching must be true; and, whatever men may do, they admit that truth ought to be believed. Jesus, therefore, appeals to this native conviction of the soul. "I am without sin; if I am without sin, I speak only truth; and if I speak truth, why do ye not believe me? Ye would believe me if ye were of God, instead of being of the wicked one." The critical editors omit the word **and** (or, *but*), in this clause.

47. He that is of God, heareth God's words. The word **heareth** means, as in verse 43, to hear and accept. And to be of **God,** is to be morally a child of God, loving

what he loves, and hating what he hates. One who is thus of God, hearkens to his words, obeys them. Ye therefore hear them not, because ye are not of God. The Jews must be taught that their unbelief in the words of Jesus was rooted in their religious character and condition. They must be made to feel, if possible, that a great change in the state of their hearts was indispensable, if they were to appreciate divine truth. But it was impossible to make them feel this. The light did not find a place in their minds. They still took it for granted that they were pre-eminently the children of Abraham, and of God. Hence their reply.

48. Say we not well, that thou art a Samaritan, and hast a devil (or, *demon*)? To call one a Samaritan, was to pronounce him a misbeliever, and a bitter enemy of the people of God. To call him a demoniac, was to represent him as a man controlled by a spirit of evil from the unseen world. The reply of **the Jews** was one of anger and contempt. They rejected the words of Jesus as completely false, and avowed their passionate hostility to him. Their language, on this occasion, may have been in the mind of Peter when he wrote, testifying of Christ, that "when he was reviled, he reviled not again," etc. (1 Pet. 2: 23.) His answer is a firm and absolute denial of their accusation.

49. I have not a devil (or, *demon*), **but I honour my father, and ye do dishonour me.** Making no reply to the first part of their charge, he calmly denies the second. 'It is not true that an unclean spirit from the other world possesses me and speaks through my lips. It is not true that what I am saying is against God, or the real people of God. For God is my Father, and my word honors him; it is the language of the true Son of God, who speaks that, and that only, which is worthy of his Father.' But he does not stop with a re-assertion of his own holiness and

198   JOHN.   [Ch. VIII.

50 And *I seek not mine own glory: there is one that seeketh and judgeth.
51 Verily, verily, I say unto you, *If a man keep my saying, he shall never see death.
52 Then said the Jews unto him, Now we know that thou hast a devil. *Abraham is dead, and the prophets; and thou sayest, If a man keep my saying, he shall never taste of death.
53 Art thou greater than our father Abraham, which is dead? and the prophets are dead: whom makest thou thyself?

50 my Father, and ye dishonour me. But I seek not mine own glory: there is one that seeketh
51 and judgeth. Verily, verily, I say unto you, If a
52 man keep my word, he shall never see death. The Jews said unto him, Now we know that thou hast a demon. Abraham died, and the prophets; and thou sayest, If a man keep my word, he shall
53 never taste of death. Art thou greater than our father Abraham, who died? and the pro-

a ch. 5: 41; 7: 18....b ch. 5: 24; 11: 26....c Zech. 1: 5; Heb. 11: 13.

union with the Father: he declares once more, their opposition to God, by saying that they dishonor the Son of God. He was before them, honoring God by the sinless words, the divine truth, which he spoke; but they were dishonoring, scorning, and falsely accusing himself.

50. And I seek not mine own glory. And, therefore, though ye dishonor, ye do not disturb me. (Compare 5: 41; 7: 18.) Indeed, my honor is not in peril, *for there is one that seeketh and judgeth.* God will provide for the glory of his Son, and will judge between him and those who dishonor his name. "He that has God for his friend need not fear to speak the truth, though men should be enraged at his words and be ready to defame his character. All true glory is from God."

51. Verily, verily, I say unto you. The repeated **verily** indicates the great importance of what is to be said. **If a man keep my saying** (see verses 24 and 31), **he shall never see death.** Some would translate the last clause: "he shall not see death forever," that is, he shall not suffer eternal death. Though he will die, and be without life for a time, death will be terminated by resurrection. But the Greek expression here used, justifies and requires the customary translation, **he shall never see death**; that is, he who keeps the word of Christ has already passed from death into life (5: 24,) and death, in its deep and full sense, as the penalty of sin, will never be experienced by him. He is alive, spiritually, and is assured of life forevermore. "Death has been swallowed up of life, and physical death is thought of, in its true sense, as an entering into life" (*Watkins*); or, more exactly, as a passage from one stage of true life to another.

52. The Jews said unto him. Notice that it is all along, **the Jews,** who criticise and defame the Holy One. **Now we know** (lit., *have known*) **that thou hast a devil** (or, *demon.*) The exact force of the Greek perfect in the New Testament is not easily reproduced in English. Alford supposes that the idea of past time is nearly or quite lost in that of present time, and this view is sometimes favored, as in the passage before us, by the addition of the adverb **now**. But the perfect tense always differs in some degree from the present. It affirms something to be true now which had its beginning at some previous time. So, here, the Jews mean to say that their present knowledge, though clearer now than ever before, is not an absolutely new thing. They have been coming to this knowledge for some time, and are now in full and absolute possession of it. **Abraham is dead** (or, *died,*) **and the prophets**—the greatest and best men the world ever saw —"the friend of God," and the most eminent servants of God—**and thou sayest, If a man keep my saying, he shall never taste of death.** To "see death" and to "taste of death" are synonymous, or nearly synonymous expressions, so that there is no reason to accuse **the Jews** of any misrepresentation of Christ's language. (Cf. Matt. 16: 28; Heb. 2: 9.) Whether they honestly or perversely assumed that he was speaking of natural death, is not so clear.

53. Art thou greater than our father Abraham, which is dead? and the prophets are dead; whom makest thou thyself? The first question is very similar to that of the Samaritan woman: "Art thou greater than our father Jacob?" (4: 12.) But the feeling with which it was uttered was doubtless more intense. The Jews here assume the absurdity of any but a negative answer. "Thou art not greater, surely, than our father Abraham?" Their last question, **whom makest thou thyself?** was probably uttered with a tone and gesture indicative of pious horror at his arrogance and blasphemy. For to affirm

Ch. VIII.] JOHN. 199

54 Jesus answered, *a* If I honour myself, my honour is nothing: *b* it is my Father that honoureth me; of whom ye say, that he is your God:
55 Yet *c* ye have not known him; but I know him: and if I should say, I know him not, I shall be a liar like unto you: but I know him, and keep his saying.
56 Your father Abraham *d* rejoiced to see my day: *e* and he saw it, and was glad.

54 phets died: whom makest thou thyself? Jesus answered, If I glorify myself, my glory is nothing: it is my Father that glorifieth me; of whom ye
55 say, that he is your God; and ye have not known him: but I know him; and if I should say I know him not, I shall be like unto you, a liar: but I know
56 him, and keep his word. Your father Abraham rejoiced 1 to see my day; and he saw it, and was

a ch. 5: 31....*b* 5: 41; 16: 14; 17: 1; Acts 3: 13....*c* ch. 7: 28, 29....*d* Luke 10: 24....*e* Heb. 11: 13.—1 *Or, that he should see.*

that those who kept his word should not die, while those who had kept the word of God in ancient times had died, was surely to put himself on a level, at least, with the Most High. Such self-exaltation they rebuke, declaring that it must be a result of demoniacal possession.

54. If I honour (or, *glorify;* for honour is too weak a term) myself, my honour (*glory*) is nothing. The emphasis is on the pronoun I. If *I, myself,* in distinction from the Father, glorify myself, etc. It is my Father that honoureth (*glorifieth*) me. The Father's love of the Son is equal to the Son's love of the Father. And as the Son delights to honor the Father, so does the Father delight to honor the Son. (See 5: 20, 22, 26, 36.) Jesus did not pass through his earthly ministry without glory, though its source was divine rather than human. Of whom ye say that he is your (or, *our*) God. By these words Jesus identifies his Father with the God of Israel. The reading *our God,* is somewhat better supported than the common text, your God; but the change is one that does not affect the meaning. "Jehovah our God" is a form of expression used in the Old Testament; and the phrase *our God,* was, doubtless, frequently on the lips of Israelites in the time of Christ.

55. Yet ye have not known him. Their professions of knowledge were loud and unhesitating; but the Searcher of hearts, who stood before them, perceived that they had never possessed any true knowledge of his Father. For no one can know the Father but by the Son, who is the Light of the world. Whoever, therefore, rejects the Son, has no love to the Father; and there can be no true knowledge of God without love to him. But I know him—by an immediate, eternal, and perfect fellowship of thought, feeling, and will; and this may be called absolute knowledge. (See Matt. 11: 27; John 1: 18; 3: 13; 5: 20, 22, 26, 36.) And if I should say, I know him not, I shall be a liar like

unto you. "It would be as false for me to say that I do not know him, as it is for you to affirm that you do know him." How direct and personal was this language! Plain, solemn, searching, but manifestly calm, and without any bitterness of spirit. But I know him, and keep his saying (or, *word*). As no one can have a true knowledge of God without having love to him, it is certain that no one can have this knowledge without keeping his word. Profoundly conscious of his personal communion with the Father, Jesus asserts, also, once more, his supreme regard to the Father's will. (4: 34; 5: 30; 7: 18; 8: 29.) His claim of moral perfection is just as unqualified as his claim of divine knowledge.

56. Your father Abraham rejoiced to see my day: and he saw it, and was glad. The Greek may also be translated: *Rejoiced that he should see my day.* (See Buttmann's "Gr. of N. T. Greek," Thayer's Transl., p. 239.) The passage is one of acknowledged difficulty, and the interpretation of it depends very greatly on the meaning which is given to the words my day. Nearly all the best interpreters suppose that these words refer to the earthly ministry of Jesus, or, at least, that his day did not antedate his birth, however long it may have continued afterwards. Hence, many of them conclude that his words in this passage imply the continued life of Abraham after death, and his knowledge, in some way, of the earthly manifestation and ministry of Christ. Others conclude that he saw the day of Christ in symbol, and by faith, at the birth or offering up of Isaac. But we see no sufficient reason for the opinion that the words my day refer to the earthly ministry and manifestation of Christ only. The period embraced by them must be determined by the connection, and there is nothing in the context to limit that period to the earthly ministry of Christ. On the other hand, the tense of the verbs he saw it and was glad points to something accomplished in a definite past time. The interpretation which the Jews

JOHN. [Ch. VIII.

57 Then said the Jews unto him, Thou art not yet fifty years old, and hast thou seen Abraham?
58 Jesus said unto them, Verily, verily, I say unto you, Before Abraham was, *a* I am.
59 Then *b* took they up stones to cast at him: but Jesus hid himself, and went out of the temple, *c* going through the midst of them, and so passed by.

57 glad. The Jews therefore said unto him, Thou art not yet fifty years old, and hast thou seen Abraham?
58 ham? Jesus said unto them, Verily, verily, I say unto you, Before Abraham was born, I am. They
59 took up stones therefore to cast at him: but Jesus ¹ hid himself, and went out of the temple ².

a Ex. 3: 14; Isa. 43: 13; ch. 17: 5, 24; Col. 1: 17; Rev. 1: 8....*b* ch. 10: 31, 39; 11: 8....*c* Luke 4: 30.——1 *Or, was hidden, and went, etc.*....2 Many ancient authorities add, *and going through the midst of them went his way, and so passed by.*

gave to his words (ver. 57) implies the same thing; and the response of Jesus to their language (ver. 58) justifies this view. This passage may therefore be relied on to prove the pre-existence of Christ in his higher nature, and the fact of salvation by him in the time of Abraham. The promise antedates the law of Moses; Christianity is older than Judaism. (Gal. 3: 15, sq.) The work of Christ as Mediator began immediately after the fall. The bloody sacrifices typified the Lamb of God. The promises led to faith in a coming Messiah. Mercy was shown in anticipation of his atoning death. And Abraham saw the dawning of the day of Christ.

57. Then said the Jews unto him. *Therefore* instead of **then**, because their words were occasioned by his last statement, and rested on a certain interpretation of it. **Thou art not yet fifty years old.** Some have inferred from this remark that Jesus must have been more than thirty-three years old at this time. But there was no occasion for exactness in their reference to his age. It was enough for them to say: "Thou art still a young man: thou hast not reached the meridian of life, the age when men begin to lay aside their heavy tasks." (Num. 4: 3, 39; 8: 24.) **And hast thou seen Abraham?** Though in the form of a question, these words were meant to be a positive rejection of his statement. They were an avowal of disbelief, not of doubt. But they prepared the way for one of the clearest and most remarkable declarations of Jesus in respect to himself.

58. Verily, verily, I say unto you: Before Abraham was, I am. This verse is much more exact and forcible in the Greek original than in the translation. For the verb which is used of Abraham, is not the same as the one which is used of Christ. The former signifies an existence which has an origin, and might be rendered in this case, *came to be;* the latter denotes existence simply and absolutely, without any reference to origin. It is called by some, as here used, the timeless present; and by it Jesus claims for himself the same eternal, unsuccessive, absolute being, which was claimed by Jehovah, when he said to Moses: "I am that I am." The reader is therefore to observe, (1) the repeated **verily**, which calls attention to the great importance of what is said; (2) the difference between the meaning of the verb translated **was**; and the meaning of the verb translated **am**; and (3) the tense of the latter verb, which suggests the idea of existence independent of time. (Compare, also, 1: 1-18; 6; 62; 17: 5; Col. 1: 17; Heb. 1: 2; 1 John 1: 2.)

59. Then (*therefore*) **took they up stones to cast at him.** To the Jews, this last declaration of Jesus appeared blasphemous; and so, in their furious zeal, they laid hold of such stones as happened to be within their reach, in the court of the temple, where they were, that they might hurl them upon him, and kill him on the spot. (Compare 10: 31; and Josephus "Ant.," 17: 9, 3.) **But Jesus hid himself.** Whether by miracle, or not, the Evangelist fails to say. It is possible that, at the moment when his infuriated enemies stooped with one impulse of wrath to seek for stones, which lay scattered about, or rushed to some part of the court where fragments of building-stone were accumulated, he passed quietly but quickly into the crowd, and out of sight; for there were, doubtless, many of his friends in the crowd. Yet, on the other hand, it is equally possible that his divine power was exercised on this occasion to render himself, for the moment, invisible. **And went out of the temple.** The word here translated **temple**, means the whole sacred inclosure, with its courts open above, and accessible to the people; and not *the temple* proper, which the common people never entered. (See "Temple," in Smith's "Dict. of the Bible.")

CHAPTER IX.

AND as *Jesus* passed by, he saw a man which was blind from *his* birth.
2 And his disciples asked him, saying, Master, *a* who did sin, this man, or his parents, that he was born blind?
3 Jesus answered, Neither hath this man sinned, nor his parents: *b* but that the works of God should be made manifest in him.

1 AND as he passed by, he saw a blind man from his birth. And his disciples asked him, saying, Rabbi, who did sin, this man, or his parents, that he should be born blind? Jesus answered, Neither did this man sin, nor his parents: but that the works of God

a ver. 34....*b* ch. 11: 4.

Ch. 9: 1-7. HEALING OF A MAN BLIND FROM BIRTH.

1. And as Jesus (*he*) passed by, he saw a man which was blind from his birth. According to critical evidence the last clause of (8: 59,) as given in the Textus Receptus, viz.: "going through the midst of them, and thus passed by"—did not belong to the autograph of John. Hence there is no reason to assume that the events narrated in this chapter took place immediately after those recounted in the foregoing chapter. And it does seem improbable that the disciples would have thought of such a question as that in verse second, just after their Master had escaped the violence of the infuriated Jews. It is better, therefore, to suppose that the giving of sight to the blind man occurred some days, or at least hours later, when the excitement produced by the scene in the temple had passed from the minds of the disciples. The narrative furnishes no information concerning the part of the city in which the blind man was, when seen by Jesus. He may have been near the temple, and so not very far from the Pool of Siloam; but this is only a conjecture. The word **saw** appears to denote an earnest looking at the blind beggar—so earnest as to attract the attention of the disciples, and lead them to propose the following question:

2. Master (*Rabbi*,) who did sin, this man, or his parents, that he was (*should be*) born blind? It may be that the disciples had seen this man or his friends before, and had thus learned that his blindness was congenital; or, it may be, that he mentioned this fact in his plea for alms, as they were passing by. At all events, the disciples knew that he had been born blind, and they were perplexed in attempting to account to their own reason for such a calamity. Sharing with others the opinion that all misfortune is due to sin, and that special misfortune must be the penalty of some special sin, they ask for an explanation of the present case, mentioning the only alternatives which at the moment occurred to them as possible. That they thought of the pre-existence, or transmigration, of souls, is not very probable. That they believed it possible for a child to sin before its birth, need not be assumed. They were perplexed, and presented the only alternative that entered their minds, asking for light from One who had claimed to be "the Light of the world," and in whose word they had full confidence. They were, no doubt, familiar with Ex. 20: 5, and similar passages, which speak of the great and terrible law of sinful and penal heredity, and they knew, perhaps, that some of their teachers believed in the theory of ante-natal sinning; but as these doctrines were, both of them, very perplexing to human reason, they desired to know which of these, if either, was true. Perhaps they were not without some hope that Jesus would offer them a better explanation than either of them, though their question does not imply this. (For the use of that (ἵνα), see Buttmann's "Gram. of N. T. Greek," Thayer's Transl. p 239. "It designates the internal causal connection, ordained by a higher power, between sin and malady.")

3. Neither hath this man sinned, (rather, *did this man sin*,) **nor his parents**; viz.: to the end *that he should be born blind.* For Jesus manifestly did not intend to say, without qualification, that this man and his parents were sinless; but only that no special sin of his own, or of his parents, was with God (ἵνα) the reason why he should be born blind. (Compare Notes on Luke 13: 1-5.) In the Old Testament, the Book of Job teaches the same doctrine as this answer of Jesus. **But that the works of God should be made manifest in him. The works of God** are the works which he performs; and the condition of this blind man was a fit occasion for show-

JOHN. [CH. IX.

4 *I must work the works of him that sent me, while it is day; the night cometh, when no man can work.
5 As long as I am in the world, *I am the light of the world.
6 When he had thus spoken, *he spat on the ground, and made clay of the spittle, and he anointed the eyes of the blind man with the clay,

4 should be made manifest in him. We must work the works of him that sent me, while it is day; the night cometh, when no man can work. When I am 6 in the world, I am the light of the world. When he had thus spoken, he spat on the ground, and made clay of the spittle, ¹and anointed his eyes with the

---

a ch. 4:34; 5:19, 36; 11:9; 12:35; 17:4....*b* ch. 1:5, 9; 3:19; 8:12; 12:35, 46....*c* Mark 7:33; 8:23.—¹ Or, *and with the clay thereof anointed his eyes.*

---

ing to the world a specimen of his works; for manifesting openly the kind of deeds he is able and willing to do. And it was according to the holy purpose of God that this very man was born blind, that he lived at this precise time in Jerusalem, that he attracted the attention of Jesus at this particular moment, and that he should be a bold and grateful recipient of sight from the Lord. Doubtless, he was ever after thankful to God for his long blindness, since it was to be so graciously and wondrously removed. Born of a sinful race, and himself a sinful man, he was not wronged by being born blind. He had received in his darkness far more of good than he had deserved. And now it appeared that God had turned misfortune into a blessing—giving him sight in such a way as to save, at the same time, his soul. All this was far from accidental. It was embraced in the plan and will of God, which Jesus had come into the world to fulfill.

4. I (or, *we*¹) **must work the works of him that sent me, while it is day.** The term **day** is here used figuratively, to denote life as the period in which Christ was to do

[¹ This is an interesting example of various readings, though there can be no doubt as to which gives the true text. (1) "We must work the works of him that sent me," is given by B D, Thebaic, Syriac of Jerusalem. (2) "We must work the works of him that sent us," by ℵ (first hand) L, Memphitic, Æthiopic (one edition), and Cyril of Alexandria. (3) "I must work the works of him that sent me," by all other documents. Now it is plain that no one would ever have wished to change (3) into either of the others, as its sense is obvious, and it presents nothing objectionable to any class of readers. But (1) accounts for both the other readings. The apparent incongruity between "we" and "me," induced the "Alexandrian" to change to "we" and "us," and the "Syrian" to change to "I" and "me." And the incongruity is, in fact, only superficial. That Jesus should associate his followers with him in accomplishing the objects of his mission, is a profound and impressive thought, and in harmony with the general spirit of his teachings. Thus, transcriptional and intrinsic evidence tend to the same result. Notice that B and D here share the honor of giving the true text.—D.]

certain works—works of God—and works that, according to the plan of God, must be terminated by his death on the cross. These works were inexpressibly important for the disciples themselves, and for the world that was to be enlightened by their ministry. **The night cometh when no man can work.** That is to say, for every one; and so for me, the night of death cometh, when no one can do the work of this life.

5. As long as (rather, *when*) **I am in the world, I am the light of the world.** "My being in the world, and my being the light of the world, are contemporaneous and inseparable." It can scarcely be doubted that the Saviour here designates himself, as in 8:12, the Light of the world, because he was in the highest and most comprehensive sense the Revealer of the Father. The natural, and especially the moral perfections of God, were manifested by him in the clearest manner. Every miracle that he wrought, every word that he spoke, every scoff that he bore, every wrong that he forgave, was a ray of light from the unseen God, revealing his nature to men.

6. He spat on the ground, etc. The details here given are simple, precise, unexplained, just as they might naturally be if coming from the pen of an attentive but reverential eye-witness. If we ask, Why this process? Why did the Lord in this instance transmit his restorative energy through a physical medium? or, at least, give the people occasion to suppose that he did so? It is difficult to answer. Of this, however, we may be confident, that neither the Jews, nor any thoughtful reader of this narrative, will imagine that the healing virtue was inherent in the material clay, in the spittle, or in both these, united. It was not by the efficacy of medicine that this congenital blindness was removed. Jesus selected such means, or perhaps symbols, as could be proved, by a thousand experiments, to be incapable of producing the effect which was then wrought. It is pos-

[Сн. IX.] JOHN. 203

7 And said unto him, Go, wash ^a in the pool of Siloam, (which is by interpretation, Sent.) ^b He went his way therefore, and washed, and came seeing.

7 clay, and said unto him, Go, wash in the pool of Siloam (which is by interpretation, Sent). He went

a Neh. 3: 15....b See 2 Kings 5: 14.

sible that he resorted to the process described, in order to prove, or to strengthen, or to man- attained by the power of God. According to the best accredited text, the pronoun *his* should

POOL OF SILOAM.

ifest the faith of the blind man. It is, perhaps, *possible*, though we have no reason to think it, in the least degree, probable—that the moist clay softened the coating of the eyes, and, in a certain measure, prepared them for the miracle; for natural means may be employed and honored, even though they go but a little way towards the effect which is to be be inserted, and the words, **of the blind man,** dropped. This change does not affect the meaning of the verse.

7. Go, wash in the pool of Siloam (which is by interpretation, Sent.) A more literal rendering would be, *Go, wash into the pool of Siloam;* meaning, as many have thought, "Go into the pool of Siloam

8 The neighbours therefore, and they which before had seen him that he was blind, said, Is not this he that sat and begged?
9 Some said, This is he: others said, He is like him: but he said, I am he.

8 away therefore, and washed, and came seeing. The neighbours therefore, and they who saw him aforetime, that he was a beggar, said, Is not this he that 9 sat and begged? Others said, It is he: others said,

and wash," or, as others have supposed, "Go, wash (the clay from thine eyes) into the pool," etc. In either case the expression is pregnant, and something must be supplied in thought to complete the sense. The latter view is ingenious, and perhaps preferable to the former.

"The name Siloah, or Siloam, which has obtained such celebrity in the Christian world, is found only three times in the Scriptures, as applied to waters: once in the prophet Isaiah, who speaks of it as running water (Isa. 8:6); again, as a pool, in Nehemiah (3:15); and, lastly, also as a pool, in the account of our Lord's miracle of healing the man who had been born blind. (John 9:7, 11.) None of these passages afford any clue as to the situation of Siloam. But this silence is amply supplied by the historian Josephus, who makes frequent mention of Siloam as a fountain, and says expressly, that the valley of the Tyropœon extended down to Siloam; or, in other words, Siloam was situated in the mouth of the Tyropœon, on the southeast part of the ancient city, as we find it at the present day. Its waters, he says, were sweet and abundant. There can also be no room for doubt that the Siloam of Josephus is identical with that of the Scriptures." It is "a small, deep reservoir in the mouth of the Tyropœon, into which the water flows from a smaller basin excavated in the solid rock a few feet higher up; and then the little channel by which the stream is led off along the base of the steep, rocky point of Ophel, to irrigate the terraces and gardens extending into the Valley of Jehoshaphat below. The distance from the eastern point of Ophel nearest this latter valley to the said reservoir, is 255 feet. The reservoir is 53 feet long, 18 feet broad, and 19 feet deep; but the western end is in part broken down. Several columns are built into the side walls, perhaps belonging to a former chapel, or intended to support a roof; but there is now no other appearance of important ruins in the vicinity. No water was standing in the reservoir as we saw it; the stream from the fountain only passed through, and flowed off to the gardens." ("Robinson's Researches," I., 335-6.) When Dr. Hackett saw it, in the spring of

1852, "it contained two feet of water." Barclay gives a more minute measurement, "fourteen and a half at the lower (eastern) end, and seventeen at the upper; its western end being somewhat bent; it is eighteen and a half in depth, but never filled, the water either passing directly through, or being maintained at a depth of three or four feet; this is effected by leaving open or closing ... an aperture at the bottom." (Smith's "Dict. of the Bible," Art. Siloam.)

John gives to his readers an interpretation of the name Siloam, probably because he wished to associate it with the Sent of God, the Saviour, by whom in reality the blind man was healed.

What a new world was revealed to the blind man as he returned seeing! With what lively interest and wonder must he have looked for the first time upon the mountains round about Jerusalem, the sky, the sun, and the numberless objects that encircled him on every side, as he returned into the city. to his home and friends! For there is no evidence that Jesus tarried at the place where he saw the blind man, or that the man sought him on his return.

8-12. RECEPTION BY HIS NEIGHBORS.
8. The neighbours therefore, etc. The Rev. Ver. represents the true text: *The neighbors therefore, and they which saw him aforetime, that he was a beggar,* etc. It is certainly noticeable, and not a little remarkable, that, according to the true text, the neighbors described the man, not as **blind,** or, "blind from his birth," but as he that "was accustomed to sit and beg." Hence, as Alford remarks, "the reading *blind* was, most likely, a correction of some one who thought *beggar* did not express plainly enough the change in him." For the same reason, a *falsarius* of the second century, intent on glorifying the divine power of Jesus, would surely have made them speak of him as blind, rather than as begging. Yet the narrative is manifestly true to nature. For the begging was quite as obtrusive a circumstance to these neighbors as the blindness.

9. Some said, This is he, etc. This

JOHN.

10 Therefore said they unto him, How were thine eyes opened?
11 He answered and said, A man that is called Jesus made clay, and anointed mine eyes, and said unto me, Go to the pool of Siloam, and wash: and I went and washed, and I received sight.
12 Then said they unto him, Where is he? He said, I know not.
13 They brought to the Pharisees him that aforetime was blind.
14 And it was the sabbath day when Jesus made the clay, and opened his eyes.
15 Then again the Pharisees also asked him how he had received his sight. He said unto them, He put clay upon mine eyes, and I washed, and do see.

10 No, but he is like him. He said, I am he. They said therefore unto him, How then were thine eyes
11 opened? He answered, The man that is called Jesus made clay, and anointed mine eyes, and said unto me, Go to Siloam, and wash: so I went away and
12 washed, and I received sight. And they said unto him, Where is he? He saith, I know not.
13 They bring to the Pharisees him that aforetime
14 was blind. Now it was the sabbath on the day when Jesus made the clay, and opened his eyes.
15 Again therefore the Pharisees also asked him how he received his sight. And he said unto them, He put clay upon mine eyes, and I washed, and do see.

a ver. 6, 7.

---

may be literally rendered: *Others said: This is he; others, No, but he is like him; but he said: I am he.* Observe the rapidity and naturalness of the recital. The look and bearing of the man may have been somewhat changed by the new and glorious power of vision, so that there was, perhaps, some little reason for the answer—He is like him, especially on the part of Jews, who could not easily believe that so stupendous a miracle had been wrought almost before their eyes.

10. Naturally, they answer the man himself by the question: **How were thine eyes opened?** In other words: "How were they made to see?" For the language is figurative, and, as usual, all the more expressive and beautiful for being so. Ordinarily it is the closed eye that does not see, and the open eye that sees. Hence to open blind eyes is the same thing as to cause them to see.

11. **He answered and said,** etc. (Or, *he answered: The man that is called Jesus, made clay, and anointed mine eyes, and said unto me: Go to Siloam, and wash: So I went and washed, and I received sight.*) This is a translation of the best supported text. It will be observed that it differs from the Common Version by omitting *and said* after *answered*, by substituting *the* for *a* before *man*, by omitting the words *the pool of* before *Siloam*, and by substituting *so* for *and*, in the last sentence. But none of these changes affect the substance of thought in the verse. Whether the blind man, now restored to sight, spoke of Christ as **a man that is called Jesus,** or, as *the man called Jesus,* would only differ in this, that the latter form of expression would imply some previous knowledge concerning Jesus in the speaker and those addressed, while the former would not.

12. **Then said they unto him: Where is he?** He said: I know not. The omission of **then** at the beginning of this verse is required by critical authorities, but does not change the meaning.

13-17. FIRST EXAMINATION OF THE RESTORED MAN BY THE PHARISEES.

13. **They brought** (rather, *bring*) **to the Pharisees him that aforetime was blind.** The general brevity of the Gospel narrative forbids one to assume that this was done before the close of the day on which the miracle was wrought. It may have been done on the next day as well, and from what follows it is natural to suppose that the Sabbath was already past. Hence the fact that the Sanhedrin was not accustomed to meet on the Sabbath, fails to prove that the man who had been made to see was not brought before that court. But, if the Sanhedrin is meant, it must have been so referred to by the Evangelist, because, in this instance, the most active and influential members of it were Pharisees. Yet there is no real necessity for the assumption that the examination was made by the Sanhedrin. The Pharisees, probably, had an association of their own in Jerusalem, whose action determined their course in the Sanhedrin, and, therefore, practically, the decisions of that body. To this association of leading Pharisees the man that was blind may have been brought by those who doubted, or wished to doubt, the miracle. For it was probably this part of his neighbors that brought him to the Pharisees.

14. **And it was the** (*a*) **Sabbath,** etc. This remark anticipates the scene that follows. Jesus had done work—had made the clay, and spread it on the eyes of the blind man, on the Sabbath; and this was regarded by the Pharisees as a violation of the law of rest on that day. (See Note on 5: 10.)

15. **Then** (or,) **again,** etc. The word *again*

16 Therefore said some of the Pharisees, This man is not of God, because he keepeth not the sabbath day. Others said, "How can a man that is a sinner do such miracles?" And *there was a division among them.

17 They say unto the blind man again, What sayest thou of him, that he hath opened thine eyes? He said, *He is a prophet.

18 *But the Jews did not believe concerning him, that he had been blind, and received his sight, until they called the parents of him that had received his sight.

19 And they asked them, saying, Is this your son, who ye say was born blind? how then doth he now see?

16 Some therefore of the Pharisees said, This man is not from God, because he keepeth not the sabbath. But others said, How can a man that is a sinner do such signs? And there was a division among them.

17 They say therefore unto the blind man again, What sayest thou of him, in that he opened thine eyes? And he said, He is a prophet.

18 And he said, He is a prophet. The Jews therefore did not believe concerning him, that he had been 19 blind, and had received his sight, until they called the parents of him that had received his sight, and asked them, saying, Is this your son, who ye say

a ver. 33; ch. 3: 2....*b* ch. 7: 12, 43; 10: 19....*c* ch. 4: 19; 6: 14.

assumes correctly that the same question had been asked before, though not by the same persons. (Ver. 10.) **He said unto them, He put clay upon mine eyes, and I washed, and do see.** A briefer answer than the one made to his neighbors (ver. 11), perhaps because he saw the purpose of his questioners, and therefore chose to use as few words as possible. For in all that follows, he proves himself to be a clear-headed and true-hearted man.

16. Therefore said (or, *were saying*) **some of the Pharisees, This man is not of** (*from*) **God, because he keepeth not the sabbath day.** From his disregard of the Sabbath law, as interpreted by the scribes, they infer that he must be a sinner, and not a messenger from God. But their premise was false, and their conclusion equally so. **Others said,** (or, *were saying*), **How can a man that is a sinner do such miracles?** (or, *signs*.) From the miracle which he had wrought, these infer the impossibility of his being a transgressor of the law. "To press the Sabbath-breaking, was to admit the miracle; and to admit the miracle, was to establish the fact that he who performed it could not be the criminal whom the others described." (Farrar, "The Life of Christ.") **And there was a division among them.** If this examination was made by the Sanhedrin, there were many besides Nicodemus in that court who reasoned soundly respecting Jesus. (8:2.)

17. They say unto the blind man again: What sayest thou of him that he hath opened thine eyes? *Thou* is emphatic. "We make our appeal to *thee*." This question may be regarded as coming from both parties. Divided among themselves, the Pharisees turn to the man whose sight had been restored, in order to learn his opinion—a majority of them certainly hoping to find in it something which they could use against Jesus. **And, he said, He is a prophet.** A very

clear, sensible, and decided answer. If any of the dominant party supposed that, having heard their words (10:s), and seen their hostility to Christ, he would hesitate about avowing his trust in Jesus as a messenger from God, they were quickly undeceived. The man with whom they now had to deal was a different person from the one who had waited at the Pool of Bethesda. (See 5: 10-15.) This man was shrewd and firm; that man, apparently, weak and simple.

18-23. EXAMINATION OF THE BLIND MAN'S PARENTS.

18. But the Jews (*therefore*) **did not believe concerning him, that he had been blind, and received his sight, until they called the parents of him that had received his sight.** But, and his, in two places, are wanting in the original, and needless in English. *Therefore* is inserted because the true text requires it. Observe (1) that the persons spoken of are called **the Jews**, meaning that part of the Pharisees most hostile to Jesus. (2) That their unbelief is voluntary; for it varies in form with the supposed necessities of their cause. The man is firm, and avows his confidence in Jesus as a prophet; *therefore*, they do not believe that he was once blind, and has been made to see. (3) That their unbelief only yielded when it *must*; that is, when the positive testimony of the blind man's parents took from them every pretext or excuse for doubt. A large part of the unbelief of mankind is voluntary. As long as they can find any plausible excuse for distrusting the word of God, they will reject it as unworthy of confidence.

19. Is this your son, who ye say was born blind? how then doth he now see? In other words, (1) Is this your son? (2) Was he born blind? (3) How then doth he now see? These questions were appropriate, if there was any need of asking them; but

20 His parents answered them and said, We know that this is our son, and that he was born blind: 21 But by what means he now seeth, we know not; or who hath opened his eyes, we know not: he is of age; ask him: he shall speak for himself. 22 These *words* spake his parents, because ᵃ they feared the Jews: for the Jews had agreed already, that if any man did confess that he was Christ, he ᵇ should be put out of the synagogue. 23 was born blind? how then doth he now see? His 21 parents answered and said, We know that this is our son, and that he was born blind: but how he now seeth, we know not; or who opened his eyes, we know not; ask him: he is of age; he shall speak 22 for himself. These things said his parents, because they feared the Jews: for the Jews had agreed already, that if any man should confess him *to be* Christ, he should be put out of the syna-

a ch. 7: 13; 12: 42; 19: 38; Acts 5: 13....b ver. 34; ch. 16: 2.

they may have been proposed with a look and tone which clearly revealed the *animus* of the speakers (inquisitors?), and boded no good to any friend of Jesus; and we cannot avoid suspecting that they were proposed with such a look and tone.

20. We know that this is our son, and that he was born blind. Thus two of the questions were answered plainly, and without evasion.

21. But by what means (*how***) he now seeth, we know not; or who hath opened his eyes, we know not.** In a certain sense, this also was true; they had no direct personal knowledge of the miracle; they were not present when Jesus anointed the eyes of their son, and commanded him to go to the Pool of Siloam and wash; and they only knew by report that it was Jesus who had wrought "the sign." Yet they must have heard their son's story; and it is evident from what follows that, however joyful they were, because their son had received sight by miracle, they wished to avoid saying anything favorable to Jesus. **He is of age; ask him: he shall speak for himself.** Thus, through fear, they cast the whole burden of responsibility as to Jesus upon their son. In view of the recent and astonishing miracle wrought for his benefit, their words seem pusillanimous; but they may have reasoned with themselves that any reference which they could make to Jesus would not assist their son, while it would call down on themselves the displeasure of the Pharisees. But evidently their hearts were not deeply touched with gratitude to Jesus; nor did they believe him to be the Messiah. There is reason to suppose that the position of the first and second clauses given above ought to be reversed; thus: *Ask him; he is of age.* And the last clause might be translated: *He himself will answer,* etc., emphasizing the thought that *he,* and not his parents; *he,* in distinction from any one else, would answer. They had reason to trust his judgment and courage—more reason, perhaps, than they had to trust their own.

22. Because they feared the Jews: for the Jews had agreed already, that if any man did confess that he was Christ, he should be put out of the synagogue. Compare the Revised Version. At what time this agreement was made by the Jews, does not appear. (See Note on 7: 49.) Whether it was ratified by a formal act of the Sanhedrin, or by that of some inferior court, cannot be certainly known. It was, however, a definite agreement made by those who controlled religious affairs, and it was known to the parents of the man who had received sight. "The Jewish system of excommunication was threefold." According to the first kind, "the excommunicated person was prohibited the use of the bath, or of the razor, or of the convivial table; and all who had to do with him were commanded to keep him at four cubits' distance. He was allowed to go to the temple, but not to make the circuit in the ordinary manner. The term of this punishment was thirty days; and it was extended to a second, and to a third thirty days, when necessary. If, at the end of that time, the offender was still contumacious, he was subjected to the second excommunication. Severer penalties were now attached. The offender was not allowed to teach or to be taught in company with others, to hire or to be hired, nor to perform any commercial transactions beyond purchasing the necessaries of life. The sentence was delivered by a court of ten, and was accompanied by a solemn malediction." . . The last excommunication "was an entire cutting off from the congregation. It has been supposed by some that these two latter forms of excommunication were undistinguishable from each other."—(Smith's "Dict. of the Bible," Excommunication.) Whether the expulsion from the synagogue here spoken, of as determined upon by the Jews was the first or the second kind of excommunication, is a matter of

208 JOHN. [Ch. IX.

23 Therefore said his parents, He is of age; ask him.
24 Then again called they the man that was blind, and said unto him, *a* Give God the praise: *b* we know that this man is a sinner.
25 He answered and said, Whether he be a sinner or no, I know not: one thing I know, that, whereas I was blind, now I see.
26 Then said they to him again, What did he to thee? how opened he thine eyes?
27 He answered them, I have told you already, and ye did not hear: wherefore would ye hear it again? will ye also be his disciples?
28 Then they reviled him, and said, Thou art his disciple; but we are Moses' disciples.

23 gogue. Therefore said his parents, He is of age; 24 ask him. So they called a second time the man that was blind, and said unto him, Give glory to 25 God: we know that this man is a sinner. He therefore answered, Whether he is a sinner, I know not: one thing I know, that, whereas I was blind, now I 26 see. They said therefore unto him, What did he to 27 thee? how opened he thine eyes? He answered them, I told you even now, and ye did not hear: wherefore would ye hear it again? would ye also 28 become his disciples? And they reviled him, and said, Thou art his disciple; but we are disciples of

a Josh. 7: 19; 1 Sam. 6: 5....*b* ver. 16.

some doubt. In either case, however, it was a serious evil and disgrace, from a Jewish point of view, and no one would be ready to incur it for a slight reason.

23. Therefore (or, *for this cause*), **said his parents, He is of age; ask him.** Having stated the precise ground for the fear which the parents had, the Evangelist reiterates his declaration that this fear was their motive for declining to speak of Jesus themselves, and referring their questioners to their son.

24-34. SECOND EXAMINATION OF THE MAN WHO WAS BLIND.

25. Give God the praise: (or,*glory*); **we know that this man is a sinner.** It is the party hostile to Jesus that recalls the man, and undertakes to make him confess that Jesus had wrought no miracle in his case. Their exhortation, Give God, assumes that by ascribing, in any way, a miracle to Jesus, and calling him a prophet (ver. 17), he had dishonored God, while, by accepting their view and denouncing Jesus as a sinner, because he had done work on the Sabbath, he would be giving glory to God. And, as if they had perfect knowledge in religious matters, they go on to say: **We—who are the religious judges, leaders, and teachers of the people—know that this man is a sinner.** Thus they attempt to overawe the man, and constrain him to say what they put in his mouth. But, fortunately, he is not the man to be overawed. He can see; he can reason; he is true; he knows what to say; and, after these eighteen hundred years, we read and rejoice that he said it.

25. Whether he be a sinner or no, I know not: one thing I know, that, whereas I was blind, now I see. A cautious, but decisive answer. Of one thing he is certain, and this one thing is really of

pre-eminent importance (comp. Mark 10: 21; Luke 10: 42) in considering the claims of Jesus. Though naturally blind, the man now sees; and no pressure of Jewish authority or of Pharisaic dogmatism can lead him to hesitate about this marvelous change. Yet he forbears to express his belief that Jesus is not, as they affirm, a sinner. He takes a position which is unassailable.

26. What did he to thee? How opened he thine eyes? Unable, as they perceive, to make him deny or conceal the principal fact, they proceed to question him again about the process—hoping, perhaps, to detect some inconsistency between his several statements, or something in the conduct of Jesus which they can criticise as wrong.

27. I have told you already, and ye did not hear (or, *and did ye not hear?*) **wherefore would ye hear it again? will ye also be his disciples?** The principal reason for making the second clause of this answer a question, is that, so understood, the word **hear** has the same sense in both clauses; while if the second clause is not made a question, the word **hear** must signify the mental act of hearkening, in the former instance, and the mere physical act of hearing in the latter. The last question is slightly ironical but the form of it in Greek anticipates a negative answer. "Ye do not wish to become his disciples?"

28. Then (strictly, *and*) **they reviled him, and said, Thou art his disciple; but we are Moses' disciples.** This language of the Jews may have been regarded by them as strictly true, and in the sight of God it was, doubtless, highly honorable to the man addressed. Yet, it was uttered in a bitter, railing, contemptuous tone, and it is properly characterized by the Evangelist, when he says: **They reviled him.** The pronoun **his**

29 We know that God spake unto Moses: *as for this fellow,* ᵃ we know not from whence he is.
30 The man answered and said unto them, ᵇ Why herein is a marvellous thing, that ye know not from whence he is, and *yet* he hath opened mine eyes.
31 Now we know that ᶜ God heareth not sinners: but if any man be a worshipper of God, and doeth his will, him he heareth.
32 Since the world began was it not heard that any man opened the eyes of one that was born blind.
33 ᵈ If this man were not of God, he could do nothing.

29 Moses. We know that God hath spoken unto Moses: but as for this man, we know not whence he is. The man answered and said unto them. Why, herein is the marvel, that ye know not whence he is, and *yet* he opened mine eyes. We know that God heareth not sinners: but if any man be a worshipper of God, and do his will, him he heareth. Since the world began it was never heard that any one opened the eyes of a man born blind.
33 If this man were not from God, he could do nothing.

a ch. 8: 14....*b* ch. 3: 10....*c* Job 27: 9; 35: 12; Ps. 18: 41; 34: 15; 66: 18; Prov. 1: 28; 15: 29; 28: 9; Isa. 1: 15; Jer. 11: 11; 14: 12; Ezek. 8: 18; Mic. 3: 4; Zech. 7. 13....*d* ver. 16.

(ἐκεῖνον) indicates very clearly that they separated themselves from Jesus. The conjunction **then,** or *therefore,* at the beginning of this verse, is not found in the best manuscripts, but several of them have the connective *and.*

29. We know that God spake (or, *has spoken*) **unto Moses: as for this fellow** (*man,*) **we know not from whence he is.** *Hath spoken unto Moses,* because God was still speaking, through the inspired writings of Moses, to them. The perfect tense of the verb brings over the act of speaking from the past into the present, and represents God as still teaching the people through their great lawgiver. The pronoun **this,** (τοῦτον), meaning **this man,** or, *this one,* is used contemptuously. (Comp. 6: 42.) **Whence he is**—that is, from whom he has come, or by whose authority he speaks. They mean to affirm that he has given them no credentials proving himself to be from God. He may be from beneath, as well as from above.

30. Why, herein is a marvellous thing, that ye know not from whence he is, and yet he hath opened (rather, *opens*) **mine eyes.** The precise connection of this response with the words of the Jews, is doubtful. The Greek term, here translated **why,** usually signifies **for,** and makes the sentence in which it stands a reason for something said before. If that is its meaning here, the reply of the man under examination was slightly elliptical, and may be completed thus: "Say not so; for in this is a marvellous thing," etc. It should also be observed that the pronoun **ye** is emphatic; "that *ye*"—who are instructed in religious matters, and able to teach others—"do not know whence he is." The word **yet** is inserted in the last clause—**and yet he hath opened mine eyes**—though there is nothing equivalent to it in the original, and though the sense does not absolutely require it. The undoubted meaning of the original is, however, more clearly expressed by inserting this word.

31. Now we know that God heareth not sinners; but if any man be a worshipper of God, and doeth his will, him he heareth. For the first proposition, see Ps. 66: 18; Prov. 15: 9-29; Isa. 1: 11-15. The second proposition is but the converse of the first, and is sustained by many passages of the Old Testament. See 1 Kings 18: 36 sq.; 2 Kings 4: 33 sq.; Ps. 25: 3. The word *sinners* is here used of those who do not truly worship God, (comp. ver. 16, 24), but disobey openly his commands. There is a sense in which all men are sinners—the best, as well as the worst—the disciple that leaned on Jesus' breast, as well as the disciple that betrayed him for thirty pieces of silver; the man that hungers and thirsts after righteousness, as well as the man that tramples deliberately on the authority of his Maker. (Rom. 3: 9, sq.) But the word is here used in another and more restricted sense.

32. Since the world began was it not heard that any man opened the eyes of one that was born blind. The man appreciates the greatness of the miracle that has been wrought for his benefit. It is unparalleled. There is no record of such a miracle in the Holy Scriptures—no tradition of such a miracle known to the people of God. Since time began such a sign has never been given.

33. If this man were not of (rather, *from*) **God, he could do nothing.** The argument is complete. Miracles are wrought by God in answer to the prayer, not of his foes, but of his servants. A great and unparalleled miracle has been wrought at the word of this man. But unless he were from God, unless he were God's servant and messenger, he could do nothing of the kind. The conclusion was one that need not be stated.

O

34 They answered and said unto him, *Thou wast altogether born in sins, and dost thou teach us? And they cast him out.
35 Jesus heard that they had cast him out; and when he had found him, he said unto him, Dost thou believe on *the Son of God?

34 They answered and said unto him, Thou wast altogether born in sins, and dost thou teach us? And they cast him out.
35 Jesus heard that they had cast him out; and finding him, he said, Dost thou believe on ¹the Son of

a ver. 2 ...b Matt. 14:33; 16:16; Mark 1:1; ch. 10:36; 1 John 5:13.——1 Many ancient authorities read, *the Son of man*.

34. Thou wast altogether born in sins, and dost thou teach us? This translation does not give the exact sense of the original. For the word **altogether** represents an adjective meaning "whole" (ὅλος), and agreeing with **thou**. Hence the meaning is: "*Thou*, as to thy whole being, body and soul, wast born in sins." And this taunt appears to rest on the assumption that he was born blind, and that his blindness was due to his utter sinfulness at birth. (Comp. ver. 2.) Thus, in their wrath and confusion, they virtually concede that the man has received sight by a miracle; and the principle on which they condemn him, as loaded with sins at birth, should lead them to believe in Jesus as a true messenger from God. **And they cast him out.** That is, as is commonly supposed, out of the place where they were—a rude and passionate expulsion from their presence. The words may signify that they excluded him from the synagogue (ver. 22); but he had not yet confessed Jesus to be the Christ, and could not, therefore, be excommunicated in pursuance of the agreement which the Pharisees had made. Yet, in their fury, they may have driven him from their presence, and may have followed up their persecution by a formal excommunication. The subsequent narrative renders this probable.

"If the narrative of this chapter is not thus far true to human nature, we may despair of finding anything in history that is. The bearing of the Pharisees is of a piece throughout —consistently hostile to Jesus, arrogant, and bitter. So, too, is that of the blind man; for, from first to last, he is modest, resolute, faithful." This comment, made by the writer fifteen years ago, agrees with that of Godet in the last edition of his work on John: "If there is any narrative whose truth is guaranteed by its simple and dramatic character, it is this. The fact has not been invented to serve as the basis for a discourse; for the discourse does not exist. This whole scene is so little ideal in its nature, that, on the contrary, it rests from beginning to end on the reality of *fact*... This whole chapter offers to modern criticism a portrait of itself. The defenders of the Sabbatic institute reasoned thus: God *cannot* lend his power to one who violates the Sabbath; hence the miracle ascribed to Jesus did *not* occur... The adversaries of miracles in the Evangelical history reason in precisely the same way, merely substituting a scientific axiom for a religious statute: The supernatural *cannot* be; and, therefore, however well attested the healing of the blind man may be, it did *not* take place."

35-38. THE BLIND MAN WORSHIPS JESUS AS THE CHRIST.

35. Jesus heard that they had cast him out; and when he had found him, he said unto him, Dost thou believe on the Son of God? It may be assumed that Jesus was aware of the character and spirit which this man had shown in his examination by the Pharisees, and that he perceived in him a heart ready to welcome the truth. On this account—though how long after the occurrences related in ver. 13-34, we do not know— he sought for him, and gave him an opportunity to honor his benefactor as the Christ. Some of the earliest and best manuscripts read *the Son of man*, instead of **the Son of God**, in the last clause. Indeed, the external evidence for the one reading is about equal to that for the other. But two considerations favor the received text: (1) That Jesus called himself *the Son of man* much oftener than he called himself **the Son of God**, and a transcriber would be more likely to substitute a frequent for an infrequent designation than the reverse. And (2) that the connection seems to make the title **Son of God** more natural and pertinent than the title *Son of man*. But, in either case, we must suppose that Jesus used a designation that would be understood by the blind man as referring to the Messiah. And, in either case, the expression **believe on** signifies a confidence or trust which terminates in a personal object.

36 He answered and said, Who is he, Lord, that I might believe on him?
37 And Jesus said unto him, Thou hast both seen him, and ᵃ it is he that talketh with thee.
38 And he said, Lord, I believe. And he worshipped him.
39 And Jesus said, ᵇ For judgment I am come into this world, ᶜ that they which see not might see; and that they which see might be made blind.
40 And some of the Pharisees which were with him heard these words, ᵈ and said unto him, Are we blind also?

36 God? He answered and said, And who is he, Lord, that I may believe on him? Jesus said unto him, Thou hast both seen him, and he it is that speaketh 38 with thee. And he said, Lord, I believe. And he 39 worshipped him. And Jesus said, For judgment came I into this world, that they who see not may 40 see; and that they who see may become blind. Those of the Pharisees that were with him heard these things, and said unto him, Are we also blind?

a ch. 4: 26.... *b* ch. 5: 22, 27; see ch. 3: 17; 12: 47.... *c* Matt. 13: 13.... *d* Rom. 2: 19.

36, 37. Who is he, Lord, that I might believe on him?... Thou hast both seen him, and it is he that talketh with thee. The words **thou hast seen him,** are to be understood of natural sight, not of spiritual discernment; and the time referred to is that of the present interview. "Thou hast already seen him, and the one who is now talking with thee is he." But how could he recognize Jesus as the man who had anointed his eyes with clay, and had sent him to wash in Siloam? How, if he had not seen him since his sight was restored? Doubtless by tones of voice—unlike those of any other man. For the sense of hearing is generally very exquisite and highly cultivated in the blind. And even with those who see, recognition by voice is quite as certain as recognition by sight. Besides, there must have been a sincerity, purity, authority, and love in the tones of the Saviour's voice, which inspired reverence and trust. Hence the effect on this true and grateful man was instant. That voice, heard by such a man, would never be forgotten.

38. And he said, Lord, I believe. And he worshipped him. In other words, he affirmed his belief in Jesus as the Messiah, the Son of God, and paid to him religious homage. Whether he comprehended the real import of the title "Son of God," it is impossible to say; but he knew enough of its meaning to bring him to his knees before Jesus. And it is to be remembered that Jesus, neither in this instance, nor in any other, refuses any degree of worship that is paid to him. He is worthy to receive all honor and praise on earth and in heaven.

39. For judgment I am come (or, *came*) **into this world, that they which see not might** (or, *may*) **see, and that they which see might** (or, *may*) **be made blind.** The ultimate and supreme end of Christ's coming into the world was to save the lost. (12: 47; 3: 16, 17.) But, in accomplishing that end, many would be hardened, and fall under greater condemnation. (Luke 2: 34; 2 Cor. 2: 16; John 12: 40.) This double effect of Christ's mission to the world was foreseen and embraced in the purpose of God. Hence it is here declared that one object and result of the Saviour's coming was judicial; to wit, that those who felt themselves to be spiritually poor and blind, like babes in their knowledge of divine things, might be made to see the truth, while those who felt themselves to be wise and prudent, masters in Israel, and needing no instruction as to the will of God, might sink, through their rejection of offered light, into ever deeper spiritual darkness. (Matt. 5: 3-6; 11: 25; 13: 13-15.) The language of Jesus is figurative, having no reference to physical blindness or sight, but using these as emblems of states of the soul in the presence of divine truth. His words may have been addressed to the man whose physical and spiritual vision had both been restored, but they were not intended for him only. Others were listening, and others responded.

40. And some (or, *those*) **of the Pharisees which were with him heard these words, and said unto him, Are we blind also?** Their question is so framed in the Greek as to show that they deemed an affirmative answer absurd or impossible. And their tone was probably one that indicated their feeling quite as clearly as the words they uttered: "You do not mean to say that we, also, as well as the people that know not the law (7: 49,) are blind and in need of religious instruction?" Thus, in spite of Christ's warning, they place themselves with "the wise and prudent," with "those that see"; and Jesus accepts their view of themselves as in a measure correct. They have knowledge, they do see; and they ought to perceive that their

41 Jesus said unto them, *If ye were blind, ye should have no sin; but now ye say, We see; therefore your sin remaineth.

41 Verily, verily, I say unto you, He that entereth not by the door into the sheepfold, but climbeth up some other way, the same is a thief and a robber.

41 Jesus said unto them, If ye were blind, ye would have no sin; but now ye say, We see: your sin remaineth.

CHAPTER X.

1 Verily, verily, I say unto you, He that entereth not by the door into the fold of the sheep, but climbeth up some other way, the same is a thief and

a ch. 15: 22, 24.

knowledge and sight are very imperfect. But of this, in their pride, they are profoundly unconscious.

41. If ye were blind, ye should have no sin: but now ye say, We see; therefore your sin remaineth. Therefore, in the last clause of the Common Version, must be omitted. Thus the Lord adapts his answer to their own view of the case. He admits that they have some knowledge of the truth. But they are satisfied with what they now have, refusing to accept of Christ as the Light of the world. Their knowledge which should lead them to him, leads them to reject him, and so their sin remaineth. For the sin referred to is the sin of unbelief in Christ. Others understand if ye were blind, as meaning, if ye were of those who see not —*i. e.*, who feel themselves to be blind, ye would come to the true Light, and your sin would be forgiven. But as ye are not of this class, as ye rather claim to see, ye refuse to come to me, the true Light, and your sin remains unforgiven.

Ch. 10: 1-5. False and True Shepherds—*i. e.*, Religious Teachers.

1. Verily, verily, I say unto you, He that entereth not by (or, *through*) the door into the sheepfold (or, *the fold of the sheep*), but climbeth up some other way, the same is a thief and a robber. The paragraph beginning with this verse is a continuation of the discourse with which the preceding chapter closed; for there are no sufficient indications of any change in time or place. The Pharisees to whom he was there speaking were, in reality, false teachers, endeavoring to lead the people astray; and the words verily, verily, are never elsewhere used at the opening of a discourse, but rather in the progress of a conversation, debate, or discourse, in order to fix attention on something specially important.

It has been supposed by many that the imagery here employed was suggested by the sight of some shepherd with his flock, drawing near, perhaps, to the fold; but there is little need of supposing this to have been the case. For the imagery was natural, expressive, and familiar to the Jews. It appears more than once in the Old Testament. (See Ps. 23; Ezek. 34; and Zech. 11).

"A fold is not, in the East, a covered structure, like our stables; it is a simple enclosure, surrounded by a palisade, or wall. Into it the flocks are brought for the night. Several flocks are, ordinarily, united in one such enclosure. The shepherds, after committing them for the night to the care of a common guard, the porter, or gate-keeper, go to their own homes. In the morning, they return, and knocking at the firmly closed door of the fold, the guard opens it. Then every one separates his own flock by calling them, and when he has brought all together, leads them forth to pasture."—*Godet.* In his work entitled "The Land and the Book," I., 299, Dr. Thomson says: "Those low, flat buildings, out on the sheltered side of the valley, are sheepfolds. They are called mârâh; and when the nights are cold, the flocks are shut up in them; but in ordinary weather they are merely kept within the yard. This, you observe, is defended by a wide stone wall, crowned all around with sharp thorns, which the prowling wolf will rarely attempt to scale."

The principal object of this first paragraph (ver. 1-5) is to contrast false and true shepherds —religious teachers that would serve themselves by means of the flock, and religious teachers that would serve the flock without regard to personal advantage. The former do not enter the fold by the door, but from some other point, and are similar to thieves and robbers. The latter seek the sheep in the appointed way, and conduct them into "green pastures," and "beside the still waters." By the sheep, must be meant the servants of God—ordinarily, it means the true servants

CH. X.]   JOHN.   213

2 But he that entereth in by the door is the shepherd of the sheep.
3 To him the porter openeth; and the sheep hear his voice: and he calleth his own sheep by name, and leadeth them out.
4 And when he putteth forth his own sheep, he goeth before them, and the sheep follow him: for they know his voice.
5 And a stranger will they not follow, but will flee from him; for they know not the voice of strangers.
6 This parable spake Jesus unto them: but they understood not what things they were which he spake unto them.

2 a robber. But he that entereth in by the door is 3 ¹ the shepherd of the sheep. To him the porter openeth: and the sheep hear his voice: and he calleth his own sheep by name, and leadeth them 4 out. When he hath put forth all his own, he goeth before them, and the sheep follow him: for they 5 know his voice. And a stranger will they not follow, but will flee from him: for they know not the voice 6 of strangers. This ² parable spake Jesus unto them: but they understood not what things they were which he spake unto them.

1 *Or, a shepherd.* ...2 *Or, proverb.*

---

of God, not including those who are merely nominal servants. Whether **the fold** represents the Theocracy, or the Christian Church, or the (invisible) kingdom of God, is less evident; and it is by no means necessary to suppose that every part of the allegory is significant of something definite in the kingdom of Christ.

2. But he that entereth in by the door is the (a) shepherd of the sheep. There is usually but one door or gate into an Oriental fold, and all the shepherds as well as flocks go in and out through that door. A shepherd would never think, for he would never have occasion to think, of entering at any other place; and therefore it is characteristic of a shepherd to enter by the door.

3. To him the porter openeth, etc. The Holy Spirit is thought by some to be represented by **the porter;** but this interpretation is doubtful. When it is said that the sheep **hear his voice**—that is, the shepherd's voice —it means that they *hearken* to it, and respond to the call made by it. In illustration of the next clause, **he calleth his own sheep by name,** the following words of Thomson may be cited: "Some sheep always keep near the shepherd, and are his special favorites. Each of them has a name, to which it answers joyfully, and the kind shepherd is ever distributing to such choice portions which he gathers for that purpose. They are the contented and happy ones." In this ideal flock, with its ideal shepherd, all the sheep are represented as objects of special care—all are contented and happy, for all have names. Hence the Saviour had in mind none but true believers; for the Lord knoweth them that are his, and their names are all written in the book of life. (2 Tim. 2:19; Rev. 3:5.)

4. When he putteth forth his own sheep (better, as in Rev. Ver., *hath put forth all his own*), **he goeth before them, and the sheep follow him: for they know his voice.** "They are so tame and so trained, that they *follow* their keeper with the utmost docility. He leads them forth from the fold . . . just where he pleases. As there are many flocks in such a place as this, each one takes a different path, and it is his business to find pasture for them."—*Thomson.* Instead of **his own sheep,** (τὰ ἴδια πρόβατα), in the first clause, the best critical authorities give *all his own* (τὰ ἴδια πάντα), and this was probably the original text.

5. And a stranger, etc. "If a stranger call, they stop short, lift up their heads in alarm; and, if it is repeated, they turn and flee. . . . This is not the fanciful costume of a parable; it is simple fact. I have made the experiment repeatedly."—*Thomson.* If Dr. Thomson intends to suggest (we do not suppose he does) that "the costume" of the Saviour's "parables" is ever "fanciful," we must dissent from his view. It would be difficult to name an instance in which any part of the costume of his parables is not true to nature.

The man who was born blind (ch. 9) recognized the voice of Jesus as that of his shepherd, and had refused to listen to the voice of the Pharisees. In him, therefore, Jesus had seen, as in a glass, the great multitude which no man can number that would, in the ages to come, acknowledge him to be their true shepherd, by hearing his voice; and with this vision of the future in his mind, he tells the Pharisees plainly that the sheep of God. the true Israel, will not follow them.

6. This parable spake Jesus unto them, etc. The word **parable** does not reproduce exactly the Greek word (παροιμία) used by the Evangelist. That word might, perhaps, be translated in this place, "similitude," or, "illustration." It does not differ, essentially, from an extended metaphor, or a brief allegory.

7 Then said Jesus unto them again, Verily, verily, I say unto you, I am the door of the sheep.
8 All that ever came before me are thieves and robbers: but the sheep did not hear them.
9 ᵃ I am the door: by me if any man enter in, he shall be saved, and shall go in and out, and find pasture.

7 Jesus therefore said unto them again, Verily, I say unto you, I am the door of the sheep. 8 All that came ¹ before me are thieves and robbers; 9 but the sheep did not hear them. I am the door; by me if any man enter in, he shall be saved, and

a ch. 14 : 6; Eph. 2 : 18.——1 Some ancient authorities omit, *before me.*

The language of Jesus was not understood. It was, no doubt, perceived to be metaphorical; but the real meaning of it was not seen. He, therefore, proceeds with his discourse, drawing attention to himself and his manifold relations to the flock. His method of teaching was full of wisdom; for, by thus clothing his doctrine in a simple allegory, the underlying sense of which was not clearly discerned by his foes, he was enabled to go on with his discourse, and give them a large amount of food for reflection.

7-10. JESUS THE DOOR TO THE SHEEP.

7. Verily, verily, I say unto you, I am the door of the sheep. The fold is the place of safety, and Jesus declares himself to be the door to that place of safety, where the sheep are, and into which the shepherds also must enter. Only through him can the sheep be found, or sheltered, or fed. This may have been spoken after an interval of time.

8. All that (ever should be omitted) **came before me are thieves and robbers.** It seems possible and best to understand, that the words, **all that came before me,** refer to those, and to those only, who had come representing themselves virtually as **the door,** or as those through whom the people could be saved. In this sense the Pharisees, who insisted with so much confidence on their knowledge of the law, were embraced in the class referred to. For they professed to teach men how to be saved without reference to the Messiah; they virtually pronounced themselves sufficient, and his coming unnecessary. The language of Christ need not be supposed to affirm that any one had already appeared claiming, in so many words, to be the Messiah. What they had done *virtually,* they had done really. Jesus was "the coming One"; but they had pitted their authority and teaching against him, making themselves the coming ones. Thus, they came. Yet, the really humble and spiritual did not hear their voice; but that of Jesus. Hence, no argument can be drawn from it in support of a post-apostolic origin of this Gospel, as if the author of it, living in the second century, had put into the mouth of Jesus words that could only have been spoken by him if he had lived fifty years later than he did. By **the sheep,** in the last clause, was evidently meant the true children of God.

9. By me if any man enter in, he shall be saved, and shall go in and out, and find pasture. These words are, doubtless, supposed by most readers to refer to the sheep, and not to shepherds. But there are strong reasons for thinking that Jesus had in mind shepherds. (1) The general object of the allegory is to distinguish between false and true religious teachers. It relates to the shepherds, and not to the sheep. It assumes that all the sheep are sheep, and not wolves; and of course they go in and out through the door. But it speaks of *professed* shepherds, who do not make use of the door, because they are, in reality, "thieves and robbers." (2) The eighth verse prepares the way for the ninth, if the latter is understood to refer to shepherds; for, by pronouncing those who taught salvation without Christ to be "thieves and robbers," he has led us, by the law of contrast, to expect a reference to genuine shepherds, and their relation to him who is the door and the way. (3) The singular number and the pronoun (τις) point to a shepherd more naturally than to one of the sheep. (4) The finding of pasture is the work of the shepherd, rather than of the sheep; while the going in and out is at least as true of the shepherd as it is of the sheep. Indeed, the allegory represents the sheep as being led in and out, rather than as going in and out of their own motion, while it represents the shepherd as going in and out of his own choice. Hence, in so far as consistency of figurative speech is concerned, a reference of this verse to shepherds is more natural than a reference of it to the sheep. (See Zech. 11: 5, 8, 17.)

The declaration that the shepherd who enters by the door will be saved, suggests that false teachers, that thieves and robbers, not only imperil the sheep, but also rush into danger themselves. (Comp. 1 Cor. 3: 15.)

JOHN. 215

10 The thief cometh not, but for to steal, and to kill, and to destroy: I am come that they might have life, and that they might have *it* more abundantly.
11 ᵃ I am the good shepherd: the good shepherd giveth his life for the sheep.
12 But he that is an hireling, and not the shepherd, whose own the sheep are not, seeth the wolf coming, and ᵇ leaveth the sheep, and fleeth; and the wolf catcheth them, and scattereth the sheep.
13 The hireling fleeth, because he is an hireling, and careth not for the sheep.

10 shall go in and go out, and shall find pasture. The thief cometh not, but that he may steal, and kill, and destroy: I came that they may have life, and
11 may ¹ have *it* abundantly. I am the good shepherd: the good shepherd layeth down his life for the sheep.
12 He that is a hireling, and not a shepherd, whose own the sheep are not, beholdeth the wolf coming, and leaveth the sheep, and fleeth, and the wolf snatcheth
13 them, and scattereth *them:* he *fleeth* because he is a

a Isa. 40: 11; Ex. 34: 12, 23; 37: 24; Heb. 13: 20; 1 Pet. 2: 25; 5: 4....*b* Zech. 11; 16, 17.——1 Or, *have abundance.*

This, too, is true; and we may, therefore, perceive in this verse a warning addressed to the Pharisees—and indeed, to all religious teachers who do not recognize Christ as the only door and way to spiritual safety.

10. The thief (or, *robber*) **cometh not,** etc. The object of the robber is his own advantage, at whatever harm to the flock, and the result of his success is destruction to the sheep. So the result of success on the part of religious pastors who do not trust in Christ, is the ruin of those who follow them. But the object of Christ's coming is the life of the sheep. He came into the world that men might have the true and eternal life—a life that consists in knowing and loving God—and that they might have an abundance of this higher life—might indeed be filled with all the fullness of God. (17: 3; 1 Cor. 3: 22; Eph. 3: 16-19.)

11-18. CHRIST THE GOOD SHEPHERD.

11. I am the good shepherd. The pronoun I is emphatic—*I*, in distinction from all others. By claiming to be **the good shepherd,** Jesus claims to have, in a preeminent degree, every quality that belongs to a shepherd's interest in his flock—watchfulness, tenderness, courage, love; so that he is the ideal and perfect shepherd. And he makes this claim in the presence of those who were accustomed to sing: "The Lord is my shepherd." How naturally would they be reminded, by his claim, of the words of their Scriptures, which speak of Jehovah as the Shepherd of Israel, and be led to reject his claim as arrogant, if not blasphemous! Without sympathy with his character, or some clear perception of the sweet and reverent, though divine spirit, which breathed in every tone of his voice, they would certainly be startled and repelled by so high a claim. Yet there is, perhaps, no saying of Jesus that has been dearer to the hearts of Christians than this. It appears very often in the writings of the Fathers, and the fact which it asserts is represented many times in the early works of Christian art. A shepherd with his crook, or with a lamb upon his shoulders or in his bosom, is found depicted more frequently than any other emblem. **The good shepherd giveth** (*layeth down*) **his life for the sheep.** This is the supreme evidence of a shepherd's fidelity to his flock, and interest in its preservation. To protect the sheep, he will meet the lion or the bear at the risk of his own life. (1 Sam 17: 34-36.) So Christ was willing to save his followers from destruction at the price of his own life; and he foresaw that this price must be paid. "The Son of man came not to be ministered unto, but to minister, and to give his life a, ransom for many." (Matt. 20: 28.) The Greek preposition translated **for** (ὑπέρ), signifies, generally, "in behalf of," "for the benefit of." though, sometimes, it means "in place of." Here, the death of the shepherd is supposed to save the sheep from death, so that, in a certain general sense, his death takes the place of theirs. Yet no reference is made to the fact of penal substitution; and we can only say that the Good Shepherd lays down his life for the benefit of the sheep—that is, to save them from destruction.

12, 13. But he that is an (a) hireling, and not the (a) shepherd, whose own the sheep are not, seeth the wolf coming, and lenveth the sheep, and fleeth; and the wolf catcheth them, and scattereth the sheep. The hireling fleeth, because he is a hireling, and careth not for the sheep. The owner of a flock does not always tend it himself, but sometimes hires another man to do this for him. And in many instances this hired servant cares only for himself, and not at all for the good of the flock. And of such a hireling Jesus speaks in this verse; that is, of one who has the spirit of a hireling, and not of a shepherd; of one who *feels* that the flock belongs to another, and

14 I am the good shepherd, and ᵃ know my *sheep*, and am known of mine.
15 ᵇ As the Father knoweth me, even so know I the Father; ᶜ and I lay down my life for the sheep.
16 And ᵈ other sheep I have, which are not of this fold: them also I must bring, and they shall hear my voice; ᵉ and there shall be one fold, *and* one shepherd.

14 hireling, and careth not for the sheep. I am the good shepherd; and I know mine own, and mine
15 own know me, even as the Father knoweth me, and I know the Father; and I lay down my life for the
16 sheep. And other sheep I have, that are not of this fold: them also I must ¹ bring, and they shall hear my voice; and ² they shall become one flock, one

a 2 Tim. 2 : 19....b Matt. 11 : 27....c ch. 15 : 13....d Isa. 56 : 8....e Ezek. 37 : 22 ; Eph. 2 : 14 ; 1 Pet. 2 : 25.——1 Or, *lead*....2 Or, *there shall be one flock*.

not to himself. When such a keeper of the flock beholds a wolf coming, he makes haste to secure his own safety, leaving the flock to be scattered, and the sheep to perish. Alas, there are many religious teachers that are in spirit hirelings. Many have undertaken the care of churches, the cure of souls, who seek their own, and not the things of Christ; who are almost indifferent to the spiritual good of those under their instruction, but ever ready to welcome personal comfort or advancement. Such pastors are sure to prove faithless in the presence of spiritual foes. Many a church has been scattered and lost by reason of selfish leaders.

It will be observed that the Revised Version has omitted two words, viz.: **the sheep,** at the close of ver. 12, and three words, **the hireling fleeth,** at the beginning of ver. 13. These omissions seem to be required by the best manuscripts, but they do not affect the meaning of Christ's language.

14, 15. I am the good shepherd, etc. The Rev. Ver. of the remainder is better: *And I know mine own, and mine own know me, even as the Father knoweth me, and I know the Father.* The knowledge here spoken of is mutual, springing from personal acquaintance and love. The point of similarity is not to be found in the degree of knowledge possessed by the shepherd on the one hand and the sheep on the other, as compared with that possessed by the Father on the one hand and the Son on the other; but it is to be found in the kind or quality of the knowledge possessed by all—a knowledge founded on mutual recognition and love. Meyer remarks that the comparison refers to "the *kind and manner*—to the holy nature of this mutual acquaintanceship. (Comp. 14: 20; 15: 10; 17: 8, 21.) As between God and Christ, so likewise between Christ and 'them that are his,' the mutual knowledge is that of innermost fellowship of life and love, in which fellowship the knowledge is implied." And Lange says that "this knowledge does not

mean *loving;* but still it is an emphatic expression by which a loving knowledge is implied." **And I lay down my life for the sheep.** The present tense of the verb points to the near future, when Christ would die for the salvation of his own "rational flock."

It will be noticed that we have adopted the Rev. Ver., founded on a text and punctuation differing slightly from those of the Common Version, and that the reading adopted adds somewhat to the clearness and force of Christ's language. But it is adopted on no other ground than that of superior manuscript authority.

16. And other sheep I have, which are not of this fold. This fold is the Jewish nation; and these words furnish a reply—whether intended or not—to the scornful question of his foes: "Will he go unto the dispersed among the Gentiles, and teach the Gentiles?" (7: 35.) For he claims to have sheep among the Gentiles. Knowing that there are many outside of Israel who will become his disciples when they hear the gospel; knowing that the ancient prophets had foretold the conversion of numerous Gentiles (*e. g.*, Isa. 53: 10, sq., 55: 5; Micah 4: 2); knowing that the plan of God is well ordered and sure, and that the names of all his elect are even now in the book of life—he anticipates the future, and speaks of them as if they were already his own in reality, as well as in prospect and purpose. **Them also must I bring**—not, indeed, by his personal ministry while in the flesh, but by that of Paul and other messengers of life, whose work will not cease till the end of time. The word **bring** points to the attractive and guiding power of Christ, drawing all his followers together, as the next words declare. **And they shall** (or, *will*) **hear my voice.** "He that receiveth you, receiveth me." To hear the voice of Christ's ambassadors, is to hear his voice; for their message is his message, in substance and spirit. Let no one who rejects the call of Jesus by the ministry of his servants imagine

17 Therefore doth my Father love me, ᵃ because I lay down my life, that I might take it again.
18 No man taketh it from me, but I lay it down of myself. I have power to lay it down, and I ᵇ have power to take it again. ᶜ This commandment have I received of my Father.

17 shepherd. Therefore doth the Father love me, because I lay down my life, that I may take it again.
18 No one ¹ taketh it away from me, but I lay it down of myself. I have ² power to lay it down, and I have ² power to take it again. This commandment received I from my Father.

a Isa. 53: 7, 8, 12; Heb. 2: 9....b ch. 2: 19....c ch. 6: 38; 15: 10; Acts 2: 24, 32,——1 Some ancient authorities read, *took it away*....2 Or, *right.*

that he would have listened to it with a different spirit, if it had come to him from the lips of the Good Shepherd himself. **And there shall be one fold, and one shepherd.** The Rev. Ver. is better. In other words: "There shall come to be one flock with one shepherd." Observe that the words of Jesus are *one flock, not one fold.* For the idea of the fold is subordinate to that of the flock. It is the flock which belongs to the shepherd, and sheep from many folds are to become one flock—instead of flocks that belong to many shepherds being sheltered in one fold, as is often the case in Palestine. The unity contemplated is one springing out of a common relation to Christ, and that relation is primarily spiritual. Only in a secondary sense can it be one of outward or formal organization. In Christ, Jew and Gentile will possess the same inward temper —the same trust and love and hope. By him, the middle wall of partition is to be broken down, and every man who recognizes him as the Good Shepherd will be recognized by him as a member of "the rational flock" which he has bought with his own blood.

17. Therefore (or, *for this reason*) **doth my Father love me, because I lay down my life, that I might** (*may*) **take it again.** The expression *for this reason* is generally supposed to look backward to what has been said in verses 14-16, and forward to a re-statement of the same thought in another form, viz.: **because I lay down my life,** etc. It will be noticed that the words of Jesus in this verse are no longer figurative, allegorical, but plain and direct; also, that his approaching death is represented as voluntary, and as about to be followed by his voluntary resurrection; and, again, that this voluntary death and resurrection are well pleasing to the Father. The words **that I may take it again,** are to be closely connected with the preceding expression, **I lay down my life.** The Father's love to the Son has one of its sources in the redeeming work of the Son. But that redeeming work depends on his resurrection as well as on his death. "The ground of the love of God lies not merely in the sacrifice, considered by itself, but in the fact that the Good Shepherd, when he gives up his life, is resolved to take it again, in order that he may continue to fulfill his pastoral office till the final goal is reached, when all mankind shall constitute his flock." —*Meyer.* Watkins remarks that "the key to the meaning is in the truth that for Christ the taking again of human life is itself a further sacrifice, and that this is necessary for the completion of the Great Shepherd's work." But if the reunion of the eternal Word with his human body glorified is of itself a sacrifice, it follows that the humiliation of the Word is eternal; for there is no reason to suppose that he will ever sunder his connection with his glorified human nature. We do not see that the view of Watkins is necessarily implied in the words of Christ, yet it is a view which would perfectly account for his words, and which, if clearly established, might powerfully move the Christian heart.

18. No man taketh it from me, but I lay it down of myself. It is better to follow the Greek exactly, and translate *no one*, instead of **no man**; for Jesus may have intended to exclude the idea that any being in the universe took from him his life, without his own absolutely free consent. This certainly was true; and the Greek term (οὐδείς) is comprehensive enough to mean this. (Sirach 18: 6, 7, 8; Luke 23: 46.) As freely as the Father gave the Son, so freely did the Son give himself—a ransom for many. But it is none the less true that he suffered a violent death by the hands of sinful men. To this death he submitted of his own accord, and thus, in a true and important sense, laid down his life; but this death was *suffered* by himself, not *inflicted* by himself. Had he been pleased to exercise his theanthropic power in retaining his own life, as he employed it in raising Lazarus, the power of man would have failed to effect his death. But himself he would not save, for he came into the world to be crucified and slain. **I have power to lay it down, and I have power to take it again.**

19 ᵃThere was a division therefore again among the Jews for these sayings.
20 And many of them said, ᵇ He hath a devil, and is mad; why hear ye him?
21 Others said, These are not the words of him that hath a devil. ᶜ Can a devil ᵈ open the eyes of the blind?

19 There arose a division again among the Jews because of those words. And many of them said, He hath a demon, and is mad; why hear ye him. 21 Others said, These are not the sayings of one possessed with a demon. Can a demon open the eyes of the blind?

ᵃ ch. 7 : 43 ; 9 : 16. ...ᵇ ch. 7 : 20 ; 8 : 48, 52....ᶜ Ex. 4 : 11 ; Ps. 94 : 9 ; 146 : 8....ᵈ ch. 9 : 6, 7, 32, 33.

It is difficult to define the word **power**, in this place. Grimm understands it to signify "power of choice, liberty to do what one pleases." That is to say, Jesus claims that he acts in this matter with perfect freedom; that it depends on himself whether he lays down his life or takes it again. If this view of the word is correct, the next clause: **This commandment I have** (omit **have**) **received of** (*from*) **my Father**, must be interpreted, with Godet, to mean a permission or commission, "to die or not to die, to rise again or not to rise again, according to the free inspirations of his own love." Others understand the word **power** (ἐξουσίαν), to signify, in this place, "full and rightful authority"; in which case the language of Jesus *implies* his perfect freedom in dying and rising again. Yet this freedom is to be used in accordance with the Father's will; and that will or **commandment** was received at the time of the incarnation. All that he is to do or to suffer will be strictly voluntary on his part; but it will be, at the same time, in pursuance of the Father's will. This interpretation assigns a more usual meaning to the word translated **power**, and is, therefore, preferable to the one first named. According to Cremer, the original word combines the two ideas of *right and might*. Sometimes the one is prominent by virtue of the context, and sometimes the other.

The resurrection of Christ from the dead is frequently ascribed to the power and agency of the Father; but in this passage Jesus appears to teach that he will not only lay down his own life, but, also, **take it again.** How is this language to be reconciled to that? Meyer says, that "the *taking* again of his life... implies the *giving* it again—i. e., the re-awakening activity of the Father." In other words, the life was restored by the act of the Father, but received by the act of the Son. But he does not explain what he means by the two acts. Watkins says that "the taking again was under the Father's authority, and was, therefore, itself the Father's gift." Compare ch. 5 : 19 sq., with the Notes. Christ seems to be intent on affirming two things: (1) The absolute voluntariness of his death and resurrection, and (2) the absolute harmony of his conduct in this matter with the plan and will of the Father. Whether he himself put forth energy in bringing to pass his own death, or his own resurrection, is not affirmed. It was the Father's plan that Christ should die and rise again for the salvation of the people; but that he should do this of his own accord, of his own choice, with no constraint but that of love. And it was because Christ freely gave himself to dying and rising again for this end, that the Father *loved* him with a special and inexpressible love.

19-21. EFFECT OF THIS DISCOURSE.

19. There was a division, etc. Or, as in the Rev. Ver. : *There arose a division again among the Jews, because of these words.* Comp. 9 : 16; 9 : 8, 9; 7 : 12, 30, 31, 40, 41. If the writer means, by **the Jews**, the leaders of the people, who were conspicuous for their bigoted attachment to the ritual of the old religion, it is plain that a considerable number of this class were favorably impressed by the sayings of Jesus. Nicodemus was not the only Pharisee who was touched by his wisdom. **Therefore,** (οὖν), of the Com. Ver., is omitted by the highest authorities.

20. And many of them said, (or, *were saying,*) **He hath a devil,** (or, *demon,*) **and is mad : why hear ye him ?** The word **many** points to a majority of the Jews present. These clung to the opinion which they had before expressed. (8 : 48.) But they were evidently disturbed by the attention and respect with which some were listening to the Saviour. Hence they were tempted to repeat their wild and bitter accusation. But their scorn did not silence those who had another temper.

21. Others said, (or, *were saying*)—that is, in response to this bitter accusation—**These are not the words of him that hath a devil** (or, *demon.*) **Can a devil** (*demon*)

Ch. X.]   JOHN.   219

22 And it was at Jerusalem the feast of the dedication, and it was winter.
23 And Jesus walked in the temple *in Solomon's porch.
24 Then came the Jews round about him, and said unto him, How long dost thou make us to doubt? If thou be the Christ, tell us plainly.

22 ¹And it was the feast of the dedication at Jerusalem: it was winter; and Jesus was walking in
24 the temple in Solomon's porch. The Jews therefore came round about him, and said unto him, How long dost thou hold us in suspense? If thou art

a Acts 3:11; 5:12.——1 Some ancient authorities read, *At that time was the feast.*

open the eyes of the blind? They repel the accusation by appealing to the words and the works of Jesus. His language was not that of a demoniac—fierce, raving, incoherent—nor was the power possessed by a demon, such as Christ exercised when he restored sight to the blind. Two convincing facts briefly and clearly stated.

22, sq. JESUS IN JERUSALEM AT THE FEAST OF DEDICATION. (Dec. 20-27, A. D. 29.)

The Evangelist now passes over, in silence, a period of about two months from the Feast of Tabernacles to the Feast of Dedication. Where was Jesus during those two months—from the second week of October to the third week of December? Meyer, Hengstenberg, and others answer, In Jerusalem, or its suburbs; for nothing is said of any departure thence, or return thither. But, against this view, it has been forcibly urged: (1) That he could not have remained there in peace, on account of the bitter enmity of "the Jews." (2) That the references which appear in the following discourse, to what he had said at the Feast of Tabernacles, are far more natural if we suppose that he had been absent from Jerusalem two months, than they are if we suppose that he had remained there and taught, meanwhile; for by the former supposition, these references were to his last discourse in that place. And (3) that events are related in the other Gospels which appear to belong to just this period of the Lord's ministry. Between the Feast of Tabernacles (Oct. 11-18, A. D. 29,) and the Feast of Dedication, (Dec. 20-27, A. D. 29,) Dr. Robinson places the following events: A lawyer instructed by parable (Luke 10: 25-37); Jesus in the house of Martha and Mary (Luke 10: 38-42); the disciples again taught how to pray (Luke 11: 1-12); the return of the seventy (Luke 10: 17-24); the giving of sight to a man born blind, etc. (John 9: 1-41; 10: 1-21). Gardiner assigns to this period of about two months several events and parables not embraced in Robinson's list; but it is not im-

portant for us to examine his reasons for so doing.

22. And it was at Jerusalem the feast of the dedication. This feast was established by Judas Maccabæus, to commemorate the cleansing and re-consecration of the temple after its destruction by Antiochus Epiphanes (1 Macc. 4:50, sq.; 2 Macc. 1:13; 10. 6, sq.; Josephus "Ant." 12:7, 7.) It was celebrated eight days every year, beginning with the 25th of Kisleu, not only in Jerusalem, but in any part of the land, and was an occasion of much joy and festivity. The writer of 2 Maccabæus says that "they kept eight days with gladness"; that "they bore branches and fair boughs, and palms also, and sung psalms unto him who had given them good success in cleansing his place." (10: 6. 7.) Josephus remarks that this festival was called "Lights," and that he supposes the name was given to it from the joy of the nation at their unexpected liberty. In the temple at Jerusalem, the "Hallel" was sung every day of the feast. (Smith's "Dict. of the Bible," Art. Dedication). And it was winter. The and is to be omitted, and this statement connected with the following.

23. And Jesus walked (*was walking*) in the temple, in Solomon's porch. The descriptive tense, *was walking*, shows that the scene was vividly present to the Evangelist's mind; and the fact that Christ was walking in a covered porch, or arcade, is accounted for by the season of the year. This arcade was on the side of the temple towards the east, nearest the wall that overhangs the Valley of Kedron, and is said to have been a relic of Solomon's days.—*Josephus*, "Antiq.," 20: 9, 7. There is a reference to the same porch in Acts 3: 11. "The mention of this particular part of the temple is one of the traces of the writer having himself been an eye-witness; events like this no doubt impressed themselves on the memory, so as never to be forgotten. (Comp. 8: 20.)"—*Meyer.*

24. Then (rather, *therefore*) came the

220   JOHN.   [Ch. X.

25 Jesus answered them, I told you, and ye believed not: *the works that I do in my Father's name, they bear witness of me.
26 But *ye believe not, because ye are not of my sheep, as I said unto you.
27 *My sheep hear my voice, and I know them, and they follow me:
28 And I give unto them eternal life; and *they shall never perish, neither shall any *man* pluck them out of my hand.

25 the Christ, tell us plainly. Jesus answered them, I told you, and ye believe not: the works that I do in my Father's name, these bear witness of me.
26 But ye believe not, because ye are not of my sheep.
27 My sheep hear my voice, and I know them, and 28 they follow me: and I give unto them eternal life; and they shall never perish, and no one shall

a ver. 38; ch. 3:2; 5:36....b ch. 8:47; 1 John 4:6....c ver. 4:14....d ch. 6:37; 17:11, 12; 18:9.

Jews round about him. Many of the prominent men, who were, for the most part, opposed to Christ, gathered around—literally, *encircled*—him, as he was walking to and fro in the porch. **And said unto him, How long dost thou make us to doubt** (or, *hold us in suspense.*—Rev. Ver.)? **If thou be (*art*) the Christ, tell us plainly.** The Greek words which are translated *hold us in suspense* literally signify, *lift up our soul,* or mind—that is, in the present case, keep our souls in a state of excitement, by leaving a question of the highest interest unsettled. But why did the Jews gather round Jesus and broach this question? It is probable that during the two months of his absence they had remained divided in sentiment, a majority of them rejecting the claims of Jesus, but some of them feeling that both his words and his works proved him to be from God. (See ver. 20, 21.) The former might ask the question with the purpose of making his answer the basis of accusation, and the latter with the desire to have all doubt removed from their minds. At any rate, they seek the interview and propose the question, which is evidence enough that the absence of Jesus had not diminished their interest in him.

25. I told you, and ye believed (*believe*) not. That is, "I declared myself to be the Christ, and though I did this, ye do not believe." That he had done this more than once is very evident from the preceding narrative. His answer is therefore equivalent to a plain assertion of his Messiahship, and a plain assertion of their unbelief, together with a pretty obvious allusion to either malice or dullness on their part, in making such a demand. **The works that I do in my Father's name, they (or, *these*) bear witness of me.** To do works in the Father's name, is to appeal to the Father in doing them, or to recognize them in some way as the Father's works, revealing his will. This agrees with the representation of 5: 19, sq. What the Father does, the Son does in like manner, and the works of the Father are wrought by the Son.

26. But ye believe not, because ye are not of my sheep. The last words of the Common Version: **As I said unto you,** are not adequately supported. If they were genuine, they would contain a distinct reference to his discourse, at the Feast of Tabernacles, two months before. He had then virtually declared that they were not his sheep (see ver. 4, 14), and it was not too much to expect that they would at once recall to mind his words at that time. At all events, the expression **my sheep** recalls that discourse. "The circumstance that Jesus should refer to this allegory, about two months after the date of ver. 1-21, has been used as an argument against the originality of this discourse (Strauss Baur); but it may be simply accounted for by the assumption that during the interval he had had no further discussions with his hierarchical opponents.—*Meyer,* freely. Some of those who then listened to him were now present, with undiminished hostility.

27, 28. My sheep hear my voice, and I know them, and they follow me: and I give unto them eternal life. The first three statements are almost verbal repetitions of what he had said at the Feast of Tabernacles (see ver. 14-16), and the last statement was implied in what he then said. For if the Good Shepherd lays down his life for the sheep, it is that they may not perish, but may have eternal life. (Comp. 3: 16.) **And they shall never perish,** etc. That is, those who are true disciples of Christ—being guided and nourished by him, will never be suffered to perish. The blessed life which they have begun to enjoy will be preserved from this time forward forever. **And no one,** etc. They are in the hands of the Chief Shepherd, and no one, however powerful or fierce, can wrest

29 ª My Father, ᵇ which gave *them* me, is greater than all; and no man is able to pluck *them* out of my Father's hand.
30 ᶜ I and my Father are one.

29 snatch them out of my hand. ¹ My Father, who hath given *them* unto me, is greater than all; and no one is able to snatch ²*them* out of the Father's hand. I and the Father are one. The Jews took

a ch. 14 : 28.....*b* ch. 17 : 2, 6, etc.....*c* ch. 17 : 11, 22.—1 Some ancient authorities read, *That which my Fath*ᵉʳ *hath given unto me*..... 2 *Or, aught.*

them out of that hand. The first clause of this verse appears to mean that believers in Christ will never, by their own carelessness or ignorance, lose that union with him which makes existence a blessing; and the latter, that no enemy, however crafty or strong, will succeed in destroying their life in Christ. (See Rom. 8: 31, sq.) The preservation of the saints is distinctly taught by the Lord in this passage.

The word **perish** is used by Christ and by Paul to denote an utter loss of true life, or blessed communion with God, and not to denote an utter loss of being. Annihilation is nowhere taught by the sacred writers. For a fuller con.ment on the Greek expression translated **never** (οὐ μὴ—εἰς τὸν αἰῶνα), see Note on 11: 26.

29, 30. My Father, which gave (rather, *hath given*) **them me, is greater than all; and no man** (*one*) **is able to pluck them out of my Father's hand. I and my Father are one.** This is added in confirmation of the last statement: "No man is able to pluck them out of my hand." For by identifying his own power with his Father's, he pronounces it absolute. In this remarkable passage Jesus claims: (1) That his Father is the greatest of all beings—*i. e.*, God; (2) that the sheep of which he is speaking have been given him by his Father; (3) that no one can pluck them out of his Father's hand; and (4) that in keeping them he and his Father are one—*i. e.*, one in action, in power, and therefore in essence. To be **one** *thing*, (ἕν), in the sense demanded by the argument, is to be one in keeping the sheep against all destroyers. The action of the Son is, therefore, declared to be inseparable from that of the Father, and one with it. But if their action is one, their power must be one; for action is but the movement of power. And if their power is one, their being or essence must be one; for power belongs to being. The language of this verse may, therefore, be said to agree with the common doctrine of the Trinity; that the Father, the Son, and the Holy Spirit are in essence one

and the same, but distinguishable in a personal respect.

In the expression **greater than all,** Meyer supposes that the word **all** refers to persons, and includes even the Son. But, as the obvious scope of the passage is to affirm the oneness of the Son's preserving agency with that of the Father, it is unnatural to suppose that Jesus meant to separate himself from the Father in this clause, and associate himself, as to greatness, with the inferior **all.** The only evidence of his subordination to be found in this place is in the words **my Father,** since sonship implies a certain subordination; and in the words **who has given them to me,** since the receiver of a kingdom is, in a certain respect, subordinate to the giver.

According to the highest textual authority, the word **greater** has a neuter form (μεῖζόν), showing that the Saviour's thought was this: "My Father.. is something greater than all," that is, a power greater than all. For a similar use of the neuter adjective, see Matt. 12: 6. Some editors make the relative pronoun neuter also: "My Father *which* gave them to me, is greater than all"; but the pronoun, as Meyer and Schaff suggest, may have been changed by transcribers, who could not understand how a neuter adjective could agree with the masculine term Father. But another construction is certainly possible, viz: "*That which my Father hath given to me, is greater than all.*" (So א B* L. Tisch, Tregel., West. and Hort. Alford, Revisers, margin.) The meaning then would be, that the power given to him by the Father was greater than all. Some MSS. read: "The Father," instead of "My Father," an unimportant variation.

"The doctrine of the saint's perseverance in holiness is here most expressly taught. (**Ver. 27 - 29.**) If one of the elect should finally perish, it would not only falsify the declaration here made by Christ, but would be a violation of the compact between the Father and the Son (see 6: 37), and contrary to the expressly declared will of the Father. (**6: 39, 40.**) Yet this great truth, which so illustrates the sov-

31 Then *a* the Jews took up stones again to stone him. 32 Jesus answered them, Many good works have I shewed you from my Father; for which of those works do ye stone me? 33 The Jews answered him, saying, For a good work we stone thee not; but for blasphemy; and because that thou, being a man, *b* makest thyself God.

31 up stones again to stone him. Jesus answered them, 32 Many good works I have shewed you from the Father; for which of those works do ye stone me? 33 The Jews answered him, For a good work we stone thee not, but for blasphemy; and because that thou,

a ch. 8: 59....*b* ch. 5: 18.

creign mercy of God through Jesus Christ, and which is the only sure foundation upon which the believer rests his hope of eternal life, must not be abused to justify any laxity of effort on his part to make his calling and election sure, by a life of prayer and holy living, such as becometh the disciples of Christ."—*Owen*, ad. loc.

31. Then the Jews (or, *the Jews therefore*) **took up stones again to stone him** (or, *that they might stone him*). If the word **therefore** belongs to the genuine text,—of which there is some doubt,—the act of the Jews is expressly declared to be a consequence of what Jesus had just said; but if it does not belong to the text, there is no reason to suppose that it misrepresents the connection between the act of the Jews and the words of Jesus. The manner in which he associated himself with the Father, filled their hearts with wrath, if not with horror. And what they did was to lift up stones from the ground, with the intention of hurling them at Jesus, and thus killing him upon the spot, without even the form of trial and judgment. (Comp. Levit. 24: 10 sq.). The word **again**, refers without doubt to the scene described in 8: 59.

But as they were in the act of stoning him, they were arrested by a remark of infinite sagacity, and, it may be. authority, compelling them to turn their thoughts to what he had done.

32. Jesus answered them, Many good works have I shewed you from my Father. The action of the Jews was most expressive; it was accusation and condemnation and execution in a breath. Hence the language of Jesus is called an answer to them. By the term **works**, he means "mighty works," or miracles; by the term translated **good** (καλά) he characterizes these miracles as divinely "fair and fit," worthy of the highest regard; by the expression, **from my Father**, he reminds them that his works are from the Father, even as he himself is from the Father, and that his own action is inseparable from the Father's: and by the words, **have I shewed you**, he affirms that these miracles were meant for "signs" to them: they were significant of the Saviour's authority as well as goodness. **For which of those works do ye stone me?** There is deep and holy irony in this question. For the Lord knew that it was his words that had provoked their wrath; but he also knew that his works and his words signified one and the same thing, brought one and the same message, asserted one and the same authority, and that in condemning him for his words they were also condemning him for his works. He, therefore, assumes that they are intelligent and self-consistent, enraged at his works, which speak the same language as his words. If there was, as we concede, a species of irony or mockery in this, it was profoundly just, fitted to open their eyes and deter them from the awful crime they were at the point of committing.

The word rendered **which** (ποῖον) cannot be easily reproduced in English, without resorting to paraphrase: for it suggests quality as well as distinction. Thus: "What is the character of that one of those works on account of which ye are about to stone me?" or, "Of those works what is the character of the one for which ye are about stoning me?" This was a question that might well make them pause.

33. For a good work we stone thee not; but for blasphemy; and because that thou, being a man, makest thyself God. Are two offences here charged against Jesus, or only one? Lange says, two: "They reproach him with two things: first, that he places God on a par with himself—and this they call blasphemy; secondly, that he makes himself God—and in this they think they recognize the false prophet." But it is difficult to discriminate between these two things, and better to suppose, with Meyer, that but one offence is charged. According to this view, **"And** connects with the general charge

34 Jesus answered them, *Is it not written in your law, I said, Ye are gods? 35 If he called them gods, *unto whom the word of God came, and the scripture cannot be broken; 36 Say ye of him, *whom the Father hath sanctified, and *sent into the world, Thou blasphemest; *because I said, I am *the Son of God?

34 being a man, makest thyself God. Jesus answered them, Is it not written in your law, I said, Ye are 35 gods? If he called them gods, unto whom the word of God came (and the scripture cannot be broken), 36 say ye of him, whom the Father ¹sanctified and sent into the world, Thou blasphemest; because I

a Ps. 82: 6....b Rom. 13: 1....c ch. 6: 27....d ch. 3: 17, 5: 36, 37; 8: 42....e ch. 5: 17, 18; ver. 30..../ Luke 1: 35; ch. 9: 35, 37.— 1 Or, *consecrated*.

a more exact definition of that on which it is based." Thus: "We stone thee for blasphemy, and indeed because thou, being man, makest thyself God." Whether they understood him to claim *essential*, or only *dynamical* unity with the Father, is of little moment; for they were certainly in a mood to pronounce either claim blasphemous, and to regard either as a claim to being God. But when he said, "I and my Father are one" (thing), it is probable that they supposed him to assert his essential oneness with the Father. "The word rendered **for** (before **blasphemy**), is not the causal, 'on account of,' which we have in the last (preceding) verse, but 'concerning,' the technical form for an indictment. For the Mosaic law concerning blasphemy, see Lev. 24: 10-16."—*Watkins*.

It is clear that the Jews were determined not to consider the words of Jesus in the light of his works, which proved that God was with him, but to consider them alone, and on the basis of the assumption that he was merely human—a man, and nothing more. It is also plain that Jesus adapted his answer to their state of mind and habits of reasoning, meeting them on their own ground, without yielding a particle of his own claim. Only by bearing in mind these points, can one perceive the wisdom of Christ's response. They had formulated, as it were, their legal accusation, and he tests it by an argument founded on the language of their law.

34. Is it not written in your law, I said, Ye are gods? By your law, is meant the Old Testament (comp. 12: 34; 15: 25; Rom. 3: 19; 1 Cor. 14: 21); and the passage here cited is in Ps. 82: 6. The Psalm is addressed to unjust judges and rulers of Israel. According to the original idea of the theocratic nation, these judges were to be representatives of God, acting for him, and doing his will. (Comp. Ex. 21: 6; 22: 8, 28; 2 Chron. 19: 5-7.) In the Psalm, God refers to his language, by Moses, as having been virtually addressed to the unjust rulers of the Psalmist's day. "I

myself have said, Ye are gods, and sons of the Most High, all of you; yet surely as men, ye shall die," etc.

35. If he—or the Scripture—called them gods, unto whom the word of God came. The phrase **unto whom the word of God came**, does not assign a reason why they were called gods, but mentions a circumstance, notwithstanding which they were so called. Though they were persons to whom God's message was sent, instead of being persons entrusted with his message to others, they were called **gods. And the Scripture cannot be broken.** Meyer connects this with the preceding clause, and makes it depend upon **if** (*ei*). "If—as is true—it called them gods to whom the word of God came, and [if] the Scripture cannot be broken." But most interpreters regard this statement as parenthetic, calling to mind an admitted truth on which the validity of his argument rested. And the more common view is probably correct. Jesus here affirms the permanent authority and divine truth of **the Scripture** in question—that is, the passage from the Psalms. **Cannot be broken** (or, *loosened*)—*i. e.*, cannot be deprived of its validity. And if this Scripture cannot be annulled, there is much reason to believe that the same is true of all other Scriptures; especially when we call to mind the circumstance that Jesus always speaks with reverence of the Old Testament. Indeed, it is possible that **the Scripture** here means the Old Testament as a whole.

36. Say ye of him, whom the Father (omit **hath**) **sanctified, and sent into the world, Thou blasphemest, because I said, I am the Son of God?** "How could they charge him with blasphemy in claiming to be *the Son of God*, when their own judges had been styled *gods*. . . . Their office was but for a time; they were mortal men, yet wearing, by divine permission, a divine name. He had been with the Father before he came into the world, was by him sealed and set apart ('sanctified'), and sent to be, not a judge,

37 a If I do not the works of my Father, believe me not. 38 But if I do, though ye believe not me, b believe the works; that ye may know, and believe, c that the Father is in me, and I in him. 39 d Therefore they sought again to take him; but he escaped out of their hand, 40 And went away again beyond Jordan into the place e where John at first baptized; and there he abode.

37 said, I am the Son of God? If I do not the works 38 of my Father, believe me not. But if I do them, though ye believe not me, believe the works; that ye may know and understand that the Father is in 39 me, and I in the Father. They sought again to take him: and he went forth out of their hand. 40 And he went away again beyond Jordan into the place where John was at the first baptizing; and there

a ch. 15: 24....b ch. 5: 36; 14: 10, 11....c ch. 14: 10, 11; 17: 21.. .d ch. 7: 30, 44; 8: 59....e ch. 1: 28.

but the Christ; not one of many sons, but emphatically the Son of God—the King of an everlasting kingdom. Both in his office and in his person he has far more right to the title, 'Son of God,' than they have to that of 'gods.'"—*Perowne*, on Ps. 82: 6. The interrogative form characterizes their charge as one that needs only to be stated in order to be rejected.

37. If I do not the works of my Father, believe me not. A remarkable word, showing that divine works, or miracles, were just what might naturally be expected of the Son of God, and that they were, in their place, a necessary part of the evidence on which Jesus rested his claim to be received as the Son of God. By it he authorized and commanded the Pharisees to reject him if he failed to do such works as only God could do. If any evidence were necessary to prove that Jesus did not intend to lower, by his criticism of their charge, the claim which he had made by calling himself **the Son of God,** and by saying **I and my Father are one,** it is furnished by this verse and the next following.

38. But if I do (*them*), **though ye believe not me, believe the works.**—That is, though my words do not come to you with a self-evidencing power, nor my spirit and life by themselves win your confidence and convince you that I am all that I profess to be, yet believe at least what my works proclaim —**that ye may know and believe** (or, *understand.*) *Understand* is a translation of the best supported text. The former verb (**know**) denotes a single, accomplished act; the latter a continuous exercise. **That the Father is in me, and I in him** (or, *the Father.*) For this is no more than could be certainly concluded and known from the works of Christ, when fairly interpreted by the light emanating from them, and from all the circumstances of the case. But, as Jesus here assumes, this inter-penetration and mutual indwelling of Father and Son is not all that his words have taught. Something more

than this was meant by the declaration, "I and my Father are one," to wit: that in their power, in their action, and in that which is the seat of power and the source of action, their mysterious and divine essence, they are one. This could only be learned from the testimony of Christ himself.

In translating the last clause, we follow the best authorities by giving, instead of **in him,** *in the Father;* though it is one of a multitude of instances where the meaning is very slightly affected, if at all, by the change of text.

39. Therefore they sought (or, *were seeking*) **again to take him.** Not now for the purpose of stoning him on the spot, but rather to have him in their power with a view to his destruction either with or without a regular trial. More than this cannot certainly be inferred from the Evangelist's remark; but this he depicts as if he were an eye-witness, and were keenly watching their movements, as they were trying to lay hold of him. Tischendorf omits the word meaning **again,** from the Greek text, but without sufficient reason. It refers, probably, to the scenes described in 7: 30, 32, 44. But (*and*) **he escaped out of their hand.** Literally, *he went forth out of their hand.* Meyer says: "*out of their hands,* which are conceived as already stretched out after him." But is it not an objection to this that the sacred writer uses the singular, **hand,** instead of the plural, "hands"? And is it not better to take the word **hand** as a figurative designation of their power? *How* Jesus escaped, the writer does not relate, and any conjecture of ours would be worthless.

40-42. TEMPORARY SOJOURN IN PEREA. Jesus had probably been traveling and preaching and working miracles in Perea, before his appearance at the Feast of Dedication in Jerusalem. This would account for **again,** in ver. 40.

40. And went away again beyond Jordan, into the place where John at first

41 And many resorted unto him, and said, John did no miracle; *but all things that John spake of this man were true.
42 *And many believed on him there.

41 he abode. And many came unto him; and they said, John indeed did no sign: but all things whatsoever 42 John spake of this man were true. And many believed on him there.

CHAPTER XI.

NOW a certain man was sick, *named* Lazarus, of Bethany, the town of *Mary and her sister Martha.

1 Now a certain man was sick, Lazarus of Bethany,

a ch. 3: 30....b ch. 8: 30; 11: 45....c Luke 10: 38, 39.

baptized; and there he abode. The Jews had rejected him in a conclusive manner, and it was therefore worse than useless to remain in the capital. But, "his hour" to be lifted up on the cross was not yet come. So he withdrew from Jerusalem to a region where the people would be benefited by his presence and ministry It is commonly assumed that the particular place to which he repaired was the Bethabara, or Bethany, spoken of by the Evangelist in 1: 28. But this is not perfectly certain; for the place where the deputation of Pharisees from Jerusalem met John may not have been the place where he *at first baptized*. Bethany and Enon are, indeed, the only two places named by the Evangelist in connection with the administration of baptism by John, and it is evident that Enon was visited after Bethany; but the narrative of this Evangelist is so fragmentary that we cannot regard it as complete in itself, with no references to events not particularly described. Yet the place to which he now repaired may have been the Bethany of 1: 28, and there is at least some probability that it was.

41. And many resorted (*came*) **unto him, and said** (or, *were saying*). The last verb is in the descriptive tense, betokening either the writer's presence, or the frequent recurrence of this remark. **John** (*indeed*) **did no miracle** (or, *sign*). "A characteristic feature of the history of John, which, in this respect also, has remained free from fanciful additions."—*Meyer*. It was natural for the people of this region to contrast the ministry of John with that of Jesus. They had been greatly moved by the preaching of the mighty harbinger of Christ, and they now compared his words respecting the Messiah with what they had seen and heard. **But all things that John spake of this man were true.** The Baptist had distinctly asserted the superior greatness of the Messiah. And as they heard of the miracles of Jesus, or witnessed them, the fulfillment by him of John's word

became a ground of faith—an additional reason why they should trust in Jesus as the Messiah.

42. And many believed on him there. "Jesus was reaping," as Bengel says, "the posthumous fruit of the Baptist's work."

Ch. 11: 1-44. LAZARUS RAISED FROM THE DEAD.

1-16. PRELIMINARY NARRATIVE.

1. Now a certain man. The connective **now,** or *but* (δέ), is used because the sickness and death of Lazarus led to an interruption of the Lord's sojourn in Perea. The name Lazarus is supposed to be a Greek modification of the Hebrew Eleazar. It is applied in this chapter to the (probably) younger brother of Martha and Mary; and in the Saviour's parable preserved by Luke (16: 20-25), to the beggar who was laid at the rich man's door. The parable is thought by many to have been spoken by Christ about this time in Perea; and an attempt has been made to connect the poor man of the parable with the one who was now sick. But there is no evidence of any connection between the two. Nor is there any sufficient reason for conjecturing that he was the young man who came eagerly to Jesus, and was loved by him, but went away sorrowful, because he was very rich. (Luke 18: 18-27.) More plausible, but at the same time wholly incapable of verification, is the hypothesis that the young man who followed Jesus, having "a linen cloth cast about his naked body" (Mark 14: 51), was Lazarus. The best interpreters now agree that the two Greek prepositions (ἀπό and ἐκ), the one before **Bethany**, and the other before **the village**, etc., denote the same relation; so that the latter clause is merely explanatory of the former, distinguishing this Bethany from another Bethany, on the east side of the Jordan. Bethany, the village of Mary and Martha, was the home and native place of Lazarus. It was afterwards known among Christians

P

2 (a It was *that* Mary which anointed the Lord with ointment, and wiped his feet with her hair, whose brother Lazarus was sick.)
3 Therefore his sisters sent unto him, saying, Lord, behold, he whom thou lovest is sick.
4. When Jesus heard *that*, he said, This sickness is not unto death, b but for the glory of God, that the Son of God might be glorified thereby.
5 Now Jesus loved Martha, and her sister, and Lazarus.

2 of the village of Mary and her sister Martha. And it was that Mary who anointed the Lord with ointment, and wiped his feet with her hair, whose brother Lazarus was sick. The sisters therefore sent unto him, saying, Lord, behold, he whom thou 4 lovest is sick. But when Jesus heard it, he said, This sickness is not unto death, but for the glory of God, that the son of God may be glorified thereby.
5 Now Jesus loved Martha, and her sister, and

a Matt. 26: 7; Mark 14: 3; ch. 12: 3....*b* ch. 9: 3; ver. 40.

as the village of Mary and Martha, at least down to the time when this Gospel went into circulation; at some later period it took the name of Lazarus, and is now called El-Azirieh, or El-Lazirich, from El-Azir, the Arabic form of Lazarus.

2. It was that (or, *the*) **Mary which anointed the Lord with ointment,** etc. This explanation distinguishes the Mary in question from others, and at the same time accounts for her being named, in this connection, before Martha (ver.1), her elder sister. (See ver. 5.) By reason of her act of love, referred to in this verse, and related more fully in chap. 12: 1-8, this Mary was well known and highly honored by the early disciples. But there is no valid reason for the somewhat current belief that she was the woman who is mentioned by Luke (7:36, sq.) as a sinner, though the act of the one was so similar to that of the other, for the act was one that might not unnaturally be repeated; or for the opinion that either of these was identical with Mary Magdalene. (See Articles on Lazarus, and on the several Marys, in Smith's "Dict. of the Bible," Am. ed.)

3. Therefore his sisters sent unto him, saying, Lord, etc. **Therefore** represents this act as a consequence of the facts just stated, namely, the sickness of Lazarus, and the affectionate confidence which the sisters had in Christ, as illustrated by the well known incident referred to. Their message was a beautiful expression of this confidence. Their request was delicately conveyed by the simple statement of their brother's sickness, and their plea as finely chosen and expressed— **whom thou lovest.** We can readily believe that this message was the language of Mary. Perhaps they hesitated to ask the Lord to visit Bethany, because they were aware of the purpose of the Pharisees, to lay hold of him and put him to death. At all events, they said just enough to show their unreserved confidence in him.

4. When (or, *but when*) **Jesus heard that** (better, *it*), **he said**—in the presence of the messenger and of his disciples—**this sickness is not unto death.** An expression which might be easily misunderstood at the moment, but which really affirmed, as the event proved, that in the divine plan the final issue of this sickness would not be death. **But for the glory of God.** In some definite and remarkable manner the glory of God was to be revealed by means of this sickness. This, instead of death, was the ultimate purpose of it. (Comp. 9: 3, 4.) But with this was embraced another end, viz: **that the Son of God might** (or, *may*) **be glorified thereby.** The glorifying of God is in order to the glorifying of the Son of God; for when the one is glorified, so also is the other. **Thereby** means by this sickness.

5. Now Jesus loved Martha, and her sister, and Lazarus. "Happy family," says Bengel. But the reason for the insertion of this remark in this place is not perfectly certain. Meyer supposes that it is introduced to account for the consolatory declaration of ver. 4. Jesus loved them, and therefore suggested to them enigmatically the blessed issue of this sickness. When this remark (ver. 4) was reported to the sisters, Lazarus was probably dead; but it may have been pondered in their hearts, and by its gracious purport they may have been comforted in some degree. Godet, and others, however, suppose that this remark of the Evangelist is anticipatory of ver. 7, explaining why, though he tarried for a time in Perea, he said: "Let us go into Judea again." The latter is, on the whole, more probable than the former, especially in view of the Greek words, ($\delta\grave{\epsilon}$) **now,** ver. 5, and ($\mu\grave{\epsilon}\nu$) **indeed,** ver. 6. The word **loved** ($\dot{\eta}\gamma\acute{a}\pi a$) is not the same in this verse as in ver. 3. ($\phi\iota\lambda\epsilon\hat{\iota}\varsigma$). It denotes a high moral and religious affection, and is used to express the love of God to men and the love of Christians to God and to one another. The word used by the

6 When he had heard therefore that he was sick, *he abode two days still in the same place where he was.
7 Then after that saith he to *his* disciples, Let us go into Judea again.
8 *His* disciples say unto him, Master, *the Jews of late sought to stone thee; and goest thou thither again?
9 Jesus answered, Are there not twelve hours in the

6 Lazarus. When therefore he heard that he was sick, he abode at that time two days in the place where he was. Then after this he saith to the 8 disciples, Let us go into Judea again. The disciples say unto him, Rabbi, the Jews were but now seeking to stone thee; and goest thou thither 9 again? Jesus answered, Are there not twelve

a ch. 10: 40....*b* ch. 10: 31.

sisters (ver. 3) denotes warm personal attachment.

6. **When he had heard therefore that he was sick,** etc.—literally, *when therefore he heard,* etc. This part of Christ's conduct has been pronounced unnatural, unaccountable, and a clear proof that the whole narrative is worthless in a historical respect. "Why," it is asked, "must Lazarus die, in order that Jesus might have some one to raise from the dead? Why did he not from a distance rebuke the disease and prevent the death of Lazarus, selecting some other person already dead to be raised?" In answer to such objections, we may refer, with Meyer, to verse 4, "according to which Jesus was conscious of its being the *divine will* that the miracle should be performed precisely under the circumstances and at the *time* at which it actually was performed. (Comp. 2: 4)." Further, it may have been already, when the message reached Jesus, too late for him to save the life of his friend by a cure of the disease. For Lazarus was probably now dead, and, indeed, by the custom of the East, laid in the tomb. For Lazarus had been dead four days when he was recalled to life. (Ver. 39.) He must, therefore, have died soon after the messenger of the sisters left them to go to Jesus beyond the Jordan. The journey must have occupied about one day, then Jesus remained where he was two days, and the fourth day was spent in returning to Bethany. Accordingly, it is not surprising that Christ abode yet two days in the place where he was; for, as he purposed to raise Lazarus from the dead, it was important to defer this act till there could be no possible doubt of his death. Besides, miracles were not wrought by Christ irrespective of moral conditions; and fit opportunities for doing such a work as it was God's will that he should now do, may not have been so numerous as some imagine. Again, he may have had important spiritual work to do in Perea—work which he could not leave unfinished for the sake of repairing to Bethany sooner than he did.

7. **Then after that** (or, *this*) **saith he to his disciples, Let us go into Judea again.** This was doubtless said to prepare the way for a more definite explanation. Hence Judea is mentioned instead of Bethany. And by Judea, the disciples probably understood Jerusalem and the surrounding villages, where Christ had been accustomed to preach the gospel of the kingdom, and to do mighty works. It was not long since he had gone thither at the Feast of Dedication, and had encountered deadly hostility; yet now he proposes to visit the same region **again,** with his disciples. But they remonstrate.

8. **Master, the Jews of late,** etc.; or, *Rabbi, the Jews were but now seeking to stone thee,* etc. The scene of peril from which he had escaped, that he might depart to the other side of the Jordan, is brought vividly to mind by his proposal; and they wonder at his purpose to venture once more into the jaws of destruction—into the stronghold of his implacable foes. Their principal anxiety is, doubtless, for *his* safety, but they are not wholly free from solicitude concerning themselves (ver. 16); for they know enough of human nature to suspect that the life of their Master would not be taken without some risk to their own. The adverb of time, **of late** (νῦν), is commonly translated *now,* but by reason of its position, it is emphatic in this verse, and is fairly represented by *even now;* or *just now.* Interpreters have sometimes inferred from it that only a very short time had elapsed since Jesus came to Perea; but the inference is by no means necessary. For as the disciples recalled the peril of their Lord in Jerusalem, at the Feast of Dedication, it might naturally have seemed to them nearer than it was. The days had passed swiftly since they had reached a place of safety, and probably a period of several weeks had passed since their return to Perea. (See 10: 41.)

9, 10. **Are there not twelve hours in** (or, *of*) **the day?** That is, of the day, as contrasted with the night. The form of the question in Greek presupposes an affirmative

228   JOHN.   [Ch. XI.

day? *a* If any man walk in the day, he stumbleth not, because he seeth the light of this world.
10 But *b* if a man walk in the night, he stumbleth, because there is no light in him.
11 These things said he: and after that he saith unto them, Our friend Lazarus *c* sleepeth; but I go, that I may awake him out of sleep.
12 Then said his disciples, Lord, if he sleep, he shall do well.

hours in the day? If a man walk in the day, he stumbleth not, because he seeth the light of this 10 world. But if a man walk in the night, he 11 stumbleth, because the light is not in him. These things spake he: and after this he saith unto them, Our friend Lazarus is fallen asleep; but I go, 12 that I may awake him out of sleep. The disciples therefore said unto him, Lord, if he is fallen asleep,

---

a ch. 9: 4....*b* ch. 12: 35....*c* So Deut. 31: 16; Dan. 12: 2; Matt. 9: 24; Acts 7: 60; 1 Cor. 15: 18, 51.

---

answer. **If any man walk in the day,** etc. By this illustration, Jesus reminds his disciples of a great law of life and action which he is observing. He reminds them that he is walking in the light; that the day of his Messianic work is not yet closed; that he sees clearly, as by the light of the sun, all the perils and obstacles in the way of his proposed return to Judea; and that he can go without harm. He also reminds them that he is perfectly aware of the perils of darkness—of the dangers into which one falls when his walk is untimely, and his hours of service are passed. Meyer explains the allegory thus: "The time appointed to me by God for working is not yet elapsed; as long as it lasts, no one can do anything to me; but when it shall have come to an end, I shall fall into the hands of my enemies, like him who walketh in the night, and stumbleth, because he is without light." We doubt whether Jesus meant to apply the latter part of the illustration. He did not go blindly or darkly to the cross. He "laid down his life" as truly as he submitted to hunger and thirst and weariness. (Comp. 10: 17, 18.) To **see the light of this world,** is equivalent to seeing by the light of the world—*i. e.*, of the sun. Whether the expression, **there is no light in him,** means any more than "the light is not in his eyes or possession," is doubtful; it may possibly mean, "he is not conscious of the light"—*i. e.*, of the effect of it, so that he may be guided by it.

11. **Our friend Lazarus sleepeth** (lit., perhaps, *is asleep*), etc. An interval had passed after the remark of verses 9, 10, and this is an explanation of his reason for going again into Judea. Meyer assumes that Lazarus had just now died. as Jesus knew by divine vision. This is certainly possible, notwithstanding what has been said under verse 6, and is, in fact, probable, if the place of Christ's retirement was north of the Sea of Galilee and east of the Upper Jordan, as Von Raumer and Caspari suppose, or only a few miles south of the Sea of Galilee, and east of the Jordan, as others have recently conjectured. For in either case the journey of Jesus to Bethany, on the eastern slope of Olivet, might naturally have occupied three or four days, and could not have been made in one. Yet the expression **is asleep** (perfect tense), does not require us to suppose that he had *just now* fallen asleep. The same word might have been used with equal propriety, if Jesus thought of him as now continuing in a sleep into which he had fallen two days before. "In all verbs," remarks Dr. J. A. Broadus, "the perfect denotes *an action standing in a completed state*. In many verbs, this will *suggest* to the mind a foregoing process which has led to this completed state, but not in all cases, and not at all necessarily." The words **our friend,** show that Lazarus had manifested good will to the disciples, as well as to Jesus, and are in special harmony with the exhortation, **Let us go into Judea again.** (Ver. 7.) The further statement, **I go, that I may awake him out of sleep,** was fitted to make the disciples understand that Lazarus was in no ordinary sleep; for there could surely be no occasion for Jesus to make a long journey to rouse him from a peaceful, restful, recuperative sleep. But a misunderstanding of his remark when first informed of the sickness of Lazarus (ver. 4), may have prevented their apprehending all that was implied in the declaration, **I go, that I may awake him out of sleep.** The word sleep appears to be used by the sacred writers in place of "death," first, because the physical phenomena of the two are somewhat similar; and, secondly, because death is to be followed by resurrection. For the same reasons, Jesus spoke of Lazarus in this place, and of the daughter of Jairus, in Matt. 9: 24, as being asleep.

12. **Then** (or, *therefore*) **said his disciples,** etc. . . **he shall do well;** or, *will be saved*—that is, from death, as threatened by

13 Howbeit Jesus spake of his death: but they thought that he had spoken of taking of rest in sleep.
14 Then said Jesus unto them plainly, Lazarus is dead.
15 And I am glad for your sakes that I was not there, to the intent ye may believe; nevertheless let us go unto him.
16 Then said Thomas, which is called Didymus, unto his fellow disciples, Let us also go, that we may die with him.

13 he will [1] recover. Now Jesus had spoken of his death; but they thought that he spake of taking 14 rest in sleep. Then Jesus therefore said unto them 15 plainly, Lazarus is dead. And I am glad for your sakes that I was not there, to the intent ye may believe; nevertheless let us go unto him. 16 Thomas therefore, who is called [2] Didymus, said unto his fellow-disciples, Let us also go, that we may die with him.

[1] Gr. *be saved*....[2] That is, *Twin*.

the disease It is sufficiently accurate to render the word (σωθήσεται) *he will recover* (Alford, Noyes), or, *he will be restored* (Bible Union Revision). Sleep was considered a favorable symptom in many diseases. It often marked and followed the turn of a fever. Hence the disciples seize upon this fact as a reason why Jesus need not repair to Bethany. But in their eagerness they misunderstood the Lord, as the Evangelist proceeds to show.

13. Howbeit Jesus spake (better, *but Jesus had spoken*) **of his death.** This verse makes it certain that the disciples did not suspect the real meaning of Christ. And in partial explanation of their failure to divine his meaning, it has been suggested that the three select disciples, Peter, James, and John, who were permitted to enter the house of Jairus with him and to hear him speak of the damsel who was dead as being asleep, were now absent. This is plausible, and might account for the prominence of Thomas, instead of Peter; but it is only a conjecture, and the style of John goes to show that in almost every instance he was a personal witness of what he relates.

14. Then (or, *therefore*) **said Jesus unto them plainly, Lazarus is dead** (or, *died*). The death of Lazarus is here distinctly set forth as a past event, though without any hint of the precise time when it took place. Yet it does not seem perfectly natural for Jesus to employ the aorist tense of the verb (*Lazarus died*), if the death of Lazarus had just occurred.

15. And I am glad for your sakes that I was not there, etc. This language implies, (1) that had Jesus been present in Bethany, he would not have suffered Lazarus to die; his miraculous power would have been used in restoring the sick to health, and not in raising the dead to life. The Saviour always paid due regard to all the circumstances of life in his conduct. His miracles were never extravagant, but always adapted to person and place with divine wisdom. (2) That Christ desired to increase the faith of his disciples, and had that end distinctly in view when doing mighty works. Meyer beautifully explains the words **to the intent** (or, *that*) **ye may believe,** by remarking, "that every new *flight* of faith is in its degree a *progress* towards faith." (3) That all miracles are not equally impressive and convincing as revelations of divine power. Raising the dead is a greater work than healing the sick, a more signal and glorious exhibition of the might of him who is over all. "If we cannot say with certainty that no miracle he ever wrought occupied beforehand so much of our Saviour's thoughts, we can say that no other miracle was predicted and prepared for as this one was."—*Hanna.*

16. Then said Thomas, which (*who*) **is called Didymus,** etc. The word **then,** or *therefore*, represents the saying of Thomas as occasioned by Christ's renewed expression of his purpose to visit Bethany, and of his desire to be accompanied by his disciples. (Ver. 15.) But so vivid was the apprehension which Thomas had of the power and enmity of the Jews, and of the almost certain death which awaited Jesus at their hands, that he failed to take in the import of his Master's language. (Ver. 15.) "I (*am glad*) rejoice for your sakes that I was not there, to the intent ye may believe." For this language certainly foreshadowed a glorious display of the Saviour's power, and forbade the thought of immediate death. But though Thomas could think of nothing but the danger which threatened the life of his Lord, his loyalty and love were deep, and he was ready to follow him into danger and death. Such at least was his feeling at this time. The name Thomas is derived from the Hebrew, and signifies *twin;* Didymus is from the Greek, and means the same. Only a few notices of this apostle occur in the New Testament. He is coupled with Matthew, in Matt. 10: 3; Mark 3: 18;

17 Then when Jesus came, he found that he had lain in the grave for four days already.
18 Now Bethany was nigh unto Jerusalem, about fifteen furlongs off:
19 And many of the Jews came to Martha and Mary, to comfort them concerning their brother.

17 So when Jesus came, he found that he had been 18 in the tomb four days already. Now Bethany was 19 nigh unto Jerusalem, about fifteen furlongs off; and many of the Jews had come to Martha and Mary, to

Luke 6: 15; and with Philip, in Acts 1: 13. "All that we know of him is derived from the Gospel of St. John; and this amounts to three traits, which, however, so exactly agree together, that, slight as they are, they place his character before us with a precision which

verse, see comments on verses 6 and 11. As it was the custom of the Jews to bury their dead on the day of their decease, and with very little delay, it would be unsafe to make much allowance for the time which may have elapsed between the death and the burial of

BETHANY.

belongs to no other of the twelve apostles, except Peter, John, and Judas Iscariot. This character is that of a man slow to believe, seeing all the difficulties of a case, subject to despondency, viewing things on the darker side, and yet full of ardent love for his Master." (Smith's "Dict. of the Bible," Art. Thomas).

17-44. THE MIRACLE PERFORMED.

17. Then when Jesus came, he found that he had lain (*been*) **in the grave** (*tomb*) **four days already.** This statement is joined to the preceding by **then,** or *therefore,* because the action which it relates resulted from the purpose there spoken of. For the different inferences which have been drawn from this

Lazarus. It is proper to insist only upon the fact that he had been dead four days. From the remark, **he found that he had** *been* **in the** *tomb* **four days already,** it cannot be inferred, with any certainty, that Jesus was ignorant of the time of Lazarus' death and burial, until he arrived in Bethany. Doubtless, this fact was reported to him by those whom he met, and was then first known by the Evangelist. There is reason to believe that Jesus knew all this, while he was still on the other side of the Jordan, and that the testimony now given was to him only the verification of his divine knowledge.

18. Now Bethany was nigh unto Jerusalem, about fifteen furlongs off. The

JOHN. [CH. XI.

20 Then Martha, as soon as she heard that Jesus was coming, went and met him: but Mary sat still in the house.
21 Then said Martha unto Jesus, Lord, if thou hadst been here, my brother had not died.
22 But I know, that even now, *a* whatsoever thou wilt ask of God, God will give it thee.

20 console them concerning their brother. Martha therefore, when she heard that Jesus was coming, went and met him: but Mary still sat in the house.
21 Martha therefore said unto Jesus, Lord, if thou hadst
22 been here, my brother had not died. And even now I know that, whatsoever thou shalt ask of God, God

a ch. 9: 31.

short distance of Bethany from Jerusalem—a little less than two English miles—is mentioned because of the number of Jews who visited Martha and Mary in that village, to comfort them for the loss of their brother.

19. And many of the Jews came (*had come*) **to Martha and Mary, etc.** The Jews most probably refer, in this place, to the leading men of the nation who resided in Jerusalem. The family of Martha, Mary, and Lazarus was so respectable, that many of the leading Jews continued their intercourse and friendship with it, even after its members were known to be disciples of Jesus. Some of these Jews were not so full of prejudice and hatred to Christ as others (see ver. 45, 46); and none of them were ringleaders in the attempts to destroy him. The Greek expression translated to **Martha and Mary**, means properly to Martha and Mary, *with the women about them*. "According to later Greek usage, it might be indicative simply of the two sisters. But the New Testament, says Meyer, contains no instance of its use in this sense, and there is here an especial *decorum* in the expression, since those who came to them were men. It reveals, moreover, an establishment of the better class." (From Lange.) Seven days was the customary period for such manifestations of sympathy. (Comp. 1 Sam. 31: 13; 1 Chron. 10: 12.)[1]

20. Then Martha, as soon as (lit., *when*) **she heard that Jesus was coming, went to meet him, etc.** The conduct of the two sisters agrees perfectly with their characters as revealed on another occasion. (See Luke 10: 38-42.) The older sister is prompt, active, practical; the younger quiet, spiritual, con-

[1] It should, however, be remarked that Lach., Treg., W. and H., adopt a reading, supported by ℵ B C* L X. 33. Pesch., Memp., and other versions (τὴν Μάρθαν καὶ Μαριάμ), which agrees with the English version, to **Martha and Mary**. But though the evidence for this text is so strong, it is difficult to account for the change to the common text from this easier reading; and therefore, it is safer to abide by the text explained above.

fiding. Martha went to meet Jesus, partly because it was her nature to act and not to wait, and partly, we imagine, because she preferred to speak with him first in the presence of his friends, rather than in the presence of his foes. "Mary, whether she hears or not, sees her sister rise and go, yet stays still in the house—the two sisters, one in her eager movement, the other in her quiet rest—here, as elsewhere, showing forth the difference of their characters."—*Hanna.* "Mary speaks less, but feels more."—*Schaff.* The word **still** in the Common Version is not the adjective meaning "silent," but the adverb *after that*, or *after Martha went out.*

21. Then said Martha unto Jesus, Lord, if thou (this pronoun is not emphatic) **hadst been here, my brother had not** (*would not have*) **died.** A sentiment in perfect accord with the most natural interpretation of Christ's language in ver. 15. From the circumstance that both sisters meet the Lord with the same words, it may be safely inferred that they had communed together on this point, and had, perhaps, expressed the same thought to each other many times since their brother's death. Why they felt this assurance, we cannot tell. It may have been the fruit of love trusting in love. But at all events it appears to have been well-founded, though it was no part of the Saviour's plan or work to heal all his friends who were sick. More remarkable are the next words of Martha.

22. But (rather, *and*) **I know, that even now, whatsoever thou wilt ask of God, God will give it thee.** There is certainly to be discovered in these words a hope that Lazarus might be restored to life. Probably two things contributed to produce this hope and to lead her to express it, though but indirectly: (1) The declaration of Jesus preserved in ver. 4: "This sickness is not unto death, but for the glory of God, that the Son of God might be glorified"; for this declaration was, doubtless, reported to the sisters by their messenger; and, (2) The restoration

23 Jesus saith unto her, Thy brother shall rise again.
24 Martha saith unto him, *a* I know that he shall rise again in the resurrection at the last day.
25 Jesus said unto her, I am *b* the resurrection, and the *c* life; *d* he that believeth in me, though he were dead, yet shall he live:
23 will give thee. Jesus saith unto her, Thy brother shall rise again. Martha saith unto him, I know that he shall rise again in the resurrection at the last day. Jesus said unto her, I am the resurrection, and the life; he that believeth on me, though

a Luke 14:14; ch. 5:29....*b* ch. 5:21; 6:39, 40, 44....*c* ch. 1:4; 6:35; 14:6; Col. 3:4; 1 John 1:1, 2; 5:11....*d* ch. 3:36; 1 John 5:10, etc.

of life to the son of the widow of Nain and to the daughter of Jairus, of which she must surely have heard. But the modesty and reserve of Martha are also noticeable. She does not expressly mention what seems to have been in her heart, but merely suggests it by a comprehensive word—**whatsoever thou wilt ask.** It will also be observed that she does not ascribe to Jesus himself any supernatural power. That power, according to her language, belongs to God, but will be exercised, as she knows, in response to the entreaty of Jesus. That this is her view is manifest from the prominence given to God—"whatsoever thou wilt ask of *God*, *God* will give it thee." Some have inferred the same thing, and even more, from the verb which she employs to express the idea of asking or entreating (αἰτέω)—a verb which is supposed to be used only by inferiors to superiors, while another (ἐρωτάω) is used by equals to equals. But this distinction is not well-founded. (See an article in the North American by Dr. Ezra Abbott, entitled Trench's Synonyms)[1]

23. Jesus saith unto her, Thy brother shall rise again. Her comprehensive whatsover is perfectly understood by the Lord, and his response has respect to its real import. But this response is itself indefinite. It may refer to the resurrection of the just at some future time called "the last day," or it may refer to an immediate re-animation of Lazarus. The latter meaning is doubted by some eminent scholars, but, as it seems to us, without sufficient reason. For in itself the verb appears to signify a rising again to physical life quite as naturally as it does any different rising; and there is no conclusive evidence that it had already become a technical term, even if it became one at a later day. Moreover, the whole previous narrative leads one to expect at this point some reference, either plain or obscure, to the miracle in pros-

pect. And still further, Martha, as we learn from her response, had no doubt of a final resurrection in the case of her brother, and it was, therefore, needless to assure her of it. We believe that Jesus wished to bind together in the mind of Martha, the final resurrection and the re-animation of her brother, and on this account used a term that was applicable to both, and might signify either. Martha perceived the indefiniteness of his declaration, but did not venture to speak out clearly the desire of her heart. She only hinted her hope of something else, by saying that she was already aware of the truth of his declaration, if it had respect to the final resurrection only.

24. I know that he shall (or, *will*) **rise again in the resurrection at the last day.** If this was uttered with a slightly rising inflection, indicative of a desire for something more definite in respect to her brother—as if she almost hoped for something in his case that would not be true of every one, the thought has been correctly explained in the comment on ver. 23. "Her words are expressive, not merely of a sad resignation, but of an indirect query—she is feeling her way." —*Lange, De Wette.* It is not necessary to suppose that Martha's knowledge of a future resurrection was derived wholly from the Old Testament, or from the scribes of her people. She may have been taught the truth by Christ himself, who had been often welcomed to her house. Yet there is ample evidence that the Pharisees believed in a future life, and in a resurrection of the just. (See Article Resurrection, in Smith's "Dict. of the Bible," Am. ed.)

25. I am the resurrection, and the life. "I am their source, their ground, their author." "*I*, no other than I.. am the personal *power* of both—the one who raises again, and who makes alive."—*Meyer.* "Without me they would be unattainable. Behold in me the being on whose will and work the resurrection of the dead and the blessed life in God absolutely depend." This is the central

---

[1] Probably (αἰτέω) is a stronger term than (ἐρωτάω), the former corresponding to the English "beg" or "entreat," and the latter to the English "ask."

26 And whosoever liveth and believeth in me shall never die. Believest thou this?

26 he die, yet shall he live: and whosoever liveth and believeth on me shall never die. Believest thou

point in the narrative, and the one great truth which it illustrates. This truth Christ proceeds to paraphrase and explain. He that **believeth in me**—that is, he who is a believer in me—he of whom trust in me is a characteristic. **Though he were dead.** The Rev. Ver. gives: *Though he die.* It is, perhaps, doubtful whether this translation is preferable to another of which the Greek is capable, viz.: *Though he have died.* If Jesus had Lazarus in mind when uttering this clause, the latter version is to be preferred, for Lazarus was now dead; but if not, the Rev. Version is better, because it agrees with the prevailing New Testament signification of verbs, in the mood and tense here used. Perhaps there was sufficient reference to Lazarus to justify the latter rendering, which is approved by Meyer, Schaff, Noyes, and Watkins. **Yet shall he live,** or, more briefly, *shall live.* That is, death will not retain him in its power, but he will be raised by Christ to a true and blessed life—he "will come forth . . . to the resurrection of life." (5:29.) Thus Christ declares himself to be the resurrection unto life to all who believe in him. They may suffer physical death, but they will be brought into a perfect life of body and spirit.

26. And whosoever—(*i. e., every one who*) **liveth and believeth in me shall never die.** The believer who is still in possession of physical life will never suffer true death—that death which is the antithesis of true life. In ver. 25, the death spoken of is physical, and the life spiritual; in this verse, the life spoken of is physical, and the death spiritual. The last clause is sometimes translated, *will not die forever*—*i. e.*, though he may die for a time. Schaff remarks that "the phrase is in itself ambiguous, and may mean either *not forever*, or *never*. The first and literal rendering would give a very plain sense: *He that liveth* (physically) *and believeth in me, will not die* (physically) *forever*—*i. e.*, will be raised again. But in all other passages in which the same phrase occurs (4:14; 8:51,52; 10:28; 13:8; 1 Cor. 8:13), it is equivalent to *never* . . . with an emphasis on the negation. We must, then, suppose that Christ, in verse 26, either spoke of *spiritual* death, or overlooked *physical* death as a vanishing transition to real and eternal life." Meyer adopts the former interpretation: "*will assuredly not die forever—i. e.*, he will not lose his life in eternity"; but it is difficult to see how this adds anything to what has been before said. To assert that a believer in Christ, though he die, or have died, will live—*i. e.*, by virtue of the resurrection, is the same as to say that a living believer will not die forever, because he will be raised again to life. But the great objection to this view is, that the phrase has a different meaning in every other passage of the New Testament, and that meaning one perfectly adapted to this place. To the woman of Samaria, Jesus said: "Whosoever drinketh of this water will thirst again; but whosoever drinketh of the water that I shall give him, *will never thirst*," etc. In contrast with *thirsting again*, is here put *never thirsting again*—a natural and perfect contrast. It was so understood by the woman, and so explained by the added metaphor of a living and upspringing fountain in the soul. In 8: 51 stand recorded the words of Jesus: "If a man keep my saying, he shall *never see death*," and in the next verse, the interpretation of the Jews: "Abraham is dead, and the prophets; and thou sayest, If a man keep my saying, he shall *never taste death.*" Here there is no question about the resurrection. As the Jews understood him to say, even so Christ really said, that one who should keep his word would never die. The Jews themselves did not believe that Abraham and the prophets had lost their lives in eternity. Christ intended to say that the true life possessed by one who keeps his word will never come to an end, but flow on forever. Again, the Lord says of his true sheep, "I give unto them eternal life; and they shall *never perish*, neither shall any man (or, *one*) pluck them out of my hand." (10: 28.) This does not mean "They shall *not perish forever*," though they may perish for a time; death may pluck them out of my hands for ages, but I will recover them at last, by the resurrection; but, as the connection requires, "they shall *never perish*: in my protection, they are safe for time and eternity. In John 13: 8, Peter uses the same expression, "Thou shalt *never wash my feet*," and of course he does not mean, "thou shalt *not wash my feet*

27 She saith unto him, Yea, Lord: *a* I believe that thou art the Christ, the Son of God, which should come into the world.

28 And when she had so said, she went her way, and called Mary her sister secretly, saying, The Master is come, and calleth for thee.

29 As soon as she heard *that*, she arose quickly, and came unto him.

30 Now Jesus was not yet come into the town, but was in that place where Martha met him.

27 this? She saith unto him, Yea, Lord: I have believed that thou art the Christ, the Son of God, *even* 28 he that cometh into the world. And when she had said this, she went away, and called Mary ¹ her sister secretly, saying, The ²Master is here, and calleth thee. And she, when she heard it, arose quickly, 30 and went unto him. (Now Jesus was not yet come into the village, but was still in the place where

a Matt. 16: 16; ch. 4: 42; 6: 14, 69.——1 Or, *her sister, saying secretly....*2 Or, *Teacher.*

---

forever, or *in eternity.*" The meaning of the phrase is unambiguous. Paul avails himself of the same expression (1 Cor. 8: 13): "If meat make my brother to offend, I will eat no flesh while the world stands, or, *never eat flesh,*" not, "I will not eat flesh *forever*, or *in eternity.*" (See, also, Matt. 21: 19; Mark 11: 14; 3: 29; Luke 1: 54, 55; John 6: 51, 58; 8: 35; 12: 34, for a similar phraseology.) **Believest thou this?** "A personal appeal, or application, very pungent by its suddenness."—*Bengel.*

27. Yea, Lord: I believe (lit., *have believed*) **that thou art the Christ, the Son of God,** etc. It is best to understand Martha's **Yea, Lord,** as her full and affirmative answer to the Saviour's question, **Believest thou this?** and the rest of her words as giving her reason for this answer. "Yea, Lord; for I have myself believed and do believe that thou art the Christ," etc. This interpretation agrees with that of Meyer, Godet, Watkins, and others. How fully she apprehended the designation—**the Son of God**—can only be conjectured; but she must have seen in him One who could raise the dead and impart true life, because he was in a wholly peculiar sense from with God. The present tense of **which should come,** (or, *cometh* (ὁ. . . . ἐρχόμενος), is a kind of ideal present, meaning one who is known in the promises of God as "the Coming One."

28. And when she had so said, she went her way (better, *away*), **and called Mary her sister secretly, saying, The Master is come, and calleth for thee.** Martha's second statement, **and calleth for thee,** is to be received with the same confidence as her first statement, **the Master** (*Teacher*) **is come.** For it is quite in accord with the Evangelical narratives to omit certain facts that are presupposed by what is written. Every powerful writing does the same. A full record of what Jesus said and did in one busy day of his ministry would, with all the related circumstances, make a large volume. Martha spoke to her sister **secretly**—*i. e.*, in a *whisper*, in order that the Jews about them might not hear what was said; for it was thought by Martha, if not by Jesus also, that Mary would prefer to meet the Master, or, *Teacher*, without the presence of unbelieving friends. Indeed, it is natural to suppose that Christ's reason for calling Mary to himself, instead of going to the house where she was, was his desire that their meeting might be as quiet and informal as possible. It may be inferred from Martha's language that the sisters were accustomed to speak of Jesus as *The Teacher.* No other teacher was, in their minds, comparable to him.[1]

29. As soon as she heard that, etc. Better, *And she, when she heard it.* An instant response to the call of her Lord! There is nearly equal authority for the more vivacious and descriptive reading: *She riseth and goeth unto him.* Godet remarks, with too much confidence, that this "certainly is the true reading."

30. Now Jesus was not yet come into the town (*village*), **but was** (or, *was still*) **in that place where Martha met him.** He appears to have remained for a while outside the village—*first*, because he was met there by Martha, and was led to pause in his journey during the conversation which had been related (21: 27); and, *secondly*, because, having learned that there were many Jewish friends at the time in the house of Martha and Mary, he preferred to meet Mary also before entering Bethany, and to say to her what he wished to say in the simplest and quietest manner possible. It is also probable

[1] The doubtful readings of this verse (τοῦτο or ταῦτα, Μαριὰμ or Μαριάν, εἰποῦσα or εἴπασα) do not affect the meaning in any important respect.

JOHN. 235

31 *a* The Jews then which were with her in the house, and comforted her, when they saw Mary, that she rose up hastily and went out, followed her, saying, She goeth unto the grave to weep there.
32 Then when Mary was come where Jesus was, and saw him, she fell down at his feet, saying unto him, *b* Lord, if thou hadst been here, my brother had not died.
33 When Jesus therefore saw her weeping, and the Jews also weeping which came with her, he groaned in the spirit, and was troubled,
34 And said, Where have ye laid him? They say unto him, Lord, come and see.

31 Martha met him.) The Jews then who were with her in the house, and were comforting her, when they saw Mary, that she rose up quickly and went out, followed her, supposing that she was going unto the
32 tomb to ¹ weep there. Mary therefore, when she came where Jesus was, and saw him, fell down at his feet, saying unto him, Lord, if thou hadst been here, my
33 brother had not died. When Jesus therefore saw her ² weeping, and the Jews *also* ² weeping who came with her, he ³ groaned in the spirit, and ⁴ was trou-
34 bled, and said, Where have ye laid him? They say

a ver. 19....*b* ver. 21.——1 Gr. *wail*.... 2 Gr. *wailing*....3 Gr. *was moved with indignation in the spirit*....4 Gr. *troubled himself*.

that the burial place of Bethany was outside the village, not far from the place where Jesus rested. To this, Meyer's objection that he did not even know where Lazarus was laid (ver. 34) is without force; for in a burial place there are usually many graves. It also appears that Mary took such a direction in going to meet Jesus as led the Jews to suppose that she might be going to the grave of her brother.

31. The Jews then which (*who*) **were with her in the house,** etc. Trustworthy observers testify that it is still the custom of Oriental women to visit often the tombs of their deceased kindred and weep there; and not alone, but with many who join them. These friendly Jews were, no doubt, anxious to do all in their power to express their sympathy with the afflicted sisters, and especially with Mary, whose sorrow was overwhelming. Whether the original text had a word that means *saying* (λέγοντες), or a word that means *thinking* (δόξαντες), is uncertain and unimportant. There is, perhaps, a slight preponderance of testimony in favor of the latter, which is, therefore, adopted by the Revised Version (*supposing*).

32. Then when Mary was come, (or, *Mary therefore, when she came,*) etc. In two respects the conduct of Mary differs from that of Martha—she falls at the feet of Jesus, evidently with a deeper feeling of grief than was experienced by her elder sister, when she met the Lord; and she utters only one sentence, relating wholly to the past, while her sister glanced with at least a ray of hope into the future. This sentence (compare ver. 21) "had unquestionably been the oft-repeated refrain of their mutual communications on the subject of their sorrow."—*Meyer*. That Mary had less confidence than Martha in Jesus, as one through whom her brother's life might

even now be restored, there is no reason to suppose; but grief choked her utterance. There is also a slight difference in the order which she gave to the words of the sentence uttered by her sister and herself, by which the pronoun *my* has been supposed to gain a slight emphasis, as if she had said in English: "My own brother would not have died."

33. When Jesus therefore saw her weeping, (or, *weep,*) etc. In explaining this very difficult verse, it must be remarked that there is no sufficient ground for the Common Version, **he groaned in spirit.** For the primary and physical sense of the verb here used, is *to snort*, and its derived sense, *to be angry*, or, *indignant*. The second meaning is not inappropriate here. For anger and grief are compatible feelings; certainly they may succeed each other in an instant. And on this occasion there was a reason for the one as well as for the other. Jesus saw before him not only Mary, whom he loved with a holy tenderness and compassion, but some of his implacable foes, who would on'y be hardened and infuriated by the miracle he was about to perform. And these self-righteous men were now weeping and groaning in professional sorrow with Mary! Men who would soon be plotting to kill, not only Jesus, but the restored Lazarus (12: 10), were there in his presence, professing their sympathy and friendship for the sisters. No wonder the spirit of the Holy One was hot within him. The next verb is yet more difficult to translate. It probably means, *he shook himself*, or shuddered a kind of voluntary shudder, expressing his indignation by an almost convulsive movement of his whole frame. The former verb describes the inward feeling, and the latter its *visible* expression. But this indignation was only for a moment.

34. Where have ye laid him? They

35 *Jesus wept.
36 Then said the Jews, Behold how he loved him!
37 And some of them said, Could not this man, ᵇ which opened the eyes of the blind, have caused that even this man should not have died?
38 Jesus therefore again groaning in himself cometh to the grave. It was a cave, and a stone lay upon it.

35 unto him, Lord, come and see. Jesus wept. The
36 Jews therefore said, Behold how he loved him! But
37 some of them said, Could not this man, who opened the eyes of him that was blind, have caused that
38 this man also should not die? Jesus therefore again ¹groaning in himself cometh to the tomb.

a Luke 19: 41....b ch. 9: 6.—1 Or, *being moved with indignation in himself.*

say unto him, Lord, come and see. It is a moment of unspeakable emotion, and the fewest words possible are uttered. Jesus speaks to the sisters, and is answered by them.

35. Jesus wept. Not aloud, as some of the Jews were doubtless weeping or wailing, but tears fell from his eyes. His grief was silent, but deep and tearful. This brief sentence teaches the perfect human sympathy of Christ. He was man, as well as God; perfectly human, as well as perfectly divine. This is the mystery of mysteries, and this is the pervading thought of the Fourth Gospel. "The Word became flesh and dwelt among us," and the genuineness of his human nature is beautifully revealed in the event commemorated by this verse. The divine-human Redeemer can be touched with the feeling of our infirmities (Heb. 2: 17; 4: 15.)

36. Then said the Jews (or, *the Jews therefore were saying*), **Behold how he loved him!** Some of the Jews, in view of the sorrow of Jesus, that was manifesting itself in tears, as he passed along towards the sepulchre, remarked more than once: "See how deep an affection he must have had for Lazarus!" There was something so natural, so human, so profound, in the grief of Jesus, that the less prejudiced Jews saw in it an evidence of extraordinary love. But not all "the Jews"—and what a part they play in this pathetic scene!—were open to the sacred influence of sorrow. The thoughts of a part of them were taking a sinister direction; for the Evangelist adds:

37. And some of them said, Could not this man, which (*who*) **opened the eyes of the blind** (or, *of him that was blind*), **have caused that even this man** (*also*) **should not have died?** That this was asked in a tone of irony, malice, and unbelief in Jesus, which assumed a negative answer, may be inferred (1) from the obvious contrast between **the Jews,** and **some of them,** expressed by the conjunction **but** (*δὲ*) (compare the same word and expression in verse 46);

and (2) from the feeling of indignation which at once arises in the soul of Jesus. (ver. 38.) This feeling is naturally occasioned by such an expression, at such a moment. Our interpretation is essentially the same as that of Meyer, Godet, Alford, Schaff, Lange, Watkins. And if the spirit and aim of their question were thus malicious, it is probable that they intended to insinuate doubt as to the truth of the report that he had opened the eyes of the blind man. "If he opened the eyes of the blind man, as some of you profess to believe, could he not have prevented the death of this friend, for whom he is now weeping? But this he could not do; what, then, must we think of his doing that?" Ah, these were men who would not be persuaded, though one should rise from the dead. They were men who *could* not be convinced, because they *would* not believe.

38. Jesus therefore again groaning (or, *being again indignant*), **cometh to the grave** (or, *tomb*). His indignation was renewed by the sneering question of the Jews just recorded. But as this feeling of holy, though unexpressed, wrath was kindled afresh in his soul, the sepulchre was reached. **It was a cave, and a stone lay upon it.** That is, **upon,** or *against*, the entrance into it. "The sepulchres of the Hebrews," says Dr. Hackett, "were generally cut out of the solid rock; sometimes below the level of the ground, but oftener above the ground, and on the sides of mountains. The natural caves with which the country abounds were also used for this purpose." "At the bottom of a ledge, in the rear of the Maronite Church at Nazareth, I noticed a sepulchre cut in the rock, which excited my interest the more, because it had a large stone rolled against the mouth of it." "The grave of Lazarus was closed with a stone." "On the contrary, most of the tombs which I examined near Jerusalem must have had doors. The grooves and perforations for the hinges that still remain, show that they were furnished with that convenience."—("Il-

39 Jesus said, Take ye away the stone. Martha, the sister of him that was dead, saith unto him, Lord, by this time he stinketh: for he hath been *dead* four days.
40 Jesus saith unto her, Said I not unto thee, that, if thou wouldest believe, thou shouldest *a* see the glory of God?

39 Now it was a cave, and a stone lay [1] against it. Jesus saith, Take ye away the stone. Martha, the sister of him that was dead, saith unto him, Lord, by this time he stinketh: for he hath been *dead* four days. Jesus saith unto her, Said I not unto thee, that, if thou believedst, thou shouldest see

a ver. 4, 23.——1 Or, *upon.*

lustrations of Scripture," pp. 97, 100.) "A doorway in the perpendicular face of the rock, usually small, and without ornament, leads to one or more small chambers excavated from the rock, and commonly upon the same level with the door. Very rarely are the chambers lower than the doors. The walls in general are plainly hewn; and there are, occasionally, though not always, niches, or resting-places, for the dead bodies."—(Robinson's "Researches," vol. I., p. 352.) In describing a visit to Bethany, he says: "The monks, as a matter of course, show the house of Mary and Martha, that of Simon the leper, and the sepulchre of Lazarus. The latter is a deep vault, excavated in the limestone rock, in the middle of the village; to which there is a descent by twenty-six steps. It is hardly necessary to remark that there is not the slightest probability of its ever having been the tomb of Lazarus. The form is not that of the ancient sepulchres; nor does its position accord with the narrative of the New Testament, which implies that the tomb was not in the town."—("Ill.," p. 432.) In confirmation of this inference from the narrative, it may be added that Jewish sepulchres were regularly located out of town. The place where Lazarus was entombed is therefore undiscovered, and there is no reason to expect that it will ever be identified. But the fact that he appears to have been placed in a tomb is generally supposed to indicate the easy circumstances of the family.

39. Jesus said (*saith*), **Take ye away the stone.** This command was probably addressed to his disciples, though it might have been addressed to any of the Jews present. It has been often used to illustrate the truth that God does not do, by miracle or otherwise, the work which properly belongs to men, and can be performed by them. The verb used seems to imply that the stone would be lifted up in removing it (ἄρατε); and, if so, it favors the view that the entrance to the sepulchre was by a descent, so that the floor of the sepulchre was lower than the surface of the ground. This, however, is by no means certain. **Martha, the sister of him that was dead,** etc. Whether Martha knew, by her frequent visits to the sepulchre, that the smell of putrefaction was already in the place, or whether she merely inferred that it must be so, from the circumstance that this was the fourth day since he was placed in the tomb, is uncertain; yet the latter view is more obviously suggested by her language than the former. For, in the one case, she says: "Decomposition has already begun, as I am certain, for this is his fourth day in the tomb"; and, in the other: "Decomposition has already begun, as I know, and as was to be expected, for this is his fourth day in the tomb." But whether she declared what she *knew* to be the case, or what she was satisfied *must* be the case, there is no reason to doubt the correctness of her statement. There is no evidence that even the wealthy Jews were accustomed to embalm their dead in such a manner as to preserve them from corruption. "It is a proverb in the Talmud and the Targum, that corruption sets in on the third day."—*Tholuck.* Martha is here described as **the sister of him that was dead,** not to account for her boldness in thus speaking, but rather to account for her peculiar shrinking at what was proposed. She shudders at the thought of having the putrefying form of her brother exposed. Hence, she did not say this for the purpose of intimating to Jesus the greatness of the work which he seemed about to attempt, or her doubt of his power to perform it.

40. Said I not unto thee, that, if thou wouldest believe (or, *believedst*), **thou shouldest see the glory of God?** This question is, on the one hand, a gentle rebuke of her weakness of faith; and, on the other hand, taken with what follows, an evidence of the sufficiency of her faith. There is no previous record of the utterance of just these words by the Saviour to Martha, but the substance of what they express had been said to her, both indirectly and directly. (See verses 4, 23, sq.)

41 Then they took away the stone *from the place where the dead was laid.* And Jesus lifted up *his* eyes, and said, Father, I thank thee that thou hast heard me.
42 And I knew that thou hearest me always: but ᵃ because of the people which stand by I said *it,* that they may believe that thou hast sent me.

a ch. 12: 30.

---

41. Then (or, *so*) **they took away the stone.** In consequence of this answer to Martha, which removed her objection, and in obedience to his previous command, some of those present, perhaps the disciples of Jesus, removed the stone which closed the opening into the sepulchre. The words, **from the place where the dead was laid,** are omitted by the best editors as an interpolation; and it is clear that they are not necessary to a proper understanding of the act; for the stone would, of course, be removed from the opening of the cave in which the dead was laid. **And Jesus lifted up his eyes and said.** The mention of the uplifting of his eyes indicates the pen of an eye-witness. The disciple whom Jesus loved, was, no doubt, one of those who accompanied him to Bethany, and followed him to the sepulchre. **Father, I thank thee that thou hast heard** (or, *didst hear*) **me.** The hearing referred to was evidently at some definite time in the past (aorist), as early, at least, as the moment when the message from the sisters reached him in Perea; for he then said (ver. 4): "This sickness is not unto death, but for the glory of God, that the Son of God might be glorified." And, when these words were uttered, he must have known that, according to his Father's will, Lazarus would die, and be restored to life; or, was dead, and would be restored to life. For all his miracles were wrought in absolute concurrence with the Father. (5:19, sq.) In them the Son glorified the Father, and the Father glorified the Son. Never did the Saviour perform them in pursuance of an impulse originating in himself, without communion with the Father. As the divine-human Mediator, every desire of his heart was laid before his Father for his approval, before it was carried into effect.

42. And I knew that thou hearest me always. The pronoun I is emphatic in the Greek—"I, for my part, knew"—though this might not be true of others. Thus, Jesus, while recognizing a certain subordination to the Father in the work which he is accomplishing, claims to have no desire which the Father does not approve; no purpose which the Father does not endorse and sustain. Their oneness of aim and action is perfect. **But because of the people** (*multitude*) **which stand by** (or, *standeth around*) **I said it, that they may believe that thou hast sent** (*didst send*) **me.** These words, then, addressed to God, were spoken aloud, that the people might hear them. Jesus was in perpetual inward communion with the Father; but he saw fit, on this occasion, to utter words to his Father aloud, that the people might perceive the holy familiarity of his intercouse with God. With a love and confidence, and divine simplicity, which could not innocently be misunderstood, he talked for a moment with the Father in the hearing of men. "Bauer calls the prayer a *scheingebet;* Weisse, a *schaugebet;* conceived by the Evangelist in the apologetic interest for the divinity of Christ. Such impious nonsense arises from utter ignorance of the singular intimacy between Christ and the Father, which is so often asserted in this Gospel, and illustrated on this occasion. By virtue of this intimacy, he, the Only Begotten, never addressed God as *our* Father; but, as *My* Father; or, Father, simply; and stood in *constant* communication with him, so that his prayers assumed, as it were, the character of reflection and mutual consultation, and were *always* answered."—*Schaff.* From the circumstance that this prayer was made *audible,* for the purpose of producing faith in the minds of the people, it has been inferred that public prayer, though offered directly to God, may properly be put in words intended to persuade men to repent and believe. But there is certainly some danger that this secondary reference will diminish the earnestness and simplicity of the primary reference. Besides, Christ does not seem to have aimed to produce faith by his prayer, in and by itself; but to establish a ground for faith in view of the miracle to be wrought.

CH. XI.] JOHN. 239

43 And when he thus had spoken, he cried with a loud voice, Lazarus, come forth.
44 And he that was dead came forth, bound hand and foot with graveclothes; and *his face was bound about with a napkin. Jesus saith unto them, Loose him, and let him go.

43 may believe that thou didst send me. And when he had thus spoken, he cried with a loud voice, Lazarus, come forth. He that was dead came forth, 44 bound hand and foot with ¹grave-clothes; and his face was bound about with a napkin. Jesus saith unto them, Loose him, and let him go.

a ch. 20: 7.——1 Or, *grave-bands*.

43. He cried with a loud voice, Lazarus, come forth! More literally, *Hither! forth!* A great voice, corresponds with the idea of death as a profound sleep, from which one can only be aroused by an extraordinary call, and at the same time with the exercise of an authority and power which belong only to God. In brevity and sublimity this cry has been likened to the creative fiat: "Let there be light!" Cyril calls it "a divine and royal command." The power of God accompanied this summons; for the dead body was instantly filled with life. The re-animation did not precede the call, as some interpreters have supposed, but followed it in an instant, as if the great voice had carried in itself the awakening energy to the dead. (Comp. 5: 28, 29; 1 Thess. 4: 16; 1 Cor. 15: 52). Moreover the words used by Jesus were in agreement with the circumstances. "He did not here call out, Arise! (as in the case of the daughter of Jairus, and of the son of the widow of Nain, Luke 8: 54; 7: 14), because the words "Hither, out!" seemed the most natural to employ in the case of a dead man already lying in the tomb."—*Meyer*.

44. And he that was dead came forth, bound, etc. Whether the limbs of Lazarus had been bound separately, as was the Egyptian custom, or the grave-clothes had been wrapped about him somewhat loosely, cannot be determined; though the latter hypothesis is more probable than the former; but there is no necessity for supposing that his walking was in itself miraculous. With the new life pulsating through his body, he was able, in obedience to the word of Jesus, to come forth slowly from the sepulchre, and to stand there in the vigor of health, though in the garments of death, before the wonder-stricken company. The **napkin**, or handkerchief, did not probably cover the whole face, but was so bound about the head as to support the chin and cover the face in part. **Loose him, and let him go.** The "loosing" consisted, of course, in so arranging or removing his grave-clothes, that he could walk freely. Thus simply does the narrative of this astonishing miracle close, and the Evangelist pass on to describe the effect which it had upon the Jews, and, through them, upon the tragic, though glorious, end of our Lord's ministry.

But the truth of this narrative has been often assailed by unbelieving critics. (1) On the ground that a person actually dead, cannot be brought to life again. This ground, however, is solid for none but atheists or pantheists; for all others it is merely "sinking sand." (2) On the ground that Jesus could not have suffered Lazarus to die, if his life was to be prolonged. As he knew of his friend's sickness, he must have chosen to heal him, rather than to let him die, and then to revivify him. How much of suffering and of sorrow would thus have been spared to the family in Bethany! And surely, if he could have healed him at all, he could have healed him from a distance, sparing himself the toil and peril of the journey. But this criticism is worthless, because it assumes that the plan and object of the Saviour's life are certainly understood by the critic, and that the resurrection of Lazarus at this juncture was no more subservient to the mission of Christ than would have been the healing of Lazarus from a distance. The whole tenor of the Gospels refutes the former assumption, and the present narrative, with the history that follows, refutes the latter. (3) On the ground that the other Evangelists knew nothing of this stupendous miracle; for if they had known of it, they would surely have described it. No other miracle was so important in itself or in its consequences; and it is therefore incredible that they should have been ignorant of it, or should have passed it by in silence, if it had been really performed. In reply to this objection it may be said, in the *first* place, that there is no sufficient ground for the opinion that any one of the Evangelists related all the important discourses and deeds of Christ with which he was familiar. Under the guiding influence of the Holy Spirit, each one of them prepared a written account of

45 Then many of the Jews which came to Mary, *a* and had seen the things which Jesus did, believed on him. | 45 Many therefore of the Jews, who came to Mary and beheld ¹ that which he did, believed on him.

a ch. 2: 23; 10: 42; 12: 11, 18.——1 Many ancient authorities read, *the things which he did.*

certain events, parables, and sayings of the Lord, which would fairly represent his ministry, but he was kept at the same time from the folly of attempting to put on record all that he knew. In the selection of particulars to be recorded, the character and object of each Evangelist may have been influential, but in every instance there must have been a selection. It may be said, in the *second* place, that the Synoptical Gospels omit nearly all the ministry of Jesus in Jerusalem and Judea, with the single exception of what he said and did at the last passover. But they do this for some other reason than ignorance, since they were aware that Christ was acquainted in Jerusalem. (Matt. 23: 37; Luke 10: 38.) "Cyril remarks that the resurrection of Lazarus furnishes the true explanation of the plaudits and hosannas of our Lord's triumphal entry into Jerusalem, as described by the Synoptists."—*Schaff.* It is by no means necessary for us to show why the earlier Gospels were limited geographically, or to the ministry of Jesus in Galilee and the regions round about; the mere fact accounts for their silence concerning this miracle. This is the view also of Meyer.

Little need be said in support of this most wonderful story to those whose hearts are open to the divine sweetness and greatness of the Saviour's character. But it may be well to notice a few points. The truthfulness of this narrative is involved in the character of the Fourth Gospel. For in spirit and style, it is of a piece with the narrative parts of the Gospel, and it is trustworthy, if they are trustworthy. But, as we have had frequent occasion to observe, they afford evidence of being written by an appreciative eye-witness. Again, the events which follow in the Fourth Gospel presuppose the truthfulness of this narrative. They must be fictitious, if this is fictitious. "How could the writer have assigned to a purely fictitious event so decisive a part in the organism of the life of Jesus?"—*Godet.* Still further, the recital is so life-like and graphic as to forbid the thought of invention. "No narrative of this apostle is pervaded by so intense a glow and rapid liveliness of description as this, in which he undertakes to set forth in one great picture the trembling of Jesus for the life of his friend, the attendant struggle with the darkness of the world, and the calmness and joy of victory, prominent over all, and undisturbed from first to last; while mingled with these are the still higher tones of his consciousness of Messianic glory, and of its powerful confirmation."—*Ewald.* "The recital of the resurrection of Lazarus is distinguished among all the narratives of the Fourth Gospel by its special vivacity and dramatic movement. The personages are sketched by a hand at once firm and delicate. Nowhere is the relation of Christ with his disciples set forth in a manner so life-like. We are initiated by this recital to this intimate communion, this affectionate exchange of thoughts and feelings which took place between the Master and his own. The disciples are presented in the most attractive manner, with their simple freedom, and their noble devotion. The Jews themselves, of whom we know little by our Evangelist save their opinionated resistance to the efforts of Jesus, here appear under an aspect less displeasing, as friends of the two afflicted sisters; and in the Jew is discovered the man. But, above all, how clear and delicate is the study of the character of the two women; with what fineness of touch and psychological depth is the difference of their conduct depicted."—*Deutinger, in Godet.* And Meyer expresses the judgment of every ingenuous student when he declares that "the narrative is distinguished for its thoughtful tenderness, certainty, and truthfulness."

45–57. EFFECT OF THE MIRACLE.

45. Then many of the Jews which (*who*) **came to Mary,** etc. If a rigid construction of the Greek be insisted on, the relative *who* does not represent **the Jews,** but **many of the Jews;** and John does not say that "of the Jews who came to Mary and beheld what Jesus did, many believed on him; but, rather, that "many of the Jews came to Mary, beheld what Jesus did, and believed on him." This interpretation is now given to the verse by Meyer, Alford, Watkins. The objection to it will be considered below. But according to any tenable interpretation of the

46 But some of them went their ways to the Pharisees, and told them what things Jesus had done.
47 a Then gathered the chief priests and the Pharisees a council, and said, b What do we? for this man doeth many miracles.

46 But some of them went away to the Pharisees, and told them the things which Jesus had done.
47 The chief priests therefore and the Pharisees gathered a council, and said, What do we? for this

a Ps. 2:2; Matt. 26:3; Mark 14:1; Luke 22:2....*b* ch. 12:19; Acts 4:16.

verse, it plainly affirms that many of the Jews were led to believe in Jesus by the resurrection of Lazarus. This was a miracle that convinced some who were by no means willing to yield.

46. But some of them went their ways (better, *away*) **to the Pharisees, and told them what things Jesus had done.** If all the Jews who came to Mary and beheld what Jesus did, believed in him, it follows (we are told) that those who went away and told the Pharisees what he had done, were believers in him at the time, and made their report to his bitter enemies with no unfriendliness to him. This is possible, without doubt, but it seems to be very improbable. And if this had been the Evangelist's meaning, he would, I think, have coupled this verse with the 45th by "and," instead of **but**. Thus: "Many of the Jews believed in Jesus, and some of them went away to the Pharisees and told them what he had done"—"with well-meaning intent, in order to put them in possession of a correct account of the act, and to bear witness to them of the miracle."—*Meyer*. As, however, the Evangelist, by means of **but,** contrasts **some of them** who went away with others who did not go away, we believe that the former were hardened instead of convinced by the miracle, and that they made their report with the expectation that it would hasten action against Jesus. But if this was the case, it will be necessary to adopt one of two alternatives. Either the writer was not formally accurate in his use of the Greek, but admitted an anacoluthon in this place (a supposition which could not be refuted by the style of the Book of Revelation), or the word **them,** in the expression **some of them,** refers to **the Jews** in general. (Ver. 45.) The latter view is maintained by Godet, who remarks: "I think it unnecessary to include the 'some' (τινὲς) of this verse in the category of the numerous visitors of Mary and Martha who became believers (ver. 45), but that the expression 'of them' (ver. 26) refers to the Jews in general ('Ἰουδαίων, ver. 45.) There were cer-

tainly other Jews than those of ver. 45, who came to visit the sisters—Jews whose sympathy with the sisters did not predispose them in favor of Jesus. These were the persons who, faithful to their *role* as *Jews,* carried without delay the great news to the Pharisees, who were the bitterest enemies of Jesus." It seems to me that either of these solutions of the difficulty is preferable to that of Meyer.

47. Then (better, *therefore*) **gathered the chief priests and the Pharisees a council.** By reason of the account thus brought to them of the resurrection of Lazarus, the Pharisees communicated with the chief priests, some of whom were Sadducees, and they at once called a meeting of the Sanhedrin. Matters, as they felt, were approaching a crisis. The great Pretender, as they would prove him to be, was at their doors again, and, according to this new report, had performed, or seemed to perform, a miracle of surpassing interest. Indeed, a considerable number of their own party had been led by it to look upon him as the expected Messiah. What less could they do than summon an extra meeting of the Sanhedrin to consider the course to be taken in such an emergency? The Sanhedrin (Συνέδριον) was the highest tribunal of the Jews, having its seat at Jerusalem, and being composed of seventy-one members—chief priests, elders, and scribes. In the time of Christ a majority of the members were Pharisees, but an influential minority, Sadducees. The high priest was generally president. It was accustomed to meet daily, except on the Sabbath, or a great feast day. Its sessions were commonly held in a hall which was "supposed by Lightfoot to have been situated in the southeast corner of one of the courts near the temple." "In special exigencies it seems to have met in the residence of the high priest." The cases that could be brought before it in the first instance were such as related to a whole tribe, to a false prophet, to the high priest, to an arbitrary war, or to blasphemy. **And said, What do we?** (or, *What are we doing?*) A

Q

48 If we let him thus alone, all *men* will believe on him; and the Romans shall come and take away both our place and nation.
49 And one of them, *named a* Caiaphas, being the high priest that same year, said unto them, Ye know nothing at all,
50 *b* Nor consider that it is expedient for us, that one man should die for the people, and that the whole nation perish not.

48 man doeth many signs. If we let him thus alone, all men will believe on him: and the Romans will come and take away both our place and our nation.
49 But a certain one of them, Caiaphas, being high priest that year, said unto them, Ye know nothing at all, nor do ye take account that it is expedient for you that one man should die for the people, and

a Luke 3:2; ch. 18:14; Acts 4:6....*b* ch. 18:14.

question of censure, designed to make them do otherwise, and finding its support in the next clause. **For this man doeth many miracles** (lit., *signs*). Watkins would unite the two clauses in a single question, thus: "What do we, seeing that this man doeth many miracles?" But the sense is nearly the same with this, as with the common punctuation. Their words show that they regard immediate action on their part as indispensable. The ground is giving way under their feet. But what they say appears inconsistent in itself; for while they refer to Jesus contemptuously as **this man**, they seem to admit the reality of his many signs. Probably, however, their words were merely an accommodation, for brevity's sake, to common speech, while their looks and tones and gestures revealed their disbelief in Jesus. It is indeed possible that they mean to concede the extraordinary character of his works, but without conceding that they are wrought by divine power.

48. If we let him thus alone, all men will believe on him, etc. In this expression of fear the Sanhedrists are, no doubt, perfectly honest. They believe that any great increase of the followers of Jesus will arouse the suspicions of Rome and lead to severe measures. By **our place,** Jerusalem is commonly supposed to be meant; for it was the seat of the Sanhedrin and the centre of its powerful influence. The members of this court claim it, therefore, as in a special sense their own. In like manner, filled with egotism, they think of the Jewish nation as *theirs*, and of any process by which the nation would be withdrawn from their religious control as a taking away of *their* nation. But the question has been raised whether the Sanhedrists would be apt to speak of the Romans as taking away their place, if they meant by their place Jerusalem. Probably not, unless it were in the sense of taking it from *them*—from their control, so that they could no longer think or speak of it as *their* place. And the same may be said of the nation. It is scarcely probable that the Sanhedrists feared the transportation of Jerusalem and the whole nation to some distant land by the Romans. "The Sanhedrists apprehend that the Romans . . . would enter Jerusalem and remove the city as well as the people . . from the rule of the Sanhedrin, because it knew so badly how to maintain order."—*Meyer*. This interpretation does not differ in result from that of Watkins, who supposes that by **our place** is meant our *standing* or *position* as leaders of the people, while it agrees better with the expression **both our place and nation;** for this expression blends together the ideas of place and nation, which are more homogeneous, if the words refer to the people of Jerusalem and the nation at large, than if they refer to the religious *position* of the speakers and to the nation at large.

49, 50. But one of them, named Caiaphas (omit **named**), **being the high priest** (omit **the**) **that year.** According to Josephus, Joseph Caiaphas was high priest eleven years, from A. D. 25 to A. D. 36, and so during the whole administration of Pontius Pilate. His father-in-law was Annas. The Evangelist says that he was high priest **that same year,** not because the high priests were then frequently changed, but because that was a memorable year—the year in which the Lord was crucified. **Said unto them, Ye know nothing at all.** This language is not wanting in force, whatever may be thought of its courtesy. Caiaphas sees no ground for hesitation. He is absolutely selfish, and the way to personal safety seems to him plain.

50. Nor consider—(*nor do ye take account.*—Rev. Ver.)—for a moment's reckoning would show what is prudent for us—**that it is expedient for us**—there is here no conscience, no inquiry as to what is right or wrong in the case; self-interest is supreme—**that one man should die for the people**—

51 And this spake he not of himself: but being high priest that year, he prophesied that Jesus should die for that nation;
52 And *a* not for that nation only, *b* but that also he should gather together in one the children of God that were scattered abroad.

51 that the whole nation perish not. Now this he said not of himself; but being high priest that year, he prophesied that Jesus should die for the nation; 52 and not for the nation only, but that he might also gather together into one the children of God that

a Isa. 49:6; 1 John 2:2....*b* ch. 10:16; Eph. 2:14, 15, 16, 17.

considered here as a theocratic community (λαός)—**and that the whole nation perish not**—or the national existence of the Jews come to an end. "This judgment," says Godet, "is made the more remarkable by the contrast between the divine truth of its content, and the diabolical purpose of him who utters it." There is nothing in the language of the high priest which tends to a favorable view of his character.

51. And (rather, *now*, or, *but*) **this he spake not of** (better, *from*) **himself)**—*i. e.*, not from himself alone. (Comp. Notes on 5: 19, 30; 8:28.) It had a source back of himself, in the Divine Mind. **He prophesied,** etc. In other words, his language was virtually a prophecy to this effect. And, therefore, if the testimony of the inspired Evangelist is to be accepted without qualification, the manifestly selfish spirit of Caiaphas was under the directing influence of God to such an extent that his judgment expressed a great truth, and foreshadowed a great event of the divine administration. But we are not told that he was conscious of any divine illumination or influence, like that which enabled Balaam to foresee the future prosperity of Israel; and we do not imagine that he thought himself to be uttering a prophecy. For his language has not the form of prophecy. This was rather a case of unconscious prediction—a case in which God "disposes," and man "proposes" accordingly—a case in which God "makes the wrath of man to praise him" (Ps. 76:10)—a case included in the apostle's declaration: "Him, being delivered according to the determinate counsel and foreknowledge of God, ye have taken, and by wicked hands have crucified and slain." (Acts 2:23.) (Comp. Gen. 50:20.) There is no valid objection to this view. Indeed, it is justified by the proper idea of God. For a being who did not and could not thus direct the actions of men without destroying their freedom, and who could not thereby bring good out of evil, would not be recognized by any servant of Jehovah as his God, and would not be able to assure our hearts of the ultimate victory of right over wrong, in a universe which sin has entered. But the Evangelist manifestly connects the prophetic character of Caiaphas' language with the fact that he **was high priest that year.** How is this to be understood? Does the expression that year simply mean, at that time, so that the whole emphasis rests on the fact of his being *high priest* when he spoke? Or does it mean, during that memorable year, so that the *particular year* is also emphasized as having something to do with the prophetic character of his words? I am inclined to the latter interpretation, especially because it gives to *that year* the sense which it has in verse 49. Accordingly, both the office of Caiaphas, and the year in which he was now holding it, were reasons why, through the guidance of God, his opinion should be prophetic of the transcendent reality which was soon to be witnessed. "In the Old Testament," remarks Godet, "the normal centre of the theocratic people is not the royal house, but the priesthood. In all moments decisive for the life of the people, it is the high priest who receives, by virtue of a prophetic gift which is imparted to him for the moment, the decision of God for the deliverance of his people. (Num. 27: 21; 1 Sam. 30:7, sq.) John does not pretend that, speaking generally, all that the high priest might say was prophetic. He only judges that at this decisive moment, Caiaphas, as an accredited organ of God with his people, performed the part that was assigned him for emergencies of this kind."

52. And not for that (lit., *the*) **nation only, but that also,** etc. This wider and higher aim of the Saviour's death is added by the Evangelist. It was not implied in the words of Caiaphas, but it was important in itself, and specially important in the apostolic age. When this Gospel was written, there was still reason to seize every opportunity to proclaim that the new religion was intended for all mankind, and that there were some of the elect in every nation. The **one,**

53 Then from that day forth they took counsel together for to put him to death.
54 Jesus *therefore walked no more openly among the Jews; but went thence unto a country near to the wilderness, into a city called ᵇEphraim, and there continued with his disciples.
55 ᶜAnd the Jews' passover was nigh at hand: and many went out of the country up to Jerusalem before the passover, to purify themselves.

53 are scattered abroad. So from that day forth they took counsel that they might put him to death.
54 Jesus therefore walked no more openly among the Jews, but departed thence into the country near to the wilderness, into a city called Ephraim; and 55 there he tarried with the disciples. Now the passover of the Jews was at hand; and many went up to Jerusalem out of the country before the passover,

a ch. 4: 1, 3: 7: 1....b See 2 Chron. 13: 19....c ch. 2: 13; 5: 1; 6: 4.

or *one thing* (ἕν), into which he would gather them together is the unity of faith, or a spiritual unity. There is here no reference to the kingdom of Christ, as organized into visible churches, or a visible church.

53. Then (or, *therefore*,) **from that day forth they took counsel,** etc. *Therefore,*— *i. e.* in consequence of the words of Caiaphas, and of the resolution that was reached at this sudden meeting of the Sanhedrin. They had long cherished a deadly hostility to Christ; they had often consulted together how they should put him out of the way; but from this time onward their purpose was more settled and their planning more open. John often uses the same word to denote a feeling or course of conduct, which varies in degree, though it is the same in kind. The persecuting spirit is not always equally firm. There is progress in mortal hatred.

54. Jesus therefore walked no more openly among the Jews. Observe the use of the familiar designation, **the Jews.** It still means the dominant party resident in Jerusalem and the suburbs of that city, and represented by the Sanhedrin. Notice, also, the tense of the verb **walked,** which might be translated *was walking.* His sphere of itinerant labor was no longer among the Jews. He did not continue to go about among them and do the work of his ministry. **But went thence** (lit., *away from there*) **into a** (*the*) **country near to the wilderness, into a city called Ephraim,** etc. The locality of Ephraim has not been satisfactorily ascertained. Dr. Robinson is in favor of regarding the Ephraim of this verse, the Ephraim of 2 Chron. 13: 19, the Ophrah of Josh. 18: 23 and 1 Sam. 13: 17, and the Ephron of Eusebius and Jerome, as the same place. "According to John 11: 54, the place in question was situated near the desert; according to the Old Testament and Josephus, it was not far from Bethel; according to Eusebius and Jerome, it lay five Roman miles from Bethel, in the eastern quarter, and nearly twenty Roman miles . . . north of Jerusalem. Now, taking all these specifications together, they apply with great exactness to the lofty site of the modern Taiyibeh, two hours northeast of Bethel, and six hours and twenty minutes north-northeast of Jerusalem (reckoning three Roman miles to the hour), adjacent to and overlooking the broad tract of desert country lying between it and the valley of the Jordan, and also along the western side of the Dead Sea; a position so remarkable, that one cannot suppose it to have been left unoccupied in ancient times. . According to Matt. 19: 1 and Mark 10: 1, our Lord's last approach to Jerusalem was by way of Perea and Jericho. At Ephraim he could overlook the whole of Perea, as well as all the valley of the Jordan; and nothing would be more natural for him than to pass over into that region, and there preach the gospel on his way back to Jerusalem for the last time. Here, then, John harmonizes with Matthew and Mark; according to whom great multitudes followed Jesus on this journey." ("Bib. Sac.," vol. II., p. 399.) The period of Christ's sojourn at this time in Ephraim cannot have been very many weeks.

55. And (or, *now*) **the Jews' passover was nigh . . . to purify themselves.** They were not required by any special law to make these purifications at Jerusalem (see Gen. 35: 2; Ex. 19: 10, 11; Num. 9: 10, sq.; 2 Chron. 30: 17, 18), but it is easy to suggest many reasons for their preferring to make them there. Especially would their liability to encounter things common or unclean on their way to the holy city through places more or less contaminated by the presence of foreigners, lead them to defer their ceremonial purifications till they reach Jerusalem. How little did they imagine their need of a higher purification, of cleansing by the blood of Jesus! By **the country** is probably meant, not that part

56 ᵃ Then sought they for Jesus, and spake among themselves, as they stood in the temple, What think ye, that he will not come to the feast?
57 Now both the chief priests and the Pharisees had given a commandment, that, if any man knew where he were, he should shew *it*, that they might take him.

56 to purify themselves. They sought therefore for Jesus, and spake one with another, as they stood in the temple, What think ye? That he will not come 57 to the feast? Now the chief priests and the Pharisees had given commandment, that, if any man knew where he was, he should shew it, that they might take him.

CHAPTER XII.

THEN Jesus six days before the passover came to Bethany, ᵇ where Lazarus was which had been dead, whom he raised from the dead.

1 JESUS therefore six days before the passover came to Bethany, where Lazarus was, whom Jesus raised

a ch. 7: 11....*b* ch. 11 : 1, 43.

---

of the country to which Jesus had gone, but the country in general as opposed to the city.

56. Then (or, *therefore*) **sought they** (*were seeking*) **for Jesus, and spake** (or, *were speaking*) **among themselves,** etc. As a result of the recent miracle in Bethany, and of its well known effect on the rulers, the people from the country were more than ever excited about Jesus, and were seeking him day by day in every new arrival of pilgrims. But they were extremely doubtful whether he would make his appearance at the festival, and were often saying to one another: "What is your opinion? Is it that he certainly will not come to the feast?" They regard it as barely possible that he will come, but as far enough from probable.

57. Now both the chief priests, etc. It is reasonably supposed that this **commandment** had been given in the name and authority of the Sanhedrin, and in pursuance of a decision reached at the meeting described in verses 47–50, or by the consultations that followed. (Ver. 53.) These it was which rendered the people so very doubtful whether Jesus would come to the feast.

Ch. 12 : 1-8. SUPPER IN BETHANY.

1. Then Jesus, six days before the passover, came to Bethany, where Lazarus was, whom he (*Jesus*) **raised from the dead.** From Ephraim, the place where Jesus had been residing a few weeks, he may have gone northward through Samaria, and then eastward through a part of Galilee into Perea (comp. Luke 17: 11; Matt. 19: 1; Mark 10: 1), or he may have gone into Perea directly, without making at this time the circuit referred to. Harmonists are not yet agreed on this point. But it is considered certain that he visited Jericho, if not also Perea, and that he returned by way of Jericho to Bethany. If we assume that he made the circuit through Samaria, Galilee, and Perea, to Jericho, and that he began this journey about the middle of March, the following events may be assigned (see Clark's "Harmony of the Gospels") to the journey, which occupied not far from two weeks, viz. : The cleansing of ten lepers (Luke 17 : 11-19); how the kingdom of God would come (Luke 17 : 20-37); parables of the importunate widow, and of the Pharisee and publican (Luke 18 : 1-14); answer concerning divorce (Matt. 19: 1-12; Mark 10: 1-12); blessing the little children (Matt. 19 : 13-15; Mark 10 : 13-16; Luke 18: 15-17); the rich young ruler (Matt. 19: 16-30; Mark 10: 17-31; Luke 18 : 18-30); parable of the laborers in the vineyard (Matt. 20: 1-16); prediction of his own death and resurrection (Matt. 20 : 17-19; Mark 10: 32-34; Luke 18: 31-34); ambitious request of James and John (Matt. 20: 20-28; Mark 10: 35-45); two blind men healed near Jericho (Matt. 20: 29-34; Mark 10: 46-52; Luke 18: 35-43); visit to the house of Zacchæus, and parable of the pounds (Luke 19: 1-27); Jesus sought at Jerusalem (John 11: 55-57); his journey from Jericho to Bethany (Luke 19: 28; John 12: 1.)

It is probable that Jesus, in company with his disciples and other pilgrims to the Passover, left Jericho on Friday, at the dawn of day, and reached Bethany in the early evening, after the Sabbath had begun. For it was lawful to go a short distance on the Sabbath; and travelers from Jericho to Jerusalem might occasionally find themselves, at the close of the sixth day of the week, so near to Bethany that they could finish their journey thither without breaking the law of rest for the seventh day. In this reckoning we assume that the Passover occurred on Friday; so that the six days here mentioned reach back from the beginning of the Friday on which Jesus suffered to the beginning of the previous Sat-

2 *There they made him a supper; and Martha served; but Lazarus was one of them that sat at the table with him.
3 Then took *Mary a pound of ointment of spikenard, very costly, and anointed the feet of Jesus, and wiped his feet with her hair: and the house was filled with the odour of the ointment.

2 from the dead. So they made him a supper there: and Martha served; but Lazarus was one of them 3 that sat at meat with him. Mary therefore took a pound of ointment of ¹pure nard, very precious, and anointed the feet of Jesus, and wiped his feet with her hair: and the house was filled with the

a Matt. 26: 6; Mark 14: 3....*b* Luke 10: 38, 39; ch. 11: 2.——1 Or, *liquid nard*.

urday. Jesus remained over the Sabbath in Bethany, and on the first day of the week made his triumphal entrance into Jerusalem. Thus, even before his resurrection, was special honor put upon the first day of the week.

The words, **where Lazarus was, whom he raised from the dead,** were added, not because they were necessary to distinguish this Bethany from another east of the Jordan (see Note on 1: 28), but because the writer's mind was full of the great event to which he refers, and because Lazarus and his sisters were prominent in the "supper" which he is about to describe. The words of the Com. Ver., **which had been dead** (ὁ τεθνηκώς), may belong to the genuine text; but the evidence of early manuscripts and versions *for* them is overbalanced by that *against* them, and they may therefore be safely omitted.

2. **There they made,** etc., (or, *therefore they made him a supper there*, etc.) The reference is to the principal meal of the day (δεῖπνον), which, though it was served at a late hour in the afternoon, answered to our dinner, rather than to our supper. The Evangelist does not mention the persons by whom this dinner was given, but from the circumstance that **Martha served,** or, *was serving*, it has been inferred that it was given by the sisters and Lazarus. Yet this inference is extremely precarious; for Martha might have served at the house of a friend, even as the mother of Jesus appears to have served thus at the wedding in Cana of Galilee. (See 2: 3, sq.) And since the anointing of Jesus by a woman, in the house of Simon "the leper" (see Matt. 26: 6-16; Mark 14: 3-11), took place near this time in Bethany, and strikingly resembled, in most of its circumstances, the anointing here described, it is reasonable to believe that the three narratives describe the same event—that the dinner was held at the house of Simon, and, perhaps (though this is hardly the best view), that John anticipates the time of it by three or four days, because it was the most important event which he asso-

ciated with this visit of the Lord to Bethany. Says Dr. Hackett: "This feast being the principal event which John associates with Bethany, during these last days, he not unnaturally inserts the account of the feast immediately after speaking of the arrival in Bethany. But having (so to speak) discharged his mind of that recollection, he then turns back and resumes the historical order, namely, that on the next day after coming to Bethany (12: 12, s.), Jesus made his public entry into Jerusalem."—(Smith's "Dict. of the Bible," Am. ed., II., p. 1372, Note a.) But "there is nothing whatever in Matthew's account to fix the *time* of the feast; and both the structure of his Gospel and the apparent links of connection, in this particular narrative, are consistent with the view ordinarily taken, that at ver. 6, he (Matthew) goes back to an earlier event, which furnished occasion to Judas for furthering the design of the rulers, as recorded in the first verses of the chapter."—*Schaff*. This Simon was known as "the leper," doubtless because he had suffered from that terrible disease, but had, perhaps, been healed by the Saviour. Hence his desire to receive Jesus into his house, and to pay him honor, even though he must have been well aware of the deadly animosity which now threatened his life.

3. **Then took Mary** (or, *Mary therefore took*) **a pound of ointment of spikenard, very costly** (or, *precious*.) If, as we suppose, the narratives of Matthew and Mark refer to the same event, they differ from this in not giving the name of the woman who anointed Jesus. This, however, is not surprising; for the reasons which led them to pass over in silence the raising of Lazarus, may have led them to speak of "a woman," instead of giving her name. The Greek (λίτρα) *litra*, and the Latin *libra*, are generally translated *pound*, and are supposed to denote a weight of twelve ounces. This cannot be far from the truth, though it is difficult to ascertain the exact value of ancient weights and measures. The

4 Then saith one of his disciples, Judas Iscariot, Simon's son, which should betray him,
5 Why was not this ointment sold for three hundred pence, and given to the poor?
6 This he said, not that he cared for the poor; but because he was a thief, and ᵃ had the bag, and bare what was put therein.

4 odour of the ointment. But Judas Iscariot, one of 5 his disciples, who should betray him, saith, Why was not this ointment sold for three hundred ¹ shillings, and given to the poor? Now this he said, not because he cared for the poor; but because he was a thief, and having the ²bag ³took away what

a ch. 13 : 29.——1 See marginal note on Matt. 18 : 28....2 Or, *box*....3 Or, *carried what was put therein*.

spikenard is described as **very costly**—the Greek word meaning, probably, "genuine," unadulterated (though the meaning is not perfectly certain); and, therefore, **very costly**, or *precious;* for then, as now, articles were cheapened by adulteration. **Anointed the feet of Jesus, and wiped his feet with her hair.** Matthew and Mark speak of an "alabaster box," which contained the ointment. Matthew says that she "poured it on his head, as he sat at meat"; and Mark, that "she broke the box, and poured it on his head." These different particulars are consistent with one another; but, at the same time, sufficiently marked to prove the independence of the witnesses. No writer of a spurious Gospel, in the middle of the second century, would have been likely to omit all notice of the well-attested pouring of the ointment on Jesus' head, and to affirm an anointing of his feet—the latter being a mere conjecture of his own. But the anointing of Jesus' feet, if it was performed in addition to the anointing of his head, would naturally enough make a deep impression on the thoughtful and loving spirit of John, who was, perhaps, reclining next his Lord; and it might, therefore, of all others, be the one feature of the anointing that he would remember and record. **And the house was filled with the odour.** A fact not unworthy of commemoration, as it probably drew the attention of all to the act of anointing. Compare Cant. 1 : 12; 4 : 13; and "spikenard," in Smith's "Dict. of the Bible," Vol. IV., p. 3103, Am. ed.

4. **Then saith,** etc., or, *But Judas Iscariot, one of his disciples, which should (was about to) betray him, saith* (Rev. Ver.) Here again the narrative of John designates, by name, the person who takes the lead in censuring Mary's act, though others appear to have joined in the censure. For Matthew says that "when his disciples saw it, they had indignation, saying"; and Mark relates that "there were some that had indignation in themselves,

and said." Possibly Matthew, who once sat at the receipt of custom, and understood well the value of money, was one of the twelve who at first sympathized with the criticism of Judas. If so, it was specially natural for him to record the fact that Christ's disciples (without meaning to say, *every one* of them) "had indignation." But John is wont to take his readers at once to the fountain-head of good or evil. Here, therefore, he names the very man with whom the censure of Mary's act began, and at whose suggestion the thought of censure came into other minds. The best textual authorities omit the words, **Simon's son.**

5. **Why was not this ointment sold for three hundred pence** (lit., *denarii*), **and given to the poor?** The translation, **three hundred pence,** gives an English reader no proper idea of the value here assigned to the ointment. For a *denarius* was worth from fifteen to seventeen cents of American money; and three hundred *denarii* from forty-five to fifty dollars—a sum which is proof, on the one hand, of the comfortable circumstances of the family; and, on the other, of the great love and devotion of Mary to Christ.

6. **This he said,** etc. (Better, *but this he said*), **not that** (rather, *not because*) **he cared for the poor;**—which would have been a Christian motive—**but because he was a thief**—the first and only statement of this fact in the Gospels—**and had the bag, and bare what was put therein.** Being the treasurer, or purse-bearer, of the disciples, he was in the habit of secretly appropriating a part of the common treasure to his private use. And now he thought, "If only the value of this ointment were in the common purse, a good percentage of it would find its way into my own pocket, and none of my companions would be the wiser for it." From whom did the Evangelist learn that Judas was a thief? Perhaps, from Jesus himself, after the work of Judas was accomplished. It is natural to suppose that the conversation of Jesus with

7 Then said Jesus, Let her alone: against the day of my burying hath she kept this.
8 For *the poor always ye have with you; but me ye have not always.

7 was put therein. Jesus therefore said, ¹Suffer her
8 to keep it against the day of my burying. For the poor ye have always with you; but me ye have not always.

a Matt., 26: 11; Mark 14: 7.—1 Or, *Let her alone: it was that she might ke p it.*

the disciples, after his resurrection, may, at some time, have turned upon Judas, and that he may have revealed to them a little of the unsuspected history of the traitor. But why did Jesus permit a thief to be the treasurer of his disciples? Did he not thereby suffer them to be wronged, and Judas to be tempted beyond what he was able to bear? Perhaps Jesus left the secular affairs of the company to his disciples, judging it best that they should be exposed to the ordinary risks of financial management, from the first. And as to the temptation of Judas, it was only what must happen to men of like spirit, in all times. Their moral strength is tested at its weakest point; if it fails there, it fails everywhere. Moral character is a unit, and it is no stronger than its weakest part. The word translated **bare**, is supposed by De Wette, Meyer, Godet, and some others, to signify, in this place, "bore away." Doubtful. (Compare 20: 15.)

7. Let her alone, etc. Read: *Suffer her to keep it for the day of my burial.* This was said before the act of anointing was finished, and it means: "Let her keep the ointment, according to her purpose, instead of selling it; let her retain and use it, without annoyance, for the day of my burial." "Thus Jesus gives this occurrence a typical importance for his burial."—*Luthardt.* It was in harmony with a divine purpose, not understood, perhaps, by Mary, but clearly perceived by Christ, that this anointing was now taking place. His body was not anointed, according to custom at the time of his death, but this part of the funeral honors was anticipated by the act of Mary. Having made this remark, checking the criticism of Judas and of his fellow disciples, who appear to have seconded it in some degree, Jesus may have paused a few moments before adding the words preserved by the other Evangelists. So that his words may have succeeded each other in the following order: "Why trouble ye the woman? Suffer her to keep it for the day of my burial." (Pause.) "For she hath wrought a good work upon me. For the poor ye have always with you, but me ye have not always. For in that she poured this ointment on my body, she did it for my burial. Verily I say unto you, wheresover this gospel shall be preached in the whole world, what this woman did will also be told for a memorial of her." (Matt. 26: 10-13.)

We have followed in this passage a reading which is much better supported than that of the common text, but which makes the interpretation of the passage more difficult.

8. For the poor ye have always with you; but me ye have not always. The Saviour assents to the propriety of giving to the poor; but he assumes that this is not the whole duty of his disciples; they are also to express their reverence and love to their Lord. Worship is no less a duty than almsgiving. Direct, and even public, expressions of loyalty and devotion to God are a part of Christian duty. But the opportunity for such an expression of love as Mary was now making, would soon be past; while the opportunity to bestow alms on the poor would be always present. "Mary, as if she knew I was soon to die, has chosen the strongest way she could of showing how much she loved me. She has done for me, as her Teacher, Messiah, and Friend, while I live, what she would soon have had to do to my dead body— she has embalmed me for the grave."—*Geikie.* According to Matthew, Jesus added the words: "For in that she poured this ointment on my body, she did it for my burial. Verily I say unto you, wheresoever this gospel shall be preached in the whole world, there shall also this that this woman hath done, be told for a memorial of her." (26: 12, 13.) And according to Mark, another expression still: "She hath done what she could." (Mark 14: 8.) The three narratives agree as to the principal circumstances. Yet only the Synoptical Gospels record the interesting prophecy that the act of Mary should be told wherever the gospel should be preached; while John's narrative is the only one that gives the name of the woman who performed this act of love, or mentions the

9 Much people of the Jews therefore knew that he was there: and they came not for Jesus' sake only, but that they might see Lazarus also, ⁿ whom he had raised from the dead.
10 ᵇ But the chief priests consulted that they might put Lazarus also to death;
11 ᶜ Because that by reason of him many of the Jews went away, and believed on Jesus.
12 ᵈ On the next day much people that were come to the feast, when they heard that Jesus was coming to Jerusalem,

9 The common people therefore of the Jews learned that he was there: and they came, not for Jesus' sake only, but that they might see Lazarus also, whom he had raised from the dead. But the chief priests took counsel that they might put Lazarus also to 11 death; because that by reason of him many of the Jews went away, and believed on Jesus.
12 On the morrow ¹ a great multitude that had come to the feast, when they heard that Jesus was coming

a ch. 11: 43, 44....b Luke 16: 31....c ch. 11: 45; ver. 18....d Matt. 21: b; Mark 11: 8; Luke 19: 35, 36. etc.——1 Some ancient authorities read, *the common people*.

presence of Lazarus at the feast, or traces the criticism of the disciples to the selfish heart of Judas.

9-11. JEWISH SENTIMENT AT THIS TIME.

9. Much people—the common people—**of the Jews therefore knew that he was there.** This verse is probably to be connected with verse first. The coming of Jesus and his disciples to Bethany on Friday evening, became generally known before the Jewish Sabbath was over. Indeed, he was now an object of such deep and varied interest that his approach to Jerusalem was sure to be noised abroad. **And they came not for Jesus' sake only, but that they might see Lazarus also, whom he had raised from the dead.** From the circumstance that the **much** (or, *common*) **people** is described as **of**—*i. e., from*—**the Jews**, it may be inferred that they were, for the most part, hostile to Jesus. Yet they were not, perhaps, of the most unyielding temper, but were willing at least to see if Lazarus were actually alive, and to examine on the spot the evidence of his resurrection. Some of them were doubtless convinced by what they saw and heard, and were ready, in the excitement of their new conviction, to join those who, on the first day of the week, spread their garments in the way, and shouted, "Hosanna!" But there was a party very differently employed.

10. But the chief priests consulted (or, *took counsel*) **that they might put Lazarus also to death.** In this consultation, we are not to suppose the whole Sanhedrin engaged; but the hierarchical members, the heads of the twenty-four classes into which the officiating priests were divided, together with the high priest, and his kindred. This influential part of the Sanhedrin was ready to resort to any measure, however desperate, in order to bring about the destruction of Jesus. But the presence and testimony of Lazarus, as the Evangelist proceeds to indicate, were doing something every day to defeat their cherished purpose.

11. Because that by reason of him many of the Jews went (or, *were going*) **away, and believed** (*were believing*) **on Jesus.** The expression, *were going away*, shows that they were, one by one, separating themselves from the extreme adversaries of Jesus; the leading faction, which would hesitate at nothing, and which was, in fact, the nucleus and centre of the Sanhedrin. And those who were thus separating themselves from this centre of hostility to Christ, and making inquiry as to the truth, were also one by one coming to believe in Jesus, on account of Lazarus. With Lazarus before them, they could not deny his resurrection, at the word of Christ; and, convinced of his resurrection, at the word of Jesus, they could not withhold their confidence from Jesus.

12-19. CHRIST'S TRIUMPHAL ENTRANCE INTO JERUSALEM.

12. On the next day much people (lit., *a great multitude*) **that were come to the feast.** It is impossible to arrive at absolute certainty in respect to the day of the week meant by **the next day;** but there is a strong probability that it was the first, or Sunday—hence called Palm Sunday. (See Note on ver. 1.) The multitude here referred to was composed, for the most part, of people who had come up to the holy city from various parts of the land, to keep the passover. They were, therefore, less prejudiced than the inhabitants of Jerusalem, and especially "the Jews." **When they heard** (lit., *having heard*) **that Jesus was coming to** (or, *into*) **Jerusalem.** By what means they heard, the Evangelist does not state; perhaps, by the report of some of "the Jews," who had visited him at Bethany, during the Sabbath, had been convinced of his divine mission (**ver. 11**),

13 Took branches of palm trees, and went forth to meet him, and cried, *a* Hosanna: Blessed *is* the King of Israel that cometh in the name of the Lord.
14 *b* And Jesus, when he had found a young ass, sat thereon; as it is written,
15 *c* Fear not, daughter of Sion: behold, thy King cometh, sitting on an ass's colt.

a Ps. 118: 25, 26....*b* Matt. 21: 7....*c* Zech. 9: 9.

and had learned of his purpose to enter the city on the morrow; or, by the report of persons who had visited Bethany on the morning of the first day of the week, and had returned to Jerusalem, with a knowledge of Christ's purpose. At such a time, the intercourse between the two places would be constant; and now, more than ever before, the movements of Jesus were a matter of universal interest.

13. Took branches of palm trees (that is, of *the palm trees*, that were standing near.) These branches were symbols of victory and peace. Dr. Robinson describes them as the "pendulous twigs and boughs of the palm tree." The word *Bethany* signifies "house of dates"; and it is, therefore, reasonable to suppose that date-palms were abundant on the sides of the Mount of Olives. The tree "was regarded by the ancients as peculiarly characteristic of Palestine and the neighboring regions." (Smith's "Dict. of the Bible." Art. Palm-tree.) **And went forth to meet him, and cried, Hosanna: Blessed is the King of Israel that cometh in the name of the Lord.** The Revised Version makes **the King of Israel** the last clause, **the King of Israel,** being in apposition with **he that cometh,** and added for the purpose of setting forth the office of this personage. The people are represented by Matthew (21:9) as crying: "Hosanna to the Son of David; blessed be he that cometh in the name of the Lord. Hosanna in the highest." where the expression, "the Son of David," is equivalent to "the King of Israel," in this passage; but, as the verb translated **cried** (*i. e., were crying,*) denotes continued action, both expressions may have been used. The word "Hosanna," means, "save, I entreat"; or, "bring salvation, I entreat"; and the language of the people was borrowed, with slight additions, from Ps. 118: 25, 26, which is thus translated by Perowne: "*We beseech thee, O Jehovah, save now; we beseech thee, O Jehovah, send now prosperity. Blessed be he that cometh in the name of Jehovah.*" And he remarks as follows, on the word "hosanna"; "*Save now;* or, rather, 'Save, I pray.' The particle of entreaty is repeated in each member of this (25th) verse, so that, altogether, it occurs four times, as if to mark the earnestness of the petition. The English word 'now,' is not, therefore, a particle of time, but a particle of entreaty, as in Eccl. 12: 1: 'Remember now thy Creator'—*i. e.*, 'Remember, I beseech thee, thy Creator.'"

14. And Jesus, when he had found a young ass. John omits the details in respect to the procuring of the young ass, which had been recorded by the other Evangelists; but we are not to infer from this that he was ignorant of them, or that he deemed them of no importance. (Comp. 20: 30, 31; 21: 25.) **He sat thereon; as it is written:**

15. Fear not, daughter of Sion: behold, thy king cometh, sitting on an ass's colt. This is a free quotation of Zechariah 9: 9, a considerable part of the original text being omitted, but enough being given to prove that the prophecy was fulfilled. The words of Zechariah may be thus translated: "Rejoice greatly, daughter of Zion! shout, daughter of Jerusalem! Behold, thy king cometh unto thee; just and having salvation is he; meek, and riding upon an ass, and upon a colt, the foal of an ass." The freedom with which the inspired writers of the New Testament treat the text of the Old Testament—sometimes quoting it with verbal accuracy, sometimes condensing two clauses into one, sometimes changing the tense of a verb to bring out more clearly its prophetic pertinency, and sometimes giving an implied thought for the one expressed—is by no means inconsistent with the highest reverence for the divine authority of that volume. This they uniformly show by the manner in which they refer to the ancient Scriptures. And so far as we can judge, they never attribute to an Old Testament writer any thought foreign to his language, or, indeed, any thought that is not fairly implied in his language. In this passage, a part

Ch. XII.] JOHN. 251

16 These things ᵃ understood not his disciples at the first: ᵇ but when Jesus was glorified, ᶜ then remembered they that these things were written of him, and that they had done these things unto him.
17 The people therefore that was with him when he called Lazarus out of his grave, and raised him from the dead, bare record.
18 ᵈ For this cause the people also met him, for that they heard that he had done this miracle.
19 The Pharisees therefore said among themselves, ᵉ Perceive ye how ye prevail nothing? behold, the world is gone after him.

16 cometh, sitting on an ass's colt. These things understood not his disciples at the first: but when Jesus was glorified, then remembered they that these things were written of him, and that they had done these things unto him.
17 these things unto him. The multitude therefore that was with him when he called Lazarus out of the tomb, and raised him from the dead, bare witness.
18 ness. For this cause also the multitude went and met him, for that they heard that he had done this sign. The Pharisees therefore said among themselves, ¹ Behold, how ye prevail nothing: lo, the world has gone after him.

a Luke 18: 34....b ch. 7: 30....c ch. 14: 26....d ver. 11....e ch. 11: 47, 48.—1 Or, Ye behold.

of the original word is omitted, and the expression, "Fear not," is substituted for "Rejoice." But joy banishes fear, and an exhortation to rejoice is virtually an exhortation to banish fear; as an exhortation to banish fear is, in many circumstances, an exhortation to rejoice.

16. These things understood not his disciples at the first, etc. The homage paid to Jesus at this time was so enthusiastic and spontaneous, and the interest of the disciples in the events of the hour was so absorbing, that they did not observe how exactly the ancient prophecy was being fulfilled. This was perfectly natural; and it was equally natural that, in reflecting upon these events after the resurrection of Jesus, they should have recalled the words of prophecy that were fulfilled by them. So, too, we can readily understand how one of the twelve, and especially one so meditative, introspective, and spiritual as John, should have put on record these facts about the disciples; but we are unable to see how a *falsarius* of the second century would have been likely to attribute to the disciples this lack of understanding. It is a stroke too delicate for a deceiver. Compare the similar statements in 2: 22; 7: 39.

17. The people (*multitude*) **therefore that was with him when he called Lazarus out of his grave, and raised him from the dead, bare record** (or, *witness*). This language is retrospective, and applies to the whole period since the resurrection of Lazarus. The verb translated **bare witness** represents an act as being in progress, and might be rendered *was bearing witness—i. e.*, repeatedly, from time to time, so that their testimony was not silenced by the authority of the priesthood, but continued to make itself heard until the public entrance of Jesus into Jerusalem. According to another reading (which gives ὅτι, instead of ὅτε), this verse should be translated: "The multitude therefore that was with him bare witness that he called Lazarus out of the tomb, and raised him from the dead"—that is, bore witness to what they had seen and heard at that time. As to sense, the two readings do not differ. But the weight of manuscript authority favors when, rather than *that*.

18. For this cause the people (or, *multitude*) **also met him, for that they heard that he had done this miracle** (or, *sign*). The report which had gone abroad as the testimony of a large number of witnesses, namely, that Jesus had raised Lazarus from the dead, led a multitude of the people who had come up to the Passover to go out towards Bethany, to meet the Lord. (See on ver. 12.)

19. The Pharisees therefore said among themselves—that is, when the multitude had fairly left the city, on their way to meet Jesus, and the Pharisees, who headed the opposition to him, were left by themselves, to meditate on the course which events seemed to be taking. **Perceive ye how ye prevail nothing?** Words spoken, without doubt, in a querulous and bitter tone; every one being ready to charge the blame of their ill success in the plot against Jesus upon others. "Thus far," they say, "your efforts amount to nothing; they are bootless, unprofitable, vain." The structure of this clause in the Greek permits us to translate it as a question: "Do ye see ye that ye prevail nothing?" but does not require this. Whether it was a question, or not, depended on the inflection of the voice with which the clause was uttered. But the meaning of these words, if they were a question, would be the same as that given above. **Behold, the world is gone after him.** As if the act were fully accomplished in the past, and they were looking back upon it as finished already. For they had observed that the

20 And there *were certain Greeks among them
b that came up to worship at the feast:
21 The same came therefore to Philip, *c* which was of
Bethsaida of Galilee, and desired him, saying, Sir, we
would see Jesus.
22 Philip cometh and telleth Andrew: and again Andrew and Philip tell Jesus.

20 Now there were certain Greeks among those who
21 went up to worship at the feast: these therefore
came to Philip, who was of Bethsaida of Galilee,
and asked him, saying, Sir, we would see Jesus.
22 Philip cometh and telleth Andrew: Andrew cometh

a Acts 17 : 4....*b* 1 Kings 8 : 41, 42 ; Acts 8 : 27....*c* ch. 1 : 44.

multitude had gone to meet Jesus, with a friendly feeling towards him, and in face of the known hostility of the Pharisees. This act seemed, therefore, to be an abandonment of the Pharisaic party for the purpose of attaching themselves to Christ. And by an exaggeration natural to their bitter and disappointed spirit, they speak of the multitude as **the world!** As if almost none were left. Would that it had been literally so!

20-22. CERTAIN GREEKS ASK TO SEE JESUS.

20. And (or, *now*) **there were certain Greeks among them that came to worship at the feast.** The word **Greeks** signifies persons of the Greek race or nation, not Hellenists, or Jews who made use of the Greek language. The present participle, which might be translated *coming up*, describes the class of persons referred to as those who were in the habit of coming up to worship at the feast. They were proselytes to Judaism, believers in the true God, like Cornelius, and they now manifested a greater interest in Jesus than did a majority of the chosen people, who had been long desiring the advent of their Messiah. The Evangelist does not mention the place where these Greeks were when they expressed their wish to see Jesus, but it is natural to suppose that they were in the Court of the Gentiles. The same silence is observed as to the time when this occurred; but there seems to be good reason, in the language of verse 36, to suppose that it was as late in the week as about the close of Tuesday. This is the time which best agrees with the series of events and discourses narrated by the other Evangelists, but which the purpose of John did not require him to repeat.

21. The same came therefore to Philip, which was of Bethsaida of Galilee, etc. Their desire, modestly expressed, was to be introduced to Jesus; doubtless for the purpose of forming a personal judgment as to his character and claims. The assistance of one of his disciples would scarcely have been needed, if their wish had been simply to look upon the face and note the bearing of the Teacher about whom so much was said. Why they came to Philip cannot be known, and why John takes occasion to say that he was from Bethsaida of Galilee is equally a matter of conjecture. Such particularity is, however, *characteristic* of this Evangelist, and it reminds us continually of his independent and minute knowledge of the disciples as well as their Master. On the address Sir, or, *Lord* (κύριε), Meyer remarks: "Not without the tender of honor, which they naturally paid, even to the disciples of a Master so admired, who truly appeared to be the very Messiah."

22. Philip cometh and telleth Andrew. Whether there was any special reason for hesitation about complying with their request that led Philip to tell Andrew, is uncertain. Perhaps the extreme sensitiveness of the Jews to intercourse with Gentiles, might render it specially dangerous for Jesus to receive the Greeks at this time, when the Pharisees were so eager to find occasions to accuse him, and to kindle the fanaticism of their followers against him. But it is also possible that Philip would have been diffident about introducing any strangers to his Master, without consulting some one of his associates, especially when that Master was surrounded by people in the court of the temple. **And again Andrew and Philip tell Jesus.** Or, as in Rev. Ver. : *Andrew cometh, and Philip, and they tell Jesus.* Probably taking the Greeks with them until they were near the place where Jesus was standing, and then approaching him alone, and making known to him the request of the Greeks. In that case, whether the Gentile strangers were introduced to Christ or not, they were near enough to hear the words which their request led him to utter, and which were, doubtless, a sufficient answer to the thoughts of their hearts.

23 And Jesus answered them, saying, *The hour is come, that the Son of man should be glorified.
24 Verily, verily, I say unto you, *Except a corn of wheat fall into the ground and die, it abideth alone: but if it die, it bringeth forth much fruit.
25 *He that loveth his life shall lose it; and he that hateth his life in this world shall keep it unto life eternal.

23 eth, and Philip, and they tell Jesus. And Jesus answereth them, saying, The hour is come, that the 24 Son of man should be glorified. Verily, verily, I say unto you, Except a grain of wheat fall into the earth and die, it abideth by itself alone; but 25 if it die, it beareth much fruit. He that loveth his life loseth it; and he that hateth his life in

a ch. 13: 32; 17: 1....b 1 Cor. 15: 30....c Matt. 10: 39; 16: 25; Mark 8. 35; Luke 9: 24; 17: 33.

23-28. GLORY THROUGH DEATH.

23. And Jesus answered (or, *answereth*) **them, saying, The hour is come, that the Son of man should be glorified.** The hour referred to is that of his propitiatory death, by which his work of humiliation and suffering would be completed, and his return to the right hand of power virtually accomplished. For with his sacrificial death was bound up his resurrection, his exaltation, and his kingship as the Son of man, together with the renovation and eternal life of his people. The hour appointed by God from eternity, that in it the Son of man might be glorified, is perhaps the exact thought expressed by the Saviour. Knowing that he was **the Son of man**, in a far more important sense than he was "the Son of David," the desire of these Greeks to see him appears to have brought to his mind the "great multitude, which no man can number, out of every tribe and tongue and people and nation," that were to be "redeemed by his blood," and to be made "kings (or, *a kingdom*) and priests unto God"; and, with them, the final, the crucial, and the all important moment and act of his ministry on earth. Of course, the word **hour** is used in the sense of time. Critical authorities favor the present tense of the verb in the first clause —*answereth*, instead of **answered**.

24. Verily, verily, I say unto you, Except a (or, *the*) **corn** (or, *grain*) **of wheat fall into the ground** (or, *earth*) **and die, it abideth alone: but if it die, it bringeth forth much fruit.** Nature and spirit are made for each other. The law of life for the one resembles in many a particular the law of life for the other. And no religious teacher has equaled Jesus Christ in setting forth spiritual truth by the aid of facts taken from the realm of nature. In the saying before us, John has preserved a sample of the Lord's power to prepare the minds of men for a great law of the kingdom of grace, by reminding them of a similar law in nature. In the latter realm, life springs out of decay and death; for death is not annihilation of being, but, normally, a process by which the very life of the seed is renewed and multiplied. Death is a process of glorification, or a process by which new glory is attained. For the vital principle is never more active than when it is casting off its worn integuments, and clothing itself anew. Instead of remaining simply what it was, it clothes itself with root and stalk and ear, multiplying itself thirty, sixty, or even a hundred fold. And Jesus sees in this law of the vegetable world a faint emblem of what he is to experience as he makes to himself a spiritual body, or becomes the principle of spiritual life in a multitude who are to be redeemed from sin and woe. But this law seen in the vegetable world is applicable, not only to Christ himself, but to all men, as related to him, and to salvation through him.

25. He that loveth his life shall lose (*loseth*) **it; and he that hateth his life in this world shall keep it unto life eternal.** The word translated **life**, in the expression, **his life**, (not in the phrase "eternal life,") is translated by some, *soul*—a meaning which it often has. But this rendering is scarcely suitable in the present case, unless we understand by "soul" the spirit in its selfish, earthward tendencies. It is better to regard it as a more emphatic term for the word *self*, a meaning which it often has in the Old Testament. Selfishness is ruin to the highest interests of him who is ruled by it, while self-denial in this world, and with reference to this world, leads to the eternal good of him who practices it. He that loves God with all the heart, and his neighbor as himself, will be called to suffer much; but it will be but for a moment, and will issue in "a far more exceeding and eternal weight of glory." (2 Cor 4:17.) He that forgets self, in his love to God and man, will be assailed, and stripped, and wounded, and left half dead by the forces of moral evil; but he will be re-animated, and crowned by the infinite grace of God, and the uplifting power of a good conscience and a

JOHN. [Ch. XII.

26 If any man serve me, let him follow me; and where I am, there shall also my servant be: if any man serve me, him will *my* Father honour.
27 *b* Now is my soul troubled; and what shall I say? Father, save me from this hour: *c* but for this cause came I unto this hour.

26 this world shall keep it unto life eternal. If any man serve me, let him follow me; and where I am, there shall also my servant be: if any man serve me, him will the Father honour. Now is my soul troubled; and what shall I say? Father, save me from this ¹ hour. But for this cause came I unto

a ch. 14: 3; 17: 24; 1 Thess. 4: 17....*b* Matt. 26: 38, 39; Luke 12: 50; ch. 13: 21....*c* Luke 22: 53; ch. 18: 37.——1 Or. *hour?*

true heart. (Compare 2 Tim. 2: 12; Matt. 10: 39.)

26. **If any man serve me, let him follow me,** etc. Observe, *first,* that the word *me* is emphatic in the first part of this verse: "If any man serve *me,* let him follow *me*"; *secondly,* that Jesus here claims service from his disciples—he does not teach them to serve the Father only, but he expects them to serve himself; *thirdly,* that true service to Christ implies following him in the way of self-denial and suffering—it is enough for the disciple to imitate his Lord, and he cannot do his Master's will without following in his steps; and, *fourthly,* that such service will issue in his being forever with the Lord, than which a greater good cannot be imagined. To be with Christ, and to reign with him!—this is fullness of joy to the Christian heart. In the last part of the verse, the emphatic words are **serve,** and **will honour.** Service to Christ will be recompensed by honor from his Father. The genuine disciple of Christ will be an heir of God, a joint-heir with Christ (Rom. 8: 17); having suffered with him, he will also be glorified with him. But now the Saviour returns to his own cross.

27. **Now is my soul troubled.** The prospect of his dreadful suffering, from which he had turned his thought for a moment, to speak of the law of true life for his followers, now re-asserts its power over his soul, and with holy simplicity and wisdom he gives expression to his dialogue with himself, in the hearing of his disciples. Observe that the perfect tense of the verb is employed, indicating that his trouble of soul had come down from a previous moment to the present. And bear in mind, also, that his human nature was never suppressed by the divine. Its appeals were every whit as strong as they would have been if his divine nature had been torpid, or unconscious. And, finally, learn that a knowledge of the blessed ministry and issue of suffering does not make it for the time being unreal. The good are far more troubled by some forms of evil than the bad. **And what shall I say? Father, save me from this hour.** That is, from the suffering of this hour—from the terrible death into whose shadow I am now entering. The words, **Father, save me from this hour,** may be understood as a question embodying the petition which human nature prompted, but which was not offered; or as an actual prayer addressed to the Father. The former interpretation makes the passage less dramatic and impassioned than the latter. But we prefer it (1) because it agrees better with the doubt expressed by the previous question. and (2) because it agrees better with the idea that Christ was conscious at the instant of the presence of his disciples. "Lücke, Meyer, and Hengstenberg suppose this to be an actual prayer: 'Deliver me from the necessity of dying.' But how, then, is the following word to be understood? It would be an instant recalling of this request. So sudden a revulsion of feeling is impossible. They appeal to the prayer in Gethsemane. But Jesus there began by saying: *If it be possible;* and then he marked impressively the contrast between the two cries by the word *nevertheless* (πλήν.) Here the contradiction would be absolute, and would remain unexplained."—*Godet.* Westcott supposes that all objection to the latter view, namely, that this is a prayer, may be removed by noticing "the exact form in which it is expressed. The petition is for deliverance *out of* (σῶσον ἐκ..), and not for deliverance *from* (ἀπο), the crisis of trial. So that the sense appears to be, 'bring me safely out of the conflict.' (Heb. 5: 7), and not simply, 'keep me from entering into it.'" But we doubt whether this would be suggested by the Greek expression to any one who was not looking for a way of escape from an interpretation which did not please him. **But for this cause came I unto this hour.** That is, "unto this hour of suffering and death I came, just because it was such an hour. If, then, I am saved from it, I shall fail of accomplishing that for which I came into the world. Every step of my course has looked to this now im-

28 Father, glorify thy name. ᵃThen came there a voice from heaven, saying, I have both glorified it, and will glorify it again.
29 The people therefore that stood by, and heard it, said that it thundered: others said, An angel spake to him.
30 Jesus answered and said, ᵇ This voice came not because of me, but for your sakes.

28 this hour. Father, glorify thy name. There came therefore a voice out of heaven, saying, I have both 29 glorified it, and will glorify it again. The multitude therefore, that stood by, and heard it, said, that 30 it had thundered; others said, An angel hath spoken to him. Jesus answered and said, This voice hath not come for my sake, but for your sakes.

a Matt. 3:17....*b* ch. 11:42.

---

pending atoning death, and deliverance from this must be fatal to the highest purpose of my incarnation and ministry." This saying of Jesus perfectly agrees with another recorded by Matthew (20:28): "Even as the Son of man came, not to be ministered unto, but to minister, and to give his life (τὴν ψυχὴν αὐτοῦ) a ransom for many"; and these expressions from his own lips account for the central place which was given to the doctrine of the cross by the apostles. (See 1 Cor. 1: 17, sq.; Gal. 3: 1.)

28. **Father, glorify thy name.** This is the actual prayer. One might have anticipated from the foregoing a prayer having special relation to himself, and perhaps to his own glorification. But self was forgotten. For the Father's glory, the Son of God "became obedient unto death, even the death of the cross." (Phil. 2:8.) Though he knew that his death was the way to his own glory, and that his own glory was one with his Father's, it was regard for his Father's glory that filled his soul. Love conquered—a love in which there was no selfishness. What a lesson for his followers! If they desire to be victorious in trial, let them think of God, and permit the flame of love to him to rise in their hearts! It will consume fear, and generate power. **Then came there** (better, *came therefore*) **a voice from** (*out of*) **heaven.** That is, in response to the prayer of Jesus. Hence the connecting particle (οὖν) is best represented by the word *therefore*. *Out of heaven* here means out of the sky, from which, according to the natural symbolism of Scripture, God's voice comes down to men. **I have both glorified it, and will glorify it again.** Hence the voice was intelligible, certainly to Jesus, probably to the disciples, and among them, to the writer of this Gospel, and possibly, to some of the people. For the Evangelist declares its meaning, without any hint that it had been interpreted to him by his Master. But to what does the first part of the expression refer? Probably to the whole

work of Christ hitherto, which is now looked upon as completed in the past; hence the Greek form which expresses completed action: "I both glorified"; though the English idiom requires us to translate as above: "I have both glorified." Christ had glorified God by his ministry among the Jews, and he was now to glorify him by his death for all men, and by the gradual spread of the gospel among all nations.

29. **The people therefore that stood by and heard it, said that it** (*had*) **thundered: others said, An angel spake to him.** "We must abide by the interpretation that *a voice actually issued from heaven*, which John relates, and Jesus confirms as an objective occurrence."—*Meyer*. But such was the nature of this voice that it was recognized by the unsusceptible multitude as a sound like that of thunder, while to others it was like speech, and was ascribed to an angel, though the words were not understood. With this voice may be compared that which Paul heard on the way to Damascus (Acts 9:7; 22:9); for it appears that the companions of Saul heard the voice, but did not recognize the words that were uttered.—*Lücke, Hackett*.

30. **Jesus answered and said, This voice came not because of me, but for your sakes** (*hath not come for my sake, but for yours*). His language is called an *answer*, because it was occasioned by the words of the people, and was intended to explain to them the true significance of the miraculous event which had arrested their attention. Some of the multitude were susceptible of holy impressions, and might be led to full trust in him; while others were already believing, but with a faith so weak that it would soon be shaken and apparently destroyed by his death on the cross. Hence he says to them: "This voice has not come to convince me that my prayer is heard and answered, for I have no need of such evidence; but it has come to conquer your unbelief, or to strengthen your faith."

31 Now is the judgment of this world: now shall *the prince of this world be cast out.
32 And I, *if I be lifted up from the earth, will draw *all men unto me.
33 ᵈ This he said, signifying what death he should die.

31 Now is ¹ the judgment of this world: now shall the ²prince of this world be cast out. And I, if I be lifted up ² from the earth, will draw all men unto myself. But this he said, signifying by what man-

a Matt. 12: 29; Luke 10 18; ch. 14: 30; 16: 11; Acts 26: 18; 2 Cor. 4: 4; Eph. 2: 2; 6: 12....*b* ch. 3: 14; 8: 28....*c* Rom. 5: 18; Heb. 2: 9....*d* ch. 18: 32.—1 Or, a *judgment*....2 Or, *out of*.

31. Now is the judgment of this world. The whole sinful world, heathen as well as Jewish, is brought before the mind of Christ. All Israel and all the Gentiles are represented by the people around; and all are pronounced guilty by his death, which is for all. For **this world** is an evil world, subject to Satan, "the spirit that now worketh in the children of disobedience." (Eph. 2: 2.) The Jews, indeed, regarded the Gentiles as under the control of the prince of darkness, but supposed themselves to be servants of God; the Saviour, however, counted all who rejected the truth as belonging to **this world**—a world which he was about to condemn; while he fell by its malice, and died for its redemption. **Now shall the prince of this world be cast out.** That is, out of his throne and kingdom, the hearts of men. He shall no longer be the ruler of mankind. His expulsion from the seat of power shall begin from the time of my death, which has now come.

32. And I, if I be lifted up from the earth, will draw all men unto me (*myself*). That the conditional clause, **if I be lifted up from the earth,** refers to the crucifixion of Jesus, is made certain by the explanation of the Evangelist (ver. 33)—an explanation which fully agrees with the preceding context. (See ver. 24-27.) But it may, at the same time, be true that Jesus thought of the cross as his pathway to glory, and associated his ignominious but atoning death with his consequent exaltation at the right hand of power. By using a conditional form, **if I be lifted up,** he does not intimate any doubt as to the certainty of his death, but he adopts this form in order to say, in the briefest manner, that he will draw all men to himself, and that his crucifixion is prerequisite to his doing this. His triumph and reign are certain, but they are conditioned on his death.

The drawing spoken of must be understood to embrace all the moral and spiritual influences by which men are led to put their trust in Christ, and to serve him with a true heart. Especially does it include the preaching of Christ, and the work of the Holy Spirit, who is given by Christ. It is an effectual drawing, by means of which the servants of Satan are led to become the servants of Christ; not an *attempt* to draw men to himself, which is resisted, and rendered unavailing. A victory is here predicted, and not simply an effort to secure victory. But the victory may not be gained at once. Divine processes seem to men very slow. Eve probably thought that her first-born son was the promised "seed"; but thousands of years passed before the Messiah was born in Bethlehem. Then, however, "when the fulness of the time was come, God sent forth his Son, made of a woman, made under the law, to redeem them that were under the law." (Gal. 4: 4.) In like manner, the casting out of the ruler of this world, and the drawing of all men to himself, have not yet been accomplished, though nearly two thousand years have passed since the words of Jesus were spoken. But the circle of the Redeemer's influence is ever enlarging, and the time will surely come when a great majority of the living will be subject to Christ—so large a part, indeed, that it will seem as if all were his friends. Then the world will be full of light. Then the broadest and deepest currents of human thought and action will be Christian. Then the heathen will be given to the Son for his inheritance, and the uttermost parts of the earth for his possession. (Ps. 2: 8.)

But in this language, properly understood, there is no reference to the generations that had passed from the earth before the death of Christ, or to the heathen who have, since that great event, lived without God and without hope in the world, or to the multitudes who have known and rejected the gospel of peace. It does not, therefore, teach the doctrine of universal salvation, but it foretells a reversal of the present religious condition of the world—a period when the reign of Christ will take the place of Satan's reign, and the spiritual forces of the world will be mainly on the side of righteousness and truth. Beyond this, the general scope of the passage does not warrant us in going.

33. This he said, signifying what death

CH. XII.] JOHN.

34 The people answered him, *We have heard out of the law that Christ abideth forever: and how sayest thou, The Son of man must be lifted up? who is this Son of man?
35 Then Jesus said unto them, Yet a little while *is the light with you. *Walk while ye have the light, lest darkness come upon you: for *he that walketh in darkness knoweth not whither he goeth.

34 ner of death he should die. The multitude therefore answered him, We have heard out of the law that the Christ abideth forever: and how sayest thou, The Son of man must be lifted up? who is this Son of man? Jesus therefore said unto them, Yet a little while is the light among you. Walk while ye have the light, that darkness overtake you not: and he that walketh in the darkness knoweth

a Ps. 89: 36, 37; 110: 4; Isa. 9: 7; 53: 8; Ezek. 37: 25; Dan. 2: 44; 7: 14, 27; Mic. 4: 7....*b* ch. 1: 9; 8: 12; 9: 5: ver. 46....*c* Jer. 13: 16; Eph. 5: 8....*d* ch. 11: 10; 1 John 2: 11.—1 Or, *in.*

(or, *by what manner of death*) **he should die.** That is, by crucifixion. No doubt, this kind of death was felt to be peculiarly ignominious and painful. Hence this allusion to it beforehand by the Saviour was recalled with deep emotion by "the disciple whom Jesus loved." See also 3: 14, where there is a similar prediction of the manner of Christ's death.

34. We have heard out of the law that (*the*) **Christ abideth forever.** Obviously the multitude failed to understand the meaning of Christ's language, as a prediction concerning the manner of his death, but gathered from it, either that he was expecting to be taken up from earth to heaven by the power of God, as was Elijah—a thought which might naturally be suggested by his words here, and by those recorded in verse 23—or that he was expecting to be removed from earth by death, according to an alleged Rabbinic use of the expression. But they were unable to reconcile *any* removal from the earth with the predictions of their Scriptures concerning the Messiah's reign; for they understood their Scriptures to teach that the Messiah would have his throne in Jerusalem, and would bring all the nations into subjection to himself as the King of Israel. (See Ps. 89: 36, 37; 110: 2-4; Isa. 9: 6, 7; Ezek. 37: 24, 25; and perhaps Dan. 7: 14.) **The law** is here used for the whole collection of the Jewish Scriptures, whose authority was recognized by the people as divine. (See Note on 10: 24.) For there is nothing in the Pentateuch which could have led the multitude to speak as they did; while the passages from the Psalms and Prophets, quoted above, sufficiently account for their language. **And how sayest thou**—with some emphasis on the pronoun **thou,** as if it were at least very strange that Jesus should array himself, while claiming to be the Messiah, against the word of God concerning the Messiah. **The Son of man must be lifted up?** They evidently borrow from the lips of Jesus (see ver. 23) his title, "the Son of man," which they had supposed him to appropriate as the Messiah, though now they hesitate whether he can have intended to do this. For if "the Son of man" is to be lifted up from the earth, he cannot surely be the Christ! **Who is this Son of man?** Meaning, "What sort of a personage is he? What is his mission, his office, his relation to the Messiah?" This appears to be the fairest interpretation of their question; for they must have been certain that Jesus had just applied the title to himself. (ver. 23.) Yet, Meyer may be right in saying that "the inquiry has in it something pert, saucy; as if they said: 'A fine Son of man art thou, who art not to remain forever in life, but as thou dost express it, art to be exalted!'" According to the former view, they are perplexed as to what Jesus can mean, and wish to be courteous in their response; according to the latter, they reject him and his word as unworthy of respectful notice. One thing is evident; that they have not the faintest idea of a suffering Messiah, or of a spiritual kingdom.

35. Then Jesus (*Jesus therefore*) **said unto them.** By *therefore* we learn that the following words were occasioned by the language of the people. Yet, Jesus does not enter into an argument with them, or attempt an explanation of what he had before said, for their satisfaction. But, as he was wont to do, he spoke with divine authority, and gave to his discourse a thoroughly practical aim. **Yet a little while is the light with you.** Spoken, of course, with reference to himself, (see 1: 4, 5, 7, 8; 7: 33; 8: 12; 9: 4, 5,) and calling their attention, in the boldest manner, to himself, as the highest, if not the only, source of religious truth. And at the same time he intimates that he, the true Light, is not to remain for any considerable period with them. The blessed privilege of learning

R

36 While ye have light, believe in the light, that ye may be *the children of light. These things spake Jesus, and departed, and *did hide himself from them. 36 not whither he goeth. While ye have the light, believe on the light, that ye may become sons of light. These things spake Jesus, and he departed and

a Luke 16: 8; Eph. 5: 8; 1 Thess. 5: 5; 1 John 2: 9, 10, 11....*b* ch. 8: 59; 11: 54.

the ways of God from the Holy One, who is "the brightness of his glory and the express image of his person" (Heb. 1: 3), will soon be withdrawn. Alas, that so many of them had closed their eyes to the light! **Walk while ye have the light.** Not while ye have the light, in the sense of "as long as," for this meaning is not well established; but, "*as*"ye have the light; that is, in harmony with the fact that ye have the light; walk as ye should walk, seeing ye have among you the perfect Teacher of divine truth. Receive his instruction; let his words enter into your hearts. "Walk according to your present state of privilege in possessing the light; which indeed can only be done while it is with you."—*Alford.* Lest **darkness come upon you** (or, as in Revised Version, *that darkness overtake you not*). Darkness is here represented as an evil ready to come down upon and take the persons addressed. (Comp. 1 Thess. 5: 4.) Light rejected is certain to be followed by thicker darkness. To refuse truth is to choose error. To turn away from the Holy One is to turn towards the wicked one. This was so in the time of Christ, and it is no less so now. **For (*and*) he that walketh in (*the*) darkness knoweth not whither he goeth.** For the meaning of the last verb, see 3: 8; 1 John 2: 11, and John 16: 5. "Thus," says Meyer, . . . "he goes away, without knowing the unhappy end, into everlasting destruction." Compare especially the words of this Evangelist: "He that hateth his brother is in the darkness, and walketh in the darkness, and knoweth not whither he goeth, because the darkness hath blinded his eyes." (1 John 2: 11.) Rev. Ver.

36. While (*as*) ye have (*the*) light. See explanation under ver. 35. **Believe in the light**—*i. e.,* "in me, who am the light of the world." To believe in the light is very much the same as to walk in the light, though in so far as the verb is concerned, this expression is more literal than that. **That ye may be the children (*become sons*) of light.** That is to say, truly enlightened. For as sons are naturally supposed to inherit the character, receive the instruction, and obey the will of their father, so, in figurative language, do men become *sons of light* when they experience the transforming influence of divine truth, and are purified and controlled by it. Observe that believing in the light is the same thing as believing in Christ, and that to believe in Christ, is to think his thoughts and to share his purposes—it is to love what he loves, and to seek what he seeks—to be identified as fully as possible with him, in feeling and motive and aim and effort. In this way men become "sons of light," pervaded and transfigured by the light which is life, and by the life which is light. For the rational and religious nature of man *lives* when it loves what God loves, and is in fellowship with him. This is the normal movement of reason, of conscience, of reverence, of devotion, out of which come peace, joy, and strength unspeakable; and none but those who become sons of light can be said to live the full and true life of the soul. The sons of darkness are the sons of death. To be ignorant of God, is to be without spiritual life or light—it is to be in "the outer darkness." **These things spake Jesus, and departed, and did hide himself from them.** These may have been, therefore, the last words of instruction and counsel which Jesus uttered in the hearing of the people. There were many who were thirsting for his blood. His lofty claims exasperated them; for they had closed their eyes to the light, and saw in Jesus nothing but an impostor and blasphemer, though he was the "Light of Light," the Word that was with God and that was God. And so he **did hide himself from them.** A most suggestive statement! From how many of "the wise and prudent" does the Christ hide himself still, because they treat his message with contempt! And is it not possible that he has hid himself from large portions of mankind, because he knew that they would reject him with scorn? Perhaps the writing of these words brought to the Evangelist's mind the language of Isaiah quoted below, and led him, under the inspiration of the Holy Spirit, who certainly honors and uses, as far as possible, the laws of mental association, to present the

37 But though he had done so many miracles before them, yet they believed not on him.
38 That the saying of Esaias the prophet might be fulfilled, which he spake, ᵃ Lord, who hath believed our report? and to whom hath the arm of the Lord been revealed?

37 ¹ hid himself from them. But though he had done so many signs before them, yet they believed not on him: that the word of Isaiah the prophet might be fulfilled, which he spake,
Lord, who hath believed our report?
And to whom hath the arm of the Lord been revealed?

ᵃ Isa. 53: 1; Rom. 10: 16.——1 Or, *was hidden from them.*

solemn and startling truth of the next paragraph (Ver. 37-43.)

37-43. REFLECTIONS OF THE EVANGELIST.

37. **But though he had done so many miracles** (or, *signs*) **before them, yet they believed not on him.** However important miracles may be as evidences that God is with him who works them, they do not convince those whose eyes are closed. For what is lacking to such persons is not clear evidence, but a willingness to consider and receive evidence. It will be noticed that John here speaks of *so many signs*, as if the number that had been wrought by Jesus in their presence had been very considerable—indeed, far greater than might be inferred from the instances specified by this Evangelist. For he mentions only six up to this time, viz.: The changing of water into wine, at Cana of Galilee (2: 1-11); the healing of the nobleman's son from a distance—Cana-Capernaum (4: 47-54); the healing of the man at the Pool of Bethesda (5: 6-15); the feeding of the five thousand, east of Genesareth (6: 5-15); the giving of sight to the man who had been born blind, in Jerusalem (9: 1-7); and the raising of Lazarus from the dead. (11: 1-46.) Of course, then, he knew of many others, but did not deem it best to describe them separately, either because they were sufficiently known through the other Gospels, or because they would add to the extent but not to the value of his narrative. (See 2: 23; 3: 2; 4: 45; 5: 36; 6: 2; 7: 31; 20: 30.)

The persons referred to as those before whom Christ had wrought so many signs, and who, in spite of them, were still refusing to trust in him as the Son of God and the Saviour of men, were the mass of the people, led on in unbelief by the influential scribes and Pharisees. All had expected the Messiah to be a Jewish prince, at the head of an earthly kingdom; and few of them could relinquish that expectation, or satisfy themselves that Jesus would fulfill it. But a general statement of this kind is not inconsistent with the evidence which all the Gospels afford, that for a time many of the people heard him gladly, and that a considerable number of them became his true disciples. The Evangelist, however, is now, at the close of Christ's public ministry, looking at the attitude of the great body of the Jews, and he perceives it to be one of persistent unbelief in him. He had proved to be "a root out of a dry ground," with no "form or comeliness," to the sinful nation in which he appeared. (Isa. 53: 2.) He had come unto his own, and his own had received him not. (1: 11.) Was the providence of God in this? or was the plan of God defeated by it?

38. **That the saying of Esaias the prophet might be fulfilled.** The plan of God was not defeated. For this very unbelief was predicted by Isaiah the prophet, and must therefore be freely indulged, in order that the word of God revealing a section of his plan might be fulfilled. For every part of that plan, even to the permission of unbelief, is regarded as holy and good by the Evangelist: and in the midst of his wonder and sadness at the rejection of Christ by the mass of the people, he can but notice the fact that their unbelief is involved, so to speak, in the omniscience and veracity of God. For God had chosen to make that unbelief serve the purpose of revealing his omniscience and supremacy, by predicting it ages before it was cherished in the hearts of Christ's contemporaries; and, therefore, when this prediction was fulfilled by their unbelief, the Evangelist could well say that, from a divine point of view, they were thus unbelieving in order that the word of God might be fulfilled. Nothing is accidental; even a particular course of sin may do something for the confirmation of faith, when it is so embraced in the plan of God that it is made to fulfill his word. But this is not, of course, a full account of the matter. The unbelief of the Jews might be contemplated from many points of view, though only one is here taken. For further remarks on

39 Therefore they could not believe, because that Esaias said again,
40 *He hath blinded their eyes and hardened their

39 For this cause they could not believe, for that Isaiah said again,
40 He hath blinded their eyes, and he hardened their hearts;

*Isa. 6:9, 10; Matt. 13:14.

the phrase, "that it might be fulfilled," see Note on Matt. 1:22.

The saying of the prophet is now quoted from Isa. 53:1: **Who hath believed our report? and to whom is the arm of the Lord revealed?** The word translated **report**, means, literally, "hearing," and then, "that which is heard." As used by the prophet in the passage cited, it denotes, not what he had heard from God, but what the people had heard from him, though the message which the people had heard from him he had previously received from God. It is plain that John regards this "saying" as a prediction of the unbelief of the Jews in the time of Christ. But whether the prophecy is typical, or, rather, direct, he does not intimate; it may be either, and yet have its supreme fulfillment in the time of Christ. The writers of the New Testament almost never distinguish between direct and typical prophecies. The one thing which may be learned from them in such a case as this is, that the language of the prophet had respect in the mind of God to events taking place at the Messiah's coming. "The lament of the prophet over the unbelief of *his* time towards *his* preaching (and that of his fellows, *our*), and towards the mighty working of God announced *by him*, has, according to the Messianic character of the whole grand oracle, its reference and fulfillment in the unbelief of the Jews towards *Jesus;* so that in the sense of this fulfillment, the speaking subject . . is *Jesus*, not the *Evangelist*, and those of like mind with him."—*Meyer*. The **arm of the Lord** is a figurative term, denoting his power; and that power had been signally revealed in the miracles wrought by Jesus, whether we consider their number or their character. The **our report** of the prophet is here fulfilled by the teaching of Christ.

39. Therefore (or, *for this reason*) **they could not believe, because that Esaias said again.** That is, because of another oracle of that prophet. But interpreters are not agreed as to the reference of the words **therefore** (*for this reason,* διὰ τοῦτο). Do they refer to that which precedes, or to that which follows? Does the Evangelist intend to say that the inability of the Jews to believe is accounted for by the fact that the prophecy just quoted must be fulfilled in the history of Christ? Or does he mean to say that this inability is accounted for by another passage in the writings of the same prophet, which reveals the method of God's providence? The expression may certainly be *anticipative* of the next clause, **because that Esaias said again,** and this affords the best meaning. (See 5:16, 18; 8:47; 10:17; 1 John 3:1, and ver. 18, above, for examples of this use of "therefore," or, rather, of the Greek words frequently represented by this conjunction.) With this view of the connection, the Evangelist may be understood to declare, first, that the unbelief of the Jews was a fulfillment of prophecy, assuring men once more of the truth and foreknowledge of God; and, secondly, by another passage, that their inability to believe was a result of their own rejection of light—and a result brought about by the innermost laws of their moral nature, which always, in the way of blessing or judgment, accomplish the holy will of God. This interpretation is suggested by the original passage, (Isa. 6:9, sq.), where the prophet is commanded, among other things, to "make the heart of this people fat, and make their ears heavy, and shut their eyes." For surely the prophet was expected to do this, not by moving upon their souls through any supernatural influence, but by declaring to them the word of Jehovah, which it was foreseen they would reject, while by the process of rejection and disobedience they would become more and more insensible and unspiritual. This, which the prophet had been commanded to effect in his day, had been effected by the preaching of Christ in a more signal manner; and therefore the Evangelist, adapting the language of the passage quoted to the circumstances of his own day, uses the past tense of the verbs, and says, as from Isaiah:

**40. He hath blinded their eyes, and hardened their heart; that they should heart; that they should not see with *their* eyes, nor understand with *their* heart, and be converted, and I should heal them.

41 "These things said Esaias, when he saw his glory, and spake of him.

Lest they should see with their eyes, and perceive with their heart, And should turn, And I should heal them.

41 These things said Isaiah, because he saw his glory;

a Isa. 6: 1.

not see with their eyes, nor understand with their heart, and be converted, and I should heal them. The pronoun **he,** the subject of the verbs **blinded** and **hardened,** must be God; but according to the import of the original passage and the connection here, he has done this blinding and hardening through a marvelously clear presentation of truth by his Son; so that, from another point of view, the blinding and hardening are wholly due to the sinful action of the people in rejecting Christ. And thus it is always. Hence Paul could say: "We are unto God a sweet savour of Christ in them that are saved, and in them that perish; to the one we are the savour of death unto death, and to the other the savour of life unto life" (2 Cor. 2: 15, 16); for he knew that the offer of divine grace to sinners was sincere, and honorable to God, even though their guilt was increased by refusing to accept it. Compare the commentary on Matt. 13: 10-15, and Acts 28: 26-28, where the same passage from Isaiah is quoted, and Romans 9: 6-33.

But while emphasizing the sinful action of men in the process by which they are blinded and hardened, there may be danger of forgetting the relation of God to this process. For this ever diminishing susceptibility to the power of truth on the part of those who willfully reject it, which becomes at last a sort of moral inability to receive it, may be looked upon as being, in a certain deep and true sense, God's judgment upon sin. For, in the first place, man's spiritual nature was originated by God, and the dreadful effect of sin in rendering that nature unresponsive to divine truth, was really provided for in the qualities of it; and, in the second place, the special environment of every human being is fixed, in a great measure, by the providence of God, and this environment has much to do with moral conduct. The signs by which God appealed to Pharaoh to let the Israelites go from the land, may have been selected and arranged with a view to bringing out the evil that was in the king's heart. The signs were such that he could nerve himself to resist them, one after another, until he was at last constrained by sudden terror to yield. Divine providence may be said to have co-operated with his own proud and selfish will in hardening his heart. The King of kings made the wickedness of this cruel monarch an occasion for revealing his own power to the nations, and especially to the chosen people, who had become disheartened by oppression. If there was anything which they specially needed, it was this —to be convinced that there was no mercy in Pharaoh, and all power in Jehovah.

41. These things said Esaias, when (rather, *because*) **he saw his glory, and spake of him. His glory**—*i. e.,* the glory of Christ in his higher nature, as he was in the beginning with God. (John 1: 1, 2.) This is evident from the whole context, and especially from verses 37 and 42, and is affirmed by the best interpreters—*e. g.,* De Wette, Lücke, Meyer, Alford, Godet, Lange, and many others. Enlightened by the Holy Spirit, the Evangelist knew that Isaiah was instructed by the same Spirit (Acts 28: 25), and that the theophany which he saw was a manifestation of the Eternal and Divine Word. (Comp. 1 Cor. 10: 4; 1 Pet. 3: 15.) Indeed, there is reason to believe that the theophanies of the Old Testament were, all of them, manifestations of the pre-incarnate Word. "John held the passage of Isaiah to be in such a sense Messianic, that, according to the method of interpretation which referred all the theophanies in the Old Testament to Christ, . . . he could only understand by the divine glory, which the prophet saw, the glory of Christ."—*Lücke.*

The earliest copies (א A B L M X. 1. 33, etc.,) read *because* (ὅτι,) instead of **when** (ὅτε,) and according to a strict interpretation of this, the best supported text, the Evangelist states that Isaiah delivered this severe oracle about the disbelieving and judicially hardened people, because he saw the glory of Christ and spoke concerning him. If then the oracle was fulfilled in Isaiah's time, that fulfillment was typical of a more striking and important fulfillment "in the fulness of the time," when

42 Nevertheless among the chief rulers also many believed on him; but ᵃ because of the Pharisees they did not confess *him*, lest they should be put out of the synagogue:
43 ᵇ For they loved the praise of men more than the praise of God.
44 Jesus cried and said, ᶜ He that believeth on me, believeth not on me, but on him that sent me.
45 And ᵈ he that seeth me seeth him that sent me,

42 and he spake of him. Nevertheless even of the rulers many believed on him; but because of the Pharisees they did not confess ¹ *it*, lest they should
43 be put out of the synagogue: for they loved the glory *that is* of men more than the glory *that is* of God.
44 And Jesus cried and said, He that believeth on me, believeth not on me, but on him that sent me.
45 And he that beholdeth me beholdeth him that

a ch. 7: 13; 9: 22....b ch. 5: 44....c Mark 9: 37; 1 Pet. 1: 21....d ch. 14: 9.——1 Or, him.

"the Word was made flesh" and dwelt among men.

Having thus referred to the unbelief of the great body of the people, the writer now remarks, that there was a considerable number who were convinced that Christ was the true Messiah, though they were too timid to confess their faith.

42. **Nevertheless among** (better, *even of*) **the chief rulers also many believed on him**. The word **rulers** probably refers to the members of the Sanhedrin, who were regarded by the Jews as pre-eminently their rulers in religious matters. The expression, **believed on him**, must be interpreted by the connection as denoting a rational conviction that he was what he claimed to be, but not a profound and saving trust in him. John uses the word "believe" to denote many different degrees of faith. Whether he refers in this place to men whose belief was as strong and practical as that of Nicodemus and Joseph of Arimathea, is doubtful; probably he has in mind persons who never took so decided a stand as these men afterwards took. (Comp. 2: 23, 24; 3: 2; 7: 48.) **But because of the Pharisees**—who were scrupulous, yea sanctimonious, in their observance of religious rites, but at the same time, bitter and powerful adversaries of Christ—**they did not confess him** (or, *it*,) **lest they should be put out of the synagogue**. See the words of Christ in Matt. 10: 32, 33; 12: 30; but compare Mark 9: 38, 40.

43. **For they loved the praise** (*glory*) **of men more than the praise** (*glory*) **of God**. By *the glory of men* is meant the glory that is from men, and by *the glory of God*, the glory that is from God. Hence these Sanhedrists were not men who had been renewed by the Spirit of God; their religion was not of the heart, but of the head; they had very little sense of the awful nature of sin, and no experience of the true peace which God imparts to those who delight in

him. For whoever cares more for human applause than for the approbation of God, is radically unlike the Saviour. (Comp. 5: 41, 44.) The heart can have but one object of supreme affection. It will be found impossible to give men the first place and God the second. Whoever attempts to do this will soon find that he is making a vain and absurd attempt, working against reason and conscience, and that he must give God the first place in his heart, or no place at all.

44-50. SUMMARY OF CHRIST'S PREACHING, AS RECORDED BY JOHN.

Having thus described, in ver. 37-43, the attitude of the Jews towards Christ during his ministry, and having shown that their course had been foreseen and predicted by God, the Evangelist now gives a resumé of what Jesus had preached, in order, it may be, to set in clearer light their hardness of heart.

44. **Jesus cried and said**. Not at any one time, but in his public preaching, and especially in his discourses to the Jews in Jerusalem, as preserved by John. While the people had been dull of hearing, Jesus had openly and plainly declared to them the way of life; and in such a manner that they had no excuse for rejecting him, who was that way. **He that believeth on me, believeth not on me, but on him that sent me**. That is to say, "I am the perfect representative of him that sent me, and he that believes in me believes in him. As the Revealer, as the Messiah, as the Light of the world, as the Saviour of men, I am inseparable in spirit and in action from the Father, and he who hears my voice, hears his voice; he who accepts my grace, accepts his grace. It is impossible for any man to trust in me without trusting in him; and every one who properly trusts in me, trusts in me because I am a revelation of the Father's love and power." (Comp. 7: 16; Mark 9: 37.) A paradox, suggestive of the deepest truth!

45. **And he that seeth** (*beholdeth*) **me**,

Ch. XII.] JOHN. 263

46 *I am come a light into the world, that whosoever believeth on me should not abide in darkness.
47 And if any man hear my words, and believe not, *I judge him not: for *I came not to judge the world, but to save the world.
48 *He that rejecteth me, and receiveth not my words, hath one that judgeth him: *the word that I have spoken, the same shall judge him in the last day.

46 sent me. I am come a light into the world, that whosoever believeth on me may not abide in the 47 darkness. And if any man hear my sayings, and keep them not, I judge him not: for I came not to 48 judge the world, but to save the world. He that rejecteth me, and receiveth not my sayings, hath one that judgeth him: the word that I spake, the

a ·h. 3: 19; 8: 12: 9; 5. 39; ver. 35, 36....*b* ch. 5: 45; 8: 15, 26....*c* ch. 3: 17....*d* Luke 10: 16....*e* Deut. 18: 19; Mark 16: 16.

seeth (*beholdeth*) him that sent me. Whoever looks upon Christ in such a way as to discern his true character and glory, beholds the divine character and glory. "In *his* working and administration, the believing eye beholds that of the *sender;* in the glory of the *Son* that of the *Father,* 1: 14; Heb. 1: 3.— *Meyer.* The language of this and of the preceding verse is in agreement with that of verse 41, in which the Evangelist represents the theophany which Isaiah saw (ch. 6) as a manifestation of Christ's glory. (See also 5: 24; 8: 19, 42; 10: 30, 38; 14; 10.) But it is surely difficult to vindicate either of these expressions (ver. 41, 44, 45) unless Jesus Christ was, in his higher nature, strictly divine. If the Word was God (1:1), but not otherwise, he could be a perfect revelation of God.

46. I am come a light into the world. The word I and light are emphatic by virtue of their position; and, perhaps, the exact force of the original would be more adequately represented by omitting the indefinite a before light. There is nothing equivalent to it in the Greek. The meaning is, "*I,* and no other, have come as in a pre-eminent sense, light, into the world of mankind, sunk in the darkness of sin." The expression is, therefore, substantially equivalent to 8: 12: "I am the light of the world." "Through me alone is it possible for men to have a true and saving knowledge of God." That whosoever believeth on me should (*may*) not abide in (*the*) darkness. That is, "my purpose in coming into the world is this, that every one who believes in me may pass out of spiritual darkness into spiritual light—out of death into life, out of error and sin into truth and holiness." (Comp. 5: 24.)

47. And if any man hear my (*sayings*) words, and believe (*keep them*) not. Or, it might be translated: "If any one shall have heard my words, and kept them not"— the speaker taking his place in thought at the last day, when the *hearing* and *keeping not* are already past. But the meaning would be

essentially the same with this rendering, as with the common one. The term hear denotes in this case the mental act of hearing, without the moral act of hearkening to or obeying, which is often implied in the use of this word. The term translated believe, or, keep, when used of doctrines, precepts, and the like, denotes keeping by *fulfillment,* and not merely guarding or holding fast in the mind.—*Meyer.* Hence, to hear the words of Christ and not keep them, is just the opposite of believing in him; for the words of Christ require belief in himself as the very root and source of acceptable service to God. "This is the work of God, that ye believe on him whom he hath sent." (6:29.) "This is the will of him that sent me, that every one which seeth the Son, and believeth on him, may have everlasting life." (6:40.) I judge him not: for I came not to judge the world, but to save the world. The word judge is here used in a *condemnatory* sense, as very often by the Lord, in his discourses recorded by John. Jesus here asserts that his object in coming into the world was to save it, not to condemn it; and that he is engaged in doing the former, not the latter— a statement which clearly proves that the fulfillment of prophecy, referred to by the Evangelist in the preceding paragraph, was not sought as an end by Christ, but was brought about by the sinfulness of the people, while he was offering them life and peace.

48. He that rejecteth me, and receiveth not my words. These two things always go together; for no one can truly receive and keep the words of Christ, without receiving him; and no one can hear the words of Christ, and receive them not, without rejecting him. For he is himself the very substance of his message. He declares himself to be the Good Shepherd, the Door of the Sheep, the True Bread from heaven. To accept his word is, therefore, to believe in him as the Way, and the Truth, and the Life. Hath one that judgeth him. The word

49 For *I have not spoken of myself; but the Father which sent me, he gave me a commandment, *what I should say, and what I should speak.

50 And I know that his commandment is life everlasting: whatsoever I speak therefore, even as the Father said unto me, so I speak.

49 same shall judge him in the last day. For I spake not from myself; but the Father who sent me, he hath given me a commandment, what I should say, 50 and what I should speak. And I know that his commandment is life eternal: the things therefore which I speak, even as the Father hath said unto me, so I speak.

a ch. 8: 38; 14: 10....*b* Deut. 18: 18.

hath seems to be emphatic. Such a one *has even now* his judge, and his trial has begun in the present life. For he is already condemned by the word which he rejects. It is a discriminating word, separating the wheat from the chaff. **The word that I have spoken, the same shall judge him in the last day.** For the voice of truth never changes; it will be the same at the last as now. He that believeth not is condemned already, and his present condemnation is sure proof of his final rejection: for the same truth which judges him now will be his judge when the heavens are rolled together as a scroll, and the elements melt with fervent heat. The **last day,** as used in this Gospel (see 6: 39, 40, 44, 54; 11: 24; and comp. "the last trumpet," 1 Cor. 15: 52), means the time of the resurrection of the dead, and of the final judgment—the time when "all that are in their graves shall hear his voice and shall come forth, they that have done good unto the resurrection of life; and they that have done evil unto the resurrection of damnation." (5: 29.) There are many last things, but "the last day" is of all others the one which men should be prepared to meet. And the last day of one's earthly life brings him judicially face to face with the last day of human history, when the Mediatorial reign will cease, and he that is unjust will be unjust still. (Rev. 22: 11.)

49. For I have not spoken (*spake not*) **of** (*from*) **myself**—*i. e.*, "not from myself, as a person acting apart from the Father." (See Notes on 5: 30; 7: 16-28; 8: 26, 28, 38.) Every word that he uttered was in harmony with the Father's will. He came to reveal the Father, but in doing this he revealed himself likewise. Of the latter fact, that he spake out of his own mind and heart, the Jews had no need of being reminded. They were all along disposed to insist upon this as the whole truth, and to deny that his message was the Father's also. Hence his continual and emphatic iteration of this thought, that his word must be traced back to a divine source—to the very mind and will of God the Father. But the **Father which sent me, he gave me a commandment, what I should say, and what I should speak.** The former expression, **what I should say,** may denote the *substance* of his teaching, and the latter, **what I should speak,** the *manner* of communicating it. The word **commandment** answers to the fact that Jesus was a theanthropic being, human as well as divine, and that he came to reveal, in his life and teaching, the Father's will. The statement does not differ in substance from that which Jesus made in Jerusalem, when "the Jews" asked in surprise: "How knoweth this man letters, not having learned?" viz.: "My teaching is not mine, but his that sent me... He that speaketh from himself, seeketh his own glory; but he that seeketh the glory of him that sent him, the same is true." (7: 16, 18; Rev. Ver. See commentary there.)

50. And I know that his commandment is life everlasting. In other words, obedience to his commandment insures eternal life. Or it may be still better to say that the word **commandment** here stands for the whole doctrine which, by the Father's will, Jesus taught—that is, for the truth which is called the gospel. This truth is a means of eternal life; this gospel, when received, is heavenly manna and living water to the spirit. Divine truth, in a soul prepared by the Holy Spirit to welcome it, is a source of holy affections—a fountain of love, joy, peace, and hope. **Whatsoever I speak therefore, even as the Father said unto me, so I speak.** In the preceding verse, Jesus is represented as declaring that God the Father had commanded him what he should say, and in this, as affirming that he speaks precisely as he has been told or commissioned to speak. (See on ver. 49.)

With these words the Evangelist closes his recapitulation of what Jesus had testified concerning himself and his teaching to the Jews

CHAPTER XIII.

NOW *before the feast of the passover, when Jesus knew that *his hour was come that he should depart out of this world unto the Father, having loved his own which were in the world, he loved them unto the end.

1 Now before the feast of the passover, Jesus knowing that his hour was come that he should depart out of this world unto the Father, having loved his own who were in the world, he loved them ¹ unto the

a Matt. 26: 2....b ch. 12: 23; 17: 1, 11.—1 Or, *to the uttermost.*

in Jerusalem. His effort to reach the people, and lead them to accept him as the Messiah, has failed. The members of the Sanhedrin, and a great part of the Jews following them as leaders, were now resolved to compass the death of Christ; and he, having taught them and wept over them, now leaves them to their doom, and speaks his last words before death to the little company of his disciples.

Ch. 13. The last appearance of Jesus in the courts of the temple, as a teacher of the people was on Tuesday, or, at the latest, on Wednesday. Then going away, as John relates, he was concealed from all but his intimate friends and disciples. (12: 36.) The place of his retirement seems to have been Bethany; and on his way thither he is supposed by Robinson (see "Harmony of the Gospels") to have foretold the destruction of the temple and the persecution of his disciples (Matt. 24: 1-14; Mark 13: 14-37; Luke 21: 5-19); to have described the signs of his coming to destroy Jerusalem, and to put an end to the Jewish State (Matt. 24: 15-42; Mark 13: 14-37; Luke 21: 20-36); to have predicted his final coming, at the Day of Judgment (Matt. 24: 43-51); to have spoken the parables of the ten virgins, and of the talents (Matt. 25: 1-30); and to have pictured the scenes of the Judgment Day. (Matt. 25: 31-46.) The supper at the house of Simon the leper, of which John has spoken already, may have taken place in the afternoon of Wednesday, or, as John's narrative suggests, in the afternoon, towards evening, of the preceding Saturday. (Matt. 26: 6-16; Mark 14: 3-11; John 12: 2-8.) During Wednesday, the rulers conspired to take Jesus by craft, that they might kill him (Matt. 26: 3-5; Mark 14: 1-2; Luke 22: 2); and from the hour of that supper, whether on Saturday or Wednesday, Judas began to seek a favorable opportunity to betray him into their hands. (Matt. 26: 16; Mark 14: 11; Luke 22: 6.) In the afternoon of Thursday, Jesus sent two of his disciples into the city, to make ready the Paschal Supper, that he might eat it with the twelve. (Matt. 26: 17-19; Mark 14: 12-16; Luke 22: 7-13.) All these events are omitted in the narrative, partly because they were well known through the other Gospels, and partly because they were not necessary to John's purpose in setting forth the divine-human personality of Christ.

1-11. JESUS WASHES HIS DISCIPLES' FEET. (*Fourth Passover*, April 7, A. D. 30).

1. Now before the feast of the passover. This note of time is indefinite. Considered by itself, it might refer to a period antedating the festival named, by the space of a moment, an hour, a day, or a month; but it might just as well refer to a period preceding and introducing the Paschal Supper. If it is to be connected with the last and principal clause of the verse, and if that clause, **loved them unto the end,** refers to the wonderful act of condescending love which the Evangelist goes on to describe, the hour intended must have been early on Thursday evening; for the supper which John proceeds to speak of took place at that time—soon after this illustrative act of condescending love. Thus far interpreters agree. But some believe that John supposed this Thursday evening to be at the close of the 13th and the beginning of the 14th day of the month—that is, one day previous to the appointed time for eating the Passover; while others believe that he supposed it to be at the close of the 14th and the beginning of the 15th day of the month—that is, at the regular time for eating the Paschal Supper. According to the former view, his narrative disagrees with the testimony of the Synoptical Gospels; according to the latter, it agrees with that testimony. For an able vindication of the latter view, see Robinson's Greek "Harmony of the Gospels," pp. 211-224. He says: "It has been the object of this Note to show that, upon all grounds, both of philology and history, the conclusion is valid and irrefragable, that the testimony of John in respect to the Passover need not be, and is not to be, understood as conflicting with that of Matthew, Mark, and Luke." **When Je-**

2 And supper being ended, *the devil having now put into the heart of Judas Iscariot, Simon's *son*, to betray him;

2 end. And during supper, the devil having already put into the heart of Judas Iscariot, Simon's *son*, to

a Luke 22 : 3 ; ver. 27.

sus knew (or, *Jesus knowing*) **that his hour was come that he should depart out of this world unto the Father, having loved his own which were in the world, he loved them unto the end.** Every clause of this verse requires explanation. But the principal statement is found in the last: **loved them unto the end.** It was the love of Jesus to his own that John saw in the significant act which he was about to describe. For the word **loved** is here used of that "singular proof of love which Jesus gave to his disciples by washing their feet."—*Grimm.* The Evangelist saw in this act perfect love, perfectly expressed—as, indeed, it was no unusual thing for him to see love itself in an act of love. (Comp. 1 John 4: 10, and 5: 3.)

The persons to whom this love was now manifested are described as **his own which were in the world**; the words **his own** referring especially to the little group of trusted followers whom he had selected from the larger number given him by the Father—to the eleven with whom he was about to observe the Passover, and to institute the Holy Supper; and the words, **which were in the world**, referring to the sphere of trial and service in which he had been with them, and in which they were still to be after his departure. But while these were, doubtless, especially in the mind of John, as those to whom the Saviour's love was at this time so tenderly expressed, there is no reason to suppose that he thought of that love as restricted to them. It embraced all who were at that time "his own," and, indeed, all who were to become his own in after ages. (Comp. 17: 20.)

The Greek words translated **unto the end,** sometimes signify "to the highest degree"; but this meaning, though preferred by some interpreters, does not agree with the clause, **having loved his own,** as well as does the one given by our translation. (Comp. Matt. 10: 22, and 24: 13.) John saw in the act of Jesus which he was about to describe the clearest evidence that the Saviour's love to his disciples continued to the last hour of his ministry on earth; he saw that in the immediate prospect of his agony, and of his consequent glory, Christ's deep and self-forgetful affection was signally revealed.

The first participial clause: *Knowing that his hour was come that he should depart out of this world unto the Father*—Rev. Ver.—has sometimes been understood to mean: *Though he knew that his hour was come,* etc.,—as if this knowledge might have been expected to turn away his mind from his disciples, and to render such an expression of love to them more improbable than it would have been at any previous moment. But it is, perhaps, more natural to find in this clause a reason for the act remembered by John. The prospect of at once leaving his own moved him to the wonderful act of love and condescension which the Evangelist relates. "Because he knew that his hour was come that he should depart out of this world unto the Father, he loved his own to the end." The second participial clause, in like manner, serves to account for the singular proof which he gave of his love. The fact that he had all along loved his own, helped to explain the depth and tenderness of his affection at the last moment. Love never faileth. It is crescent and immortal.

2. **And supper being ended** (rather, *as supper was taking place.*) This latter is a literal rendering of the first clause, according to the now accepted text. By it the writer points out more exactly the time when Jesus rose from his place to wash his disciples' feet. According to the preceding verse it was "before the feast of the passover" had actually begun; and according to this it was while supper was, in some sense, taking place—perhaps, soon after the preliminary cup of wine had been drunk, and while the principal course of food was brought on for the guests who had already taken their places at the table. Then, instead of beginning the meal, Jesus "riseth," etc. (ver. 4.) The clause before us has been variously translated: by Noyes, "And supper being served"; by Alford, "And when supper was begun"; by Davidson, "And when supper was ready"; by Meyer, "And whilst it is becoming supper time"; by Watkins, "And it now becoming supper time"; in the Bible Union Revision,

3 Jesus knowing *that the Father had given all things into his hands, and *that he was come from God, and went to God ;
4 *He riseth from supper, and laid aside his garments; and took a towel, and girded himself.

3 betray him, *Jesus,* knowing that the Father had given all things into his hands, and that he came forth from God, and goeth unto God, riseth from supper, and layeth aside his garments; and he took

a Matt. 11:27; 28:18; ch. 3:35; 17:2; Acts 2:36; 1 Cor. 15:27; Heb. 2:8....b ch. 8:42; 16:28....c Luke 22:27; Phil. 2:7, 8.

"And supper being served"; in the Revised English Version, "And at supper time." The Common Version, "And supper being ended," represents a different reading, which had the participle in the past tense instead of the present (γενομένου, instead of γινομένου.) **The devil having now** (*already*) **put into the heart of Judas Iscariot, Simon's son, to betray him.** This remark is inserted by the Evangelist, in order to show the wonderful depth of Jesus' love; for the traitor was one of those whose feet the Saviour stooped to wash, and a knowledge of the dreadful crime which darkened the soul of this man, did not quench the ardor or modify the expression of Christ's love. Meyer remarks that the full name of the traitor "contains a shuddering emphasis." This Evangelist does not tell us when Satan first put into the heart of Judas Iscariot the purpose to deliver Jesus into the hands of his enemies; but from the words of Mark (14:10) it is natural to conclude that this Satanic purpose was formed soon after, if not during, the supper at Bethany, in the house of Simon, when Mary anointed Jesus, and the money for which the ointment might have been sold was coveted in vain by the traitor. If so, the heart of Judas had been filled with the purpose to betray his Master for at least a full day, probably five days, and Jesus was perfectly aware of that purpose, together with all that had been done to accomplish it.

3. The word Jesus is to be omitted at the beginning of this verse. **Knowing that the Father had given all things into his hands, and that he was come** (or, *came forth*) **from God, and went** (or, *goeth*) **to God.** Here the knowledge of Jesus is so described as to exhibit in a clearer light his condescension and love in washing the disciples' feet, and the sense would be given by translating the verse: "Though he knows that the Father gave all things into his hands," etc. The Lord of all, stooping to menial service, out of love to his own! This is the point of view from which John here looks at the scene which he is about to describe. And it is certainly well chosen. From no other point can the amazing wisdom and love of the Saviour be more clearly seen.

4. He riseth from supper. For they had already taken their places around the table, though the supper had not yet begun. In what spirit the disciples had come to the table, may perhaps be inferred from the language of Luke 22:24: "Then arose a strife among them, which of them should be accounted greatest." If so, the rising from the supper, here mentioned, probably took place, as noted above, soon after the preliminary cup of wine had been drunk (Luke 22:17,) which was followed by ablutions, by bringing on the bitter herbs, the unleavened bread, the roasted lamb, etc. Whether the strife among the disciples was occasioned by the necessity that some one of them should wash his companions' feet, because there was no servant provided, cannot be known; but their contention may have been one of the occasions for the Saviour's act. **And laid aside his** (*outer*) **garments.** For the word here used signifies properly the outer garments, as do the words *coat* and *cloak* in English. **And took,** etc. ; or, rather, *taking a towel, he girded himself.* With what feelings did the disciples observe this? Why did they not all spring to their feet to take their Lord's place in the service which he was preparing to render? Was there in his countenance and bearing a holy purpose and authority that overawed them, and made it impossible for them to do aught but wonder and wait? Or, were they so filled with the spirit of rivalry that no one was willing at the moment, even for his Lord's sake, to waive his own claims and take the place of a servant? It is difficult to account for their remaining unmoved, unless we suppose that reverence or ambition prevented them from asking to do the menial service which they saw their Master undertaking. Possibly, in their surprise and confusion, they knew not what to say, or to do; but there is some reason to suspect that they may have been, one and all, unwilling to take the lowest place.

5 After that he poureth water into a bason, and began to wash the disciples' feet, and to wipe *them* with the towel wherewith he was girded.
6 Then cometh he to Simon Peter: and Peter saith unto him, Lord, *dost thou wash my feet?*
7 Jesus answered and said unto him, What I do thou knowest not now; *b* but thou shalt know hereafter.
8 Peter saith unto him, Thou shalt never wash my feet. Jesus answered him, *c* If I wash thee not, thou hast no part with me.

5 a towel, and girded himself. Then he poureth water into the bason, and began to wash the disciples' feet, and to wipe them with the towel wherewith he was
6 girded. So he cometh to Simon Peter. He saith
7 unto him, Lord, dost thou wash my feet? Jesus answered and said unto him, What I do thou knowest not now; but thou shalt understand hereafter.
8 Peter saith unto him, Thou shalt never wash my feet. Jesus answered him, If I wash thee not, thou

a See Matt. 3:14....*b* ver. 12....*c* ch. 3:5; 1 Cor. 6:11; Eph. 5:26; Tit. 3:5; Heb. 10:22.

5. After that (or, *then*) **he poureth water into a (*the*) bason.** That is, *the bason* that had been provided for such a purpose, and was, therefore, at hand. Hence the article. How distinctly is the scene portrayed! The narrative bears upon its face the clearest evidence that it was written by an eye-witness. **And began to wash the disciples' feet, and to wipe them with the towel wherewith he was girded.** From this language it appears that Jesus made an actual beginning in washing his disciples' feet, and, probably, with no remonstrance from them. With whom he began, the Evangelist does not say; but certainly not with Peter.

6. Then cometh he (or, *so he cometh*, or, lit., *he cometh therefore*) **to Simon Peter.** *Therefore,* (or, *so*)—*i. e.,* in pursuance of the task which he had undertaken to perform. This task brought him naturally to Simon Peter. **And Peter** (*he*) **saith unto him.** The words and, and Peter, do not belong to the true text, and are omitted in the Revised Version; but the question itself shows that it was addressed by Peter to Jesus. **Lord, dost thou wash my feet?** This was evidently spoken in a tone of remonstrance. Peter means to say that the manifest intention of Jesus is surprising to him. The emphatic words of his question are **thou** and **my.** He wondered that such a one as Jesus, the Lord, should purpose to wash the feet of such a one as Peter, the disciple. His question, therefore, with whatever feeling it may have been asked, contains a virtual affirmation that it would be far more suitable for the disciple to wash the Master's feet than for the Master to wash the disciple's feet. But it does not imply that even this disciple was ready to take his Master's place and finish the humble service that he was performing.

7. What I do thou knowest not now; but thou shalt know (or, *understand*) **hereafter.** Peter could not have been ignorant of the outward service which Jesus had been rendering to some of the disciples, and was now about to render to him; but the spiritual significance of that service—what it was morally and religiously—he failed to perceive. There was in it a depth of meaning, a lesson of condescending love for the sanctification of believers, which Peter did not now apprehend, but which was to be made plain to him afterwards. This promise may refer to the explanation recorded in verses 12-17, below; but it may also refer to the Holy Spirit, who, by his work in the souls of the disciples, was to reveal to them the full significance of the Saviour's life. The latter was, at least, included in the Redeemer's thought.

8. Thou shalt never wash my feet. This is the correct version of Peter's reply: "Neither now, nor ever, to eternity, shalt thou wash my feet." The negation is absolute; and, according to the true text, a secondary emphasis falls on the pronoun **my.** Is not this Peter our old acquaintance of the first three Gospels? Here, as there, his respect for Jesus is clouded by assumption. His intended confession of inferiority is dictatorial. Good is mingled with evil in his character, and we are pleased and offended by the same act. Are there not Peters in every age? **If I wash thee not, thou hast no part with me.** This is a second intimation (see ver. 7) that there was a deeper meaning in his act than Peter imagined. It signified more than a removal of dust from the feet; it was emblematic of the continued renewal (2 Cor. 4:16) by which the believer is made meet for an inheritance with the saints in light. (Col. 1:12.) For, though a persistent refusal to yield to his Lord's will in any matter, however external or trivial it might appear, would have separated Peter from the Saviour's kingdom and fellowship, it is far more natural to suppose that Jesus here referred to a spiritual cleansing, represented by the act of feet-washing, than to suppose that he referred to the mere physical act in question. For the former sup-

9 Simon Peter saith unto him, Lord, not my feet only, but also *my* hands and *my* head.
10 Jesus saith to him, He that is washed needeth not save to wash *his* feet, but is clean every whit: and ᵃ ye are clean, but not all.

9 hast no part with me. Simon Peter saith unto him, Lord, not my feet only, but also my hands and my 10 head. Jesus saith to him, He that is bathed needeth not ¹ save to wash his feet, but he is clean every

a ch. 15:3.—¹ Some ancient authorities omit, *save*, and *his feet*.

position best agrees with his language in verse 10, and well accords with the profound and suggestive, and, sometimes, enigmatical character of his teaching. (Comp. 2: 19-21; 4: 10, 13; 7: 37, 39.) To *have part with Christ*, is to share in his reign and glory and love (comp. Matt. 24: 51; Luke 12: 46; Rom. 8: 17; John 14: 3); to have **no part** with him, is to be forever separated from all that is capable of satisfying the soul. This threatening word of Christ, revealing to Peter the possible loss of all that he anticipated and longed for in the kingdom of his Master, caused an instant revulsion of feeling.

9. Lord, not my feet only, but also my hands and my head. That is, all the exposed parts of his body. The reaction of feeling carries Peter too far. He asks for something that Jesus had not done or proposed to do. His frank, bold, impulsive nature is not easily trained to obey the will of another. But the wisdom and love of Jesus are equal to the task of guiding this honest, though impulsive and powerful man.

10. He that is washed (rather, *bathed*). It may mean: *He that hath bathed himself,* as was probably true of the disciples, before coming into the city to eat the Paschal Supper. For bathing the whole body was customary in preparing for special religious services. **Needeth not save to wash his feet,** which must naturally have been soiled with dust in passing through the streets to the house where they had met to eat the Paschal Supper. Observe that the word translated *bathe* (λούω) is different from the one translated *wash* (νίπτω); the former denoting an ablution of the whole body, and the latter an ablution of a part of the body, as the hands or the feet. By rendering both the words **wash,** the Common English Version has obscured the meaning of the passage. "A symbolical significance is attached, in John 13: 10, to washing the feet, as compared with bathing the whole body, the former being partial (νίπτω), the latter complete (λούω); the former oft-repeated in the course of the day, the latter done once for all."—(Smith's "Dict. of the Bible," Art.,

Washing the Hands and Feet.) **But is clean every whit.** That is, in his entire body—a statement of the disciples' case at the moment when these words were spoken. For having bathed, as we may assume, before coming into the city, they needed but the washing of their feet to be virtually clean. **And ye are clean**—save as to the feet—**but not all.** This is added with reference to Judas; and, no doubt, as Meyer says, with deep grief. Moreover it shows that Jesus is not speaking of ritual purity merely, but also of the spiritual state which it represents. For the outward symbolizes the inward; and in speaking of ceremonial or bodily cleansing, he thinks of the purification of soul which it signifies. With one awful exception, the disciples had been renewed in heart. They had passed from death into life. They had been "saved by the washing (or, bath) of regeneration" (Titus 3:5), and their sins had been forgiven. But they were not yet delivered from all evil. It was still necessary for them to contend with sinful inclinations, and to mortify the deeds of the body. (Rom. 8:13.) Every day they had reason to offer the petition: "Forgive us our debts, as we forgive our debtors." (Matt. 6:12.) And this process of daily sanctification, by which believers are continued in fellowship with Christ, is here symbolized by washing the feet. Says Godet: "Peter is clean, for he has sincerely believed in Christ. What Jesus now does with him has not, then, for its end to reconcile him with God, but, by the example of humility which he would give him, to remove a particular stain which Jesus observed at this time in his own—the desire for greatness and earthly dominion. With this vicious tendency, Peter would not know how to do the work of God, or ever to have place at the table of Christ. Every Christian ought, therefore, to apply this saying to his own daily purification from the evil desires whose presence he detects in his heart. The word, the example, and the spirit of Jesus are the means of this growing purification, which is a necessary complement of the initial justification."

11 For *he knew who should betray him; therefore said he, Ye are not all clean.
12 So after he had washed their feet, and had taken his garments, and was set down again, he said unto them, Know ye what I have done to you?
13 *b* Ye call me Master and Lord: and ye say well; for so I am.
14 *c* If I then, *your* Lord and Master, have washed your feet; *d* ye also ought to wash one another's feet.
15 For *e* I have given you an example, that ye should do as I have done to you.

11 whit: and ye are clean, but not all. For he knew him that should betray him; therefore said he, Ye are not all clean.
12 So when he had washed their feet, and taken his garments, and *l* sat down again, he said unto them,
13 Know ye what I have done to you? Ye call me *2* Master, and, Lord: and ye say well; for so I am.
14 If I then, the Lord and the *2* Master, have washed your feet, ye also ought to wash one another's feet.
15 For I have given you an example, that ye also should

a ch. 6: 64....*b* Matt. 23; 8. 10; Luke 6: 46; 1 Cor 8: 6; 12: 3; 12: 3; Phil. 2: 11....*c* Luke 22: 27....*d* Rom. 12: 10; Gal. 6: ,, 2; 1 Pet. 5: 5....*e* Matt. 11: 29; Phil. 2: 5; 1 Pet. 2: 21; 1 John 2: 6.——1 Gr. *reclined*....2 Or, *Teacher*.

11. For he knew who should betray him (lit., *him that was delivering him up*); **therefore said he, Ye are not all clean.** Judas had already agreed with the chief priests to deliver Jesus up to them for a certain sum of money, and was waiting for a safe opportunity to fulfill his engagement. It came sooner than he expected. It is to be observed that John regards him as one who was already engaged in his traitorous undertaking.

12-20. CHRIST'S APPLICATION OF THIS SYMBOLICAL LESSON.

12. So after (or, *when therefore*) **he had washed their feet, and had taken his** (*outer*) **garments, and was set down** (*reclined*) **again, he said unto them.** Notice the enumeration of particulars, every one of which would be interesting to the disciple whom Jesus loved, but which would be likely to have no interest to one who was not present as a personal friend of the Lord. The several verbs, **had washed, had taken,** *had reclined*, and **said,** are in the same Greek tense, and they might be translated (with Davidson) "washed," "took," "reclined," and "said"; but the act of speaking referred to, certainly followed the other acts named, and, therefore, the sense of the narrative is best given by translating the first three verbs as if they were in the pluperfect tense, and the last verb, in the past, or aorist. **Know ye what I have done to you?** That is, the true meaning and intent of what I have done. This question is asked for the purpose of calling their attention to what he is about to say. For Jesus waits for no answer, but proceeds at once to speak of his act in such a way as to reveal its deeper sense. And no teacher ever availed himself more skillfully of all proper means of gaining the attention of his hearers, than did Jesus Christ. "He that hath an ear, let him hear." "Take heed how ye hear." "Verily, verily, I say unto you," etc.

13. Ye call me Master (lit., *the Teacher*) **and Lord** (or, *the Lord*), **and ye say well; for so I am.** Though Christ was "meek and lowly in heart" (Matt. 11: 29), having no love of human applause, no vain desire for the glory that cometh from men, he never reproved any one for ascribing to him the highest, even divine, wisdom or authority. (See Matt. 16: 16, 17; John 1: 50; 6: 69; 20: 28; 21: 27.) On the contrary, for the truth's sake, and for the glory of the Father, whom he represented, he sometimes directed the minds of his disciples, or hearers, to his divine prerogatives. The reference which he makes in this place to his Messiahship adds greatly to the force of his example and appeal.

14. If I then, (*the Lord and the Teacher*) **have washed** (or, *washed*) **your feet, ye also ought to wash one another's feet.** That is to say, in similar circumstances and for like ends, ye ought to render to one another such a service. For a service that is not too humble for the Lord to perform, cannot be too humble for the servant to perform. Moreover, it is the end sought by an act of service which determines the moral character and dignity of that act, and therefore if the end sought by an act which is servile in form and appearance is worthy of God, the act itself must be noble and divine.

15. For I have given you an example, that ye should do as I have done to you. There is no reason to suppose that Jesus intends by these words to make feet-washing a Christian ordinance, like baptism and the Lord's Supper. Had this been his purpose, the other Evangelists would have been almost certain to mention the Saviour's act of washing his disciples' feet at the Paschal Supper, and there would have been some traces of the practice as a solemn rite, in the Acts of the Apostles and in the Epistles of Paul. But there is no mention of this act by the other

16 ^a Verily, verily, I say unto you, The servant is not greater than his lord; neither he that is sent greater than he that sent him.
17 ^b If ye know these things, happy are ye if ye do them.

16 do as I have done to you. Verily, verily, I say unto you, A ¹servant is not greater than his lord; neither 17 ²one that is sent greater than he that sent him. If ye know these things, blessed are ye if ye do them.

_{a Matt. 11 : 29; Phil. 2. 5; 1 Pet. 2 : 21; 1 John 2 : 6....b Matt. 10 ; 24; Luke 6; 40; ch. 15; 20.——1 Gr. bondservant....2 Gr. an apostle.}

Evangelists, and no trace of such a rite among Christians of the apostolic age. The reference to "washing the saint's feet," in 1 Tim. 5: 10, is to an act of hospitality, and not to an ecclesiastical rite. "To abase one's self in order to serve, and to serve in order to save, is the moral essence of the act."—*Godet.* "It is the inward spirit of Christ, not the mere outward act, that is an example for us to follow; the cleansing love, not the girded garment and the washing of feet, that is our pattern. For the spiritual significance of this declaration, see ch. 17: 18; 1 John 3: 16."—*Abbott.* "The unwillingness to perform the act of feet-washing had been on the side of the disciples an 'example' of selfishness; the action of Jesus was an 'example' of condescending love. . . . It is clear that the idea that a sacrament is instituted here, is entirely out of the question; nor, furthermore, is the action linked with a promise."—*Tholuck.* It may also be added, that baptism and the Lord's Supper are expressly represented by the Saviour as rites to be observed till the end of the gospel age: "Baptizing them . . . . teaching them . . . and lo, I am with you alway, even unto the end of the world—or, *until the end of the age."* (Matt. 28: 19, 20.) The commission to make disciples, and baptize and teach them, was given with reference to all the nations and to the whole Christian period—till the coming of the Son of man to judge the world. In like manner, the Lord's Supper was made a permanent ordinance: "For as often as ye eat this bread, and drink this cup, ye do shew the Lord's death, till he come." (1 Cor. 11: 26.) But nothing of this kind is said in respect to feet-washing. Besides, it may be worthy of consideration, that immersion and the Lord's Supper are natural and self-interpreting rites, the world over; while feet-washing is only natural and necessary, as a frequent act, in hot climates, and with such methods of clothing the feet as prevail in such climates.

16. Verily, verily, I say unto you, The servant is not greater than his lord, neither he that is sent greater than he that sent him. A most solemn affirmation of the fact that they ought to perform the humblest service to their brethren, if by so doing they can promote their sanctification; for such a service their Lord had just performed. They were to be his apostles, sent forth by him to preach the good news of salvation, and direct men in the way of life: how unnatural and inconsistent for them to decline such a service as he was willing to render! Yet they had, within an hour, given evidence of a spirit which would lead them to do this. They had striven together as to who should be greatest, and were not yet prepared to be esteemed less than nothing for Christ's sake.

17. If ye know these things, happy (*blessed*) **are ye if ye do them.** With this saying may be compared the words of Jesus, in response to the exclamation, "Blessed is the womb that bare thee, and the paps which thou hast sucked!" "Yea, rather, blessed are they that hear the word of God and keep it." (Luke 11: 27, 28.) But this saying, which speaks only of good, has a tone of sorrow in it. For had not the disciples been unwilling to do **these things?** Could they fail to perceive that the love which their Lord had just revealed by his words and conduct was wanting, or very weak, in their hearts? Must not his assurance of blessedness, in case they should do **these things,** have awakened more of fear than of hope, at that moment? Perhaps they recalled his words on a former occasion: "Not every one that saith unto me, Lord, Lord, shall enter into the kingdom of heaven; but he that doeth the will of my Father which is in heaven" (Matt. 7: 21), or his declaration that the "servant which knew his Lord's will, and prepared not himself, neither did according to his will, shall be beaten with many stripes" (Luke 12: 47); and so, were alarmed, rather than comforted, by what he now said. "To him that knoweth to do good, and doeth it not, to him it is sin." (James 4: 17.) There are some who hear but to obey, and they are blessed; but there are many who hear without being willing to obey, and their condemnation is just. God's pleasure in the

18 I speak not of you all; I know whom I have chosen; but that the scripture may be fulfilled, *He that eateth bread with me hath lifted up his heel against me.
19 *Now I tell you before it come, that, when it is come to pass, ye may believe that I am *he.

18 I speak not of you all: I know whom I¹ have chosen: but that the scripture may be fulfilled, He that eateth ²my bread, lifted up his heel against me.
19 From henceforth I tell you before it come to pass, that when it is come to pass, ye may believe that I

a Ps. 41:9; Matt. 26:23; ver. 21....*b* ch. 14:29; 16:4.——¹ Or, *chose*...²Many ancient authorities read, *his bread with me.*

former is matched by his displeasure with the latter. From the blessedness which follows those who obey, may be inferred the misery of those who disobey. And these results of conduct are not chiefly rewards, or inflictions from without, having no natural connection with the conduct itself, but they are rather, for the most part, the proper fruits of that conduct, flowing out of the moral condition of the soul as unavoidably as the qualities of a particular fruit flow out of the qualities of the seed from which it derives its life.

18. I speak not of you all. The mind of Jesus turns to the traitor, and he feels keenly his presence. But these words, at the same time, imply his confidence that the rest of the disciples would prove, on the whole, faithful. He knows them to be sincere, and foresees that, though they may be weak, and fail "to do these things," uniformly they desire and endeavor to do them. But he also knows that one of the twelve is radically and thoroughly untrue to his Master. **I know whom I have chosen** (rather, *chose*). The I is emphatic. "Though you may not understand it, I for my part know whom I chose. And Judas is one of them." **But—I chose them, Judas included—that the scripture may be fulfilled, He that eateth bread with me hath lifted up his heel against me.** (Ps. 41:9.) That is, Jesus gave to Judas a place among the twelve with a view to the fulfillment of the "determinate counsel" of God, revealed in the Scriptures. The character of Judas was known from the first; and he was numbered with the twelve—not, however, against his own will, or for the purpose of hardening his heart—but because God could use the wickedness of a hypocrite and a thief in accomplishing a holy and gracious work. Christ knew that he must die; for he came into the world, "not to be ministered unto, but to minister, and to give his life a ransom for many." He knew, also, that one of his professed friends, who had received from him nothing but good, would betray him. He therefore chose one who was a hyp-

ocrite and a thief to be an apostle, offering him all good, and never tempting him to evil; but aware from the beginning that he was untrue in his professions of trust, and fit for villainous deeds, like that of delivering up his Master to those who were seeking his life. (6:64.) This appears to be the most natural meaning of the language here used, and the course of action which it ascribes to Jesus agrees with many statements of Scripture as to the use which God sometimes makes of men whose hearts are bent upon evil. (Ex. 7:2-5; Isa. 10:5-15; Ps. 76:10.)

The words, **He that eateth bread with with me hath lifted up his heel against me**, are quoted from Ps. 41:9, in which David is supposed to have described the treachery of Ahithophel, or of some other pretended friend, though David's experience was meant by the Spirit of God to be typical of the experience of his greater Son. Hence Jesus quotes but a part of the verse, namely, that which was, in a pre-eminent sense, fulfilled in his own experience; while he omits the words: "Yea, mine own familiar friend, in whom I trusted," because, if our interpretation is correct, these were not, strictly speaking, fulfilled in his own experience, since Judas was never one in whom he *trusted*. By quoting these words from the Forty-first Psalm, Jesus reveals his sense of the baseness and treachery of Judas, in the course he was taking. "Judas, so near to an act of treason, is like him who has already lifted up his heel in order to kick another."—*Meyer*.

19. Now (rather, *from henceforth*) **I tell you before it come** (*to pass*), **that, when it is come to pass, ye may believe that I am he.** Thus he takes every proper measure to confirm the faith of his disciples in himself, as being all that he had claimed to be, the true Messiah, the Son of God, and the Light of the world. By calling attention to his reason for predicting the treachery of one of his own disciples, he made it more certain that they would recollect this prediction when it was fulfilled, and see in it fresh evidence that he

20 a Verily, verily, I say unto you, He that receiveth whomsoever I send receiveth me; and he that receiveth me receiveth him that sent me.
21 b When Jesus had thus said, c he was troubled in spirit, and testified, and said, Verily, verily, I say unto you, that d one of you shall betray me.

20 am he. Verily, verily, I say unto you, He that receiveth whomsoever I send receiveth me; and he that receiveth me receiveth him that sent me.
21 When Jesus had thus said, he was troubled in the spirit, and testified, and said, Verily, verily, I say

a Matt. 10: 40; 25: 40; Luke 10: 16....b Matt. 26: 21; Mark 14: 18; Luke 22: 21.....c ch. 12: 27....d Acts 1: 17; 1 John 2: 19.

was the Messiah. *From this time*, is the only correct reading of the Greek expression (ἀπ' ἄρτι) here used, though it has sometimes been translated in this place *now*, or *even now*. It will be seen that he repeated the prediction a few moments later (ver. 21), thus taking away all objection to the view that the expression which he employs has its customary sense in this verse.

20. Verily, verily, I say unto you, He that receiveth whomsoever I send, receiveth me; and he that receiveth me, receiveth him that sent me. The connection of this saying with what precedes is not perfectly obvious; but it may be stated as follows: In predicting openly the crime that was soon to be perpetrated by one of the twelve, Jesus had in mind the future needs of his disciples, who were to be witnesses for him in perilous circumstances, first among the Jews, and then among the Gentiles. He desired to lay the foundations of their faith in himself as deeply as possible, for they were to be his representatives in teaching; and, if his representatives, then the representatives of his Father. In other words, Jesus wishes them to have strong faith in him (ver. 19), because they are to be his ambassadors, and so the ambassadors of his Father. (Ver. 20.) The meaning would not have been changed, if he had said: "*For* verily, verily, I say unto you," etc. This appears to me a better view of the connection than that proposed by Lücke, viz.: "Jesus wishes to encourage his disciples, who were disheartened, either by the thought of treachery originating among themselves, or yet more, perhaps, by the prospect of their Master's departure from them (comp. 14: 1); and he does this by setting before their minds in whose name and with what dignity they were to be sent out. (Comp. Matt. 10: 40-42; Luke 9: 48.)" Equally unsatisfactory is that of Godet: "If we consider verses 18 and 19 to be a simple parenthesis, occasioned by the contrast between the lot of Judas and the blessedness of the faithful disciples (ver. 17), we cannot easily doubt that a prominent trait of

this blessedness is promised, in verse 17, to the disciple who is humble and devoted, like his Master. Jesus had said: '*The servant is not greater than his lord*'; he now seems to say: 'The servant is *not inferior in greatness* to his Master.' To receive him, is to receive Jesus, and the Lord himself. (Comp. Matt. 18: 4, 5.)" Alford presents yet another view of the connection: "I believe that the saying sets forth the dignity of that office from which Judas was about to fall—*q. d.*, 'not only was he in close intercourse with me (ver. 18), but invested with an ambassadorship for me, and in me, for the Father; and yet he will lift up his heel against me.'" But this, again, is less natural and forcible, after verse 19, than the connection first stated.

21-30. ANNOUNCEMENT OF HIS BETRAYAL BY JUDAS.

21. When Jesus had thus said, he was troubled in (*the***) spirit.** These words imply a sudden accession of sorrow, a great disturbance of soul, as his mind turned again to the faithless one who was about to betray him. The human nature of Jesus was subject to agitation, conflict, and grief; for it was a real human nature—one that made him liable to temptation. The sight of Judas, unmoved by his act of condescending love, the washing the disciples' feet; unmoved by his reference to the betrayal, in verse 18; and wearing still a mask of hypocrisy which deceived his fellow disciples, filled the spirit of Jesus with grief and indignation. **And testified, and said, Verily, verily, I say unto you, that one of you shall betray me.** On these words, Lange remarks: "The inmost life of his human spirit was invaded by horror at the unprecedented fact of his approaching and imminent betrayal; the sight of the crafty one, and of his connection with the circle of disciples . . . tempted him to despise the whole race of mankind (?), and tended to produce in him an exasperation of spirit which he must summon all his energies to resist." It may be doubted whether just this is suggested by the expression, **troubled in**

22 Then the disciples looked one on another, doubting of whom he spake.
23 Now *there was leaning on Jesus' bosom one of his disciples, whom Jesus loved.
24 Simon Peter therefore beckoned to him, that he should ask who it should be of whom he spake.
25 He then lying on Jesus' breast saith unto him, Lord, who is it?

22 unto you, that one of you shall betray me. The disciples looked one on another, doubting of whom he spake.
23 There was at the table reclining in Jesus' bosom one of his disciples, whom Jesus loved. Simon Peter therefore beckoneth to him, and saith unto
25 to him, Tell us who it is of whom he speaketh. He leaning back, as he was, on Jesus' breast saith unto

a ch. 19: 26; 20: 2; 21: 7, 20, 24.

spirit. The feeling of Jesus was probably one of mingled indignation and sorrow; and the moment had now come when he could properly reveal the cause of that feeling, as well as the feeling itself. By the order of words in the Greek, the emphasis falls on **one of you**, rather than on **shall betray me**. It was the circumstance that one of his own followers, who had so often eaten with him, and listened to his words of love, was to deliver him up, that made his sorrow so deep.

22. Omit **then**, and read: **The disciples looked** (or, *were looking*) **one on another, doubting of whom he spake.** This, again, is one of the graphic touches which distinguish the Fourth Gospel, and prove that it was written by a most sensitive and appreciative eye-witness. According to Matthew, the disciples " were exceeding sorry, and began each one of them to say unto him, Lord, is it I?"; according to Mark, "they began to be sorry, and to say unto him, one by one, Is it I?"; and according to Luke, "they began to inquire among themselves which of them it might be that was about to do this thing." (Matt. 26: 22; Mark 14: 19; Luke 22: 23, Davidson's Transl.) But John remembers the look of surprise, of doubt, and of painful inquiry, with which the disciples turned one to another. The expression which was seen in their countenances was more significant to him than any words which they addressed to one another, or to Jesus. Yet he deems it proper to mention Peter's special appeal to himself, and the manner in which Christ answered the question which was asked in response to that appeal.

23. Omit **now**, and read: **There was (at the table) leaning on Jesus' bosom one of his disciples, whom Jesus loved.** "The custom was to lie with the left arm supported on the cushion, and the feet stretched out behind, so that the right hand remained free for eating. The one who lay next, reached, with the back of his head, to the *sinus* of the girdle of the first, and had the feet of the first at his back; in like manner, the third in the bosom of the second."—*Meyer.* The pronoun **whom** refers only to the one who was reclining in Jesus' bosom, and the clause denotes that this disciple was loved by the Saviour with a special love. The repetition of the word **Jesus**, in this clause, is singularly natural and expressive, showing how the grateful disciple appreciates the personal affection of his Master, and loves to repeat his name in speaking of his affection. It is not the fact that he is loved, but the fact that he is loved by Jesus, which fills the heart of the Evangelist with a joy and gratitude that, with all his modesty, he cannot repress. He is constrained to say, without mentioning his own name, that there is a disciple who will wonder and rejoice forever that he was loved by Jesus with a great and special love; and this disciple was reclining in the bosom of Jesus when the latter said: "One of you shall betray me."

24. Simon Peter therefore beckoned, etc. (Better, as in Rev. Ver., *beckoneth to him, and saith unto him, Tell who it is of whom he speaketh*). That is, *tell us who it is*, etc. "Peter was unable to restrain his sorrow and impatience. Eager to know and to prevent the treachery—unseen by Jesus, whose back was turned to him as he reclined at the meal—he made a signal to John to ask 'who it was.'"—*Farrar.* According to the best authorized reading, Peter expected that John could tell him which of the disciples was meant, either because he supposed that Jesus had already pointed out the person to the disciple whom he loved, or because he supposed that Jesus would do this privately at John's request. By beckoning to John, Peter gains his attention, and is able to address him in a whisper.

25. He then lying, etc., (or, *he leaning back thus*, or, *as he was*) **on Jesus' breast, saith unto him, Lord, who is it?** The first clause presents a very exact picture of the scene. John, leaning his head backward so as to touch the breast of Jesus, is able, unobserved by others except Peter, to whisper in his ear

Cн. XIII.]   JOHN.   275

26 Jesus answered, He it is, to whom I shall give a sop, when I have dipped it. And when he had dipped the sop, he gave it to Judas Iscariot, *the son* of Simon.
27 ᵃ And after the sop Satan entered into him. Then said Jesus unto him, That thou doest, do quickly.

26 him, Lord, who is it? Jesus therefore answereth, He it is, for whom I shall dip the sop, and give it him. So when he had dipped the sop, he taketh and 27 giveth it to Judas, *the son* of Simon Iscariot. And after the sop, then entered Satan into him. Jesus therefore saith unto him, That thou doest, do quick-

a Luke 22:3; ch. 6: 70.

the question which had been asked by his fellow disciple. With some of the best editors, I have recognized an adverb, meaning *thus*, as belonging to the text after the words *leaning back*. For though the manuscripts and versions are nearly equally divided in respect to it, the omission of this adverb by a copyist is more easily accounted for than its insertion. Its effect on the sense is only to hold the attention a little longer on the scene as it was present to the mind of the writer. *Leaning back* THUS—*i. e.*, as he was, in a reclining posture, and as he would naturally do, being in such a posture. A copyist would not perceive that anything was lacking to the sense, if he accidentally omitted this word; and the same fact would make it improbable that he supplied it by a natural law of mental action. It is a word that might be added by an eye-witness of the scene (comp. 4: 6), but by no other. I am, therefore, persuaded that it is genuine, and that it affords another evidence of the apostolic origin of this Gospel.

26. Jesus answered, etc. The Rev. Ver. is better: *Jesus therefore answereth, He it is for whom I shall dip the sop, and give it to him*. Both the question of John and the answer of Jesus were probably uttered in a low voice, not distinctly heard by the other disciples. The **sop** was a morsel, or small piece of bread, probably of the thin, flexible, unleavened loaf eaten at the Passover. Westcott says: "It is an Eastern custom, at present, for the host to give a small ball of meat to the guest whom he wishes to honor. The reference here may be to this custom." But there is little reason to suppose that Jesus meant to put any special honor on Judas. The most that can be said in this direction is, that his act was friendly, making one more appeal to the traitor's heart. It was an act of "sorrowful good will."—*Meyer*. The translation given in the Revised Version is made from the best authorized text, which differs slightly from that on which the Common Version is based. **And** (*so*) **when he had dipped the sop, he gave it** (*taketh and giveth it*) **to Judas, the**

son of Simon (*Iscariot*). From this language, it may be inferred that Judas was reclining so near his Master that, without rising or leaving his place, he could receive the morsel directly from the Saviour's hand; but it does not follow that he must have been next to Jesus on the left. That, which would have been the place of honor, as related to Jesus the Master, was probably filled by Peter. "Jesus first declares that one of the twelve shall betray him. (Ver. 21; comp. Matt. 26: 21; Luke 22: 21; Mark 14: 18.) They, in amazement, inquire: 'Lord, is it I? is it I?' (Matt. 26: 22; Mark 14: 18; Luke 22: 23), and Peter makes a sign to John, leaning on Jesus' bosom, that he should ask who it was. (Ver. 24.) John does so; and Jesus gives him privately a sign by which he may know the traitor, viz.: the sop. (Ver. 25, 26.) The amazement and inquiry still continuing, Jesus gives the sop to Judas (ver. 26); who, then conscience-smitten, but desiring to conceal his confusion, asks, as the others had done: 'Lord, is it I?' (Matt. 26: 25.) Jesus answers him (Matt. 26: 25; John 13: 27), and he immediately goes out."—(Robinson's "Harmony," § 135.) We have inserted in parentheses the references not given by Robinson.

27. And after the sop Satan entered into him. That is, after Jesus had given him the morsel, his spirit, under the influence of Satan, was turned against the Lord with a final and unalterable purpose to deliver him up. But this was not an instance of demoniacal possession. Judas was as free, and as truly responsible, as ever. **Then said Jesus** (or, *Jesus therefore saith*) **unto him, That** (or, *what*) **thou doest, do** (*more*) **quickly.** *Therefore*, namely, because of Satan's entering into him, and of his purpose to go on in the work of betrayal. Perceiving this, *Jesus saith unto him*, **That thou doest**—*i. e.*, "What thou art doing already, in spirit and purpose"; for, in the deepest sense, Judas was now engaged in betraying his Master. *More quickly*, or, *quicker*, may be understood as a comparative adverb, meaning "more quickly than thou art planning to do it"; for Judas was "linger-

JOHN. [Ch. XIII.

28 Now no man at the table knew for what intent he spake this unto him.
29 For some *of them* thought, because *a* Judas had the bag, that Jesus had said unto him, Buy *those things* that we have need of against the feast; or, that he should give something to the poor.
30 He then, having received the sop, went immediately out; and it was night.
31 Therefore, when he was gone out, Jesus said, *b* Now is the Son of man glorified, and *c* God is glorified in him.

28 ly. Now no man at the table knew for what intent he spake this unto him. For some thought, because Judas had the [1]bag, that Jesus said unto him, Buy what things we have need of for the feast; or, that
30 he should give something to the poor. He then having received the sop went out straightway: and it was night.
31 When therefore he was gone out, Jesus saith, Now [2]is the Son of man glorified, and God [2]is

a ch. 12: 6....*b* ch. 12: 23....*c* ch. 14: 13; 1 Pet. 4: 11.—1 Or, *box*....2 Or, *was*.

ing, and pretending (Matt. 26: 25) to share in the general doubt."—*Alford.*

The command is, not to do a deed about which Judas hesitated, but to do, in a certain way, a deed which was fully resolved upon by the traitor. Jesus knew that delay was useless—that his hour was come; and he now wished to be alone with his true disciples. Hence it appears that he was Lord over the *manner* of his betrayal and death.

28. Now no man at the table knew for what intent he spake this unto him. The Evangelist includes himself in this remark. And it is no way surprising that neither he nor any of his fellow disciples suspected the mission on which Judas was sent. How could they imagine that Jesus should hasten a traitor in his work? But Judas understood the meaning of Christ's language, for his soul was full of the dark purpose referred to.

29. For some of them thought, because Judas had the bag, that Jesus had said unto him, Buy those things that we have need of against (or, *for*) the feast; or, that he should give something to the poor. The word *for* is used because the actual thoughts of some show that they, at least, did not know what Jesus had in view when he said: "What thou doest, do (more) quickly." The words, **Buy those things that we have need of against (or, *for*) the feast,** have been supposed to prove that the meal which they were now observing was not the *Paschal Supper*, or, if it was, that the regular time of eating it was anticipated by Jesus. But in reply to this, Dr. Robinson remarks: "The disciples thought that Judas was to buy the things necessary for the *festival* on the fifteenth and following days. If now our Lord's words were spoken on the evening preceding and introducing the fifteenth of Nisan, they were appropriate; for some haste was necessary, since it was already quite late to make purchases for the next day. But if they were uttered on the evening preceding and introducing the fourteenth of Nisan, they were not thus appropriate; for then a whole day was yet to intervene before the festival."

30. He then having received the sop, went immediately out: and it was night. One cannot help feeling that the Evangelist added the last clause, partly at least, because of the harmony between the darkness without and the person who went forth into it. "This *conclusion* of the narrative respecting Judas presents, unsought, something *full of horror,* and precisely in this simplest brevity of expression something that profoundly *lays hold of the imagination*."—*Meyer.* The words of Christ after Judas had gone out may be said to form three groups: (1) His words to the eleven in the upper room (13: 31; 14: 31;) (2) His words to them on the way to Gethsemane (15-16;) and (3) His words of prayer to the Father for himself and his flock. (17.)

13: 31—14: 31. His Words to the Eleven in the Upper Room.

31. Therefore when he was gone out. Davidson translates this clause: "When therefore he went out"; but this translation introduces a Greek idiom into a language to which it is foreign. "Had gone out" is the proper English equivalent for the Greek expression. **Jesus said, Now is the Son of man glorified.** By sending forth Judas to his traitorous work, Jesus consented afresh to encounter the awful death by which he was to be glorified; he made this death a certain, and, as it were, an accomplished fact. And it was by this death that the perfect moral excellence of his character and mission was to be revealed. **And God is glorified in him.** In and by the Son of man, becoming obedient unto death, was also revealed the love, the holiness—indeed, the entire moral perfection of God. And this truth the Son of man declares in the plainest terms. As

32 a If God be glorified in him, God shall also glorify him in himself, and b shall straightway glorify him.
33 Little children, yet a little while I am with you. Ye shall seek me; c and as I said unto the Jews, Whither I go, ye cannot come; so now I say to you.
34 A d new commandment I give unto you, That ye love one another; as I have loved you, that ye also love one another.

32 glorified in him; and God shall glorify him in himself, and straightway shall he glorify him.
33 Little children, yet a little while I am with you. Ye shall seek me: and as I said unto the Jews, Whither I go, ye cannot come; so now I say unto 34 you. A new commandment I give unto you, that ye love one another; 1 even as I have loved you,

a ch. 17:1, 4, 5, 6....b ch. 12:23....c ch. 7:34; 8:21....d Lev. 19:18; ch. 15:12, 17; Eph. 5:2; 1 Thess. 4:9; James 2:8; 1 Pet. 1:22; 1 John 2:7, 8; 3:11, 23; 4:21.—1 Or, even as I loved you, that ye also may love one another.

death drew near, the reason for it filled his soul with light and strength.

32. If God be glorified in him, God shall also glorify him in himself, and shall straightway glorify him. The first clause of this verse is wanting in most of the very early manuscripts, and may, therefore, be no part of the inspired text. But, whether it be retained or omitted, the meaning of the verse is the same. Westcott (after Lachmann and Tregelles) omits this clause and gives the following as "a literal rendering" of the Saviour's words in verses 31 and 32: "Now was glorified the Son of man. And God was glorified in him: And God shall glorify him in himself. And straightway shall he glorify him." And he thus expounds the thought: "Even as God was glorified in the Son of man, as man, when he took to himself willingly the death which the traitor was preparing, so also it followed that God would glorify the Son of man in his own divine being, by taking up his glorified humanity to fellowship with himself." (Acts 7:55.)

Having spoken of his death as it was to affect himself, he next refers to the same event as it must affect his disciples. Notes of triumph are quickly followed by notes of sadness, which are at the same time notes of love.

33. Little children. A form of address peculiarly tender and affectionate, found nowhere else in the Gospels—and now, perhaps used for the first time by the Saviour. John employs the designation frequently in his First Epistle, e. g. (2:1, 12, 18, 28; 3:7, 18; 4:4; 5:21,) and it is possible that the memory of this scene endeared the word to his heart. Yet it is a very appropriate word, in perfect accord with the theology of John; for by derivation it points to a vital or spiritual sonship rather than to legal adoption. **Yet a little while I am with you.** As if he had said: "Only a little while am I with you," the moment of separation is at hand. **Ye shall seek me—** referring to their desire for personal union and communion with him—a desire which seems to have remained in their hearts to the end of life, and to have given a remarkable glow to their language in respect to his future appearing. **And as I said unto the Jews, Whither I go, ye cannot come**—see 8:21, and compare also 7:34—**so now I say to you.** For the departure of Christ would separate him temporarily from his disciples, as it would separate him eternally (7:34) from his foes. In going to his Father, through the dreadful pathway of death, he would enter upon a life distinct from the present, and inaccessible to "his own" in their earthly state. In view of this impending separation, he proceeds to enjoin upon them love to one another, making his own love to them the example and motive and standard of that love.

34. A new commandment I give unto you, That ye love one another; as I have loved you, that ye also love one another. Lange, with whom Schaff seems to agree, holds that the **new commandment** here spoken of was the institution of the Lord's Supper. Accordingly, he translates the verse as follows: "A new commandment give I unto you, in order that ye may love one another— even as I loved you, in order that ye may love one another." If this were a correct interpretation, it would follow that the object for which the Lord's Supper was established was to increase brotherly love among Christians. A noble object, indeed, but one that is nowhere else declared to be the purpose of this ordinance. Besides, it will be remembered that John (2:8) speaks of a "new commandment," having in mind, probably, this saying of Christ, but without alluding to the Lord's Supper at all. And still further, it will be felt by every reader that, if the words, **a new commandment,** in our passage, refer to the Lord's Supper, the reference is exceedingly obscure. This interpretation must, therefore, be rejected. But if the **new commandment** is explained by the following words, **that ye**

35 *a* By this shall all *men* know that ye are my disciples, if ye have love one to another.
36 Simon Peter said unto him, Lord, whither goest thou? Jesus answered him, Whither I go, thou canst not follow me now; but *b* thou shalt follow me afterwards.
37 Peter said unto him, Lord, why cannot I follow thee now? I will *c* lay down my life for thy sake.

35 that ye also love one another. By this shall all men know that ye are my disciples, if ye have love one to another.
36 Simon Peter saith unto him, Lord, whither goest thou? Jesus answered, Whither I go, thou canst not follow me now; but thou shalt follow afterwards.
37 Peter saith unto him, Lord, why cannot I follow thee even now? I will lay down my life for thee.

a 1 John 2:5; 4:20....*b* ch. 21:18; 2 Pet. 1:14....*c* Matt. 26:33, 34, 35; Mark 14:29, 30, 31; Luke 22:33, 34.

love one another, why is it called a *new* commandment? Is it not simply the old commandment: "Thou shalt love thy neighbor as thyself?" (Levit. 19:18; Luke 10:27.) We think not. It is rather a command to love those who are in Christ, *because* they are in him, and with a love which springs from devotion to him. As the Saviour himself had a love for "his own," distinguishable from his love to the ungodly, so "his own" should have a love for one another distinguishable from their love to mankind in general. It is a love rendered peculiar by a sense of union in Christ, and of supreme devotion to his will.

35. By this (or, *in this*) shall all men know that ye are my disciples, if ye have love one to another. This prediction was signally fulfilled in the early church. Nothing was more surprising to the heathen world, in the second century, than the love of Christians to one another. "Behold, they say, how they love one another! For they themselves hate one another; and how they are ready to die for each other! because they themselves are more ready to kill each other. And they defame us because we call each other brethren, for no other reason, I suppose, than this: that among themselves every expression of kinship is merely feigned. Yet we also call you brethren, in virtue of the nature which is our one mother, though ye are scarcely men, because ye are evil brethren. But how much more worthily are they called and considered brethren who recognize one Father, God, who have received the one Spirit of holiness, and who have awaked from one womb of the same darkness into one light of truth!"—(Tertullian, "Apol.," c. 39.) The last clause might be translated more literally, and perhaps more exactly, thus: *If ye have love among one another*, or, *if among one another ye have love*—the reference being to the love which they have within the limits of Christian brotherhood, or of those who are servants of Christ.

36. Simon Peter said (*saith*) unto him, Lord, whither goest thou? Peter was more deeply moved by the Saviour's assertion, that he was about to leave them, going where they could not come, than he was by the "new commandment," or by the effect which obedience to that commandment would have upon mankind. His love was now so warm, and his ardor so kindled, that he was preparing to deny the existence of any obstacle that he would not surmount in following his Lord. Probably he imagined that Jesus was about to assert by force his Messianic authority as King of Israel, and that his words were meant to remind the eleven of their lack of military prowess and courage to meet death on the battle field for him. **Jesus answered him, Whither I go, thou canst not follow me now; but thou shalt follow me afterwards.** Thus the Master answered the thought of the disciple, though not his question. For Peter's question was asked because he thought his Master could name no place nor danger into which he was not ready to follow him. And Jesus, perceiving this underlying thought, the real motive to his question, made his reply to it, reiterating his statement, that Peter could not follow him now; and then graciously adding that he would follow afterwards. The separation was, therefore, to be only temporary.

37. Lord, why cannot I follow thee now? I will lay down my life for thy sake (or, lit., *for thee*). Hence he has no suspicion that there is a divine plan which requires the separation of his Lord, by means of death, from the circle of his disciples. He imagines that their inability to follow him must be, perhaps, a want of courage to face death, or of fortitude to endure sufferings; and, if that be all, he makes bold, in the warmth of his affection, to assure his Master that one, at least, of his disciples is ready to die for him. This is Peter, as we have learned his character from the other Gospels—impulsive, self-confident, and a little apt to overestimate his own strength.

38 Jesus answered him, Wilt thou lay down thy life for my sake? Verily, verily, I say unto thee, The cock shall not crow, till thou hast denied me thrice.

38 Jesus answereth, Wilt thou lay down thy life for me? Verily, verily, I say unto thee, The cock shall not crow, till thou hast denied me thrice.

CHAPTER XIV.

LET not your heart be troubled: ye believe in God, believe also in me.

1 Let not your heart be troubled: [1] believe in God,

a ver. 27; ch. 16: 22, 23.——1 Or, *ye believe in God.*

38. Jesus answered, Wilt thou lay down thy life for my sake (or, *me*)? The Master repeats the very words of his overconfident disciple, so that the contrast between them and his prediction of this disciples' conduct in the hour of trial may be felt. **Verily, verily, I say unto thee, the cock shall not crow, till thou hast denied me thrice.** Far from laying down his life for Jesus, Peter would even disown him again and again before to-morrow's dawn. Doubtless, the spirit of Peter was such as to render this emphatic declaration necessary; for it is very noticeable, in all the Gospels, how perfectly the words of Christ are adapted to the moral state of those addressed.

Luke adds some particulars to this account. (See Luke 22: 31-38.) Matthew and Mark speak of a dialogue resembling this, as occurring after the company had left the upper room, and were on their way to Gethsemane; but the substance of the conversation may have been repeated under slightly different circumstances. Mark represents Jesus as saying: "Verily, I say unto thee, that thou, to-day, this night, before a cock crow twice, will deny me thrice." And it will be observed that, as the day began at sunset, Mark gives first the longest period, "to-day"; then a shorter one, "this night," and then the shortest, "before a cock crow twice"—*i. e.*, first at midnight, and then at three in the morning. The other Evangelists refer only to the cock-crowing at the hour of three A. M., for this was the oftenest heard, and the best known. There is no real discrepancy, therefore, between the four Evangelists as to the import of Christ's language to Peter.

At this point, probably, the Lord's Supper was instituted; and after it Jesus uttered the words of ch. 14.

Ch. 14. 1-6. JESUS COMFORTS HIS DISCIPLES IN VIEW OF THEIR FUTURE LIFE WITH GOD.

1. Let not, etc. Whether the Lord's Supper was instituted before Jesus uttered the words recorded in 13: 36-38, or not till after his prediction of Peter's fall, in the last verse of that paragraph (ver. 38.) cannot be certainly ascertained. Andrews and Gardner assign it to the former position, Robinson and Clark to the latter: and the latter seems to us slightly more probable than the former. But, according to either hypothesis, it is easy to see that the hearts of the disciples must have been troubled; in the one case, because the death of their Lord had been distinctly announced and set apart as an event to be commemorated by a solemn rite to the end of time; and in the other, because his immediate departure, amid circumstances that would lead the foremost disciple to a cowardly denial of his Master before another sun should rise, had been plainly foretold. How sweetly, then, must these words of comfort and of promise have found their way into the soul of the Evangelist who was reclining by the side of Jesus! **Let not your heart be troubled.** The word **heart** is frequently employed to denote the spirit when affected by joy or sorrow, hope or fear, peace or trouble, exultation or contrition. (Comp. John 16: 22; Acts 2: 26; John 14: 27; 16: 6; Rom. 9: 2; 2 Cor. 2: 4.) A little knowledge of human nature, assisted by a vigorous effort of imagination to reproduce in thought the scene, will enable one to realize, in some degree, the agitation and sorrow which the eleven felt at the words of Jesus declaring the crisis to have come, and the gracious influence of his assurance that, nevertheless they had ample grounds for peace, and trust, and hope. **Ye (?) believe in God, believe also in me.** The Greek original is here ambiguous. For the word **believe** may be imperative in both clauses, as we would translate it; or, indicative in the first clause, and imperative in the second, as the Common Version has it; or, indicative in both clauses, reading thus: "Ye believe in God; in me also ye believe." And any one of these three

2 In my Father's house are many mansions: if *it were not so*, I would have told you. ª I go to prepare a place for you.
3 And if I go and prepare a place for you, ᵇ I will come again, and receive you unto myself; that ᶜ where I am, *there* ye may be also.

2 believe also in me. In my Father's house are many ¹ mansions; if it were not so, I would have told you; 3 for I go to prepare a place for you. And if I go and prepare a place for you, I come again, and will receive you unto myself; that where I am, *there* ye

ª ch. 13: 33, 36....ᵇ ver. 18, 28; Acts 1: 11....ᶜ ch. 12: 26; 17: 24; 1 Thess. 4: 17.——1 Or. *abiding-place*..

translations gives a meaning pertinent to the circumstances and occasion. According to the first, which we prefer, Jesus exhorts his disciples to peace, to trust in God, and to trust in himself, also. According to the second, he exhorts them to peace, recognizes their trust in God, and calls upon them to trust in himself, also. And according to the third, he exhorts them to peace, recognizes their faith in God, and their faith in himself, also. In favor of the second view, it is said that the disciples certainly had faith in God, but they were still deficient in faith in Christ. We think, rather, that they had a certain degree of faith in Christ as well as in God, but that in both cases it needed to be strengthened.

2. **In my Father's house,** etc. God is here spoken of by Jesus Christ as being, in some peculiar sense, his Father, but also by implication as being, in another sense, the Father of his disciples. (Comp. 8: 35, and especially 20: 17.) Moreover, the heavenly home of his Father is represented as spacious, having many dwelling places. **Many** is the word emphasized. The family of God's redeemed ones will be large, but there will be no lack of abodes for them. And those abodes will be abiding places, places where they will remain (μοναί,) homes. When these are reached, the time of pilgrimage will be over. But the word **many** does not, as has been conjectured by some, imply variety in **the mansions,** and so point to gradations of happiness among the saved. That thought, however true it may be, is not contained in the words used by Christ. **If it were not so,** etc. Jesus thus claims to be, and to have been, absolutely frank with his disciples; so open and sincere that he would not have allowed them to entertain false expectations; much less, then, would he excite expectations which would not be fulfilled. This was said with the utmost simplicity and tenderness, as if to children, for the purpose of creating in their hearts the deepest confidence in his words.

For, (as in Rev. Ver.), **I go to prepare a place for you.** A reason for the preceding statement. If there had been no room for them in his Father's house, he would have told them, for he was going to prepare a place for them. If heaven, his Father's house and his own blessed home, could not be theirs also, he who was now leaving them to prepare a place for them would have notified them of that fact, lest "his own" might suffer disappointment at last. This appears to be the most obvious interpretation of the clause. Yet it may possibly refer to the exhortation to peace and trust: "Let not your heart be troubled," etc.—the clause "If it were not so, I would have told you," being virtually a parenthesis. The doctrine of the sentence is, that Jesus, by going to the Father in the way he was about to go, and by presenting himself before his Father in heaven, would make heaven a blessed home for all his disciples. All heaven would be ready to receive them, when "the Lamb of God that taketh away the sin of the world" should be exalted to the right hand of power. It would be "a prepared place for a prepared people." The word translated for, seems to have been a part of the original text, and has, therefore, been taken into account in explaining the verse.

3. **And if I go and prepare,** etc. Not as if there were any doubt about his doing this. The words only assume that his going and doing what he had promised, would be no more than a natural prelude and preparation for something that was to follow. The prepared place must not remain without the people for whom it is prepared. **I will come again.** When and how? Many hold that this points to a single event, to take place at one and the same time for all the disciples, that is, to the Second Advent of Christ at the end of the present age, or dispensation. But it may be observed that the Greek original of **will come** is in the present tense, and may, therefore, denote a process as well as a single act. Indeed, this is the proper tense of the Greek verb to express the continuance of a

4 And whither I go ye know, and the way ye know.
5 Thomas saith unto him, Lord, we know not whither thou goest; and how can we know the way?

4 may be also. ¹ And whither I go, ye know the way.
5 Thomas saith unto him, Lord, we know not whither

---

¹ Many ancient authorities read, *And whither I go ye know, and the way ye know.*

---

given act or process, and, in the present instance, might be represented by the literal version, *I am coming again*. Says Westcott: "Christ is, in fact, from the moment of his resurrection ever coming to the world and to the church, and to men, as the risen Lord." (Comp. 1 : 9.) Yet it may doubtless be said also, with Clark: "The promise of his coming again will only be realized in its fullness at his second advent at the end of the world; for not until then do Christ's people enjoy all the fruits of his completed redemption." **And receive you unto myself.** The Greek verb is here in the future tense, and may, therefore, refer to some particular event, as that of death, by which the believer is taken to the home of his Lord. (Comp. Phil. 1 : 23.) On this and the foregoing clause, Alford says: "The *coming again of the Lord* is not one single act, as his resurrection, or the descent of the Spirit, or, his second personal advent, or the final coming to judgment, but the *great complex* of all these, the result of which shall be, his taking his people to himself to be where he is. This "coming" is begun (ver. 18) in his resurrection—carried on (ver. 23) in the spiritual life (see also ch. 16 : 22 ff.) the making them ready for the place prepared; further advanced when each, by death, is fetched away to be with him (Phil. 1 : 23;) fully completed at his coming in glory, when they shall forever be with him (1 Thess. 4 : 17) in the perfected resurrection state." **That where I am ye may be also.** The word *there* may be supplied (as in the Common Version and the Revised Version,) before **ye**, but it is scarcely necessary. With this language may be compared the words of his intercessory prayer, 17 : 24, and the language of Paul quoted above. (Phil. 1 : 23; also 2 Cor. 5 : 8.) The comment of Godet on this verse deserves to be repeated: "With what touching simplicity and dramatic life are here expressed the ideas, so profound and so new, of the celestial glory of the believer and of the spiritual union with Christ here below, which is its indispensable condition! The house of my Father, the preparation of abodes, the return, the 'I will receive you to myself'—this familiar and almost infantile language is like a sweet music with which Jesus seeks to calm the anguish of separation." If anything could have brought peace into the perturbed and sorrowful hearts of the eleven, it must have been such words as these, assuring them of reunion with himself, their gracious and loving Master.

4. And whither I go ye know, and the way ye know. Rather, *and whither* (lit., *where*) *I go, ye know the way*—or, in customary English: "Ye know the way where *I* am going." The pronoun I is emphatic. What he had just said was, virtually: "I am going to my Father's house; you cannot follow me now, but the time will come when you shall follow me thither. For, as I have shown you, my body and blood are to be given for you in death (1 Cor. 11: 26), and the way I am going must therefore be known to you." It is not, then, necessary to suppose that Jesus was mistaken as to their knowledge. He only used the language of common life, ascribing to them a knowledge of that which he had told them, and which they must have understood, if they had been willing to receive his word. The disciples *could* have known, and *ought* to have known, that which Jesus assumes that they knew. Thus, we may say that he held them responsible for a knowledge of the way that he was going—that is, the way through death to the Father. And there is a deep truth in such language. Many are the men who know and who do not know at the same moment—many are the men to whose minds truth has been brought, but who have refused to look at it, and accept it. (Comp. 3 : 19-21.) This is oftenest done because their deeds are evil; and always because, for some reason, they are unwilling to receive the perfect truth.

5. Lord, we know not whither thou goest; and how can we know the way? Unable to accept, in their natural sense, the Saviour's words concerning his approaching death, Thomas had missed the import of his language respecting the Father's house. (ver. 2, 3.)

6 Jesus saith unto him, I am *the way, b the truth, and c the life: d no man cometh unto the Father, but by me.

6 thou goest; how know we the way? Jesus saith unto him, I am the way, and the truth, and the life.

a Heb. 9: 8....*b* ch. 1: 17; 8: 32....*c* ch. 1: 4; 11: 25....*d* ch. 10: 9.

Unable to comprehend his Lord's words concerning his Father's house, Thomas very naturally feels that he knows nothing of the way thither. For, ordinarily, a knowledge of the way to any place, implies some knowledge of the place to which the way leads. But Thomas feels himself to be ignorant of both place and way. His Master's words are very dark and enigmatical to him. Their obvious meaning is one that he will not and cannot receive; and rejecting that as impossible, his mind is full of perplexity and doubt. Indeed, the one great misapprehension which he will not surrender —that Jesus is to be a temporal prince, and therefore cannot literally suffer death, renders it quite impossible for him, or for his fellow disciples, to understand the mind of Jesus. Peter and the other disciples may have caught a passing glimpse of it (comp. 13: 37; Mark 14: 31), but no more than a glimpse; for they did not give up their vain expectation of a temporal reign till they were compelled to do so.

6. **I am the way, the truth, and the life.** Here, again, we have the emphatic *ego*. Jesus summons his disciples to look upon *himself* as the beginning and end of their salvation. Westcott quotes the paraphrase of Thomas á Kempis: "*Sine via non itur, sine veritate non cognoscitur, sine vita non vivitur. Ego sum via quam sequi debes; veritas cui credere debes; vita quam sperare debes.*"—("De Imit.," III. 56); which may be rendered, with much loss of flavor: "Without the way, we cannot go; without the truth, we cannot know; without the life, we cannot live. I am the way which you ought to follow—the truth which you ought to believe—the life which you ought to hope for."

Because of sin, men are separated from God; and only through Jesus Christ, who is giving his life for their life, can they draw near to God, and obtain pardon, purity, and peace. He is **the way**—*i. e.*, the one and only way—to fellowship with God. By his mediation, if at all, will they be saved. Through him, if at all, will they enter the house of many mansions.

Again; because of sin, men are ignorant of the highest truth; they know not God; his wisdom, holiness, goodness, compassion, are hidden from them; and no light of nature is clear enough to reveal to their souls these perfections of his being. But Christ, and especially Christ "the Lamb of God, that taketh away the sin of the world," is a perfect revelation of Jehovah. Christ Jesus, as he passes through suffering to glory, is the holy and the whole substance of **truth,** bringing to light the very heart of God. He is, so to speak, the sole and sufficient Word of God concerning himself, as merciful to sinners; and therefore he who receives this truth will never walk in darkness.

Still further; according to this profound saying of Jesus, he is himself **the life**—*i. e.*, the source, or fountain-head, of spiritual life for sinful men. And so the apostle who wrote this Gospel says, in his First Epistle (5: 12): "He that hath the Son, hath (the) life; and he that hath not the Son of God, hath not (the) life." Of course, the "life" is here more than conscious existence—it is "righteousness and peace and joy in the Holy Ghost," (Rom. 14: 17.), it is the sum and substance of all good to a moral and religious being—perfect communion with the "Father of lights." For this is what Christ enjoyed; and those who derive their life from him will be partakers of his joy.

The whole saying of Jesus declares what men may have in him, namely, the only way to God; the only perfect revelation of God; the only source of life with God. As soon as they accept the way, they accept the truth and the life. As soon as they begin to follow the way, they begin to know the truth, and to share the life. The consummate blessing is future; the incipient blessing is present. Those who believe in Christ have passed from death into life. The **I am** is therefore no mere prediction; it describes a relation that is present and permanent. Communion with God, through Christ, begins, but never ends. **No man (or, *no one*) cometh unto the Father but by (*through*) me.** If there were any reason to doubt the view which we have given of the way, the truth, and the life, namely,

7 • If ye had known me, ye should have known my Father also: and from henceforth ye know him, and have seen him.
8 Philip saith unto him, Lord, shew us the Father, and it sufficeth us.
9 Jesus saith unto him, Have I been so long time with you, and yet hast thou not known me, Philip? *b* he that hath seen me hath seen the Father; and how sayest thou *then*, Shew us the Father?

7 no one cometh unto the Father, but ¹by me. If ye had known me, ye would have known my Father also: from henceforth ye know him, and have seen 8 him. Philip saith unto him, Lord, shew us the 9 Father, and it sufficeth us. Jesus saith unto him, Have I been so long time with you, and dost thou not know me, Philip? he that hath seen me hath seen the Father; how sayest thou, Shew us the

a ch. 8: 19....*b* ch. 12: 45; Col. 1: 15; Heb. 1: 3.——1 *Or, through.*

that Jesus claims to be the *only* way and truth and life for sinful men, it would be removed by this clause. For here it is explicitly taught that no one comes to the Father, unless he comes through Christ. No wonder, therefore, that when Peter, filled with the Holy Ghost, stood before the rulers of Israel, he said unto them: "Neither is there salvation in any other: for there is none other name under heaven, given among men, whereby we must be saved." (Acts 4: 12.)

In this expression Jesus passes also from the thought of a heavenly home to that of a heavenly Father. He represents the "life" of men as attained by coming to the Father. A knowledge of God as their Heavenly Father—a sight of his glory in peace, is evidently regarded as the supreme good—as the **"life"** for which human souls were made; and he affirms that through himself alone is this filial access to God, and this real knowlege of God, to be gained—a thought which forms the nucleus of the next paragraph. (Ver. 7-11.)

7-11. GOD THE FATHER, PRESENT AND REVEALED IN CHRIST.

7. If ye had known me, etc. That is, *had come to know me.* Jesus had been living a truly divine life for many months in the presence of his disciples. The holiness and love of the Father had appeared in all his words and deeds. (5: 19-21.) But the eleven true disciples had not clearly perceived this. In spite of their intimate association with Jesus, they had seen but little of his divine perfection. For their eyes had been holden by prejudice and sin. Endeavoring to recognize in him the Messiah of their early hopes, and of the national expectation, they had apprehended very imperfectly the true glory of his character, the profound unity of his life with the life of God. But if they had truly known him, they would have known his Father also; and in so far as they had known him, they had known his Father. **And from henceforth ye know him, and have seen him.** So

near was the time of their true illumination, that Jesus speaks of it as already present. The great event of his own death and resurrection and ascension, together with the outpouring of the Spirit, was so near, so vividly present to the mind of Christ, that he uses the present tense in describing the effect of it all on the spiritual view of his disciples. We should omit the connective **and,** as probably an addition to the original text—principally because the sentence is more fluent and natural with than without it, and therefore it was more likely to be inserted by a transcriber, if absent from the text, than to be omitted, if present in the text. The evidence in early manuscripts and versions for insertion and for omission is pretty evenly balanced.

8. Lord, show us the Father, etc. Just what Philip meant by this expression, we do not know. Perhaps he desired some visible manifestation of the divine glory, such as was made at times to the ancient prophets. He may have imagined that, at the Saviour's request, the Father would appear in the Shekinah, and by his supernatural presence expel every doubt from their minds. But whatever he may have wished, it is plain that he did not understand the language of Jesus; and it is probable that the words, "from henceforth ye . . . have seen him," suggested the thought of a supernatural manifestation of the Father. How tender and loving, but, at the same time, how solemn and mysterious, must have seemed these sayings of the Lord to minds not yet open to the whole truth! We may wonder at their dullness; but, in their time and place, we should have been, without doubt, as dull as they.

9. Have I been so long time with you, and yet hast thou not known me, Philip? This may have been uttered either in a tone of gentle reproof or in one of sorrowful surprise. It is always difficult to penetrate the soul of a human being by the light of a single brief expression; how much more difficult is

10 Believest thou not that "I am in the Father, and the Father in me? the words that I speak unto you b I speak not of myself: but the Father that dwelleth in me, he doeth the works.
11 Believe me that I *am* in the Father, and the Father in me: *or* else believe me for the very works' sake.

10 Father? Believest thou not that I am in the Father, and the Father in me? the words that I say unto you I speak not from myself: but the Father abiding in me doeth his works. Believe me that I am in the Father, and the Father in me: or else believe

a ch. 10: 38; 17: 21, 23; ver. 20....*b* ch. 5: 19; 7: 16; 8: 28; 12: 49....*c* ch. 5: 6; 10: 38.

it to penetrate that of a being at once human and divine! Perhaps, then, the Lord's question was equivalent to the words: "As I have been so long with you, Philip, you ought surely to have known me; but you do not." Yet, when we bear in mind the true humanity of Christ, it is not improper to suppose that a feeling of sorrow mingled with surprise filled his heart at the words of Philip. Let us ever speak with cautious reverence in respect to that mysterious world—the divine-human consciousness of our Lord! Of this, however, we are certain, that Philip had not yet seen the full glory of Christ's character, nor perceived how near he himself had been to the Father. Ah, if but the eyes of his spirit had been opened! as the eyes of the prophet's servant were opened. (See 2 Kings 6: 17.) "Blessed are the pure in heart, for they shall see God." (Matt. 5: 8.) A prejudiced and sinful soul cannot see the presence of God, even in the holy person of Jesus. He that hath seen me hath seen the Father. Meaning, of course, not the essential nature of God, nor the Father as personally distinct from the Son, but the Father's mind and will, the Father's moral glory and grace, the Father's abhorrence of sin and purpose to save the lost—in a word, all the Father's perfection. For Jesus Christ, even while here in the flesh, was "the brightness of his (Father's) glory and the express image of his person," (Heb. 1: 3.)—*i. e.*, the true and adequate manifestation of the invisible Godhead. And being this, we conclude that he was divine as well as human. For if such a claim were put forth by any other being who ever trod the earth in human form, he would surely be pronounced insane, or blasphemous. That we do not and cannot think of Jesus save as the greatest and holiest being that has appeared among men, is proof of his deity as well as of his humanity. Observe, too, that this claim does not stand by itself; it is the basis of an appeal, the promise, as it were, of a reproof: **How sayest thou then, Shew us**

the Father? "Why ask for what you have received? Why seek to see what ye have already seen, and what you now behold? In me you look upon the brightest possible image and revelation of the Father; his whole heart, and life, and power are in me; why then do you say, 'Show us the Father, and it sufficeth us?'"

10. Believest thou not, etc. The mutual indwelling of the Father and the Son had been previously asserted by the Lord (see 10: 38), and Philip might, therefore, be presumed to believe it. Moreover, the Saviour had used language, on several occasions, which pointed to a perfect unity of will and action in the Father and himself, and which would naturally lead to the thought of mutual interpenetration and perfect communion of life—*e. g.*, (5. 19, 20, 30; 8: 16, 18; 10: 25-30.) But the disciples had failed to apprehend the full meaning of his words, and, therefore, he was now compelled to repeat them. **The words that I speak,** etc. This, too, is but a repetition of what he had often said before. (See 7: 16, 17; 8: 16, 18, 26, 28, 29.) Not from himself, as one separate from the Father, had Jesus spoken, but always in perfect union with the Father, and as one doing his will. **But the Father that dwelleth** (or, *abiding*) **in me, he doeth the works.** This transition from words to works is peculiar and characteristic. No one can read the Gospels without perceiving that the words and the works of Jesus are in perfect accord. They seem to flow from the same will and to reveal the same spirit. No shock is felt by the reader in passing from one to the other. Every sentence in his Sermon on the Mount is as full of authority as is his command to the winds sweeping over the Sea of Tiberias, or his words at the grave of Lazarus, in Bethany. And so, in a very important sense, his words were deeds, and it was perfectly natural for him to glide from the former to the latter, in such a case as the one before us.

11. Believe me, etc. How often does the

12 "Verily, verily, I say unto you, He that believeth on me, the works that I do shall he do also; and greater works than these shall he do; because I go unto my Father.

12 me for the very works' sake. Verily, verily, I say unto you, He that believeth on me, the works that I do shall he do also; and greater works than these

a Matt. 21:21; Mark 16:17; Luke 10:17.

word **believe** fall from the lips of Jesus in this Gospel! A hundred times does it appear in the record, and generally in the sayings of Christ. How strongly, then, must he have set his heart upon producing belief in the hearts of men, and upon strengthening it in the hearts of his disciples! "Believe in God, believe also in me," is the key-note of his preaching. But how often, too, was he obliged to admit a lack of proper belief, even in his most trusted followers! in the sifted wheat of the eleven who had been with him constantly for three years! Especially was this the case when he referred to his peculiar relations with the Father, or to the spiritual nature of his reign. It was so now. With the deepest love and sincerity, with tones of voice that were as impossible to fanaticism as they were to vanity or conscious deception, he said: "Believe me, accept my solemn and repeated testimony, that I am in the Father and the Father in me; but if you find this impossible—if, after all you have seen of me, my word is not enough, consider the mighty works, the signs and wonders which I have wrought, and, in view of these, believe me when I say, that 'I am in the Father, and the Father in me,' for these are manifestly works which none but God could do." To think that he must appeal to miracles once more! that he must array the *evidence*, as it were, before the minds of his disciples, *proving*, as well as asserting the truth! But we must not forget how stupendous a truth it was; how difficult for a few to receive; how seemingly incompatible with what Jesus had just now been saying as to his own death. All the contrasts involved in the being and the work of Christ were reflected in this profound discourse with his disciples, as the early evening was deepening into the night. Never were his infinite love and tenderness to his chosen more needed or more clearly revealed. He was all care for them, though the garden and the cross were just before him.

12-24. THE FAITH AND LOVE OF THE DISCIPLES ENCOURAGED BY THREE GREAT PROMISES.

Faith and love are inseparable Christian virtues, and their fruit is obedience. For faith cannot live without love, or love without obedience. We do not say, without *perfect* obedience; for neither faith nor love is perfect in this life, and therefore obedience remains imperfect. But obedience will keep pace with faith and love, improving as they improve; and when, in a better state, they become perfect, it will become perfect also.

12-14. FAITH ENCOURAGED BY THE PROMISE OF DIVINE HELP AND SUCCESS.

12. Verily, verily, etc. By the repeated **verily,** Christ seeks to give his disciples the utmost assurance of the truth of what he is about to say—partly, perhaps, because of its intrinsic importance to the full establishment of his reign over men, and partly, perhaps, because of its surprising character, rendering it a saying difficult to believe or receive. **He that believeth on me.** Observe, it is not believeth me—that is, believeth my word—the truth of what I say, but, definitely, **believeth on me,** or, *in me*—that is, trusts in me as the true Messiah and Son of God—makes me the personal object to which his faith is directed, and in which it terminates and rests. "Belief *on him,*" says Weiss, "includes the full conviction of his specific relation to the Father, and with this, of his Messianic calling in the highest sense." **The works that I do,** etc. The term **works** has just been used with special reference to miracles, and on this account we must not exclude miracles from its meaning here. But it should not be forgotten that Jesus appears to have regarded his miracles as secondary and subsidiary to his teaching. Their evidential value was, indeed, great to the Jews, and their significance, as acts of divine compassion, was clear; but they were mere sporadic flashes of light, and not the steady beams of the sun. They were intended to prepare the minds of men for his spiritual teaching, and not to hold an equal place with that teaching. And therefore, interpreting his words here by what he says in other places, and by the history of his people, we understand by **works,** all that he did in draw-

13 ᵃAnd whatsoever ye shall ask in my name, that will I do, that the Father may be glorified in the Son.
14 If ye shall ask anything in my name, I will do it.

13 shall he do; because I go unto the Father. And whatsoever ye shall ask in my name, that will I do,
14 that the Father may be glorified in the Son. If ye shall ¹ask anything in my name, that will I do.

a Matt. 7: 7; 21: 22; Mark 11: 24; Luke 11: 9; ch. 15: 7, 16; 16: 23, 24; James 1: 5; 1 John 3: 22; 5: 14.—¹ Many ancient authorities add, me.

ing men to himself, and implanting in their hearts true faith. These works were to be continued by his disciples, and, indeed, not merely by those who were listening to him at that moment, but by believers in him in every age and every land. **And greater than these shall** (or, *will*) **he do**—*i. e.*, "he that believeth on me will do greater works than those which I have done." A very wonderful promise! But has it been fulfilled? We think it has. For if we look at the wonders of the Day of Pentecost, together with the events that followed in the rapid spread of the gospel during the apostolic age, it does not seem extravagant to regard them as greater than any which took place during the ministry of Christ. And if we compare the spiritual results of the three most fruitful years of the ministry of Paul, of Luther, of Whitefield, or of Spurgeon, with the spiritual results of Christ's preaching and miracles for three years, we shall not deem his promise vain. And if it be urged against the latter instances that miracles are wanting, it may be replied that supernatural works in the realm of spirit are superior, rather than inferior, to those in the world of sense—that to raise a soul from death unto life is really a greater act than to raise a dead body from the grave. **Because I go unto my** (lit., *the*) **Father.** This clause is to be connected with the following verse, and the whole must be understood as depending on the word **because**, and as furnishing the reason why the believer in Jesus will do greater works than were done by his Lord in the flesh—of course, not including his sacrificial death. The presence of Christ with his Father will be the reason and pledge of extraordinary grace to his followers.

13, 14. And whatsoever ye shall ask in my name, that will I do, etc. These verses present several things worthy of note. (1) Their connection with the first part of verse 12 is important. The works to be done by believers in Christ, are to be done by divine help, in answer to their prayers. More definitely, they are to be done by help coming from Christ—**that will I do.** (2) This help is in some way dependent on his going to the Father—that is, on his glorification through death. In other words, the manner in which he is about to finish his earthly mission and go to the Father, is to make him a perfect Advocate with the Father. (See 1 John 2: 1.) Thus these verses are closely connected with the last part of verse 12, and should be separated from it by a comma only. (3) Their effectual prayers are to be offered *in the name of Jesus Christ.* This is clearly expressed: **Whatsoever ye shall ask in my name.** And this seems to have been the first occasion on which it was mentioned. (Comp. 16: 24.) What, then, is it to ask in the name of Christ? Some expositors take the name of Christ to be the element in which the prayer is offered, and regard *in the name of Christ* as substantially equivalent to *in Christ.* But an examination of the passages where the former expression occurs (namely, John 5: 43; 10: 25; 14: 26; 15: 16; 16: 23, 24, 26; and Mark 9: 38; 16: 17; Luke 10: 17; Acts 3: 6; 4: 10; comp. 2: 28), leads to the following view: (1) To ask in the name of Christ, is to ask as a servant of Christ, honoring his authority, trusting in his grace, and seeking to do his will. (2) Whatever a true believer in Christ—who rests not on his own authority, but on the authority of his Lord, and who seeks not his own glory, but the glory of his Lord—shall ask God to do, he may expect will be done. (3) Hence, asking in the name of Christ presupposes being in Christ; but the two expressions, asking in the name of Christ, and asking in Christ, are not precisely equivalent to each other. (4) The end contemplated by Christ in answering the prayers of his own is, **that the Father may be glorified in the Son.** The things which he will therefore do at their request will be those, and it may be those only, which tend to manifest the grace and glory of the Father. This furnishes another limit to the meaning of **whatsoever ye shall ask.** Only that which is asked in Christ's own name, and which, if done by him, will tend to reveal the glorious

CH. XIV.]   JOHN.   287

15 ᵃ If ye love me, keep my commandments.
16 And I will pray the Father, and ᵇ he shall give you another Comforter, that he may abide with you for ever;
17 Even ᶜ the Spirit of truth; ᵈ whom the world cannot receive, because it seeth him not, neither knoweth him: but ye know him; for he dwelleth with you, ᵉ and shall be in you.

15 If ye love me, ye will keep my commandments.
16 And I will ¹pray the Father, and he shall give you another ²Comforter, that he may be with you
17 for ever, even the Spirit of truth: whom the world cannot receive; for it beholdeth him not, neither knoweth him: ye know him; for he abideth

---

ᵃ ver. 21, 23; ch. 15: 10, 14; 1 John 5: 3....ᵇ ch. 15: 26; 16: 7; Rom. ⁸: 15, 26....ᶜ ch. 15: 26; 16: 13; 1 John 4: 6....ᵈ 1 Cor. 2: 14.... ᵉ 1 John 2: 27.—¹ Gr. make request of....² Or, Advocate; or, Helper. Gr. Paraclete.

---

character of his Father, does the Saviour here promise to do. But these are limits which every true Christian will approve. To suppose one dissatisfied with them, is to suppose him either thoughtless or self-willed, and so a stranger to the very spirit and reign of Christ.

According to the reading of verse 14, adopted in the Revised Version, and probably correct, it should be translated: *If ye shall ask me anything in my name, that I will do.* An emphatic repetition of the promise just given in verse 13. Yet with one modification; for the prayer is here represented as not only offered in the name of Christ, but also as addressed to *Christ.* This may seem at first sight inconsistent with another statement of Jesus in the same interview (16: 23,) but it is not (see Note on that verse), and it is quite certain that the apostles and early Christians did pray to their ascended Lord, (see Acts 7: 59; 9: 14, 21; 22: 16; 1 Cor. 1: 2), as well as quite certain that his own claims of unity with the Father in the work of human salvation, and of special headship over his people, were sufficient warrant for this. Notice also, that the pronoun I, (ἐγώ,) is expressed, and therefore, in some degree, emphatic. "It is I, myself, who, after my departure, will do this great work for you and with you." But the special way in which he will do this is not yet stated; only that it is to be done by himself in answer to prayer.

15-17. THE HOLY SPIRIT PROMISED TO THOSE WHO LOVE THE SAVIOUR.

15. If ye love me, keep, etc. According to the true text, the Revised Version gives— *If ye love me, ye will keep my commandments.* Love produces obedience. Indeed, it is itself the truest and deepest part of obedience, and the spring from which all other obedience flows. This inward movement of the soul to Christ in heartfelt appreciation and devotion, is the practical source of all outward action in accordance with his will. "The subject of the love of the disciples for Christ (comp. 8:

42), is peculiar to this and the following section. (15-31.)"—*Westcott.* Yet there is no true faith without love, and, therefore, whenever Jesus speaks of faith in himself he implies love to himself. Hence this section is closely connected with the preceding. By **my commandments,** must be meant all the precepts and directions which the Saviour gave to his followers, thus, not merely the "new commandment," but all his demands upon heart and life in their relations to God, to himself, to their fellow Christians, and to their fellow men, including all that he said of Christian ordinances and of church life.

16, 17. And I will pray (or, *ask*) the Father. The word (ἐρωτῶν) which we would translate *ask,* is not the word (αἰτεῖν) so translated in verses 13 and 14. In the Revised Version it is rendered *pray,* and by this change the reader is at least reminded that there are two words in the original. But scholars are not yet agreed as to the precise distinction between the two. Westcott (see his Note on 16: 29) holds that ἐρωτῶν has a peculiar sense in John, "expressing a request made on the basis of fellowship, and is used in the Gospel only of the petitions of the Lord. (Contrast αἰτεῖν 11: 22, Note.)" The same distinction is affirmed by Trench ("New Testament Synonyms," under the word αἰτέω.) But there is reason to question the correctness of it. Dr. Ezra Abbot, in an article of the "North American" for January, 1872, comes to the following result: "*Αἰτέω* (Αἰτέω) is, in general, to ask for something which one desires to *receive,* something to be *given,* rarely for something to be *done;* it is therefore used when the *object sought* is prominent in the mind of the writer; hence, also, it is very rarely employed as exhortation. *Ἐρωτάω* (Ἐρωτάω), on the other hand, is to request or beseech a person to *do* something, rarely to give something; it refers more directly to the *person* of whom the favor is sought, and is, therefore, naturally used in exhortation and entreaty."

It may be said with some confidence, that *erotan* (ἐρωτᾷν) is fairly represented by the word "ask," with its two meanings of putting a question and of making a request, while *aitein* (αἰτεῖν) is often used in the more urgent sense of seeking by earnest entreaty or petition for some good. **And he shall** (or, *will*) **give you another Comforter** (*Advocate* or *Helper*). The word **Comforter** is retained in the Revised Version, but it does not represent adequately, in this passage, the Greek term Paraclete (Παράκλητος.) For, notice (1) that Christ speaks of the Spirit whom the Father was about to give them, at his request, as *another* (ἄλλον) Paraclete, but not as a *different sort of* (ἕτερον) Paraclete. This implies that Jesus had been a Paraclete to his disciples, and that the Spirit would do for them substantially the same thing which he had been doing. But Jesus had not been chiefly a Consoler of his disciples, but the Father's Representative and Advocate with them, even as he was now to be their Representative and Advocate with the Father. (2) The Paraclete is here described as **the Spirit of** (*the*) **truth,** as if a principal part at least, of his service to the disciples would consist in imparting to them the truth of God, or, the truth as it is in Jesus; and this agrees with the account which Christ gives of that service in other parts of this discourse. (See 14: 26; 15: 26; 16: 8-15.) But the end for which Christian truth was revealed to the disciples was not simply, or even chiefly. to console them. Comfort was but a secondary object; the primary object was to make them true servants of Christ, lovers of righteousness and haters of evil, able to endure hardness as good soldiers of Jesus Christ, "steadfast, unmovable, always abounding in the work of the Lord." (3) The word Paraclete, as used by John in his first Epistle (2:1,) evidently signifies *Advocate*—*i. e.*, one who acts, pleads, intercedes with the Father for his own, who have sinned. And there appears to be no sufficient reason why the term should be supposed to have a different meaning here. For, certainly, the Holy Spirit may be said to act or plead for Christ with his people, and with mankind in general. He recalls and reveals the truth pertaining to Christ and to the Father, that men may be convicted, converted, enlightened, sanctified, and made strong in the Lord. He acts as the representative of Christ, inducing and enabling men to receive him as their Saviour and to obey him as their Lord. And there is, perhaps, no better term with which to express this than Advocate. If we were to select any other, it would be the more general term Helper; but we prefer to abide by that used in 1 John 2: 1. **That he may abide** (*be*) **with you forever.** By these words is described the fellowship of the Spirit. For **with** (μετά, properly *among*) is used with the genitive "in reference to personal association (John 3: 22; 19: 2; Acts 9: 39), and alternate action (John 4: 27; 6: 43; Matt. 18: 23), especially of intellectual or moral (Matt. 20: 2; 2: 3; 1 John 1:6.") (See also, Thayer's "Winer," Rev. Ed., p. 376.) Thus the Spirit would be associated with them in holy intercourse, as Christ had been. Really, though invisibly, he would be their Mentor and Guide, by reminding them, as their Lord's Advocate and Representative, of his works and words, character and claims, even to the end of time. Yet, observe that this is not promised as a fellowship of the Spirit with the church, or with the churches, but rather as his fellowship with individual disciples; primarily, with the clever. to whom he was speaking, but constructively, with all who should believe through their word. **Whom the world cannot receive, because it seeth him not** (*for it beholdeth him not*—Rev. Ver.), **neither knoweth him.** The unbelieving world cannot receive the "Spirit of truth," because it has no direct perception or mediate knowledge of him. The former is meant by *beholdeth*, and the latter by **knoweth. The world** has neither that knowledge of the Spirit which comes by inward experience, nor that which is gained by a candid weighing of testimony, or other evidence from without. And so, through culpable ignorance, it refuses to welcome his presence, even as his own people refused to welcome the Lord of life, when he came to them. (1:11.) **But ye know him.**[1] A blessed privilege and distinction, separating them forever from the unbelieving world! The present tense of

---

[1] The conjunction **but,** is probably to be rejected as forming no part of the original text. It is wanting in ℵ B Q, and it is much easier to account for its insertion than for its omission.

18 *I will not leave you comfortless: ᵇI will come to you.
19 Yet a little while, and the world seeth me no more; but ᶜye see me: ᵈbecause I live, ye shall live also.

18 with you, and shall be in you. I will not leave
19 you ᶠdesolate: I come unto you. Yet a little while, and the world beholdeth me no more; but ye behold me: because I live, ᵉye shall live also.

a Matt. 28: 20....*b* ver. 3: 28.....*c* ch. 16: 16....*d* 1 Cor. 15: 20.——1 Or, *Orphans*....Or, *and ye shall live.*

the verb is not, in the opinion of Weiss, to be understood as anticipating the future, but as "denoting a characteristic relation of the disciples to the Spirit, without regard to a definite time." And nearly the same view is expressed by Westcott. But whatever the Spirit may have been to the disciples, up to this moment (and we do not question his presence in their hearts), Jesus appears to have had in mind a greater manifestation of his presence and power in the future. The whole context favors a *proleptical*, or anticipatory, use of the present tense. In a very important sense, the characteristic relation of the disciples to the Spirit, was to begin after the Saviour's departure. (Comp. ver. 25, 26; 15: 26; 16: 7). **For he dwelleth** (or, *and he abideth*) **with you, and shall be in you.** The expression **with you** (παρ' ὑμῖν, literally, *beside* you), though different from the one used in verse 16, has nearly the same meaning. It may possibly suggest the personality of the Spirit a little more distinctly than that, but both of them point to intimate connection and association. The Spirit was to remain with them permanently, and by his presence qualify them for all their work. (Comp. Ex. 3: 12.) Nay, he was to be *in* them—a Spirit in their spirits, illuminating, quickening, encouraging, by a most immediate, though mysterious, action on mind, heart, and will, taking and presenting to them the things of Christ with such clearness, that Christ's glory would be seen by them more perfectly than it had ever been seen while he was walking beside them in bodily form.

18-24. JESUS HIMSELF AND THE FATHER WILL BE PRESENT WITH THEM BY THE SPIRIT.

18. I will not leave you comfortless (*orphans*). Jesus had already, in this discourse, called his disciples "little children." (13: 33.) His love for them at this moment was like a father's love to his children. But he was able to say to them words which no dying father can say to his little ones: "I will not leave you in the condition of orphans, alone, unprotected, comfortless." **I will come** (lit., *come=am coming*) **to you.** "The presence of the Advocate will be my presence. He will come with all my power, grace, and truth, and so, in a spiritual sense, I shall be with you. To your minds and hearts, I shall be nearer by his agency than I am now by my bodily presence and words of love. My person and my work, as the Son of God and Saviour of men, will be presented to your souls as never before; and my power will be with you in every time of need." Some interpreters hold that this promise of coming to his disciples was fulfilled when Jesus "showed himself to them alive, after his passion, by many infallible proofs, being seen of them forty days." (Acts 1: 3.) But, not to insist on the brief and sporadic character of those manifestations, the following verses, especially 21 and 23, do not agree with this view. (Comp. Matt. 28: 20.) Others hold that the promise refers to the second coming of Christ. But against their interpretation may be urged the prediction that, at his second coming, "every eye shall see him" (Rev. 1: 7), while verse 19 shows that "the world" will not behold him at the return to his disciples which is here predicted.

19. Yet a little while, etc. "The world can now see me in bodily form, but after a few hours I shall be withdrawn from its sight." The hostile world will not behold him, for it has no spiritual vision—it cannot behold, or know, or receive the promised Advocate, the Spirit of truth, in and by whom the Saviour is coming back, with richer blessing, to his own. **But ye see** (*behold*) **me.** Again the present in the sense of the future: "Ye will behold me at my coming, through the Spirit." The Day of Pentecost witnessed the fulfillment of these words. **Because I live, ye shall live also.** The words may also be translated, *for I live, and ye shall live.* This construction is defended by Watkins and Weiss, but is rejected by most interpreters. It gives a feebler sense than the usual construction, and it is not required by the context. As to the life promised to the disciples, it can be no other than the new and blessed

20 At that day ye shall know that *I am in my Father, and ye in me, and I in you.
21 ᵇHe that hath my commandments, and keepeth them, he it is that loveth me: and he that loveth me shall be loved of my Father, and I will love him, and will manifest myself to him.

20 In that day ye shall know that I am in my Father, and ye in me, and I in you. He that hath my commandments, and keepeth them, he it is that loveth me: and he that loveth me shall be loved of my Father, and I will love him, and will manifest

a ver. 10; ch. 10: 38; 17: 21, 23, 26....*b* ver. 15: 23; 1 John 2: 5; 5: 3.

life of fellowship with God, which begins here, and reaches perfection hereafter. But this life of the disciples is represented as dependent on the life of Jesus: **Because I live,** etc. Is there any objection to the view that Jesus claims for himself, at this point, just such a life of fellowship with God? Of the rightfulness of this claim, his resurrection from the dead would soon furnish overwhelming evidence. And because this life had been, and would continue to be, perfect in himself; because his union with the Father was perfect, and his doing the Father's will, even to the suffering of death, perfect—he could be the Author of life to every one that believeth. And this spiritual life was the necessary condition of beholding Christ in and through the Paraclete. The sense, therefore, is: "Ye will behold me again when the Paraclete is given; for, though I go from you to the Father, by way of the cross, I shall have uninterrupted fellowship with him, accomplishing his purpose of redemption; and through me, you will also be in fellowship with the Father and the Son."

20. **At (or, in) that day, ye shall know,** etc. A profound description of the life just promised to the disciples! When the Spirit should be given, they, in contrast with the unbelieving world, and perhaps in distinction from their present selves, should know by his illumination the perfect fellowship uniting the Son of God with his Father, and with his true followers. Notice the double expression of the fellowship between himself and his chosen—ye in me, and I in you; ye sharing my purposes, and seeking my honor, and I sympathizing with your infirmity, and strengthening your hope.

21. **He that hath my commandments, and keepeth them, he it is that loveth me.** Christ here assumes that he has given commandments to men. He therefore virtually claims to be their Lord. Moreover, he declares that true obedience to these commands is proof of love to himself. Hence such obedience can spring from no other affection; for if it could spring from any other affection, or be rendered without any affection, it would be no certain evidence of love. (Comp. ver. 15 and Note.) And may we not infer from the emphatic **he it is that loveth me,** that one who fails to obey Christ's commandments is destitute of love to him? Does it not imply that he, and only he, who keeps his Lord's commandments, can be said to love him? **And he that loveth me shall be loved of my Father.** The Father's love to the Son renders it certain that his love will flow forth to all who love and honor the Son. The same thing had been said, in other words, months before, to the Jews (5: 20-23.) And it agrees with all that is written about the character of Christ. For as the Son is "the brightness of his (the Father's) glory, and the express image of his person" (Heb. 1: 3), as Jesus could say, "he that hath seen me, hath seen the Father" (ver. 9, above); it follows that love to the Son, in his true character, is identical in moral quality with love to the Father, and must, therefore, call forth responsive love from him. **And I will love him.** For whom the Father loves, the Son will love, not only because he is always and absolutely of one mind with the Father; and because, loving the Father with a perfect love, he delights in all who honor and obey him—but also because he appreciates the love of his own to himself, and wishes to assure them again and again of his own love to them—a love which, as they will soon know, is stronger than death. **And will manifest myself to him.** The word translated **manifest** (ἐμφανίζειν), is found also in Matt. 27: 53, and Heb. 9: 24; while the corresponding adjective (ἐμφανής) occurs in Acts 10: 40, and Rom. 10: 20. "The exact force of the word," remarks Westcott, "is that of presentation in a clear, conspicuous form." Yet Jesus does not here refer (see ver. 23) to any visible manifestation of himself in bodily form after his resurrection, but rather to the very distinct view of himself which he would give to the disciples by the Spirit. Through the Spirit's agency, he himself, in all the glory of

22 a Judas saith unto him, not Iscariot, Lord, how is it that thou wilt manifest thyself unto us, and not unto the world?
23 Jesus answered and said unto him, b If a man love me, he will keep my words: and my Father will love him, and c we will come unto him, and make our abode with him.
24 He that loveth me not keepeth not my sayings: and d the word which ye hear is not mine, but the Father's which sent me.

a Luke 6:16....b ver. 15....c 1 John 2:24; Rev. 3:20....d ch. 5:19, 38; 7:16; 8:28; 12:49; ver. 10.

his character and work, would be presented to their minds. (Comp. Gal. 3:1.) And this higher manifestation of Christ, though spiritual, would "more than supply the place of his presence under the conditions of earthly life." (See Westcott's excellent Note.)

22. Judas saith unto him, not Iscariot. Except in the catalogues of the apostles (see Matt. 10:2-4; Mark 3:16-19; Luke 6:14-16), this is the only place in the Gospels where this apostle is mentioned. In the catalogues, his name always stands as one of the four which compose the last group. He seems to have had two additional names, Lebbeus and Thaddeus; and to have been the son (or brother) of James, though it is not certain of what James. (See Art. Judas, Lebbeus, in Smith's "Dict. of the Bible.") **Lord, how is it that,** etc., (or, *what is come to pass that*, etc.) Evidently Judas has not understood the words of his Master. What he has gathered from them is that Jesus purposes to withdraw from public life, and cease his efforts to win the people to his cause, while he still associates with his little band of disciples, and reveals to them his will. In a word, he is trying to bring his Lord's language into harmony with his own Jewish idea of the Messiah's reign. And the best he can do is to suppose that something of which he is ignorant has occurred, which has led Jesus to decide against presenting himself any more to the people. His question is probably an index of the degree of understanding which the other apostles had at this moment, though it would doubtless be unjust to Peter, James, and John, to place them on just the same spiritual plane as that occupied by Judas Thaddeus.

23. If a man love me. The same presupposition as in ver. 15 and 21. **My Father will love him.** A repetition of his statement in ver. 21. **And we will come unto him.** How could any words prove more clearly that the coming spoken of was spiritual? For One of those about to come was the invisible God, the Father of Spirits; and not even Judas could expect to see him and live. **And make our abode with him.** The plural form of the Greek word which is here translated **abode,** is translated "mansions" in ver. 2. Its literal meaning is "an abiding-place"—*i.e.,* a place where one remains, or dwells. Jesus therefore says that he and his Father will make for themselves (as is indicated by the middle voice of the verb) permanent homes, or dwelling-places, with every loving and obedient disciple. But this abiding of the Father and the Son with Christians was to be accomplished by the coming and agency of the Spirit. For the Advocate, the Paraclete, was to be the representative of Christ, and so, of the Father. As Christ, in his earthly life, presented the Father to the hearts of his disciples, so was "the Spirit of truth" to present Christ, and with him, the Father, to their hearts. And we know that in Christian experience the presence of the Father and the Son is as real and distinct, to the eye of the believing soul, as is that of the Spirit—so that the promise of Jesus has been fulfilled. The Advocate has presented, not himself, but the Saviour, and with him, the Father; and therefore many Christians have far clearer views of the Father and the Son than they have of the Holy Spirit.

24. He that loveth me not keepeth not my sayings (or, *words*). An explicit statement that without love to Christ there is no obedience to his commands (see Note on ver. 21); for, plainly, the *words* of Christ include his commands. **And the word which ye hear,** etc. A truth often before expressed, but aptly repeated in this place; for it rests on the same principle as that which supports the language of ver. 23. The work of the Spirit is said to present the Father and the Son to believers, on the same principle, or from the same point of view, as the word of

25 These things have I spoken unto you, being yet present with you.
26 But ᵃthe Comforter, *which is* the Holy Ghost, whom the Father will send in my name, ᵇ he shall teach you all things, and bring all things to your remembrance, whatsoever I have said unto you.
27 ᶜ Peace I leave with you, my peace I give unto you: not as the world giveth, give I unto you. ᵈ Let not your heart be troubled, neither let it be afraid.

25 These things have I spoken unto you, while yet abiding with you. But the ¹Comforter, *even* the Holy Spirit, whom the Father will send in my name, he shall teach you all things, and bring to your remembrance all that I said unto you. Peace I leave with you; my peace I give unto you: not as the world giveth, give I unto you. Let not your

a Luke 24: 49; ver. 16; ch. 15: 26; 16: 7....b ch. 2: 22; 12: 16; 16: 13; 1 John 2: 20, 27....c Phil. 4: 7; Col. 3: 15....d ver. 1.——1 Or, *Advocate.* Or, *Helper.* Gr. *Paraclete.*

Christ is said to present, not his own will, in distinction from the Father's, but the Father's will, with which his own is in perfect accord; and therefore a statement of the former leads, by a natural law of association, to a restatement of the latter. "Thus," says Godet, "have been gradually set forth the motives for encouragement offered by the Lord: You will be received with me into my Father's house... You have already in me seen the Father... You will continue my work here below... Another divine Helper will give you power... In this inward Helper, I myself will return to be in you... And with me, the Father himself will be with you."

25, sq. REASONS FOR ENCOURAGEMENT REPEATED AND ENFORCED.

25. These things have I spoken unto you, being yet present (better, *while abiding*) **with you.** Thus he reminds them, in the principal clause, of the precious truths which he had uttered during the evening, and lends them, by the subordinate clause, to infer that he is expecting to leave them soon.

26. But the Comforter (or, *Advocate*), etc. Observe that in repeating his promise of the Paraclete, he applies to him the full designation, **Holy Spirit**—a name which points to his special work of implanting and nourishing a holy disposition in the hearts of men. Here only, in this Gospel, is this name given to the Divine Spirit. Observe, also, that the Advocate is to be sent by the Father in the name of Christ—that is, to speak of Christ and for Christ—to reveal the fullness of his nature and the greatness of his sacrifice—to manifest his glory, and lead men to trust in his grace. Observe lastly, that the Advocate is (1) to teach the disciples **all things**—*i. e.,* all things pertaining to the Son of God, and salvation through him—all the truths of the Christian religion which are to be revealed to men in their present state; and (2) to bring to their remembrance all that Christ had said to them during the years of their special discipleship.

This work of the Spirit, commonly called inspiration, was unspeakably important to the eleven; for they were to give authoritative expression to the principles of Christianity, and the sayings of their Lord, for the benefit of all generations, till the end of time. And it is not going too far to suppose that the same Spirit who should enable them to recall the sayings of Jesus, would enable them to recall his deeds of power—the signs which he wrought, especially as these signs were revelations of divine grace, as well as of power.

27. Peace I leave with you. "These are last words, as of one who is about to go away, and gives his good-night, or blessing." —*Luther.* We may compare 1 Sam. 1: 17; 20: 42; 20: 7; Mark 5: 34; Luke 7: 50; 8: 48; Acts 16: 36; James 2: 16; Eph. 6: 23; 1 Pet. 5: 14; 3 John 14. But we feel at the same time that these words are no mere friendly adieu, expressive of ordinary hope or desire; they assert a fact and furnish assurance of what is to be done. And, therefore, Jesus proceeds to define this peace as his own peace. **My peace I give unto you.** The legacy which he thus bequeaths to his disciples is the calmness, the quietness, the repose of spirit, which he himself possesses, and which is characteristic of the true life in God. This subjective sense of the expression **my peace,** is to be preferred, because it presents itself first and most naturally to the reader's mind, because it is suggested by the exhortation which follows in the last part of the verse, and because it is in perfect harmony with the occasion. Jesus would have "the high blessed peace" (*Weiss*) which filled his own soul in prospect of death, fill the souls of his loved disciples in times of peril and suffering, and this greatest gift he, therefore, solemnly affirms to be theirs when he leaves them. A foretaste of it may have gladdened their hearts as he uttered these words; but the blessing in its fullness was not received before the Day of Pentecost. **Not**

CH. XIV.] JOHN. 293

28 Ye have heard how *I said unto you, I go away, and come *again* unto you. If ye loved me, ye would rejoice, because I said, *b* I go unto the Father: for *c* my Father is greater than I.

28 heart be troubled, neither let it be fearful. Ye heard how I said to you, I go away, and I come unto you. If ye loved me, ye would have rejoiced, because I go unto the Father: for the Father is

a ver. 3: 18....*b* ver. 12; ch. 16: 16; 20: 17.....*c* See ch. 5: 18; 10: 30; Phil. 2: 6.

as the world giveth, give I unto you. The precise difference between the giving of the world, and the giving of Jesus, is not specified, but the disciples were able to feel or imagine it with sufficient clearness. Perhaps it was revealed by the tones of his voice more impressively than it could have been by the strongest words. For they were not ignorant of the world, of its formal and professional, but reluctant, niggardly, and self-interested, giving; and as they listened to the deep and loving words of their Master—words coming up from the infinite heart of the Holy One, in tones of perfect affection, they would feel the contrast between the world's giving and his giving. And this was enough. And so, in view of such a bequest he exhorts to peace, and rebukes their fear. **Let not your heart be troubled, neither let it be afraid.** With these words he returns to the beginning of his discourse after instituting the Holy Supper. But how much had been said, meanwhile, to prepare their hearts to receive this exhortation! It is, therefore, no idle repetition that we meet here, or elsewhere in the Fourth Gospel, but repetition in altered circumstances and with augmented force, and repetition where the expression already used is better than any that can be substituted for it.

28. Ye have heard (strictly, *heard*) **how I said unto you, I go away, and come again** (or, *I come*) **unto you.** See ver. 2–4. This form of recalling to their minds what he had said, is somewhat deliberate and emphatic. "Ye heard, indeed, what I said to you a few minutes ago, of my going away and coming to you, and it filled your hearts with sadness; but it should have had an opposite effect; for, **If ye loved me, ye would rejoice** (or, *have rejoiced.*—Rev. Ver.), **because** (omit **I said**) **I go unto the Father: for my** (*the*) **Father is greater than I.** The principal object of this language is not, we suppose, to reprove the disciples for their sorrow because it was selfish, though it appears to have been so, but to remind them of a brighter side of the event which he had

pressed upon their attention, of the fact that his going away from them was a return to the divine state, a resumption of his seat at the right hand of power. If, therefore, they understood the case, love to himself would lead them to rejoice in his departure, since by that departure alone could he be glorified again with the Father, who, because remaining in the divine state, was greater than he. (Comp. 17: 5). The implication of the passage seems to be that, by his exaltation, the Son would resume a condition of being essentially the same as that of the Father. (See Phil. 2: 6 sq). And if this be a correct view, the contrast is not really between the intrinsic and essential nature of the Father and the Word, who became incarnate in the Son, but between the Father in his divine state and the Word in his state of humiliation. This seems to us the most obvious interpretation of the Lord's words. Weiss remarks: "While the going to the Father does not of itself involve a participation in his power, but only a participation in his heavenly life, withdrawn from all the limits and imperfections of this earthly existence, this alone can be meant. On this hypothesis only should their joy have respect to his personal departure, and that there would be something selfish in demanding such a joy (*Meyer*) is certainly no objection, inasmuch as a friend can desire that his friend should rejoice in his joy." Again, in a Note at the bottom of the page, he says, very justly: "The superiority (μειζοτητης) of the Father is not to be found in the superiority of the Unbegotten to the Begotten (*Athan., Faustin., Gregor., Naz., Hilar., Enth., Zig.*, and n.any others, also *Olsh*), to which special view the text gives absolutely no occasion, nor again in the essential subordination of the Eternal Word as the exalted Christ to the Father, on the ground of the absolute monotheism of Jesus, 17: 3 (*Meyer*), also, not certainly upon the distinction of the human and the divine nature of Christ (*Gerhard*). For, without doubt, Jesus is not speaking here of the relation of the Father and the Son in themselves,

29 And *now I have told you before it come to pass, that, when it is come to pass, ye might believe.
30 Hereafter I will not talk much with you; *for the prince of this world cometh, and hath nothing in me.
31 But that the world may know that I love the Father; and *as the Father gave me commandment, even so I do. Arise, let us go hence.

29 greater than I. And now I have told you before it come to pass, that, when it is come to pass, ye 30 may believe. I will no more speak much with you, for the prince of the world cometh: and 31 he hath nothing in me; but that the world may know that I love the Father, and as the Father gave me commandment, even so I do. Arise, let us go hence.

a ch. 13: 19; 16: 4....*b* ch. 12: 31; 16: 11....*c* ch. 10: 18; Phil. 2: 8; Heb. 5: 8.

but of the relation of God to Christ in his temporal humiliation (*Cyrill., August., Ammon., Luther, Melancthon, Calvin, Beza*, and many others, also, *De Wette, Thol.*), and Hengstenberg is perfectly correct, when he says that only such a superiority of the Father can be meant as would 'come to an end' by the going of the Son to the Father. But that the eternal, God-like nature of the Son is presupposed by the statement, appears clearly from this, that such a comparison of himself with God by any created being would be folly, bordering on blasphemy."

29. And now I have told you before, etc. How wise and loving this foresight of Jesus! How perfectly were the means adapted to secure the end! For the time would soon come when the disciples' recollection of this hour, and of the words now spoken and presently fulfilled, would strengthen their faith. And what they needed more than all else, to qualify them for their great mission, was an increase of faith. "*Believe* in God; *believe* also in me." (Ver. 1.) **That, when it is come to pass, ye might** (or. *may*) **believe.** The belief here contemplated is belief in God, and in Jesus Christ, the Sent of God, or belief as comprehensive as the gospel requires—though its proximate object would naturally be Christ himself.

30. I will not talk (or, *no more speak*) **much with you.** A few last words only can be said before the dreadful conflict begins; and by reminding them of this fact, he rivets their attention more closely to what he says. It is a more emphatic "verily, verily, I say unto you." **For the prince of this** (or, *the*[1]) **world cometh. The world** is here put for the unbelieving and far greater part of mankind—the part which seems to outward observation well-nigh the whole; and **the prince of** *the* **world** is the same ungodly being who is described by Paul as "the prince of the power of the air—the spirit that now worketh in the children of disobedience." (Eph. 2: 2.) Jesus therefore intends to represent Judas Iscariot (comp. 13: 2, 27), and all who are seeking his life, as being influenced in their course by the worst of beings. In them and by them, Satan renews his assault upon the Son of man. The words of Jesus have also been thought to afford some intimation of a more inward and terrible approach of the wicked one, accompanying this outward assault, and serving to explain the agony of the garden; but on the method of Satan's coming we are left to conjecture, except so far as it may be indicated by the language concerning Judas, and by what is said of the suffering of soul endured by Christ. **And hath nothing in me**—*i. e.*, nothing that pertains to him as prince of the world. Jesus is, in no respect, in no degree, subject to him. This is probably the most obvious and satisfactory interpretation of the words. But they imply, if they do not formally express, the sinlessness of Jesus. The fact that nothing in Jesus belongs to the prince of the world, shows that he has never been under the moral control of that evil being. As the reign of that prince is the reign of a rebel against God, over a world in rebellion against God, Christ is independent of the prince, because he is morally separate from the world. The words in **me** are emphatic, and antithetical to **the world.** Jesus thus intimates that what he is about to suffer he will not suffer because Satan has any authority over him, or power to bring this evil upon him, against his own will.

31. But that the world may know, etc. There are three possible ways of construing this verse, viz.: (1) "But that the world may know that I love the Father, and [that] as the Father gave me commandment, even so I do: Arise, let us go hence"—to encounter death: the apodosis beginning with "Arise." (2) "But that the world may know that I love

---
[1] We omit **this**, before **world**, in deference to the oldest manuscripts.

CHAPTER XV.

I AM the true vine, and my Father is the husbandman.
2 *Every branch in me that beareth not fruit he

1 I am the true vine, and my Father is the husbandman. Every branch in me that beareth not fruit, he taketh it away: and every *branch* that

a Matt. 15: 13.

the Father, even as the Father gave me commandment, so I do. Arise, let us go hence"—the apodisis beginning with "even as" (καὶ καθὼς), and being expressed by the words **so I do**. (3) "But [I suffer what I suffer through the coming of the prince of the world] that the world may know that I love the Father, and [that] as the Father gave me commandment, even so I do. Arise, let us go hence." The simplicity of style which characterizes this Gospel is an objection to the first two constructions, while the third has been exemplified more than once already—(*e. g.*, at 13: 18.) We therefore accept this as probably correct. Yet the meaning of the verse will remain very nearly the same, whatever view may be taken of the construction. Christ declares his purpose to meet the conflict before him, in order that the world may know his love and obedience to the Father. It is a free act of his own; he has power to lay down his life, and to take it again; but at the same time it is the will of his Father that he should give his life for the world; and in no other way can he so clearly reveal to the world his love to the Father, as by making his soul an offering for sinners. **Arise, let us go hence.** These words were doubtless followed by corresponding action. Yet it has been said: "They do not, indeed, rise. An interesting fact [?], to be accounted for only by the deep, vivid effect produced upon their minds by the Lord's previous words and deeds, and by his whole bearing, (Comp. Luke 24: 29.) They were riveted to the spot, and seemed unable to move—as if they would hear more. To this silent invitation, the Lord yields, and proves that he had not yet said the best he could say—more of heaven now drops from his lips than his followers had ever tasted before."—("The Gospels from the Rabbinical Point of View," by Rev. G. Wildon Pieritz, M. A., p. 23.) Only there is no satisfactory evidence of the alleged fact—it is rather an inference from the writer's neglect to state where they went upon leaving the room.

Ch. 15. If we suppose that the word **arise** (14:31), was followed by the act of rising up from a sitting posture, we must, for the same reason, suppose that the words, **let us go hence**, were followed by the act of leaving the room where the Lord's Supper had been instituted. Hence the following discourse and prayer were not, we think, uttered in the "guest chamber," or "large upper room" (Mark 14:15; Luke 22:12). But it is impossible to ascertain where they were uttered. On their way to Gethsemane, Jesus and his disciples may have turned aside into the temple courts, and there, in the late and silent evening hour, the sacred words of the three following chapters may have been spoken; and, if so, the golden vine upon the gates (see Jos. "Ant." xv. 11. 3; "B. J." v. 5. 4) may have suggested the parable or illustration used (15:1-8) by the Lord. But it is also barely *possible* (see on 18: 1) that the words of these chapters were spoken outside the city and temple, as Jesus paused, with his disciples, in sight of some noble vine on the hill-side sloping down to the Kedron. This, however, is far from probable.

1-3. THE UNION BETWEEN CHRIST AND CHRISTIANS SIMILAR TO THAT BETWEEN A VINE AND ITS BRANCHES.

1. I am the true vine. The true vine (ἡ ἄμπελος ἡ ἀληθινή) is one that realizes perfectly the idea of a vine. (Comp. Notes on 1: 9; 4: 23; 6: 32). In this brief statement, the word vine does not mean the mere vine stock, but the stock with its branches. **And my Father is the husbandman.** That is, the vine planter and vine dresser. "He it is," says Godet, "who attends to the preservation of this divine organism, and guides its development on earth. While Jesus is the inner life of it, the Father gives it providential care and culture... What is here said is not inconsistent with the view that this work, ascribed to the Father, is accomplished through the agency of Christ. Only the figure employed forbids a reference to this aspect of the truth."

2. Every branch. Jesus here refers to

taketh away; and every *branch* that beareth fruit, he purgeth it, that it may bring forth more fruit. 3 ª Now ye are clean through the word which I have spoken unto you. 4 ᵇ Abide in me, and I in you. As the branch can- beareth fruit, he cleanseth it, that it may bear more 3 fruit. Already ye are clean because of the word 4 which I have spoken unto you. Abide in me, and

a ch. 13: 10; 17: 17; Eph. 5: 26; 1 Pet. 1: 22....*b* Col. 1: 23; 1 John 2: 6.

processes well known to his disciples. For two operations are included in the proper culture of the vine—(1) that of removing sterile branches, and (2) that of cleaning fruitful branches. The latter is accomplished by taking from the fruitful branches useless shoots, in order that the sap may concentrate in the shoots which are loaded with clusters. Thus, "to him that hath is given, and from him that hath not is taken away even that which he hath." In like manner, two classes of persons are connected with Christ—(1) those who are united with him by intellect and profession merely, and (2) those who are united with him in heart also. Those of the first class may exhibit the form of godliness, but they know nothing of its power. They promise, but do not perform; they bear leaves, but not fruit; they are like the fig tree which the Lord cursed. At death, if not before, the tie which unites such persons with Christ will be sundered. It is frequently broken in this life, by tribulation or persecution, which the nominal Christian finds it difficult to bear; or by the cares of this world and the deceitfulness of riches, which turn away the mere professor from even thoughts of God. It is sure to be severed, first or last. But those of the second class, being united with Christ by love, are to be disciplined with a view to abundant fruitfulness in the divine life. For by **fruit**, is here meant spiritual life and action; or, in the words of Paul, "love, joy, peace, longsuffering, gentleness, kindness, goodness, faith, meekness, temperance." (Gal. 5: 22.) To secure this blessed fruit, they may be stripped of worldly possessions, subjected to heavy burdens, exposed to severe trials, made to drink the cup of their Master, so that it may be truly said of them, "They that are Christ's have crucified the flesh, with the affections (or, *passions*) and lusts." (Gal. 5: 24.) The eleven were soon to know a great deal about this cleansing process, and, purified by it, were to become zealous of good works. Yet it is not by means of suffering or burden-bearing only, that the fruitful branches, the true friends of Christ, are prepared for their work. The knife by which they are pruned of useless leaves and shoots, is often the pure word of God.

3. Now (*already*) **ye are clean through** (*because of*) **the word,** etc. This is a timely word of encouragement, assuring the disciples that they were recognized by their Lord, not as sterile, but as fruitful branches. The Greek adjective translated **clean** (καθαροί), is a kin to the verb "cleanseth" (καθαίρει) in ver. 2, which, however, is translated **purgeth**, in the Common Version; and it means in this place, those who are prepared to bear fruit, like vine branches made clean by pruning. Yet, Jesus does not intend to pronounce the eleven morally perfect, or, indeed, perfectly qualified for their work. Their ambition and worldliness had been too recently manifested to allow of this interpretation of his language. But he does mean to say that they were in spiritual union with himself; that they were connected with him, not merely by intellectual conviction, but also by faith and love, as affections of the heart; and that by the influence of his word, many of their errors, prejudices, and selfish aims had been removed, so that there was reason to expect from them spiritual fruit. More than this the word **clean,** as here used, cannot be said to imply. But this recognition was enough to cheer the hearts of the disciples.

It is also noticeable that they are said to be clean through, or *because of the word* which Christ had spoken to them. Christian truth is therefore employed by the Most High in qualifying his people for service, and Jesus Christ is not only the inward source of life to his own, but, in his Father's name and behalf, he teaches, disciplines, and purifies them for holy conduct and usefulness among men. (Comp. 8: 31, 32; Eph. 5: 26; James 1: 18.)

4, 5. CONTINUANCE AND APPLICATION OF THE PARABLE.

4. Abide in me, and I in you. Jesus assumes the existence of a most intimate fellow-

not bear fruit of itself, except it abide in the vine; no more can ye, except ye abide in me.
5 I am the vine, ye are the branches. He that abideth in me, and I in him, the same bringeth forth much *fruit; for without me ye can do nothing.

I in you. As the branch cannot bear fruit of itself, except it abide in the vine; so neither can ye, 5 except ye abide in me. I am the vine, ye are the branches: He that abideth in me, and I in him, the same beareth much fruit; for apart

a Hos. 14:8; Phil. 1:11; 4:13.

ship between himself and his disciples. He implies that its continuance is dependent on their action, as well as his own. And he exhorts them to cherish and preserve this fellowship, with the promise, if they do, of maintaining it himself. (Weiss interprets the clause, "and I in you," as a promise equivalent to, "and I will abide in you." Westcott says that "both parts are imperative in conception: Do ye abide in me . . . and let me abide in you." Improbable. Godet, better: "Jesus suppresses the verb in the clause, 'and I in you,' because the second act is conceived of as the immediate and necessary consequence of the first; if the first is accomplished, the second cannot fail to be realized.") Thus he recognizes the moral freedom of his disciples in matters pertaining to their salvation—a point which could not be represented in his similitude. So it must often be. For no metaphor, simile, parable, or allegory, borrowed from the realm of nature, can be perfect in relation to spiritual beings. It would be absurd to exhort the branches to abide in the vine. But the union between Christ and his disciples, the members of his spiritual body, is voluntary, reciprocal, progressive. It is therefore natural for Jesus to urge his followers to avoid everything that might tend to separate them in spirit from him, and to do everything in their power to preserve and increase their fellowship with him. **As the branch**, etc. Every one knows that the branch cannot bear fruit from itself alone, or "by any power of its own which it may have apart from the vine."—*Grotius.* It can bear fruit only by abiding in the vine, and drawing vital force from the stock. Godet considers the clause, **except it abide in the vine**, as an explanation of the words **from itself**—thus: "As the branch cannot bear fruit from itself"—*i. e.,* "if it abide not in the vine." That is to say, bearing fruit from itself, and bearing fruit when not in the vine, are equivalent expressions. **No more** (or, *so neither*) **can ye, except ye abide in me.** Though the connection between Christ and his own is

voluntary, and spiritual, consisting in mutual love, their dependence upon him to whom they are thus united, and therefore upon the conservation of the union, is every whit as absolute as is that of the vine branch upon the vine. A good reason, surely, for the exhortation in the former part of the verse! Union with Christ is indispensable to usefulness in his service. The stream must draw from the fountain, or it will become dry. How closely would Jesus bind the disciples to his heart! How sweetly does he urge them to drink of the fountain of his love! He is more than ready to take these poor, weak, unworthy, trembling followers to himself, and fill their entire being with light and peace. Could such a man as John ever forget such an appeal as this?

5. I am the vine, ye are the branches. According to this Gospel, Jesus often repeats the cardinal words or sentences of a discourse, thus fixing them more deeply in the minds of his hearers. Yet he almost always repeats with some variation or addition. So here the words used are a resumption of the theme (ver. 1), with an express statement, not given there, that his disciples are represented by **the branches. He that abideth in me, and I in him.** Observe that Christ does not restrict his view to the eleven. For **he that abideth in me** is equivalent to "every one that abideth in me." The language of Jesus refers to Christians of every age and nation. Notice, also, that he speaks of the individual, not of the church. Notice, again, that the indwelling is mutual, like that of verse 4. **The same** (or, *this one*) **bringeth forth** (lit., *beareth*) **much fruit.** By the present tense of the verb, the fruit-bearing is described, not as a single act, performed once for all, but as a process no less enduring than the union on which it depends. Note, also, the expression, **much fruit.** The man who abides in Christ, and in whom Christ abides by his Spirit, he it is who bears, not a little fruit—a small cluster, scarce discernible amid the leaves—but **much fruit**—grapes of Eschol, in heavy clusters;

6 If a man abide not in me, *he is cast forth as a branch, and is withered; and men gather them, and cast *them* into the fire, and they are burned.

6 from me ye can do nothing. If a man abide not in me, he is cast forth as a branch, and is withered; and they gather them, and cast them into the

a Matt. 3: 10; 7: 19.

he it is, and he alone, whose life is a great blessing to the world. But do all who abide in Christ fulfill this saying? Do not some of this class bear very little fruit, and some very poor fruit? Does not Paul teach that there are believers whose work will not stand the test of fire, even though they themselves will be saved, yet so as by fire? (1 Cor. 3: 15.) *First*, it is certain that not all true Christians are Peters, or Johns, or Pauls, or Luthers, or Calvins, or Judsons, in ability and devotion combined. But ability may be left out of the account in speaking of fruitfulness in Christian life. For the poor widow who cast into the treasury of the Lord but two mites, is said to have cast in more than all the rich, because they gave out of their abundance, and she gave out of her deep poverty. By this rule of judging, many Christians who seem to men weak and comparatively useless, bear much fruit. *Secondly*, it is certain that not all Christians are equally devout. There are some who make very slow progress in everything that pertains to godliness. So weak is their faith, so languid their affection, and so irresolute their conduct, that they seem to be in constant danger of falling away from Christ. These, surely, cannot be said to bear much fruit. Even the gracious judgment of the Lord will condemn their slothfulness and inefficiency, because they do not use the talent entrusted to them. *Thirdly*, there are degrees of union with Christ, and spiritual fruit increases as union with him becomes more intimate. When the believer and his Saviour are one in feeling, desire, and aim, in so far at least as the disciple is let into the counsels of his Master, then will the fruits of holiness abound in his life. Only as one is united with Christ, does he bear fruit; and in proportion to the completeness of the union, will be the abundance of fruit. Being in Christ, is the condition of bearing much fruit. This is the principal thought, and Jesus does not pause to explain the qualifications or limitations of it. For without (*apart from*) me ye can do nothing. An explicit statement of the negative implied in the previous clause, by giving the reason for that implied negative. "This, and

no other, beareth much fruit," "because apart from me ye can do nothing"—*i. e.*, no Christian work, no deed acceptable to God. Hence this saying has no direct reference to the ability or inability of unrenewed men to obey the moral law, or to believe in Christ. Its primary application is to those who are in Christ. Yet it is difficult to resist the conviction that it is equally true of all men; and therefore that nothing acceptable to God can be done by any person who is still out of Christ. "I hear a voice of song and sweet content within my text: 'Without me ye can do nothing.' I pick up my text and hold it to my ear, as many a child has held a shell; and as within the shell the child hears the rolling of the sea ... so within my text I hear a sweet, sweet sound. Put it to your ears and try it: 'Without me ye can do nothing.' Lord, what is there that I want to do without thee? Lord, thou hast tied and tethered me to thyself by this blessed text, which is so sweetly bitter, so intensely precious to my heart, when I come to get into its depths. What could I want to do without thee? Suppose there were something I could do without thee! then there would be a little crown for my head; but now I can do nothing without thee. Then there is one great crown for thy brow, and thou shalt have all the glory. ... Oh, God, we thank thee that we can do nothing without Christ, for of all things, I should dread success apart from Christ."—*C. H. Spurgeon*.

6. CONSEQUENCE OF NOT ABIDING IN CHRIST.

6. If a man abide not in me, etc. Does this refer to one who has been in vital, fruit-bearing union with Christ? Or to one who, like the sterile branch of ver. 2, is only united to Christ by a public profession, resting on a merely intellectual belief? Even if the former is taken to be the correct view of Christ's language here, the premise is hypothetical, and may have been assumed, not as actual, or even probable, but simply as *possible*. For, if so deplorable an act is possible, it ought to be prevented by a revelation of the dreadful result that must follow its becoming actual. But the latter view may be correct.

7 If ye abide in me, and my words abide in you, • ye shall ask what ye will, and it shall be done unto you.

7 fire, and they are burned. If ye abide in me, and my words abide in you, ask whatsoever ye

a ver. 16; ch. 14: 13, 14; 16: 23.

Says Weiss: "Since fruit-bearing, according to ver. 4, 5, depends on abiding in Jesus, the Lord here speaks of the doom of the unfruitful branch, which, according to ver. 2, the vine-dresser cuts off. If Luther insists against Lampe, that one can, therefore, have been actually (spiritually) in Christ, and yet have fallen away, it is very doubtful, according to 1 John 2: 19, whether this Evangelist would have regarded a 'being in Christ,' which was not followed by an 'abiding in him,' as real." **He is cast forth as a** (or, *the*) **branch, and is withered. By a branch,** must be understood the unfruitful branch, which is here represented as being cast out of the vineyard (ἔξω, *outside*—i. e., of the vineyard), where it withers away and becomes dry. But why are the Greek verbs (ἐβλήθη and ἐξηράνθη) in the past tense (aorist), though translated as if they were in the present? Meyer, Alford, Godet (last ed.), Watkins, Weiss, Abbott, account for it by supposing that the point of view assumed by Jesus is that of the gathering together and casting into the fire of unbelievers at the last judgment. "Jesus places himself at the point of time when the last judgment is being carried into effect, when those who fell away from him are gathered together and cast into the fire, after having been *previously* cast out of his community, and become withered."— *Meyer.* This is, perhaps, the best explanation of the tense of the verbs, which might be translated "*was cast out,*" and "*became withered.*" But others hold that the past tense is here used to express an effect that follows instantly upon its cause. Thus Westcott: "This happens simultaneously with the cessation of the vital union with Christ... It is an inevitable accompaniment of the separation." Similarly, Winer (Thayer's Transl., § 40, 5, 6, p. 277: "The not abiding in Christ has this as its instantaneous consequence: whoever has severed himself from Christ, resembles a branch broken off and thrown away." (See also, Buttmann's "Grammar of the N. T. Greek," Thayer's Transl., on the *Proleptic,* and the *Gnomic* Aorist, § 137, 4, 8). **And men** (or, *they*), **gather them, and cast them into the fire, and they are burned.** This imagery is borrowed from the course taken with fruitless branches, and is not to be pressed as literally applicable to unspiritual men. But without insisting on the literal sense of these words, it is to be maintained without wavering, and on the authority of such teaching, that the doom of all who are found out of Christ at the last day will be very dreadful. "The Lord leaves the image, just as it is, to work its proper effect."— *Westcott.* And the reality which calls for the use of such an image, must be something from which a rational being ought to shrink with horror; something more terrible than aught else in the universe, save the sin which merits this awful doom. A reader of Scripture cannot too seriously bear in mind that, for every figurative expression of God's word, there must be a corresponding reality.

7, 8. The Result of Union with Christ Re-affirmed.

7. The condition here stated differs in form, but scarcely in substance, from that recognized in verse 5. For it is said there: "He that abideth in me, and *I in him,*" while it is said here: **If ye abide in me, and my words abide in you.** But Christ and his words are inseparable in the believer's heart. By his words Christ presents *himself* to his people. As he, the Eternal Word, is the revelation of the Father, presenting the Father to us, so his word, the sum of his sayings, is a revelation of himself—a revelation by which he presents to us his inmost nature; and, therefore, by retaining his word, and meditating upon it, we retain him in our minds and hearts. And this is presupposed in acceptable prayer. When this condition is fulfilled, prayer will be according to the will of Christ, and will be surely answered. As Godet remarks: "A prayer so inspired is a daughter of heaven; it is the promise of God transformed into a supplication; and upon this condition the answer is certain." It may be remarked also, (1) that **what ye will,** is by position emphatic, indicating the freedom of the believer's choice as long as it accords with the teaching of

8 a Herein is my Father glorified, that ye bear much fruit; b so shall ye be my disciples.
9 As the Father hath loved me, so have I loved you; continue ye in my love.
10 c If ye keep my commandments, ye shall abide in my love; even as I have kept my Father's commandments, and abide in his love.

8 will, and it shall be done unto you. Herein 1 is my Father glorified, 2 that ye bear much fruit; and so 9 shall ye be my disciples. Even as the Father hath loved me, I also have loved you: abide ye in my 10 love. If ye keep my commandments, ye shall abide in my love; even as I have kept my Father's com-

a Matt. 5: 16; Phil. 1: 11....b ch. 8: 31; 13: 35....c ch. 14: 15, 21, 23.——1 Or, was....2 Many ancient authorities read, that y bear much fruit, and be my disciples.

Christ. (2) That the best text reads: *ask*, in the imperative, instead of **ye shall ask,** in the future—**what** (or, *whatsoever*) *ye will ask,* etc. (3) That the words, **and it shall be done unto you,** represents an expression meaning, literally, *and it shall come to pass to you,* or, *become yours.*

8. Herein (*in this*) **is my Father glorified, that,** etc. If the word **that,** (ἵνα) at the beginning of the second clause, has its usual signification, viz., in order that, the word *this* (*in this*), must refer to what is said in verse 7—*i. e.*, to God's answering the prayers of those who abide in Christ. The Father is glorified in answering their prayers, for he gives these answers in order that they may bear spiritual fruit; and such fruit is always to the glory of his name. This fruit is in reality the life which men ought to live—a life of righteousness and peace and joy in the Holy Spirit, a life of devout love to God, and of beneficent love to men. But it is possible that the word *this* looks forward to the latter part of the verse, beginning with **that,** (ἵνα); and, if we assume this to be the case, we do not change the general meaning of the passage, though we fail to connect this verse as closely as before with the seventh, and give a less usual meaning to the Greek word translated **that.** The tense of the verb which is here rendered **is glorified,** must be either the *proleptical* or the *gnomic* aorist; if proleptical, it denotes what is to be true henceforth, when the process described in verse 7 is realized; if *gnomic*, it denotes a result which always accompanies or follows that process, **So shall ye be my disciples.** Or, *and ye shall become disciples to me.* The latter rendering is more exact, and is on that account to be preferred. Discipleship is never complete, any more than knowledge. It is always becoming truer, deeper, more intimate. Paul, speaking of himself, says: "The inward man is *renewed day by day*" (2 Cor. 4: 16), and, speaking of "the new man" in the Colossians, declares that it "*is being renewed*" unto knowledge after the image of him that created him." (3: 10, Rev. Ver.). *Disciples to me—i. e.,* belonging to me, is a more forcible expression in the original than "disciples of me," commonly translated "my disciples."

9–17. CHRIST'S LOVE TO HIS OWN, AND HOW IT IS TO BE RETAINED.

9. As (or, *even as*) **the Father hath loved me, so have I loved you.** Stronger language could not have been used. Jesus compares his love with that of the infinite God to his only begotten Son, and assures his disciples that they are now in the possession of his love—living under its influence. The tense of the verbs suggests that the act of loving them is looked upon as one that became complete and perfect in the past. He loved them with a divine love when he called them to be his own. **Continue ye in my love.** That is, *abide* in it; so live that the sunshine of my love will surround you as an atmosphere. "The exact form of the phrase, which is found here only (ἡ ἀγάπη ἡ ἐμή), as distinguished from that used in the next verse (ἡ ἀγάπη μου), emphasizes the character of the love as Christ's: *the love that is mine*—the love that answers to my nature and my work."—*Westcott.* Is it possible to over-estimate the privilege of abiding in such love?—a love divine, unchangeable, and stronger than death? Must not the hearts of the eleven have thrilled with joy at these words? As they stood there, a listening group, about their Master, with the mighty sky above their heads, the Valley of Kedron at their feet, and the Garden of Gethsemane at the base of Olivet beyond, must they not have felt, as never before, the spiritual glory, the unutterable love of Jesus? Must they not have deemed his love "the pearl of great price?"

10. If ye keep my commandments, ye shall abide in my love. Westcott considers this promise "the exact converse of that in 14: 15": "If ye love me, keep (or, *ye will keep*) my commandments." It would be so, if **my** love here meant "love to me"—*i. e.*, if the

JOHN.

11 These things have I spoken unto you, that my joy might remain in you, and *a that* your joy might be full.
12 *b* This is my commandment, That ye love one another, as I have loved you.

11 mandments, and abide in his love. These things have I spoken unto you, that my joy may be in 12 you, and *that* your joy may be made full. This is my commandment, that ye love one another, even

a ch. 16: 24; 17: 13; 1 John 1: 4....*b* ch. 13: 24; 1 Thess. 4: 9; 1 Pet. 4: 8; 1 John 3: 11; 4: 21.

---

love of the disciples to Christ, and not his love to them, were intended by the expression, "my love." But we think it signifies his love to them. Accordingly Jesus affirms that, by cheerful obedience to him, his disciples will continue to enjoy the blessing of his love. If they bear fruit, they will abide in the vine; if they are willing and obedient, they will live in the light of their Lord's countenance. **Even as I have kept my Father's commandments, and abide in his love.** "The perfect love of complete devotion to God is the highest conceivable good."—*Westcott*. Possibly; but it is not, we think, the good here described; for **his love,** is the Father's love to the Son, not the Son's love to the Father. The perfect obedience of the Son rejoices with exceeding joy in the absolute approval and love of the Father. At the same time it is to be understood that obedience springs from love, and is perfected by love. "He that dwelleth in love" is the one who "dwelleth in God, and God in him." But love expresses itself in acts of obedience, and so obedience is here made the condition of abiding in the enjoyment of Christ's love.

11. These things ... that my joy might (or, *may*) **remain in you.** By the expression **my joy,** Jesus means "the joy which I have" —"the joy which fills my heart." A joy identical in kind with this he would have his disciples possess; and for this reason he has spoken to them so tenderly and sweetly, laying open to them the depths of his own heart. But is the joy of which he speaks as **my joy,** that of loving obedience to the Father's will, or that of knowing his Father's love to himself? If the former, the Christian's peculiar and chief joy should spring directly from conscious love and obedience to the Saviour; if the latter, the Christian's peculiar and highest joy should spring from a grateful appreciation of the Saviour's love to him. The latter seems to us the true interpretation of Christ's language, and of Christian experience. The joy of Christ arises from his consciousness of his infinite Father's love, and the joy of the Christian from his assurance of his divine Redeemer's love. **And that your joy might** (or, *may*) **be full,** or *complete*. The joy of Christ was complete, but that of his disciples was yet imperfect; and his words had been spoken for the purpose of laying a foundation for the purest and highest joy which it was possible for them to experience. Whether these things include all that Jesus had spoken since the Supper, or all that he had said for their comfort in this chapter (ver. 1-10), or only what is recorded in verses 9 and 10, is doubtful. Perhaps the last supposition is more probable than either of the others, though there seems to be no decisive objection to the second.

12. This is my commandment, etc. That is, the commandment "that answers to my nature and my mission."—*Westcott*. See the exposition of 13: 34, where precisely the same commandment is characterized as "a new commandment." Here, as there, the clause, **that ye love one another,** etc., is a statement of what the command is, rather than a statement of the end to be reached by it. Yet the end to be reached by a command is often expressed, as here, in and by the command itself—a fact which accounts for the use of a conjunction (ἵνα) whose primary import is *final,* rather than *expository*. "The content of the command is represented as the purpose of giving it."—*Weiss*. "The predicates after which it (ἵνα) stands are still, in the main, of such a nature that the dependent clause can be regarded as a statement *akin to a specification of purpose.*"—(Buttmann's "Gr. of the N. T. Greek," p. 237.) **As I have loved you.** Thus Christ makes his own love to his followers the model and standard of their love to one another; for a proper view of his love to them would give them the clearest conception possible of the fraternal love which they ought to cherish, and the best incentive to a constant exercise of it. And the degree of his own love to them he now proceeds to suggest.

JOHN. [Ch. XV.

13 ᵃGreater love hath no man than this, that a man lay down his life for his friends.
14 ᵇYe are my friends, if ye do whatsoever I command you.
15 Henceforth I call you not servants; for the servant knoweth not what his lord doeth: but I have called you friends; ᶜfor all things that I have heard of my Father I have made known unto you.

13 as I have loved you. Greater love hath no man than this, that a man lay down his life for his friends. Ye are my friends, if ye do the things which I command you. No longer do I call you ¹ servants; for the ¹servant knoweth not what his lord doeth: but I have called you friends; for all things that I heard from my Father I have made

ᵃ ch. 10: 11, 15; Rom. 5: 7, 8; Eph. 5: 2; 1 John 3: 16....ᵇ See Matt. 12: 50; ch. 14: 15, 23....ᶜ See Gen. 18: 17; ch. 17: 26; Acts 20: 27
—1 Gr. bond-servants....2 Gr. bond-servant.

13. Greater love hath no man than this, that, etc.,—*i. e.*, there is no love greater than that which leads one to give up his life for those whom he loves. "All that a man hath will he give for his life" (Job 2: 4); and an affection which freely surrenders life for the good of others cannot be surpassed. Of course, such love commonly presupposes intimate friendship; and as Jesus recognizes his disciples as friends, his language naturally takes the form here given. "Love is contemplated on the side of him who feels it, so that the objects of it are spoken of as friends—that is, 'loved by him.'"—*Westcott*. "According to Rom. 5: 6-8, there is a yet greater love of Christ—his sacrifice of himself for sinners—for enemies. And, in fact, the work of Christ's love appears in its full greatness only under this point of view. But the love wherewith Christ, according to Paul, dies for sinners, is at the same time the love whereby, according to John, he makes the disciples his friends. Only because, full of love, he thinks of sinners as his friends, does he die for them."—*Lücke*. Dying love for enemies is more surprising, but is it stronger than dying love for friends? Godet finds an expression of end or purpose in the clause, **that a man lay down his life for his friends**—thus: We say that the Greek word for **that** (ἵνα) "retains the notion of end—the highest point to which love can *aspire* in this relation, is that," etc. But this is changing the expression, and I prefer the interpretation of Weiss: "*This* (ταύτης) does not point back to the love expressed by '*even as I have loved you*' (ver. 12), but it looks forward, and is explained by the words, 'that a man lay down his life,' etc." (Comp. Buttmann' "Gr. of the N. T. Greek," p. 239.)

14. Ye are my friends, if ye do whatsoever (=*the things which*) **I command you.** The pronoun *ye* is emphatic; and the meaning is: "I regard you and treat you as my friends." But there is added a condition:

"If you are obedient to me." It is the Master who speaks, though he speaks in love. "What more affecting in domestic life than that a master, finding a servant truly faithful, should give him in the house the rank and title of friend?"—*Godet*. Abraham is called the "friend of God" (James 2: 23), because God treated him as a friend, and admitted him to the intimacy of friendship. So to be counted a friend by Christ, is to be honored with his friendship. The following verse illustrates the method of friendship, as distinguished from that of lordship.

15. Henceforth (*no longer*) **I call you not servants,** or, *bond-servants*, as in the margin of the Revised Version. That they were his servants is true—purchased, as would soon appear, with his blood (comp. 1 Cor. 6: 20; 7: 23; 1 Pet. 1: 18; Rev. 5: 9); and that he had spoken of them as servants that very evening, they knew (see 13: 14, 16); but a faithful servant may be treated as a friend or a brother, and such recognition and treatment would the Saviour accord to his disciples in time to come. **For the servant knoweth not what his Lord doeth.** A glimpse is afforded by this saying of the ordinary relation of bond-servants to their masters. The former were usually ignorant of the thoughts, plans, or cares of the latter; and their service was therefore constrained, not willing. Their life was separated from that of their masters by a wide chasm. Love, friendship, fellowship, were almost wholly wanting. All this is implied in the saying of Jesus. And though his disciples must be his servants, under infinite obligation to do his will, he was ready to give them, if faithful, all the blessing and honor of his friendship, letting them into his counsels, and communicating to them the plans of his love. **But I have called you friends.** The **you** is emphatic: "but *you* have I called friends"—**you,** my disciples, I have treated as friends, and not as servants, unworthy of confidence. **For all things,**

16 • Ye have not chosen me, but I have chosen you, and ordained you, that ye should go and bring forth fruit, and *that* your fruit should remain; that *whatsoever ye shall ask of the Father in my name, he may give it you.

16 known unto you. Ye did not choose me, but I chose you, and appointed you, that ye should go and bear fruit, and *that* your fruit should abide; that whatsoever ye shall ask of the Father in my name, he may

a ch. 6: 70; 13: 18; 1 John 4: 10, 19....*b* Matt. 28: 19; Mark 16: 15; Col. 1: 6....*c* ch. 14: 13; ver. 7.

etc. Or, as in Rev. Ver.: "*For all things that I heard from my Father I made known to you.*" If this be understood as relating to the past, it must be taken with the limitation suggested by 16: 12. Nothing had been kept back from them on the principle and in the spirit with which the more servant is denied a knowledge of his master's plans and reasons, but all things which they could receive without being offended had been freely imparted. The limitation was in them, not in their Lord. But the language may be understood as anticipatory, descriptive of what would be done through the Spirit. Yet even with this interpretation it would still be extravagant to suppose that the words **all things** are to be taken with no restriction whatever. Jesus might surely assume that his disciples would understand him to mean all things which it was desirable and possible for them to know. Taking this view of his meaning, he had already taught them, by pregnant sayings, or parables, all the essential principles of the gospel; but his teaching was to be explained and confirmed by his death and resurrection, as well as by the illumination of the Spirit. "It was the work of the Spirit to interpret afterwards, little by little, what he had revealed in word and life, implicitly, once for all. (14: 26; 17: 26.)"—*Westcott.*

16. Ye have not chosen (or, *did not choose*) **me, but I have chosen** (or, *chose*) **you,** etc. The object of what is said in this verse is to increase the confidence of the disciples in the love of Christ, and so to bind them to him by a trust that would never die out of their hearts. The "choosing" here spoken of is generally referred to his selection of them for apostles. (See Luke 6: 13). But this does not agree with the first clause, *Ye did not choose me.* What pertinence has this, if he had in mind their selection to be apostles? How could they choose him with reference to the apostolate? But they might choose him as a teacher, even as Jewish pupils sometimes selected their teachers; and, on the other hand, he might choose them "out of the world" (**ver. 19**), to be his followers, or out of a larger company of adherents, to be his constant attendants. Hence we do not think that Jesus has special reference to the apostolic office in the words, *but I chose you.* That special reference may lie in the next clause, **and ordained** (or, *appointed*) **you;** but we are not perfectly certain that it does, since all the followers of Christ receive an appointment from him to bear spiritual fruit, in this way or in that. Yet it is natural, on the whole, to suppose that Jesus has some regard to their apostolic mission in this clause. For he is speaking directly to the *eleven*, and their Christian service, their fruit bearing, consisted largely in their apostolic work. **That ye should go**—*i. e., go away* from immediate personal connection with me to a service comparatively distinct. **And bring forth fruit**—resuming the figure of the vine and its branches, and therefore implying their continued union with him in their more distinct work after the Day of Pentecost. **And that your fruit should remain.** The result of their service is to be permanent. A distinct service, productive of good that will endure! This is the promise which cheers their hope in a trying hour. "They were to go into all the world and bring forth fruit, by their godly lives and earnest teaching winning souls to Christ, founding churches, instructing and confirming believers in the faith. The fruit they thus gathered in their personal ministry was unto 'eternal life,' but the fruit of their labors, as apostles, remains for us in the Scriptures of the New Testament."—*G. W. Clark.* **That whatsoever ye shall ask of the Father in my name,** etc. See Notes on 14: 13, and 15: 7. The passages are very similar to one another. In the first, Jesus declares that he himself will do for his disciples what they ask. In the second, he says that the thing which they ask shall come to pass for them. And in this, the third, he represents the Father as about to give that which is asked of him. Again, in the first and third passages, the prayer is said to be offered in the name of Christ, while in the second, it is said to be offered by those who abide in Christ,

17 *These things I command you, that ye love one another.
18 ᵇIf the world hate you, ye know that it hated me before *it hated* you.

17 give it you. These things I command you, that ye love one another. If the world hateth you, ¹ye know

a ver. 12....b 1 John 3:1, 13.——1 Or, *know ye.*

and have his words abiding in them. It may then be inferred from these representations, (1) That both the Father and the Son (as well as the Spirit) may be looked upon as concerned in answering true prayer. What is heard by the Father is heard by the Son, and what is answered by the Father is answered by the Son. This instance comes, therefore, under the more general law that, "whatsoever things he (*the Father*) doeth, these also doeth the Son likewise (*in like manner.*) (5:19). And (2) that there is no promise of answers to prayer, unless those who offer it are in union with Christ and ask according to his will. Hence the need of divine grace in prayer, and the preciousness of the apostle's testimony: "Likewise the Spirit also helpeth our infirmities: for we know not what we should pray for as we ought; but the Spirit itself maketh intercession for us, with groanings which cannot be uttered" (Rom. 8:26); that is to say, the Spirit moves believers in Christ to pray for what is pleasing to God, and, through their acceptable praying, interposes in their behalf. A Christian, then, need not be troubled by the thought that he assumes, in prayer, to enlighten and direct the All-wise. His prayers will never be answered by the gift of what he asks, unless that gift can be conferred in harmony with the principles of the holiest and best moral government. Acceptable prayer is not, therefore, dictatorial, but humble, trustful, and ready to bow to the divine will. This, however, is no denial of the efficacy of prayer. Admitting all this, it is still true that prayer is a real antecedent and occasion of blessing from God, a reason for the bestowment of gifts that would otherwise be withheld. Prayer is not omnipotent, but it is an appeal of weakness to omnipotence, of a dependent child to an independent and Almighty Father, and its request will be granted, if love permits.

For what are men better than sheep or goats,
That nourish a blind life within the brain,
If, knowing God, they lift not hands of prayer
Both for themselves and those who call them friends?
For so the whole round earth is every way
Bound by gold chains about the feet of God.

Observe, also, the two ends or purposes for which Jesus chose and appointed his disciples—(1) "That ye should go and bring forth fruit," etc., and (2) "That whatsoever ye shall ask of the Father in my name, he may give it you." Are these ends—bearing spiritual fruit and obtaining answers to prayer—represented by Christ as co-ordinate? or, as dependent, the former upon the latter, or, the latter upon the former? or, as closely connected and mutually dependent? There is no grammatical objection to any one of these views, but the last seems to us preferable to either of the others. So interdependent are Christian life and Christian prayer, so necessary is fruit bearing to prayer, and prayer to fruit bearing, that the mind naturally associates them together as things inseparable and equally important.

17. These things I command you, etc. The expression, **these things,** cannot refer to the single precept that follows; but it may naturally refer to the precepts directly or indirectly given in ver. 9-16, such as: "abide in my love," "keep my commandments," "love one another, even as I have loved you," "bear fruit," and "offer prayer in my name." And, if this be the correct interpretation, Jesus declares that his purpose in giving these precepts is, **that ye** (*may*) **love one another.** So important is brotherly love in the mind of Christ, that he devotes a considerable part of these last moments with his disciples to an explanation of the duty and privilege of such love. This verse is a resumption of what has been said before, and an introduction to what follows.

18-25. HATRED OF THE WORLD TO THE DISCIPLES OF CHRIST, BECAUSE OF ITS HATRED TO CHRIST, AND TO HIS FATHER.

18. If the world hate you. A supposition according to fact, though the disciples themselves had as yet experienced very little of that hatred. But the time was soon to come when, in the absence of their Master, that hatred would be turned fiercely against them. Of course, **the world,** is the unbelieving, unspiritual mass of mankind, so des-

19 a If ye were of the world, the world would love his own; but b because ye are not of the world, but I have chosen you out of the world, therefore the world hateth you.
20 Remember the word that I said unto you, c The servant is not greater than his lord. If they have persecuted me, they will also persecute you; d if they have kept my saying, they will keep yours also.

19 that it hath hated me before it hated you. If ye were of the world, the world would love its own: but because ye are not of the world, but I chose you out 20 of the world, therefore the world hateth you. Remember the word that I said unto you, A¹servant is not greater than his lord. If they persecuted me, they will also persecute you; if they kept my word,

a 1 John 4: 5....*b* ch. 17: 14....*c* Matt. 10: 24; Luke 6: 40; ch. 13: 16....*d* Ezek. 3: 7.——1 Gr. *bondservant.*

ignated from the majority. **Ye know** (or, *know*) **that it hated** (rather, *hath hated*) **me before it hated you.** The Greek word translated **know** (γινώσκετε), has the same form in the present indicative and imperative; but in this place it is probable imperative. (Comp. "Remember," in ver. 20). The disciples were not yet fully aware of the deadly hate that was even now seeking the life of their Lord. **Hath hated**—perfect tense, to denote enduring enmity. It was no sudden, effervescent passion, but a deep-seated, inveterate jealousy and bitterness of spirit against the Holy One of God that he saw in the hearts of men, and that was so soon to find expression in their conduct. **Before it hated you**—literally, *first of you.* Compare 1: 15, where the same idiom occurs. It may imply that he was "first" hated, and that they were related to him in the matter spoken of, that he was temporally and causally head of the series to which they also belonged. Weiss rejects this view, and says that "after this example the hatred of the world should be nothing new, surprising, or stumbling to them." We incline to the view first mentioned.

19. If ye were of the world. To be of the world, is to belong to it in character and conduct, to partake of its spirit, and yield to its influence. (Comp. 17: 14, 16; 1 John 4: 5; John 8: 44; 1 John 3: 8, 10, and Grimm "N. T. Lexicon," s. v. εἰμί, 3. d). **The world would love his** (*its*) **own.** Not merely because everywhere "like rejoices in like" (Euth., Zig.), but also, because in sinful men, selfishness reigns, and leads them to favor those who are on their side. As Weiss remarks, the language of Jesus presupposes that self-love is characteristic of the world. Hence there is said to be a kind of honor among thieves. They will befriend those whom it is their interest to befriend. Even the most self-seeking will speak well of men who strengthen their hands or flatter their vanity. **But because ye are not of the world**—in the sense explained above, **but I have chosen** (*chose*) **you out of the world.** Here, certainly, whatever may be thought of the expression, "but I chose you," in verse 16, the choice spoken of is not the election to the apostolic office, but the election to discipleship and salvation, to spiritual and eternal life; for the choice, or election, is one by which they were separated from the world, and not from the general body of disciples. "It is dogmatic artifice," says Weiss, "if Luthardt, and Ebrard after Hofmann, assert that there is no reference in this language to others who are not chosen, but only to the collection of a holy band, since the expression, 'out of the world,' points directly to the community to which they had belonged, and the rest of whose members remain what they were, because not chosen, as these. But it by no means follows that this choice was made according to a *decretum absolutum,* and not in view of something which made them suitable for his purposes." It may be added, that the word *chose*, both here and in verse 16, represents a Greek verb in the middle voice, and may be translated, strictly, "chose for myself." **Therefore the world hateth you. Therefore**—*i. e.,* on account of this. The disciples must not be surprised at the world's hatred; for it is due to the great fact that they are no longer at one with it in aim or spirit, in creed or conduct; they have been called out of it, and now belong to a kingdom "not of this world." In union with Christ, they must of necessity share his destiny as one rejected by the world. And surely this thought will be a comfort to them whenever they are made to suffer by the world's hatred.

20. Remember the word, etc. Probably he intends to recall what he had said to them earlier in the evening, for another purpose (see 13: 16); for the same truth may be pertinent in more than one connection. The fact

21 But *all these things will they do unto you for my name's sake, because they know not him that sent me. | 21 they will keep yours also. But all these things will they do unto you for my name's sake, because they

a Matt. 10:22; 24:9; ch. 16:3.

that the servant is not greater than his Master, is a good reason why he ought cheerfully to perform any task, however lowly, which his Master is willing to perform; and the same fact is an equally good reason why he should expect that men who will maltreat his Master, will not hesitate to maltreat him, if faithful to that Master. But the words of Christ on another occasion, when he sent forth the twelve on a brief mission to the lost sheep of the house of Israel, are not only identical with these, but were employed to teach the same lesson. (See Matt. 10: 24, sq.). **If they have persecuted me, they will also persecute you. Have** is to be omitted before **persecuted.** This is only another and stronger statement of the case presented in the foregoing verse; for whom the world hates it will find means to persecute. But it is interesting to observe that Jesus here speaks of his disciples as truly devoted to him, and as distinct from the world, by virtue of their moral affinity to him. For merely nominal disciples are in little danger of persecution. Only those who are true to their Lord are likely to suffer from the malignity of his foes. **If they have** (omit have) **kept my saying, they will keep yours also.** A plain assumption that their word would be substantially the same as his—a word giving the same view of him and of his spiritual reign which he had so patiently endeavored to instill into their minds, but which they had proved so incapable of receiving until this hour. Yet they were to receive it, as the Saviour knew, with the gift of the Spirit at the first Pentecost after his resurrection, and were to preach it so purely that God would confirm their message by signs following. Moreover, this saying of Jesus has been verified by the entire history of the Christian religion. Those who have reverenced the word of Christ as holy and true, have also, with few exceptions, reverenced the word of the apostles as holy and true. And those who have rejected the divine authority of the apostles' teaching, have also, sooner or later, rejected that of Christ's teaching in the Gospels.

21. But all these things will they do unto you for my name's sake. Notice (1) that Jesus takes for granted the truth of the former of the two alternatives mentioned by him in the last part of verse 20, and means by the expression, **all these things,** persecution and other manifestations of hatred. (2) That he points out the deepest reason for this hatred and persecution of his disciples. Because the world hates the name of Jesus Christ—*i. e.*, the character and work represented by that name, it will seek to vex and destroy those who honor and worship it. (See Acts 4: 17; 9: 14; 26: 9.) That Jesus claimed to be "the Son of God" was counted blasphemy by the Sanhedrin, and was the ostensible reason for his condemnation; but, in reality, his holy and unworldly spirit, together with the aim and character of his work, was a disappointment to their expectations, a rebuke to their pride, and a condemnation of their life, which filled them with wrath. (3) That this is no new doctrine of Jesus. He had suggested the same thing in his Sermon on the Mount: "Blessed are ye when men shall revile you, and persecute you, and shall say all manner of evil against you falsely, for my sake." (Matt. 5:11.) And it is certainly safe to presume that Jesus, by suggesting this, intended not only to show his disciples the *inevitableness* of persecution, but to furnish them also with *comfort* in bearing it. "Rejoice, and be exceeding glad: for great is your reward in heaven: for so persecuted they the prophets which were before you." (Matt. 5:12.) The assurance that they were suffering for the name of Christ, whom they adored as their Saviour, and that they were but drinking the cup which he had drained before (Matt. 20:22), would be their greatest consolation in the dungeon, or on the cross. **Because they know not him that sent me.** Thus Jesus attributes the hostility which was seeking his life, and which would seek that of his friends, to ignorance of God. And by ignorance of God is meant want of love to his character. For to know God, in the highest and only adequate sense, is to love him. Not to love him, is to be ignorant of him. If the Jews had understood and ap-

22 "If I had not come and spoken unto them, they had not had sin: but now they have no cloke for their sin.
23 He that hateth me hateth my Father also.
24 If I had not done among them ᵈthe works which none other man did, they had not had sin: but now have they both seen and hated both me and my Father.

22 know not him that sent me. If I had not come and spoken unto them, they had not had sin: but now they have no excuse for their sin. He that hateth
24 me hateth my Father also. If I had not done among them the works which none other did, they had not had sin: but now have they both seen and

a ch. 9: 41....*b* Rom. 1: 20; James 4: 16....*c* 1 John 2: 23....*d* ch. 3: 2; 7: 31; 9: 32.

preciated the God of their fathers, they would have been won to Christ, and would have seen in him the Son of the Highest, the image of the invisible God. The same is true of those to whom the gospel is preached. A rejection of Christ, is a rejection of the Father who sent him; and a rejection of the Father is due to a want of love.

22. If I had not come and spoken unto them, they had not had sin. The coming here referred to, is the coming from heaven, by way of the incarnation. It was the condition of Christ's speaking to men, and revealing to them the Father with unprecedented clearness. Jesus here affirms that the sin of the world is without excuse, because of his teaching and miracles. (Ver. 22, 24.) All previous revelations were starlight when compared with the noonday brightness of the one made by Christ, and therefore, without this, the Jews would have been comparatively innocent. For the guilt of rejecting God is always in proportion to the means of knowledge furnished. To *have sin*, means to be a sinner; in other words, it is to have sinned, and hence to be guilty of sin. Sin is conceived of as belonging to the sinner, just as truly as a wound, or a sense of pain belongs to one who has it. (Comp. 19: 11; 1 John 1: 8.) *Bearing sin* is a similar expression; for the guilt of it is conceived of as resting upon the wrong-doer, and exposing him to just punishment. (Num. 9: 13; 14: 34; 18: 22.) Of course, the second clause, **they had not had sin,** must be taken in a qualified, not an absolute sense. Their sin would, in that case, have been as nothing compared with what it now is. **But now they have no cloke (*or, excuse*) for their sin.** As knowledge, and, indeed, knowledge in its purest form and greatest spiritual beauty, has been placed within their reach, and they have refused to welcome it, their sin is without excuse. "To him that knoweth to do good, and doeth it not, to him it is sin." (James 4: 17.) Observe (1) that ignorance may sometimes be a plausible or partial excuse for evil conduct, though it is never, perhaps, a perfectly sufficient one. (Comp. 1 Tim. 1: 13; Acts 17: 30; 1 Pet. 1: 14.) (2) That this ignorance must be due to a lack of the means of knowledge, as well as of knowledge itself, or it will be of no avail as an apology for wrong-doing. *Only* in case it were absolute, involuntary, and wholly due to the providence of God, would it be a valid excuse for evil conduct. And such ignorance of duty does not probably anywhere exist (comp. Rom. 1: 19, sq.; 2: 12-15); certainly it did not prevail among the Jews in Christ's day.

23. He that hateth me hateth my Father also. The Son is one with the Father, is the image of the Father, is the clearest possible revelation of the Father, and, indeed, as clear a revelation of the Father as of himself—the Son. And he is this down to the present hour, by his teaching and personal bearing; by the divine purity and authority; by the soul-awakening and soul-illuminating power of his words and life. But he knows himself to be hated—steadily, deeply, and even bitterly hated—by many of the people, and in this hour of most solemn and holy feeling, he deliberately affirms that hatred of himself is hatred of his Father—that hatred of the Son of God is hatred of God. And if it was so then, is it not so now?

24. If I had not done among them the works which none other man did. The mighty works of Jesus, viewed in all their circumstances and characteristics, were more evidently and indisputably divine than any works ever performed among men. They were "signs" which ought to have convinced the most cautious and conservative that God was with him. (Comp. 3: 2; 9: 30-33.) Judged by them, as well as by his teaching, Jesus ought to have been welcomed as the long expected Messiah and Holy One of God (6: 69), instead of being accused of serving Beelzebub, and blaspheming Jehovah. Profoundly as they were disappointed in their expectations of a civil ruler, and shocked as they

25 But *this cometh to pass*, that the word might be fulfilled that is written in their law, *They hated me without a cause. 26 *But when the Comforter is come, whom I will send unto you from the Father, *even* the Spirit of truth, which proceedeth from the Father, *he shall testify of me:

25 hated both me and my Father. But *this cometh to pass*, that the word may be fulfilled that is written 26 in their law, They hated me without a cause. But when the ¹Comforter is come, whom I will send unto you from the Father, *even* the Spirit of truth, who ²proceedeth from the Father, he shall bear

a Ps. 35: 19; 60: 4....*b* Luke 24: 49; ch. 14: 17, 26; 16: 7, 13; Acts 2: 33,....*c* 1 John 5: 6.—1 Or, *Advocate.* Or, *Helper.* Gr. *Paraclete*....2 Or, *goeth forth from*.

were by his disregard of their Sabbath scruples, and provoked as they were by his outspoken condemnation of their hypocrisy, they ought to have received the holy and self-evidencing truth which he proclaimed with divine authority, and to have been convinced by the miracles which he wrought. But they were filled with a deep moral enmity to God, which evidence could not overcome. Their unbelief was a matter of the heart, and was, therefore, proof against reason. How many in every age have been like them! The world did not come to an end with the destruction of Jerusalem. **But now have they both seen and hated both me and my Father. Seen**—*i. e.*, in and by the works of which he is speaking. These works were no less a revelation of his Father than of himself. They "revealed outwardly the majesty and will of God, and of Christ, as the representative of God."—*Westcott.* With this language may be compared that of 14: 9: "He that hath seen me hath seen the Father" **25. But this cometh to pass, that the word might** (or, *may*) **be fulfilled that is written in their law, They hated me without a cause.** The ellipsis after **but,** is properly filled, we believe, with the words, *this cometh to pass.* But why an ellipsis here, and in 13: 18? Weiss suggests that we "may assume a painful *aposiopesis*, in which Jesus forbears to declare what it was that took place, in order that the prophecy might be fulfilled." Of course Jesus does not mean that the world hated him with a view to fulfilling a prediction of the Scripture, or that God had either moved or permitted the world to hate him in order to thus fulfill a prophecy of Scripture. But God made the prediction because he foresaw the events which it described, and because he would have his people know that he foresaw these events, and so was not taken with surprise by them. There was, therefore, a good *end* accomplished by the fulfillment of these predictions—an end which God had in view when he made them,

an end which the Saviour recognized as accomplished by them. And by calling attention to the fact that, in a comprehensive sense, God's knowledge and plan of government took into account from the beginning all these dark and perplexing events, Jesus removes doubt from the mind of his disciples. The emphatic words of the quotation are, probably, the last, **without a cause.** (Comp. ver. 22, 24). Their enmity to Christ was gratuitous, undeserved, unprovoked. The quotation is thought to be from Ps. 69: 4. (Comp. Ps. 35: 19). In his introduction to this Psalm, Perowne says: "Enough, however, remains to justify the Messianic sense of the Psalm, provided our interpretation be fair and sober. The broad principle laid down in the introduction to the Seventy-second Psalm applies here. The history of prophets and holy men of old is a typical history. They were, it may be said, representative men, suffering and hoping, not for themselves only, but for the nation whom they represented. In their sufferings they were feeble and transient images of the Great Sufferer, who by his sufferings accomplished man's redemption." And on the fourth verse, as cited in part by Jesus, he remarks: "The manner of citation plainly shows how we are to understand *that it might be fulfilled* (ἵνα πληρωθῇ); what was true, in some sense, even of the suffering Israelite under the law, was still more true of Him in whom was no sin, and whom, therefore, his enemies did indeed hate without cause." And the Spirit of God foresaw the antitype in the type. Observe that the Psalms are evidently embraced in **their law,** as the words are here used. The whole Old Testament was, in fact, regarded by the Jews as **their law, in** so far as it was their rule of duty towards God and man. Jesus does not seem to call it their law by way of contrast with a different law now binding on his followers, but simply as a law which they recognized as divine.

26. But when the Comforter (*Advocate*)

27 And *a* ye also shall bear witness, because *b* ye have | 27 witness of me: ¹and ye also bear witness, because
been with me from the beginning. | ye have been with me from the beginning.

a Luke 24: 48; Acts 1: 8, 21, 22; 2: 32; 3: 15; 4: 20, 33; 5: 32; 10: 39; 13: 31; 1 Pet. 5: 1; 2 Pet. 1: 16....*b* Luke 1: 2; 1 John 1: 1, 2.—
¹ *Or, and bear ye also witness.*

is come, etc. The word **but** should probably be omitted. Notice (1) that the purpose for which the Spirit of truth is here said to come to the disciples, is to bear witness concerning Christ. The hatred of the world is not to prevail against Jesus and his followers, by putting them to silence after putting him to death, but his honor and cause are to be maintained by the Divine Advocate, who is to take his own place with the disciples. (2) That Jesus himself engages to send this Advocate and Witness from the Father; for the pronoun **I** is emphatic, as if he had said in English, "Whom I myself will send to you," etc. Twice before he has claimed a part in this sending of the Paraclete, first, by saying, "I—*i. e., I myself* will pray the Father, and he shall give you another Comforter, (Advocate)" (14: 16); and, secondly, by speaking of the Spirit as One "whom the Father will send *in my name*" (14: 26); but here he makes his own authority more prominent, though in perfect harmony with his claim to be one with the Father in all action for the salvation of men. (Comp. 5: 19 sq.; 6: 44; 12: 32; 10: 28-30). (3) That the Advocate is to come **from the Father**—*i. e., from with the Father*, even as he is characterized as One "who proceedeth from with the Father." Westcott remarks: "The preposition (παρά) which is used in both clauses, expresses, properly, position ('from the side of'), and not source (ἐκ, 'out of')." There is, therefore, no sufficient basis in the expression, "which proceedeth from the Father," for the doctrine of the eternal Procession of the Spirit from the Father. Especially important is it, as Westcott has noted, "that the Greek Fathers who apply this passage to the eternal Procession instinctively substitute 'out of' (ἐκ) for 'from' (παρά) in their application of it." Why then is the present tense employed in this clause? or why is this clause added to the promise, **I will send,** etc.? We answer, to connect the working of the Spirit in every age or dispensation with the Father's will. And this appears to be the view of Weiss (in Meyer). He says that the word "proceedeth" (ἐκπορεύεται), "expressing action in a general way, without temporal limits, does not refer to the essence of the Spirit (*Lücke*), or to the imminent relation of the divine subsistences (*Stier, Godet*) . . but, according to the context, to the effective communication from the Father *ad extra*, through which, in every case that occurs, the Spirit is received." And Westcott says again: "The use of the present (*proceedeth*), in contrast with the future (*I will send*), brings out the truth that the mission of the Spirit consequent on the exaltation of the Son, was the consummation of his earlier working in the world." It is certainly rash to affirm that this language has any direct reference to the inner and essential relations of the Godhead. It shows, however, that in the economy of grace, the work of the Son and of the Spirit cannot be regarded as separate from that of the Father. (4) That the work of the Paraclete in bearing witness respecting Christ, is to be effected in and through his disciples—unless, perhaps, the testimony of miracles be regarded as external to them, though connected with their faith and confirmatory of their mission and word. In support of this statement, we appeal to the words, "whom I will send *unto you*," and to the fact that the Spirit was not only to quicken the memory of the disciples as to what Jesus had taught them, but was also to teach them himself, and guide them into all the truth (14: 26; 16: 16 sq). Besides, as a matter of history, it appears that the Spirit's witness concerning Christ has always been closely connected with that of the apostles in preaching, or the written word. The experience of Christian men under the influence of the Spirit is dependent on the testimony of Scripture as to the life of Christ. Hence the importance of the next verse.

27. And ye also shall bear witness. Bear witness, instead of **shall bear witness,** appears to be the true reading in this place. But to translate it as an imperative (though the form allows this) breaks the connection and mars the harmony of the passage. It is better to account for the present indicative by supposing that Jesus would recognize, with all possible honor, their actual relation

CHAPTER XVI.

THESE things have I spoken unto you, that ye ªshould not be offended.
2 ᵇThey shall put you out of the synagogues: yea, the time cometh, ᶜthat whosoever killeth you will think that he doeth God service.

1 These things have I spoken unto you, that ye 2 should not be made to stumble. They shall put you out of the synagogues: yea, the hour cometh, that whosoever killeth you shall think that he

a Matt. 11:6; 24:10; 26:31....b ch. 9:22, 34; 12:42....c Acts 8:1; 9:1; 26:9, 10, 11.

to him. For the eleven were loyal, though weak. They had often testified of the wisdom and power of their Master, and they were now ready to repeat their testimony. Jesus therefore describes them as doing what they have done, are prepared to do, and will spend their lives in doing. "Ye, too, are my witnesses," is the purport of his language. Because ye have been (rather, are) with me from the beginning. A case of breviloquence, meaning, "Ye are now, and have been, from the beginning of my public work, with me." (Comp. Luke 1:2; Acts 1:22; and John 8:44; Acts 26:4). Godet remarks: "The apostles will not be more passive instruments of the Spirit. They will continue to be free and personal agents. Along with the action of the Spirit they will have their special part to do in bearing testimony. For they possess a treasure which is their own, and which the Spirit could not have communicated to them—their *historical* knowledge of the ministry of Jesus from its origin even to its end. The apostles were to be the witnesses of the *historic* Christ. But the Spirit does not teach the facts of history; he unfolds its true meaning. The apostolic testimony, and the testimony of the Spirit, form, therefore, a single act, but they contribute each a different element—one the historic narrative, the other its internal evidence and victorious force." If Godet means to deny the agency of the Spirit in quickening the memory of the apostles, his denial is nullified by the express declaration of Christ (14:26); but if he only means that the Holy Spirit did not reveal to them historic facts in the life of Christ which they had never learned by natural means, by sight or hearing, his statement may be correct. At all events, it directs us to what may be called the distinctive elements of the double testimony of the Spirit and the apostles.

Ch. 16: 1-4. Religious Persecution Because of the World's Hatred, Graciously Foretold.

1. These things have I spoken unto you. These things, may comprise all that is recorded in the preceding chapter, but especially in the last part of it. (Ver. 18-27). That ye should not be offended, (better, as in Rev. Ver., *that ye may not be made to stumble*). By forewarning them of the inexcusable hostility of "the world"—a hostility directed against Jehovah and his Anointed (Ps. 2: 2), even when it is aimed at them—Jesus seeks to prepare them for what is to come, and so to prevent them from falling into doubt or despair. For the rejection of the gospel by the bulk of the Jewish nation, was sure to prove one of the sorest trials of their faith. If the confidence of the elect in him could be broken by anything, it would be broken by the utter failure of the chosen people to recognize their King, and by their bitter enmity to him as an alleged impostor and blasphemer. For the use of the word (σκανδαλίζειν), *to cause to stumble*, see Matt. 5: 29, 30; 11: 6; John 6: 61; and Matt. 13: 21, compared with Luke 8: 13. In the New Testament it never denotes causing one to stumble or fall, physically, but always morally; in other words, it is always used in a tropical sense, meaning, to cause one to fall into sin, apostasy, or the like.

2. They shall (better, *will*), put you out of the synagogue. See Note on this form of excommunication at 9: 22. "And this, which you might naturally anticipate, if the people reject the gospel, is not the worst; "*but an hour cometh.*" This gives the sense more exactly than the version, Yea, the time, etc. For but (ἀλλά) "introduces the contrast of a much worse, a bloody issue."— *Weiss.* If no attempt is made to supply (as above) the unexpressed thought which accounts for the contrast expressed by this connective, the customary version, yea, is the best approximate rendering of the original. (See Winer, p. 451). That whosoever killeth you, etc. What must be said of the conjunction that (ἵνα)? Does it retain in this place the idea of purpose or end? So Winer believes (p. 330:) "*the time is come in order*

3 And *these things will they do unto you, because they have not known the Father, nor me.
4 But *these things have I told you, that when the time shall come, ye may remember that I told you of them. And *these things I said not unto you at the beginning, because I was with you.

3 offereth service unto God. And these things will they do, because they have not known the Father, 4 nor me. But these things have I spoken unto you, that when their hour is come, ye may remember them, how that I told you. And these things I said not unto you from the beginning, because I was with

a ch. 15: 21; Rom. 10: 2; 1 Cor. 2: 8; 1 Tim. 1: 13....*b* ch. 13: 19; 14: 29....*c* See Matt. 9: 15.

to—that is, the time appointed for the purpose, that, etc." So, also, Meyer and Weiss. "What will happen in the 'hour,' is regarded as the object of its coming." In other words, this dreadful violence in persecuting the disciples of Christ will have its day and hour, a period provided for it in the holy plan of God.[1]
By saying **whosoever**—*every one*, etc., Jesus declares that the deadly persecutions to be anticipated by his followers would be animated by religious fanaticism, by an opinion on the part of those who should conduct them, that killing the servants of Christ is rendering a strictly religious service to God, (like offering an appointed sacrifice). So, then, an impure and ignorant zeal of God would embitter the hearts of men against his most faithful servants. (Comp. Acts 26: 9; Gal. 1: 13 sq). Many commentators refer, in illustration of Christ's saying, to the Midrash on Num. 20: 12, (where Phinehas is said to have *made an atonement* for the children of Israel): "Was this said because he offered an offering (*Korban*)? No; but to teach them that every one who sheds the blood of the wicked is as he that offereth an offering." See also, the view of heathen writers, in Tacitus, "Ann." xv. 44; and Suetonius, "Nero," 16. Alas, the day has not yet dawned, when religious persecution, even unto death, is seen by all to be evil.

3. And these things will they do unto you (omit **unto you**), **because they have not known the Father, nor me.** Perhaps

[1] The writer is indebted to Dr. Broadus for the following Note: "*An hour is coming, and has come, for you to be scattered*, etc. I think this is a pretty exact rendering. It does not mean that an hour *has come for that purpose*, but that an hour suited and appointed for that has arrived. There are in this Gospel many delicate *non-final* uses of (ἵνα). Meyer insists on making them all strictly final, which is often extremely awkward and forced, and Winer only half extricated himself from that notion. It is frequently very difficult to render, or to determine, the exact shade of meaning in such cases, but that the (ἵνα) is very often not final is certain."

the stricter rendering, *because they knew not*, would be justified in this case by supposing that the mind of Jesus passes forward to the time of persecution (**will they do**), and from that point views the failure to recognize the Father and Christ as something already complete in the past. But with either translation the principal thought of this clause remains the same. The *knew not;* or, **have not known**, is not mentioned by way of excuse for their conduct. It is rather a part of their sin, but a part which accounts for the rest. That when light came into the world, they loved darkness rather than light (3: 19), was in a high degree sinful, and was the occasion of other sin, even the unrelenting severity with which they tried to exterminate those who were willing to walk in the light. How evident it is that one who supposes God to be pleased with religious persecution, has no correct view of his character! How clear that one who imagines Jesus Christ to be pleased with such a use of force and violence, is a stranger to his love! Yet how uniformly and fiercely have the persecutors of good men claimed that they were doing their terrible work for the Lord's sake! Is there not danger of palliating their sin, by the plea that they were doing what they supposed to be right? Was not the light offered to their minds? And did they not reject it? With the knowledge which had been brought to mankind by the Saviour, they had no excuse for being ignorant of the true God, or for persecuting his servants.

4. But these things have I told you (or, **spoken unto you**). The word **but** is most naturally explained as denoting a sharp interruption of the account of what *the world* would do, and a recurrence to the thought of verse 1: **But**—to say no more of this—**these things**, etc. **That when the time shall come** (lit., *their hour is come*). *Their hour* is the hour of these events, the time when they will come to pass. **Ye may remember that I told you of them.** The best supported text reads: *Ye may remember them*, *that I myself told you.* Few things would be more comforting to the disciples in times of distress, produced by the hatred of men, than a remembrance of Christ's own prediction of the events by which they were distressed—a prediction uttered in the immediate presence of his agony in the garden! That he foresaw it all, that he told them of it in love, that their suffering was for him, and that he had suffered far more for them—all this would give them patience and strength. **And these things I said not unto you at** (rather, *from*) **the beginning, because I was with you.** Observe, (1) that Jesus does not deny having spoken of **these things** before the present hour; he simply denies having spoken of them to his disciples **from the beginning** of his public ministry. This denial is not inconsistent with an occasional reference in the course of his ministry to the sufferings which they would be called to bear. "The future fate of the disciples had not been unfolded little by little in unbroken order as a necessary consequence of their relation to Christ. Here and there it had been indicated before, but now it was shown in its essential relation to their faith."—*Westcott.* (2) That while the Synoptists appear to affirm that Jesus spoke previously on one occasion with much fullness of the sufferings which would overtake the disciples, of the hatred of the world as the source of those sufferings, and of the name of Christ as the occasion of that hatred, they do not say that he spoke with the same fullness (as here) of the Holy Spirit as their Teacher and Helper in time to come. (See Matt. 5: 10; 10: 16, sq.; Luke 6: 22, sq.) " 'These things,' in this verse," says Watkins (comp. ver. 3 and 1, and chap. 15: 21), " refers to the full account he has given them of the world's hatred and the principles lying at the foot of it, and the manner in which it was to be met by the Spirit's witness and their witness of him." On the other hand, Weiss maintains (1) that Matthew inserts in Christ's address to the twelve (Matt. 10), predictions as to their future sufferings through persecution which, as Luke 12 proves, were not uttered at that time, the Evangelist bringing together in that address the substance of what Jesus had said at different times on the matter referred to. (2) That John also appears to have brought together in this section, either consciously or unconsciously, whatever according to his recollection Jesus had foretold concerning the destiny of his disciples in the world. In proof of this he remarks: "Therefore in this place occur such sayings as 15: 20, sq., which are undoubtedly the same as Matt. 10: 24, 25, sq.; therefore the being hated for my name's sake 15: 21, comp. Matt. 10: 22; therefore above all the somewhat mechanically (and here surely by the writer's combination of materials) introduced 26, 27, which are certainly nothing else than a genuine Johannic reproduction of Matt. 10: 19, sq." But this criticism of John's record seems to me to overlook the circumstance that every great teacher is wont to repeat the same truth again and again with slight variations of language, gathering up the results in some final lesson which is more complete or impressive than any one that preceded it. In this way, I would account for the similarity of thought and language in the first two instances (viz., John 15: 20, sq., compared with Matt. 10: 24, 25, sq., and John 15: 21, compared with Matt. 10: 22). And as to the insertion of 15: 26, 27, where they stand, it seems to me far more probable that Jesus put them there in a free, tender, spontaneous address to his disciples—an address adapting itself moment by moment to the varying emotions reflected from the countenances of the little circle of friends about him—than that the reflective skill of the writer put them there, though out of their true place. But whatever may be thought of the probability that the apostle John has unconsciously brought into this address something that belongs elsewhere, it is manifestly very improbable that a *Falsarius,* writing in the third, fourth, or fifth decade of the second century, when the Synoptical Gospels were already well known and highly esteemed, would have ventured upon even a seeming contradiction of what they teach, such as we are supposed to have in the words: "These things I said not unto you from the beginning." Would not such a writer have been extremely solicitous to avoid every appearance of inconsistency with the earlier testimony? Besides, what conceivable motive could have led him to make this statement, with no evidence of its truth in his possession, and to expose his narrative thereby to criticism?

CH. XVI.]   JOHN.   313

5 But now *I go my way to him that sent me; and none of you asketh me, Whither goest thou?
6 But because I have said these things unto you, *sorrow hath filled your heart.
7 Nevertheless I tell you the truth; It is expedient for you that I go away: for if I go not away, *the Comforter will not come unto you; but *if I depart, I will send him unto you.

5 you. But now I go unto him that sent me; and none of you asketh me, Whither goest thou? But because I have spoken these things unto you, sorrow 7 hath filled your heart. Nevertheless I tell you the truth; It is expedient for you that I go away: for if I go not away, the *Comforter will not come unto

a ch. 7: 33; 13: 3; 14: 28; ver. 10: 16....b ch. 14: 1; ver. 22.. .c ch. 7: 39; 14: 16, 26; 15: 26....d Acts 2: 33; Eph. 4: 8.—1 Or. Advocate. Or. Helper. Gr. Paraclete.

5-15. PROMISE OF THE PARACLETE'S COMING AND WORK.

5. But now I go my way (better, *go away*, or *depart*) to him that sent me. The idea of withdrawal or retirement from the company of his disciples, if not from the world, is expressed by the word (ὑπάγω) here used, while the words, to him that sent me, describe the goal to be reached by that withdrawal. And none of you asketh me, Whither goest (or, *withdrawest*) thou? They had given some attention to the thought of his leaving them, and had been troubled by it. But they seem to have considered its effect upon themselves, not upon him. In other words, they had not asked *whither* he was going, or what would be the *home* that he would reach. Their concern for themselves had filled their hearts, and prevented any interest in respect to his glory and joy with the Father.

6. But because I have said (or, *spoken*) these things unto you, sorrow hath filled your heart. They should have rejoiced. Love to him should have filled their hearts with exceeding gladness, because he was about to resume his divine estate (comp. 14: 28). But instead of this they were sad. The shadow of a great disappointment was gathering about them. While they still clung with desperate tenacity to the hope that he would in some way escape the malice of his foes and restore the kingdom to Israel, every sentence which he uttered pointed to a different issue, and tended to increase their sorrow. Doubtless this was very manifest in their looks and gestures, if it was not also expressed by audible sighs. A sorrowful company they were at this moment.

7. Nevertheless I tell you the truth. Purely as a matter of taste in reproducing the simplicity of John's style, we should prefer *yet* to nevertheless, as a translation of the Greek word (ἀλλά) in this place; and the same rendering would be better than the almost obsolete *howbeit*, in John 7: 27, and Acts 7:

48. It is also noteworthy tat the I is emphatic in the original; probably to contrast his own correct view with their false view. Thus: "You have a wrong view of my departure, deeming it your greatest calamity, and, therefore, sorrow fills your hearts. But I, on the contrary, tell you the truth, in respect to this event," etc. It is expedient for you that I go away. Thus Jesus declares that if they were to disregard his condition and look only at their own good, they had more to gain than to lose by his departure. Their intense self-care was, therefore, unwise as well as ungenerous, though he only says this by implication. What he does say directly, after gently reminding them of their disregard of his interest in the case, is, that henceforth his presence was not the highest blessing they could have. Not that his presence was anything less than gracious, uplifting, and sanctifying, but that his going away would bring to them light and help more powerful, more spiritual, and better adapted to their condition in days to come. This he proceeds to explain: for if I go not away, the Comforter (or, *Advocate*) will not come unto you. What is to be understood by this? Could not the Holy Spirit work in the hearts of men, to renew and sanctify them, while Christ was in the flesh? We believe that he could, and did. But for two reasons, at least, he could not, without violence to the principles of human nature, do for them all that he did after the return of Jesus to his Father. (1) The visible and natural presence of Christ was an obstacle to the fullest influence of the Spirit in certain directions. For, while Jesus was there in bodily form, a true man, it was extremely difficult for them to think of his reign as purely spiritual. As we have seen all along, they shared, with the bulk of their nation, the expectation that the Messiah would be a temporal prince, whatever else he might be. And obviously nothing short of his departure from earth by death, would thoroughly destroy

8 And when he is come, he will reprove the world of sin, and of righteousness, and of judgment:

8 you; but if I go, I will send him unto you. And he, when he is come, will convict the world in respect of sin, and of righteousness, and of judgment:

that expectation. Moreover, the visible presence of Christ, as a teacher, to whom they could resort for answers to every question, would tend to prevent their gathering up and pondering, with suitable care and prayer for divine help, all that he had said to them. It was time for the young eagles to be left alone. (2) The departure of Christ by crucifixion, burial, resurrection, and ascension, were parts of his work, as Mediator between God and men, which the Holy Spirit was to use, and which could not be used with full effect, until they had been accomplished. Hence the new and mightier work of the Spirit after the departure of Jesus, is described as his coming from the Father, sent by the Son; and as that greater work could not be performed until Christ had been crucified and glorified, thus furnishing the truth to be employed, the coming of the Spirit for that work is represented as dependent on the previous departure of Christ. **But if I depart** (better, *go*), **I will send him unto you.** Observe that Christ here employs a word which signifies merely to go, to make a journey, not to go away. Observe also, that he says again (see 15: 26), **I will send him unto you.**

8. And when he is come, etc. A more formally exact translation would read: *And, having come, he will convict* **the world** *concerning*, etc. The questions to be answered by the interpreter of this verse relate solely to the meaning of the words. (1) The Greek word (ἐλέγξει), is translated in the Com. Ver. **reprove,** in the Rev. Ver. *convict*, and by many scholars, *convince.* Does it here signify *will reprove,* or *will convince,* or *will convict?* The first definition may be given to the verb in Luke 3: 19; 1 Tim. 5: 20; Titus 1: 13; Rev. 3: 19. But it does not satisfy the demands of this passage. For, while it is natural to speak of reproving one in respect of sin, it is less natural to speak of reproving one in respect of righteousness, and unnatural to speak of reproving one in respect of judgment. Besides, mere reproof expresses but a small part of the Holy Spirit's work in relation to the world, especially if that work is performed in great measure through the inspired teaching of the apostles. (Comp. Notes on 15: 26, 27). This definition of the word is, therefore, unsatisfactory. The second meaning is given to the verb in 1 Cor. 14: 24: "If all prophesy, and there come in one that believeth not, or one unlearned, he is convinced of all," etc. But against this meaning, it has been urged that "the chief part of the world is still without the pale of the church, and that, even within the church, the number of those in whom a living spiritual conviction of sin and righteousness and judgment has been wrought, is by no means the largest." (Hare, in "Mission of the Comforter"). There is weight in this consideration. Moreover, this rendering carries the mind of the reader directly to the effect of the Paraclete's work in the hearts of men—that is, to the subjective influence of the Spirit, while the Greek term gives quite as much prominence to the intrinsic force of the argument or evidence employed. Thus the word *reprove,* directs attention almost exclusively to the objective side of the action, and the word *convince,* to the subjective, while the Greek original seems to embrace both. The third definition is supported by the use of the word in ch. 8: 46: "Which of you convicteth me of sin?" and in James 2: 9: "But if ye have respect of persons, ye commit sin, and are convicted by the law as transgressors." Rev. Ver. Yet the legal use of this English word has a tendency to restrict its meaning, and on this account, Noyes's translation, namely: "Shall bring conviction to the world, etc.," is, perhaps, as free from objection as any. Lücke remarks that, "In the Greek verb used by Christ is always implied the refutation, the overcoming of an error, or wrong, by the truth and the right. And when, by means of the conviction (ἔλεγχος), the truth detects the error, and the right the wrong, so that a man becomes conscious of them—then arises the feeling of *guilt,* which is ever painful. And hence this office has been called the Punitive Office of the Spirit. The effect of conviction wrought by the Divine Spirit in the world, may be to harden; but its *aim* is the deliverance of the world." With the last statement of Lücke may be compared the words of Paul in 2 Cor. 2: 15, 16.

(2) By **the world,** must be understood

9 *a* Of sin, because they believe not on me; | 9 of sin, because they believe not on me; of righteous-

a Acts 2: 22-37.

the yet unbelieving part of mankind, so denominated because it was the far larger part, when these words were spoken, as it still is. Only a few of the Jews, and a still smaller number of the Gentiles, gave any evidence of saving faith in God. "If Luthardt and Hengstenberg maintain that the Jewish world is primarily meant, this is certainly correct as to the mind of Jesus, but not as to that of the Evangelist."—*Weiss.* We enter our protest against this oracular style of criticism. How any one can know what was intended by Jesus, in distinction from what the Evangelist understood him to mean, is left without explanation by Weiss, and is incomprehensible to us. That Jesus did not restrict his own kingdom, or the work of the Spirit, absolutely and forever, to the seed of Abraham after the flesh, is clear from many passages; and if he looked beyond the Israelites at all, there seems to be no reason why he should not have done this in his last protracted interview with his disciples, and especially when speaking to them of the work of the Spirit.

(3) The words **sin, righteousness, and judgment,** are used in a general sense, and therefore without the article; but a conspicuous example of each is made use of by the Spirit, according to the next verse, in demonstrating to the world the nature of sin, of righteousness, and of judgment. The Note of Westcott is very suggestive: "The three conceptions, sin, righteousness, and judgment, are given first in their most abstract and general form. These are the cardinal elements in the determination of man's spiritual state. In these, his past and present and future are severally summed up. Then, when the mind has seized the broad divisions of the spiritual analysis, the central fact in regard to each is stated, from which the process of testing, of revelation, of condemnation, proceeds. In each case the world was in danger of fatal error, and this error is laid open in view of the decisive criterion to which it is brought." Again: "The three subjects are placed in a natural and significant order. The position of man is determined first; he is shown to have fallen. And then the position of the two spiritual powers which strive for the mastery over him is made known; Christ has risen to the throne of glory; the prince of the world has been judged."

(4) The preposition translated **of,** signifies, in this place, *concerning,* or, *in respect of.* The conviction of the world will have respect to the nature of sin, as well as to the fact of its own sinfulness, etc.

9. Of sin, because they believe not on me. This does not mean that the Holy Spirit, through the preaching of the apostles, or otherwise, will demonstrate to men that their sin remains unforgiven, because they do not believe in Christ—that, like the venom of the fiery flying serpent, it will continue in them, working death, because they reject the only cure, the Saviour lifted up on the cross. Such a truth is plainly taught by the Lord himself (ch. 3: 14, 15,), but it is hardly found in the most natural interpretation of this verse. Nor does it mean that nothing but unbelief in Christ is now reckoned as sin, so that the only way in which the Holy Spirit can bring conviction of sin to the mind of man, since the death of Christ, is by proving to him that he does not believe in the Lamb of God that taketh away the sin of the world. The words of Jesus assume that unbelief in him is sin, and therefore proof of sin in all those who entertain it; but they do not say or imply that it is the only sin of which men are guilty. This is self-evident. If a devout father were to hear his son blaspheme the name of God, he might attempt to bring conviction to that son concerning the presence and nature of sin in his heart, by directing his attention to the particular and awful sin of blasphemy; for all blasphemy is sin, and illustrates the nature and power of sin; but the father would not be likely to think that proving his son a sinner because a blasphemer, was equivalent to proving, or assuming, that he was a sinner in no other way.

And this leads to the true interpretation of Christ's language in this clause. The Holy Spirit will bring conviction to mankind concerning sin, because they believe not in Christ, which is a great and fatal sin. In other words, the reason or argument which

10 ᵃ Of righteousness, ᵇ because I go to my Father, and ye see me no more; 11 ᶜ Of judgment, because ᵈ the prince of this world is judged.

10 ness, because I go to the Father, and ye behold me no more; of judgment, because the prince of this world

ᵃ Acts 2 : 32....ᵇ ch. 3 : 14 ; 5 : 32,...ᶜ Acts 26 : 18,...ᵈ Luke 10 : 18 ; ch. 12 : 31 ; Eph. 2 : 2 ; Col. 2 : 15 ; Heb. 2 : 14.

the Spirit will use in convicting them of sin, will be their unbelief in Jesus. For unbelief in him is unbelief in God; since he is the perfect manifestation of God, and especially of the love of God. And unbelief in God is the central principle of alienation from him. Now that Christ has come and revealed the moral perfection of the Father, a rejection of him is a rejection of the only true God, and an exaltation of self to the throne. "The Spirit, therefore, working through the written and spoken word, starts from the fact of unbelief in the Son of man, and through that, lays open what sin is."—*Westcott*. Whether Jesus intends by this language to predict any direct work of the Spirit in the hearts of ungodly men, leading them to receive the truth, it is, perhaps, impossible to know; but there is nothing in his words incompatible with such a view. Yet it cannot be rightly inferred from the expression "will convict *the world*," that every person who was then living, or who has since lived, was to be shown that he had sinned by rejecting Christ. "The world" is a general expression, denoting the sphere of the Spirit's direct or mediate operation. (Comp. 12 : 32.)

10. Of righteousness, etc. (Lit., *And of righteousness, because I go to the Father*.) The work of the Spirit here described, though separable in thought, is inseparable in fact from the work which is spoken of in the previous verse. For unbelief in Christ cannot be a sin, or an illustration of all sin, unless he is what he claims to be—the Holy One of God. His righteousness is therefore presupposed in the sinfulness of rejecting him. And in order to bring home to conscience and heart the sin of not trusting in him and not obeying him, his moral perfection, his sinless character as the Son of God, must be clearly established. Moreover, in exhibiting and proving his moral perfection, the clearest possible light is cast upon the nature and beauty of righteousness itself. He was ever at one with his Father, ever ready to do his Father's will, ever illustrating divine truth, goodness, and mercy, in his conduct. He was holy, harmless, undefiled, proving himself to be absolutely righteous, whether regarded as the Son of God, or as the Son of man.

But what was the ultimate verification of all his claims, the invincible proof that he was the "only begotten of the Father, full of grace and truth?" It was his going to the Father. And observe that *to the Father* are the emphatic words, made so by their position in the Greek sentence,—and *to the Father* I go." This fact will be used by the Spirit in demonstrating the righteousness of Christ. By his voluntary and sacrificial death in obedience to the Father's will, by his glorious resurrection from the dead and his manifestation of himself to his disciples at sundry times during forty days, by his separation from them on the Mount of Olives, and his ascension towards heaven, till a cloud received him out of their sight, and by the coming of the Spirit with mighty power on the Day of Pentecost, according to his promise, will that Spirit, speaking through the apostles, convict the unbelieving world of the righteousness of him who had been slain as a malefactor, convict the unbelieving people that they had "denied the Holy One and the Just One," asking for "a murderer to be granted" them. (Acts 2 : 36 ; 3 : 14.) The words, **and ye see** (or, *behold*) **me no more,** are probably added for the purpose of showing that his departure to the Father would be a permanent withdrawal from his earthly and visible connection with them, and a permanent return to a higher state of being. Is it too much to say that he did not wish them to expect any renewal of this sensible communion with him on earth? and that he would have them welcome communion with him by the Spirit as a greater blessing? It was "expedient" for them that he should go away, and the Advocate come in his place; for, be it said with all reverence, the Advocate could hereafter give them more of Christ than could Jesus himself by his bodily presence.

11. Of judgment, etc. (Lit., *and of judgment, because the prince of this world hath been judged*.) By reason of the perfect tense,

Ch. XVI.] JOHN. 317

12 I have yet many things to say unto you, *but ye cannot bear them now.
13 Howbeit when he, *the Spirit of truth, is come, *he will guide you into all truth: for he shall not speak of himself; but whatsoever he shall hear, *that* shall he speak: and he will shew you things to come.

12 world hath been judged. I have yet many things to say unto you, but ye cannot bear them now.
13 Howbeit when he, the Spirit of truth, is come, he shall guide you into all the truth: for he shall not speak from himself; but what things soever he shall hear, *these* shall he speak: and he shall declare unto you the things that are to come.

a Mark 4:33; 1 Cor. 3:2; Heb. 5:12....*b* ch. 14:17; 15:26....*c* ch. 14:26; 1 John 2:20, 27.

this language signifies that the prince of this world has been and is condemned. The point of view is naturally that of the Spirit's agency after the Pentecost in convicting the world. Then Christ's work on earth will have been completed; and that work, all along a perfect expression of divine holiness and grace, but culminating at last in the gift of his life as a ransom for sinners, and approved by God through his resurrection from the dead and enthronement at the right hand of the Father, will be made by the Spirit to appear in its true character, as a permanent, irreversible condemnation of Satan, the prince of this world. "This passage differs in form only from 12: 31, 32; the three actors mentioned the world, Satan, and Jesus, are the same, as well as the parts which are assigned to them. Our passage adds only this idea: that it is the Holy Spirit who will unfold to men the grandeur of the invisible drama accomplished on the cross. Thenceforth some remain in the *sin* of unbelief, and share the *judgment* of the prince of this world. Others take their stand on the side of the *righteousness* of Christ, and are withdrawn from the judgment pronounced upon Satan."—*Godet.*
Observe, also, (1) The world has a prince. Men who are not the servants of Christ are the servants of Satan, whose personality is clearly assumed in this language. (2) The fact that their prince has been condemned is evidence that those who follow him will be condemned likewise, unless they repent. The decision against the prince will prove to be a decision against all who maintain his cause. (3) The act expressed by the word translated **judged** (κρίνω), is always, in the Gospel of John, *the premise to a judicial punitive act.—Cremer.* In other words, judgment looks forward to punishment. Those who persist in rejecting Christ will at last hear the sentence: "Depart from me, ye cursed, into everlasting fire, prepared for the devil and his angels." (Matt. 25:41).

12-15. THE INSPIRATION OF THE SPIRIT PROMISED TO THE ELEVEN.

12. I have yet many things, etc. A natural introduction to the following promise, which assures them of all needed instruction through the Holy Spirit. Much as Jesus has taught them in public with others, and in private for their special benefit, there is much more which he has forborne to teach, because of their prejudice and lack of spiritual discernment. There is a fullness of truth in Christ which he cannot even now impart to them. Just what these **many things** are, the Saviour does not of course specify, but they all pertained, no doubt, to his spiritual reign over mankind; and many of them were revealed to the apostles by the Paraclete. Some of them may be, redemption by the sacrifice of Christ, the relation of the Mosaic law to grace, the acceptance of the heathen upon repentance and faith without submission to the Levitical law, the ultimate turning of the Jews to Christ, and the great apostasy before the end of the Christian Dispensation. Germs of nearly all these doctrines may, indeed, be found in the sayings of Christ, but they were more fully developed by the apostles under the teaching of the Spirit.

13. Howbeit when he, the Spirit of truth, is come, etc. *But* is a simpler and more intelligible rendering of the Greek connective here employed (δέ), than **howbeit.** So Noyes, Am. Bible Union, Revised English Bible, and others. Here again, for the third time, is the Advocate described as **the Spirit of truth.** Wherefore? In the first instance (14:17), there is nothing but the expression itself to suggest its meaning. In the second (15:26), the accompanying statement, **shall testify** (or, *he will bear witness of me*), points to his office as the Revealer of truth in respect to Christ. And in the present connection, all that is said represents him as the Revealer of Christian truth to the apostles. With these passages, compare 1 John 5: 6, which says: "*It is the Spirit that beareth witness, because the Spirit is truth.*" Compare also the language of John in his First Epistle (1 John 4:6), where "*the spirit of truth*" is contrasted with "*the spirit of error*," though some do not admit that the Holy Spirit is referred to; and his language in Rev. 19: 10, "*for the testimony of Jesus is the spirit of prophecy*," where again it is doubtful whether "*the spirit of prophecy*" refers to the Holy Spirit. It is, however, certain that the gift of prophecy is represented by the sacred writers as a gift imparted by the Spirit (*e. g.*, Acts 1:16; 2:4, 17; 19:6; 21:11; 28:25; 1 Cor. 12: 8, 10; 14:1). We understand, therefore, that the revelation of Christian truth is here set forth as a characteristic attribute or function of the Holy Spirit; indeed, as so characteristic of him, that it is represented as a quality of his nature. Revealing *the truth* may be regarded as a part of his normal action. So important is a correct view of this matter, that we subjoin the explanations of a few eminent commentators. "*The Spirit of truth*—*i. e.*, the Spirit of God, and the principle of truth, who teaches it (16:13). and by its power imparts self-reliance, decision, and firmness (Matt. 10:19, sq.), who, therefore, takes the place of Christ as Helper."—*De Wette*. "The Holy Spirit, who is possessor, bearer, and dispenser of the divine truth. He is the divine Principle of revelation, by whose action in human hearts the redemptive truth given by God in Christ—that is, *the* truth by way of preeminence—is transformed into knowledge, is vitally appropriated, and is brought to powerful expression.—*Meyer*. "This expression certainly implies, not merely that the Spirit communicates the truth (*Luth., Godet*), or possesses and communicates it (*Hengst.*), but the genitive (*of truth*) is one of quality, only the truth is not a subjective attribute, which the Spirit has, but the objective divine truth which [so to speak] constitutes his nature, because it belongs to that nature to possess the knowledge of the truth, and so to be the bearer of the revelation of God."—*Weiss*. "The Spirit by whom the truth finds expression, and is brought to man's spirit."—*Westcott*. "He is called the Spirit of truth, because part of his special office is to bring truth home to the hearts of men, to carry it from the material to the moral sphere, to make it something more than a collection of signs seen or heard—a living power in living men."—*Watkins*. **He will guide you into all truth.** A very significant promise! For,

First—the domain into which apostles are to be guided is *the whole truth;* that is, Christian truth in its totality. The Spirit will lead them into the truth as it is summed up in Jesus Christ; he will open to them *the mystery of God, and of Christ, in whom are hid all the treasures of wisdom and knowledge* (Col. 2:2, 3). From the promise of Jesus, as well as from the nature of the case, it may be inferred that the various truths of the Christian religion are self-consistent, and that, if clearly apprehended, they will be seen to form a single, harmonious system. From this promise it may also be inferred that, sooner or later, the Eleven were brought into such a state of mind and heart as to profit by a knowledge of Christian truth in its completeness. For the Spirit would not show them the way to this before they were prepared in the temper of their hearts to follow that way.

Secondly—in accord with what has now been said, the verb **will guide,** suggests a gradual and progressive work—a work that presupposes a teachable spirit in the disciples, and that adapts itself, with absolute wisdom, to their inward condition. And this condition must, in the nature of the case, be affected by the ever changing demands of their ministry. Hence we conclude that the Spirit was not to bring the whole sum of Christian truth to the minds of the apostles in a moment, and, as it were, without effort or inquiry on their part. No doubt that a great light shone into their minds on the Day of Pentecost—a light which revealed to them very clearly the meaning of Christ's death and resurrection; but there was much truth to be revealed when that day of wonders closed. The central truth of their Lord's redemptive victory was enough to fill their minds and hearts. If they could think of more than this, the fulfillment of prophecy in the miracle before their eyes was likely to absorb their attention. How the Gentiles were to be made partakers of the great salvation, whether with or without submitting to the Mosaic ritual, was a question which did not, perhaps, enter their minds. And the same might be said of many other questions not unimportant to the purity and progress of the new religion.

Thirdly—if the work of the Spirit in showing the apostles the way into the whole truth, as it is in Jesus, was thus gradual and progressive, adapting itself evermore to their spiritual capacity and need, it is more than probable that some of them were outstripped by others in the attainment of knowledge, and, indeed, that some died without reaching the same heights and depths of spiritual understanding as others. Can it be reasonably assumed that James the Less, who suffered martyrdom at Jerusalem, in A. D. 44, was as profoundly versed in the whole system of Christian truth, as was Paul at his death, in A. D. 66, or John at his death, in A. D. 98? If not, it is easy to account for the apparently different degrees of doctrinal development attained by the writers of the New Testament, even without insisting upon the obvious fact that several of them have not written enough to give us anything more than fragments of their belief. It is sufficient to find that every one appears to hold the truth, as far as his knowledge extends, and that together they present to us the facts and principles of a great system. **For he shall not speak of himself.** (Rather, *for he will not speak from himself*); and the meaning is, not that the Spirit will refrain from saying anything about himself—e. g., as to his own knowledge (1 Cor. 2:10), or power (1 Cor. 2:4; Heb. 2:4), or divinity (1 Cor. 12:8-11)—but that he will not speak from his own impulse or will, apart from the will of God. (Comp. 5: 19, 30). Godet remarks: "The infallibility of this guide springs from the same cause as that of Jesus himself (7:17,18), namely, from the absence of all egoistic and therefore evil productivity. All his revelations will be drawn from the treasure of objective divinity; and so his teaching will be only an initiation into the divine reality of things. Satan is a liar just because he proceeds according to a wholly different method, drawing that which he speaks from his own source. (8:44)." **But whatsoever he shall hear, that shall he speak.** Or, more strictly, *but whatsoever he shall hear will he speak*. The insertion of *that* or *these*, before **will he speak**, seems to be unnecessary; as is also the insertion of *things*, unless it be to indicate that the word represented by **whatsoever** is plural (ὅσα). **Shall hear;** from whom? Probably from the Father, or the Son; for he comes as the Representative of both, and all things that are the Father's are the Son's also. Both have the same thoughts, plans, affections, desires. In nature, in power, and in aim, they are one. The commentators call attention to the fact that the hearing and speaking here predicted do not refer to single acts, accomplished once for all, but to a series of acts, or, rather, to continuous action of the kinds specified. This agrees with the interpretation given above to the verb **will guide.** Of course, hearing and speaking are used in a figurative sense, to denote that what the Spirit imparts to the minds of the apostles by a process inscrutable, but equivalent in effect to speaking, is from the Father's mind as really as it would be if heard by the Spirit in words uttered by the Father or the Son. **And he will show you things to come.** More exactly, *will declare unto you the things that are to come.* None but God sees the end of all things from the beginning. The Omniscient alone can foreknow the course which will be taken in every particular emergency by beings truly free. Hence, the prediction of future events which are contingent on human action is impossible to any but those who are divinely taught. But Jesus here promises his disciples that the Spirit of truth will announce to them the things that are to come, and thus enable them to preach the same things to other men. What, then, is to be understood by *the things that are to come?* Certainly not all future events in time and eternity; for it would never occur to the Eleven to give the words so comprehensive a meaning. Nor can they signify all the events connected with the reign of Christ or the last judgment; for this interpretation would be equally absurd. Westcott, however, goes too far by way of limitation, when he says: "The reference is, no doubt, mainly to the constitution of the Christian church, as representing hereafter the divine order, in place of the Jewish economy." It is far more natural to find the fulfillment of this promise in the revelations made to the apostle John in Patmos, together with such as were made to Paul—e. g., (1 Thess. 4: 15 sq.; 2 Thess. 2: 1-12; 1 Cor. 15: 23-28, 52; Rom. 10: 11-25), and other apostles. Godet remarks that "the words of 14: 26 contain the formula of the inspiration of our Gospels, while this verse, the 13th, gives that of the inspiration of the Epistles and the Apocalypse."

14 He shall glorify me: for he shall receive of mine, and shall shew *it* unto you.
15 *All things that the Father hath are mine: therefore said I, that he shall take of mine, and shall shew *it* unto you.

14 He shall glorify me: for he shall take of mine, 15 and shall declare *it* unto you. All things whatsoever the Father hath are mine: therefore said I, that he taketh of mine, and shall declare *it*

a Matt. 11: 27; ch. 3: 35; 13: 3; 17: 10.

14. He shall (or, *will*) **glorify me.** The me is emphatic. Bengel says: "The Son glorifies the Father, and the Holy Spirit the Son." This is true, but it is also true that the Father glorifies the Son (see 8: 54; 13: 32; 17: 1, 5; Acts 3: 13); and that the Son glorifies the Spirit (see ver. 7 and 14: 18 sq.). It is evident from these words, especially when they are compared with 17: 1, 5 and Heb. 12: 2, 3, that Jesus Christ, though he was the most unselfish being that ever walked the earth, was keenly alive to the reproaches heaped upon him, and painfully conscious of his name being cast out as evil. And now, as he draws near the conflict in Gethsemane and the mocking and buffeting that followed, as he feels more deeply, perhaps, than ever before, the ignominy of being "despised and rejected of men," as he sees himself assailed by the treachery of Judas, the denials of Peter, and the implacable hatred of the rulers, he appears to welcome the certainty that his character will be loved, his work appreciated, and his name honored by an ever-increasing multitude of disciples, as the ages come and go. He foresees, not without joy, that through the Spirit's work in the apostles, his name will at last be exalted above every name. But how would such words sound, if they fell from the lips of Peter, or John, or Paul? What should we think of any mere man, however great his ability, or high his office, or remarkable his services, who should predict that the Spirit of God would be sent into the world to glorify him? Should we not be filled with pity, or horror? Should we not pronounce him either insane or profane, either a madman or a blasphemer? Why then do we not think this of Jesus, the Christ? Why does every candid reader of the Gospels refuse to accept either of these alternatives? Is it not because the whole record of Christ's life proves that he was more than simply man?—that he was divine as well as human, and therefore entitled to glory and praise without limit?

But how will the work of the Spirit glorify Jesus? The reason is given in the next clause:

for he shall (or, *will*) receive of mine, and shall (or, *will*) declare it unto you. The word mine need not be restricted. The term itself and the compass of the apostolic message concerning Christ justify the broadest sense. Jesus might have unfolded its meaning by saying: "My existence as the Eternal Word with the Father, my birth into human nature, my perfect communion with God, my perfect sympathy with men, my works and words of power and wisdom, of love and compassion, my propitiatory sufferings and death, my resurrection and ascension, my priestly intercession and regal authority, my second coming to raise the dead, and judge the living and the dead." These things, and such as these, are comprehended in the single word mine. Says Luthardt: "The Spirit, therefore, which proceeds from the Father, has Christ for the substance and aim of all his activity. And all progress of the church in knowledge will only consist in greater study of Christ, in deeper, more comprehensive understanding of Christ, as all growth in holiness will consist only in the more thorough, more manifold representation of the image of Christ."

15. All things that (whatsoever) the Father hath are mine. "This verse," it has been remarked, "solves the contradiction, that in ver. 13, the speaking of the Spirit was traced back to his hearing from the Father, and in ver. 14, to his taking of what belongs to Christ." But there is no contradiction to solve; for the thirteenth verse merely affirms that "whatsoever (*things*) he shall hear, (not, hear from the Father), that shall, or *will* he speak." It is never wise to make a contradiction, in order to solve it. Whether, as some suppose, "all things that **the Father hath,**" refers only to the treasures of the Father's knowledge, may be doubtful; it seems to embrace at least all the great facts, as well as the spiritual principles, or doctrines, involved in the salvation of men. These all centre in Christ—and Christ, in his person and work, is a revelation of the Father's mind and will. Moreover, if the knowledge of Christ is the same as that of the Father, so is his will, and so is his love. It is better, therefore, to understand by **all things that the Father hath,** all the Father's purposes and deeds of grace, accomplished, or yet to be accomplished, by the Saviour in his mediatorial office. These belong to the Son, as well as to the Father, and of these the Spirit **taketh** (the present denoting a constant relation) and will declare unto the disciples.

"In this section, (ver. 5-15)," remarks Weiss, "everything is brought together which Jesus had said in respect to the sending of the Paraclete, and in ver. 5-7 is preserved the recollection that this belonged to the farewell discourse of Jesus to his disciples. We have already seen, in the remark on 14: 24, that Jesus must have said more than is preserved in the Synoptical tradition Matt. 10: 19, sq., (=John 15: 25 sq. Comp. the remark on 16: 4), concerning the sending of the Spirit. What the Evangelist has inserted by way of anticipation from these communications in 14: 15-17, is only the reverse side of ver. 8-11. The Spirit has no immediate relation to the world; but on the ground of the definite exaltation of Jesus, he will convict the world, through the testimony of the apostles, of its sin of unbelief, in such a way as must win from it whatever is to be won. The highly original manner in which this is drawn out in ver. 8-11, argues for the essential genuineness of this saying of Christ, which has its substantial analogon in the word respecting the sign of Jonah. (Matt. 12:39 sq.; compare John 8: 28.) Even so is 14: 26 only an anticipation of 16: 12-15, where the relation of the Paraclete to the progressive knowledge of the disciples is developed. But, however certain it is that Jesus must have spoken also on this matter, it is equally certain that precisely these sayings of his were only reproduced as the apostle's own experience had taught him to understand them. Under the guidance of the Spirit he was conscious of having gained a fuller and deeper understanding of the person and work of Christ, and that this was nothing else than what the testimony of Christ himself already contained, although in a form (for pedagogic reasons), more obscure and limited. On this very account he must reproduce the same, as the Spirit, who was his guide into all truth, had taught him to understand it. This reproduction of the Paraclete's promise is the key to his peculiar treatment and reproduction of the discourse of Jesus in his gospel."

We are ready to grant that the aged Evangelist was conscious of having gained by experience a fuller and deeper knowledge of the person and work of Christ, than he had when listening to his words in the evening before his betrayal. We are also ready to grant that he was conscious of having heard from Christ testimonies concerning the Spirit which seemed to him to predict and account for this increase of knowledge which he had gained. But we do not discover the proof that he enlarged or clarified the promise of Jesus into conformity with his own experience, that he laid hold of some dark saying of Jesus, and, clothing it in a garb furnished by his own spiritual experience, presented it transfigured to his readers. Much less do we perceive that Matt. 12: 39 sq., is any proper analogon of John 16: 8-11, or that there is any improbability in supposing that Jesus anticipated in a brief saying (14: 26) what at a later moment he repeated and expanded. That John would not have consciously modified the teaching of Jesus in such a way as to make it agree with his own experience, may be safely inferred from all that is known of his character, and especially of his reverence for Christ, and also from his habit of recording and explaining dark sayings—(e. g. 2: 21, 22; 7: 38, 39; 12: 32, 33). And further, if some great promise of the Spirit's mission was really made to the disciples on their way to the garden, as Weiss admits. what reason is there for the assumption that it was very brief or obscure? What ground for thinking that it was given in a single saying, instead of being presented at three different points in the Lord's conversation with his troubled friends? Our judgment is, that if the Evangelist has unconsciously transformed the discourse of Jesus, the fact cannot be learned from his record of the Saviour's words in respect to the coming and ministry of the Paraclete, but must be discovered somewhere else.

Combining now the statements respecting the Paraclete in the record of John (14: 16, 17, 26; 15: 26, 27; 16: 7-15), we learn that he was to be (i) a messenger from the Father and the Son, —*i. e.*, sent by the Father and the Son, (ii) at

16 a A little while, and ye shall not see me: and again, a little while, and ye shall see me, b because I go to the Father.
17 Then said *some* of his disciples among themselves, What is this that he saith unto us, A little while, and ye shall not see me: and again, a little while, and ye shall see me: and, Because I go to the Father?

16 unto you. A little while, and ye behold me no more; and again a little while, and ye shall see me. Some of his disciples therefore said one to another, What is this that he saith unto us, A little while, and ye behold me not; and again a little while, and ye shall see me: and, Because I go to the Father.

a ch. 7: 33; 13: 33; 14: 19; ver. 10....b ch. 13: 3; ver. 28.

the request of the Son, Jesus Christ, and (iii) for the purpose of taking the Son's place with the disciples, as an Advocate or Helper. Fulfilling this office he was (1) to bring to their remembrance all the teachings of Christ, (2) to show unto them the things that were to come, and (3) to guide them into all Christian truth, some part of which they were not yet able to bear. By the help of the Paraclete they were (A) to bear witness in respect to Christ, both as to his works and as to his words, (B) to receive from him, through the Spirit, other truth, nay, *the whole truth,* to be used in their ministry, and (C) to convict the world by their preaching, (a) in respect to sin, as illustrated by the world's rejection of Christ, (b) in respect to righteousness, as illustrated by Christ's character and work, and (c) in respect to judgment, as illustrated by the condemnation of the Prince of this world.

16–24. CHRIST'S WITHDRAWAL AND RETURN; THE DISCIPLES' SORROW AND JOY.

16. A little while, and ye shall not see me. (Better, *and ye behold me no more*). That is—"after a little while ye will no longer behold me, as ye now do, with the eye of sense"—a saying which refers to his approaching death and return to the Father. But does not this saying contradict 14: 19: "Yet a little while, and the world seeth (beholdeth) me no more, but ye see (behold) me"? The same verb, indeed, is found in both passages; but words must be interpreted in the light of the connection in which they stand. There are different kinds of beholding, as there are of seeing. In 14: 19, the word *behold* is applied to an act purely spiritual; in this verse, to an act dependent on the sense. In comparison with the world, the disciples never ceased to behold Jesus; for the wondering gaze of their souls was directed to him by the Spirit, who brought his words and deeds to their remembrance. But here they are said to behold him no more—*i. e.,* with their bodily senses. They are no longer to watch with admiration the changing expression of his countenance, or to listen with rapt attention to the familiar tones of his voice. Such beholding was presently to cease. **And again a little while, and ye shall** (or, *will*) **see me;** for it is difficult to ascertain whether the force of the Greek future is better represented in this case by *shall see,* or by *will see.* **Again a little while.** This second brief period, though longer than the first, only extended from his death to the Day of Pentecost. The seeing here predicted or promised is not the same as that referred to in 14: 19, where the word translated in Rev. Ver *behold* (θεωρεῖ) is used. The interpretation of Grimm is as follows: "The apostles are said to see (ὄψεσθαι) Christ, because they were about to perceive his invisible presence through his action in their hearts by the Holy Spirit." In support of this view Godet remarks: "If the seeing promised refers directly to the manifestations of Jesus after the resurrection, to his disciples, there is no connection between ver. 15 and 16. But *the omission of any connective* suggests a tie of profound sentiment binding together the two verses. This proves it necessary to apply the 'seeing' [promised] to the illumination of the Pentecost; thus the relation to the preceding presents no more difficulty. Filled with the idea of his glorification by the Spirit, in the hearts of the disciples (ver. 14), Jesus calls this return a mutual 'seeing again.' " The last clause of the Common Version, **because I go to the Father,** is probably an interpolation occasioned by ver. 17, where it is undoubtedly genuine. It is omitted in this place by Tischendorf, Tregelles, Westcott and Hort, and bracketed by Lachmann. Several of the earliest MSS.—*e. g.,* א B D L, and some of the earliest versions, do not have it.

17. Then said some of his disciples among themselves. The Revised Version —*Some of his disciples therefore said one to*

18 They said therefore, What is this that he saith, A little while? we cannot tell what he saith. | 18 the Father? They said therefore, What is this that he saith, A little while? We know not what he saith.

another, is a more exact translation of the Greek text. We may reasonably infer from this statement that the perplexity which is described in the following words was not expressed, if it was felt, by all the disciples. Moreover, those who felt it did not go to Jesus with it, but spoke of their difficulty to one another, aside and in a low voice, probably at a pause in the discourse of their Master. How distinctly does the Evangelist recall the scene, and how precisely does he describe it! **What is this that he saith unto us,** etc. That is, "What does this mean?" They hear his words, but they do not really understand them. Nor is this very strange; for surely there was something contradictory in his language, if all of it was taken in a literal sense. How could he depart to the Father, so that they should see him no more, if, after a little while, they were again to see him. (ver. 10 and ver. 16)? We sympathize with their perplexity, and can readily understand their questioning. But no great teacher always employs words in their primary, literal, and semi-physical sense. That which is natural is first; afterwards that which is spiritual. The lower form of knowledge is a type and shadow of the higher; the common signification of words is but the vestibule to their higher and holier signification. Thus, seeing by means of the bodily eye is analogous to seeing with the mind's eye—*i. e.*, with the mind itself. And probably no teacher ever employed language in a figurative and spiritual sense more frequently than Jesus Christ. Many of his sayings were, therefore, misunderstood, or very imperfectly comprehended, at first. This he knew; but he was not deterred from uttering them by his knowledge of the way they would be received.

The remainder of the verse is translated in the Revised Version somewhat more exactly than in the Common Version; for the former substitutes *behold me not*, for **shall not see me**—a manifest improvement, since the verb is in the present tense, and is a different word (θεωρεῖτε) from the one translated **shall see** (ὄψεσθέ), in the next clause. Yet neither version gives the exact meaning of the last clause. For the verb in that clause (ὑπάγω) signifies *to depart*, or, *go away*, rather than simply *to go*. The disciples repeat the very terms used by Jesus (see ver. 5, 6, 10), and if the several verbs employed by him were each represented by a different English verb, this fact would be more obvious. Thus: *What is this that he saith unto us, A little while and ye behold me not; and again a little while, and ye shall (or, will) see me; and because I depart to the Father?*

18. They said therefore, (or, *they were saying*.) The scene rises before the mind of the writer, and he repeats, more briefly, the substance of the comment which some of the disciples were making in a low tone to one another; but adding to what he had before noted, their explicit confession of inability to understand their Lord's words: **We cannot tell** (or, *know not*) **what he saith**—*i. e.*, the meaning of what he saith. From what follows it is clear that these whispered questionings and confessions of perplexity were not the mutterings of a querulous spirit. Why, then, did not the disciples, who were thus commenting to one another on their Master's words, turn rather at once, and at first, to him for an explanation? Because he was felt by them to be their Lord and Teacher; one to whom they looked up with peculiar reverence, and not infrequently with awe. None of them, save Peter, who was naturally bold, even to rashness, in personal intercourse, had been wont to approach him without a sense of his mysterious greatness. The sweetness and lowliness of his spirit must have been mingled with a divine authority and dignity, which rendered easy familiarity impossible. And, doubtless, the spiritual glory of Jesus had been very conspicuous during the last few hours, and while he was uttering the sayings which perplexed them. A careful student of the Apostolic Epistles will perceive that no one of their writers, not even Peter, was accustomed to place himself on such a level of personal intimacy and familiarity with the Lord Jesus, as has been assumed in prayer and conversation by some Christians of the present day. And this fact, if it be a fact, suggests a grave doubt whether the tone of modern piety is in as perfect accord as it should be with the whole nature of Christ, whether the element of reverence is not wanting, or, at

19 Now Jesus knew that they were desirous to ask him, and said unto them, Do ye inquire among yourselves of that I said, A little while, and ye shall not see me: and again, a little while, and ye shall see me?
20 Verily, verily, I say unto you, That ye shall weep and lament, but the world shall rejoice: and ye shall be sorrowful, but your sorrow shall be turned into joy.

19 Jesus perceived that they were desirous to ask him, and he said unto them, Do ye inquire among yourselves concerning this, that I said, A little while, and ye behold me not, and again a little while, and 20 ye shall see me? Verily, verily, I say unto you, that ye shall weep and lament, but the world shall rejoice: ye shall be sorrowful, but your sorrow

least, feeble, to the serious injury of religious life.

19. Now Jesus knew. The word translated **now** (οὖν), is omitted by Tischendorf, Tregelles, Westcott and Hort, in agreement with the oldest MSS. א B D L, 1, 33, 157. **Knew**—*i. e.*, perceived by the power which he had to read the hearts of men (comp. 2: 25); though it is quite possible that their looks and tones of voice may have been observed by him, while their words were too indistinct to be heard. **That they were desirous to ask him.** See the remarks on ver. 18, for the probable reason why they refrained from doing what they desired to do. Observe, also, that "he knew, not only the whisperings of the disciples, and their inquiries among themselves, but also the sense of his words, but, also, their secret desires to ask him concerning it."—*Gill.* It was not because of "a dark presentiment" (*Weiss*), but because of their reverence for the Lord; and they spoke of their perplexity to one another, rather than to him, with such a spirit that he was willing to remove that perplexity, as far as possible. "Yet, as usual, he gives in the following no exposition of his meaning, but describes the succession of pain and joy which the 'not-seeing' and the 'seeing-again' will bring, for the purpose of preparing them practically for that which was ready to take place."—*Weiss.*

20. Verily, verily, I say unto you. This emphasis of expression is, as we have before remarked, peculiar to the Fourth Gospel, and to the sayings of Christ in this Gospel. It is a solemn call to the disciples to give heed to what he is about to say, by notifying them beforehand of its great practical importance. By such turns of expression, as well as by its wonderful dignity and simplicity, does the record of John reflect, as from the surface of a polished mirror, the theanthropic life of the Lord. **That ye shall weep and lament.** The words **weep** and **lament**, refer to the unrestrained expression of grief by means of tears and wailing, "by mournful gestures and doleful voice," which has always been customary in the East upon the death of kindred or friends. (Comp. Gen. 50: 10, 11; Luke 23: 27; John 11: 31-33; Mark 5: 38, 39. "How exactly, at the moment of the Saviour's arrival, did the house of Jairus correspond with the condition of one, at the present time, in which a death has just taken place! It resounded with the same boisterous expressions of grief, for which the nations of the East are still noted."—*Hackett.* Of course, these open manifestations of grief are, in this case, revelations of the heart The ye is emphatic, in contrast with **the world. But the world shall rejoice.** Better, *will rejoice;* for this is simply a prediction of what will be the feeling of unbelieving men, the foes of Jesus Christ, at his crucifixion. (Comp. Matt. 27: 28-31, 39-44; Mark 15: 29-32; Luke 23: 35-39). "Not only the common people, but the chief priests, with the scribes and elders, mocked at him, insulted him, and triumphed over him, when on the cross, being glad at heart they had got him there; imagining now, that it was all over, the day was their own, and they should be no more disturbed by Christ and his followers."—*Gill.* Yes, "the world will rejoice" at the crucifixion of Jesus of Nazareth. The leaders of the people will exult, for a brief period, in the accomplishment of their purpose. With hearts full of religious pride, bent upon retaining power, angry at reproof, and blind to the transcendent purity and loveliness of the Saviour's character, they will cry: *His blood be upon us and upon our children,* and will glory in his bitter death as in victory over a relentless foe. Alas, there have been some in every age who have walked in the footsteps of these leaders of the people—some, who, in the name of God and religion, have persecuted the saints of the Most High, some who have thought that in killing men of whom the world was not worthy, they were presenting an acceptable offering to God (ver. 2), as well as confirming their own power. **And ye shall be sorrowful.** Omit **and**, with the Revised Version, the critical editors,

21 *A woman when she is in travail hath sorrow, because her hour is come: but as soon as she is delivered of the child, she remembereth no more the anguish, for joy that a man is born into the world.
22 *And ye now therefore have sorrow: but I will see you again, and *your heart shall rejoice, and your joy no man taketh from you.

21 shall be turned into joy. A woman when she is in travail hath sorrow, because her hour is come: but when she is delivered of the child, she remembereth no more the anguish, for joy that a man is born 22 into the world. And ye therefore now have sorrow: but I will see you again, and your heart shall rejoice, and your joy no one taketh away from you.

a Isa. 26: 17....b ver. 6....c Luke 24: 41, 52; ch. 14: 1, 27; 20: 20; Acts 2: 46; 13: 52; 1 Pet. 1: 8.

L., T., Treg., W. & H., and the early MSS. ℵ* B D A, etc. The sense is not affected by the omission. Being sorrowful differs from weeping and lamenting, as heart-grief differs from the cry of sorrow or the funeral dirge by which it is expressed. Weak as the disciples might prove to be in the first great trial of their faith, their love was genuine, and the Saviour knew that he would have in them real mourners. Their lamentation would be no formal act, no perfunctory wailing for custom's sake, but a cry as of children bereaved of their father, and left orphans in the world—a bitter cry of disappointed hope and wounded affection. **But your sorrow shall be turned into joy.** That is, not merely succeeded by joy, but turned into joy. The very fountain of their sorrow will become a fountain of joy. The very ground of their lamentation will become a ground of rejoicing. They will, ere long, glory in the cross of Christ. (Gal. 6: 14.) What they have deprecated as the greatest possible calamity, and what they will mourn over for a little while, as the end of all their hopes, namely, their Lord's voluntary submission to death, will become their inspiration and strength; and, as the central act of redemption, the keynote of their sweetest song; nay, the very heart of their message to a world lying in the wicked one. This change of grief into joy, is next set forth by a striking illustration.
21. **A woman, when she is in travail.** Literally, *the woman*, whoever she may be, because the experience is universal. But the English idiom for generic nouns calls for the indefinite article, or for none at all. Hence, in the present case, **a woman, when she is in travail** (present tense, τίκτῃ), refers to the protracted anguish of child-birth, when great physical pain and mental anxiety must be borne. **Her hour**—the hour of parturition, which is so decisive and important to the mother. **For joy that a man is born into the world.** She forgets the anguish of child-birth in the joy of maternity. The same

illustration is employed by the prophets. (See Isa. 21: 3; 26: 17, 18; 66: 7, 8; Jer. 4: 31; 22: 23; 30: 6; Hos. 13: 13, 14; Mic. 4: 9, 10). **The child**, (lit., *the little child*, τὸ παιδίον), to whom she has given birth is a human being, possessing already, in the mother's eye, all the mental and moral qualities which will be unfolded by years of discipline and experience; a human being worthy of a place in the great world-order, and certain to continue in existence forever. "As the pains of a woman in travail are very sharp and severe, and the distress of her mind about the issue of things respecting herself and her offspring is very great, so would be the grief and trouble of the disciples on account of the death of their Lord and Master; but, as when a woman is safely delivered of a child, she is so filled with joy that her sorrow is remembered no more; so should it be with them, when Christ should appear to them."—*Gill*.
22. **And ye now therefore have sorrow. Therefore**—that is, in harmony with this illustration, which shows that great sorrow is often changed into great joy. According to Lachmann, supported by some of the early MSS.—(*e. g.*, ℵ A D L, 33), we ought to read *will have*, instead of **have**; but Tischendorf, Tregelles, Westcott and Hort, with the Anglo-American Revisers, supported by better manuscript authority—(*e. g.*, ℵ* B C Y T Δ Λ II, etc.), retain **have** as the original text. Probably the future tense was substituted for the present by some transcriber who thought it a more exact expression of the fact. But this was a mistake; for the sorrow of the disciples at the prospect of their Lord's withdrawal from them, had already begun to weigh them down; and its greatest pressure, at the actual death of Jesus in the near future, was as distinctly present to his mind, as if they were now sinking to the earth under it. Some interpreters endeavor to find a distinction between *having sorrow* and *being sorrowful*, but without much success. The two forms of expression are equivalent each to the other.

23 And in that day ye shall ask me nothing. *Verily, verily, I say unto you, Whatsoever ye shall ask the Father in my name, he will give it you.

23 And in that day ye shall ¹ask me nothing. Verily, verily, I say unto you, if ye shall ask anything of the Father, he will give it you in my name.

a Matt. 7: 7; ch. 14: 13; 15: 16.——1 Or, *ask me no question.*

But I will see you again. Implying, doubtless, that in some true sense of the words, they also should see him again. But how? In his resurrection body, during the forty days before he was taken up? Such a view does not agree with the following context. At his *parousia,* or second advent, in visible form? Neither does the context favor this. It remains for us, then, to suppose that he had in mind his return through the Holy Spirit from the Day of Pentecost, onward. Westcott remarks on the promise, **I will see you again,** as distinguished from the promise, "Ye shall see me" (ver. 19), that "the highest blessing lies, not in the thought that God is the object of our regard, but that we are objects of God's regard. (Comp. Gal. 4: 9; 1 Cor. 8: 3; John 10: 14, 15)." There may be psychological truth in this remark, but there is certainly no evidence that Jesus had any such distinction in mind when he uttered the words, **I will see you again. And your heart shall rejoice.** Joy of heart is real, inward joy; and this form of expression is just as full of meaning as the form "your heart will have joy." It signifies the full realization of joy. **And your joy no man taketh from you.** "Your sorrow will be brief, your joy permanent and secure. Enemies may assail you, and even put you to death; but they cannot rob you of that "joy in the Holy Spirit which I will impart to you." There is considerable manuscript authority for the future *will take,* instead of the present **taketh;** (viz., for the future, B* D T, Vulg., Cop., Arm., Aeth., and for the present ℵ A C D¹ L Y ∆ Λ Π, Early Latin, Syr.); but the predominance of testimony favors the common text, and a copyist would be more likely to substitute the future for the present, than the present for the future; not because the future is the stronger form of statement, but because it is more exact to a prosaic mind.

23. And in that day ye shall ask me nothing. Or, *will* ask—the sentence being, not a prohibition, but a prediction. The word **me** is emphatic, in contrast with **the Father,** in the next clause. **That day was** to begin with the outpouring of the Spirit at the next Pentecost. From that time forward they were to be taught by the Paraclete, and would no more come to Jesus, personally, with their questions and perplexities. The word **ask** (ἐρωτᾶν), seems to be used in the same sense as in ver. 19, viz., to ask for information, explanation, instruction, to propose a question. His seeing them again will not, then, be of such a nature as to restore their present relations to him as a Teacher. This change in their relations may be due to the circumstance that Jesus will be no longer visibly present with them, and to the circumstance that the Holy Spirit will then be, in a special sense, their Teacher. The discourse of Peter, Acts 2: 14 sq., illustrates the change which took place in the disciples when the Spirit came upon them with power. Their views of the kingdom of Christ were thenceforth clear and consistent. Verily, verily, I say unto you—thus calling their attention to the importance of what he was to say. **Whatsoever ye shall ask the Father in my name, he will give it you.** According to Tisch., Treg., W. & H., and the Anglo-American Revisers, the true text requires the following translation: *If ye shall ask the Father anything, he will give it you in my name.* Two reasons justify the position here given to the words, **in my name:** (1) A preponderance of early manuscript evidence (ℵ* B C T., etc., requiring the change, and A C³ D T, etc., forbidding it); and (2) the probability of a transposition, by which this clause would be connected with praying to God, as in 14: 13; 15: 16, and the improbability of a transposition, by which it would be connected (in this case only) with God's act in answering prayer. But if the Revised Version represents the original text, how is the expression, **he will give it you in my name,** to be understood? When a believer prays in the name of Christ, he prays with a full recognition and acknowledgment of the mediatorship of Christ, or in living fellowship with Christ. (Comp. on 14: 13). So, when the Father, in the name of Christ, answers prayer, he gives the blessing which is asked, in recognition of the mediatorship of Christ. The Saviour and

24 Hitherto have ye asked nothing in my name: ask, and ye shall receive, ᵃ that your joy may be full. | 24 Hitherto have ye asked nothing in my name: ask, and ye shall receive, that your joy may be made full.

ᵃ ch. 15: 11.

his work are, so to speak, the moral sphere in which all is done, and so the condition on which all depends. If this be correct, the doctrinal significance of Christ's language in this passage is very great, amounting to no less than this: that by every answer to prayer, the Father honors the Son, or that the interposition of Christ in behalf of sinners is recognized in every answer to prayer. This interpretation of the clause is supported by Grimm: "God is said to do something 'in the name of Christ'—*i. e.*, *mindful of the name of Christ*, moved by the name of Christ, on account of Christ" (s. v. ὄνομα, 2) e). The same view is probably intended by Winer: "Something takes place 'in a person's name,' when it is comprehended or embraced in his name, is to be set down to his personal activity," even though he is not the nearest or immediate subject of the action. (See p. 390).

24. Hitherto have ye asked nothing in my name. This language is important as a clue to the precise import of the last clause, **in my name.** For these eleven disciples were certainly men of prayer. Imperfect as they were in Christian knowledge and faith, they must have been renewed and devout men, who are never prayerless men. Moreover, they had said to Jesus: "Lord, teach us to pray, as John also taught his disciples," and in response to their request, he had given them a model of prayer, very nearly identical with that contained in the Sermon on the Mount. (Comp. Luke 11: 1-4 with Matt. 6: 9-13). But this model had in it no allusion to himself, and there is reason to believe, apart from this statement of Christ, that they had not heretofore offered prayer to God in the name of Christ.

These disciples were true followers of Christ. He counted them his friends. He was assured of their love. They were *in him*, by virtue of a living fellowship, as truly as the branch is in the vine. Therefore, during the two years or more of their special discipleship, they had prayed in spiritual union with him. To have a Christ-like spirit in prayer, is not, then, what is meant by praying in the name of Christ. Such a temper had been possessed, in some measure, by the Eleven, for months, as, indeed, it had been possessed by the saints of earlier ages. These disciples had known Jesus as a Divine Teacher, the true Messiah, the Holy One of God, the Son of the living God, but they had not known him as their high priest and sin-offering, as "the Lamb of God which taketh away the sin of the world." (1: 29). They had not seen in him "a propitiation for our sins, and not for ours only, but also for the sins of the whole world." (1 John 2: 2). They had not yet comprehended his words affirming that he "came, not to be ministered unto, but to minister, and to give his life a ransom for many." (Matt. 20: 28). This was one of the "many things" which they had been unable to bear (ver. 12), and which could not be taught them effectually, save by his death and resurrection, and the illumination of the Spirit.

From that time forward, to ask **in the name of Christ,** would be to recognize and honor him as One who had purchased them with his blood (Acts 20: 28), who was their "Advocate with the Father" (1 John 2: 1), and whose mediation through sacrifice was the great reason why their petitions for pardon and life should be heard. And now all who know Jesus Christ as the "one Mediator between God and men," who "gave himself" for them (1 Tim. 2: 5), must gratefully acknowledge his sacrifice in their behalf, in order to find favor with his Father. Every prayer should have upon it the name of the Lord Jesus. This seems to be a just conclusion from the statement under consideration, and this statement is, therefore, of much doctrinal importance. **Ask, and ye shall receive, that your joy may be full.** That is, ask in my name, ask continuously in my name (present tense), and ye shall receive, to the end that your joy may be made full. "The fullness of joy," remarks Westcott, "is the divine end of Christ's work, according to the Father's will." Consider, then, the goodness of God in the perfect joy which is provided for his people. Consider, also, the connection between frequent prayer and the attainment

328   JOHN.   [CH. XVI.

25 These things have I spoken unto you in proverbs: but the time cometh, when I shall no more speak unto you in proverbs, but I shall shew you plainly of the Father.
26 *a* At that day ye shall ask in my name: and I say not unto you, that I will pray the Father for you:

25 These things have I spoken unto you in ¹dark sayings: the hour cometh, when I shall no more speak unto you in ¹dark sayings, but shall tell you plainly of the Father. In that day ye shall ask in my name: and I say not unto you, that I

a ver. 23.—1 Or, *parables*.

of that joy. And consider, finally, that this joy comes through Christ, and by a constant recognition of his perfect work.

25–33. SUMMARY OF HIS WORDS TO THE ELEVEN; OR, REASON FOR "DARK SAYINGS"; THE ELEVEN UNDERSTAND HIS MEANING; LAST WARNING AND ANNOUNCEMENT.

25. These things have I spoken unto you in proverbs (or, *parables*). **These things,** must comprehend all that he had said to them since leaving the room where the holy Supper was instituted. A glance back will show the reader that a considerable part of all this had been clothed in figurative speech. On the word translated **parables** (παροιμίαις), see the Note to 10: 6. The Revised Version renders it *parable* in the text, and *proverb* in the margin of 10: 6, while here it is rendered by the American Revision *dark sayings* in the text, and *parables* in the margin. It is applied to language which is highly figurative or allegorical, and, therefore, obscure. Sometimes the figurative character of the language is principally referred to, and at others, the obscurity resulting from that character. The former reference seems to prevail in 10: 6, and the latter in the passage before us. It is, therefore, difficult to find a single word that will reproduce in English the force of the Greek term in different connections. But it is here applied to figurative expressions as *obscure*, and is fairly represented by *dark sayings*. **But the time cometh. But** is omitted by Tisch., Treg., West. and Hort., and Anglo-Am. Revisers, according to ℵ A B C* D* L X Y II, 1, 33. Moreover, there appears to be no sufficient reason for the insertion of the definite article before **time** (lit., *hour*), as there is no good reason for translating *hora* (ὥρα), **time,** instead of *hour*. A literal translation would be, *an hour cometh*. The period referred to began with the outpouring of the Spirit on the Day of Pentecost, and will continue until the return of Christ at the last day. **When I shall no more speak unto you in proverbs** (or, *dark sayings*). Everything may be good in its time, but dawn should be followed by the clear shining of the sun. Having done their work, types and shadows must give way to realities. *Dark sayings*, are not the best for all periods of religious life. The face of truth need not always be covered by a veil. **But I shall show you plainly of the Father.** To *show*, means in this place to *declare* (ἀπαγγελῶ Lach., Tisch., Treg., West. & Hort., after ℵ A B C* L, etc.), "marking the origin, rather than the destination, of the message." —*Westcott.* **Plainly**—*i. e.*, clearly, openly, without concealment. Observe that the teaching of the Holy Spirit is claimed by the Saviour as his own teaching. Jesus expected to speak unto his people in and by the Spirit of truth. In taking from the things of Christ, the Spirit was to take his words, his will, and make them known to the church. Thus Jesus would continue to be the Divine Word, or, Revealer, though he should speak through the Spirit, his Advocate with men.

26. At that day. Rather, *in that day*, is the meaning of Christ's language. And *that day*, is the period mentioned above, ver. 25, the word *day*, in this verse standing for the same idea as the word *hour*, in that. Both signify, as here used, a long period of time, a Dispensation, or æon. Yet these two words should be literally translated, since their English use corresponds with their New Testament use, and since much would be lost by substituting for them the utterly indefinite, unlimited word *time*. **Ye shall** (or, *will*) **ask in my name**—*i. e.*, offer your petitions (αἰτήσεσθε) in my name. For the expression, **in my name,** see Notes on 14: 13, 14, and on verses 23, 24, above. **That I will pray the Father for you.** Better, *will ask the Father about you;* for the word rendered **pray** (ἐρωτήν), means to *ask*, either for information, instruction, or for a blessing, privilege, favor of some kind, while the words **for you**, do not precisely represent the Greek (περὶ ὑμῶν),

27 a For the Father himself loveth you, because ye have loved me, and b have believed that I came out from God.
28 c I came forth from the Father, and am come into the world: again, I leave the world, and go to the Father.

27 will ¹ pray the Father for you; for the Father himself loveth you, because ye have loved me, and have believed that I came forth from the Father. I came out from the Father, and am come into the world: again, I leave the world, and go unto the Father.

a ch. 14: 21, 23....b ch. 3: 13; 17: 8; ver. 30....c ch. 13: 3.——1 Gr. *make request of.*

which means, *about you*, or, *concerning you*. To ask about them when they pray, would be to inquire after the Father's will in respect to them, and in so doing, to lay their case before him. Three things are noticeable in this saying of Jesus: (1) It betrays no thought of diminished interest on his part in the welfare of his followers. See the reason for it in the sequel. (2) It does not predict a closing up of his personal interposition in their behalf. That interposition will cease only so far as it is needless. In certain cases it may be relied upon—(*e. g.*, 1 John 2: 2). (3) It assumes the continued virtue of his influence in their behalf, by the words, ye *will* ask in my name. For prayer in the name of Christ is, in reality, prayer endorsed by him, and it will be heard as if it were offered by him.

27. For the Father himself loveth you. And he will surely answer the petitions of those whom he loves. The Father himself, is the Father, as personally distinguishable from the Son. And the love here spoken of, is like that which springs from natural relationship (φιλεῖ); it is a spontaneous affection, going out to those who are, as it were, his children in Christ. (Rom. 8: 15; comp. Rev. 3: 19.) Because ye have loved me. The perfect tense represents the love of the disciples to Christ as an affection which began in the past and had continued into the present. And the verb is the same as that used in the previous verse to denote the Father's affection for them. Only here in the Gospels is it chosen to characterize the affection of the disciples for Christ, unless Peter's language in 21: 15-17, be counted another instance. Probably its selection may be partly owing to the use of the same verb in speaking of God; for Jesus evidently desired to associate his Father's love to them with their love to himself, the Son. Moreover, the affection which they felt for him was not purely religious, but to some extent natural and personal. Yet their consciousness of it would do much to make the Father's love to them intelligible. That I came out from God. Better, *that I came forth from the Father*. This reading is adopted by Tisch., Treg., West. & Hort., Anglo-Am. Revisers, after ℵ^{ca} B C* D L X, etc. *From the Father*, means *from with the Father*, or, *from a position by the Father's side*. It would not have been enough for the disciples to have felt a warm personal attachment to Jesus, as a noble and sincere man; they must also recognize his relation to the Father before his appearance among men, and his mission from the Father, as the promised Messiah.

28. I came forth from the Father. More precisely, *I came out from the Father*; not from the Father's side (παρά), but, as it were, out from (ἐκ) the inner being, the very life and love of the Father. The language is exact, and strong enough to be appealed to in proof of the essential unity of the Father and the Son, or at least of the Father and the Word. But it does not suggest the doctrine of eternal generation; for the coming out from the inner sphere of the Father's life, is represented as an act of Christ (not of the Father), performed at a definite moment in the past. "This, his coming forth from the Father, is to be understood, not of his eternal filiation; nor of his coming forth in a way of grace, towards his own people in the council and covenant of grace and peace; nor of his constitution, as Mediator, from everlasting; but of his coming in the flesh, in the fullness of time; which supposes that he was, that he existed as a divine person before; that he was with the Father before; that he came forth from him with his knowledge, mind, and will," etc.—*Gill*. And am come into the world. Would it not be still better English to translate: and *have come* into the world? This language does not refer exclusively to his incarnation in the womb of Mary, and so to his incorporation into the world of mankind; but rather, to the whole process by which he entered into human life and society, to be a teacher of the divine will, and to give his life a ransom for many. It refers to his manifestation in human history. (Comp. 1:

29 His disciples said unto him, Lo, now speakest thou plainly, and speakest no proverb.
30 Now are we sure that ᵃthou knowest all things, and needest not that any man should ask thee: by this ᵇ we believe that thou camest forth from God.

29 Father. His disciples say, Lo, now speakest thou plainly, and speakest no ¹dark saying. Now know we that thou knowest all things, and needest not that any man should ask thee: by this we believe

a ch. 21: 17....*b* ver. 27; ch. 17: 8.—1 Or, *parable*.

9-11; 3: 19; 9: 39; 12: 46). **Again, I leave the world.** The original verb (ἀφίημι), signifies *to send from, to dismiss, to relinquish, to leave*, and does not, therefore, differ, essentially, from the word *withdraw* (ὑπάγω), (ver. 5, Note). The suggestion of Westcott (on 4: 3), that "the general idea which it conveys seems to be that of leaving anything to itself, to its own wishes, ways, fate; of withdrawing whatever controlling power was exercised before," is not sustained by its use in this passage. For, in leaving the world to go unto the Father, Jesus did not desert it, did not leave it to itself; he continued to care for it, and to draw it unto himself. (Comp. 12: 32). **And go to the Father.** "As surely as this is to be understood of his exaltation to the heavenly existence, so surely is the 'came out from' to be understood of his leaving an existence with God in the heavenly life."—*Weiss*. Meyer speaks of this verse as "a simple and grand summary of his entire personal life." It is so worded as to affirm directly, or by assumption, his pre-existence with God, his incarnation and life among men, and his return to the divine state with the Father. And this language is so plain that his disciples seemed to themselves to comprehend it. His words had answered the question of their hearts, and convinced them afresh of his divine knowledge. Hence their language in the following verses, 29, 30.

29. His disciples said unto him, etc. According to the best editors this should read: *His disciples say*, **Lo, now speakest thou plainly, and speakest no proverb** (or, *parable*). For the meaning of the words plainly and *parable*, see Notes on ver. 25. The interjection Lo (ἰδε), which appears twice in this connection, is characteristic of the Fourth Gospel, being found in it a greater number of times than in all the other books of the New Testament. **Now** is emphatic; as if the Lord's promise of clearer light in the future had been found true in the present. Of course they had no thought of claiming that what they now perceived was all the truth which he had promised to give them through the ministry of the Spirit, but the "rays and beams of light which were darted into their minds," awaken surprise and joy. "In responding directly to the thoughts which profoundly agitated their hearts, Jesus gave them a standard by which they could measure the truth of all his words, and the certainty of all his promises."—*Godet*.

30. Now we are sure. More precisely: *Now we know* (οἴδαμεν). The evidence seems to them complete. Not a doubt remains. Belief has risen to certainty, and is spoken of as knowledge. But how stupendous the fact which they profess to know! **That thou knowest all things.** Do they mean this in an absolute sense? Or is it a case of bold exaggeration, without much regard to the proper use of words? The occasion was not likely to beget extravagant speech in that direction. Moreover, the disciples must have been impressed by the mysterious penetration of their Lord, and they probably felt at this moment that nothing, however secret, was hidden from him; nay, that his knowledge was divine. **And needest not that any man should ask thee.** Their special ground for confidence in his supernatural knowledge, was the answer which he had given to the unexpressed desire of their hearts for an explanation of his words (ver. 19). To this instance of his discernment, therefore, they specially refer, as a proof or illustration of their general statement. By (or, *in*) **this we believe that thou camest forth from God** —*i. e.*, "Our belief that thou camest forth from God, is grounded in the knowledge which thou hast manifested of the secret feelings of our hearts," or, "we believe that thou camest forth from God with a belief that has its source and support in the knowledge of our hearts which thou hast shown." Not that they now first believed this truth, but that they now believed it with fresh assurance, in the light of his heart-searching discernment. "For their present faith in the divine origin of Christ they confess that they have found a new and special ground of certainty in that which they have just men-

31 Jesus answered them, Do ye now believe?
32 *a* Behold, the hour cometh, yea, is now come, that ye shall be scattered, *b* every man to his own, and shall leave me alone: and *c* yet I am not alone, because the Father is with me.

31 that thou camest forth from God. Jesus answered 32 them, Do ye now believe? Behold, the hour cometh, yea, is come, that ye shall be scattered, every man to his own, and shall leave me alone; and *yet* I am not alone, because the Father is with me.

a Matt. 26:31; Mark 14:27....*b* ch. 20:10....*c* ch. 8:29; 14:10, 11.

tioned."—*Weiss*. It is characteristic of this Gospel to treat words as elastic, and especially the word *believe*. Thus a lower and a higher degree of confidence is expressed by the same term, and any fresh sense of trust is spoken of, as if the feeling were now experienced for the first time. Moreover, though the disciples merely avow their belief that their Master had come to them from God, we may assume that they also accepted the corresponding statement, "Again, I leave the world, and go to the Father." (ver. 28.) Yet their reluctant lips failed to utter what they knew. And it is not, perhaps, amiss to suppose that Jesus had respect to that reluctance in the response which follows. Rejoicing that he had brought them on so far in their spiritual course, he yet perceives with natural sadness the practical weakness of their faith.

31. Do ye now believe? Words which imply doubt as to the steadfastness or permanence of their faith, but not as to its reality. For the exact bearing of these words must be inferred from what follows. Rightly understood, they are a hearty recognition of present belief on the part of his disciples, and at the same time a hint that more should be said, that there is another aspect of the case, since to-morrow may not be with them as to-day. Thus the question is a natural preface to the prediction that follows.

32. Behold, the hour cometh, yea, is now come. More exactly: *Behold, an hour cometh, and has come.* For the definite article, which is not in the original, need not be inserted before the word **hour,** and the latest editors (Lach., Tisch., Treg., Anglo-Am. Rev., West. & Hort, after ℵ A B C* D* L X 33), omit the adverb **now.** *And has come,* is added, because it was *so near!* The very day had arrived. Before the night should pass, their weakness would appear. Nay, it is possible, though not probable, that the literal hour which was to witness their dispersion had begun. Westcott remarks, that "this clause, as contrasted with 'and now is' (*4: 23*), presents rather the fulfillment of condition than the beginning of a period," but we cannot discover any solid ground for his opinion. **That ye shall be scattered, every man to his own.** Yet Jesus himself secured for his disciples the opportunity of separating and retiring to their homes (see 18:8), but they would not have seized it as promptly as they did, if they had possessed a martyr spirit. His course was marked by condescension to the weakness of their faith. Westcott translates: "that ye may be scattered," etc., because the conjunction rendered "that" (ἵνα), introduces a final clause—*i. e.*, a clause which states an end for which something is done or occurs. Hence he adds: "Even this was part of the divine counsel." The doctrine is true, but it is difficult to determine the exact force of this conjunction in many passages of our Gospel. Certainly Jesus intended to predict the scattering of his disciples in the hour referred to, but we are not sure that he intended to represent the hour as coming, and as already come, *for the purpose* of their being scattered. **Every one to his own**—*i. e.*, to his own possessions and pursuits. Thus Peter and some of his companions returned to their employment as fishermen on the Sea of Galilee. (21:3.) **And shall leave me alone.** A pathetic word, surcharged with human sweetness and sorrow, revealing, on the one hand, how precious was their presence and love to him, and, on the other, how weak their love would prove to be in the hour of trial. If Westcott's view of the introductory conjunction, as meaning "in order that," be correct, this clause should be translated, "and leave me alone," for it is in the same construction as the preceding one, "may be scattered." **And yet I am not alone, because the Father is with me.** Yet is supplied by the translators, but it represents fairly well what must have been the meaning of Christ—a meaning that may have been conveyed by uttering the word **and,** pausing for a moment, and then pronouncing, with suitable intonation, the words that follow. Thus: **and—I am not alone, because the Father is with me.** Such breviloquence is often the most effective speech. The

33 These things I have spoken unto you, that *a* in me ye might have peace. *b* In the world ye shall have tribulation: *c* but be of good cheer; *d* I have overcome the world.

33 These things have I spoken unto you, that in me ye may have peace. In the world ye have tribulation: but be of good cheer; I have overcome the world.

a Isa. 9: 6; ch. 14: 27; Rom. 5: 1; Eph. 2: 14; Col. 1: 20....*b* ch. 15: 19, 20, 21; 2 Tim. 3: 12....*c* ch. 14: 1....*d* Rom. 8: 37; 1 John 4: 4; 5: 4.

look, the pause, the tone, are more impressive than words. So now the satisfaction of Jesus is too deep for any but the simplest expression. The presence of the Father is a source of joy too sacred and precious for description in the language of men. Alone—and not alone! Deserted by men—supported by God! Meyer speaks of the feeling here expressed as "the calm, clear consciousness of the Father's protection, raised above all human desertion." Never, perhaps, was there a person on earth who felt so keenly the loss of human sympathy; never, surely, was there one who prized so highly the continuance of divine fellowship. Yet, for a moment, he seemed to be left without the latter. (Matt. 27: 46.) Paul was permitted to follow, at a distance, no doubt, in the footsteps of his Lord. "At my first defence no one took my part, but all forsook me: may it not be laid to their account! But the Lord stood by me and strengthened me." (2 Tim. 4: 16, Rev. Ver.) But neither had the apostle to the Gentiles such claims on the fidelity of his companions as Jesus had on the love of his disciples, nor did he ever have such perfect intercourse with the Lord, as Jesus now had with his Father.

33. **These things,** etc. Namely, all that he had said to the Eleven since Judas, the betrayer, had left the upper room. One general purpose had been in the mind of Christ in all that he had spoken—**that in me ye might have peace.** Better, *may have peace.* Compare the comments on 14: 27; 15: 11; 16: 1, 4. True peace, rest of soul, has its source in Christ; and those who are in him, as the living branches are in the vine, will have this true peace. Out of him, men are tormented with discord and strife and unrest of soul; in him they have love, hope, and joy. **In the world ye shall have tribulation.** Notice, *first,* that the text approved by the best editors (Tisch., Treg., West. & Hort, Anglo-Am. Revisers), and supported by the principal early MSS. (א A B C L X Y Γ Λ Π), requires the translation: *In the world ye have tribulation*—showing that the hostility of the world had already begun to assail them, or, better, perhaps, that in their relations with the world, tribulation would be their permanent lot. They were to meet with contradiction, reproach, persecution, so that an apostle would say, nearly forty years later, "Yea, and all that will live godly in Christ Jesus, shall suffer persecution." (2 Tim. 3: 12.) But persecution and spiritual peace are perfectly consistent. Of course, **in the world,** does not mean in harmony with the world, but the world in which they live is regarded as the source in which their tribulation takes its rise. **But be of good cheer.** "Take heart, be encouraged." **I have overcome the world.** The pronoun **I** is emphatic. "He does not say, 'Be of good cheer, you have overcome the world'; but this is your consolation, that I, I have overcome the world; my victory is your salvation."—*Luther.* But, in what did the victory of Jesus consist? In what way had he overcome the world? Weiss replies, that "he neither has suffered, nor does suffer himself to be led into sin by the world, nor to be disturbed in his peace." Meyer holds that the perfect, **have overcome,** "states the victory immediately impending, which is to be gained through his glorification, by means of death, as already completed. (Comp. 12: 31; 13: 31)." It seems to me that the perfect is best explained by supposing a reference to the victory which Christ had been gaining, and was now gaining, and was certain of making perfect in the garden and on the cross; a victory which consisted of an inward triumph over temptation, and a giving of his life a ransom for many. It was subjective and objective at the same time. It began as early as the day when he was led by the Spirit into the wilderness, to be tempted by the devil, and was completed on the cross, when he cried, "It is finished," and gave up the ghost, or, at the latest, when he rose from the dead, and took his place at the right hand of God. From first to last he was victorious. At every point, even the darkest, he conquered. And, through him, his followers will overcome as well.

CHAPTER XVII.

THESE words spake Jesus, and lifted up his eyes to heaven, and said, Father, ªthe hour is come; glorify thy Son, that thy Son also may glorify thee:

1 These things spake Jesus; and lifting up his eyes to heaven, he said, Father, the hour is come; glorify—

a ch. 12: 23; 13: 32.

Ch. 17. The prayer which the Evangelist now records, was offered in the presence and hearing of the disciples with whom Jesus had been conversing; and there is no sufficient reason for calling in question the substantial accuracy of the Evangelist's record. A more suitable or sublime ending of his personal work for the Eleven, by way of teaching and encouragement, cannot be imagined. Such an ending was not likely to be forgotten by the beloved disciple. For his spirit was one that would be deeply impressed by it; that would cherish with affectionate interest through all his ministry the memory of it; and that, assisted by the Spirit of truth, would put it on record, with holy reverence, for the people of God. "It is impossible," says Alford, "to regard the following prayer otherwise than as *the very words of our Lord himself, faithfully rendered by the beloved apostle, in the power of the Holy Spirit.* The Greek form of them only can be regarded as bearing evidence of the style and manner of John."

This prayer may be fitly called the Lord's Prayer—(1) for himself (1-8), (2) for the Eleven (9-19), and (3) for all believers, to the end of time (20-26). "But," according to Godet, "when Jesus prays for himself, it is not merely his own person which he has in view, it is *the work of God* (ver. 1 and 2); when he prays for his apostles, it is for the *organs* and continuers of the same work; and when he commends to God, believers, present and future, it is as *objects* of this work, and because these souls are the theatre wherein the glory of his Father ought to shine."

As to the place where the little group, of which Jesus was the centre, was now standing—whether it was a court of the temple, or a more secluded spot on the western slope of the Kidron valley—we are in doubt. The words of 14: 31 suggest that they had left the upper room; and the words of 18: 1 suggest that they had not passed over the Kidron; but they do not, separately, or together, furnish any clue to the precise locality. Perhaps they favor the view that he was still in the city, and if so, probably in the precincts of the temple.

1-8. JESUS PRAYS FOR HIS APPROACHING GLORIFICATION.

1. These words spake Jesus. By these words (or, *these things*, as the Greek word is usually rendered), the Evangelist may mean all that had been said by the Lord during the evening, or, possibly, the last sentences uttered by him. (16: 32, 33.) The former is a more probable view than the latter. **And lifted up his eyes to heaven, and said.** Better, *and lifting up his eyes to heaven, he said;* for this more exact reproduction of the Greek idiom (since it translates the participle by a participle), is even better English than the Common Version. Lifting up the eyes to heaven, is a natural act in prayer, especially when filial confidence is strong; for God is conceived of as dwelling in heaven, and the eyes of a trustful Son spontaneously turn towards the Father, who is addressed. **Father, the hour is come.** Has come, would be a still more exact representation of the original word. **By the hour,** is meant the time when the Son was to be glorified. This is evident from the request that follows. It was a time fixed in the eternal purpose of God, and was, therefore, called by Jesus, simply and sublimely, **the hour. Glorify thy Son.** That is, by receiving him into the heavenly glory. (Comp. 7: 39; 12: 16). This glory was to be reached through suffering, by way of the cross; but the eye of Christ seems to be directed, for the moment, to the goal itself, rather than to the way that must be trodden in coming to it. The pronoun **thy,** may be considered as itself a plea for what is asked. "*Thy Son* it is whom thou art requested to exalt into glory;" or "Glorify me, for I am *thy Son.*" **That thy Son also may glorify thee.** Omit thy (with Tisch., Treg., West. & Hort, Anglo-Am. Revisers, after ℵ B C*, etc.), and **also** (with Tisch., Treg., West. & Hort., Anglo-Am. Revisers, after ℵ A B C* D, etc.), leaving the clause, *that the Son may glorify thee.* Which

334   JOHN.   [Ch. XVII.

2 *As thou hast given him power over all flesh, that he should give eternal life to as many *as thou hast given him.
3 And *this is life eternal, that they might know thee *the only true God, and Jesus Christ, *whom thou hast sent.

2 fy thy Son, that the Son may glorify thee: even as thou gavest him authority over all flesh, that whatsoever thou hast given him, to them he should give 3 eternal life. And this is life eternal, that they should know thee the only true God, and him

a Dan. 7:14; Matt. 11:27; 28:18; ch. 3:35; 5:27; 1 Cor. 15:25, 27; Phil. 2:10; Heb. 2:8....b ch. 6   37; ver. 6:9, 24.....c Isa. 53:11; Jer. 9:24.....d 1 Cor. 8:4; 1 Thess. 1:9....e ch. 3:34; 5:36, 37; 6:29, 57; 7:29; 10:36; 11:42.

means, "that the Son may reveal, with greater clearness than heretofore, thy perfection or glory." More than this cannot be intended; for Christ had been revealing the Father during all his earthly ministry. Observe that Jesus desires his own glorification in order that he may make manifest his Father's glory. Confident of his Father's love to him, he is conscious of supreme love to the Father.

2. As thou hast given him power, etc. The Revised Version is better: *Even as thou gavest him authority over all flesh, that whatsoever thou hast given him, to them he should give eternal life.* Even as, marks the correspondence between what is now asked (ver. 1), and what the Father had given the Son when he sent him into the world. (Comp. 13:3). The authority which the Father then gave the Son, and the end for which it was given, harmonize with the glorification of the Son at this time. For only by that glorification can the end proposed be accomplished. Observe (1) that by **all flesh,** is meant all mankind, in their natural state, as coming short of the glory of God. (Rom. 3:23.) And authority over all mankind would scarcely have been given to the Son, unless many outside the Jewish nation were to receive the gift of eternal life from him. But while in the flesh, his work was chiefly with the Jews. That he might approach all men with the same blessing, it was necessary that he should be glorified. (2) That the word **whatsoever, or, all which** (πᾶν ὅ), represents the whole body of believers, given to Christ by the Father, as a unity, while the clause, *to them he should give eternal life*, represents the spiritual life of these believers as Christ's gift to them as individuals. He expects to save those, and those only, whom the Father has given him. (3) That by giving to them eternal life he will glorify the Father, who has given them to him. Godet points out the connection of thought as follows: "The second proposition of verse 2, *that he should*

give eternal life, is parallel to the second of verse 1; *that he may glorify thee*. The true means of glorifying God, is that of communicating eternal life. For life eternal consists in *knowing God*. (ver. 3.) By presenting his request in this new form, Jesus urges it in a manner the most pressing: 'Glorify me, in order that, in accordance with the trust committed to me, I may be able to give eternal life to all that believe.' That is to say: 'Grant me the ascension, that I may effect the Pentecost.'" It is worth while to notice also the expansion of the second clause of this verse by Gill. "Eternal life is a gift, and not owing to the merits of men... (It) is Christ's gift;.. it is put into his hands, and he came into this world that his people might have it; he has procured it, and has removed what lay in the way of their enjoyment of it; he has a right to bestow it, and their right unto it comes by him, through his blood and righteousness; the persons on whom he confers this gift are not all men, but such as the Father, in the everlasting covenant, has given to him as his people and portion.... his jewels and his treasure, to be saved and enjoyed by him;.. to these, and every one of them, Christ gives this great blessing; nor shall any of them come short of it; and 'tis for the sake of this, that all creatures and things, all power in heaven and earth, are given to him."

3. And this is life eternal, that they might know, etc. We regard this as a definition of the eternal life referred to in the preceding verse as Christ's gift. It is a statement, at once brief and profound, of that in which eternal life consists. But the knowing spoken of is more than intellectual, it is spiritual; comprehending in itself love, appreciation, communion. "Every one that loveth is begotten of God, and knoweth God. He that loveth not, knoweth not God, for God is love." (1 John, 4:7, 8.) Godet says: "The Scripture always (?) employs the word *know* in a sense most profound. When speaking of the connection between two persons, this word denotes the perfect view which each one has of the moral being of the other, their close spiritual contact in the same luminous medium." Weiss remarks: "The knowledge here meant is not to be regarded as a purely theoretical function of the understanding, but, as ever with John, a spiritual intuition, a sinking one's self into the supreme object of knowledge, by means of which that object is inwardly appropriated and made the central and controlling principle of the whole spiritual life." It may be noticed, also, that the verb to know conveys a slightly different meaning from that which would be conveyed by the noun knowledge. For the one represents eternal life as the highest form of present and continuous spiritual action, while the other represents it as a spiritual possession. Moreover, it is characteristic of this Gospel to make use of verbs rather than of nouns—*e. g.*, to speak of believing rather than of faith or belief, the verb occurring ninety-eight times and the corresponding noun not once; of knowing rather than of knowledge, the verb occurring fifty-five times and the corresponding noun not once; and of loving rather than of love, the verb (ἀγαπᾶν) occurring thirty-six times, and the corresponding noun (ἀγάπη) only seven times. Such a choice of words flows naturally from the conception of true religion as *a life*—a conception which pervades the Fourth Gospel and the First Epistle of John.

With this view of the first part of the verse, the translation **might know**, is incongruous. Hence, instead of **might know**, the Revised Version reads, *should know*, Westcott and McClellan *may know*, the Bible Union and Davidson, *know*, Alford and Noyes, *to know*. (Tisch. and Treg. give the Greek verb in the indicative present, after A D G L Y Δ Λ, 33. West. & Hort, with Anglo-Am. Revisers, give it in the subjunctive present, after א B C X Π, etc). If the conjunction **that,** (ἵνα) here retains its ordinary sense, *in order that*, we must adopt the version of Westcott and McClellan, *may know*. But the language is then dark. For to say, "This is the eternal life," namely, "in order that they may know," etc., is, by no means, a natural or clear expression of thought. It begins to state what eternal life *is*, but ends by stating what it is *in order to*, or what is the end contemplated by it. We are satisfied that the conjunction, as here used, is employed to introduce a definite clause, explanatory of **this;** and if so, the best English translation is by the infinitive, *to know*. **Thee, the only true God, and Jesus Christ, whom thou hast sent.** This rendering is less exact than that of the Revised Version: *Thee, the only true God, and him whom thou didst send, even Jesus Christ*. Here the Father is described as **the only true God**—i. e., as the only being in whom the idea of God is perfectly realized. This language has been considered by many incompatible with the proper deity of Christ; and, if taken altogether by itself, it has an appearance of being so. But it should be observed, (1) that the association of himself with the Father, as one of the two personal objects of that knowledge which is life eternal, does not accord with any view which denies his own deity. It seems well nigh incredible that Jesus should have said that it is eternal life to know the only true God, *and an inferior being*, sent by him as a messenger to men. If it be said, that knowing the messenger sent, is the only means of knowing the true God who sent him, it is impossible to see how the messenger could be an adequate revealer of One whose nature he did not share. "He that hath seen me hath seen the Father." Jesus was then a perfect manifestation of the Father. "Glorify thy Son, that thy Son also may glorify thee." In such language there is the plain assumption of some real, though mysterious, alliance of the Son with the Father, which seems inconsistent with the exclusive deity of the Father, in contrast with the Son. Indeed, Cyril of Alexandria remarks, that "the knowledge of God as the Father really involves a knowledge of the Son as God" (from Westcott.) (2) That Jesus intended to represent the deity of the Father as exclusive of his own deity, is an idea foreign to the context, and, therefore, improbable. Lücke, certainly an impartial scholar, says: "The passage is neither trinitarian nor anti-trinitarian, because its standpoint is not that of the Logos (1: 1 sq.), but of the historical appearance and revelation of Christ. It is the combined anti-polytheistic and anti-Judaistic expression of Christian truth." Westcott has in mind the same view when he writes: "The primary reference is, no doubt, to the respective trials of Gentile and Jew; but these include in themselves the typical trials of all ages." On the other hand, Weiss holds that "Jesus designates the Father (see ver. 1) as the One who alone is truly God, because God is only truth, if he is known as the Father of Christ." So, also, Lange: "It is the God of revelation in Christ, the God and Father of our Lord Jesus Christ, Eph. 1: 3; not in antithesis to the Old Testament idea of God, or to the idea of Christ, but in antithesis to all false and obscure belief in God; hence God, as he reveals himself in Christ, distinct as to his divine consciousness, and distinguished from Christ." (3) If it were distinctly taught in this passage that the being and position of the Father alone fulfill, in every respect, the complete idea of God, it would not follow that the Eternal Word or the Divine Spirit must be separate in essence from the Father, or inferior to him in any natural or moral perfection. The difference might be one of position, rather than one of nature; it might be owing to the humiliation of the Son, and to the mission of the Spirit, rather than to derivation of being or inferiority of knowledge. And there can be no doubt of the fact that both Jesus and his apostles do assign a certain precedence in order and rank to the Father, while at the same time they teach the true divinity of the Son and Spirit, together with the unity of the Godhead.

But another question presents itself. Is it reasonable to believe that the Saviour actually called himself, in this connection, **Jesus Christ?** Must we not rather suppose that the beloved disciple has, by mistake, put these words into his mouth? Or, at least, has added them by way of explanation as the personal and official names of the Sent of God? Many interpreters, including Westcott, feel constrained to adopt this view. The Note of Mr. Westcott deserves to be copied without abbrevintion: "The complex name, 'Jesus Christ,' appears to answer exactly to the corresponding clause, 'the only true God.' These two clauses are thus, most naturally, taken to define the persons indicated before, (viz.), 'Thee' and 'Him whom thou didst send.' If we accept this construction, we have then to consider whether the definitions are to be treated as literally parts of the prayer, or as words used by the Evangelist in his record of the prayer, as best fitted, in this connection, to convey the full meaning of the original language. In favor of the latter view it may be urged (1) that the use of the name 'Jesus Christ' by the Lord himself, at this time, is, in the highest degree, unlikely, while the compound title, expressing, as it did at a later time, the combination of the ideas of humanity and of divine office, may reasonably be supposed to give the exact sense of the Lord's thought; (2) that the phrase, 'the only true God,' recalls the phrase of St. John, 'the true God' (1 John 5: 20), and is not like any other phrase used by the Lord; (3) that the clauses, while perfectly natural as explanations, are most strange if they are taken as substantial parts of the prayer. It is no derogation from the truthfulness of the record that St. John has thus given parenthetically and in conventional language (so to speak) the substance of what the Lord said probably at greater length."

Every one will see the force of these considerations. But they seem to me to over-state the objections to the assumption that John's record is faithful to the expression, as well as to the thought of Jesus. It may be unlikely, but is it "in the highest degree unlikely," that the compound name "Jesus Christ" was used by the Lord himself? Do we know all the circumstances of the case, all the motives, all the spiritual conditions of this prayer, well enough to affirm this? Jesus was offering a prayer in the presence of his disciples. It was proper for them to hear and remember it. For it was adapted to give them a just conception of his relations to the Father, as well as to them. Moreover, he was referring to himself in the third person, as being, along with the Father, the object of that knowledge which is eternal life. Still further, the compound name applied to himself was significant, in both its parts, of that for which he was sent into the world. Jesus—Saviour, and Christ—Anointed One, pointing to his mediatorial work (comp. 1 Tim. 2: 5. 6), which might naturally be referred to in this connection. In this solemn hour, it is by no means clear that he might not have applied to himself, once for all, the great compound name, which the apostles were to use so often. Nor is it altogether probable that the Holy Spirit

4 *a* I have glorified thee on the earth: *b* I have finished the work *c* which thou gavest me to do.
5 And now, O Father, glorify thou me with thine own self with the glory *d* which I had with thee before the world was.

4 whom thou didst send, *even* Jesus Christ. I [glorified thee on the earth, having accomplished the 5 work which thou hast given me to do. And now, O Father, glorify thou me with thine own self with the glory which I had with thee before the

a ch. 13:31; 14:13....*b* ch. 4:34; 5:36; 9:3; 10:30....*c* ch. 14:31; 15:10....*d* ch. 1:1, 2; 10:30; 14:9; Phil. 2:6; Col. 1:15, 17; Heb. 1:3, 10.

would have left the Evangelist to inject his own explanations into this extraordinary appeal of Jesus to his Father. It may also be mentioned, that only a few hours later, Jesus publicly declared himself the Messiah. We adhere, therefore, to the view that this is the language of Christ himself.

4. I have glorified thee on the earth. Better: *I glorified thee*, etc.; for Jesus places himself, in thought, at the end of his earthly ministry, including his voluntary sacrificial death, and looks back upon it as a completed service. In and by it he has already revealed the character of the Father, thus glorifying him in the only possible way. Looking at his work on earth as virtually accomplished, he perceives in it no defect, as the next clause expressly affirms. **I have finished the work**, etc. Here, too, the form of the Revised Version is more exact, viz.: *having accomplished the work which thou hast given me to do*. The participle *having accomplished*, etc. (Substituting the aorist participle for the personal verb, with Lach., Tisch., Treg., West. & Hort, Anglo-Am. Revisers, after ℵ A B C L Π, 1, 33, etc.), states the way in which he had glorified the Father—*i. e.*, by completing the work committed to him. *Having accomplished* expresses more precisely the force of the Greek term than *having finished*, for the term (τελειώσας) means to make perfect, complete, to bring to a true end, rather than simply to finish, to bring to an end. (Comp. 4: 34; 5: 36; 17: 23; 1 John 2: 5; 4: 12, 17; Heb. 2: 10; 5: 9; 7: 28.) Weiss remarks: "*Having accomplished;* because Jesus stands at the goal of his earthly course; he has accomplished his life-work, in so far as it could be accomplished in the calling of his earthly life; but this does not prevent its being still further accomplished in his death, though we must not here include that further accomplishment." The expression used by Jesus might, very naturally, refer to his work in preaching the gospel of the kingdom, in gaining disciples from the people, and in training a select company of these by special instruction to carry forward his work after his return to glory; but the analogy of certain passages already considered, leads rather to the view stated above, that he anticipates the moment of his death, and looks back upon his work as brought to a perfect end by that propitiatory sacrifice. (Comp. 13: 31; 16: 11.)

5. And now. Since the appointed hour has come. **Glorify thou me.** The correspondence between **I . . thee, verse 4, and thou me,** in this verse, is much more striking in the Greek than in the English; for the Greek pronouns are emphatic in both cases, and they follow each other with no intervening word (ἐγώ σέ . . με σύ). The language is, therefore, in form and spirit, a plea for reciprocity: "I glorified thee on the earth—glorify thou me in heaven." **With thine own self.** The sense of the preposition, in such a construction as this, is said to be always, in the Fourth Gospel, local, either literally (1:39; 4:40; 14:25; 19:25), or figuratively (8:38; 14:17, 23.) In the latter case, it expresses a direct spiritual connection (Westcott). This expression points to life in the immediate presence of God in heaven as contrasted with life among men on earth. **With the glory,** etc. Jesus here refers to what has been called his threefold state—to a state of glory, in which he lived with the Father, before the creation of the world, to a state of humiliation among men, into which he entered at birth, and in which he was still living, and to a state of re-assumed glory with the Father, to which he was now looking forward as his just reward. Hence, this language is a full warrant for the Evangelist's testimony in 1: 1, as to the pre-existence of the Word, and in 1: 14, as to his incarnation. For Jesus seems to speak, in this place, of his pre-existence with the Father, in possession of divine glory, as if it were a matter of personal consciousness. His *kenosis*, or, humiliation, did not, therefore, interrupt the continuity of his higher life as the Divine Word; did not extinguish, in his higher nature, the light of

W

6 *I have manifested thy name unto the men which thou gavest me out of the world: thine they were, and thou gavest them me; and they have kept thy word.

6 world was. I manifested thy name unto the men whom thou gavest me out of the world: thine they were, and thou gavest them to me; and they have

a Ps. 22:22; ver. 26....b ch. 6, 37, 39; 10: 29; 15: 19; ver. 2, 9, 11.

memory, as to the past. In the spiritual centre of his being he was one and the same before and after his incarnation.

But what is meant by the **glory which I had?** The same thing, perhaps, which is called in Phil. 2: 6, "the form of God,"— i. e., a mode of existence corresponding with the proper idea of God, one in which the attributes of the Godhead are exercised and revealed in the highest and freest manner possible. To such a state of existence or life, Jesus now asks to be restored. Yet the Eternal Word was not to be reinstated in glory without his human nature. He was to be exalted to the right hand of power, not as a divine being merely, or as a human being merely, but as a theanthropic Prince and Saviour. Clothed in humanity, the Word was to ascend into heaven. (Acts 1:3, 9.) And so at the resurrection of the just, he will "fashion anew the body of our humiliation, that it may be conformed to the body of his glory." (Phil. 3: 21, 22. Rev. Ver.)

6-8. TRANSITION TO HIS PRAYER FOR THE ELEVEN. These verses may be regarded, with Weiss, as an expansion of what is recorded in the fourth verse, or as an introduction to the intercessory prayer which follows. (Ver. 9-19.) The latter is commonly supposed to be their object. But we see no reason why they may not be regarded as serving both purposes.

6. I have manifested thy name. It would be safer to translate, as in the Revised Version: *I manifested thy name;* for Jesus is, doubtless, thinking of this manifestation as something completed in the past. By thy **name,** is meant "all that thy name signifies to those who believe on thy Son, and have learned from him thy character." Hence, that name must be far more significant to Christians than it was to the ancient Israelites —than it can be to any who know not God as the Father of our Lord Jesus Christ. Unto **the men which thou gavest me out of the world. Which,** ought to be *whom.* Whether the giving here mentioned is merely another expression for the drawing of 6: 44 (comp. 6: 37, 39), or is an act of the Father in the coun-

sels of heaven, has been considered doubtful. The latter view must not be rejected as inconsistent with free moral agency on the part of man. For if God could know in eternity that any persons would believe in Christ (whether with or without the influence of special grace), he could give these persons to his Son. And such a giving in purpose and promise, would naturally be followed in time by influence tending to bring them to faith in Jesus. Jesus now has in mind his immediate disciples, whom God, the Father, had given to him in the latter sense, as well as in the former, in time, as well as in eternity. The words, **out of the world,** show the moral character of the people from whom the Father had taken these disciples. They had been part of a sinful multitude, and from that multitude they had been separated and given to Christ. **Thine they were, and thou gavest them me.** In what sense were they the Father's before they were Christ's? (1) Scarcely in the sense of their having been members of the chosen people, Israelites, before they were Christians. For they were taken **out of the world,** and given to Christ; nothing is said of their Jewish descent or nationality; this thought seems to be wholly foreign to the context. (2) Perhaps, in the sense that, even before they believed in Christ, they were true servants of God—"Israelites in whom there was no guile." In favor of this view may be urged two considerations: *first,* that the Eleven seem to have been already devout men, "waiting for the consolation of Israel," when they first saw Jesus; and, *secondly,* that, if so regarded in this passage, they belonged to the Father in the same full, spiritual sense in which they afterwards belonged to Christ. But we cannot go as far as a writer who says: "Evidently the gift in this case is that which turns them over to Christ as his actual disciples, and the meaning of the **thine they were,** is, that in the act of conversion, the fundamental relation affected is that to the Father, and that they therefore become his children; and that he then, having acquired a right to

Ch. XVII.] JOHN.

7 Now they have known that all things whatsoever thou hast given me are of thee.
8 For I have given unto them the words *which thou gavest me:* and they have received *them*, *and have known surely that I came out from thee, and they have believed that thou didst send me.

7 kept thy word. Now they know that all things 8 whatsoever thou hast given me are from thee: for the words which thou gavest me I have given unto them; and they received *them*, and knew of a truth that I came forth from thee, and they believed that

a ch. 8 : 28 ; 12 : 49 ; 14 : 10....*b* ch. 16 : 27, 30 ; ver. 25.

them that he did not have before, gives them to Christ." The idea that conversion affects, primarily and directly the sinner's relation to the Father, and only through the Father his relation to Christ, is not, we think, contained in these words; but it may be probable that the Eleven were actually converted before they knew Jesus the Christ, and, therefore, probable that *their* conscious relation to God was changed at conversion, while their conscious relation to Jesus began with their latergained knowledge of him, and faith in him. (3) In the sense that they were the Father's, by virtue of his eternal purpose of creation and redemption, in which things that are not are counted as though they were. Having been given to the Son, in consideration of his death for them, they were in due time drawn to him, and made, in a practical sense, "his own," so that it was possible for them to sing:

From everlasting we are his,
In love's eternal counsel given;
And he himself our portion is,
The glory of our promised heaven.

This broader view of the Father's ownership of his people agrees with the doctrine of the Fourth Gospel (10: 15, 16, 26, 27; 11: 52; 12: 32; 17: 20, 24; comp. Acts 18: 10), with the statement of Paul, that believers were chosen in Christ before the foundation of the world (Eph. 1: 4), and with the apostolic preaching of repentance toward God, and faith in the Lord Jesus (Acts 20: 21) as necessary to salvation. Hence, we may suppose that the fundamental relation to the Saviour, as well as to the Father, is immediately determined by conversion. **And they have kept thy word.** That is, "the word which I have spoken to them, and by means of which I have made known to them thy name. This word they have heard and obeyed. My giving it to them has, therefore, been for thy glory." Like Paul, Jesus was most generous in commending whatever was worthy of approval.

7. Now they have known. Now, is an adverb of time. The perfect, **have known,** is probably correct, being retained by Lach.,

Tisch., Treg., West. & Hort, after א B C D L Y, etc. The sense is, they have now learned, or come to know. For the verb used may signify the process of acquiring knowledge, as well as the result of that process; and it seems to be used here in the former sense. **That all things whatsover thou hast given me.** Jesus appears to be thinking of his entire ministry on earth as given to him; not as a succession of actions, which, though intended to manifest the Father's will, have nevertheless sprung from himself alone, but as words and deeds, which he has been commissioned by his Father to accomplish. In this clause, the perfect, **hast given,** is supported by Tisch., Treg., West. & Hort, though there is some authority (A B) for the simple past, *gavest.* **Are from thee.** In all things Christ is conscious of having done the very things which have been given him, as it were, from the presence and mind of the Father; and this the disciples have now learned to know. In no saying or miracle had he acted independently of the Father's plan and commission, but always in perfect harmony with the same.

8. For I have given unto them the words which thou gavest me. In this instance it would be well to preserve the order of the Greek words in translation, (as is done in the Revised Version); for that order corresponds with the order of events, and is, at the same time, consistent with the genius of our language, thus: "*For the words which thou gavest me I have given unto them.*" By this verse, Jesus may be said to justify and explain ver. 7, or, to give the reasons why his disciples have learned that his ministry is from God. The first of these was the faithfulness of his own teaching. The second, that his teaching was the Father's teaching. His words, from first to last, had been his Father's words, fresh from the mint of heaven. They could, therefore, be recognized as divine. "On the truth of this saying stands the whole fabric of creeds and doctrines. It is the ground of authority to the

9 I pray for them: *I pray not for the world, but for them which thou hast given me; for they are thine.
10 And all mine are thine, and *b* thine are mine; and I am glorified in them.

9 thou didst send me. I ¹ pray for them: I ¹ pray not for the world, but for those whom thou hast given me; for they are thine: and all things that are mine are thine, and thine are mine: and I am

a 1 John 5: 19....*b* ch. 16: 15.—1 Gr. *make request.*

preacher, of assurance to the believer, of existence to the church. It is the source from which the perpetual stream of Christian teaching flows. All our testimonies, instructions, exhortations, derive their first origin, and continuous power, from the fact that the Father has given to the Son, the Son has given to his servants, the words of truth and life."—*Bernard.* **And they have received them.** More strictly: *And they received them;* that is, when I gave to them these words, from time to time. **And have known surely.** Again, the simple past would be a better rendering of the Greek: *and knew surely—i. e.,* truly, or of a truth, as in Revised Version. By receiving in faith the words of Jesus, they gained a true knowledge of this fact, adds the Lord, **that I came out from thee**—*i. e., from with thee.* For the Greek prepositions (*ἐκ* in composition and *παρά*), do not signify "out of," but "from the presence of," or, "from companionship with." Of this, his coming from his divine condition with the Father, he had often testified; and it now appears that the Eleven had received his testimony as true. And, believing that he had come from his place with God, they naturally believed that he was God's messenger to men. Hence, the words: **and they have believed that thou didst send me.** Accordingly, the words of Jesus were believed to be God's message to them, and whenever the Saviour bore witness to his being sent from the Father, they received his testimony. **Have,** ought to be omitted, as in the Revised Version; for the original verb is not in the perfect tense.

9-19. PRAYER FOR THE ELEVEN (1) THAT THEY MAY BE DIVINELY KEPT (9-16), AND (2) THAT THEY MAY BE SANCTIFIED (17-19.)

9. I pray for them. The pronoun I is emphatic. The verb translated **pray,** would be adequately represented by the English term *ask,* and the preposition translated **for,** signifies, properly, *in respect to.* The sense, then, is: "I myself present a request in respect to my disciples, who have thus believed

my words, and recognized my mission from thee." **I pray not for the world.** By the **world,** is meant the unbelieving part of mankind. And the clause brings into bold relief the special object of the Saviour in the petition here offered. It shows the concentration of his thoughts upon the welfare of his disciples. His request is not general, but specific; offered for a particular class of persons, and supported by reasons drawn from their relations to his Father and himself. But it cannot safely be inferred from this, that he never prayed for the world at large, or for persons who would finally perish in their sins. That he could not pray for them in the same terms as for his own, is natural; that the blessings which he would ask for his enemies, must be different, in some respects, from those which he would ask for his friends, is certain; but this passage does not warrant the assertion that he forbore on all occasions to pray for mankind as ruined by sin and needing salvation. **But for them which thou hast given me, for they are thine.** The fact that they are Christ's is itself a reason why he should pray for them, and why his Father should listen to his request. The fact that they had been given him by the Father, adds force to that reason. And the fact that they are still the Father's, though given to Christ, completes the appeal. This appeal could not have been made, in this form, for the ungodly world.

10. And all mine are thine. Literally, with the Revised Version: *and all things that are mine are thine.* The pronouns are not in the masculine, but in the neuter form, and their meaning is as comprehensive as possible; it allows no exception. Whatever belongs to Christ belongs to God also; whatever belongs to the Son belongs to the Father as well. The two have no separate possessions or interests; they have, so to speak, all things common. More than once, according to this Evangelist, had Jesus affirmed the inseparable unity of his knowledge, will, and action, with the Father's; now he affirms that he has nothing which does not belong to the Father also.

11 *And now I am no more in the world, but these are in the world, and I come to thee. Holy Father, *keep through thine own name those whom thou hast given me, *that they may be one, *as we are.

11 glorified in them. And I am no more in the world, and these are in the world, and I come to thee. Holy Father, keep them in thy name, whom thou hast given me, that they may be one even as we

a ch. 13: 1; 16: 28.....b 1 Pet. 1: 5; Jude 1.....c ver. 21, etc.....d ch. 10: 30.

And thine are mine. Or, *and that are thine are mine.* An expression just as comprehensive as the preceding. The possessions of the Lord Jesus are identical and co-extensive with those of the infinite Father. "The words are all-inclusive, and assert absolute community in all things between the Father and the Son."—*Watkins.* The feelings of Christ are therefore certain to be in perfect harmony with those of his Father. Hence, it is impossible for him to overlook any part of the universe, in his prayer for a special blessing on his disciples. The bearing of this language upon the question concerning the divinity of Christ, is too obvious to escape notice, and whoever comprehends its real significance will perceive how well it agrees with many other passages in this Gospel. (*e. g.*..1: 1-4; 5: 19, 20.) **And I am glorified in them.** Them, may refer to *all things that are mine,* and *all that are thine,* in the preceding clauses of this verse, or to the pronoun **they,** in the last clause of verse 9. If the latter reference be intended, as I suppose, the intervening words "and all mine are thine and thine are mine," are a sort of parenthetic expansion of the thought, "for they are thine"—*i. e.*, a further thought in the same direction, but not essential to what precedes and follows. Again, the verb, which is in the perfect tense, may be translated *have been* **glorified,** instead of **am glorified;** for it binds together the past and the present, and represents the spirit of trust, of love, and of obedience, which had been for months in the disciples, as abiding in them still, and doing honor to their Lord. For the glory of Christ is revealed in the character and life of "his own." Weiss appears to restrict the verb to a conscious recognition and appreciation of Christ's divine origin and mission by the disciples, saying: "They recognized him in his glory (ver. 7, 8), and, therefore, he was glorified in their hearts (11: 4; 12: 28; 13: 31.)." But the wider reference spoken of above, agrees better with the general tenor of Scripture as to the way in which the Saviour is glorified by his followers, and is equally suited to the context here.

11. And now I am no more in the world. "The declaration of the grounds on which the prayer is urged is followed by the statement of the circumstances which made the prayer necessary."—*Westcott.* **Now,** must be stricken from the Common Version, because it represents nothing in the original. The simple words are: **and I am no more in the world**—where I have been the Teacher and Guide of the Eleven for nearly three years. **But these are in the world.** These—not they; these who are by my side, and are my own,[1] these are in the world, a "world that lieth in wickedness," or, "in the wicked one" (1 John 5: 19.) Whether the world is here thought of as hostile or as seductive, as persecuting the disciples of Christ because of their union with him (15: 18, 19; 16: 2), or as enticing them to forsake him for the pleasures of sin, may not be certain; possibly it is contemplated as both seductive and cruel, though the former characteristic seems, by the sequel, to be more in the mind of Jesus. **And I come to thee.** Notice the present tense of the verbs in this verse. The future is so near and so real to the mind of Jesus, that he speaks of it as present. "I am no more in the world; these are in the world. I am coming to thee." How vivid and intense, yet calm and simple and tender is this language! No merely human teacher ever so talked and prayed with his pupils. Heaven and earth were brought together by this high priestly intercession. **Holy Father.** A most reverent and significant form of address! The epithet **holy,** seems to anticipate the great petition for the sanctification of his disciples, by recognizing as supremely excellent the moral purity of God. Weiss accounts for this epithet by saying that "it belongs to the holy God, in his separation from the world, with its impurity, to preserve the disciples also, in a like separation, from its polluting

[1] Yet the text is uncertain. Tisch., West. & Hort, after א. B, and a few cursives, substitute αὐτοί, *they,* for οὗτοι, *these,* which is retained by Lach., Treg., and Anglo-Am. Revisers, after C Dgr L X Y, and many cursives.

12 While I was with them in the world, *a* I kept them in thy name: those that thou gavest me I have kept, and *b* none of them is lost, *c* but the son of perdition; *d* that the Scripture might be fulfilled.

12 *are.* While I was with them, I kept them in thy name whom thou hast given me: and I guarded them, and not one of them perished, but the son of perdition; that the scripture might be fulfilled.

a ch. 6:39; 10:28; Heb. 2:13....*b* ch. 18:9; 1 John 2:19....*c* ch. 6:70; 13:18....*d* Ps. 109:8; Acts 1:20.

influence." The word **Father** appeals to all that is benignant, tender, and loving in the divine nature; but, as used by Jesus, it cannot be affirmed to have any greater significance here than in other places. **Keep through thine own name those whom thou hast given me.** The best accredited text (Lach., Tisch., Treg., West. & Hort, after ℵ B C L Y Γ Δ Λ Π, etc.), requires a different version, viz.: *keep them in thy name which thou hast given me.* The expression is remarkable, but nevertheless intelligible and profound. It is thus explained by Weiss: "The name itself, which has been manifested to them (ver. 6), in so far as it denotes the nature of God revealed in Christ, has become, in consequence of faith (ver. 8), their life-element, from which, as long as they are kept in it, they draw all the incentives and powers for their new life and work, and so, that name separates the holy sphere in which they move from the world around them." Just as the lame man was healed " in the name of Jesus Christ of Nazareth" (Acts 4:10), and just as there is no "other name under heaven, that is given among men, in which we must be saved" (Acts 4:12, Bib. Un. Vers.), so God, the Father, is asked to keep in his own name, which he had given to Jesus, his own servants, who were also Christ's. The name stands for the whole character, for the purity and power, the love and grace of the Being denoted by it. And the name of the Father had been given to Christ, in this sense at least, that he was to make known, and had made known, by his life and teaching, the true character of God. Hence, the name of God was in him. Hence, too, he could say: "He that hath seen me hath seen the Father." And so the prayer of Jesus is, that the disciples may be kept in union with God, as revealed by himself, that their "life," as an apostle afterwards wrote, may be "hid with Christ in God." (Col. 3:3.)¹ That they

may be one, as we are. Or, more exactly, *even as we.* This is the end sought, viz., the unity of all the disciples. But, what kind of oneness is here meant? "The unity," remarks Westcott, "is not only of will and love, but of nature, perfectly realized in absolute harmony *in Christ.*" If by "nature," Westcott means inward disposition, or character, his language is evidently correct; but, if he means by it something more, namely, an *essential* oneness of being, there is reason to doubt its correctness.

12. While I was with them in the world. Jesus, therefore, now looks back upon his earthly ministry as finished. He has reached the end. He thinks of himself as no longer with his disciples, preserving them from apostasy by his wisdom, watchfulness, and care. **In the world,** is probably an addition to the text, repeated from the preceding verse; for it is omitted by the best editors, in agreement with the earliest manuscripts. (ℵ B C* D L, etc.). **I kept them in thy name.** The I is emphatic. It was by his own personal care and influence that they had been preserved during his intercourse with them. And it may be noticed that the tense of the verb translated **kept,** describes a continuous process, not an act performed once for all. Moreover, according to the best supported text, there should be no pause after **name,** but the sentence should be completed, as in the preceding verse: **which thou hast given me.** See interpretation of this expression in ver. 11. McClellan adopts a slightly different reading here, and in ver. 11, (namely, ᾧ, instead of ᾧ), and supposes that the pronoun represents the disciples (**them**) in their "*corporate unity.*" He says: "Now, with the reading 'that which' (ὅ), how affectingly does the intercession rise in fervor and power! How tenderly it pleads! How earnestly it wrestles! Yes, much more so even than with

¹ There is no doubt that ver. 11 must read "in thy name which (ᾧ) thou hast given me," as found in ℵ A B C L, eleven other uncials, most cursives, Peshito, Harklean and Jerusalem Syriac, Thebaic, Armenian, some Fathers; and with a merely formal difference (ὅ) in D (first hand) X U, several cursives. The other reading, "whom thou hast given me" (οὕς), is here supported by no uncial but D (second hand), by only a few cursives, and Old Latin (some copies), Vulgate, Memphitic, Æthiopic, Gothic. It is obvious that

JOHN. [Ch. XVII.

13 And now come I to thee; and these things I speak in the world, that they might have my joy fulfilled in themselves.

13 But now I come to thee; and these things I speak in the world, that they may have my joy made full in themselves.

the *whom* of the Authorized Version, which yet happily retained the correct *personal* application: *Holy Father, preserve them in thy name—them, that gift of thine to me—that body, that little flock, which thou hast given me—that they may be one as we are.*" But the preponderance of testimony in favor of the other reading, forbids us to accept this view. The best authenticated reading requires another change, thus: *and I guarded them.* Godet suggests that the verb *kept,* refers to the result gained, and the verb *guarded,* to the means employed. But Weiss holds, with greater reason, that "preserving them in the right element of life was accompanied by guarding them from hostile influences, which might draw them away from that element" — (a free translation.) **And none of them is lost, but the son of perdition.** Better: *was* **lost.** The word **perdition** (ἀπωλείας), is from the same root as the word *was* **lost** (ἀπώλετο), and this fact may be imperfectly represented by translating as follows: *and no one of them went to perdition, except the son of perdition.* Was Judas, then, one of those given to Jesus, and kept by him? This is the most obvious sense of the words, and is distinctly affirmed by many interpreters. Thus, Watkins: "He, then, was included in 'them which thou gavest me.' For him there was the same preservation, and the same guardianship as for those who remained in the fold. The sheep wandered from the flock, and was lost by his own act." On the other hand, Westcott remarks, that "the excepting phrase (εἰ μή), does not, necessarily, imply that Judas is reckoned among those whom the Lord *guarded.* The excep-

tion may refer simply to the statement, *not one perished.* Compare Matt. 12: 4; Luke 4: 26, 27; Gal. 1: 19; 2: 16; Rev. 21: 27. Contrast 18: 9." Winer also says (§ 67, 1. e): "Of two parallel members of a sentence, the first is sometimes expressed in such terms as to appear to comprehend the second, though, from the nature of the case, that is impossible"; and he cites under this remark, Acts 27: 22; Gal. 1: 19; Rev. 21: 27. If the words *kept* and *guarded,* describe what was done effectually by Jesus, and this seems to be the only natural interpretation of them, then, "from the nature of the case it is impossible" that Judas was meant to be included, and this expression is, therefore, in a grammatical respect, parallel to Luke 4: 26, 27, and Gal. 1: 19. By a **son of perdition,** is to be understood one who is subject to, or an heir of perdition, (comp. 2 Thess. 2: 3; Matt. 23: 15; Luke 10: 6; Matt. 8: 12; 13: 38), one that is about to perish. Such a man was Judas. **That the scripture might be fulfilled.** See Notes on 12: 38; 13: 18. The reference may be to Ps. 41: 9, or to 109: 8. At all events, the sin of Judas was included in the wise and holy plan of God, and had been foreseen and foretold long before by the prophetic Spirit. But the sin of Judas was without excuse, drawing after it the dreadful doom which is signified by the word perdition. It was none the less his own free act because it was embraced in the foreknowledge and plan of God.

13. And now come I to thee. *But* would represent, in this place, the original conjunction (δέ) much better than **and.** For Winer says of this particle (§ 53, 7) that it

---

"**which**" is the difficult reading, likely to have been changed to "**whom**," and yet, upon reflection, yielding a good sense. So in ver. 11, the case is clear. But the evidence stands far otherwise in ver. 12. Here "**which**" (ὅ) is found in B C (first hand) L, 33, 64, Cyril of Alexandria, and (ὅ) in ℵ (third corrector), Memphitic, Thebaic, Jerusalem Syriac, Armenian, while "**whom**" (οὕς) is read by A D X Y Γ Δ Λ Π, and eight other uncials, most cursives, and Old Latin, Vulgate, Peshito, and Harklean, Syriac, Æthiopic, Gothic. Now it would be easy to call this a "Western and Syrian" reading. But how explain the fact that so very many authorities have "**whom**" here, and "**which**" in the immediately preceding and exactly similar sentence? Are not the phenomena best accounted for by supposing that in ver. 12 the Saviour's language returns to the expression of ver. 6 and 9, and that so the true reading is "**which**" in ver. 11 and "**whom**" in ver. 12? Then "**which**" in the latter case would be an "Alexandrian" correction, sustained by the well-known group of C L, Egyptian versions, Cyril, with the addition of B, which is not wholly a stranger either to "Alexandrian" or to "Western" readings.—B.

14 ᵃI have given them thy word; ᵇand the world hath hated them, because they are not of the world, ᶜeven as I am not of the world. 15 I pray not that thou shouldest take them out of the world, but ᵈthat thou shouldest keep them from the evil.

14 in themselves. I have given them thy word: and the world hated them, because they are not of the world, 15 world, even as I am not of the world. I ¹pray not that thou shouldest take them ²from the world, but that thou shouldest keep them ²from ³the evil

a ver. 6....*b* ch. 15: 18, 19; 1 John 3: 13....*c* ch. 8: 23; ver. 16....*d* Matt. 6: 13; Gal. 1: 4; 2 Thess. 3: 3; 1 John 5: 18.—1 Gr. *make request*....2 Gr. *out of*....3 Or. *evil*.

"connects while it contrasts—*i. e.*, adds another particular different from what precedes;" and Grimm describes it as "an adversative, distinctive, discretive particle." In most cases, then, it should be translated "but," while it may sometimes be rendered, approximately, by the conjunction "and." Jesus represents himself as now going to the Father, yet he has not quite left the scenes of earth. His point of view seems to fluctuate between a work that has been closed, and one that is about to be closed. Here, it is the latter, a work at the point of being closed. **That they might have my joy fulfilled in themselves.** This clause should be read as in the Revised Version: *that they may have my joy made full in themselves.* And the joy of Christ was perfect; it was the joy of perfect purity, perfect love, and perfect communion with the Father. Inward peace, trust, hope, were associated with wise, far-seeing, fruitful activity for the honor of God, and the welfare of men, and the result was joy unspeakable.

14. I have given them thy word. Observe, (1) that the pronoun **I** receives a certain emphasis in the original which it is difficult to reproduce in English. "I have not failed in my mission; in accordance with thy will, I have myself, by my life and teaching, delivered unto them thy word. By a process, begun long ago and continued down to the present hour, this has been accomplished by me." (2) That the expression **thy word,** represents all the teachings or sayings of Jesus as an organic unity, as one message. Informal, unsystematic, and spontaneous as they are, they are nevertheless self-consistent, harmonious, and interdependent, to a most wonderful degree. One spirit pervades them all. In like manner, Christians now speak of the sacred Scriptures as "the word of God," and are justified in so doing by the example of Jesus. **And the world hath hated them.** More exactly: *the world hated them.* As if the hatred of the world broke out decisively and at once against them. Instruction is a process; the manifestation of hatred may be concentrated into an act, which is, as it were, complete in itself, though it may be repeated again and again. For a different representation, see 15: 18, 24. **Because they are not of the world.** To be of the world, is to draw one's life and spirit, aims and motives, from the world. And this had ceased to be the case with the Eleven. They had broken with the unbelieving world, and had become allied to Christ. Their truest life, their ruling motives, were drawn from a divine source. **Even as I am not of the world.** Thus graciously and lovingly does he associate them with himself, presenting them, imperfect as they were, to his Father, as standing on the same plane of life with himself, and drawing their inspirations from above.

15. I pray not that thou shouldest take them out of the world. This might have seemed the readiest way to deliver them from evil, and to render perfect their joy. To take them with himself into glory, would be to remove them from trial and conflict; but with them, as with him, the conflict must precede the victory, the cross must come before the crown. If the Captain of their Salvation must be made perfect through suffering, so, also, must his followers. Therefore, they must be in the world for a season, but not of it; must live as strangers and pilgrims among those whose spirit they do not share, whose way of life they condemn, and who, by reason of this, hate them and persecute them. **But that thou shouldest keep them from the evil.** Are we to consider **the evil** (τοῦ Πονηροῦ), as neuter, or as masculine? In support of the former view, Godet urges the meaning of the preposition, which signifies, he says, *out of*, and refers to a domain rather than to a person. But to this Westcott furnishes a reply, by saying: "Just as Jesus Christ is himself the medium or sphere in which the believer lives and moves (ἐν Χριστῷ),

16 ᵃ They are not of the world, even as I am not of the world.
17 ᵇ Sanctify them through thy truth: ᶜ thy word is truth.
18 ᵈ As thou hast sent me into the world, even so have I also sent them into the world.

16 one. They are not of the world, even as I am 17 not of the world. ¹ Sanctify them in the truth; thy 18 word is truth. As thou didst send me into the

a ver. 14....*b* ch. 15:3; Acts 15:9; Eph. 5:26; 1 Pet. 1:22....*c* 2 Sam. 7:28; Ps. 119, 142, 151; ch. 8:40....*d* ch. 20:21.—1 Or, consecrate.

---

so the prince of the world, the evil one, is the medium or sphere in which they live and move, who are given up to him (ἐν τῷ πονηρῷ)." Others have urged that it would have "been unfitting for Jesus to have thought of the devil in this prayer." To this, Luthardt replies: "It would be much more correct to say that, considering the decided and persistent manner in which Jesus places himself and his work, and the Fourth Gospel places both, in opposition to the devil, it would necessarily have been most striking if there had been no mention of the devil, either in the summation of all Christian prayer, in the Lord's Prayer, or in the summation of all Christ's prayer in the high-priestly prayer." On the whole, it seems to me probable that Jesus here refers to the adversary of good, and that the Revised Version is correct. (Comp. 1 John 5: 18, 19; 2 Thess. 3: 3; 1 John 2: 13, 14; 3: 12.) If, however, the expression be neuter, the article should be omitted in translation.

16. They are not of the world, etc. A repetition of the last part of the 14th verse. Thus the Lord associates his disciples once more with himself; but now, as an argument for the request he is about to make. Emphasis is given to **the world,** by the position which is assigned to it in the Greek text: *Of the world they are not, even as I myself am not of the world.* I *myself*, because the insertion of the Greek pronoun involves a certain degree of emphasis not suggested by the simple pronoun in English.

17. Sanctify them through thy truth. Rather, with the Revised Version: *Sanctify them in the truth.* For the critical editors omit the pronoun **thy** (with אֵ* B C* D L, etc.), and the leading interpreters give to the preposition (ἐν) its primary sense of *in*. **The truth** —*i. e.*, Christian truth, as embodied in Jesus Christ, and revealed by him, is the element or atmosphere in which sanctification is accomplished. But what is the blessing expressed by the word **sanctify**? It may mean

either to devote or consecrate one to a holy service, or to make one holy in character, and thus fit for a holy service. The former meaning prevails in the 19th verse, but the latter here. What the Eleven needed above all things was a profounder apprehension of Christian truth, and a holier character; "the equipment with divine illumination, power, courage, joyfulness, love, inspiration, etc., for their official activity (ver. 18) which should ensue, and did ensue, by means of the Holy Spirit—14: 17; 15: 26; 16: 7 sq." —*Meyer*. "By saying, '*sanctify them,*' Jesus asks for them a will wholly devoted to the task which they would have to accomplish in the world. It was necessary that all their powers, all their talents, all their life, should be consecrated to this great work—the salvation of men. . . . It is the sublime idea of Christian *holiness*, but envisaged here, where the apostles are referred to, as fulfilling itself under the special form of the Christian *ministry.*"—*Godet*. **Thy word is truth. Thy word**—whatever *thou* hast spoken is truth; and truth is the proper element for a believing soul. "The word which is thine" must partake of thy character, must be holy, divine, and supremely important. If we have the word of Christ, we have the word of the Father; and if we have the word of the Father, we have truth, without any mixture of error. Such truth Christ had communicated to his disciples; such truth were they to receive from the Holy Spirit; by such truth were they to be qualified for their work; and with such truth they were to testify of Christ.

18. As thou hast sent me, etc. The Revised Version gives the tense of the verbs more correctly than the Common Version; but Davidson's translation represents still better the original. It reads as follows: *Even as thou didst send me into the world, I also sent them into the world.* The precise time when Jesus was sent into the world was that of his incarnation, though thirty years elapsed

19 And *for their sakes I sanctify myself, that they also might be sanctified through the truth.
20 Neither pray I for these alone, but for them also which shall believe on me through their word;

19 world, even so sent I them into the world. And for their sakes I ¹ sanctify myself, that they themselves 20 also may be sanctified in truth. Neither for these only do I ² pray, but for them also that believe on

a 1 Cor. 1:2, 30; 1 Thess. 4:7; Heb. 10:10.—1 Or, *cons* crate....2 Gr. *make request*.

before he entered on his public ministry. So the definite time when the apostles were sent into the world was that of their temporary mission (Matt. 10:5; Mark 6:7; Luke 9:2) to the lost sheep of the house of Israel. (Matt. 10:6.) Many of his instructions and predictions at that time had reference, without doubt, to their later life-work. **The world**, as referred to in this verse, is the unbelieving world—men alienated from the love and service of God, men who knew not the Father and the Son. (Ver. 3.)

19. And for their sakes. The entire mission of Christ was for the benefit of mankind, and especially for the good of his true disciples, represented at this moment by the Eleven. **I sanctify myself.** This seems to refer, above all, to his sacrificial death, which now remained to be accomplished. "A way stands before him from which nature shrinks back—the way of sacrifice. The word is not, therefore, to be understood of Jesus' entrance into the divine manner of being. . . but certainly of the sacrificial consecration of Jesus; only that this is to be viewed as the acme of his entire consecration of his life to the service of God."—*Luthardt*. Yet Godet, (in his valuable work, "Defence of the Christian Faith," p. 251), appears to regard the words of Jesus as referring equally to every part of his life, from the cradle to the cross. "Holy is not [here] to be contrasted with *impure*, but with *profane*, ordinary, unconsecrated, natural. Jesus sanctified himself by offering to God, step by step, all the elements of his being, as they successively unfolded themselves; all the faculties of his body and of his soul, as they came into play; every domain of his existence, as soon as he set his foot in it." This is all true; but it is at the same time natural to suppose that the consecration of Jesus for and in that supreme event, his propitiatory death, was especially in his mind. For the shadows of Gethsemane were already darkening his pathway; and his words at this moment would forever be connected in the minds of his disciples with the scene that followed. **That they also might be sancti-**

fied through the truth. *That they also themselves may be sanctified in truth*, is a more exact rendering than that of the Common Version. The purpose for which Jesus consecrates himself to his last and crowning act of love is this, that "his own" may become like unto himself, consecrated to the holy work which he has given them to do. And this was rendered possible by his self-consecration in their behalf. Only thus could they be united to him as a perfect Saviour, be filled with his spirit, and live in the domain and service of truth instead of error. Many interpreters understand *in truth* as equivalent to the adverb *truly*; but this is a doubtful meaning of the words.

20-26. PRAYER FOR ALL BELIEVERS IN HIS NAME.

20. Neither pray I for these alone. The expression is like that in the ninth verse, and may, therefore be translated: *Yet not in respect to these only do I ask*. By these, is meant the apostolic group, standing around him in silent reverence, and listening to the words which he poured out, with filial trust, into the Father's ear. **But for them also which shall believe on me through their word.** According to the earliest manuscripts and versions, the word **believe** is here in the present, not the future tense; so that the clause may be properly translated : *But in respect to them also that believe on me through their word*. Whether the present is used as a *timeless* expression, including the future, or whether all who are to believe in ages to come stand, as it were, in spirit, before him, may be uncertain; but several things are clear—*e. g.*: (1) That Jesus does not limit his asking to blessings for those only who are listening to his words, and who may, therefore, be helped by those words; but he prays for the absent and the unborn, and thus shows that prayer is a means of reaching God, and securing a blessing from him. (2) That Jesus represents himself as the object of faith—**on** me. And believing *in* or *on* Christ is more than giving full credit to the truth of his words; it is accepting him as Saviour, honor-

[Сн. XVII.] JOHN. 347

21 ªThat they all may be one; as ᵇthou, Father, art in me, and I in thee, that they also may be one in us: that the world may believe that thou hast sent me.
22 And the glory which thou gavest me I have given them; ᶜthat they may be one, even as we are one:

21 me through their word; that they may all be one; even as thou, Father, art in me, and I in thee, that they also may be in us: that the world may believe 22 that thou didst send me. And the glory which thou hast given me I have given unto them; that

a ch. 10:16; ver. 11, 22, 23; Rom. 12:5; Gal. 3:28....*b* ch. 10:38; 14:11....*c* ch. 14:20; 1 John 1:3; 3:24.

ing him as Son of God, and drawing from him spiritual life. (3) That this belief is to be produced by means of the apostles' word. The gospel preached by them is to be the power of God and the wisdom of God unto salvation.

21. That they all may be one. Of course, one in character and spirit, one by virtue of a common faith, a mutual love, and a tender sympathy. Gill remarks that a "unity in affection may be here designed—a being knit together in love to each other, which is the bond of perfectness, the evidence of regeneration, the badge of the Christian profession, the beauty of church communion, and the barrier and security from the common enemy." But even more than this seems to be intended, namely—a unity like that which the branches have with one another by virtue of their connection with the vine—a unity which depends as much upon the indwelling Spirit as it does upon the implanted word. For, as Lange says: "Unity in the one Holy Spirit, who is the same in all, is indeed more than moral unity." (Comp. 1 Cor. 6:16, 19; 12:12, 13; Rom. 8:9-11; 15:5, 6; Eph. 2:14-22.) **As thou, Father, art in me, and I in thee, that they also may be one in us.** According to the judgment of the soundest scholars, **one** should be dropped in the last clause, so that it would read, **that they also may be in us.** But the practical end of this unity, as respects the world, must not be overlooked in judging of its character, namely, **that the world may believe that thou hast sent me.** Rather: *that thou didst send me.* And such a result presupposes a certain degree of unity in the visible life of Christians, while this unity of outward life must spring from unity of inward life, from unity of conviction, spirit, aim, and hope. Hence, a perfect agreement in views of Christian doctrine and duty, manifesting itself without disturbance in worship, business, and social life, would seem necessary, in order to a perfect visible unity of believers; yet less than this will convince the world that Christians are in Christ and for Christ; that the current of their faith, hope, and love is bearing them all in the same direction; that with many points of diversity, they are not only servants of the same Master, but animated by the same hopes, and seeking the same end. Divided as Protestant Christians are into many bands, they are, nevertheless, in a most profound and novel sense, one. "This unity," says Alford, "has its true and only *ground* in faith in Christ, through the word of God, as delivered by the apostles; and is, therefore, not the mere outward uniformity, nor can such uniformity produce it. At the same time, its effects are to be real and visible, such that the world may see them."

22. And the glory which thou gavest me I have given them. According to the best copies (א B C L, etc.), the first, as well as the second verb, is in the perfect tense; hence, the Revised Version is correct: *And the glory which thou hast given me I have given unto them.* The pronoun **I** is emphatic, and signifies "I on my part," or, "I in turn." But what is the glory here spoken of? A satisfactory answer to this question is not readily found. Meyer, and others, suppose it to be the heavenly glory. "This, once already possessed by him before the incarnation, the Father has *given* to him, not yet, indeed, *objectively*, but as a secure possession of the *immediate future*. . . In like manner has *he given* this, his *glory*, in which the eternal *life*, ver. 2, 3, is consummated, to his *believing ones* (them), who will enter into the real possession at the Parousia." (Rom. 8:30.) But the words used, **have given,** naturally suggest that this glory had been already imparted to them, so that they were now possessors of it, to some degree, at least.

Weiss, and others, assert that it must be the power of working miracles. "In behalf of the conversion of the world, he has given to them the power to confirm the message which

23 I in them, and thou in me, a *that they may be made perfect in one; and that the world may know that thou hast sent me, and hast loved them, as thou hast loved me.*
24 b *Father, I will that they also, whom thou hast given me, be with me where I am; that they may behold my glory, which thou hast given me; c for thou lovedest me before the foundation of the world.*

23 they may be one, even as we *are* one; I in them and thou in me, that they may be perfected into one; that the world may know that thou didst send me, and lovedst them, even as thou lovedst me.
24 Father, 1 that which thou hast given me, I desire that, where I am, they also may be with me; that they may behold my glory, which thou hast given me: for thou lovedst me before the foundation of

a Col. 3: 14....*b* ch. 12: 26; 14: 3; 1 Thess. 4: 17....*c* ver. 5.——1 Many ancient authorities read, *those whom.*

they bring to the world by miracles and signs, as he did." But this view is unsatisfactory, because it makes **them** mean the Eleven, and not all believers.

Alford, and others, hold that the glory here meant is that of Sonship to God. "The glory is . . . *the glory of Christ as the only begotten Son* (ch. 1: 14), full of grace and truth . . . which, by the virtue of his exaltation and the unity of all believers in him through the Spirit, has become (not, *shall be*) theirs (Eph. 1: 18; 2: 6; Rom. 8: 30), not yet fully, nor *as it is his;* but as each can receive and show it forth." And Godet remarks: "The end of verse 23 guides us to a little different sense (from one that he had been explaining). As the essence of the glory of Jesus consists in his dignity as *Son,* as *well-beloved* Son, so the glory of believers, which he has communicated to them, is the filial dignity, the state of *adoption* (1: 12) by which they have *become* what the Son *is* eternally—children of God, objects of his perfect love." But Jesus speaks of a glory which the Father has *given* him. If, then, it is the glory of Sonship, it is that of his Sonship as the theanthropic Christ Jesus, rather than of his Sonship as the eternal Word. (Comp. Luke 1: 35.) With this explanation, we are better satisfied with the view than with any other. **That they may be one, even as we are one.** See Notes on the first clause of verse 21. This repetition of the thought is deeply impressive. The Saviour returns to it again and again, showing how much he had at heart the unity of his followers.

23. I in them, and thou in me, that they may be made perfect in one. Better: *that they may be perfected into one;* that is, "into one thing," though in what respects one, must be determined by the nature of the case. (See under verse 21.) In other words, the Saviour has given them the glory in question with a view to making them perfect by means of a process which issues in spiritual oneness, in a life springing from himself, and the same in all. Moreover, the words, **I in them and thou in me,** do not begin a new sentence, but rather intimate by the way, as it were, the means by which this perfection into one must be accomplished. Hence, the meaning would be expressed by saying: "I being in them and thou in me, that," etc. With what importunate love does Jesus plead for this unity of his followers! "See how his mouth overflows with one kind of words."—*Luther in Luthardt.*

Omitting the **and,** which did not belong to the original text, the next clause corresponds with the last part of verse 21: **that the world may know that thou hast sent me.** Rather: *didst send me.* But here there is an important addition, namely: **and hast loved them, as thou hast loved me.** Better: *lovedst them even as thou lovedst me.* Thus the love of the Father to believers in Christ is virtually affirmed to be like his love to Christ himself. And the prayer of Jesus is, that this wonderful love may be made known to the world through the oneness of believers in character and life—a oneness which could only spring from the workings of divine love in their hearts. (Comp. Rom. 5: 5.)

24-26. Final Request, That His Disciples Be Ultimately Joined With Him in Heaven—and Reasons Therefor.

24. Father, I will . . . where I am. The Revised Version (see above) follows the Greek more closely than is consistent with the best English style. I therefore prefer the translation of Alford and Davidson: *Father, I will that what thou hast given me, even they may be with me where I am.* For the pronoun *what,* must, in deference to manuscript evidence, be substituted for **they whom,** especially as it is a more difficult reading, and as a transcriber would be very likely to change the neuter singular to the masculine plural, but not at all likely to change the masculine plural to a neuter singular. Yet the neuter form is very significant; for it represents all the disciples as a

25 O righteous Father, *the world hath not known thee; but *I have known thee, and *these have known that thou hast sent me.
26 *And I have declared unto them thy name, and will declare it; that the love *wherewith thou hast loved me may be in them, and I in them.

25 the world. O righteous Father, the world knew thee not, but I knew thee; and these knew that
26 thou didst send me; and I made known unto them thy name, and will make it known; that the love wherewith thou lovedst me may be in them, and I in them.

a ch. 15 : 21 ; 16 : 3....*b* ch. 7 : 29 ; 8 : 55 ; 10 : 15.. ..*c* ch. 16 : 27 ; ver. 6....*d* ch. 15 : 15 ; ver. 6....*e* ch. 15 : 9.

single body, or flock, a collective whole; and then the plural, *even they*, recognizes the same body as made up of individual saints, whom he would have with him where he should be. For the expression, **where I am,** refers, without doubt, to his place in glory. Hence, though he leaves his disciples for a little time in the world, to carry forward his work, he asks to have them ultimately with himself in heaven. **That they may behold my glory, which thou hast given me.** The glory referred to is that of the Incarnate Son, and not that of the divine Logos. Yet, in a very important sense it is the glory which the divine Logos had with the Father, before the world was. (See ver. 5, and comp. 1 : 1, and Phil. 2 : 6-9.) For, in personal union with the Word, human nature is now to be exalted to the right hand of God, and he who is the Servant of Jehovah is to be made Head over all things to the church. (Eph. 1 : 22.) To be with him, and to behold his glory, must, then, be the highest joy of believers. (Comp. Rev. 5 : 6-14 ; 22 : 1-5.) Paul was certain of this when he was in a strait betwixt the two, having the desire to depart, that he might be with Christ, which would be for him very far better, but knowing that to abide in the flesh was more needful for the disciples (Phil. 1 : 23); and he was equally certain of it when he wrote, saying, that "our light affliction, which is but for a moment, worketh for us a far more exceeding and eternal weight of glory." (2 Cor. 4 : 17.) It is impossible to imagine just what will be the nature of the vision of Christ, but it will surely be a source of unspeakable delight; and, while giving such delight, it will also transform his disciples more and more into his own likeness, and impart to them some of his glory. (1 John 3 : 2, and Rom. 8 : 17 ; 2 Tim. 2 : 11, 12.) **For thou lovedst me before the foundation of the world.** The glory of the exalted Jesus is, therefore, the gift of eternal love. For, Jesus who is now about to be glorified as the God-man, is conscious of having enjoyed the Father's love, before the world was. It is possible, moreover, though not certain, that he intends to represent that love as resting upon him, in view of his foreseen incarnation and death, for the redemption of man. For the whole work of redemption was embraced in the holy purpose of the triune God, that antedated the first act of creation. The words of this passage naturally suggest a *covenant* of redemption between the Father and the Son.

25. O righteous Father. It is commonly supposed that the expression, **I will,** in verse 24, signifies more than simple desire; that it presents a rightful claim (comp. Mark 6 : 25); and, if this is a correct view, that expression is in special harmony with the plea involved in the epithet **righteous,** here employed. But, this epithet is also perfectly suited to what follows, which refers to the sinful ignorance of the world and to the fidelity of Jesus, together with his disciples. **The world hath not known thee,** etc. The Revised Version is an improvement on the Common Version, thus: *The world knew thee not, but I knew thee; and these knew that thou didst send me.* The conjunction *and*, precedes **the world,** in the original, but cannot be represented properly in English. According to Westcott, "it serves to co-ordinate the two main clauses, which bring out the contrast between the world and the disciples. The force of it is as if we were to say: Two facts are equally true; it is true that the world knew thee not; it is true that these knew that thou didst send me." *And yet*, would be the best rendering, if the word (καὶ) is reproduced at all.

26. And I have declared unto them thy name. More exactly: *And I made known unto them thy name.* As if he had given them, in the past, a knowledge of the Father; which was, indeed, true; for nothing could well be clearer than the revelation which he had made of the character and will of God. Yet this was a work that must be continued, directly or indirectly, until the end of time; and, therefore, he adds the assurance: **and will declare it,** or, *make it*

350 JOHN. [Ch. XVIII.

CHAPTER XVIII.

WHEN Jesus had spoken these words, *he went forth with his disciples over *b* the brook Ce′ron, where was a garden, into the which he entered, and his disciples.

1 When Jesus had spoken these words, he went forth with his disciples over the ¹brook ²Kidron, where was a garden, into the which he entered,

a Matt. 26:36; Mark 14:32; Luke 22:39....b 2 Sam. 15:23.——1 Or, ravine. Gr. winter-torrent.....2 Or, of the cedars.

known. That is, probably, through the agency of the Holy Spirit, and (if the pronoun **them** embraces all future converts to the truth), through the subordinate agency of the apostles and of all other Christian teachers. This revelation of the Father is finally said to have its end or purpose in this: **that the love wherewith thou hast loved me may be in them, and I in them.** In other words, that the love which the Father has to the Son may be shed abroad in their hearts, or experienced by them, as a fountain of joy, and purity, and strength. Going from them, he would still be with them and in them.

Such is the prayer which Jesus is said to have offered, in the evening after the institution of the Holy Supper—a prayer of matchless dignity, simplicity, depth, and love. The words of Luther respecting it, have been often quoted: "So plainly and simply it sounds, so deep and rich and wide it is, that none can fathom it"—(taken from Meyer). Yet, several objections have been pressed against its genuineness, and two or three of them deserve notice. (1) It is said to be incredible that John could have remembered the words of so long a prayer through so many years. What he has given, must, therefore, be at best the fruit of his own meditation on a prayer mostly forgotten. This objection is certainly plausible, but before accepting it as conclusive, it will be wise to consider, (a) That the "Spirit of truth" had been promised to the Eleven for the express purpose of enabling them to recall the words of their Lord. (b) That such words as are found in this prayer would sink down into the mind and heart of "the disciple whom Jesus loved" with peculiar sweetness and power; (c) That the order of thought in the prayer is extremely natural and logical, while the different words to be remembered are not numerous; (d) That the whole prayer is singularly adapted to the occasion, as well as singularly rich and spiritual: forbidding the assumption that it was not believed to be genuine by the Evangelist; and (e) that,

even when the style of a translation reminds one of that of the translator, the record may be trustworthy, giving correctly the thoughts of the original.

(2) It is said that the tone of this prayer is inconsistent with the dreadful sorrow which soon after filled the soul of Jesus, and found utterance in the cry, "If it be possible, let this cup pass from me." (Matt. 26:39.) Such alternations of joy and sorrow are held to be incredible in the case of Jesus. But to this it may be replied, (a) that the human nature of Christ was like that of other men, sinfulness excepted. Accordingly it is said of him at one time, that he rejoiced in spirit, and at another time, that he groaned in spirit. And why should not one who was capable of joy and of grief, be susceptible, at times, of sudden alternations of feeling? (b) That the adversary of all good appears to have renewed his assaults in the garden, bringing on a sudden revulsion of feeling. Having tempted the Lord in the wilderness, without success, he had departed from him for a season (Luke 4:13); but there is reason to suppose that he repeated his attacks when Jesus entered the garden, soon after this prayer (see 14:31; comp. 13:2, 27), perhaps in a very different and more terrible form. That John does not refer to the agony of Jesus may be accounted for by the purpose of his Gospel, which allowed him to omit many things that were well known to Christians by other testimony.

Chap. 18: 1-11. THE ARREST OF JESUS THROUGH THE TREACHERY OF JUDAS. (Parallel passages, Matt. 26:30, 47-56; Mark 14:26, 43-52; Luke 22:47-53.)

1. When Jesus had spoken these words. That is, the words of his prayer, and, more generally, of chapters 14-16. **He went forth with his disciples over the brook Cedron.** The expression, **went forth** (ἐξῆλθε), naturally presupposes a definite place, like the city, or the upper room—from which he went out; and as there is no conclusive argument against the view that the communications of Christ to his disciples, recorded in chapters 15, 16, and his prayer, preserved in chapter 17, were made in the outer court of the temple, we may fix upon this as the probable point of departure. The word rendered **brook**, signifies a "winter torrent," and properly characterizes the Kidron, which is thus described by Dr. Robinson ("Researches," I. p. 273): "The channel of the valley of Jehoshaphat, the brook Kidron of the Scriptures, is nothing more than the dry bed of a wintry torrent, bearing marks of being occasionally swept over by a large volume of water. No stream flows here now, except during the heavy rains of winter, when the waters descend into it from the neighboring hills. . . . Like the wadys of the desert, the valley probably served of old, as now, only to drain off the waters of the rainy season." The reader will certainly be pleased to trace as accurately as possible the way that was followed by the little company which now left the city by the gate of St. Stephen, as we suppose. "A path winds down from the gate on a course southeast by east, and crosses the water-bed of the valley by a bridge; beyond which are the church with the tomb of the Virgin, Gethsemane, and other plantations of olive trees. . . The path and bridge are on a causeway, or rather, terrace, built up across the valley, perpendicular on the south side; the earth being filled in on the northern side up to the level of the bridge. The bridge itself consists of an arch, open on the south side, and seventeen feet high from the bed of the channel below; but the north side is built up, with two subterranean drains entering it from above; one of which comes from the sunken court of the Virgin's tomb, and the other from the fields further in the northwest. The breadth of the valley at this point, will appear from the measurements which I took from St. Stephen's gate to Gethsemane, along the path, viz.: (1) From St. Stephen's gate to the brow of the descent, level, 135 English feet; (2) [to] bottom of the slope, the angle of descent being 16½°, 415 feet; (3) [across] bridge, level, 140 feet; (4) [to] northwest corner of Gethsemane, slight rise, 145 feet; (5) [to] northeast corner of the same, 150. The last three numbers give the breadth of the proper bottom of the valley at this spot, viz.: 435 feet, or 145 yards." (Robinson's "Researches," etc., I. p. 270 sq.) [1] **Where was a garden, into the which he entered, and his disciples.** Better, as in the Revised Version: *himself and his disciples.* John simply affirms that this garden, or orchard, was beyond the Kidron, as one goes from the city. Luke (22:39) shows that in going to it, Jesus went to the Mount of Olives. But neither of them informs us whether it was at the foot, or on the side, or on the summit, of this mount. The small farm to which the orchard belonged, or, perhaps, the orchard itself, is called Gethsemane,

[1 We cannot think the Greek should here read τῶν Κεδρῶν, as in Tex. Rec. and W. & H., but rather, τοῦ Κεδρών. The former is supported by ℵ (third corrector) B C L X, ten other uncials, and most cursives, and several Fathers; but *no ancient version* translates "of the cedars." It is also found in the Septuagint of 2 Sam. 15: 23 (twice); 1 Kings 2: 37; 15: 13, *i. e.*—the article τῶν is inserted by some manuscripts, in two cases by B. and two by A., while omitted by others. (See Hort.) The other, τοῦ Κεδρών is read by A S Δ, 123, several important copies of the Old Latin, the Vulgate, Gothic, Armenian (apparently), and some Latin Fathers; while τοῦ Κεδρου is given by ℵ (first hand) D, some copies of the Old Latin, the Memphitic, Thebaic, Æthiopic. And Josephus (see Grimm, s. v.) three times uses the genitive Κεδρῶνος, showing a nomative Κεδρών, and once has the nomative Κεδρών itself. The word is Hebrew, *Kidron* (see the Old Testament passages), and there is a familiar Greek word κέδρος, cedar. Now how easily would scribes unacquainted with Hebrew suppose that the ravine τοῦ Κεδρών was a mistake for either τῶν κέδρων, "of the cedars," or, τοῦ κέδρου, "of the cedar" (the Greek word being apparently sometimes masculine, see L. and S.) Thus the reading τοῦ Κεδρών, *accounts for* both the others, and answers to the Hebrew form, which is commonly understood to mean *dirty, turbid*, said of a torrent. And the introduction of τῶν by some MSS. in some passages of the Septuagint would be explained in the same way; it is not said to appear at all in 2 Kings 23: 4, 6; Jer. 31: 40. Dr. Hort thinks it likely that the Greek word κέδρος, cedar, was of Phenician origin, and perhaps from the same root as the Hebrew *kidron*, meaning "dark," said of the tree, and that so the ravine *Kidron*, meant "ravine of the cedars," being so called from possible surviving clumps of that tree. But the theory will suppose that the Evangelist knew this to be the etymology of *Kidron*, and gave τῶν κέδρων, as a translation; and it would then be surprising that Josephus did not know it. The *strong* transcriptional probability, and the, at least, tacit support of all the early versions, require us to follow ℵ A D, etc., rather than B C L, etc., the later group here giving a correction of the "Alexandrian" sort.—B.]

2 And Judas also, which betrayed him, knew the place: *for Jesus ofttimes resorted thither with his disciples.
3 ᵇJudas then, having received a band *of men* and officers from the chief priests and Pharisees, cometh thither with lanterns and torches and weapons.

2 himself and his disciples. Now Judas also, who betrayed him, knew the place: for Jesus oft-times resorted thither with his disciples.
3 resorted thither with his disciples. Judas then, having received the ¹ band *of soldiers*, and officers from the chief priests and the Pharisees, cometh thither with lanterns and torches and weapons.

a Luke 21:37; 22:30....b Matt. 26:47; Mark 14:43; Luke 22:47; Acts 1:16.——1 Or, *cohort*.

i. e.—"Oil-press" (Matt. 26:36; Mark 14:32), doubtless because there was, some time, such a press connected with it. Speaking of the traditional site of this garden, Dr. Hackett says: "The original garden may have been more or less extensive than the present site, or have stood a few hundred rods further to the north or the south; but far, certainly, from that spot it need not be supposed to have been. We may sit down there and read the narrative of what the Saviour endured for our redemption, and feel assured that we are near the place where he prayed, saying, 'Father, not my will, but thine be done,' and where, 'being in an agony, he sweat, as it were, great drops of blood, falling down to the ground.' It is altogether probable that the disciples, in going back to Jerusalem from Bethany, after having seen the Lord taken up into heaven, passed Gethsemane on the way. What new thoughts must have arisen in their minds, what deeper insight into the mystery of the agony must have flashed upon them, as they looked once more upon that scene of the sufferings and humiliation of the crucified and ascended One." (Smith's "Dict. of the Bible," p. 908.)

Passing over, without notice, the agony of Jesus and his threefold prayer, which are so fully described in the Synoptical Gospels (see Matt. 26:36-46; Mark 14:32-39; Luke 22: 40-46), John now relates the principal circumstances of his apprehension, showing that he *permitted* himself to be taken and led away to judgment. Doubtless the Evangelist was convinced that no Christian would forget, when reading this record, the momentous and tragic scene in the garden, with which he was familiar in the well known writings of Matthew, Mark, and Luke. And if anything might safely be omitted, it would certainly be a scene which had been so deeply imprinted on the hearts of all who knew the Gospel. In the account which follows, he mentions several particulars not found in the earlier Gospels.

2. And Judas also, which betrayed him, knew the place. The meaning may be more exactly given as follows: *Now* (δέ) *Judas also, who was betraying him, knew the place.* For the present participle used as an imperfect with the article (ὁ παραδιδούς), describes Judas as one who was then engaged in the work of delivering Jesus over into the hands of his foes, and not as one whom the Evangelist remembers and characterizes as the man who once perpetrated this crime. In other words, Judas is set before us, graphically, after the manner of John, as one who was then carrying into effect his treacherous plan. (See Note on 13:11). And the circumstance that Judas knew the place proves that Jesus did not go there with his disciples for the purpose of concealment from his enemies. If there can be any doubt about this, it must disappear before the next statement: **for Jesus ofttimes resorted thither with his disciples.** Judas knew the place, because it was one where Jesus had often met with his disciples. Such a place would not have been selected by the Lord, if he had wished to elude the search of foes, that were to be led on, as he knew, by one of his own followers. For how long a time, or for what sufficient reasons, Jesus had been accustomed to meet with his disciples in this garden, is nowhere stated. Yet some of those visits to the place were probably made before the present passover, and the owner of the estate was, doubtless, friendly to him. It was evidently a quiet, retired spot, where he could commune with "his own," and seek the blessing of his Father.

3. Judas then, having received a band of men. More exactly: *having received the band—i. e.,* the cohort of Roman soldiers, stationed as a garrison in Antonia. (See Matt. 27:27; Mark 15:16; Acts 21:31 sq.; Joseph. "Ant." 21:4, 3; 'B. J.: 5, 8.) The Greek term here used (σπεῖρα), properly denotes a "cohort," numbering 600 soldiers, though it is used by Polybius to denote a *manipulus*, numbering about 200. The band, or cohort, was probably, in this case, represented by a

Ch. XVIII.] JOHN. 353

4 Jesus therefore, knowing all things that should come upon him, went forth, and said unto them, Whom seek ye?

4 Jesus therefore, knowing all the things that were coming upon him, went forth, and saith unto

detachment, led by their commander. **And officers from the chief priests and Pharisees.** Better: *the Pharisees*, since important manuscripts have the definite article before the word **Pharisees,** as well as before the word **chief priests.** Some of these officers from the chief priests, who were at the head of the Sadducean party, and from the Pharisees, who were powerful in religious affairs, may have been sent once before on a similar errand. (7:46.) Observe that Gentiles and Jews were united in this movement against Christ. Observe, also, that both wings of the religious army, the rationalistic and the ritualistic, joined hands in the effort to destroy Jesus. **Cometh thither with lanterns and torches and weapons.** Better: *with torches and lamps and weapons.* As the moon was full at this time, it has been supposed that no other light could have been necessary. But, not to insist on the remark of John, that it was "night,"—*i. e.*, dark, when Judas went out of the upper room (13:30), because that was an earlier hour of the night, nor to insist that the light of the moon is sometimes obscured by clouds, it is obvious that torches and lamps may have been taken with a view to the possible necessity of exploring shady recesses or rock-caverns and tombs, where the supposed fugitive might have concealed himself.

The other Evangelists do not mention the Roman cohort, which may have been present as a reserve, in case of need, and may, therefore, have taken no active part at the outset in seizing Jesus, and leading him away; but they speak of the people who went out after Jesus as a "great multitude" (Matt. and Mark), or as "a multitude" (Luke), and they specify "swords and staves" (or, "clubs"), as the weapons which they bore.

4. Jesus therefore. Therefore—*i. e.*, in consideration of the approach, or arrival of, this hostile company. For the multitude must have been already near the entrance to the garden. **Knowing all things that should come upon him.** More exactly: *All the things coming upon him.* **The things,** are represented as already *coming upon him,* although they were mostly in the immediate future, and had not yet reached him in the way of physical violence. This testimony to the perfect foreknowledge of Jesus is in deepest harmony with the whole tenor of our Gospel. **Went forth;** either from the garden, as an enclosed space, or from a secluded spot in the garden; possibly, even, from the group of disciples. This act of coming forth, is naturally to be placed directly after the saying: "Arise, let us be going: lo, he is at hand that betrayeth me." (Matt. 26:46; Mark 14:42.) "While they pause, perchance, and stand consulting how they may best provide against any possibility of escape, he whom they were seeking, with all the holy calm of prescience, comes forth from the enclosure, and stands face to face with the apostate and his company."—*Ellicott*. The suggestion of Hackett would require us to suppose that a period of perhaps ten or fifteen minutes elapsed between the summons: "Arise, let us be going," etc., and the simultaneous arrival of Judas, with his company, and of Jesus with his disciples, near the entrance to the garden, where they encountered each other. "As I sat beneath the olives, and observed how very near the city was, with what perfect ease a person there could survey, at a glance, the entire length of the eastern wall, and the slope of the hill towards the valley, I could not divest myself of the impression that this local peculiarity should be allowed to explain a passage in the account of the Saviour's apprehension. Every one must have noticed something abrupt in his summons to his disciples—'Arise, let us be going: see, he is at hand that doeth betray me.' (Matt. 26:46.) It is not improbable that his watchful eye, at that moment, caught sight of Judas and his accomplices, as they issued from one of the eastern gates, or turned round the northern or southern corner of the walls, in order to descend into the valley."—("Illus." p. 257.)

It is difficult to fix the precise order of the events which are mentioned by the different Evangelists, in connection with the arrest of Jesus. But it seems probable that Judas, seeing the Lord, left the multitude a little behind, and approaching Jesus, saluted him with a traitorous kiss; that Jesus said, in

x

5 They answered him, Jesus of Nazareth. Jesus saith unto them, I am he. And Judas also, which betrayed him, stood with them.
6 As soon then as he had said unto them, I am he, they went backward, and fell to the ground.
7 Then asked he them again, Whom seek ye? And they said, Jesus of Nazareth.

5 them, Whom seek ye? They answered him, Jesus of Nazareth. Jesus saith unto them, I am he. And Judas also, who betrayed him,
6 was standing with them. When therefore he said unto them, I am he, they went backward,
7 and fell to the ground. Again therefore he asked them, Whom seek ye? And they said, Jesus

response to this cruel and hypocritical act: "Friend, wherefore art thou come?" (Matt. 26: 50.) "Betrayest thou the Son of man with a kiss?" (Luke 22: 48); and that, awed by the tone and look of Christ, he drew quickly back and stood with his own company. Jesus then, advancing before his disciples, may have asked the question preserved by John. Observe the change to the present tense in the verb ("saith") according to the best text. And said (*saith*) **unto them, Whom seek ye?** This question was probably asked for the purpose of shielding his disciples, by drawing the attention of all upon himself; but there is no reason to imagine anything very unusual or authoritative in the manner of Jesus. This may be inferred from the answer which he received.

5. . . . **Jesus of Nazareth.** Presumably with a tone which would be suggested, in some degree, to an English reader, by the literal translation: *Jesus the Nazarene.* (Comp. 19: 19; Matt. 26: 71.) This quality of the answer is probable, in view of what follows, and of the known temper of the Jewish leaders, provided there was nothing extraordinary in the manner with which Jesus proposed the question, nothing which inspired awe in the minds of those who replied to it. But if, as we believe, there was a certain tone of assurance, and even contempt, in the answer of those priest-sent constables, who, with Judas, headed the company—(there being nothing to prevent this in the question of Jesus, nothing but the self-poise and serenity which bespeak a soul at peace with God and itself, and which might scarcely be noticed by a crowd of men who knew not the speaker)—the relation of the parties was instantly reversed by the next utterance of the Lord. For it was an utterance which, for the moment, proved him Lord. **I am he!** (Comp. 6: 20; 8: 24, 28, 58; 13: 19.) This brief avowal must have been made in a tone of moral dignity and assurance which none but Jesus could use. But before describing its effect upon those addressed, the Evangelist interjects a remark which serves to heighten our interest in the scene, and, perhaps, to render it more intelligible. **And Judas also, which betrayed him, stood with them.** In this case, again, Judas is described as engaged in the awful business of betraying the Lord Jesus; for the relative clause signifies properly, *who was betraying him.* So, too, the sense of the last clause would be represented more clearly by the expression, *was standing with them.*

6. **As soon,** etc. The Revised Version is better: *When therefore he said unto them, I am he, they went backward and fell to the ground.* The effect was immediate, as well as powerful. It is, of course, impossible for any one to be certain as to all the causes of the consternation which fell suddenly upon this crowd of armed men. Judas may have spoken with some of them, as they were coming from the city, of the miracles of Jesus, and may thus have unintentionally prepared them to shrink with terror from his word of power. Or, Judas may have been himself overcome with fear at a tone of his Master's voice which he recognized as the tone of divine authority, and his sudden fear may have communicated itself to others. At all events, the words of Jesus, enforced by his bearing and tone, in connection with the circumstances of the hour, filled the hearts of Judas and his accomplices with irresistible consternation, so that those in front pressed suddenly back, and many fell to the ground. And this effect was intended by the Lord. He would have his assailants understand that only by his free consent could they accomplish their purpose. (Comp. Matt. 26: 53.) This was a remarkable scene, which, as we can easily believe, John could never forget. It was, also, one of the incidents in the life of Jesus which would contribute to the very end for which his Gospel was written. (20: 31.)

7. **Then asked he them again.** The word translated **then,** means, generally, and in this place certainly, *therefore,* and the precise effect of the Greek expression is given in the Revised Version: *Again therefore he asked them.* The object of Jesus was not to

8 Jesus answered, I have told you that I am *he:* if therefore ye seek me, let these go their way:
9 That the saying might be fulfilled, which he spake, a Of them which thou gavest me have I lost none.

8 of Nazareth. Jesus answered, I told you that I am *he:* if therefore ye seek me, let these go 9 their way: that the word might be fulfilled which he spake, Of those whom thou hast given

a ch. 17: 12.

save himself from the hands of his enemies, but to save his disciples. But the tone of the first answer to his question made it necessary for him to reveal his ascendency over them. For their answer disclosed a temper which was not likely to spare, at his request, the disciples whom they were not specially charged to seize. Now, therefore, having established his moral ascendency over them, he repeats his inquiry. **Whom seek ye?** In other words, the state of mind into which they have been brought, leads him to ask the same question once more; and though they answer it in the same words as before: *Jesus the Nazarene,* perhaps because they were wont to speak of him thus, their answer was changed in tone, showing that they were prepared to listen with respect, if not reverence, to what he might say. Admitting in such a spirit that they were sent to arrest *Jesus the Nazarene* (the commission from their superiors may have designated him thus), they would be ready to admit that they had no right to arrest any others, and the object of Jesus would be gained. Observe, too, that it was gained by just as brief and slight a display of his divine ascendency as would accomplish his gracious purpose.

8. . . . **I have told you.** Or, *I told you*—*i. e.,* a moment ago. This was more effective than a mere repetition of the words, **I am he,** without any reference to the awe-inspiring manner in which he had uttered them before, could have been. **If therefore ye seek me. Therefore**—*i. e.,* in accordance with your own declaration. He founds his claim upon their statement. Observe, too, that the pronoun **me,** is emphatic. If ye are seeking *me,* in distinction from others, **let these go their way.** In other words: "Let these withdraw" without molestation. It seems, therefore, that the disciples had followed their Master to the entrance of the garden, and were now gathered about him. But whatever they had said about cleaving to him, and however ready they may have been at this moment to encounter peril for his sake, they were still unstable, their courage was

still fitful, and the Lord, in kindness, provided for their safety. In this, John perceives a fulfillment of Christ's own words, in the prayer which is recorded above. (17: 12.)

9. **That the saying might be fulfilled, which he spake. Saying,** is here a translation of the Greek term *logos,* which might be rendered, as in so many other places, *word.* A regard to English idiom would lead us to write, *that the word which he spake might be fulfilled,* and this version would fairly represent the meaning of the original. **Of them which thou gavest me have I lost none.** (Comp. 17: 12.) Language which was used by Jesus with direct reference to the past, but which may be said to have contained in itself implicitly an assurance as to the future. This assurance, the Evangelist perceived, was fulfilled by the action of his Master at this time; for by it the escape of the disciples was brought about. In this case, the Revised Version is more exact than the one to which we have been long accustomed. The former reads: *Of those whom thou hast given me I lost not one.* The improvement is in a more correct reproduction of the tenses of the Greek verbs, and in substituting *whom* for **which,** the reference being to persons. The verbal changes are certainly important.

It is worthy of notice that John does not here quote from his own record with literal exactness. For, according to that record, Jesus said: "*I guarded them, and not one of them perished.*"—Rev. Ver. The quotation is made *ad sensum,* and not *ad literam,* and in this respect it agrees with many quotations from the Old Testament, by the apostles, and their associates, who wrote the books of the New Testament. But such a method was safer in the hands of inspired men than it is in those of ordinary teachers of truth.

Jesus now, by his own word, stood revealed to his pursuers, and virtually pledged to make no resistance to his arrest. So they began to press upon him, in order to fulfill their commission. But the disciples were about him, and the impetuous spirit of one

10 *Then Simon Peter having a sword drew it, and smote the high priest's servant, and cut off his right ear. The servant's name was Malchus.
11 Then said Jesus unto Peter, Put up thy sword into the sheath: ᵇthe cup which my Father hath given me, shall I not drink it?
12 Then the band and the captain and officers of the Jews took Jesus, and bound him,

10 me I lost not one. Simon Peter therefore having a sword drew it, and struck the high priest's ¹servant, and cut off his right ear. Now the ¹servant's name was Malchus. Jesus therefore said unto Peter, Put up the sword into the sheath: the cup which the Father hath given me, shall I not drink it?
12 So the ²band and the ³chief captain, and the offi-

a Matt. 26 : 51 ; Mark 14 : 47 ; Luke 22 : 49, 50.....b Matt. 20 : 22 ; 26 : 39, 42.——1 Gr. bondservant....2 Or, cohort....3 Or, military tribune. Gr. chiliarch.

of them manifested itself in a rash attempt to repel, by force, his assailants.

10. Then Simon Peter. (Or, *Simon Peter therefore.*) *Therefore—i. e.*, because Peter was influenced by the purpose of Christ not to protect himself (ver. 8), and by the movement of his pursuers to effect his capture. The incident is related by the other Evangelists also, (Matt. 26 : 51-53; Mark 14 : 47; Luke 22 : 49-51), one of whom mentions a question: "Lord, shall we smite with the sword?" (Luke 22 : 49,) which immediately preceded the act of Peter, and indicated that he was not, in his own opinion, the only one of the Eleven who thought of forcible resistance. Peter, however, did not wait for an answer from his Lord, but, **having a sword, drew it, and smote the high priest's servant, and cut off his right ear.** It must be regarded as probable that this servant was one of the foremost of those who rushed towards Jesus to seize him, and that he narrowly escaped losing his life. For the suggestion that Peter judiciously avoided a fatal stroke, is absurd. The next remark of John shows his familiarity with the scene, and his knowledge of the persons affected. **The servant's name was Malchus.** The earlier Evangelists do not mention the names of Peter and of Malchus, though they must have known that it was Peter who used the sword on this occasion, even if they did not know the name of the man whom he wounded. There may have been good reasons for not giving the name of either in the early preaching of the gospel.

11. Then said Jesus unto Peter. (Or, *Jesus therefore said unto Peter.*) For the words of Jesus were occasioned by the act of his impatient disciple, and prompt rebuke and restraint were necessary if the Eleven were to escape seizure. **Put up thy sword into the sheath.** The best text reads, *the sword*, instead of **thy sword. The cup which my Father hath given me, shall I not drink it?** Though John omits any account of the Saviour's agony and prayer in the garden, he inserts here a saying which proves that prayer to have been answered, and proves it in language repeated from the prayer itself. (Comp. Matt. 26 : 39, 42; Mark 14 : 36; Luke 22 : 42.) The cup did not pass away from him, but he received strength to drink it freely. This undesigned coincidence is highly favorable to the truth of the several narratives. Matthew reports some other expressions of the Saviour, thus: "Put up again thy sword into his place: for all they that take the sword shall perish with the sword; thinkest thou that I cannot now pray to my Father, and he shall presently give me more than twelve legions of angels? But how then shall the Scripture be fulfilled, that thus it must be?" Luke adds the interesting circumstance concerning Malchus, that Jesus "touched his ear and healed him," and, in almost verbal agreement with Matthew and Mark, makes this record: "Then Jesus said unto the chief priests and captains of the temple, and the elders which were come to him: Be ye come out as against a thief, with swords and staves? When I was daily with you in the temple, ye stretched forth no hands against me: but this is your hour and the power of darkness." Mark relates that at this point "they all forsook him and fled," and Matthew testifies that it was "all the disciples" who forsook him and fled. But for an account of "a certain young man" who followed with him for a little way, see Mark 14 : 51-52, with the Notes of Dr. Clarke.

12-23. PRIVATE EXAMINATION OF JESUS. DENIALS OF PETER.

12. Then the band, etc. Observe the emphatic enumeration of the several parties concerned in the action. The word *chiliarch*, translated *captain*, or, *chief captain* (Rev. Ver.), signifies, literally, "leader of a thousand,"—*i. e.*, a prefect or tribune of a Roman cohort. (See on ver. 3.) Yet, as was there remarked, it is not necessary to assume that

13 And led him away to Annas first; for he was father in law to Caiaphas, which was the high priest that same year.
14 Now Caiaphas was he, which gave counsel to the Jews, that it was expedient that one man should die for the people.

13 cers of the Jews, seized Jesus and bound him, and led him to Annas first; for he was father in law to Caiaphas, who was high priest that year. Now Caiaphas was he who gave counsel to the Jews, that it was expedient that one man should die for the people.

a See Ma't. 26: 57....b Luke 3: 2....c ch. 11: 50.

the whole cohort was present on this occasion. **Took Jesus.** Perhaps the stronger term, *seized,* represents the original verb better; for, according to its composition and primary sense, it refers to the act of bringing the hands together in seizing or clutching an object. **And bound him.** A very natural, though needless precaution against escape. Is it possible that their momentary terror and confusion (ver. 6) made them anxious to see the manacles on their prisoner's hands? Or, was it the customary way of securing persons arrested for alleged crime? The other Evangelists do not mention this binding of Jesus— (from which he may have been released to appear before Annas and the Sanhedrin), but they speak of his being bound, in order to be sent by the Sanhedrin to Pilate. (Matt. 27: 2; Mark 15: 1.) "Perhaps this later binding was a special binding, in token of condemnation; so early tradition represents, affirming that he was led to Pilate with a cord around his neck."—*Clarke.* If this was the case, it need not be supposed that he was released before Annas or the Sanhedrin.

13. And led him away to Annas first. The word **first,** assumes the fact that he was led elsewhere afterwards, but it is unnecessary to regard it as a "tacit correction" of previous narratives that had failed to notice this part of the history. **For he was father-in-law to Caiaphas.** This circumstance is mentioned to account for the fact related. "The relationship of Caiaphas is not mentioned by any writer except St. John, and yet this relationship alone explains how Caiaphas was able to retain his office by the side of Annas and his sons."—*Westcott.* For Annas appears to have been a politic and powerful man. Josephus says ("Ant." 20. 9. § 1). "that he had five sons who had all performed the office of high priest to God, and he had himself enjoyed that dignity a long time formerly," etc. Annas was high priest seven years (A. D. 7 to A. D. 14); Joseph Caiaphas was high priest twelve years (A. D. 25 to A. D. 37); and during the long period in which the office was filled by himself, his sons, and his son-in-law, he was probably a ruler *de facto,* if not *de jure.* Luke speaks of the high priesthood of Annas and Caiaphas (3: 2), doubtless because Annas was recognized by the people as virtually sharing the high priesthood with his son-in-law. It is therefore probable that he had an office in the palace of the high priest, and that his personal influence and control were greater than those of Caiaphas. To him, then, was Jesus **first** led and subjected to an informal examination, with the purpose, no doubt, of ascertaining what would be the best method of procedure in the legal, or at least, formal, process before the Sanhedrin. **Who was the high priest that same year.** Caiaphas was high priest twelve years, and it is therefore necessary to suppose that the Evangelist had some reason for adding the words, **that same year;** otherwise it would have been more natural to say, simply, **who was high priest.** Why does he add the expression, **that same year?** Evidently because that was a most memorable year to the Evangelist, and to his readers. It was the year of all years to "the disciple whom Jesus loved." (Comp. 11: 49.)

14. Now Caiaphas was he, etc. Why this reminiscence and identification? To prepare the reader's mind for what was to follow, or at least, to put what was to follow in its proper relation to the spirit and principles of one of the chief actors. Jesus was to be judged by Caiaphas and his father-in-law, Annas, together with others, who would be more or less subject to their influence; and there could be no prospect of a fair trial and just decision when the high priest was prepared to sacrifice the life of one man (though innocent) for the people, when the judge had already decided the case, without legal examination, against the accused. Lange remarks somewhat sharply, but in probable harmony with truth: "It is also characteristic of the enmity of old Annas that Jesus was led to him even before he was brought to

15 *a* And Simon Peter followed Jesus, and *so did* another disciple: that disciple was known unto the high priest, and went in with Jesus into the palace of the high priest.
16 *b* But Peter stood at the door without. Then went out that other disciple, which was known unto the high priest, and spake unto her that kept the door, and brought in Peter.
17 Then saith the damsel that kept the door unto Peter, Art not thou also *one* of this man's disciples? He saith, I am not.

15 And Simon Peter followed Jesus, and *so did* another disciple. Now that disciple was known unto the high priest, and entered in with Jesus into the court of the high priest; but Peter was standing at the door without. So the other disciple, who was known unto the high priest, went out and spake unto her that kept the door, and brought in Peter.
17 The maid therefore that kept the door saith unto Peter, Art thou also *one* of this man's disciples?

a Matt. 26: 58; Mark 14: 54; Luke 22: 54....*b* Matt. 26: 69; Mark 14: 66; Luke 22: 54.

Caiaphas; the announcement of this fact is appropriately accompanied by the statement that he was the father-in-law of that murderous Caiaphas."

15-18. SIDE VIEW. INTRODUCTION AND FIRST DENIAL OF PETER.

15. And Simon Peter followed Jesus. The verb, in the imperfect tense, describes the action in progress. The writer recalls the scene, and therefore paints it as it rises before his mental vision out of the fountain of memory. Though all the disciples had fled at the arrest of Jesus, Peter soon regained courage to return and follow the Lord, as the latter was taken to the palace of the high priest, in the city. **And so did another disciple.** Modestly added, and meaning, without doubt, the writer of this Gospel. (20:2.) **That disciple was known unto the high priest.** This remark prepares the way for what follows, namely, first, the statement that he went into the court of the high priest with Jesus; and, secondly, the statement that he obtained the admission of Peter. His acquaintance with the high priest was such as to account for his doing these things. Hence, it implies some degree of personal respect or regard on the part of the high priest. For the sense of the word translated **known**, in such a connection as this, see Luke 2: 44, and 23: 49. By the term **high priest**, we are probably to understand Caiaphas, of whom the Evangelist has just remarked that he was "high priest that same year." (ver. 13.) The circumstance that Annas, though an ex-high priest, was sometimes called high priest (*e. g.*, in Luke 2: 3 and Acts 4: 6), is no sufficient reason for supposing that he can be meant by that title here, so soon after the statement that Caiaphas was high priest. **Went in with Jesus**—*i. e.*, with the company that brought in Jesus, being admitted as an acquaintance of the high priest.

16. But Peter stood at the door without. The verb has the force of an imperfect —*was standing*. Evidently John, looking back, saw Peter through the open door, or noticed his absence and went back to find him, easily conjecturing where he might be. What were the feelings that led Peter to remain at the door when he was not suffered to enter, no man knows; or how long he waited there before John came to bring him, can only be conjectured; but the period must have been short. Then (οὖν—*so*, or *therefore*)—*i. e.*, because Peter was standing thus—**went out that other disciple, which was known unto the high priest**—and, naturally, also to his servants—**and spake unto her that kept the door** (comp. Acts 12: 13), asking her, no doubt, to admit his friend, who was standing without—**and**—with the consent of the door-keeper—**brought in Peter.** But the maid who had charge of the door was aware of the reason why Jesus had been seized and taken to her master's court; she therefore scrutinized Peter as he entered, and either because he was a friend of John, whom she knew to be a disciple of Jesus, or because of something in his looks or bearing, she suspected him to be a disciple, and questioned him on the point.

17. Art not thou also—as well as John—**one of this man's disciples?** Either from a feeling of courtesy, or because she was quite uncertain as to the fact, the damsel's question was so framed as to show that she looked for a negative answer; as if she had said in English: "Thou art not, I suppose, one of this man's disciples?" And, alas, Peter answered, **I am not.** This was his first denial, made to the door-keeper as he was passing by her, into the court. What did Peter think of himself when he uttered these words? And what did the true-hearted John think of his friend when he heard this denial?

Ch. XVIII.] JOHN. 359

18 And the servants and officers stood there, who had made a fire of coals; for it was cold: and they warmed themselves: and Peter stood with them, and warmed himself.
19 The high priest then asked Jesus of his disciples, and of his doctrine.
20 Jesus answered him, ᵃ I spake openly to the world; I ever taught in the synagogue, and in the temple, whither the Jews always resort; and in secret have I said nothing.

18 He saith, I am not. Now the ¹servants and the officers were standing *there*, having made ²a fire of coals; for it was cold; and they were warming themselves: and Peter also was with them, standing and warming himself.
19 The high priest therefore asked Jesus of his disciples, and of his teaching. Jesus answered him, I have spoken openly to the world; I ever taught in ᵈ synagogues, and in the temple, where all the Jews

ᵃ Matt. 26: 55; Luke 4: 15; ch. 7: 14, 26, 28; 8: 2.——1 Gr. *bondservants*....2 Gr. *a fire of charcoal*....3 *synagogue*.

18. And the servants and officers stood there. More exactly: *And the servants and officers were standing there*, in the open court, which Peter had now entered with John. **Who had made a fire of coals**—literally, *having made a charcoal fire*—**for it was cold**. Note that the Roman soldiers are not mentioned; perhaps they had returned to Antonia; the bond-servants of the high priest and the officers of the Sanhedrin, or temple-police, are the persons meant. The coldness appears to have been unusual for the time of the passover. For it is said that the nights are generally warm in Palestine at this season of the year. That the Evangelist saw anything symbolic of Peter's condition or conduct, is by no means certain, though it has been supposed. **And Peter stood with them, and warmed himself.** This is best rendered in the Revised Version : *And Peter also was with them, standing and warming himself*. The picture is clearly drawn. In the dim court is the charcoal fire, with dark-browed men surrounding it. The light of the coals is just sufficient to reveal the features of the men when they turn to look upon the fire. Peter is there, seemingly indifferent to the trial taking place within sight. John, too, is there, probably on the side of the fire toward the place where his Master stands, glancing now and then at Peter, but listening chiefly to the examination of Jesus by the high priest. And to this he now directs our attention.

19-24. The High Priest Questions Jesus Before Annas.

19. The high priest then, etc. Better: *therefore*, (οὖν) *the high priest. Therefore*—i. e., because he was such a man as could utter the saying recalled in verse 14; for the Evangelist now returns in thought to what was said in that verse. Standing, as John probably did, between the group about Peter and the group about Jesus, he turns from one

party to the other in his narrative, presenting the scene in a remarkably simple and vivid manner. Here the character and spirit of the question are supposed to flow out of the character and spirit of the man. **Asked Jesus of his disciples**—i. e., *concerning* them. Just what he asked concerning them, is not said; perhaps, who they were, or how numerous they were, or what was their character, or what they had done, or what they proposed to do. **And of his doctrine,** or *teaching*—i. e., what it had been. The object of this preliminary examination was, doubtless, to obtain materials for the more public trial to follow. But the wisdom of Christ was more than a match for the craft of his foes.

20. I spake openly to the world. The pronoun I is emphatic, and may imply a contrast between himself and his adversaries, who had secretly plotted his destruction. The Greek verb should be translated *have spoken*, instead of **spake. To the world**, because his teaching had been intended for mankind generally. It had not been delivered cautiously to a few, who were at the same time charged to keep and transfer it as an esoteric doctrine; but it had been proclaimed openly to the people, so that whoever would might know it. Even the parables were the best form of teaching to those to whom they were addressed. Spiritual sympathy with the truth would have made them intelligible to the people. **I ever** (or, *always*) **taught in the synagogue.** There is no article before **synagogue,** in the Greek text, and the expression **in synagogue,** may be understood as we would understand *in church*, or, *in meeting*, at the present time. **And in the temple.** There were many synagogues and but one temple—*the* temple at Jerusalem; and to this Jesus resorted on the great festivals, teaching boldly in its courts. Of course, Jesus does not mean to say that he never

21 Why askest thou me? ask them which heard me, what I have said unto them: behold, they know what I said.
22 And when he had thus spoken, one of the officers which stood by *struck Jesus with the palm of his hand, saying, Answerest thou the high priest so?
23 Jesus answered him, If I have spoken evil, bear witness of the evil: but if well, why smitest thou me?

21 come together; and in secret spake I nothing. Why askest thou me? ask them that have heard me, what I spake unto them; behold, these know the
22 things which I said. And when he had said this, one of the officers standing by struck Jesus ¹ with his right hand, saying, Answerest thou the high priest
23 so? Jesus answered him, If I have spoken evil, bear witness of the evil: but if well, why smitest

a Jer. 20: 2; Acts 23. 2.——1 Or, *with a rod.*

taught in a private house, or by the wayside; but, rather, that constantly, habitually, and, as far as circumstances might permit, he taught in public assemblies. His teaching was characteristically unreserved and public. **Whither the Jews always resort,** should be, according to the best supported text (ℵ A B C* L X Π, vulg. Syr. Copt.), *where all the Jews come together.* That is, in the openest manner possible, in the place of all others where the devout Jews and the ecclesiastical rulers of the people are wont to assemble. **And in secret have I said nothing.** More literally, *And in secret spake I nothing.* That is, with the purpose of concealment. What he had sometimes spoken to the twelve in private, had been spoken to them alone, because others were not yet prepared to receive it. Moreover, the disciples were expected to proclaim what they thus heard to all the people, or on "the house tops." (Matt. 10: 27.)

21. Why askest thou me? It is a case which offers no apology for questioning his accused, and Jesus perceives very clearly, that the only object of the high priest is to draw from him some expression that can be turned against him in the approaching trial. **Ask them which heard me,** etc. The Revised Version is more accurate: *Ask them that have heard me, what I spake unto them.* The Saviour would have the trial conducted in a regular and proper manner, by hearing the testimony of competent witnesses. **Behold, they** (or, *these*) **know what** (or, *the things which*) **I said.** The pronoun *these,* indicates the presence of suitable witnesses; for it refers to those near, as contrasted with those at a distance. The same fact is, perhaps, suggested by the use of the perfect tense, **have heard,** in the preceding clause. This language of Jesus is a dignified remonstrance against the method adopted by the high priest; perhaps it was felt by Jesus to imply a degree of hypocrisy on his (the high priest's) part. At any rate it was interpreted by some as disrespectful to the high priest.

22. Neither the Common version, One of the officers which stood by, nor the Revised Version, *One of the officers standing by,* represents decisively the meaning of the Greek; for neither version shows that **stood by** (in the former), or, *standing by* (in the latter), refers, not to the body of officers, but merely to that one of them who struck Jesus. The ambiguity may be removed by translating as follows: *One of the officers who was standing by;* the sense being, that this officer was standing beside Jesus. **Struck Jesus with the palm of his hand.** The Greek expression used by the Evangelist, may signify, either that the soldier gave the face of Jesus a rude slap with his hand, or, that he struck him with a rod. In either case, the blow was an insult, and it was probably given with such force as to occasion severe pain. But it did not disturb the holy serenity and patience of Christ, as his response clearly shows.

23. If I have spoken (rather, *spake*) **evil, bear witness of the evil.** Does Jesus here refer to his answer to the high priest, which had provoked the officer, or to the teaching of his ministry, which the high priest had asked him to explain? Some interpreters have supposed him to mean the latter, because he calls upon the officer to **bear witness** of the evil—an expression which is believed to suit the latter reference better than the former. There is force in this reasoning, but it seems to be overcome by the circumstance that the officer's blow was given because of the Lord's answer to the high priest; while the reproof of Jesus was called out by that blow. Accordingly, the words of Jesus mean: "If what I just spake to the high priest was wrong, bear solemn testimony againt it as wrong; that would be right and fitting." **But if well, why smitest thou me?** The primary sense of the word translated **smite,** is, *to skin, to flay;* "in the N. T.," says Dr. Robinson, "*to beat, to smite, to scourge,* properly, so as to take off the skin."

24 a Now Annas had sent him bound unto the high priest.
25 And Simon Peter stood and warmed himself. b They said therefore unto him, Art not thou also one of his disciples? He denied it, and said, I am not.
26 One of the servants of the high priest, being his kinsman whose ear Peter cut off, saith, Did not I see thee in the garden with him?

24 thou me? Annas therefore sent him bound unto Caiaphas the high priest.
25 Now Simon Peter was standing and warming himself. They said therefore unto him, Art thou also one of his disciples? He denied, and said, I am not.
26 One of the 1 servants of the high priest, being a kinsman of him whose ear Peter cut off, saith, Did not

a Matt. 26: 57....b Matt. 26: 69, 71; Mark 14: 69; Luke 22: 58,— 1 Gr. *bondservants*.

It is perhaps safe to infer from the Saviour's use of this word that the officer's blow was a severe one; and it is perfectly certain that Jesus here claims to have spoken well in his answer to the high priest. It is interesting to compare his bearing on this occasion with his words as preserved in Matt. 5: 39, and with the bearing of Paul under similar provocation. (Acts 23: 2-5.)

24. Now Annas had sent him, etc. The Revised Version is here probably correct: *Annas therefore sent him bound unto Caiaphas.* Thus far the investigation had been unofficial, or private, and the result of it was scarcely favorable to the design of the accusers. Meantime, the prisoner had been relieved of his fetters But now Annas sends him probably across the inner court, where the charcoal fire was burning, to another room in the same edifice, where Caiaphas, with the Sanhedrin, would subject him to a formal trial. For it has been well said, in the "Popular Commentary," that "Annas and Caiaphas may have occupied apartments in the same house, surrounding the 'court' of our narrative. The structure of higher-class houses in Palestine, the relationship of the persons themselves, and the customs of the East, lead, not unnaturally, to such a view; and it was very early entertained. But if so, though Jesus was really taken to Annas, Caiaphas would, in all probability, be present at the examination; and, thus present, his more youthful years, and the passionateness of his rage against Jesus, would lead him to act the prominent part which is assigned to him."

25-27. ANOTHER SIDE VIEW. SECOND AND THIRD DENIALS OF PETER.

25. The Evangelist now returns to Peter. **And Simon Peter stood and warmed himself.** Literally, *was standing and warming himself.* By these words he recalls to the reader's mind the precise situation of this disciple when last referred to (ver. 18), a situation which he retained for some time. Meanwhile, the members of the Sanhedrin were probably coming together, that they might take part in the more formal trial of Jesus. **They said therefore unto him.** This may have occurred while Jesus was being led across the open court to another apartment of the building. The plural form of the verb translated **said,** is best explained by supposing that several persons expressed, more or less positively, their suspicion that Peter (as well as John) was one of Christ's followers. It suggests, therefore, a very obvious explanation of certain differences between the narrations of the several Evangelists at this point. For Matthew relates, that *another maid (ἄλλη) said. . . This man was also with Jesus of Nazareth;* Mark relates, that *The maid (ἡ παιδίσκη) began to say. . . This is one of them;* while Luke relates, that *another man (ἕτερος) said, Thou also art one of them.* According to Matthew and Mark, Peter went, at this time, toward the gate by which he had entered. This change of place would have been very natural in the excited state of his mind, and could have required but a few steps. The substance of what **they said** to Peter, as heard by this Evangelist, could be summed up in the question: **Art not thou also one of this man's disciples?** The form of the question is like that in verse 17: "It cannot be, can it? that thou also art one of his disciples!" The word **also,** may imply that the questioners were aware of the presence of John, and knew him to be a disciple of Jesus. **He denied it, and said, I am not.** The **it,** after **denied,** represents nothing in the Greek text, and is unnecessary to the proper expression of the writer's thought in English. For this reason, it is omitted in the Revised Version. Matthew says that Peter *denied again, with an oath* (saying), *I do not know the man.* Of course, the stronger form includes the weaker, while the weaker does not exclude the stronger. Indeed, it is very probable that both were used.

26. One of the servants of the high

27 Peter then denied again; and *immediately the cock crew.
28 bThen led they Jesus from Caiaphas unto the hall of judgment; and it was early; cand they themselves went not into the judgment hall, lest they should be defiled; but that they might eat the passover.

27 I see thee in the garden with him? Peter therefore denied again; and straightway the cock crew.
28 They led Jesus therefore from Caiaphas into the 1 Prætorium: and it was early; and they themselves entered not into the 1 Prætorium, that they might

a Matt. 26: 74; Mark 14: 72; Luke 22: 60; ch. 13: 38....b Matt. 27: 2: Mark 15: 1; Luke 23: 1; Acts 3: 13....c Acts 10: 28; 11: 3.—
1 Or. palace.

priest. In the open court, about the fire, were servants and officers (see ver. 18), that is, servants of the high priest, and officers of the Sanhedrin. It is one of the former who is now referred to. **Being his kinsman**, etc. Better: *Being a kinsman of him whose ear Peter cut off.* (Ver. 10.) This description of the questioner prepares the reader for the sharper form of the question, and, at the same time, shows that the writer had an accurate knowledge of the high priest's household. For the form of the question in Greek is one that anticipates an affirmative answer, while the words, **Did not I see thee in the garden with him?** implies that a denial will be against the personal knowledge of the questioner. Note the truth to nature in this question, and the life-like particularity of the narrative.

27. Peter then denied again. The Revised Version substitutes *therefore* for *then*, as a translation of the Greek conjunction (οὖν.) The repeated temptation is represented as accounting for the repeated sin. The charge of discipleship was made anew, and *therefore*, as Peter had entered the way of disloyalty and falsehood, his denial of Christ was renewed. The second step in sin is easier to take than the first, and the third still easier than the second. **And immediately the cock crew.** There is no article in the Greek text before the noun, and, perhaps, the exact meaning of the Evangelist would be given by omitting it in English—*and immediately a cock crew.* Thus John has recorded the fulfillment of his Master's word, spoken the evening before, in the upper room. (See 13: 38.) But he does not here speak of the repentance of Peter, though that repentance is presupposed by his subsequent narrative. (See 20: 3-10, and especially 21: 7, 15-17.) Nor does he speak of the later and more public trial of Jesus before the Sanhedrin, which is described in the Synoptic Gospels. (See Matt. 26: 59-68; Mark 14: 55-65; Luke 22: 63-71.) His reasons for this omission may have been, on the one hand, the circumstance that the preliminary examination had illustrated sufficiently both the spirit of Christ and the *animus* of the hierachy toward him, and, on the other, the circumstance that the later trial had been sufficiently described by the earlier Evangelists.

28-40; 19: 1-16. THE CIVIL TRIAL.

Westcott remarks, that "the narrative falls into several distinct sections, corresponding to scenes without and within the prætorium: 1. Without the prætorium. The Jews claim the execution of their sentence. (18: 28-32.) 2. Within the prætorium. The good confession.' Christ a King. (33-37.) 3. Without the prætorium. First declaration of innocence. Barabbas. (38-40.) 4. Within the prætorium. Scourging; mockery. (19: 1-3.) 5. Without the prætorium. Second and third declarations of innocence. 'Ecce homo,' 'Son of God.' (4-7.) 6. Within the prætorium. The source of authority, and from this the measure of guilt. (8-11.) 7. Without the prætorium. Conviction overpowered; the king abjured; the last sentence. (12-16.)"

28-32. THE CLAIM OF THE JEWISH RULERS REFUSED BY PILATE.

28. Then led they Jesus, etc. The Revised Version is more exact: *They lead Jesus therefore from Caiaphas into the palace.* Better, *unto the prætorium.* Who are the persons represented by the word **they?** It had been decided by the highest ecclesiastical court of the Jews that Jesus was worthy of death. (Matt. 26: 65-67.) But the members of that court had no authority, at that time, to inflict capital punishment. This authority had been taken from them by the Roman government. Hence, they lead Jesus to Pilate, hoping that the latter, a somewhat unscrupulous magistrate, would confirm and execute the sentence which they had passed. Whether the prætorium, or official residence of Pilate, was the palace built by Herod, on the western hill of Jerusalem, or a part of the Castle of Antonia, at the northwest corner of the temple area, is not certainly known; but the latter view is, on the whole, more probable than the former. **And it was early.** The word translated early (πρωία, sc. ὥρα, lit., *an early hour*), is used in a technical sense to denote the fourth watch, from 3–6 A. M. (Mark 13:35.) Pilate, who was acquainted with the intense religious prejudice of the Jews, and by whose permission the Roman cohort had been employed in seizing Jesus and taking him bound to the house of Annas and Caiaphas, had probably kept himself informed of the general course of events during the night, and was therefore prepared for the accusation that was to be made against the prisoner. **And they themselves**—in contrast with Jesus, who was doubtless delivered into the hands of soldiers, and led into the prætorium—**went not into the judgment hall** (or, *prætorium*), **lest they should be defiled** (or, *that they might not be defiled*); **but that they might eat the passover.** What light does this cast upon the day when the Lord ate the passover with his disciples? The Evangelist's words imply that these conspirators against the life of Jesus supposed that, by entering the court of Pilate, they would be so defiled as to be unable to cleanse themselves, ritually, in time to eat the passover. But if we assume that Jesus anticipated the regular time of eating the paschal lamb by one day, these conspirators were afraid of being so polluted by entering the prætorium that they could not purify themselves before the next evening, and then eat the paschal lamb. Yet such a fear is unaccountable. For the hour of sunset was between them and the time when they, on this hypothesis, would wish to eat the passover, and at the time of sunset "uncleanness of a much more serious kind than that produced by entering into the house of a Gentile was removed by the simple process of washing with water." (Lev. 15:5-11, 16-18; 22:5-7.) The language of the Evangelist cannot, therefore, be safely used as an argument for the somewhat popular view, that the supper described in chapter 13 of this Gospel, occurred twenty-four hours before the regular time for eating the paschal lamb. But in what other way can this language be explained? Many scholars answer: By the fact that *the passover* may denote the whole festival, as well as the paschal supper, and that *eating the passover*, may refer to partaking of food during any part of the festival. The Note of Dr. Gardiner is brief, and may be copied: "The phrase *to eat the passover*, occurs five times in the New Testament (Matt. 26:17; Mark 14:12, 14; Luke 22:11, 15), and once in the Old Testament (2 Chron. 30:18), and in all these places it means to eat the *Paschal Supper*, strictly. As all the instances in the New Testament, however, refer to one and the same occasion, this recurrence does not go very far to prove that the expression must be limited to this. Now the word passover (πάσχα), is used in the New Testament in a variety of significations: (1) For the paschal lamb—Mark 14:12; Luke 22:7; and (metaph.) 1 Cor. 5:7. (2) For the paschal supper—Matt. 26:18, 19; Luke 22:8, 13; Heb. 11:28, etc. (3) For the whole paschal festival of the seven days of unleavened bread—Luke 22:1; 2:41-43; Matt. 26:2; John 2:23. (4) Indefinitely, in such a way that it may be understood either as in (2) or as in (3), and yet, the latter meaning having been established, more naturally in that—John 2:13; 6:4; 11:55; 12:1; 13:1. In John 18:28, 29; 19:14, the meaning is in dispute. It will be observed that all the instances in (4) are from St. John, and that all the passages in St. John in which the word occurs, fall under this head, or under (3.) It is apparent that he uses the word in its most general sense. The phrase, therefore, *that they might eat the passover*, as used by him, would seem naturally to refer to the feast during the seven days, or any of them, and not specially to the paschal lamb." Some of these would occur during the day just dawning, and it is not surprising that the ecclesiastical rulers were "unwilling to defile themselves by entering beneath the roof of the Gentile procurator."

But this is not the only substitute for the first interpretation. (See Edersheim, "The Life and Times of Jesus the Messiah," II. pp. 565, 6.) It is possible that the Jewish rulers had been too much absorbed by their success in capturing Jesus and their efforts to secure his condemnation, to partake of the paschal supper at the usual time in the evening before, and were hoping to partake of it at the last moment possible. This is Prof. Milligan's view. "They were scrupulous, because they desired to eat *without an hour's delay*. They had lost time already; the night was flying fast; the morning light would soon appear; it would be too late then; no interrup-

29 Pilate then went out unto them, and said, What accusation bring ye against this man?
30 They answered and said unto him, If he were not a malefactor, we would not have delivered him up unto thee.
31 Then said Pilate unto them, Take ye him, and judge him according to your law. The Jews therefore said unto him, It is not lawful for us to put any man to death:

29 not be defiled, but might eat the passover. Pilate therefore went out unto them, and saith, What accusation bring ye against this man? They answered
30 and said unto him, If this man were not an evildoer, we should not have delivered him up unto
31 thee. Pilate therefore said unto them, Take him yourselves, and judge him according to your law. The Jews said unto him, It is not lawful for us to

tion that can be escaped must be allowed; they would not go into the palace, 'that they might not be defiled, but might eat the passover.' It may, perhaps, be said in reply, that if this was their intention, it failed. Morning broke before they left Pilate, and they lost the opportunity of eating. Precisely so. It is probably one of the very thoughts that John wishes us to carry from his story, as he tells it. Instead of welcoming the true Paschal Lamb, these Jews rejected him. What thought more in the manner of our Evangelist than to let us see that, seeking to retain the shadow, and sacrificing the substance for its sake, they lost not only the substance, but the shadow too (comp. 11 : 48)?" I see no insuperable obstacle to this exposition, and either this or the preceding one is preferable to any view which makes the narrative of John inconsistent with that of the Synoptic Gospels.

29. **Pilate then** (*or therefore*)—that is, because the Jews were unwilling to enter the prætorium, **went out unto them.** The text might be translated literally, *went forth without unto them*, the circumstance that Pilate went quite outside the prætorium being stated with emphasis. **What accusation bring ye against this man?** Whatever he may have known of their proceedings in the Sanhedrin, or of the grounds of their enmity to Christ, he properly demanded a formal statement of their charge, that he might judge the accused in a legal manner. Perhaps the message of his wife had been received, awakening in his heart a desire to avoid any decision against Jesus. But it is by no means necessary to suppose this in order to account for his demand. He was a ruler, and it was his duty to condemn no man without definite accusation and proof of crime.

30. **If he were not a malefactor.** Better, *If this man were not an evil doer.* A wholly indefinite charge, affording evidence that they knew of no civil offence which he had committed. But they hoped, by putting on a bold face and persisting in their demand, to obtain the condemnation of Jesus. **We would not have delivered him up unto thee.** "Of course not. Are we not honorable men, rulers of the people, incapable of uttering a false accusation? You may take our word for it, that this man is an evil-doer. What need of further proof?" But Pilate, perceiving their inability to bring any proper charge against Jesus, and discovering, perhaps, the cause of their hatred of him; at all events influenced by their reply, said unto them:

31. **Take ye him,** (or, *Take him yourselves*), **and judge him according to your law.** From these words of the Roman procurator, two things may be inferred : (1) that he did not believe Jesus to have committed any crime against the laws of the State, and (2) that he did not believe him to have done anything worthy of death, even if he had broken some Jewish law. For he would not have delivered a man guilty of a civil offence into the hands of the Sanhedrists for trial and punishment, nor would he have committed any man whom he thought worthy of death to a court which had no right to inflict capital punishment. There may have been a touch of irony in the language of Pilate, especially if he knew already, or suspected, that they were seeking the life of Jesus. At all events, his words constrained them to avow their purpose, and to confess their dependence on him for its accomplishment. **It is not lawful for us to put any man to death.** This language is unqualified. And, according to the Talmud, the Jews had been deprived of the right to inflict capital punishment forty years before the destruction of Jerusalem. Whether this statement is correct as to the matter of time or not, the language of the Jews in this passage proves that they could not in their own right inflict the punishment of death. The passages which are sometimes alleged to prove that they had this power (viz., John 8: 3, 59 ; 7: 25, Acts 5: 33; 7: 57, sq.; 21 : 27, sq.), merely show that the

32 *That the saying of Jesus might be fulfilled, which he spake, signifying what death he should die.
33 *Then Pilate entered into the judgment hall again, and said unto him, Art thou the king of the Jews?
34 Jesus answered him, Sayest thou this thing of thyself, or did others tell it thee of me?
35 Pilate answered, Am I a Jew? Thine own nation and the chief priests have delivered thee unto me; what hast thou done?

32 put any man to death: that the word of Jesus might be fulfilled, which he spake, signifying by what manner of death he should die.
33 Pilate therefore entered again into the *Prætorium, and called Jesus, and said unto him, Art thou the King of the Jews? Jesus answered, Sayest thou this of thyself, or did others tell it thee concerning me? Pilate answered, Am I a Jew? Thine own nation and the chief priests delivered thee unto me:

a Matt. 20: 19; ch. 12: 32, 33....*b* Matt. 27: 11.—1 Or, *palace*.

Roman governors sometimes winked at acts of violence.

32. That the saying of Jesus might be fulfilled, etc. The Greek term, translated **saying,** may be rendered *word,* and the word of Jesus, to which the Evangelist refers, may probably be seen in 12: 32 f., or, possibly, in Matt. 20: 19. Note how careful the Evangelist is to remind his readers of the infallible truth of all that Jesus had said. Edersheim remarks that this statement "seems to imply that the Sanhedrin might have found a mode of putting Jesus to death in the same informal manner in which Stephen was killed, and they sought to destroy Paul. The Jewish law recognized a form of procedure, or rather a want of procedure, when a person who was caught *in flagrante delicto* of blasphemy, might be doomed to death without further inquiry." But in such a case the process was not crucifixion, but stoning. Hence the answer of the Jews to Pilate was an important link in the chain of events by which the prediction of Jesus as to the manner of his death was fulfilled.

33-37. IN THE PRÆTORIUM.

33. Then Pilate (or, *Pilate, therefore*), **entered into the judgment hall again.** His doing this was a result of the persistency of the Jews, and of their confession that they could not legally punish Jesus as they affirmed he ought to be punished. Jesus was already in the prætorium, but Pilate, taking his official seat, called him near and asked this question, **Art thou the king of the Jews?** The order of the Greek words is striking. "*Thou*—so humble, modest, gentle, peaceable, unarmed —**art the king of the Jews?** The emphasis falls on the first word, **thou;** but whether the tone was one of wonder simply, or of surprise, mingled with contempt, it is impossible to say.

34. Sayest thou this thing of thyself, or did others tell it thee of me? By these words Jesus calls Pilate's attention to the source from which the charge which he had virtually made (ver. 33,) had come to him, that is, not from his own knowledge and judgment, but from the Jews; and for this reason it should be suspected by him. As if he had said to Pilate: "Am I to consider this question, (and accusation), as one that has sprung from your own mind, in view of my conduct, or as something which would not have occurred to yourself, but has been put in your lips by others?" Thus interpreted, there seems to be in the question of Jesus a courteous suggestion that Pilate was already allowing himself to be made a tool of by the Jews, and at the same time a virtual appeal to his self-respect and sense of justice as a magistrate. Meyer says that "Jesus merely insists on his *right to know the author of the accusation* which lay in the words of Pilate"; but this he already knew, and it is not easy to see what object would be gained by having Pilate formally admit the fact. Other interpreters, mindful of the following context, think that Jesus sought by his response to direct the governor's mind to the ambiguity of the charge, to the possibility of a double sense in the title, *the king of the Jews,* which he had borrowed from others—thus preparing the way for the distinction which Jesus himself was about to make between civil and spiritual kingship. This, however, does not seem to be the most obvious sense of the Lord's answer, and there is no sufficient reason for departing from that sense.

35. Am I a Jew? With a measure of contempt; as if the idea that *he,* the Roman procurator, had the character or spirit of a *Jew,* were absurd; and as if none but a Jew could feel any concern about a vain aspirant, an unarmed pretender to the throne of Israel. Thus Pilate virtually admits that Jesus had done nothing which a Roman governor would be likely to fear or punish; had raised no sedition, created no disturbance, broken no law. And, as if he, the haughty Roman, would make some excuse for even repeating

36 ᵃJesus answered, ᵇMy kingdom is not of this world: if my kingdom were of this world, then would my servants fight, that I should not be delivered to the Jews: but now is my kingdom not from hence.
37 Pilate therefore said unto him, Art thou a king then? Jesus answered, Thou sayest that I am a king. To this end was I born, and for this cause came I into the world, that I should bear witness unto the truth. Every one that ᶜis of the truth heareth my voice.

36 what hast thou done? Jesus answered, My kingdom is not of this world: if my kingdom were of this world, then would my ¹servants fight, that I should not be delivered to the Jews: but now is my 37 kingdom not from hence. Pilate therefore said unto him, Art thou a king then? Jesus answered, ²Thou sayest it, for I am a king. To this end have I been born, and to this end am I come into the world, that I should bear witness unto the truth. Every one

a 1 Tim. 6: 13....b Dan. 2: 44; 7: 14; Luke 12: 14; ch. 6: 15; 8: 15....c ch. 8: 47; 1 John 3: 19; 4: 6.——1 Or, *officers:* as in ver. 3, 12, 18, 22....2 Or, *Thou sayest that I am a king.*

such an accusation, he reminds Jesus that it originated with his own people. **Thine own nation**—who may certainly be supposed unwilling to injure one of their race, **and the chief priests**—who are the leaders of the people and men of high repute among you—**have delivered thee unto me.** This, assuredly, was a plausible justification of his course; but it was far enough from being even a hint that he supposed Jesus to be guilty of any crime against the State. Yet, there must be some explanation of the charge; Jesus must have done something which had moved the chief priests to conspire against him and deliver him up as a criminal to the civil power. And, therefore, Pilate again questions the prisoner before him. **What hast thou done?** "That is, to turn those who would naturally favor thee, into relentless enemies?"—*Westcott.* There seems to have been nothing unjust or overbearing in this question, and it gave to Jesus a favorable opportunity to set forth briefly the nature of his mission, his claims, and his authority. Of course, the *form* of his answer was determined by the accusation which had been made.

36. My kingdom is not of this world. This is equivalent to saying: "I have a kingdom, one that is emphatically and distinctly mine (observe the Greek, ἡ βασιλεία ἡ ἐμή), but it is not of this world—its source and character are unlike those of any earthly kingdom." By this language Jesus sought to accomplish two things: *first,* to suggest to Pilate a reasonable explanation of the enmity which led the chief priests to seek his life, and also of the form which they had at last given to their accusation; and, *second,* to convince Pilate that he had made no claim to civil authority. And we may be certain that the simplicity, sincerity, and holy dignity of Jesus, gave peculiar force to his testimony. Yet, having in mind the character of Pilate, and especially his lack of spiritual insight, Jesus proceeded

to show that his words in disclaiming political aims must be true, because they were confirmed by the conduct of his followers. **If my kingdom were of this world, then would my servants fight.** "Therefore, it cannot, as I have said, be of this world." The expression, translated, **would—fight,** describes a continuous and violent struggle for superiority (ἠγωνίζοντο): they "would be striving," (comp. Luke 13: 24; 1 Cor. 9: 25; 1 Tim. 6: 12; 2 Tim. 4: 7); that is, acting the part of soldiers in a fierce conflict. "They would have resisted my arrest at the outset, and would have continued their resistance until now." This was a simple appeal to facts, such as Pilate ought to have comprehended, and probably did comprehend. For he knew that the servants of Jesus had not used force or violence to prevent his arrest, and were not using force to rescue him from the Jews. And this ought of itself to have satisfied the procurator that Jesus was not seeking to establish an earthly kingdom. This, too, is what Jesus solemnly re-affirms in the last clause of the verse: **but now is my kingdom not from hence.** After reminding Pilate of what his servants would have done if his kingdom had been of an earthly nature, he denies again that it has such an origin or nature: "but in reality, as the case stands, my kingdom is not from this earthly source." This, indeed, is wholly negative in form; but if we bear in mind all the circumstances known to Pilate and the transparent sincerity of Christ, it will be impossible to doubt that it had also a positive significance, that it suggested an authority whose origin was divine—a kingdom which was religious, instead of secular. But, how little appreciation of such a kingdom had the Roman governor! For, in consequence (οὖν) of what Jesus had said, he addressed him with these words, containing a spice of irony:

37. Art thou a king, then? Meaning:

"Thou considerest thyself a king, then, dost thou?" For Jesus had evidently assented to the charge so far as to assume that he had some sort of kingly position, though it was "not of this world." And, looking at the man before him, unarmed, unsupported, deserted, the proud officer could not, or did not, repress the feeling of contempt which such a claim excited. For there is reason to infer from the position of the pronoun *thou*, at the end of the Greek sentence, that it was added contemptuously: "Thou, a helpless prisoner, a poor Jew, without friends, even among thine own people—*thou*, a king!" How little, then, could Pilate have seen in the prisoner before him! How faint an impression of that divine love and life which dwelt in the Son of God, was made on his worldly nature! How impossibe for this representative of Cæsar to conceive of moral supremacy! The world in which he lived was almost infinitely distant from the world in which Christ lived. But, though with a tone of contempt, he had nevertheless uttered the truth, and Jesus had but to assert this in order to assert his kingship. **Thou sayest that I am a king.** Thus Jesus adopts the language of Pilate as an expression of the truth. Paying no attention to the sarcastic tone of the governor's remark, he promptly and calmly assents to it as correct. But several interpreters—(*e. g.*, Meyer, Alford, Luthardt)—maintain that the last part of this sentence is confirmatory of the first, thus: *Thou sayest* —(*i. e.*, rightly), *because I am a king*—interpreting the Greek particle (ὅτι) as meaning *because*, rather than *that*. We regard this interpretation as improbable; nay, the words of Westcott concerning it are scarcely too positive, that it "seems to be both unnatural as a rendering of the original phrase, and alien from the context." With either version, however, (viz., the common or the one proposed), the meaning of Jesus is substantially the same; for, with either version, he claims to be a king, and repeating his claim, proceeds to explain the real nature of his regal authority and control over men. **To this end**—that is, for this very purpose, namely, that I might be a king—**was I born,** or, *have I been born*. (Rev. Ver.) Jesus evidently means to say, that his birth as a man was with a distinct view in the divine mind to his kingly office, that he was a predestined ruler, and that, should he fail of exercising regal authority over men, he would fail of accomplishing the end of his being. This clause is, therefore, as we understand it, an emphatic, though brief, confirmation of his previous statement. "Christ not only affirms the fact of his kingship, but also bases the fact upon the essential law of his being."— *Westcott*. **And for this cause:** the same Greek expression as before (εἰς τοῦτο), and meaning, for this end, purpose, object; more briefly, **for this: came I into the world.** In this clause, also, the verb is in the perfect tense, and should be translated (as in the Rev. Ver.), *am I come into the world*. The expression differs from the foregoing, in that it assumes the fact of Christ's pre-existence and the fact of his superhuman nature as well. **That I should bear witness to the truth.** This clause is also declarative of the purpose for which he had come into the world, and is, therefore, equivalent to his reigning as king. He came into the world in order to reign as king: he came into the world to bear witness to the truth. And these two purposes are one. The latter specifies the way in which the former is to be done. "He has indeed a kingdom; but . . . his kingdom is to be established by his witness of the eternal truth, which he had known with his Father, and which he alone could declare to men."—*Watkins*. In other words, Christ came to reign over men by the power of truth. Hence, all those who are willing to be governed by the highest truth, submit joyfully to him. **Every one that is of the truth heareth my voice.** To be of the truth is to draw one's inspiration from it, just as to be of God, is to be controlled by influences coming from him. But *the* truth is precisely that part of all truth which reveals God and his salvation; that part of all truth which is of supreme interest to man, as a moral and religious being, capable of knowing and loving the Most High. And to hear the voice of Jesus is, of course, to hearken to his words and obey his will. Over every one who thus hears his voice he reigns as king, in a far higher and more absolute sense than any earthly monarch rules over his subjects. "The nature of Christ's kingdom may be expressed in a word, by calling it *spiritual*. It embraces

38 Pilate saith unto him, What is truth? And when he had said this, he went out again unto the Jews, and saith unto them, *I find in him no fault *at all*.
39 *b*But ye have a custom, that I should release unto you one at the passover: will ye therefore that I release unto you the King of the Jews?

38 that is of the truth heareth my voice. Pilate saith unto him, What is truth?
And when he had said this, he went out again unto the Jews, and saith unto them, I find no crime 39 in him. But ye have a custom, that I should release unto you one at the passover: will ye therefore that

a Matt. 27:24; Luke 23:4; ch. 19:4, 6....*b* Matt. 27:15; Mark 15:6; Luke 23:17.

those, and only those, who are poor in spirit, who have been born of the Spirit, ... and who worship God in spirit and in truth. (Matt. 5:3; John 3:3, 5; 4:24; Rom. 8:9.) The kingdom of God is not eating and drinking, but righteousness and peace and joy in the Holy Ghost. (Rom. 14:17.) It is not of this world. (Ver. 36.) It is related to heaven, rather than to earth, in its principles and spirit, and its consummation here would make the society of earth as loyal to God and as blessed in his service, as that of heaven." (Matt. 6:10.)

38. What is truth? The motive and spirit of this question can only be conjectured. But from all that is known of Pilate's character, as well as from the circumstance that he waited for no answer, it may be regarded as probable that he now thought of Jesus as a harmless enthusiast, whom he could dismiss with an impatient intimation of his own skepticism as to the possibility of any man's knowing truth from falsehood, or as to the importance of truth, if it could be known. Of course, he referred to truth in itself, to truth as an objective reality, and not to veracity in the intercourse of man with man; for of the importance of the latter, no practical Roman could well speak with contempt. "Some critics have asserted that the writer of this Gospel must have drawn upon his imagination for the colloquy between Pilate and Jesus in the prætorium. But there is no sufficient reason for this assertion. John may not have shared the scruples of the Sanhedrists about entering the judgment-hall of Pilate, but, influenced by his great love for Christ, may have followed him quietly into the hall, and have listened there to all that was said. Or, he may have learned the substance of the governor's questions, and of his Master's answers, from some of Pilate's attendants. Hence, there is no special reason for denying the accuracy of his narrative in this place."

Outside the prætorium. Having thus terminated his examination of Jesus, **he went out again unto the Jews,** who had remained near the prætorium, awaiting impatiently the result of his interview with the object of their hatred. **And saith unto them, I find in him no fault.** The Revised Version translates this clause, *I find no crime in him*. And the word *crime* represents the original word more accurately than the word *fault*, (comp. Matt. 27:37; Mark 15:26; Acts 13:28; 28:18, with 19:4, below). It is also noticeable that the pronoun, I, is emphatic, so that Pilate contrasts his own judgment with that of the Jews. "*You* have accused him of evil-doing worthy of death, but I, upon examination, find in him no ground for your accusation, no crime deserving punishment."

At this point, as is generally supposed, took place the sending to Herod, related by Luke (23:4-12). "The sending to Herod, which Luke adds to this declaration of innocence, and by which Pilate tries to withdraw himself from the business which is so annoying to him, is passed over by John, because it was only an episode, which had no significance for the real progress of the case, and which produced no change in Pilate's mood. Hence, John could proceed without interruption to the offer Pilate made."—*Luthardt.*

39. But ye have a custom—though this custom is not mentioned by profane historians. Yet, the passover was certainly a very appropriate time for showing mercy and letting the prisoner go free; and the uncontradicted testimony of the Evangelists is ample proof of its existence, during the governorship of Pilate. According to the narrative of Mark, the people first applied to the procurator for the release of a prisoner to them, "as he had ever done unto them," (Mark 15:8), and it has been thought that some of them, as well as Pilate himself, may have hoped that Jesus would be selected, and his life saved. Vain hope! As to this expedient for saving the life of Jesus, Alford says, none too sharply: "His conduct presents a pitiable specimen of the moral weakness of that spirit of worldly power which reached its culminating point in the Roman Empire." Alas, there is reason to

40 *Then cried they all again, saying, Not this man, but Barabbas. *Now Barabbas was a robber.

40 I release unto you the King of the Jews? They cried out therefore again, saying, Not this man, but Barabbas. Now Barabbas was a robber.

CHAPTER XIX.

THEN *Pilate therefore took Jesus, and scourged him.

1 Then Pilate therefore took Jesus, and scourged

a Acts 3: 14....*b* Luke 23: 19....*c* Matt. 20: 19; 27: 26; Mark 15: 15; Luke 18: 33.

believe that many a ruler in modern times has just as little firmness in maintaining the right as was exhibited by this pagan magistrate in dealing with the Jews. He was ready to do justice, if it would not cost him too much; but he was not ready to do justice at a very great personal sacrifice. **Will ye therefore that I release unto you the king of the Jews?** There is certainly contempt in calling Jesus "the king of the Jews." And probably the contempt was for the Jews, who had undertaken to treat as a serious matter the claims of so upright and harmless an enthusiast for truth, as Jesus had appeared to be in the eyes of Pilate. According to Matthew, Pilate himself suggested the name of Barabbas, a notorious criminal, as an alternative to that of Jesus—in the hope, no doubt, that the people would be ashamed to ask favor for such a man, rather than Jesus. (Matt. 27: 17.) There, also, we are informed that "the chief priests and the elders persuaded" the people to ask Barabbas instead of the Christ. It is, therefore, plain that "the multitudes" were not all of one mind at first, and that the narrative of John is extremely condensed.

40. Then cried they all again: or, *They cried out therefore again.*—Rev. Ver. The word **all** is not found in the earliest manuscripts, and is probably an addition to the text. The word **again** implies that this was not the first time they had shouted forth their answer to nearly the same question; and, as this is the first instance *mentioned* by John, it implies also the condensation of his narrative referred to under verse 39. Many particulars, evidently known to the writer, were omitted for the sake of brevity, some of them, perhaps, because they were familiar to Christians through the other Gospels. For this portion of the trial of Jesus, see also Matt. 27: 15-26; Mark 15: 6-15; Luke 23: 13-25. **Now Barabbas was a robber.** Meyer calls this "a tragic comment." Its very brevity is significant. How, then, could he have been selected by the people? It is possible that

this notorious criminal was a Jewish zealot, whose lawless violence was half atoned for in the eyes of his countrymen by his bitter hatred of foreign domination. From Mark 15: 7, we learn that he had been joined with others in sedition and murder; yet, this may have been, in the circumstances, what seemed to his brethren an apology for his conduct. In reality, however, he was a robber and a murderer; for not only Mark in his Gospel, but Peter in his address to the people in the temple (Acts 3: 14), affirms this: "Ye denied the Holy and Righteous One, and asked for a murderer to be granted unto you."—Rev. Ver. And here John, with crushing simplicity, says, "Now Barabbas was a *robber*"—a case of *meiosis*, in which the writer says less than he might, knowing that his readers will fill out the meaning.

Ch. 19: 1-3. Scourging and Mocking of Jesus.

1. Then Pilate therefore took Jesus, and scourged him. The word **therefore**, represents the action of Pilate as a consequence of his failure to induce the Jews to make choice of Jesus, instead of Barabbas, as the object of their passover clemency. By selecting Barabbas, they virtually insisted on the condemnation and death of Jesus. And, according to the first three Evangelists, did this in express terms, calling out passionately for the crucifixion of Jesus. (See Matt. 27: 22, 23; Mark 15: 13, 14; Luke 23: 21, 23.) But the procurator did not yield to them so far as to sentence Jesus at once to the death of the cross, yet he did yield to them so far as to order the scourging *preliminary* to crucifixion, as if he intended to comply with their demand for the latter. As the sequel shows, he hoped that "the horrors of the scourging might still move the people to desist from the ferocious cry for the cross."—*Edersheim.* But his consent to injustice demonstrated his moral weakness; and, however heart-rending might be the suffering caused by scourging,

Y

2 And the soldiers platted a crown of thorns, and put *it* on his head, and they put on him a purple robe,
3 And said, Hail, King of the Jews! and they smote him with their hands.

2 him. And the soldiers plaited a crown of thorns, and put it on his head, and arrayed him in a purple garment; and they came unto him, and said, Hail, King of the Jews! and they struck him [1] with their

[1] Or, *with rods.*

---

there was no good reason to expect that it would satisfy the infuriated populace. Spurred on by the priests, they had cried out again and again for the most ignominious and terrible punishment, and nothing less than this would now meet their demands. As to the position for being scourged, we are told by Edersheim that, "stripped of his clothes, his hands tied and back bent, the victim would be bound to a column or a stake, in front of the prætorium." Wescott says, that "recent investigations at Jerusalem have disclosed what may have been the scene of the punishment. In a subterranean chamber, discovered by Captain Warren, on what Mr. Ferguson holds to be the site of Antonia—Pilate's prætorium—stands a truncated column, no part of the construction; for the chamber is vaulted above the pillar, but just such a pillar as criminals would be tied to to be scourged." Is it well to associate the sufferings of Christ with such material objects, when we can only say that those objects *may* have been connected with him?

2. However dreadful may have been the physical pain endured by Jesus, at this time, it did not probably exhaust his strength, or disturb the equanimity of his spirit. With holy patience and submission to his Father's will, "he was wounded for our transgressions, he was bruised for our iniquities." (Isa. 53: 5.) He was a silent sufferer; and when released from the pillar of scourging, was doubtless able to stand without support from others. **The soldiers platted a crown of thorns.** The Greek word signifying, *thorn*, or *thornbush* (ἄκανθα), is not sufficiently definite to authorize any positive statement as to the kind of shrub or tree from which the **crown** was made. But, most scholars have fixed on the *Zizyphus Spina Christi*, called in Palestine the Nebk or Nubk, as the plant employed. Geike says, that "One of them, running to the nearest open space, heightened the coarse and shameful merriment by bringing in some of the tough twigs of the thorny Nubk, which he twisted into a mock laurel wreath, like that worn at times by the Cæsars, and forced down, with its close, sharp thorns, on our Saviour's temples." And Watkins remarks, that "the shrub was likely enough to be found in the garden of the prætorium." **They put on him a purple robe.** Compare Matt. 27 : 28. Plumptre says, that the "purple" of the ancients was "crimson," and the same color might easily be called by either name. He also conjectures, rather strangely, that this robe "was probably some cast-off cloak of Pilate's own," while Geike assumes, that "instead of his plain abba of linen, they threw over his shoulders a scarlet sagum, or soldier's cloak—as a rough burlesque of the long and fine purple one, worn only by the Emperor." Matthew adds another feature, saying, that they put "a reed in his hand," evidently as a mock sceptre.

3. **And said.** According to the best manuscripts (ℵ B L U X A Π), and the Revised Version, this should read: *And they came unto him, and said.* Probably the first clause was omitted from some of the early manuscripts, because it was understood to affirm that the soldiers now came to Jesus from some remoter point, whereas, the meaning is, that they approached Jesus one after another, or, *kept coming to Jesus,* though they were all present in, or near, the prætorium. As they approached Jesus, they bowed the knee, in mock reverence, and said, **Hail, king of the Jews!** Matthew says, expressly, that they *mocked him,* with these words. He also relates, as further indignities, that *they spit upon him,* and *took the reed,* which they had put in his hand, *and smote him on the head.* But the language of John, **and they smote him with their hands,** may mean the same as that of Matthew: for the expression translated, *smote him with their hands,* signifies, literally, *were giving him blows* (ῥαπίσματα), either with the hand, or with a stick. (See Note on 18: 26.) Notice also the tense of the verb, which justifies the translation, "were giving," or "kept giving" him blows, as they continued their insulting homage. As usual, the narrative of John, though brief, is very vivid and powerful.

4 Pilate therefore went forth again, and saith unto them, Behold, I bring him forth to you, *that ye may know that I find no fault in him.
5 Then came Jesus forth, wearing the crown of thorns, and the purple robe. And *Pilate* saith unto them, Behold the man!

4 hands. And Pilate went out again, and saith unto them, Behold, I bring him out to you, that ye may know that I find no crime in him. Jesus therefore came out, wearing the crown of thorns and the purple garment. And *Pilate* saith unto them, Behold.

a, ch. 18: 63; ver. 6.

4-7. PILATE'S THIRD ATTEMPT TO AVOID CONDEMNING JESUS.

As a ruler, Pilate doubtless felt himself bound to deal justly with the people, sentencing criminals to punishment, and absolving the innocent. Convinced that Jesus was guilty of no civil offence, he was, therefore, reluctant to sentence him to the terrible death of the cross. But there is no reason to suppose that he was moved by humane feelings. He had probably witnessed the scourging, and had not interposed to prevent the mockery and insult that followed. Yet, it is possible, that he permitted the latter, as well as ordered the former, with a view to satisfying the vengeance of the Jews, and thus escaping further importunity to condemn the prisoner, whom he felt to be innocent.

4. Pilate therefore went forth again. According to the text followed in the Revised Version, the word *and* should be substituted for **therefore,** reading, *And Pilate went out again.* This reading is probably correct, being supported by A B K L X Π, and nine other uncial manuscripts. The word **again,** refers to what is related in the preceding chapter, verse 29. Many of the Jews had remained without, while Jesus had been with Pilate in the prætorium. They had not, therefore, witnessed the mocking of Christ by the soldiers, and, indeed, it is by no means certain, though perhaps probable, that they had been spectators of the scourging. **Behold, I bring him forth to you, that ye may know that I find no fault in him.** The word *crime* (Revised Version), reproduces more exactly the sense of the original, than the word **fault** (Common Version.) By scourging Jesus, Pilate had given the people to understand that he considered him guilty, and was about to crucify him. But by bringing him before them once more, instead of letting the execution go forward, he virtually said that the case was not yet finally settled; that he himself had not found the accused worthy of death, or guilty of any crime. Thus he confesses before all the people that, influenced by their demand, he had inflicted a dreadful punishment on one whom he believes innocent. It was a shameless confession. And it was not fitted to accomplish his purpose, to pacify the people, or to make them desist from their efforts to destroy Jesus. Nothing but the rock-like firmness of an upright ruler is of any avail against such hatred as then burned in the hearts of the Jews.

5. Then came Jesus forth, wearing the crown of thorns, and the purple robe. At the call of Pilate, Jesus came out of the castle into the open court before the people. No ignominy was too great for him to bear. The crown of thorns and the purple garment testified plainly of the mockery to which he had been subjected. Were there any that beheld him with reverence and love? We may presume that "the disciple whom Jesus loved" was within sight of his Master. But how many others were there, whose love to the Christ was true and steadfast, we cannot even conjecture. Nor is it possible for any one to say, that, if there were any true hearts in that agitated throng, they were comforted or moved by a glance of recognition from the patient sufferer. But, as Jesus appeared, with the badges of mock royalty upon him, and signs of terrible suffering in his countenance and bearing, **Pilate saith unto them, Behold the man! Behold,** is not a verb, but an interjection—*Ecce Homo! Lo, the man!* "The man, whom you have asked me to crucify; the man, scourged, mocked, abused, yet gentle. silent, enduring! Lo, there he stands. an object of pity, rather than of fear." "These words of half-contemptuous pity were designed to change the fierceness of the spectators into compassion."— *Westcott.* "A man who allows himself to be treated thus, is surely a harmless fanatic, whom there is no reason for killing."—*Meyer.* "See this man who submits to and has suffered these indignities—how can he ever stir up the people, or set himself up for king? Now cease to persecute him: your malice

JOHN. [Ch. XIX.

6 ᵃ When the chief priests therefore and officers saw him, they cried out, saying, Crucify *him*, crucify *him*. Pilate saith unto them, Take ye him, and crucify *him*: for I find no fault in him.
7 The Jews answered him, ᵇ We have a law, and by our law he ought to die, because ᶜ he made himself the Son of God.

6 the man! When therefore the chief priests and the officers saw him, they cried out, saying, Crucify *him*, crucify *him*. Pilate saith unto them, Take him yourselves, and crucify him; for I find no crime in him. The Jews answered him, We have a
7 law, and by that law he ought to die, because he

a Acts 3: 13....b Lev. 24: 16....c Matt. 26: 65; ch. 5: 18; 10: 33.

surely ought to be satisfied."—*Alford.* Geikie's description of the scene is graphic: "Then (Pilate) turning to the figure at his side, drawn together with mortal agony, and looking at the pale, worn, and bleeding face, through which there yet shone a calm dignity and more than human beauty, that had touched his heart, and might touch even the heart of Jews, he added, 'Behold the man!' Would they let the scourging and mockery suffice after all?" But the effect was not what the governor had hoped. He did not succeed in ridding himself of further responsibility by causing Jesus to be scourged, by permitting him to be mocked, and by presenting him to the people as an object of compassion rather than of dread. For religious animosity is bitter and unrelenting, and there were still in the crowd many whom Christ's gentleness and patience under the cruelest suffering could not mollify. They had sworn to compass his death, and they were determined to make it as painful and ignominious as possible.

6. **When the chief priests therefore and** (*the*) **officers saw him.** *The* officers here mentioned were not those of the governor, but those of the chief priests, or of the Sanhedrin, and they were naturally of one mind with their superiors. **They cried out, saying, Crucify him, crucify him.** According to the highest critical authorities, Tischendorf, Tregelles, Westcott and Hort, the Revised Version, and the Common Text, there is no pronoun after the word **crucify**, though as to sense, it is correctly supplied in translation. But in fact, the cry was compressed into one word, *crucify, crucify!* And there is good reason to believe that intense and concentrated passion was put into that terrible word. These ring-leaders of the hostile party were bent upon the accomplishment of their object, and their angry shout must have convinced Pilate that his movement was a failure. His next word, therefore, was: **Take ye him, and crucify him; for I find no fault in him**:

or, as in the Revised Version: *Take him yourselves, and crucify him; for I find no crime in him.* This may have been uttered in such a tone as to imply that they would do it at their peril. At any rate, it was a manifest refusal, on the governor's part, to do their will, and a distinct declaration that they had not yet made out a case against Jesus. Weiss maintains that "the procurator could have given them the right to inflict capital punishment (*Ewald*), but crucifixion was no legal capital punishment, and they had sought it merely in order to cast the odium of the execution upon the Romans. He, therefore, gives the permission in a form in which they could not accept it, and the more, because he assigns as his motive the fact that he regards Jesus as innocent, and so, must give into their hands the act of slaying a guiltless man." This answer of Pilate led them to bring forward a new charge against the Saviour.

7. **The Jews answered him.** That is, probably, the leaders of the people, who had just cried vehemently, crucify! crucify! For, as has been frequently observed, this Evangelist commonly means by **the Jews**, those leaders of the people who were partizans of Judaism and enemies of Christ. **We have a law.** The pronoun **we**, is slightly emphasized, because they know and feel that the law to which they refer is purely Jewish, and in no sense binding on a Roman. Yet, as the governor had pronounced their former accusation vain, they venture to bring forward a law of their own religion, in the hope that it will be regarded as a justification of their urgency in calling for the crucifixion of Jesus, and as a prudential reason, if no more, for yielding to their demand. For they must have noted his half measures and vacillating course, both in referring the case to Herod, and in causing Jesus to be scourged; and they were determined to leave no stone unturned in their effort to secure the death of Jesus by his authority. **And by our law he ought to die, because he made himself the Son of**

8 When Pilate therefore heard that saying, he was the more afraid;
9 And went again into the judgment hall, and saith unto Jesus, Whence art thou? a But Jesus gave him no answer.

8 made himself the Son of God. When Pilate therefore heard this saying, he was the more afraid; 9 and he entered into the ¹Prætorium again, and saith unto Jesus, Whence art thou? But Jesus

a Isa. 53: 7; Matt. 27: 12, 14.——1 Or, *palace*.

God. The law to which they referred may be seen in Lev. 24: 16: " He that blasphemeth the name of the Lord, he shall surely be put to death." For they held that any one who claimed for himself divine prerogatives, dishonored and reproached thereby the name of God. Compare Matt. 26: 63-66; Mark 14: 61-64. The principal editors omit **our,** before **law,** so that the clause reads: *And by that law,* or, more literally, *according to the law* —in question. But the meaning is not much affected by this slight change in the text. Again, there is no article before **Son,** in the Greek original, and, therefore, the last clause may be rendered: *because he made himself God's Son.* Or, *Son of God,* or, even, *a Son of God.* But there is no probability that either Jesus himself or the Jews meant by it the last. They used the expression to signify a special divine Sonship, based upon a special union of Christ with God. Weiss supposes that the Jews intended by this reply "simply to defend themselves against the reproach of desiring the death of an innocent person." Westcott thinks that they took up Pilate's challenge in an unexpected manner. " He had said, *Take him yourselves.* They answer, If you appeal to us, we have a power which we have not yet invoked. **We have a law—** to which you are bound to give effect, whatever you may think of it, **and according to the law he ought to die.** The emphatic 'we,' answers at once to the emphatic 'ye,' and to the emphatic 'I,' of the governor." It would have been more satisfactory if Dr. Westcott had produced some evidence that a Roman governor was "bound to give effect" to every religious law of a subject people, or that the Jews would have asserted this in so high a tone, if he was not bound to do it by some Roman law or imperial decree.

8-12. PILATE QUESTIONS JESUS AGAIN, AND TRIES TO RELEASE HIM.

8. When Pilate therefore heard that (or, *this*) **saying, he was the more afraid.** That he was **the more afraid,** implies some degree of fear previous to his hearing this saying. Evidently the words and bearing of the accused had made an unusual impression on his mind—an impression of incipient fear. He had perceived something extraordinary and mysterious in the prisoner by his side, and living in an age of superstition as well as of skepticism, the procurator was doubtless more or less influenced by both. He had before recognized in Jesus a spirit unlike that of other men, and now, learning that he claimed to be God's Son, he was the more afraid, thinking that there might be something real back of this claim. Perhaps the message from his wife: "Have thou nothing to do with that just man; for I have suffered many things this day in a dream because of him" (Matt. 27: 19), had contributed something to his first impression of fear; for dreams were often supposed to be from the gods. That his fear " was not a fear *of the Jews,* nor *of acting unjustly,* but of the person of Jesus, is evident from what follows."—*Alford.*

9. Whence art thou ? Having returned with Jesus into the judgment hall, Pilate asked him this question, expecting to hear from his lips a statement concerning his origin. For the accusation, that he *made himself Son of God,* suggested to the governor the thought, that Jesus might claim to be of heavenly origin, or, rather, perhaps, of divine origin. the reference being not to *place,* but to *source.* **But Jesus gave him no answer.** Why this silence? Only a conjectural reply can be given. Perhaps it was, because the true answer to this question would be misunderstood by Pilate. Perhaps it was, because the true answer to this question had no proper relation to the governor's duty at the time. Perhaps it was, because the true answer would have tended to strengthen Pilate's superstitious feelings, without serving any good purpose. Perhaps it was, because the Saviour knew that his Father's will would be accomplished by silence, since Pilate was to be the instrument of his crucifixion. Weiss thinks the silence of Jesus is most simply explained, by supposing "that an affirmative answer

10 Then saith Pilate unto him, Speakest thou not unto me? knowest thou not that I have power to crucify thee, and have power to release thee?
11 Jesus answered, *Thou couldest have no power at all against me, except it were given thee from above: therefore he that delivered me unto thee hath the greater sin.

10 gave him no answer. Pilate therefore saith unto him, Speakest thou not unto me? knowest thou not that I have ¹power to release thee, and have ¹power to crucify thee? Jesus answered him, Thou wouldest have no ¹power against me, except it were given thee from above: therefore he that delivered me unto thee hath greater sin

a Luke 22: 53; ch. 7: 30.——1 Or, *authority*.

would have been understood by Pilate in a superstitious way only, and that all the prerequisites to further explanations were wanting."

10. The silence of Jesus was surprising to Pilate, and was construed as disrespectful. Fully conscious of his authority as a magistrate representing the emperor, Pilate reminded Jesus without delay of that authority, as if its very extent must show him the temerity of his silence when questioned. **Speakest thou not unto me?** Observe that the word **me** is emphatic, anticipating the account of his authority which follows. **Knowest thou not that I have power to crucify thee, and have power to release thee?** "Reason enough why I should be treated with respect! Hope of life and fear of death, should certainly lead a subject, and especially a subject accused of wrong-doing, to answer every question of his judge with the utmost deference." The word *power* signifies *authority*, legal authority, as well as ability, and here refers to the legitimate authority of the procurator to release or condemn the accused. Of course, the clear and sharp antithesis by which he described the extent of his power was suggested by the case in hand, and he doubtless imagined that the prisoner would be touched deeply by this particular description of his power. How true to nature is this language of the procurator! Though vacillating in purpose, and moved with some degree of fear at the extraordinary claims and bearing of Jesus, he was a proud Roman governor, ready to assert the greatness of his authority, and surprised that a prisoner should seem indifferent to it.

11. To this boastful, if not threatening, language, Jesus saw fit to reply. Yet not in a strain of apology or entreaty, not in words expressive of either fear or hope, but in terms that refer to others rather than to himself, and that do not yield their full sense with readiness to the interpreter. **Thou couldest** (or, *wouldest*) **have no power at all against me, except it were given thee from above: therefore he that delivered me unto thee hath the greater sin.** There should be no article before **greater sin**, in the English, as there is none in the Greek original. And as to the meaning, we find less difficulty in comprehending the object of the first part of this answer than in seeing how the last part is a natural inference from the first. Pilate had claimed the power of life and death over Jesus, and in such language as intimated that any disrespect to himself might bring evil on the prisoner, even though he were innocent. Christ implicitly concedes the governor's official power to crucify him, but explicitly reminds him that his power was not self-originated and absolute—a power that he might use according to his own will or caprice—but, on the contrary, that his legal right to proceed against his prisoner, being involved in the office which he providentially held, had been given him from above—even from God, the source of all rightful authority. Only under the Divine Ruler was he a legitimate judge, entitled to act in the case against Jesus —a view which certainly implied that he would *have* sin if he should punish the guiltless by crucifixion. But, how is the next statement an inference from this? From what point of view did Jesus regard this as a reason for that? For he added: **therefore** (that is, *on account of this* fact, which I have now stated), **he that delivered me unto thee hath the greater sin.** The comparison involved in the word *greater*, may be with the sin of Pilate, or with the sin that would have been involved in the high priest's action, if Pilate's authority had not been from above. Let us suppose that the comparison intended was with the sin of Pilate; for this is the opinion of most interpreters. On this hypothesis Jesus virtually said to Pilate: "Because you have no official power against me, save that which has been given you as a sacred trust from above, (the misuse of which is sinful), the high priest who, with perfect indif-

12 And from thenceforth Pilate sought to release him; but the Jews cried out, saying, "If thou let this man go, thou art not Cesar's friend; *b* whosoever maketh himself a king speaketh against Cesar.

12 Upon this Pilate sought to release him; but the Jews cried out, saying, If thou release this man, thou art not Cæsar's friend: every one that maketh

a Luke 23: 2.... *b* Acts 17: 7.

---

ference to your abuse of that sacred trust, has delivered me up to you, demanding without cause, my crucifixion, is guilty of greater sin than you commit by yielding to his demand. I recognize him as the leader in this desecration of God-given authority, and his sin as even greater than yours, though yours must be great." This interpretation supposes that the expression, **delivered me unto thee**, covers, and includes all the implacable enmity and recklessness with which the chief priests, (Caiaphas at their head), handed over Jesus to the Roman governor, and called for his crucifixion, even though the governor found no crime in him. They urgently and persistently *tempted* the governor to misuse his power; he slowly and reluctantly *yielded* to their temptation. Both sinned; but, the divine sufferer, who is to be the final Judge of men, did not hesitate to tell the vacillating Pilate that, in the present transaction, some of the Jews were more guilty than he. Yet, Pilate had, without cause, inflicted on him the awful punishment of scourging! Surely the words of Jesus must have appeared to him a most impartial judgment, at once fearless and true. For the governor well knew that no crime had been proved against Jesus, and that he, himself, had no right to punish an innocent man; but he also knew that he had been sorely pressed by the Jews to do worse than he had yet done, and that he had attempted to withstand their importunity, though with too little moral firmness. Such, we believe, is the true sense of this difficult passage. It does not assume that Jesus charged his Jewish enemies with greater sin, because they had greater knowledge of God and righteousness; for this would have had little meaning to Pilate; but, calling attention to the divine origin and function of civil power—which the Roman, as well as the Jew, could understand—he charged upon Caiaphas (and his associates), *greater sin*, because they were the primary, the moving, the determined party in bringing about the desecration of a power from God, intended for the good of man. And this reference to the nature of civil authority, and its abuse, was specially appropriate as a reply to the words of Pilate, who had intimated that he could use his judicial power as he pleased. Indeed, their appropriateness may be inferred from their effect on the governor's mind.

12. And from thenceforth. Literally, *from this* (ἐκ τούτου), meaning either, *from this time*, marking a date, or, *from this response*, regarded as a source or reason. The Revised Version has *upon this*, which reproduces, in English, the ambiguity of the Greek. We incline to the view that John uses the phrase here to point out the reason or occasion of Pilate's conduct, and thus the influence of Christ's remark upon his mind. **Sought to release him.** By what means, the Evangelist does not state, or how strenuous he was in his attempt. Perhaps, the tense of the verb (imperfect) was meant to characterize his seeking as a "mere attempt, that came to nothing, because of the peculiar form which the Jews gave to their protest against it."— *Weiss.* If so, he must have expressed in words, to the people without, his purpose or desire to release Jesus. **But the Jews cried out, saying, If thou release this man, thou art not Cæsar's friend: whosoever maketh himself a king, speaketh against Cæsar.** Nothing in the life of Jesus gave the slightest occasion for this language. He had scrupulously avoided intermeddling with civil affairs. (**Luke 12: 14.**) He had gone away into a mountain alone, when the people sought to take him, and make him king. (**John 6: 15.**) He had expressly sanctioned the payment of tribute to Cæsar. (**Matt. 22: 21.**) Indeed, one of their chief reasons for rejecting his Messianic claims, was the certainty that he would not head a rebellion against Rome, and re-establish the Kingdom of Israel. But false as was the purport of their language, it served their end as well as if it had been true. Pilate knew something already of the temper of Jews, and he feared that they would make what they were now saying heard in Rome, if he did not comply with their demand. With him, selfishness was stronger than duty, and

13 When Pilate therefore heard that saying, he brought Jesus forth, and sat down in the judgment seat in a place that is called the Pavement, but in the Hebrew, Gabbatha.
14 And *it was the preparation of the passover, and about the sixth hour: and he saith unto the Jews, Behold your King!

13 himself a king ¹ speaketh against Cæsar. When Pilate therefore heard these words, he brought Jesus out, and sat down on the judgment seat at a place called The Pavement, but in Hebrew, Gabbatha.
14 tha. Now it was the Preparation of the passover; it was about the sixth hour. And he saith unto the

a Matt. 27: 62.——1 Or, *opposeth Cæsar.*

it did not take him long to decide upon his course. By no means over-anxious to please the Jews, he was exceedingly desirous of standing well with the Emperor, and reluctant to do anything that would look like indifference to his supremacy. At last, the enemies of Christ have carried their point—but only by arousing the selfish fear of the procurator, through a false charge that might be repeated where it would work his recall to Rome in disgrace.

13-16. CONDEMNATION OF JESUS BY PILATE.

13. When Pilate therefore heard that saying. Or, according to the earliest manuscripts and the best editors, *these words:* "Every word was for Pilate an arrow."— *Hengstenberg.* **He brought Jesus forth**—that is, out of the prætorium—**and sat down in** (rather, *on*) **the judgment seat, in a place called the Pavement, but in Hebrew, Gabbatha.** It was customary (see Josephus "De Bell. Jud.," 2, 9, 3; 2, 14, 8,) to pronounce formal judgment in the open air. Hence the action of Pilate, when he had made up his mind what to do. The particular spot outside the prætorium, where the governor's seat, or tribunal, was placed, was somewhat elevated, and on that account bore the Aramaic name, Gabbatha; it was also paved with stones, and for that reason bore the Greek name, Lithostroton, a pavement. The mention of these names is in harmony with the general minuteness and evident accuracy of the narrative, proving that it must have been written by an eye-witness of the events recorded. But so long as the question, Where was the prætorium of Pilate? in Herod's palace, or in the castle of Antonia? remains unanswered, we cannot point to any spot in modern Jerusalem and say: Here was the tribunal of Pilate when he delivered Jesus to be crucified.

14. And it was the preparation of the passover. The Revised Version is preferable: *Now it was the preparation of the pass-*

over. The word translated **preparation**, being virtually a proper name for Friday, as the day of preparation for the Sabbath; and as this was the Friday of the passover week, it was the preparation day belonging to the passover, regarded as a weekly festival. (See Robinson, "Greek Harmony of the Gospels," p. 219 sq.; McClellan, "The Four Gospels," p. 485, and context; Wieseler, "A Chronological Synopsis of the Four Gospels," p. 325 sq. of Bohn's transl.) **And about the sixth hour.** Since, according to the best manuscript authority (א A B D L M U X Δ Π) the original Greek text had the verb *was* (ἦν) instead of the conjunction **and** (δέ), the Revised Version, *it was about the sixth hour*, must be accepted as correct, though it mars the smoothness of the verse in English. But, how can John's notation of time be reconciled with the statement of Mark (15: 25), that the crucifixion took place *at the third hour?* Alford says, that "there is an insuperable difficulty in the text as it now stands." And if we assume that both the Evangelists used the same starting point in reckoning the hours of the day, the difference between their records is very marked, and seems at first an obvious contradiction. It was the third hour when they crucified him; it was about the sixth hour when Pilate delivered him up to be crucified. It was nine o'clock in the morning when they nailed him to the cross; it was about twelve o'clock when he was handed over to the soldiers to be led to Calvary. Is there, as thus stated, a more glaring contradiction in the records of any event? Much depends upon the habits of the people in referring to time. After a cautious statement of the case, Andrews, in his "Life of our Lord," p. 533, says: "We conclude, then, that the sixth hour of John was the twelfth hour with us, or midday. But it is to be noted that he says, 'about the sixth hour,' (ὡς ἕκτη), which implies that he gives no exact note of the time. It is rendered by Norton: 'it was toward noon,' and this very well expresses the meaning. Mark's words, 'it was the third hour, and they crucified him,' need not be taken as a specific designation of the hour when he was nailed to the cross, but as marking the time when, the sentence having been pronounced, he was given up to the soldiers, and the preparatory steps to the crucifixion began. Our exact divisions of time were wholly unknown to the ancients."

Dr. Robinson (with Alford, and others) supposes a corruption of the text. "The *third hour* of Mark, as the hour of crucifixion, is sustained by the whole course of the transaction and circumstances; as also by the fact stated by Matthew, Mark, and Luke, that the darkness commenced at the *sixth* hour, after Jesus had already for some time hung upon the cross. . . . The reading *sixth* in John is, therefore, probably an early error of transcription for *third* (F for Γ.) Indeed, this last rendering is found in Codex Bezæ and Codex Regius 62, as well as in several other authorities; so that its external weight is marked by Griesbach as nearly or quite equal to that of the common reading; while the internal evidence in its favor is certainly far greater." It may certainly be conceded that, if the numerals were denoted by letters, a *gamma* may easily have been mistaken for a *digamma*, and thus the word *sixth* may have been substituted for the word *third*. But against this explanation it may be remarked: (1) That no critical editors have ventured to substitute *third* for *sixth* in this passage; (2) that the external testimony for *third* is greatly inferior to that for *sixth*—it being only five uncials of second rate importance, four cursives of no special value, and a reported statement of Eusebius, that *third* is the reading of the "accurate copies," and of the Evangelists' autograph, preserved in Ephesus (!), against more than fourteen uncials (including ℵ° A B), all cursives except four, and all the early versions; and (3) that transcribers, noting the discrepancy between this statement and that of Mark, would have been more likely to seek harmony by changing *sixth* to *third* than to introduce discord by changing *third* to *sixth*.[1]

Still another explanation of the difference between John and Mark, has been defended by such scholars as Wieseler, Tholuck, McClellan, and Westcott. It is, that the Romans reckoned their civil day from midnight to midnight, and that John, writing for Christians in Asia Minor, followed that usage. A careful study of the other passages in which John mentions the hour of the day when any event took place (viz., 1:39; 4:6,52), is favorable to the view that he counted the hours from midnight to midnight. "It must, however, be admitted," says Westcott, "that this mode of reckoning hours was unusual in ancient times. The Romans (Mart. IV. 8) and Greeks, no less than the Jews, reckoned their *hours* from sunrise. But the Romans reckoned their civil *days* from midnight (Aul. Gell. III. 2; comp. Matt. 27:19, 'this day') and not from sunrise, or from sunset (as the Jews.) And there are also traces of reckoning the hours from midnight in Asia Minor. Polycarp is said (Mart. Pol. c. 21) to have been martyred at Smyrna 'at the eighth hour.' This, from the circumstances, must have been at 8 A. M. Pionius again is said to have been martyred (at Smyrna, also) 'at the tenth hour,' which can hardly have been 4 P. M., since such exhibitions usually took place before. These two passages furnish a sufficient presumption that St. John, in using what is the modern reckoning, followed a practice of the province in which he was living, and for which he was writing."—*Westcott.*

But, was there time between the sending of Jesus to Pilate and the hour of 6 or 6.30 A. M. for all the events related by the Evangelists? The *terminus a quo* may, perhaps, be put as early as 3.30 A. M. For we are told by John that is was "morning" (πρωία, 18:28; see also Matt. 27:1; Mark 15:1). The Jews were naturally anxious to secure the death of Jesus at the earliest moment possible, for it was a feast day, and they wished to take part in the religious services of the day. We may, therefore, presume that the Sanhedrin met at the earliest practicable hour. But the word used in the passages cited, is applied specifically to "the fourth watch of the night, that is, to the

---

[1] Allowing my own statement to remain, I will add that of Dr. Broadus, who has given special study to textual criticism, and of whose learning and judgment I have been permitted to avail myself often, as the reader must have observed.

[Instead of ἕκτη "sixth," we find τρίτη "third, in ℵ

378 JOHN. [Ch. XIX.

15 But they cried out, Away with *him*, away with *him*, crucify him. Pilate saith unto them, Shall I crucify your King? The chief priests answered, ᵃ We have no king but Cesar.

15 Jews, Behold, your King! They therefore cried out, Away with *him*, away with *him*, crucify him. Pilate saith unto them, Shall I crucify your King? The chief priests answered, We have no king but

ᵃ Gen. 49: 10.

---

time *from three to six* A. M., in our way of reckoning."—*Grimm.* Let it then be assumed that Jesus was sent to Pilate at 3.30 A. M. A half hour would be ample time for the public charges made by the Jews and their subsequent examination of Christ in the prætorium by Pilate. (Matt. 27: 1, 2, 11-14; Mark 15: 1-5; Luke 23: 1-5; John 18: 28-38.) Again, the residence of Herod may have been very near the prætorium, so that half an hour would have been sufficient for the episode of sending Jesus to Herod, including the questions and mocking there, and the return to Pilate; for Herod could not have spent a long time in questioning a prisoner who would make no answer at all to his inquiries. (Luke 23: 9.) At half-past four, Jesus would therefore have been with Pilate again. The governor, therefore, repeats his declaration that he finds no cause of death in Jesus (even as Herod had found none), and offers them the alternative of saving Jesus or Barabbas. During this process, the message from his wife is delivered to him. Half an hour, reaching to five o'clock, would be more than enough for all that was done before the scourging. (Matt. 27: 15-26; Mark 15: 6-15; Luke 23: 13-25; John 18: :9, 40.) For the scourging and mocking, three-quarters of an hour may be allowed (Matt. 27: 26-30; Mark 15: 15-19; John 19: 1-3), bringing us to a quarter before six. Less than a quarter of an hour would be needed for the presentation of "the man" to the people and their cries for his crucifixion (John 19: 4-8), and not more than another quarter for the return into the prætorium, the brief conversation there, and the re-appearance of Pilate on his tribunal in the open air. (John 19: 9-14.) Thus, all these events might surely have taken place before the hour of 6.30 A. M.

Pilate had now resolved to yield to the clamors of the Jews for the blood of an innocent man, rather than incur the risk of being accused of disloyalty to Tiberius. But he was irritated by their fierce persistency, and with bitter sarcasm called their attention to the prisoner—still wearing the purple robe and crown of thorns—by the words, **Behold, your king!** The view which Weiss takes of this expression, is ingenious: "It was meant to show that, owing to the pressure of their demands, he will recognize the crime alleged against Jesus as actual; but, intentionally, he does this, not in the form of an ordinary judicial sentence, which would have asserted the fact that Jesus had endeavored to secure regal authority in Israel, because he does not believe this now any more than before, but with a mocking turn of expression, which, on the one hand, would set forth very clearly the absurdity of such an assertion, and on the other would leave open the interpretation that he recognized not only his guilt, but also his guilty claim." There can be little doubt of Pilate's mingled displeasure and scorn at this moment, and they were probably manifest enough in his countenance and tone of voice.

15. But they cried out. Following a slightly different, but well supported text, the Revised Version, reads: *They, therefore, cried out.* This Version represents the Greek as given in the critical editions of the New Testament: see Treg., Tisch., Westcott and Hort.

(third corrector) D (matter supplied to fill gaps, as late as the tenth century.—Tisch.) L X Δ, four cursives. Eusebius and several late Fathers propose to solve the apparent striking contradiction between this passage and Mark 15: 25, by the supposition that the Greek Γ, three, third, has been here accidentally changed into F, six, sixth. This suggestion much more readily explains the occurrence of τρίτη in the above MSS. of John; and also that of "sixth," in one cursive, margin of Harklean Syriac, and Æthiopic of Mark 15: 25; both being obvious attempts to explain a discrepancy, and thus entitled to no serious attention. We might well leave the apparent contradiction between the two Gospels unsolved, as we still have to do in some cases. But the suggestion of Ewald, and many others, that the Fourth Gospel, written in Asia Minor, long after the destruction of the Jewish State, counts the hours in the Greek and Roman method, from midnight and noon, removes all the difficulty: for John's time will then be 6 A. M., and the "third hour" of Mark, clearly a good while later, will be 9 A. M. This mode of reckoning seems necessary in John 20: 19, compared with Luke 24: 29, 33; and in every other passage of John giving the hour of the day, it is entirely suitable. Whatever may be thought of this explanation, the text ἕκτη, must stand fast, beyond all question.—B.]

16 a Then delivered he him therefore unto them to be crucified. And they took Jesus, and led *him* away.
17 b And he bearing his cross c went forth into a place called *the place* of a skull, which is called in the Hebrew Golgotha:

16 Cæsar. Then therefore he delivered him unto them to be crucified.
17 They took Jesus therefore: and he went out, bearing the cross for himself, unto the place called The place of a skull, which is called in Hebrew

a Matt. 27 : 26, 31 ; Mark 15 : 15 ; Luke 23 : 24.... b Matt. 27 : 31, 33 ; Mark 15 : 21, 22 ; Luke 23 : 26, 33....c Num. 15 : 36 ; Heb. 13 : 12.

Away with him! Away with him! crucify him! Away with him, is but a single word in the original, so that the cry was brief, intense, showing that the sarcasm of Pilate had struck deep; the whole crowd felt it. Hence, he repeats it; for if he must yield, he will not conceal his contempt for the Jews who had compelled him to do so. **Shall I crucify your king?** Here, again, the sting of the original is not fully preserved in translating. For by the order of words in the Greek sentence, *your king*, is thrust forward as the emphatic part: "*Your king*, shall I crucify?" "For it is only on the ground that he claims to be your king, that I consent to crucify him." It was for the chief priests to answer this; perhaps the people did not join in their words: **We have no king but Cæsar:** words well fitted to accomplish their immediate purpose, but singularly alien to the ordinary Jewish temper and hope. "They, who gloried in the Theocracy, and hoped for a temporal Messianic reign, which should free them from Roman bondage; they who boasted that they 'were never in bondage to any man' (8: 33); they, who were 'chief priests' of the Jews, confess that Cæsar is their only king!" One cannot help being thankful that it was not the whole multitude that made this profession, but only the chief priests. And it may be well to bear in mind, that the family of the high priest, and, doubtless, many of the chief priests, were of the Sadducæan party.

16. Then delivered he him therefore unto them to be crucified. With what words, the Evangelist does not say; but, the end contemplated was crucifixion, and the persons to whom Jesus was delivered were the chief priests, under whose direction Roman soldiers were to perform the dreadful act. Westcott remarks, positively, that "Pilate pronounced no sentence himself. He simply let the chief priests have their way (comp. Matt. 27: 26; Mark 15: 15; Luke 23: 25). He had conceded a little against justice in false policy (ver. 1), and he was driven to concede all against his will. From St. Matthew it appears that he typically abjured the responsibility for the act, while the Jews took Christ's blood upon themselves. (Matt. 27 : 24, 25.)" In all these scenes there is but one perfect man concerned —namely, the prisoner, mocked, scourged, and delivered up to be crucified. In all this raging sea of human passions, there is but one pure and steadfast soul. The holy sufferer does not change, or fail in the dread emergency. And only because HE is there, do we feel any interest in the Jewish priests and Roman governor. But for *his* sake every movement of theirs, on this tragic morn, has been studied by millions, and will continue to be studied until the end of time.

16-22. THE CRUCIFIXION OF JESUS.

16. The last part of this verse should be connected with what follows, beginning a new paragraph. **And they took Jesus:** better, *they took Jesus, therefore.* The word translated **took,** is the same as that translated "received," in 1: 11: "He came unto his own, and his own received him not." In itself it does not point to any particular way of taking or receiving. Here it means that the chief priests received Jesus from Pilate's charge into their own charge; so that the soldiers who guarded him and might crucify him were under their command. The words, **and led him away,** are now supposed to be an interpolation.

17. And he bearing his cross, etc. The Revised Version is an improvement: *And he went out*—that is, from the place where he was in the city—*bearing the cross for himself, unto the place called, The place of a skull, which is called in Hebrew, Golgotha.* Though Jesus, as was customary, bore his cross at first, and perhaps, the larger part of the way, the first three Evangelists (Matt. 27: 32; Mark 15: 21; Luke 23: 26), relate that those who led him out of the city compelled a man of Cyrene, Simon by name, who was coming out of the country, to bear the cross of Jesus after him, doubtless because the latter had become so weak and faint, through agony of soul and pain of body, that he was no longer able to sustain the burden. The author of "Ben Hur," thus describes the scene: "He was nearly dead. Every few steps he staggered, as if he would fall. A stained gown, badly torn, hung from his shoulders over a seamless under-tunic. His bare feet left red splotches upon the stones. An inscription on a board, was tied to his neck. A crown of thorns had been crushed hard down upon his head, making cruel wounds, from which streams of blood, now dry and blackened, had run over his face and neck. The long hair, tangled in the thorns, was clotted thick. The skin, where it could be seen, was ghastly white. His hands were tied before him. Back somewhere in the city, he had fallen exhausted, under the transverse of his cross, which, as a condemned person, custom required him to bear to the place of execution; now, a countryman carried the burden in his stead. Four soldiers went with him as a guard against the mob, who sometimes, nevertheless, broke through, and struck him with sticks, and spit upon him. Yet, no sound escaped him, neither remonstrance nor groan."

A sad and slow procession! How long it was in forming, after Pilate delivered Christ to the chief priests? how numerous was the multitude that went out to witness the spectacle? how many were the women who bewailed and lamented him (Luke 23:27)? how much time was consumed on the way? are questions that cannot be answered. But Luke informs us that two malefactors were led with him to be put to death. These criminals may, perhaps, have been tried and condemned after the more difficult case of Jesus had been settled; if so, we can understand why, on the hypothesis that we have supposed to be correct as to the sixth hour (ver. 14), so long a time elapsed between the condemnation of Christ and his crucifixion. The soldiers, with their victims, did not start for the place of crucifixion, until everything was completed by way of preparation. And that place, Golgotha, was outside the city walls, though the site of it is not certainly known. Its name is thought to have been suggested by its resemblance, in contour, to a human skull. But, Capt. C. R. Conder, says: "It may reasonably, however, be supposed that Golgotha ('the skull') was the ordinary place of execution for criminals, which is mentioned in the Mishna, under the name Beth-

SUPPOSED SITE OF CALVARY.

18 Where they crucified him, and two others with him, on either side one, and Jesus in the midst.

18 Golgotha: where they crucified him, and with him two others, on either side one, and Jesus in the midst.

has-Sekilah—'The House of Stoning:' for there is no reason to think that the Roman procurator would have made use of a different place of execution to that established by the Jewish Sanhedrin, although that assembly had been debarred by the Romans from the power of inflicting capital punishment only a little before the date of the crucifixion." After showing that the "House of Stoning" was also a recognized place of crucifixion, he proceeds thus: "A tradition is current amongst the Jews of Jerusalem, which places this 'House of Stoning' at the present knoll north of the Damascus Gate, in which is a cave, known since the fifteenth century as the 'Grotto of Jeremiah,' with a cliff, the maximum height of which is about 50 feet, facing southwards towards the city." "The site is one well-fitted for a place of public execution. The top of the knoll is 2,550 feet above the sea, or 110 feet above the top of the Sakhrah rock in the Haram. It commands a view over the city walls to the temple enclosure, and the Holy Sepulchre Church. A sort of amphitheatre is formed by the gentle slopes on the east; and the whole population of the city might easily witness from the vicinity anything taking place on the top of the cliff. The knoll is just beside the main north road. It is occupied by a cemetery of Moslem tombs. which existed as early as the fifteenth century, at least; and the modern slaughter-house of Jerusalem is on the north slope. The hill is quite bare, with scanty grass covering the rocky soil, and a few irises and wild flowers growing among the graves. Not a tree or shrub is visible on it, though fine olive groves stretch northward from its vicinity." ("Survey of Western Palestine—Jerusalem," p. 430, sq.). We regard the "House of Stoning" as meeting the conditions found in the New Testament for Golgotha far better than they are met by the traditional site at the Church of the Holy Sepulchre. Of it, Edersheim, says: "It is a weird, dreary place, two or three minutes aside from the high road, with a high, rounded, skull-like, rocky plateau, and a sudden depression or hollow beneath, as if the jaws of that skull had opened. Whether or not the tomb of the Herodian period in the rocky knoll to the west of Jeremiah's Grotto, was the most sacred spot upon earth—the 'Sepulchre in the Garden'—we dare not positively assert, though every probability attaches to it."[1]

18. Where they crucified him. These few words signify a most cruel infliction, a punishment that was invented to make death as painful and protracted as possible. Edersheim describes it thus: "First, the upright wood was planted in the ground. It was not high, and probably the feet of the sufferer were not above one or two feet from the ground. Thus could the communication, described in the Gospels, take place between him and others; thus, also, might his sacred lips be moistened with the sponge attached to a short stalk of hyssop. Next, the transverse wood (*antenna*) was placed on the ground, and the sufferer laid on it, and his arms were extended, drawn up, and bound to it. Then (this, not in Egypt, but in Carthage and Rome), a strong, sharp nail was driven, first into the right, then into the left hand (the *clavi trabales*). Next, the sufferer was drawn up by means of ropes, perhaps ladders; the transverse either bound or nailed to the upright, and a rest or support for the body fastened on it—(the *cornu* or *sedile*). Lastly, the feet were extended, and either one nail hammered into each, or a larger piece of iron through the two. We have already expressed our belief that the indignity of exposure was not offered at such a Jewish execution. And so might the crucified hang for hours, even days, in the unutterable anguish of suffering, till consciousness at last failed." **And with him two others, on either side one, and Jesus in the midst.** Matthew (27:38), and Mark (15:27), call these two men *robbers* (Λησται)

---

[1] The last word on the "Site of Calvary," is from the pen of Dr. Selah Merrill, American Consul at Jerusalem, in the *Andover Review*, for November, 1885, p. 484: "If a person, wholly ignorant of any question in connection with the Site of Calvary, were asked to select a spot, without the walls of the city for the public execution of criminals, the only two conditions being that the place should be a slightly one and convenient to the Castle of Antonia, he would not hesitate a moment in choosing this hill for that purpose." Again, on p. 488: "The strong probabilities are in favor of regarding the hill above Jeremiah's Grotto, as the place of the crucifixion of our Lord."

382   JOHN.   [Ch. XIX.

19 'And Pilate wrote a title, and put *it* on the cross. And the writing was, JESUS OF NAZARETH THE KING OF THE JEWS.
20 This title then read many of the Jews: for the place where Jesus was crucified was nigh to the city; and it was written in Hebrew, *and* Greek, *and* Latin.

19 midst. And Pilate wrote a title also, and put it on the cross. And there was written, JESUS OF NAZARETH, THE KING OF THE JEWS. This title therefore read many of the Jews: ¹ for the place where Jesus was crucified was nigh to the city; and it was written in Hebrew, *and* in Latin, *and* in Greek.

a Matt. 27 : 37 ; Mark 15 : 26 ; Luke 23 : 38.—1 Or, *for the place of the city where Jesus was crucified was nigh at hand.*

—not *thieves*—for thieves take that which belongs to others, secretly, while robbers do the same thing by open violence and murder. The Evangelists have given us no information, beyond the meaning of this designation, concerning the previous life or criminal conduct of the "malefactors" (Luke) crucified with the Saviour. But, Matthew and Mark testify that the robbers joined with the chief priests in reproaching Christ, while Luke asserts that one of them relented, confessed the injustice of his punishment and the blamelessness of Christ, and entreated the latter to remember him when he should come in his kingdom. (Matt. 27 : 44 ; Mark 15 : 32 ; Luke 23 : 39-43.) Thus these two dying criminals were equally near the Saviour; but one of them rejected him bitterly, while the other sought his favor with penitence.

19. And Pilate wrote a title. Add the word *also*, with the Revised Version, to make the English represent exactly the Greek. The word *title* is said to have been the technical name for such a statement as was placed on the cross. Matthew and Mark call it *his accusation.* It was "the bill, or placard, showing who the condemned person was, and why he was punished."—*Plumptre.* **And put it on the cross:** probably, above the head of Jesus, on the upright shaft. **And the writing was:** more literally, *and there was written.*—(*Rev. Ver.*), but the meaning is the same. **Jesus of Nazareth, the King of the Jews.** It is easy to imagine several reasons why Pilate put just this title on the cross. It would be, in some sense, an adequate reason for capital punishment, at least, in Roman eyes. It would keep before the Jews the charge on which Pilate acted; and the more of reality there was back of the claim of Jesus, the more disgraceful was the transaction on the part of the Jews, and the less culpable on the part of the governor. It would, perhaps, suggest that Jesus had impressed Pilate as one who had some sort of religious pre-eminence which the Jews were bound to honor. Says Plumptre: "There was, apparently, a kind of rough tenderness towards the man whom he had condemned in the form which Pilate had ordered. He would, at least, recognize his claims to be in some sense a king. The priests obviously felt it to imply such a recognition, a declaration, as it were, to them and to the people that One who had a right to be their king, who was the only kind of a king they were ever likely to have, had died the death of a malefactor." Attention has been called by writers on inspiration to the difference between the superscription over Jesus given by one Evangelist and that given by another. No two of them are alike. Matthew says it was: *This is Jesus,* THE KING OF THE JEWS; Mark: THE KING OF THE JEWS; Luke: *This is*—THE KING OF THE JEWS; and John: *Jesus of Nazareth,* THE KING OF THE JEWS. It is admissible to suppose that the title in full, read: *This is Jesus of Nazareth,* THE KING OF THE JEWS. In copying it, Mark thought it sufficient to give only the essential part, the accusation, omitting the introductory words; Luke also thought it unnecessary to give the name, and therefore copied the accusation, with the introductory words, *this is;* Matthew gave all but the adjective signifying *of Nazareth;* and John omitted the less important *this is,* giving the name in full and the accusation. No one of them added anything to what was written; no one omitted any word of the accusation. Historians of perfect veracity are doing the same thing continually. To say that this or that was said, is not, ordinarily, to affirm that this or that is *all* that was said. If nothing is omitted which changes the meaning of what is repeated, there is often no reason for saying that anything is omitted. We regard, therefore, such differences as appear in the several copies of this title made by the Evangelists as entirely consistent with the doctrine of *plenary* inspiration.

20. This title then (*therefore*) (οὖν) **read many of the Jews.** The reading of it was a natural consequence of its being placed on the cross, and also, of its being placed there by au-

21 Then said the chief priests of the Jews to Pilate, Write not, The King of the Jews; but that he said, I am King of the Jews.
22 Pilate answered, What I have written I have written.
23 *Then the soldiers, when they had crucified Jesus, took his garments, and made four parts, to every soldier a part; and also *his* coat: now the coat was without seam, woven from the top throughout.

21 The chief priests of the Jews therefore said to Pilate, Write not, The King of the Jews; but, that he said, I am King of the Jews. Pilate answered, What I have written I have written.
23 The soldiers therefore, when they had crucified Jesus, took his garments, and made four parts, to every soldier a part; and also the ¹coat: now the ¹coat was without seam, woven from the top

a Matt. 27 : 35 ; Mark 15 : 24 ; Luke 23 : 34.—1 Or, *tunic.*

thority, and not less, perhaps, of its character, so displeasing to the Jews. For the first priest that read it, would be likely to speak of it to his companions with keen dissatisfaction, and so the knowledge of it would spread. **For the place where Jesus was crucified was nigh to the city:** and, therefore, many visited Golgotha, and when there, read the superscription. The nearness of the place was a reason why so many read the offensive title. **And it was written in Hebrew,** *and* **Greek,** *and* **Latin.** So that all who passed by could read it for themselves, if they could read at all. The natives of Palestine were, of course, familiar with their mother tongue— the Aramaic, here called the Hebrew. Jews born in foreign lands, but sojourning at this time in Jerusalem (see Acts 2: 8-11), would be likely to know the Greek, as would many of other nations. And some of the Romans connected with Pilate's army would probably know how to read the Latin only. It is possible that the full superscription was written in but one of these languages, while only the more important part of it was written in the others. But there is no evidence of this in the Gospel narratives.

21. Then said the chief priests of the Jews. The Revised Version is probably correct in rendering the conjunction (οὖν), *therefore,* instead of *then;* for the sequence is logical rather than temporal. John conceives of the remonstrance of these Jewish priests as occasioned by the case with which all who passed that way could read the title over Jesus, as it was written in three languages. The expression, "chief priests *of the Jews,*" is not found elsewhere in the New Testament, but may be accounted for by the writer's desire to emphasize the fact that they belonged to the leading Jewish party that had compassed the death of Christ. **Write not, The King of the Jews; but that he said, I am King of the Jews.** This request of the priests was natural, and indeed, plausible.

But it did not fairly represent what Jesus had said of himself, either to them or to the governor. When conjured by the high priest, in answer to the question, "Art thou the Christ, the Son of God?" he had said, "I am; and ye shall see the Son of man sitting at the right hand of power, and coming with the clouds of heaven." Upon this, the high priest had rent his clothes and accused him of blasphemy. (See Matt. 26: 63-66; Mark 14: 61-64; Luke 22: 67-71; John 10: 7.) Taking this answer of Jesus as it was understood by the Sanhedrin, we must deny that it was a claim to being king of the Jews, in any ordinary sense of that expression. In answer to Pilate's question, "Art thou a king, then?" he affirmed that he was; but proceeded to explain his kingship, not as placing him over the Jews, as a people, but as clothing him with authority as a witness to the truth over all genuine lovers of the truth (John 18: 36, 37). It is clear, then, that these "chief priests of the Jews" wished to have the title changed, not for truth's sake, but to escape the sting that was felt to be in it.

22. Pilate answered, What I have written I have written. In other words: "The thing is done and cannot be changed; the word is spoken and cannot be revoked; I have written once for all, and the matter is settled." For the procurator has no desire to gratify these Jewish zealots. On the contrary, he is pleased to show them his independence.

23, 24. THE SOLDIERS DIVIDE HIS GARMENTS AMONG THEMSELVES.

23. This verse resumes the narrative of the crucifixion by the soldiers at the point reached in verse 18—the narrative concerning the *title* over Christ having taken the writer along to a somewhat later point. The connecting particle (οὖν) should be rendered *therefore,* instead of *then.* For, as a consequence of their having crucified Jesus, **the soldiers took his garments**—"the head-gear, the outer

24 They said therefore among themselves, Let us not rend it, but cast lots for it, whose it shall be: that the Scripture might be fulfilled, which saith, *They parted my raiment among them, and for my vesture they did cast lots. These things therefore the soldiers did..

24 throughout. They said therefore one to another, Let us not rend it, but cast lots for it, whose it shall be: that the scripture might be fulfilled, which saith, They parted my garments among them, And upon my vesture did they cast lots.

a Ps. 22: 18.

cloak-like garment, the girdle, and the sandals."—*Edersheim.* **And made four parts, to every soldier a part:** from which it appears that they were but four in number—a quaternion. (Acts 12: 4.) If, as many infer from Matt. 27: 54; Mark 15: 39; Luke 23: 47, there was a centurion over the four, he did not share in the division of raiment. "It is generally stated, that this [division of the criminal's raiment among the executioners,] was the common Roman custom. But of this there is no evidence, and in later times it was expressly forbidden (Ulpianus 'Digest,' 48, 20, 6). I cannot see how *Keim*, and, after him, *Nebe*, infers from this as certain, that the law had formerly been the opposite."—*Edersheim.* But a prohibitory law implies a more or less prevalent *custom*, against which it was aimed, and this custom explains the word *therefore*, by which John connects the division of the garments with the act of crucifixion. **And also his coat**, or *tunic* (χιτων), the garment worn next the skin, and covering the whole body from shoulder to ankle. **Now the coat was without seam, woven from the top throughout.** "Besides these four articles of dress, there was the seamless, woven, inner garment, by far the most valuable of all, and for which, as it could not be partitioned without being destroyed, they would specially cast lots."—*Edersheim.* "Specially"—because, as Edersheim thinks, they had previously cast lots for their several portions in the four less important garments. But this is by no means certain. Matthew, says, that *they parted his garments, casting lots;* and Mark, *they parted his garments, casting lots upon them, what every man should take;* and even the words of Mark might be used, we think, by one who intended to characterize the division, briefly, as one in which lots were used, though not, perhaps, for every article. Edersheim remarks, still further: "It is deeply significant, that the dress of the priests was not sewed, but woven (Sebach. 85a), and especially so, that of the high priest." Having quoted so freely from Edersheim, "The Life and Times of Jesus, the Messiah"—a work of great value—it may not be out of place to add, that we see no reason for his statement regarding the *time* when this division of the Saviour's garments was effected, viz.: "Before nailing him to the cross, the soldiers parted among themselves the poor, worldly inheritance of his raiment." It was *after*, rather than *before*, according to the obvious meaning of all the narratives.

24. Note the particularity of this description, as if the writer had been present, seeing and hearing. **That the Scripture might be fulfilled.** Nothing was unforeseen or unprovided for in the plan of God. "Him, being delivered up by the determinate counsel and foreknowledge of God, ye, by the hand of lawless men, did crucify and slay," (*Rev. Ver.*,) said Peter, to the men of Israel, on the Day of Pentecost. And, therefore, the apostles were not surprised to find the events of Christ's death foreshadowed or foretold in the Old Testament. The Scripture quoted is the eighteenth verse of the twenty-second Psalm —a Psalm which must be interpreted as referring to Christ. Perowne believes that reference to be typical, but adds: "Whether, however, we take the Psalm as typical or predictive, in any case, it is a prophecy of Christ, and of his sufferings on the cross." On the other hand, Weiss affirms that it was understood by John as a direct prediction: "*that the Scripture*, etc., namely, Ps. 22: 18, verbally according to the Septuagint; yet, not understood typically, of the old theocratic sufferer (*Meyer*), or of David (*Luthardt and Godet*), but directly, of Christ." Westcott seems to agree with Weiss: "The central thought in the original context is that the enemies of the Lord's Anointed treated him as already dead, and so disposed of his raiment." For other citations from Psalm 22, see Matt. 27: 39, 43, 46; John 19: 28, below; and Heb. 2: 12. **These things therefore the soldiers did. Therefore,** that is, because they were predicted in Scripture, or, looking a little more deeply, because they were included in the purpose God as made known in part by the Holy Scriptures.

JOHN.

25 a Now there stood by the cross of Jesus his mother, and his mother's sister, Mary the *wife* of b Cleophas, and Mary Magdalene.
26 When Jesus therefore saw his mother, and the disciple standing by, whom he loved, he saith unto his mother, d Woman, behold thy son!
27 Then saith he to the disciple, Behold thy mother! And from that hour that disciple took her e unto his own *home*.

25 These things therefore the soldiers did. But there were standing by the cross of Jesus his mother, and his mother's sister, Mary, the *wife* of Clopas, and
26 Mary Magdalene. When Jesus therefore saw his mother, and the disciple standing by, whom he loved, he saith unto his mother, Woman, behold,
27 thy son! Then saith he to the disciple, Behold, thy mother! And from that hour the disciple took her unto his own *home*.

a Matt. 27: 55; Mark 15: 40; Luke 23: 49....b Luke 24: 18....c ch. 13: 23; 20: 2; 21: 7, 20, 24....d ch. 2: 4....e ch. 1: 11; 16: 32.

25-27. JESUS COMMITS HIS MOTHER TO THE CARE OF JOHN.

25. Now there stood. Better: *but there were standing.* See Revised Version, above. **By the cross of Jesus.** Mark speaks of a group of three women, apparently the same as these, with the exception of the mother of Jesus, as *beholding from afar.* (Mark 15: 40; Matt. 27: 55, 56.) This has been pronounced inconsistent with what is here said by John. But unwarrantably; for *by* and *from afar*, are terms of uncertain force. As seen from the city the women might be properly described as standing by the cross, when, as seen from the cross itself, they might be described as looking on from a distance. Besides—and this is of special importance—the women may not have remained all the time at the same point. After John had taken the mother of Jesus away, the rest of the group may have taken a position farther from the cross. His **mother**—who is not mentioned by the other Evangelists, perhaps because she had gone away with John at the time they refer to—**and his mother's sister**—probably Salome (Mark) "the mother of" James and John, "Zebedee's sons" (Matthew.)—**Mary the wife of Cleophas**—identical with "Mary the mother of James the less, and Joses" (Mark)—**and Mary Magdalene**—mentioned also by name in the first two Gospels. Many interpreters identify **Mary the wife of Cleophas** with **his mother's sister;** so that only three women are mentioned by John. . But it is improbable that there were two sisters of the same name in a family; it is also improbable that John has made no mention of one of the three women standing with the Lord's mother. On the other hand, if Salome was his mother, it would be like him to designate her indirectly as here, and by her relation to the Lord's mother rather than by her relation to himself.

26. It was reserved for John to relate this beautiful and touching incident. Why the earlier Evangelists passed it by in silence is no more perplexing than their silence in respect to many other events in the life of Christ. A great deal must be omitted in their narratives; but only the Spirit of God could guide each one of them in deciding what it was best for him to insert or to omit. Yet that Spirit certainly adapted his influence to the mind and heart of every writer, making holy use of tender recollections and peculiar experiences, whenever this could be done in furtherance of truth. In the light of this principle we can see why John would be moved to put on record this incident. He remembered it perfectly. The words of his suffering Master were few, and freighted with kindness. No wonder he referred to himself in such a connection, as "the disciple whom Jesus loved." "Criticism," says Weiss-Meyer, "finds in this designation of himself an evidence of *vanity (Scholten)*, or of assumption, offensive self-exaltation (*Weiss*). But a consciousness of being specially loved by the Lord, true, clear, and still glowing with inward strength in the heart of the grey old man, is inconceivable without the deepest humility, and has found its fittest expression and its holy right in the simple description, *whom he loved.*" **Woman, behold thy son!** The address, **woman,** was entirely respectful (see Note on 2: 4), and no doubt true to the divine-human feeling of Jesus as well as profoundly kind to his mother. **Behold thy son!** "Lo, this man is to be thy son; showing to thee all the care and kindness of a son"; or, perhaps, "Lo, thy son," let this man be regarded by thee as a son; expect from him a son's care and love." But no paraphrase can be so appropriate and significant as the words of Jesus.

27. Behold thy mother! "Let her receive from thee the love and tender care which thou wouldest render to a mother." **And from that hour that disciple took her unto his own home.** *The disciple*, not

28 After this, Jesus knowing that all things were now accomplished, *that the Scripture might be fulfilled, saith, I thirst.

28 After this Jesus, knowing that all things are now finished, that the scripture might be accomplished,

a Ps 69: 21.

that disciple, is the correct rendering; but *the disciple* means, of course, the one just mentioned by the writer, and as addressed by the Saviour. **From that hour,** etc., may signify the removal of the Lord's mother at once from her place by the cross to his own residence in the city. If so, it was done in order to withdraw her from a spectacle of suffering which it was unwise for her longer to witness. But the language does not require us to believe that she was led away at once from Calvary. It may only mean that thenceforth John received the mother of Jesus into his family; giving her a home and such care as he would have given had she been his own mother. If, however, he conducted her immediately to his abode in Jerusalem, he soon returned to Golgotha. Yet absence for even an hour might account for his omitting to record some of the Lord's words on the cross, as preserved in the other Gospels; for this Evangelist limits his narrative, for the most part, to what he had himself seen or heard. But why did Jesus select John, rather than one of "his brethren," to have care of his mother? Possibly because his brothers were not in circumstances to give her a home. Possibly, because they did not yet believe on him. But, probably, because John was specially loved by the Saviour, and had just those qualities of mind and heart which fitted him to render the service contemplated, in the most satisfactory manner.

28-38. CIRCUMSTANCES OF THE LORD'S DEATH.

Jesus was nailed to the cross about 9 A. M. (Matt. 15: 25.) From 12 M., until 3 P. M., a supernatural darkness covered the land. (Matt. 27: 45.) About 3 P. M. was heard the cry: "My God, my God, why hast thou forsaken me?" (Matt. 27: 46.) Then followed the events which John proceeds to relate.

28. After this, does not signify "directly after this," but allows of an interval between the events related. In this case, several hours had passed since Jesus committed his mother to the care of John—at least, the three hours of darkness. **Jesus knowing that all things were now accomplished.** Better,

with the Revised Version, *that all things are now finished;* for thus the parallelism between this expression and the words of Jesus: It is finished, in verse 30, is preserved. The same form of the same Greek verb is used in both cases, viz.: (τετέλεσται.) By "all things is here naturally meant his whole life work (17:4), including his giving himself up to death, which was already accomplished before death entered."—*Weiss.* The words, *that the Scripture might be accomplished,* (Rev. Ver.), may be connected, either with the preceding clause: *that all things are now finished;* or, with the following: *saith, I thirst,* etc. With the former connection, the words, **saith, I thirst,** and the act consequent upon them, are not here regarded as a part of the fulfillment of Scripture; with the latter, they are a final act in that fulfillment. Christ's labor and suffering being finished, he completes the fulfilment of prophecy by seeking an instant's relief from thirst—and then expires. This seems to us the true sense of the passage, though the Greek formula, translated **that the Scripture might be fulfilled,** elsewhere refers to a preceding rather than to a subsequent clause. Westcott pertinently remarks: "The incident loses its full significance unless it be regarded as one element in the foreshadowed course of the Passion. Nor is there any difficulty in the phrase 'are now finished,' as preceding it. The 'thirst' was already felt, and the feeling included the confession of it. The fulfillment of the Scripture (it need scarcely be added) was not the object which the Lord had in view in uttering the word, but there was a necessary correspondence between his acts and the divine foreshadowing of them." This word of Jesus, viz: **I thirst,** seems to have followed very closely on the cry, "My God, my God, why hast thou forsaken me?" so that both had an influence upon the bystanders, leading to the act which is next described. For Mark, after recording the great cry of Jesus, says, that "some of them that stood by, when they heard it, said: Behold, he calleth Elijah. And one ran, and filling a sponge full of vinegar, put it on a reed, and gave him to drink."—(Rev. Ver.)

CH. XIX.] JOHN. 387

29 Now there was set a vessel full of vinegar: and they filled a sponge with vinegar, and put *it* upon hyssop, and put *it* to his mouth.
30 When Jesus therefore had received the vinegar, he said, *b* It is finished: and he bowed his head and gave up the ghost.

29 saith, I thirst. There was set there a vessel full of vinegar: so they put a sponge full of the vinegar 30 upon hyssop, and brought it to his mouth. When Jesus therefore had received the vinegar, he said, It is finished: and he bowed his head, and gave up his spirit.

a Matt. 27: 48....*b* ch. 17: 4.

(Mark 15: 35, 36; comp. Matt. 27: 47, 48.) It is, however, observable that neither Matthew nor Mark mentions any direct connection between the cry of Jesus and the act of offering him "vinegar" to drink; nor is it obvious why that cry, of itself alone, should have suggested the idea of intolerable thirst. But that cry revealed extreme agony, and when the Saviour added presently, with a lower voice, **I thirst**, there was some one ready to respond. Thus the Gospel of John incidentally provides a "missing link" to the narratives of Matthew and Mark.

29. Now there was set a vessel full of vinegar. The Revised Version omits the copula **now**, as not supported by the earliest manuscripts; but the omission leaves the meaning of the clause unchanged. The **vinegar** here spoken of, is supposed to have been a kind of sour wine mingled with water, used by the soldiers—not a stupefying drink, like that which the Saviour had previously refused. (Matt. 27: 34; Mark 15: 23.) *So they put a sponge full of the vinegar upon hyssop, and brought it to his mouth.*—(Rev. Ver.) Scholars are not yet agreed as to what particular plant was called hyssop by the Jews. Alford expresses very well the prevailing opinion, describing it "as an aromatic plant, growing on walls, common in the south of England, and on the Continent, with blue or white flowers, and having stalks about one foot and a half long, which would, in this case, be long enough; the feet of the crucified person not being ordinarily raised above that distance from the ground." See the Bible Dictionaries under "Hyssop." The first two Gospels speak of "a reed" merely, as used to raise the moistened sponge to the sufferer's lips; but John specifies the kind of reed employed. It was "hyssop."

30. When Jesus therefore had received the vinegar. As the words "I thirst," were virtually a request for drink, to relieve for a moment the intolerable thirst produced by hanging on the cross, so these words of the Evangelist show that he accepted the vinegar, given for his relief and refreshment. **It is finished: and he bowed his head, and gave up the ghost** (or, *his spirit.*) All that he was to do and suffer in his earthly life, was now completed. Knowing this, he appears to have uttered, strongly, the single word which signifies: *It is finished.* Whether Matthew refers to this word, when he says, that "Jesus cried again with a loud voice" (27: 50), and Mark, when he says, that "Jesus uttered a loud voice (15: 37), must be considered somewhat doubtful; but Jesus undoubtedly added to this cry the saying preserved by Luke (23: 46): "Father, into thy hands I commend my spirit." Geikie writes: "A moment more, and all was over. The cloud had passed as suddenly as it rose. Far and wide, over the vanquished throngs of his enemies, with a loud voice, as if uttering his shout of eternal victory, before entering into his glory, he cried, It is finished! then, more gently, came the words: Father, into thy hands I commend my spirit. A moment more, and there rose a great cry, as of mortal agony: the head fell. He was dead." But if the cry was distinct from the word, *It is finished*, it must have followed that word and preceded the sentence, "Father, into thy hands I commend my spirit"—unless, indeed, with the marginal reading of the Revised Version, we identify the "cry with a loud voice" with the saying, "Father, into thy hands," etc. This seems to us a less probable interpretation; but Geikie's is impossible. On the whole, we reject the view that Jesus uttered any loud, inarticulate cry, "as of mortal agony," before expiring. His physical nature never conquered his soul, either in the garden or on the cross. *Gave up his spirit*, is clearer than **gave up the ghost.** The word translated **gave up** (παρέδωκεν), signifies properly, *delivered up*, and indicates a perfectly conscious, voluntary act. Says Prof. Milligan: "The choice of the word leaves no doubt as to the meaning of the Evangelist. However true it is, that by the cruelty of man the death upon the cross was brought about as by its natural cause, there

31 The Jews therefore, *a* because it was the preparation, *b* that the bodies should not remain upon the cross on the sabbath day, (for that sabbath day was an high day,) besought Pilate that their legs might be broken, and *that* they might be taken away.
32 Then came the soldiers, and brake the legs of the first, and of the other which was crucified with him.

31 The Jews therefore, because it was the Preparation, that the bodies should not remain on the cross upon the sabbath (for the day of that sabbath was a high *day*), asked of Pilate that their legs might be broken, and *that* they might be taken away.
32 The soldiers therefore came, and brake the legs of the first, and of the other who was crucified with

a Mark 15: 42; ver. 42....*b* Deut. 21: 23.

was something deeper and more solemn in it, of which we must take account. It was his own free will to die. There is in him an everpresent life and power, and choice, in which he, even at the very last moment, offers himself as a sacrifice." (Heb. 9: 14.) And the Weiss-Meyer Commentary says: "The expression, 'he gave over (to God) his spirit,' characterizes his dying as voluntary, since the separation of the soul (or, spirit) from the body, took place by his consciously and freely entering into the will of his Father, though it was nevertheless accomplished in accordance with natural law." That is to say, Christ at this moment, in harmony with his Father's will, allowed his body to succumb to the destructive natural forces assailing it, and delivered up his spirit to God. He did not take his own life; but he freely decided no longer to prevent its being taken by sinful men. So his natural life ended; but his life in the spirit continued. And thus were fulfilled his own words: "I lay down my life, that I may take it again. No one taketh it away from me, but I lay it down of myself." (Rev. Ver.) (10: 18.) The essential fact is this: that in the supreme act of his atoning work, Jesus made his Father's will his own will, and offered himself in sacrifice to God. To the very last moment, and in the parting of soul from body, he was free, consciously and perfectly free, doing all and suffering all without constraint, save that of love to God and man.

31. **The Jews therefore**—namely, the leading men who had sought the death of Jesus. **Because it was the preparation.** The word **preparation** has no article before it in the Greek text, because it is used as a proper name. Hence, the Revised Version begins the word with a capital—*Preparation.* And here, certainly, it means a day of preparation for the Sabbath, not for the passover. "Preparation" was, therefore, a name for the Christian Friday. "These words, therefore, so far from supporting the view of those who think that the legal passover had not yet been celebrated, tend rather in the opposite direction."—*Schaff.* It was a Roman custom to leave the bodies of criminals to decay on the cross; but the law of Moses provided, that if the body of an executed criminal were hung on a tree, it should not remain all night upon the tree, but should be buried the same day, lest the land be defiled. (Deut. 21: 23.) This rule may have been often disregarded. Indeed, the Jews are not said to have been influenced by it in the present case, but by the fact that a specially holy Sabbath was at hand. Yet the ritualistic principle determined their action. **For that sabbath day was a high day.** Literally: *for great was the day of that Sabbath.* Its greatness was due to the fact that it was the Sabbath of the passover festival. **That their legs might be broken.** Evidently, in this case, for the purpose of hastening death. For persons generally survived the sufferings of the cross more than one day, and sometimes several days. The breaking of the legs was sometimes employed by the Romans as a distinct punishment (Sueton, "August" 67; Seneca, "De Ira." III. 32; Euseb. "H. E." V. 21.) But Lactantius speaks as if the *crucifragium* were customary, with a view to an early death. His words are these: "Therefore, because fastened to the cross, he had delivered up his spirit, the executioners did not think it necessary to break his bones, *as was their custom* (sicut mos eorum ferebat), but they only pierced his side" ("Inst. Div." IV. 26.) **And that they might be taken away:** it being assumed that they would soon be dead, and their removal consistent with Roman justice.

32. **Then came the soldiers**—(or, *The soldiers therefore came.*) For Pilate had yielded to the request of the Jews, and had given them authority to employ the soldiers in this way also. We understand by the **soldiers** the four who had attended to the crucifixion of Jesus and his two fellow-sufferers. Probably these soldiers were still on guard, near the place of crucifixion, possibly two on either

33 But when they came to Jesus, and saw that he was dead already, they brake not his legs:
34 But one of the soldiers with a spear pierced his side, and forthwith *came there out blood and water.

33 him: but when they came to Jesus, and saw that he was dead already, they brake not his legs: howbeit one of the soldiers with a spear pierced his side, and straightway there came out blood and

a 1 John 5: 6, 8.

wing of the line of crosses, though at a little distance, so as not to be annoyed by the ordinary groans of the sufferers. Naturally, then, two of them would break the limbs of one robber, and two of them those of the other robber, when they might all draw near the body of Jesus, now perfectly still in death. It was cruel and ghastly work; but they were familiar with blood, and cared little for human life. In the arena, and on the battle field, they had learned to despise pain, and almost honor ferocity.

33. But when they came to Jesus, and saw that he was dead already, they brake not his legs. Thus the certainty of Christ's death is vouched for; in the first place, by the unambiguous statement of John (ver. 30), next, by his declaration that the soldiers, who would not be likely to err in such a case, saw that he was dead, and, finally, by his account of their treatment of his body. Moreover, there is no reason to doubt the presence of John near the cross of his Master, at this time, enabling him to bear personal witness to everything which he relates. To reject this part of his Gospel is to reject it all.

34. If, as we are told, the soldiers saw that he was dead, why did one of them thrust his spear into the side of Jesus? Would not such an act have been motiveless and absurd? We think not. The soldiers were rough men, not unwilling to use their arms on slight occasion. Though they considered Jesus dead, it is not surprising that one of them, to make his death doubly sure, thrust a spear into his side. Paulus supposes that the spear wounded very slightly the side of Jesus. But the Commentary of Weiss-Meyer correctly shows, that "neither the word itself (since νύσσειν is commonly the violent thrust or stab), nor the person of the rude soldier, nor the weapon (a lance belonging to heavy armor), nor the design of the thrust, nor the size of the wound, as suggested by 20: 27, nor the 'pierced' (ἐξεκέντησαν) of ver. 29, allow the view required in the interest of a 'seeming death,' that the wound inflicted was only a scratch." **And forthwith came there out blood and water.** This statement of the Evangelist has been a source of perplexity to Biblical scholars, chiefly because blood does not flow from a wound inflicted on a dead body. Hence, some have inferred that Jesus was not quite dead until the spear reached his heart. But this inference is contradicted by the plain testimony of the Evangelist. (ver. 30, 33.) Others have inferred that the process of change from a natural to a spiritual body began at the instant of death, so that "the issuing of the blood and water from his side, must be regarded as a sign of life in death."—*Westcott.* But it is certainly difficult to believe that any such thought was in the mind of the sacred writer. Indeed, the death of Christ seems to have been regarded by all the New Testament writers as a real and complete death. And he was raised on the morning of the third day, not by a process going on while he was in the tomb, and completed the third day. Of this modern theory, the Scriptures know nothing. Dr. Schaff has suggested, that the spear wound may have been inflicted the *instant after death*, that the region of the heart may have been penetrated by the spear, that the importance of the "blood and water," in the eyes of John, was *wholly* due to their symbolical meaning, that the quantity of "blood and water" having nothing to do with their meaning, may have been very small, and that it has never been proved that a *small* quantity might not issue from a wound thus inflicted. For the symbolical import of "blood and water," in the eyes of John, we must look into the writings of this apostle. And doing this, we find, that *blood* represents life surrendered; in the case of Christ, life surrendered in sacrifice for sin (1:29), or, life laid down for the life of the world. (6:51-56; 10:15.) We also find that *water* represents the Holy Spirit, as given by Christ, for the quickening and purifying of men. (4:13, 14; 7:38, 39.) "Cleansing from sin [in the sense of forgiveness] and quickening by the

35 And he that saw *it* bare record, and his record is true; and he knoweth that he saith true, that ye might believe.
36 For these things were done, *a* that the scripture should be fulfilled, A bone of him shall not be broken.
37 And again another scripture saith, *b* They shall look on him whom they pierced.
38 *c* And after this Joseph of Arimathea, being a disciple of Jesus, but secretly *d* for fear of the Jews, be-

35 water. And he that hath seen hath borne witness, and his witness is true: and he knoweth that he saith true, that ye also may believe. For these things came to pass that the scripture might be fulfilled, A bone of him shall not be ¹ broken. And again another scripture saith, They shall look on him whom they pierced.
39 And after these things Joseph of Arimathea, being a disciple of Jesus, but secretly for fear of

---

a Ex. 12: 46; Num. 9: 12; Ps. 34: 20....*b* Ps. 22: 16, 17; Zech. 12: 10; Rev. 1: 7....*c* Matt. 27: 57; Mark 15: 43; Luke 2: 50....*d* ch. 9: 22; 12: 42.—1 Or, *crushed.*

Spirit are both consequent on Christ's death." — *Westcott.* Whether or not this passage is to be associated with 1 John 5: 5, is doubtful.

35. And he that saw it bare record, etc. Better, as in the Revised Version: *And he that hath seen hath borne witness, and his witness is true; and he knoweth that he saith true, that ye also may believe.* In this verse, John speaks of himself in the third person, and without giving his name. See other passages where he evidently does the same thing. (e. *g.* ¶ 40; 1*n*: 15 *sq*.) He also affirms of the witness he bears, that it is *true* (ἀληθινή), that is, genuine, real, fulfilling the proper idea of testimony—"all that testimony can be." The word in the next clause is different in the original, denoting the truthfulness or veracity of the witness. In other words, the Evangelist assures his readers that his testimony is that of an eye-witness, whose circumstances enabled him to know accurately that whereof he has testified, and who is conscious of having stated the exact truth. And to this he adds the object which has moved him to bear witness to the events of Christ's death, and to assure them so positively of the trustworthy character of his testimony, namely—that his readers might believe—not merely in the facts which he has related concerning Christ, but also, and chiefly, through those facts, in Jesus Christ himself, as the Son of God and the Saviour of men.

36. For these things were done (or, *came to pass*) **that the scripture should be fulfilled, A bone of him shall not be broken.** Evidently the Apostle John believed that the peculiar features of Christ's death had been embraced in the purpose of God, and foreshadowed by the language of Scripture. The language quoted is, we suppose, derived from Ex. 12: 46: "Neither shall ye break a bone thereof," and Num. 9: 12: "They shall leave none of it unto the morning, nor break any bone of it." In the former passage, the reference is to the lamb of pass-

over, slain in Egypt; in the lattter passage, it is to the paschal lamb, eaten at the yearly passover. But John could not have found in the circumstance that the legs of Jesus were not broken, a fulfillment of either of these passages, unless he had seen in the paschal lamb a type of the Messiah. (Comp. Ps. 34: 20.)

37. They shall look on him whom they pierced. See Zech. 12: 10, which Henderson translates: "They shall look unto me whom they have pierced." In the original passage, *me* refers to Jehovah. Hence, probably, the reluctance of Jewish interpreters to allow that the pronoun *whom*, stands for *me*; hence, also, the change of texts in several manuscripts from *me* to *him*. John substitutes him for me, because he is speaking *of* the One to whom they were looking. He does not change the meaning of the original expression, but merely adjusts it to his narrative. And he follows the Hebrew rather than the Septuagint Version, because the latter does not give the sense of the former. The passage seems to be quoted by John as partly fulfilled by the thrust of the soldier's spear, piercing the side of Jesus; for this act he regards as the act of the Jewish people, to whom Jesus had been delivered up for crucifixion. (Comp. Acts 2: 23.) Of course, their looking to him for blessing was expected in the future; for the people were now piercing him, and the language of Zechariah supposes that the *looking* would be subsequent to the *piercing*. We may therefore see, in John's use of this Scripture, evidence that he regarded it as in some true sense Messianic, that he considered Jesus the true Messiah and proper representative of Jehovah, who was the subject of the ancient prophecy quoted, and that he also, as well as Paul, expected the ultimate conversion of Israel.

38-42. THE BURIAL OF JESUS BY JOSEPH OF ARIMATHEA AND NICODEMUS.

38. And after this, should be, *And after*

sought Pilate that he might take away the body of Jesus: and Pilate gave *him* leave. He came therefore, and took the body of Jesus.

39 And there came also ᵃ Nicodemus, (which at the first came to Jesus by night,) and brought a mixture of myrrh and aloes, about an hundred pound *weight*.

the Jews, asked of Pilate that he might take away the body of Jesus: and Pilate gave *him* leave. He 39 came therefore, and took away his body. And there came also Nicodemus, he who at the first came to him by night, bringing a ¹ mixture of myrrh and aloes, about a hundred pound *weight*.

a ch. 3: 1, 2; 7: 50——b Some ancient authorities read, *roll*.

these things—referring, doubtless, to the events related in the preceding paragraph, though the phrase is one that may have a more general reference to the whole scene of the crucifixion. **Joseph of Arimathea, being a disciple of Jesus, but secretly, for fear of the Jews.** Luke speaks of Arimathea as "a city of the Jews," meaning probably a city of Judea. It is thought to have been identical with Ramah, the birthplace of Samuel the prophet (see 1 Samuel 1: 1, 19), which is called by the Seventy, Armathaim, and by Josephus, Armatha. ("Ant." V. 10, 2.) It was situated about five miles north of Jerusalem, on the way to Bethel. Matthew calls Joseph a "rich man" (27: 57), Mark, an "honourable counsellor, which also waited for the kingdom of God" (15: 43), and Luke, "a counsellor, and he was a good man and just; the same had not consented to the counsel and deed of them." (23: 50, 51.) From John's remark, that he was a **disciple of Jesus, but secretly, for fear of the Jews,** we conclude that he considered the character of Joseph very similar to that of Nicodemus. Both were members of the Sanhedrin. Both were drawn to Jesus by his spirit and teaching. Both were convinced that he was from God, and, perhaps, the promised Christ. Both refused to take any part in persecuting him. (See John 7: 50, 51, and Luke 23: 51.) Both testified their respect and perhaps reverence for Jesus after his crucifixion. Yet, both were afraid to make a public avowal of their discipleship, because they dreaded the fierce fanaticism of their associates in the Great Council. **Besought Pilate.** The word translated **besought**, might, with equal or greater propriety, have been translated *asked;* for there is nothing in the word itself, or in the circumstances related, which points to entreaty, or, indeed, to anything more than a simple request. There was no law or custom violated by the act of Joseph; and, if he had watched the course of events during the day, he had no reason to suppose that Pilate would be unwilling to grant his request. If he had any one to fear, it was not the governor, but the chief priests. When, therefore, Mark says, that "he boldly went in unto Pilate, and asked for the body of Jesus," we take the word "boldly" to be expressive of his spirit and bearing, in view of all the circumstances of the hour, but do not regard it as implying that his request was likely to provoke the anger of Pilate. The governor was probably at the time glad to show any possible favor to the friends of Jesus, as a further token of his displeasure with the Jews. Accordingly, having assured himself that Jesus was already dead (Matt. 15: 44), he gave Joseph leave to take away his body; and Joseph, in consequence of this permission, "**came therefore and took the body of Jesus.**" This is the simple record: unimpassioned, unadorned, natural, trustworthy.

39. But Joseph of Arimathea was not alone in showing respect to his crucified Lord by attending to the burial of his body. **There came also Nicodemus (which at the first came to Jesus by night), and brought a mixture of myrrh and aloes, about a hundred pound weight.** Thus John takes occasion, in a quiet way, to recall the bearing of this "teacher of Israel," when he first came timidly to Jesus. Then he came by night; now he testifies openly his regard for the crucified One. The quantity of myrrh and aloes—**about a hundred pound weight**—has been thought unreasonable. But there seems to have been no rule, save that of affection or ability, by which the amount of aromatics used in burial should be determined. The more exalted and beloved the person whose body was to be laid away in a tomb, the greater, as a rule, would be the costliness and amount of the spices used. Thus in 2 Chron. 16: 14, it is said of Asa the king, that "they buried him in his own sepulchre, which he had made for himself in the city of David; and laid him in the bed which was filled with sweet odours and divers kinds of spices, prepared by the apothecaries' art." Jesus was loved and honored by Nicodemus, and we

40 Then took they the body of Jesus, and a wound it in linen clothes with the spices, as the manner of the Jews is to bury.
41 Now in the place where he was crucified there was a garden; and in the garden a new sepulchre, wherein was never man yet laid.
42 b There laid they Jesus therefore, c because of the Jews' preparation day; for the sepulchre was nigh at hand.

40 So they took the body of Jesus, and bound it in linen cloths with the spices, as the custom of the Jews is to bury. Now in the place where he was crucified there was a garden; and in the garden a 42 new tomb wherein was never man yet laid. There then because of the Jews' Preparation (for the tomb was nigh at hand) they laid Jesus.

a Acts 5: 6....b Isa. 53: 9....c ver. 31.

need not hesitate to say, with Westcott: "His intention was, without doubt, to cover the body completely with the mass of aromatics; for this purpose the quantity was not excessive as a costly gift of devotion."

40. Then took they, etc. Better: *Therefore, or, so they took the body of Jesus.* For this act was a natural consequence of what they had done before, as related in ver. 38, 39. The style of John is remarkable for its logical coherence, and when he uses connectives it is generally easy to account for his selection of one rather than another. **And wound it in linen clothes with the spices, as the manner of the Jews is to bury.** The verb in the last clause may be paraphrased, *to prepare for burial,* (as Schaff), though the expression, *to bury,* may fairly be said to include such preparation as is here described. If **the Jews** has the same shade of meaning in this passage which it commonly has in the Fourth Gospel, John means to say that the preparations for burial were, in this case, such as were made by leading Jews at the death of a friend or relative. Jesus was buried as carefully and lovingly, and with as free an expenditure, as custom would justify when persons of wealth and distinction were laid in their costly tombs. He was with the rich in his death. (Isa. 53: 9.) Geikie thus describes the scene: "The whole body, stained as it was with blood, was tenderly washed, and then wrapped in broad bands of linen, within which were thickly strewn powdered myrrh and aloes, which had been provided by Nicodemus, for the imperfect embalmment practiced by the Jews. The ends of the bandages were apparently secured on the inner side with gum, as in the case of the Egyptian dead. A white cloth was finally laid over the face, after a last kiss, the pledge of undying love."

41. Now in the place where he was crucified there was a garden. The word **place** is indefinite. It may denote a larger or a smaller area, according to circumstances. In the present instance, we have nothing to guide us, unless it be the fact that the place of crucifixion was near the city, but outside its walls. In and near cities, particular places, having names of their own, are relatively small; and we are therefore led to think that one spot would scarcely be described as near another, if it were many rods distant. **And in the garden a new sepulchre, wherein was never man yet laid.** Matthew describes this as Joseph's "new tomb, which he had hewed out in the rock." (27: 60.) Mark describes it as "a sepulchre which was hewn out of a rock." (15: 46.) Luke describes it as "a sepulchre that was hewn in stone" (23: 53), adding, with John, "wherein never man before was laid." This last point is probably mentioned, in order to call the reader's attention to the honor which was providentially, yet most willingly paid to Jesus, in the place of his burial. "It was in 'the court' of the tomb that the hasty embalmment—if such it may be called—took place. None of Christ's former disciples seem to have taken part in the burying. . . . Only a few faithful ones, notably among them, Mary Magdalene, and the other Mary, the mother of Jesus, stood over against the tomb, watching at some distance where and how the body of Jesus was laid. It would scarcely have been in accordance with Jewish manners, if these women had mingled more closely with the two Sanhedrists and their attendants. From where they stood they could have had only a dim view of what passed within the court; and this may explain how, on their return, they prepared 'spices and ointments' for the more full honors which they hoped to pay the dead after the Sabbath was past."—*Edersheim.*

42. There laid they Jesus therefore, because of the Jews' preparation day: for the sepulchre was nigh at hand. See the Revised Version above. This has been thought to show that they did not intend to

CHAPTER XX.

1 THE *first day* of the week cometh Mary Magdalene early, when it was yet dark, unto the sepulchre, and seeth the stone taken away from the sepulchre.

1 Now on the first *day* of the week cometh Mary Magdalene early, while it was yet dark, unto the tomb, and seeth the stone taken away from the

a Matt. 28 : 1 ; Mark 16 : 1 ; Luke 24 : 1.

leave him in that tomb as his permanent burial place. It seems to us rather that the circumstances of the hour led to his being placed in that new tomb. Two reasons are brought together by John. It was the Jews' preparation day; therefore the need of haste; and the place was near, and could be used without waste of time in going to a remote burial-place. The Revised Version follows the order of the Greek text more closely than the Common Version. *There therefore. . . . they laid Jesus.* The whole sentence is more impressive when it is made to close with the principal act.

Ch. 20: 1-10. THE TOMB OF JESUS FOUND EMPTY.

1. The first day of the week cometh Mary Magdalene early, when it was yet dark, unto the sepulchre. This verse is introduced by a particle in the Greek text which may be translated *but* or *now.* John passes over a great many particulars mentioned by some of the other Evangelists. Thus, he says nothing in respect to the putting of a large stone at the door of the sepulchre (Matt. 27: 60; Mark 15: 46), or the sealing of the stone and the setting of a watch by the chief priests and Pharisees (Matt. 27: 62-66), or the earthquake, the rolling away of the stone by an angel, and the terror of the keepers (Matt. 28: 2-4), or the purchase of spices by the women after the Sabbath, with a view to anointing Jesus' body (Mark 16. 1; comp. Luke 24: 1), or the coming of these women, including Mary Magdalene, in a group to the tomb with the spices early on the first day of the week. (Matt. 28: 1; Mark 16: 2-4; Luke 24: 1-3.) Why he omits so much, we need not attempt to explain; why he inserts just what he does, can only be a matter of speculation. It is noticeable that John speaks of the time when Mary Magdalene came to the sepulchre as **early, when it was yet dark.** But Mark speaks of the women as coming to the sepulchre *very early . . . when the sun was risen.—Rev. Ver.* John says, **early;** Mark, *very early;* John says, **when it was yet dark;** Mark, *when the sun was risen.* If Mark, then, contradicts John, does he not also contradict himself? But the latter is not to be supposed. "He must therefore have employed the expression, *when the sun was risen,* in a broader and less definite sense than a literal interpretation of the words would give." "As the sun is the source of light and day, and his earliest rays produce the contrast

STONE AT A JEWISH SEPULCHRE.

between night and dawn, so the term, *sunrising,* might easily come, in popular usage, by a metonomy of cause for effect, to be put for all that earlier interval when his rays, still struggling with darkness, do yet usher in the day. Accordingly, we find such a popular usage existing among the Hebrews and in the Old Testament."—Robinson's "Greek Harmony of the Gospels," p. 230 sq. "But, it is also possible that Mark refers by the words, 'very early,' to the time when the women started from their lodgings to repair to the tomb; and by the words, 'when the sun was risen,' to the time when they were all

2 Then she runneth, and cometh to Simon Peter, and to the other disciple, whom Jesus loved, and saith unto them, They have taken away the Lord out of the sepulchre, and we know not where they have laid him.
3 ᵇ Peter therefore went forth, and that other disciple, and came to the sepulchre.

2 tomb. She runneth therefore, and cometh to Simon Peter, and to the other disciple, whom Jesus loved, and saith unto them, They have taken away the Lord out of the tomb, and we know not where they have 3 laid him. Peter therefore went forth, and the other

a ch. 13: 23; 19: 26; 21: 7, 20, 24....b Luk 24: 12.

assembled at the tomb. This interpretation is defended at length by Gilbert West, in his treatise on the 'Resurrection of Christ,' and it is far more reasonable than the hypothesis of a contradiction between two expressions of Mark, found in one and the same verse." (See the writer's treatise on the "Miracles of Christ as Attested by the Evangelists," p. 281-2.) And seeth the stone taken away from the sepulchre. This remark presupposes the placing of a stone at the door of the sepulchre, as related by Matthew and Mark, though not by John.

2. Then she runneth, and cometh to Simon Peter, etc. The connective (οὖν), should be translated *therefore*, instead of *then;* for the running to tell Peter and John was a consequence of what she saw, and of the inference which she drew from the sight. She did not stop to examine the tomb; but concluded from the taking away of the stone that the body of Jesus had been carried away. But the other women (who had come to the tomb with her, Mary the mother of James and Joses, and Salome the mother of James and John), appear to have tarried awhile to examine the place more carefully. Indeed, they went into the sepulchre, but did not find the body of Jesus. Yet they were permitted to see a vision of angels Matthew and Mark speak of one—the former calling him "the angel," and the latter, "a young man sitting on the right side, clothed in a long white garment" (Matt. 28: 5; Mark 16: 5); but Luke says, that "two men stood by them in shining garments." (24: 4.) Probably, one of the two was prominent, saying the words that are reported. (Matt. 28: 5-7; Mark 16: 6-7; Luke 24: 5-7.) Yet, even these women did not long remain in the sepulchre. Admonished by the angel, they quickly departed from it "with fear and great joy," and ran to announce the resurrection to the disciples. On their way Jesus met them, crying, "Hail!" And drawing near, they held him by the feet and worshiped him. (Matt. 28: 8-10; Mark 16: 8; Luke 24: 9-11.) In this group there was one woman not before named, Joanna

(Luke 24: 4); perhaps there were a few others. Meanwhile, Mary Magdalene had doubtless found Peter and John, and they were hastening to the tomb. For if, as we suppose, the close of Mark's Gospel is genuine, the statement that Jesus appeared *first* to Mary Magdalene must be regarded as relative to the other appearances there related, especially to "after that" in Mark 16: 12; and "afterward" in Mark 16: 14. (Comp. "Robinson's Harmony," p 232.) **They have taken away the Lord out of the sepulchre, and we know not where they have laid him.** This language indicates very clearly that the thought of Christ's resurrection had not entered her mind while returning to the city, and confirms the view that she had left before the other women entered the tomb and saw the vision of angels; for the angel had said to them: "I know that ye seek Jesus, which was crucified. He is not here: for he is risen, as he said." Possibly her words, **We know not where they have laid him,** point to some brief communication of views to one another by the women, as they drew near the tomb and saw that the stone was taken away—these views being represented by the expression, "*We* know not," etc. If so, the first impression on all their minds was the same. They all supposed that the body of Jesus had been removed from the tomb by the hands of his foes. And it is certainly possible, that the scenes of the trial and crucifixion had so deeply impressed on their minds the weakness and mortality of his physical nature as to make his resurrection almost incredible to any of them. Death had triumphed so completely and terribly, as it seemed, over his lacerated and exhausted body, that they could not think of that body as restored to life.

3. **Peter therefore went forth, and that other disciple, and came to the sepulchre.** Notice the precedence given to Peter in this narrative, as almost everywhere else in the Gospel. For the construction is not: "Peter and the other disciple went forth"; but, "Peter went forth, and the other dis-

4 So they ran both together: and the other disciple did outrun Peter, and came first to the sepulchre.
5 And he stooping down, *and looking in*, saw ᵃ the linen clothes lying; yet went he not in.

4 disciple, and they went toward the tomb. And they ran both together: and the other disciple outran
5 Peter, and came first to the tomb; and stooping and looking in, he seeth the linen cloths lying; yet

a ch. 19: 40.

ciple" (Rev. Ver.), the verb being singular, as if the writer thought at first of Peter only. "The other examples of this construction in the Fourth Gospel tend to show that here John intends to set forth Peter as the main person in the narrative: thus the whole ground is cut away from those who hold that the design of this section is to bring 'the other disciple' into peculiar prominence."—*Schaff*. Perhaps the words rendered, **came to the sepulchre,** would be more exactly represented by *were coming toward the sepulchre,* unless it would be still better to say, *were going toward the sepulchre.* For there appears to be no good reason why the first verb (ἐξῆλθεν) should be rendered "*went* forth," and the second verb, (ἤρχοντο) be rendered "*were coming.*" The mental stand-point of the writer probably remained the same in writing the whole verse.

4. So they ran both together. *And*, rather than **so,** is the literal meaning of the connective. The verb **ran,** is in the imperfect tense—*were running*. John recalls the scene perfectly and pictures it to our minds. **And the other disciple did outrun Peter, and came first to the sepulchre.** It has generally been supposed that John was younger than Peter, and that his greater fleetness was due to his comparative youth. But, two men of the same age would not commonly be able to run with equal swiftness; and considerable difference of age would be necessary to account for difference of speed in running. It seems to us, therefore, that we neither have, nor need, any explanation of the fact that John outran Peter. Probably, it was mentioned on account of what follows, and, especially because Peter, though later in reaching the tomb, was first to enter it.

5. And he stooping down, and looking in. The reader will observe that the words, *and looking in*, are italicised in the Common Version, to show that there is nothing answering to them in the original text. On the other hand, these words appear in the Revised Version as a part of the proper translation. Which, then, is more faithful to the original, the Common Version, or the Revised? The answer will illustrate a difficulty often met by translators. The single participle of the Greek text (παρακύψας), signifies, in classic writers, according to Liddell and Scott: 1. "*To stoop sideways;* 2. *To stoop for the purpose of looking at.*" In the New Testament, according to Grimm, it signifies "*to bend towards an object in order to behold it; to look at, with head inclined, to look at, with body inclined,*" that is, stooping or bending towards an object for the purpose of inspecting it. In the one participle, then, we have the two ideas of stooping towards and looking at, distinctly, though not separately, expressed; and nothing is really added to the sense of the original by translating, with the Revised Version, *stooping and looking in.* At the same time, it is evident that the words may be wholly omitted in translating, without obscuring the thought, because the looking is presupposed by the next words: **saw the linen clothes lying.** *Cloths* is preferable to **clothes;** for the reference is to the bandages in which the body was wrapped, and not to any articles of raiment. **Yet went he not in.** Language perfectly characteristic of this Evangelist: certainly not the language of egotism, but rather of vivid recollection. If "the other disciple," is the writer, and he remembers that he outran Peter, coming first to the sepulchre, he also remembers that he only ventured to stoop down and look into the sepulchre. Why he paused just there, and allowed his companion to go before him in the more thorough examination of the vacant tomb, he does not intimate. We may reasonably conjecture that he was arrested for the time by a feeling of awe and reverence at the mystery which was opening itself slowly to his mind. Perhaps he felt somewhat as Moses did when he heard the voice out of the flames: "Put off thy shoes from off thy feet, for the place whereon thou standest is holy ground." (Ex. 3: 5.) But John simply describes the events as they occurred. We cannot see in this narrative any, even the slightest, trace of rivalry between himself and Peter, or of any, even the slightest desire to exalt himself. He is in-

6 Then cometh Simon Peter following him, and went into the sepulchre, and seeth the linen clothes lie,
7 And *the napkin, that was about his head, not lying with the linen clothes, but wrapped together in a place by itself.
8 Then went in also that other disciple, which came first to the sepulchre, and he saw, and believed.
9 For as yet they knew not the *scripture, that he must rise again from the dead.

6 entered he not in. Simon Peter therefore also cometh, following him, and entered into the tomb;
7 and he beholdeth the linen cloths lying, and the napkin, that was upon his head, not lying with the linen cloths, but rolled up in a place by itself. Then entered in therefore the other disciple
8 also, who came first to the tomb, and he saw, 9 and believed. For as yet they knew not the scripture, that he must rise again from the dead.

a ch. 11. 54....b Ps. 16: 10; Acts 2: 25-31; 13: 34, 35.

tent upon one thing—that is, upon showing, by the most certain proofs, that Jesus rose from the dead.

6, 7. Then cometh Simon Peter, etc. The Revised Version is, in some respects, an improvement of the Common Version: *Simon Peter therefore also cometh, following him, and entered into the tomb.* Fearless and unhesitating, Peter, observing the tomb to be open, entered into it without a moment's delay, prepared to scrutinize everything there, and learn the correctness or incorrectness of Mary's report. **And seeth the linen clothes** (*cloths*) **lie.** Evidently the same *cloths* which John had seen, looking into the sepulchre. But the verb used is not the same. To describe his own sight of the *cloths*, John uses a verb (βλέπει), which denotes simple sight as distinguished from intent regard; but in describing Peter's sight of them, he employs a verb (θεωρεῖ), which signifies a more earnest observant gaze. The change of word seems to have been intentional. Peter's survey of the tomb was more searching and exact than that of John. He was now, as ever in his best moments, the prompt, keen-sighted, practical man, suffering nothing which had any bearing on the removal of Jesus from the tomb to escape his notice; while the mind of John was, perhaps, already rising to higher and more spiritual questions. At any rate, he gives a certain precedence to the scrutiny of the place by Peter, as if it were more intentional and thorough than his own. Accordingly, Peter beholds not only *the cloths lying*, but also **the napkin that was about his head, not lying with the linen clothes** (*cloths*), **but wrapped together in a place by itself.** "There were no traces of haste. The deserted tomb bore the marks of perfect calm. The grave-clothes had been carefully removed, which would be a work of time and difficulty, and laid in two separate places. It was clear, therefore, that the body had not been stolen by enemies; it was scarcely less clear that it had not been taken away by friends."—*Westcott.* For why should either enemies or friends remove the winding-sheets from the body, or roll together the cloth upon the head and lay it in a place by itself?

8. Then went in also that other disciple. *Therefore* should be inserted. as in the Revised Version; for the act of John in entering the tomb, was due to the example and influence of Peter. Dr. Bushnell made this verse the text of a beautiful sermon on the power of unconscious influence. Peter said nothing to John, probably thought nothing about influencing him; yet by his example he led John to enter the tomb, and observe with himself all the particulars which, sixty years afterwards, that disciple would have occasion to relate. **Which came first to the sepulchre :** and might, therefore, have entered it first, though, for some reason, he failed to do so—a failure which may possibly have been thought of by him as a neglect of duty, or of privilege, especially when remembered in connection with Peter's action, to the influence of which he had properly yielded. **And he saw and believed. Believed,** that is to say, in the resurrection of Christ as an accomplished fact; for this interpretation is required by the next verse. Were it not for the context, and especially for that verse, it would be natural, with many of the best interpreters, to give the word **believed** a broader and more spiritual sense, making it signify, after the manner of John, a special accession to his faith in Jesus as the Son of God, and the Saviour of mankind. But, while this may be involved as a consequence in the believing here spoken of, it is not directly specified. Probaby Peter did not yet believe, or at least, express his belief.

9. For as yet they knew not the scripture, that he must rise again from the dead. John was convinced by what he *saw*, that his Master had risen from the dead, and not by the testimony of Scripture; for

10 Then the disciples went away again unto their own home.
11 ᵃBut Mary stood without at the sepulchre weeping: and as she wept, she stooped down, *and looked* into the sepulchre,
12 And seeth two angels in white sitting, the one at the head, and the other at the feet, where the body of Jesus had lain.

10 So the disciples went away again unto their own home.
11 But Mary was standing without at the tomb weeping: so, as she wept, she stooped and looked
12 into the tomb; and she beholdeth two angels in white sitting, one at the head, and one at the feet,

a Mark 16:5.

neither he, nor the rest of the disciples, yet knew that he must rise again. By **the scripture,** is probably meant some one passage of the Old Testament, which was understood by the Evangelist to predict the resurrection of the Messiah. That passage may have been the one to which Peter appealed on the Day of Pentecost (Acts 2:27), that is, the tenth verse of the sixteenth Psalm: "For thou wilt not leave my soul to Sheol; neither wilt thou suffer thine Holy One to see corruption." (Rev. Ver.) The event was needed to interpret the prophecy. And to this day the same is true. The predictions of Scripture are best understood in the light of their accomplishment.

10. Then the disciples, (or, *the disciples therefore*), **went away again.** They had seen all that remained in the tomb, with careful observation. There was no more to be learned respecting their Lord in that place; therefore, they returned to their home in the city; but whether in silence, each one meditating on what he had seen, or in subdued conversation, John expressing his belief in the Lord's resurrection, and Peter frankly avowing the doubts which still lingered in his mind, we know not. They had seen no vision of angels. John needed none, and before the evening hour Peter was to see the Saviour himself. Surely their hearts burned within them by the way, whether they walked in silence or uttered freely their rising hopes.

11-18. JESUS APPEARS TO MARY MAGDALENE.

11. But Mary stood without at the sepulchre, weeping. *Was standing,* is a better rendering of the verb than stood. It appears that Peter and John did not tarry long in the tomb. A careful survey of the place cannot have occupied many minutes, and when that was accomplished they would naturally hasten away to their friends with a report of what they had seen. Meanwhile, Mary Magdalene was returning to the tomb, having been unable to keep pace with them

as they ran thither out of the city. Whether she arrived before their examination was finished, is uncertain; but when the Evangelist brings her into his narrative again she had already come back to the sepulchre, and was standing without the same, weeping. Probably the two disciples had gone into the city without meeting her; certainly John had not told her of his belief in the resurrection of their divine Friend, for her impressions were still the same as when she said to them (ver. 2), "they have taken away the Lord out of the sepulchre, and we know not where they have laid him." **And as she wept, she stooped down, and looked into the sepulchre.** On the expression **stooped down and looked,** see comment on ver. 5; for the verb in this place is the same as the participle in that, (here, παρέκυψεν, there, παρακύψασ).

12. And seeth two angels in white sitting. Better: *And she beholdeth,* etc. For while the Greek verb here used (θεωρεῖ, compare note on ver. 6) does not commonly signify a purely mental act, independent of the senses, it does appear to denote a seeing in which the mind of the person who sees is consciously and purposely engaged—a directed and appreciative vision; it is, therefore, represented in the Revised Version by the English word, *beholdeth.* **In white**—*i. e.,* garments. Luke says, that "two men stood by them"—*i. e.,* by the women who first entered the tomb—"in shining garments" (21:4), and, doubtless, those "two men" were identical with the "two angels," whom now, at a later morning hour, Mary Magdalene *beholdeth;* for the form in which angels were manifested aforetime was generally human, **The one at the head, and the other at the feet, where the body of Jesus had lain.** More literally, *one at the head, and one at the feet.* Not only are the sitting posture and the shining raiment mentioned, but the exact position of the two angels is also carefully stated, after the manner of this Evangelist.

13 And they say unto her, Woman, why weepest thou? She saith unto them, Because they have taken away my Lord, and I know not where they have laid him.
14 *And when she had thus said, she turned herself back, and saw Jesus standing, and *knew not that it was Jesus.
15 Jesus saith unto her, Woman, why weepest thou? whom seekest thou? She, supposing him to be the gardener, saith unto him, Sir, if thou have borne him hence, tell me where thou hast laid him, and I will take him away.

13 where the body of Jesus had lain. And they say unto her, Woman, why weepest thou? She saith unto them, Because they have taken away my Lord, and I know not where they have laid him.
14 When she had thus said, she turned herself back, and beholdeth Jesus standing, and knew not that
15 it was Jesus. Jesus saith unto her, Woman, why weepest thou? whom seekest thou? She, supposing him to be the gardener, saith unto him, Sir, if thou hast borne him hence, tell me where thou hast laid

a Matt. 28: 9; Mark 16: 9....*b* Luke 24: 15, 31; ch. 21: 4.

13. The angels first speak: **Woman, why weepest thou?** Their question being asked, as so many others are, not for the sake of gaining information, but to secure a definite avowal of her sorrow, that would render their testimony more natural and less abrupt to her mind. For it is scarcely supposable they were in any doubt as to the occasion of her weeping. Her answer shows that she had no idea of what had really taken place. Her thoughts were not yet moving in the direction of truth. **Because they have taken away my Lord, and I know not where they have laid him.** It is almost the same language which she used to Peter and John, though slightly more personal. And, bearing in mind the ardor of her love to the Saviour, who had delivered her from an awful and mysterious affliction (Luke 8: 2), we can imagine this language to be an expression of the one thought that filled her heart. Had a hundred persons questioned her, this would have been her answer to them all. But her sorrow was soon to vanish away before the light of a great joy. If not the *first*, then certainly the *second* appearance of the risen Christ was to this grateful woman. Peter and John might wait a little longer, but Jesus showed himself very soon after his resurrection to this devoted and weeping follower.

14. **And when she had thus said, she turned herself back.** The more important early manuscripts and versions have no **and** at the beginning of this verse, but read simply: **When she had thus said,** etc. The mind of Mary was so completely filled with the idea of her Lord's removal to some unknown place by human hands, that the spectacle of two angels clothed in white seems not to have riveted her attention for any length of time. Yet, it is possible that the angels perceived the presence of Jesus without, and paused, before giving their response, to see what he would do. It is possible, too, that Mary heard the sound of his footsteps, and rose from her stooping posture to see who might be drawing near. Nay, it is possible that the very question which the angels asked, led Mary to believe them ignorant of the one thing which she longed to know. At any rate, without waiting for their response, **she turned herself back, and saw** (or, *beholdeth*) **Jesus standing.** Here again the verb is *beholdeth,* not **seeth.** It was not a merely casual glance that she gave her risen Lord, but an observant look which sought to read the countenance of the man who stood near, with a view to learning whether he was likely to know and make known the place to which the body of Jesus had been removed. **And knew not that it was Jesus.** Her look must have been earnest enough to recognize the Lord, if her soul had not been intent on learning one thing—the place to which his body had been carried, or, if her eyes had not been suffused with tears. It is unnecessary to suppose that he appeared to her in "another form" (Mark 16: 12), or, that her "eyes were holden that she should not know him." (Luke 24: 16.) And, as the causes of non-recognition were entirely natural, so likewise were the means employed to secure recognition. As none but the clearest evidence was fitted to dispel the prepossession which controlled her mind, that evidence was graciously furnished for her sake, and for ours; and we can trace its operation without difficulty.

15. **Jesus saith unto her, Woman, why weepest thou? whom seekest thou?** The first question is identical with that which the angels asked (ver. 13), and may be explained in the same way. For Mary was still weeping, and even human sympathy would fain do something to remove the cause of that weeping. But to do this in a natural manner, the cause must first be revealed by the sufferer.

16 Jesus saith unto her, Mary. She turned herself, and saith unto him, Rabboni; which is to say, Master. 16 him, and I will take him away. Jesus saith unto her, Mary. She turned herself, and saith unto him in Hebrew, Rabboni; which is to say, [1] Master.

[1] Or, *Teacher.*

But the second question implies a certain degree of knowledge as to that cause. Yet, no more knowledge than a man belonging to the place and aware of the removal of the body from the tomb, might well be supposed to have in the circumstances. A weeping woman, a ravished tomb, and a friendly man seeing the former and cognizant of the latter, are all that is needed to account for this question. Jesus, indeed, knew all; but his question need not have suggested to Mary a knowledge on his part beyond that which a gardener could have possessed. But if there was nothing in the tenor of this question to reveal the person of Jesus to Mary, is it not at least very surprising that she did not recognize his voice as soon as heard? For, in every human voice there is some peculiarity of tone or timbre, of accent or cadence; and it is commonly imagined that the utterance of Jesus was singularly perfect, and, therefore, easily distinguishable from that of other men. True; but there is no testimony in support of the latter hypothesis; and, unless it be correct, we are not justified in affirming that the asking of the two brief questions recorded by John, if done in a kindly, unemphatic manner, would bring out perceptibly any peculiar quality of his voice. Besides, we are to bear in mind that Mary did not suppose it possible for Jesus to be standing before her. She was searching for his lifeless body, and was as utterly unprepared as any human being could have been to recognize his presence among the living. So she did not catch the tone of his voice; but, **supposing him to be the gardener, saith unto him, Sir, if thou have borne him hence, tell me where thou hast laid him, and I will take him away.** The pronoun **thou** is slightly emphatic, probably in contrast with her prevailing thought that he had been removed by enemies. The questions of the man whom she conjectures to be the gardener were friendly, and it occurs to her that, for some cause, he may have taken away the body, and, if so, that he might consent to give it up to the disciples. "Mary makes no answer to the inquiry. Her heart is so full of the Person to whom it referred that she assumes he is known to her questioner. . . . The trait is one of those direct reflections of life which mark St. John's Gospel."—*Westcott.*

16. **Jesus saith unto her, Mary.** We assume that Jesus threw into his utterance of this name all that had been most characteristic of his tone and accent in the past: that he pronounced it with a holy tenderness and authority possible to no other person. Westcott supposes that there must have been a short pause between her word to him and his utterance of her name, during which she had resumed her former position, and become lost in grief. But it is quite unnecessary to suppose that she had become "lost in her grief again." It was enough that she had failed to recognize him. Seeing this, Jesus resorted to the most natural and effective way of enabling her to do this. He put into the clear and deep utterance of her name all that was peculiar and inimitable in his manner of speaking it. And the effect was instantaneous; the recognition perfect. Never was there a more sudden and complete revulsion of feeling. Her sorrow was changed into joy: **she turned herself, and saith unto him** (*in the Hebrew tongue*) **Rabboni; which is to say, Master.** Farrar suggests that, while making her appeal to the supposed gardener (ver. 15), "she had turned her head aside, perhaps, that she might hide her streaming tears," and that now, recognizing Jesus by his voice, she turns her face towards him again, every line of sadness passing, as it were, into light and joy. The word **Rabboni**, is explained by John himself as equivalent to Master or Teacher. Doubtless, it was uttered with the utmost reverence and love; but expositors call attention to the circumstance that this appears to have been the last time he was addressed or denominated by any one of his disciples, Master. From the hour of his resurrection onward, the divine element of his being filled a larger place in their souls, and they spoke of him as their Lord, or the Son of God, etc. *In the Hebrew tongue,* is accepted by the highest critical authorities, as a part of the original text, and the fact that Mary made

17 Jesus saith unto her, Touch me not; for I am not yet ascended to my Father: but go to ᵃmy brethren, and say unto them, ᵇI ascend unto my Father, and your Father; and to ᶜmy God, and your God.

17 Jesus saith to her, ¹Touch me not; for I am not yet ascended unto the Father: but go unto my brethren, and say to them, I ascend unto my Father, and your Father, and my God and

a Ps. 22 : 22; Matt. 28 : 10; Rom. 8 : 29; Heb. 2 : 11....b ch. 16 : 28....c Eph. 1 : 17.——1 Or, *Take not hold on me.*

use of the Aramaic language at such a moment, is, perhaps, an evidence that it was commonly employed by Jesus and his disciples in their familiar intercourse. (Comp. Mark 10: 51—Rev. Ver.; Acts 22: 2; 26: 14.)
17. Touch me not: for I am not yet ascended unto my (Rev. Ver. *the*) **Father: but go to my brethren, and say unto them, I ascend unto my Father, and your Father, and to** (Rev. Ver. omits *to*) **my God and your God.** It is not an easy matter to ascertain the precise thought of this verse. Grimm explains it thus: "Do not seek to learn by touching me, whether I am even now clothed with a body: there is no need of this search, for I have not yet ascended to the Father"—and am, therefore, still in the flesh—"but go unto my brethren," etc. This view of the passage is drawn out very satisfactorily by Dr. Hackett, thus: "It should be observed that this imperative present form (μὴ ἅπτου) implies an incipient act either actually begun, or one on the point of being done, as indicated by some look or gesture. Mary, it may well be supposed, was in the same perplexed state of mind on the appearance of Christ to her, which was evinced in so many different ways by the other disciples after the resurrection. She had already, it is true, exclaimed, in the ecstacy of her joy, ' Rabboni'; but she may not yet have been certain as to the precise form or nature of the body in which she beheld her Lord . . . In this state of uncertainty she extends her hand to assure herself of the truth. She would procure for herself, by the criterion of the sense of touch, the conviction which the eye is unable to give her. The Saviour knows her thoughts and arrests the act. The act is unnecessary; his words are a sufficient proof of what she would know. He had 'not yet ascended to the Father,' as she half believed, and consequently has not the spiritual body which she supposed he might possibly have . . . Her case was like that of Thomas, and yet unlike his; she wished, like him, to touch the object of her vision, but, unlike him, was not prompted by unbelief."

A second interpretation is defended by Weiss, Westcott, and others. Dr. Weiss assumes that "Mary indicated her wish to renew, by hand-pressure or something of the kind, the close, human fellowship which she had formerly had with him. But Jesus declined this renewal of intimate human fellowship on the ground that, though he had not yet ascended to the Father, he was about to do this. Hence, his appearing to his disciples could not have for its object a resumption of his earlier human intercourse with his own." Weiss refers the *for* to the whole sentence that follows, and especially to the message which Mary was commanded to bear to the disciples, "I ascend unto my Father and your Father, and my God and your God." In this case, as Westcott remarks, "the imminent, though not realized, ascension of the Lord would be regarded as forbidding the old forms of earthly intercourse." But this writer refers the *for* to the first clause only—"I am not yet ascended to the Father"—and says that in "this case the ascension would be presented as the beginning and condition of a new union . . . Mary substituted a knowledge of the humanity of Christ for a knowledge of his whole person . . . She thought that she could now enjoy his restored Presence as she then apprehended it. She assumed that the return to the old life exhausted the extent of her Master's victory over death. Therefore, in his reply, Christ said: 'Do not cling to me, as if in that which falls under the senses you can know me as I am; for there is yet something beyond the outward restoration to earth which must be realized, before that fellowship towards which you reach can be established as abiding." Dr. Schaff says, that "the meaning has been made more difficult by a want of sufficient attention to the force of the words, 'Touch me not'; for these words do not express the touch of a moment only, but a touch that continues for a time. They are equivalent to 'Keep not thy touch upon me,' 'Handle me not,' 'Cling not to me.' Mary would have held her Lord fast with the grasp of earthly affection and love.

18 ^aMary Magdalene came and told the disciples that she had seen the Lord, and *that* he had spoken these things unto her.
19 ^bThen the same day at evening, being the first *day* of the week, when the doors were shut where the disciples were assembled for fear of the Jews, came Jesus and stood in the midst, and saith unto them, Peace be unto you.

18 your God. Mary Magdalene cometh and telleth the disciples, I have seen the Lord; and *how that* he had said these things unto her.
19 When therefore it was evening, on that day, the first *day* of the week, and when the doors were shut where the disciples were, for fear of the Jews, Jesus came and stood in the midst, and saith unto

<small>a Matt. 28: 10; Luke 24: 10....b Mark 16: 14; Luke 24: 36; 1 Cor. 15: 5.</small>

She needed to be taught that the season for such bodily touching of the Word of Life was past. But, as it passed, the disciples were not to be left desolate: the season for another touching—deeper, because spiritual—began. Jesus would return to his Father, and would send forth his Spirit to dwell with his disciples."

It has been considered an objection to the former view, maintained by Grimm, Hackett, and others, that Christ's treatment of Mary differed from his treatment of Thomas; but to this it is replied, that Mary only doubted; she did not disbelieve with Thomas, and therefore she did not need the same evidence as Thomas. It has also been objected to the latter view, maintained by Weiss, Westcott, Plumptre, Schaff, and others, that Christ's treatment of Mary Magdalene differed from his treatment of the other women (Matt. 28:9), who were permitted to hold his feet; but to this it may be answered, that Mary's longing for the visible Christ, as a human Friend and Teacher, may have been stronger than that of the other women, leading the Saviour to deny her a privilege that was safely granted to them. Besides, their act was evidently one of lowly homage or worship, while hers would have been distinctly one of pure, but human affection. From all that is said of Mary in the Gospels, we think it more likely that she erred by undue devotion to the human personality of Jesus than by doubting the reality of his resurrection body. For this reason, we regard the latter interpretation as more likely to be correct than the former. It is worthy of notice that Jesus here speaks of the disciples, for the first time, as his *brethren*. Before his death he had called them friends as well as servants, but now he directs Mary to go to his "brethren." And in what sense they were his brethren, appears by the message which she is to deliver: *I ascend unto my Father and your Father, and my God and your God.* Thus, he pronounces them children of his Father and his God. Yet, he dis-

tinguishes his Sonship to God from theirs. He does not say, "I am ascending, or about to ascend, unto *our* Father and *our* God," thus, putting them in precisely the same relation to the Father with himself, but he says, "My Father and your Father, and my God and your God," leaving room for a great difference between the nature and origin of his own Sonship and theirs. (Comp. 1 John 3: 1; Gal. 3: 26, 27.)

18. In obedience to the Saviour's word, **Mary Magdalene came and told the disciples.** A more exact rendering is found in the Revised Version, *cometh and telleth*, and, a yet more literal translation in the Bible Union Revision, *Mary the Magdalene comes, bringing word to the disciples*. Davidson gives the same translation. And Westcott deems it significant that the *telling* is expressed by a participle, and thus made to be a mere accompaniment of the coming—the principal point in the writer's mind being the promptness of Mary in leaving Jesus to go to his disciples. **That she had seen the Lord.** According to the critical editors, this should be, *I have seen the Lord*—the Evangelist recalling and repeating the very words in which Mary testified to her having seen the Lord, but passing to the indirect style of narration, when referring to what had already been recorded in the precise language of Jesus. **And (*that*) he had spoken these things unto her:** namely, the things recorded in ver. 17. *Touch me not*, etc.

19-23. JESUS' FIRST APPEARANCE TO HIS DISCIPLES ASSEMBLED IN A CLOSED ROOM.

19. In conformity with his plan, John omits some of Christ's appearances to his followers. After appearing twice in the early morning—once to a group of women, who had been among his faithful disciples, and once to Mary Magdalene, who had been forgiven much and therefore loved much—he also appeared twice during the day, once to Simon Peter, as we learn from Luke 24: 34,

2A

and 1 Cor. 15: 5, and again to two disciples on their way to Emmaus—one of them, Cleopas. (Luke 24: 13-35.) It would be natural to conjecture that John omitted to describe Christ's manifestation of himself to Peter, and later, to the two disciples, because these three were present at both the interviews of Jesus with his disciples, described by him in the present chapter; but there is really no good reason why we should trouble ourselves about the Evangelist's grounds for deciding to omit this and insert that. The result of his work as a whole is such as to justify the conclusion that he was guided by the Spirit of Truth, according to the promise of his Master, and that his record is perfect for the ends which it was intended to serve. **Then the same day at evening,** etc.—or, as in Revised Version, *When therefore it was evening, on that day, the first of the week.* By that day, John points with emphasis to the day of Christ's resurrection. It was in almost every respect the day of days to those who had truly believed in Jesus. The narrative of Luke (24: 29 sq.) renders it probable that this appearance of Jesus was late in the evening, though not necessarily very late. It was "toward evening, and the day" was "far spent" when the two disciples sat down with Jesus to a repast in Emmaus, a village about eight miles from Jerusalem. He was made known to them in the breaking of bread, and they rose up that very hour and returned to Jerusalem. **When the doors were shut where the disciples were assembled, for fear of the Jews.** The word **assembled,** is wanting to the oldest manuscripts—(e. g., א A B D L A *, and others). The doors were therefore shut for fear of the Jews. This circumstance is mentioned, not for the purpose of showing the peril to which the disciples were exposed, but for the purpose of giving the reader a view of the supernatural manner in which Jesus revealed himself to his own. A certain "air of mystery clothed his person and movements after his resurrection. No man knew whence he came, or whither he went, or how he lived. He seemed to hover over the pathway of his disciples, visible or invisible at will. His body was real, yet not subject to the common laws of matter. With 'new properties, powers, and attributes' (*Ellicott*), it was a perfect servant of the spirit. Nowhere do the Evangelists hint at any reason for this change in the bearing of Christ after his resurrection, but with nice agreement do all their accounts reveal the change itself." (See the author's work on the "Miracles of Christ as Attested by the Evangelists," p. 46). In other words, the Evangelists simply state the facts—facts which they knew, and of which they, and they alone, in some cases, could bear witness; and it seems to us that their witness is singularly harmonious as to the extraordinary character of the Lord's resurrection life. **Came Jesus and stood in the midst.** No one could tell how he came. "All that is set before us is, that he was not bound by the present conditions of material existence which we observe."—(*Westcott.*) The comment of Weiss is more positive, though looking in the same direction: "It is not indeed said that he came *through* the closed doors, as many Fathers, Calvin, and others, interpret it (comp. against this Hengstenberg), but the representation is not therefore obscure."—(*De Wette.*) The current representation, that the bodily nature of Jesus was only on the way to glorification, and, therefore, although yet material, was not bound to the limitations of space (*Meyer*)—for which view reference is made to his walking on the sea (*Godet*, and perhaps *Hengstenberg* and *Luthardt*)—cannot be carried through. From his resurrection, onward, Christ was in his glorified body, as this coming, in spite of closed doors, shows (comp. Luke 24: 31, 36); and if he appears to the disciples in a body apprehensible by the senses (ver. 20), this takes place for the very purpose of making them certain of his having a bodily nature, and so of his resurrection." For the opposite view of Christ's resurrection body, see an able article in the *Bib. Sac.* for May, 1845, by Dr. Edward Robinson. That his body was real, material, having flesh and bones, as before the crucifixion, we are fully assured; but whether such a body may not be at the same time a perfect organ of the spirit, and subject to its will to a degree almost incredible before it is experienced, is a question not yet answered to the satisfaction of all. We are inclined to think it may be such an organ, and to believe, though not with absolute confidence, that the body of Jesus was changed when he first left the tomb, that it was raised incorruptible (1 Cor. 15:

20 And when he had so said, he shewed unto them his hands and his side. *a* Then were the disciples glad, when they saw the Lord.
21 Then said Jesus to them again, Peace be unto you: *b* as my Father hath sent me, even so send I you.

a ch. 16: 22....*b* Matt. 28: 18; ch. 17: 18, 19; 2 Tim. 2: 2; Heb. 3: 1.

20, 41, 52.) Peace be unto you. This was, and is, a customary form of salutation. But it was peculiarly appropriate at this moment. All that the words literally mean was in them as they fell from the lips of Jesus. Fearful of being misled in so vital a matter, astonished at what they had heard from the women and from Peter, perplexed by the report which the two disciples were bringing from Emmaus, anxious, agitated, and all but four of them still despondent, distrustful—into what breathless silence and awe must they have been hushed, as they saw One like unto the Son of man taking his place visibly and serenely in the midst of them! And with what feelings of wonder and joy must they have heard the voice of him who spake as never man spake, in the salutation, **Peace be unto you!** It was a word never to be forgotten, full of love and authority; a word from heaven as truly as from earth. Now, if never before, they must have felt that the God-man was with them.

20. And when he had so said (or, *said this*) **he shewed unto them his hands and his side.** To convince them beyond the reach of doubt that he was with them alive, in the very body that had been nailed to the cross and pierced with the soldier's spear. "Literally," says Westcott, "according to the most ancient text, *both* his hands and his side"; but this is surely too strong a statement. The only authority for *both*, cited by Tischendorf, is that of A B and the Peshito, while the other uncials and early versions omit this word. The difference is unimportant, except as a matter of emphasis; but that is no reason why the preponderance of testimony should be overruled in favor of a pleasing text. **Then,** (or, *therefore*) **were the disciples glad when they saw the Lord.** This testimony agrees with that of Luke, though the latter states that, at first, "they believed not for joy." (24: 41.) He mentions a number of particulars not referred to by John. Thus, at the Saviour's salutation, "they were terrified and affrighted, and supposed that they had seen a spirit" (ver. 37)— this being true of some in the room. "And he said unto them, Why are ye troubled? And why do thoughts arise in your hearts? Behold my hands and my feet, that it is I myself: handle me and see; for a spirit hath not flesh and bones, as ye see me have. And when he had thus spoken, he shewed them his hands and his feet. And while they yet believed not for joy, and wondered, he said unto them, Have ye here any meat? And they gave him a piece of a broiled fish, and of an honeycomb. And he took it, and did eat before them." Without enumerating all these items of evidence, so instructive to Luke, John relates a part of them, sufficient for his purpose, and then passes on to acts and words of profound spiritual significance, which he had treasured up in his heart through a long life of devotion to his Lord.

21. There is no indication of haste or confusion in the action of Jesus. Every movement and word is orderly, deliberate, re-assuring, full of wisdom and love and authority. Not until he has convinced them of his identity in body and spirit with their crucified Master, not until their wonder and joy have settled down into a fixed and rational belief, founded on indubitable proof, that he is their Lord—victorious over death and the grave— did he renew his benediction and pronounce them his missionaries and representatives to mankind. **Then said Jesus to them again, Peace be unto you: as my Father hath sent me, even so send I you.** *Therefore*, instead of **then;** for the disciples were now prepared for that which the Evangelist relates. By the solemn renewal of the benediction with which he first greeted them he prepares them for the words and act which were to follow. The words: **As my Father hath sent me, even so send I you,** were not absolutely new, though they may have been unexpected. For, in his high priestly prayer (17: 18) Jesus had used the same language with respect to his disciples, in addressing the Father, which he now uses in speaking to

22 And when he had said this, he breathed on *them*, and saith unto them, Receive ye the Holy Ghost:
23 a Whosesoever sins ye remit, they are remitted unto them; *and* whosesoever *sins* ye retain, they are retained.

22 even so send I you. And when he had said this, he breathed on them, and saith unto them, Receive ye the Holy Spirit: whose soever sins ye forgive, they are foregiven unto them; whose soever *sins* ye retain, they are retained.

a Matt. 16: 19; 18: 18.

them. Only one word, translated *sent*, is found in both clauses of 17: 18, while two words of nearly the same meaning are used in this verse (ἀποστέλλω, πέμπω). Schaff argues that there is a slight distinction between the two words, the former word directing attention to the sending as a *commission*, the latter emphasising it as a *mission*. "When the first is used, our thoughts turn to a special embassy, and special instructions which the ambassador receives; the second brings into view rather the authority of the sender and the obedience of the sent." But the use of the same word in both clauses in 17: 18, renders it doubtful whether any distinction is intended here. The passages differ in one respect, it is true; for there the Saviour declared what he had done virtually, rather than in fact and form; while here the sending is direct and complete in form, though the hour of action for the disciples has not yet fully come. And how greatly does the comparison, **even so**, exalt their mission! How distinctly does the clause, **even so I send you**, imply the divine authority of Jesus! He is to be obeyed as Head over all to the church. And if we follow out the analogy between the mission of Jesus and that of his disciples, to its utmost limit, both will be seen to involve self-denial and suffering, as well as triumph and glory, a cross here, and a crown hereafter.

22. But to be *the sent* of the Anointed One, they would need themselves to be anointed; to be heralds of spiritual truth, they would need illumination by the Spirit of truth. We are therefore prepared for the further record of John. **And when he had said .this, he breathed on them, and saith unto them, Receive ye the Holy Ghost.** The act of breathing upon them was intended to symbolize the fact that the Holy Spirit was, or was to be, imparted to them by him, just as the giving of life to man at first was represented by the act of God, when he "breathed into his nostrils the breath of life." (Gen. 2: 7.) The symbolism of the act, teaches also that the Holy Spirit abides in Jesus, as truly as in the Father. But, whether the words, "Holy Spirit," should have the article or not in this passage, is doubtful. There is no article in the original text; but, Greek words that have become, in effect, proper names, may take or omit the article on grounds very difficult to discover. (See Winer § 19, Thayer's Trans., p. 119-122; Buttmann, § 124, b. p. 89.) If, however, a distinction is made between Holy Spirit, and the Holy Spirit, the former must naturally signify the influence, and the latter, the person of the Spirit. But we consider it unsafe to rely upon such a distinction.

23. Whosesoever sins ye remit, they are remitted unto them; and whosesoever sins ye retain, they are retained. The words **and**, and **sins**, in the last clause, do not represent any thing expressed in the original text, and may be omitted without detriment to the sense. The Revised Version reads: *Whosesoever sins ye forgive, they are forgiven unto them; whosesoever sins ye retain, they are retained*—supplying unnecessarily, the words "sins," in the second clause. These words of Jesus seem to be very plain, but they offer a serious difficulty to a conscientious student of the Bible. Taken in their most literal sense, they signify that those addressed would be so enlightened by the Holy Spirit as to read the hearts of men, and, acting as judges in the kingdom of God, to forgive or condemn with infallible wisdom those who might appear before them—their decision being accepted in every case by the Lord as his own decision. But there is very little in the history of the Apostolic Church which favors the view that any, even though apostles, were accustomed to exercise this judicial function over individuals. Only in a few instances, and those of an extraordinary character, like that of Ananias and Sapphira, or that of Simon Magus, was such a decision pronounced. The Acts of the Apostles and the Epistles of Paul furnish clear evidence that unworthy members were sometimes received into the churches, notwithstanding the presence of apostles or the possession of extraordinary spiritual gifts by other members. But, may not the Saviour refer to a fallible action of his disciples, that would represent to a degree the divine judgment as to individuals? Thus, Alford writes: "The words, closely considered, amount to this: that with the gift and real participation of the Holy Spirit, comes the conviction, and, therefore, the *knowledge* of *sin,* of *righteousness,* and *judgment;* —and this knowledge becomes more perfect, the more men are filled with the Holy Ghost. Since this is so, they who are pre-eminently filled with his presence, are pre-eminently gifted with the discernment of sin, and repentance in others, and hence, by the Lord's appointment, authorized to pronounce pardon of sin and the contrary. The apostles had this in an especial manner, and by the full indwelling of the Spirit were enabled to discern the hearts of men, and to give sentence on that discernment. (See Acts 5: 1-11; 8: 21; 13: 9.) And this gift belongs to the church in all ages . . . in proportion as *any disciple* shall have been filled with the Holy Spirit of wisdom." Against this interpretation the following considerations may be raised : 1. That the practice of giving a positive decision as to the spiritual state of individuals, was infrequent with the apostles, and was apparently due to some extraordinary illumination and impulse, like that which led to the working of miracles. 2. That any similar practice, since the apostolic age, has generally been associated with acts of fanaticism which soon discredited it in the eyes of thoughtful Christians. 3. That even the Roman Catholic priesthood virtually disclaims a knowledge of human hearts, by conditioning the validity of its remission of sins on the sincerity and penitence of the person forgiven. Thus understood, the Roman priesthood really does little more than solemnly declare the conditions of pardon, and the certainty of judgment if those conditions are not fulfilled. 4. That this interpretation represents Jesus as linking his commission to the disciples, and his gift of the Holy Spirit, not with their *principal work—* the proclamation of the gospel and the persuading of men to receive it—but with a very subordinate, and—may we not say ?—unimportant part of their work, that of pronouncing judgment on characters formed. Thus interpreted, the drift of this promise is entirely different from that of the prediction in 16: 7-15, and entirely inconsistent with the best life of the church for eighteen centuries. For these reasons we do not believe that Jesus referred, in these words, to any formal judicial action of his disciples. To what then did he refer? To the work of his disciples as qualified by the Holy Spirit to declare without error the conditions of forgiveness or condemnation under the reign of Christ. Men were to learn from their lips the heaven-appointed terms of life and death. "What our Lord here commits to his disciples, to his church, is the right authoritatively to declare, in his name, that there is forgiveness for man's sins, and on what conditions he will be forgiven."—*Schaff.* The language of Watkins really amounts to the same thing. "Sent, as he was sent, they are not sent to condemn the world, but that the world through him might be saved; but in their work, as in his, men are condemned because the light is come into the world, and men love darkness rather than light. The ultimate principles upon which this power rests, are those stated above—the being sent by Christ, and the reception of the Holy Ghost. God has promised forgiveness wherever there is repentance; he has not promised repentance wherever there is sin. It results from every declaration of forgiveness made in the name of the Father, through Jesus Christ, that the hearts which, in penitence accept it, receive remission of their sins, and that the hardness of the hearts which willfully reject it is by their rejection increased, and the very words by which their sins would be remitted become the words by which they are retained."

Many commentators suppose that "the disciples," referred to in this paragraph, were not the apostles, but the followers of Jesus then in Jerusalem, or at least, a considerable portion of them. This seems to them a natural inference from the fact that two who were not of the Eleven, were certainly admitted, namely, Cleopas and his companion, to whom the Lord had made himself known in Emmaus. But it is more probable that John had in mind the apostles, even though a few others were present; for he speaks of them as "the disciples," and such were the apostles in a pre-eminent sense and by the prevailing use of the expression in the Gospels; moreover, they, beyond all others, might deem it necessary to meet with closed doors for fear of the Jews; and, lastly, the words addressed to

24 But Thomas, one of the twelve, *called Didymus, was not with them when Jesus came. 25 The other disciples therefore said unto him, We have seen the Lord. But he said unto them, Except I shall see in his hands the print of the nails, and put my finger into the print of the nails, and thrust my hand into his side, I will not believe. 26 And after eight days again his disciples were within, and Thomas with them: then came Jesus, the doors being shut, and stood in the midst, and said, Peace be unto you.

25 But Thomas, one of the twelve, called ¹Didymus, was not with them when Jesus came. The other disciples therefore said unto him, We have seen the Lord. But he said unto them, Except I shall see in his hands the print of the nails, and put my finger into the print of the nails, and put my hand into his side, I will not believe. 26 And after eight days again his disciples were within, and Thomas with them. Jesus cometh, the doors being shut, and stood in the midst, and said,

a ch. 11:16.—1 That is, Twine.

them in ver. 21-23, suggest the idea of inspired teachers, rather than of ordinary Christians. Perhaps we ought to add, that the only one whose absence is mentioned was an apostle.

24-29. SECOND APPEARANCE OF JESUS TO THE ASSEMBLED DISCIPLES.

24. But Thomas, one of the twelve, called Didymus, was not with them when Jesus came. No reason is given for the absence of Thomas, but it is natural to conjecture that he had given up the cause of his former Master as lost beyond recovery. Keensighted, but despondent, he had looked upon Jesus as coming to certain death when he returned from Perea to Bethany and Jerusalem. (11:16.) His worst fears had been more than realized; his Master had suffered the horrors of crucifixion; and now it was vain to think of his return to life. His tomb might be vacant, as some had reported, but this was no solid ground for hope. Moreover, it would be useless to meet and commune together; the otherthrow of their Christ had been as utter as death could make it; let every one mourn apart, and go down in despair to the grave.

25. The other disciples therefore said unto him, We have seen the Lord. His absence led them to bear this testimony, and doubtless they accompanied the brief statement recorded by John with such particulars as confirmed their own faith. But the testimony of others did not move him. His despondency or despair was too deep. They might believe, but he could not. **Except I shall see in his hands the print of the nails, and put my finger into the print of the nails, and thrust my hand into his side, I will not believe.** It is difficult, when reading these statements, to suppress a feeling that the unbelief of Thomas was willful as well as unreasonable. For he refuses to accept the testimony of his fellow-disciples who had known the Lord as long and as intimately as he himself—even, though a number of them had seen the Saviour at the same time and place, and though he had shown them his hands and his side, and, calling for food, had eaten in their presence. He refuses also to receive the evidence of his own sight and hearing, unless it is confirmed by that of touch. And this evidence of touch, he insists, shall be applied, not only to the body of the supposed Christ, to verify its reality, but also to the scars or wounds of that body—to identify it as the body of his crucified Master. Proof shall be raised to the highest possible grade of personal verification before he will surrender his unbelief. Indeed, he demands a kind and degree of evidence which could never be given to any but the little group of disciples that had followed Christ through most of his public ministry. That his demand was unreasonable, must be at once perceived; that it was willful, we do not affirm: charity requires us to withdraw the epithet. For, at heart, he had been a true disciple, and the Saviour condescended to offer him every "jot and tittle" of the evidence which he required. Moreover, though it would be wrong to excuse his unbelief, it is right to adore the wisdom and love of Christ, in overcoming that unbelief. Nay, it is well that there was a Thomas among the Eleven—a man who could not, or would not, believe without incontestable evidence that Jesus Christ had risen from the dead. If all the disciples had possessed the spiritual insight of John, our evidence that Jesus rose on the third day, would probably have been less satisfactory than it now is. Hence, for our sakes, it was needful that such a man as Thomas should be one of the apostles.

26. And after eight days again his disciples were within, and Thomas with them. A full week has elapsed, or eight days, reckoning from Sunday to Sunday, inclusively, as the Greek expression naturally signifies. Why they were again assembled

27 Then saith he to Thomas, Reach hither thy finger, and behold my hands; and reach hither thy hand, and thrust it into my side; and be not faithless, but believing.
28 And Thomas answered and said unto him, My Lord and my God.

27 Peace be unto you. Then saith he to Thomas, Reach hither thy finger, and see my hands; and reach hither thy hand, and put it into my side: and 28 be not faithless, but believing. Thomas answered

a 1 John 1:1.

on the first day of the week, we need not inquire. Probably they had met every day during the week, but Jesus had not appeared to them in that interval. Whether Thomas was with them for the first time, or not, we have no means of deciding, and what had been his state of mind through the week, is equally unknown. But that he was with them on this occasion is, perhaps, an evidence that his heart was not at rest in unbelief. He may have longed for proof that would restore his confidence in Jesus as the Messiah. A week's reflection may have taught him the misery of skepticism as contrasted with the joy of faith, especially if he met occasionally any of his former companions in the service of Christ. But his unbelief was not dispelled, whatever moral preparation may have been going on in his heart with a view to its removal. It was best that he should be left to himself in darkness for a full week, that on the first day of the second week light might break into his understanding, and adoring love fill his soul. Thus at least would the first day of the week become still more emphatically the Lord's Day. It has been considered strange that the disciples did not leave Jerusalem as soon as possible after Christ's message to them, appointing a meeting in Galilee. (Matt. 28:7, 10; Mark 16:7.) But the unbelief of Thomas may have detained the rest for a time, especially if his character was one that commanded their respect, and if they perceived his unbelief to be honest, though obstinate. They would linger a while in the hope of taking him with them to meet the Lord in Galilee. Then came Jesus (or, Jesus came), the doors being shut, etc. See exposition of the same language in ver. 19, above. The mysterious manner of his appearing was the same as before. His salutation, which was at the same time a benediction, was addressed, as in the previous meeting, to all who were present—therefore to Thomas with the rest. That voice! Did he recognize it? That countenance! Did he see in it the lines of him whom he last saw on the cross? But there was more to come. The mysterious Twelfth in that group was fixing his eye upon the disciple who had demanded the evidence of his own senses before he would believe.

27. Then saith he to Thomas, Reach hither thy finger, and behold my hands. Better: and see my hands. The word see is often used to denote knowledge gained by hearing or touch. And be not faithless, but believing. Literally, Become not unbelieving, but believing. "By the expression: Become not, Jesus makes him see that he is at a critical point, where two ways diverge, the one of settled unbelief, the other of complete faith."—Godet. "Through his doubt in the resurrection of Christ, which had actually taken place, Thomas was in danger of becoming unbelieving (in Jesus), while he could only become, in the full sense, believing, by the certainty of his resurrection."— Weiss.

28. Thomas answered and said unto him, My Lord and my God. Jesus offered to Thomas the very evidence which he had demanded, and the language in which he did this was in itself a proof of his knowledge, supernaturally acquired, of the words which Thomas had used. The form and countenance of Jesus, the sound of his voice, and the evidence of divine knowledge afforded by his words, appear to have swept away, as by a flood, the unbelief of Thomas. He did not probably need the evidence of touch. He could not withhold the exclamation of adoring confidence that leaped from his heart to his lips. "In the resurrection of Jesus, Thomas rightly sees a pledge of his so often promised—going to the Father and partaking of the divine glory. The word is certainly one of deep and powerful emotion, and no dogmatic formulated confession of faith; but not on that account an exaggeration, since Jesus accepts it." (Ver. 29.) "The last becomes, for a moment the first, and the faith of the apostles, as Thomas professed it, reaches finally the whole height of the divine truth expressed in the prologue."—Godet. Every attempt to weaken

29 Jesus saith unto him, Thomas, because thou hast seen me, thou hast believed: *a* blessed *are* they that have not seen, and *yet* have believed.

29 and said unto him, My Lord and my God. Jesus said unto him, Because thou hast seen me, ¹thou hast believed: blessed *are* they that have not seen, and *yet* have believed.

a 2 Cor. 5 : 7 ; 1 Pet. 1 : 8.——1 Or, *hast thou believed?*

the force of this testimony to the Deity of Christ is broken before the perfect clearness of the words used by Thomas, the explicit record that they were addressed to Jesus himself, and the definite recognition of their truthfulness by him. Beyond question, John was a witness of what he relates; and whoever rejects this part of his Gospel as unworthy of confidence, must, if consistent, reject it all.

29. Jesus saith unto him, Thomas, because thou hast seen me, thou hast believed. The word **Thomas** does not belong to the text. All the important uncials (including א A B C D), and early versions, want it. Again, the clause translated, **thou hast believed,** may be either declarative or interrogative. Meyer, Weiss, Godet, Watkins, prefer the interrogative form, on the ground that it gives more vividness to the gentle reproof involved in the Saviour's response. Westcott says it is half exclamatory and half interrogative. But the meaning is substantially the same, whether it be considered a declaration, an exclamation, or an interrogation. In either case, Jesus recognizes the fact that Thomas has passed from unbelief into a state of belief; for he uses the perfect tense, denoting an action that, begun in the past, is continued in the present. His belief is also genuine and satisfactory in character. In either case, too, the proximate cause of his faith was *sight.* Thomas had not been convinced by the testimony of his fellow-disciples, or by their testimony with the predictions of Jesus, or by both these with the holy life and teaching of his Lord, but only by sensible evidence superadded to all he knew of Christ, and all he had heard from the apostles. Yet, the words of Jesus, "because thou hast *seen* me," have been considered favorable to the view, that Thomas believed without putting his finger to the wounds of Christ, that he was convinced as soon as he saw the Saviour standing visibly before him. We do not think there is much force in this argument, but nevertheless admit the want of *proof* that Thomas did actually touch the wounds of Jesus. **Blessed are they that have not seen, and yet have believed.** This language is not exclusive. Jesus does not intend to say that Thomas is not accepted by him and will not be permitted to rejoice henceforth in his love. His language is rather comparative, and signifies that those who believe on suitable testimony, but without sensible evidence, are specially approved by the Lord. On such evidence men are to receive the gospel, or perish; on such evidence the business of life must be conducted, or society will dissolve. By its treatment of such evidence moral character is proved. The evidence of sense is often compulsory. Bad men accept it as readily as good men. It is, therefore, in most instances, no proper test of character. But the evidence of testimony, of the inner moral consistency of religious truth, and of its fitness to meet and satisfy the needs of spiritual life, is not compulsory. The acceptance of it is a free act of the soul in view of what that soul approves. These words of Jesus, though addressed to Thomas, and occasioned by his conduct, will never lose their interest to Christians, till their Lord returns, "without sin unto salvation." They teach that the first disciples of Christ, who were witnesses of his resurrection-life, have no preeminence on that account. We who believe on their testimony the facts pertaining to Christ, which they believed on the evidence of sense, may have as true and acceptable a faith as was theirs. Nay, in so far as they were disposed to insist upon a verification of facts by their own senses before they would believe, was their faith inferior in spiritual power to that of Christians who are satisfied with such evidence as apostolic testimony and the nature of the gospel message afford. For all the ends of religious life, our knowledge of the gospel is even better than theirs; our knowledge of Christ is even better suited to moral training than theirs. For this reason, it was expedient that he should go away, presently, and be seen no more. (16: 7, 10.)

30 ᵃ And many other signs truly did Jesus in the presence of his disciples, which are not written in this book:
31 ᵇ But these are written, that ye might believe that Jesus is the Christ, the Son of God; ᶜ and that believing ye might have life through his name.

30 Many other signs therefore did Jesus in the presence of the disciples, which are not written in 31 this book: but these are written, that ye may believe that Jesus is the Christ, the Son of God; and that believing ye may have life in his name.

a ch. 21 : 25....*b* Luke 1 : 4....*c* ch. 3 : 15, 16 ; 5 : 24 ; 1 Pet. 1 : 8, 9.

30, 31. PURPOSE OF THE WRITER IN PREPARING THIS GOSPEL.

30. And many other signs, etc. The Revised Version may be followed with advantage in reading these verses. *Many other signs therefore did Jesus in the presence of the disciples, which are not* **written in this book.** This Gospel, then, according to the explicit testimony of its author, contains but a selection of events from the life of Christ. Not all his miracles are described, nor is there any reason to suppose that any attempt is made to preserve all his sayings or discourses. Moreover from the general resemblance of this Gospel to the Synoptical Gospels, as well as from a study of their characteristics, we infer that they also are selections. The materials were so abundant that they could be used in no other way. Is it not, then, surprising that critics, like Baur and Strauss, have been wont to say, whenever a miracle or word of Jesus is recorded by only one or two of the Evangelists, that the others *knew* nothing of it? Just as if we might expect to find all they knew about the ministry of Christ written out in their narratives! "The facts which John has omitted differ from those which he has put into his narrative, not only in quantity (*many*), but also in quality (*other*). Consequently, if he has not given specimens of all kinds of miracles; if, for instance, he has related no cures of lepers or of demoniacs, it will be directly against his intention if one infers from this silence that he wishes to deny them."— *Godet.* But why are *signs* spoken of, and not discourses also? Did John undervalue the evidential, convincing power of his Master's teaching as compared with his wonderful works? By no means. He has given a large place in his Gospel to the words of Christ, and has recorded more than one saying which represents the testimony of Jesus as sufficient of itself to convince the honest hearer. But to a very unusual extent the *signs* and the teaching of Christ are linked together in this Gospel—the sign being the text, and the discourse an exposition of the truth expressed by the text. Observe, also, that these "signs" were wrought **in the presence of his disciples;** for the disciples were chosen witnesses, not merely of his resurrection, but also of his whole public life, from its beginning with the baptism of John until its close, when he was received up into heaven. (15 : 27 ; Acts 1 : 21, 22.)

31. But these are written that ye might (or, *may*) **believe that Jesus is the Christ, the Son of God; and that believing ye might** (or, *may*) **have life through his name.** The end for which the Evangelist wrote this Gospel is here plainly declared; and it is in perfect accord with the structure and contents of the book. But to apprehend the force of this statement we need to bear in mind the spiritual condition of those for whom the Gospel was primarily written. They were undoubtedly Christians, and particularly the Christians of Asia Minor. Hence, we must suppose them to have been believers in Jesus as the Christ, and, indeed, as the Son of God. There is no impropriety in supposing this; for, according to John's use of language, there are degrees of faith. The belief of a true disciple is sometimes very weak—so weak that when a higher degree is attained, the lower degree seems to have been a sort of unbelief—the increased faith being alone worthy of the name. The twilight is darkness when compared with noon-day. If, through a fuller knowledge and deeper apprehension of Christ, a believer reaches a higher degree of trust in him, he may be spoken of as now believing, as if he had never done so before. But it is possible that many Christians of Asia Minor were becoming lukewarm and skeptical in regard to the person of Christ. It is possible that Ebionites or Cerinthians were undermining the faith of some, so that John had special occasion to write this Gospel at the time when it was written. Yet this hypothesis is by no means necessary to account for the language here used. The explanation given above is equally pertinent, and the perverse doctrine of Cerinthus may not have been disseminated when this Gospel was written.

CHAPTER XXI.

AFTER these things Jesus shewed himself again to the disciples at the sea of Tiberias; and on this wise shewed he *himself*.
2 There were together Simon Peter, and Thomas called Didymus, and *a* Nathanael of Cana in Galilee, and *b* the *sons* of Zebedee, and two other of his disciples.
3 Simon Peter saith unto them, I go a fishing. They say unto him, We also go with thee. They went forth, and entered into a ship immediately; and that night they caught nothing.

1 AFTER these things Jesus manifested himself again to the disciples at the sea of Tiberias; and he manifested *himself* on this wise. There were together Simon Peter, and Thomas called 1 Didymus, and Nathanael of Cana in Galilee, and the *sons* of Zebedee, and two other of his disciples. Simon Peter saith unto them, I go a fishing. They say unto him, We also come with thee. They went forth, and entered into the boat; and that night they took

a ch. 1: 45....*b* Matt. 4: 21.—1 That is, *Twin*.

The last clause refers to the true life of communion with God, begun here, and perfected hereafter. Probably the expression, **might** (or, **may**) **have life through his name**, denotes a higher degree of union with God and blessedness in him, to be gained by a better knowledge of Jesus as the promised Messiah and the Son of God.

Ch. 21: 1-14. JESUS APPEARS TO A COMPANY OF HIS DISCIPLES BY THE SEA OF GALILEE.
1. Shewed himself. Perhaps it would be better to translate—*manifested himself;* for the Greek word (ἐφανέρωσεν) seems to imply that he now appeared, by an act of his own, out of an invisible state. Weiss asserts, possibly with too much confidence, that "he came out of the sphere of the unseen, in which as glorified he already dwelt, for the purpose of making himself known through a self assumed visible form." This is a less probable view than one which he rejects, namely: that the glorified body of Jesus was of such a nature that it could be made visible by him at will. Schaff remarks that the verb here used "expresses more than that Jesus showed himself after the resurrection. In these manifestations he really revealed himself out of the entirely new state which had begun at the resurrection." Similarly Godet: "Hitherto Jesus had manifested *his glory;* now he manifests *himself;* for his person has entered for the future into the sphere of the invisible." The expression, **after these things,** is too indefinite to be of much use in fixing the date of this manifestation. But the direction which Jesus gave his disciples on the very day of his resurrection to meet him in Galilee, and the lack of any notice of his appearing to them at Jerusalem from the eighth day after his resurrection until about the time of his ascension, lead us to think that they repaired to Galilee soon after the manifestation described in the last chapter. (Ver. 6-29.) He is said to have manifested himself to his disciples at (or, *upon*) **the sea of Tiberias;** meaning that there, on the shore of that sea, was the place of his appearing; not that his disciples were upon the sea, although this was the case at first. Only John calls the sea of Galilee the "sea of Tiberias," from the name of a city built by Herod on its western side. The late date of his Gospel accounts for this designation, especially if taken with the persons to whom it was addressed, and the writer's long residence in Asia Minor before it was written.

2. There were together Simon Peter, etc. Here only in this Gospel is John referred to distinctly in connection with his brother James, and this reference is very unobtrusive —**the sons of Zebedee.** Such a reference is strikingly favorable to the view that the chapter was written by John. For if it had been added by any other writer, surely the names of James and John would have been inserted, and, perhaps, immediately after that of Peter, instead of being placed below those of Thomas the Twin, and of Nathanael of Cana of Galilee—unless, indeed, we assume that the writer copied the style of John in the Gospel for the purpose of deceiving the readers —a most gratuitous and improbable assumption. The two unnamed disciples did not, probably, belong to the circle of the apostles, and for that reason were noticed in this indefinite manner.

3. Simon Peter saith unto them, etc. It is the language of common life. This group of faithful disciples had repaired to Galilee, perhaps to Capernaum, where Peter seems to have had a home and business. While there in waiting for the appearance of Jesus, the impulse to resume for a night his former occupation, led Peter to say, **I go a fishing.** And the others, very naturally, propose to

4 But when the morning was now come, Jesus stood on the shore: but the disciples *a* knew not that it was Jesus.
5 Then *b* Jesus saith unto them, Children, have ye any meat? They answered him, No.
6 And he said unto them, *c* Cast the net on the right side of the ship, and ye shall find. They cast therefore, and now they were not able to draw it for the multitude of fishes.

4 nothing. But when day was now breaking, Jesus stood on the beach: howbeit the disciples knew 5 not that it was Jesus. Jesus therefore saith unto them, Children, have ye aught to eat? They 6 answered him, No. And he said unto them, Cast the net on the right side of the boat, and ye shall find. They cast therefore, and now they were not able

a ch. 20: 14....*b* Luke 24: 41....*c* Luke 5: 4, 6, 7.

accompany him. The act needs no further explanation, though the events of the morning may be symbolical and very instructive. As once before, the disciples caught nothing during the night, which was the best time for fishing in that clear, inland sea. Whether such want of success was very unusual, we cannot tell; perhaps not, but it was somewhat dispiriting to fishermen, like Peter, James, and John, resuming for a night their former life.

4. But when the morning was now come, Jesus stood on the shore. Literally: *But when the morning was now becoming*, that is, dawning or breaking, before the light was perfect. The word translated *shore*, signifies *beach*. It "denotes a smooth shore, as distinguished from one precipitous or rocky."—*Hackett.* Compare Matt. 13: 2; Acts 21: 5; 27: 39, and Herodotus VII. 59, 188. The word *stood* (ἔστη) indicates a sudden appearance. (See 20: 26.) **But the disciples knew not that it was Jesus.** Possibly because it was not yet perfectly light. This, however, is not the most obvious sense of the Greek, for the word translated *but* (μέντοι), signifies *yet*, or *nevertheless*, as if his standing there might have been expected to secure his recognition. "The clause," remarks Westcott, "is added as something strange. It is vain to give any simply natural explanation of the failure of the disciples to recognize Christ. After the resurrection he was known as he pleased, and not necessarily at once." But was it not natural for John to recognize him sooner than any one else in the boat? (**Ver. 7.**) The ordinary and the extraordinary, the natural and the spiritual, were very closely united in the intercourse of Jesus with his disciples after the resurrection.

5. Then Jesus saith unto them, Children, have ye any meat? They answered him, No. Compare the Revised Version above. *Therefore*, (instead of *then*), implies that John considered this question a consequence of the disciple's failure to recognize Jesus. The question itself is so constructed as to anticipate a negative answer—proving that Jesus either knew or suspected them to have been unsuccessful in their fishing. The word (προσφάγιον) rendered *meat* in the Common Version, and *aught to eat*, in the Revised Version, signifies "anything eaten with other food," as fish with bread. Here the reference is certainly to fish. Westcott holds that the original word for **children** (παιδία), "marks the difference of age or position, and notes the tie of relationship"; but Grimm thinks it to be used here as a term of endearment, like the Latin *Carissimi*, or the English, "dearly beloved." It is difficult to decide between these two tropical uses of the word. If Jesus wished to be revealed by the extraordinary draught of fishes, he doubtless uttered the word in such a tone as to give it the former meaning; but if he aimed to reveal himself by his manner of addressing the disciples, he doubtless uttered this word in such a tone of voice as gave it the latter meaning.

6. Cast the net on the right side of the ship (or *boat*), **and ye shall find.** Their net had been on the left side of the boat—of course not very far from the place into which they were now directed to cast it, yet far enough to make their labor and watching useless. With all their knowledge of the lake, they were in need of divine guidance in order to fish with any success. And this was a typical lesson with reference to their future work. They were to follow the beckoning hand of Providence. If the Jewish synagogue rejected the Christ, his gospel must be preached in the Pagan school. **They cast therefore**—not yet indeed recognizing Jesus, but yielding to the word which he spoke— **and now they were not able to draw it for the multitude of fishes.** Literally: *They were no longer able*—as before—*to draw it*—i. e., to draw it up into the boat; for it appears that they drew it, afterwards, in the water, to the shore. Assuming, as we must, the typical character of this event, it is plain

7 Therefore *a* that disciple whom Jesus loved saith unto Peter, It is the Lord. Now when Simon Peter heard that it was the Lord, he girt *his* fisher's coat *unto him*, (for he was naked,) and did cast himself into the sea.
8 And the other disciples came in a little ship; (for they were not far from land, but as it were two hundred cubits,) dragging the net with fishes.
9 As soon then as they were come to land, they saw a fire of coals there, and fish laid thereon, and bread.

7 able to draw it for the multitude of fishes. That disciple therefore whom Jesus loved saith unto Peter, It is the Lord. So when Simon Peter heard that it was the Lord, he girt his coat about him (for 8 he [1] was naked), and cast himself into the sea. But the other disciples came in the little boat (for they were not far from the land, but about two hundred 9 cubits off), dragging the net full of fishes. So when they got out upon the land, they see [2] a fire of coals there, and [3] fish laid thereon, and [4] bread.

a ch. 13: 23; 20: 2.——1 *Or, had on his under garment only.*....2 *Gr. a fire of charcoal.*...3 *Or, a fish.*....4 *Or, a loaf.*

that the apostles were to have great success in bringing men into the kingdom of Christ, provided they should carry forward their work under his direction. Nor can we suppose that this lesson was meant for apostles only. It is a lesson for all the servants of Christ. The time will never come when they will be able to conquer the world without him; the day will never dawn when, directed by him, they will spend their strength for nought. Only under the great Leader can they overcome; but strengthened by his presence they will go forth to complete victory.

7. How true to all other representations of Peter and John are the incidents of this verse. The scene is briefly, but vividly sketched. The net full of great fishes—the disciples pulling in vain to draw it up over the side of the boat—the true-hearted John perceiving in all this the hand of his Lord and making known his discovery to Peter—Peter recognizing at once the truth of John's remark, girding on his outer garment without delay, and plunging into the sea to reach the shore and the Lord as soon as possible:—all this is in perfect accord with what is said of these two remarkable men in other parts of the New Testament. "When they recognized the Lord," says Chrysostom, "again do the disciples display the peculiarities of their individual characters. The one, for instance, was more ardent, but the other more elevated; the one more eager, but the other endued with finer perception. On which account John was the first to recognize the Lord, but Peter to come to him." The comment that Peter was *naked*, does not signify that he was wholly destitute of clothing, but rather that he was comparatively so, having laid aside his coat—the Greek word here used (ἐπενδύτης), meaning properly, any kind of over-garment.

8. The boat in which all the disciples, save Peter, remained, and came to the beach, is here called a **ship,** (or, *little boat*), and the distance which it had to pass over to reach the land was about two hundred cubits. The writer remembers the distance, as it could be measured roughly by the eye, and the time occupied in rowing to the shore, and states it as exactly as possible. There was probably no delay in starting the boat for the shore, though it did not reach that point as soon as Peter. **Dragging the net with fishes**—literally, *the net of fishes,* that is to say, the net full of fishes. Thus those in the boat drew the net after them in the water until they came to the shore, but they did not draw it out of the water.

9. John describes the scene as he saw it. When Peter had girded on his coat and plunged into the sea to go to Jesus, John remained in the boat and gave his attention with the rest to bringing it ashore and dragging the net after it. He may not have followed with his eye the course of Peter, and, therefore, he says nothing as to his swimming or as to his meeting the Lord. **As soon then as they were come to land,** (or, *So when they got out upon the land*), **they saw a fire of coals there,** etc. The verb **saw,** should rather be *see,* to correspond in tense with the original; for the present tense is more vivid than the past. **And fish laid thereon, and bread.** With equal correctness this might be rendered, *and a fish laid thereon, and a loaf.* Those interpreters who regard this meal as in some sense analogous to the Lord's Supper, prefer the latter translation. But we doubt the value of their reason for this preference, since other fish appear to have been added, and since there is nothing said in this passage which points to the food as emblematic of the Lord's body. Of the word *fish* (ὀψάριον), Watkins remarks: "In this passage and in ver. 13 only it occurs in the singular, but it seems clear that it may be collective, as our word "fish." The fire here, as in 18: 18, was of "charcoal" (ἀνθρακία). Grimm defines the word, *strues prunarum ardentium*—"a pile of burning coals." Observe the customary precision or definiteness of John's narrative.

10 Jesus saith unto them, Bring of the fish which ye have now caught.
11 Simon Peter went up, and drew the net to land full of great fishes, an hundred and fifty and three: and for all there were so many, yet was not the net broken.
12 Jesus saith unto them, *Come and dine*. And none of the disciples durst ask him, Who art thou? knowing that it was the Lord.

10 Jesus saith unto them, Bring of the fish which ye have now taken. Simon Peter therefore went [1]up, and drew the net to land, full of great fishes, a hundred and fifty and three: and for all there were 12 so many, the net was not rent. Jesus saith unto them, *Come and* break your fast. And none of the disciples durst inquire of him, Who art thou, know-

a Acts 10: 41.——1 Or, *aboard*.

Weiss believes that this narrative does not in the least suggest a miracle, "since Peter was already with Jesus, and on the shore of a sea alive with fishermen, whatever was needed for the morning meal could easily have been procured by direction of Jesus. That the Lord himself prepared it, because he wished the disciples to be *his guests* at the meal, the narrative does not at all intimate." But does the record suggest that Peter reached the shore —(a distance of about three hundred feet)— very much sooner than those in the boat? Or, that the coast was at that early hour alive with fishermen? Or, that the beach on which Jesus stood was near a city where bread and fish could be obtained at any hour of the day? All this may have been, as Weiss supposes; but we think it could not have been in the mind of the writer of this Gospel, and that an unprejudiced reader would at once ask, Did not John look upon these preparations as accomplished by Jesus in a supernatural way? That Peter had any share in making them, is quite improbable. That Jesus may have made them by the use of natural means, is certainly credible. The real question seems to be this: Does the narrative of John, read in the light of all that is said by the Evangelist concerning the movements of Jesus after his resurrection, fairly imply at this point something miraculous? We are half persuaded that it does, but leave the matter to be decided by every one for himself—only calling attention to the special awe which seems to have filled the disciples' minds.

10. Bring of the fish which ye have now caught (or, *taken*). It is an almost certain inference, that this was to be done for the purpose of adding some of the fish which they had taken to those already broiling on the coals of fire. But the fish in the net were obtained by the extraordinary intervention of Jesus, by a miracle of knowledge, if not of power: may not the same thing have been true in respect to those on the fire? Yet Weiss judges otherwise: "Precisely this necessary complementing of the fish already found on the fire excludes the miraculous or symbolical character of the meal." At all events, the materials of that morning repast were the gift of Christ to the disciples as really as if they had been created on the spot. And, besides, it is difficult to see how the addition of fishes caught in the manner described, excludes the "symbolical character of the meal," even should it be thought to exclude its miraculous character.

11. Simon Peter went up, etc. There is sufficient authority for the insertion of *therefore* after *Simon Peter*, as in the Revised Version, thus connecting the act of Peter formally and expressly with the word of Christ. The expression **went up,** refers to the prow of the boat as rising above the beach on which it rested. If the net, as may be supposed, was fastened to the stern, Peter entered the boat at the prow and going to the stern drew the net along side, until it reached the shore and was pulled out on the dry land. Probably he was assisted by some of the other disciples; as the direction of Christ (ver. 10) was addressed to the disciples, in the plural. The fish were now counted, as John remembers, and numbered one hundred and fifty-three. They were also of great size, yet the net was not broken. When they had been taken from the net and counted, some of them were probably added to those on the fire, or were broiled in addition to them, and the meal was ready.

12. Come and dine. Rather: *Come, breakfast;* that is, take breakfast, or, *break your fast;* for the verb denotes partaking of the morning meal. There is no intimation of Christ eating with them, unless it be in the word *come* (δεῦτε), which can scarcely be relied upon to prove that Jesus was standing by the food. (See ver. 13.) Great was the reverence as well as the joy that filled the disciples' hearts. They were afraid to question him freely. Though they knew it was the Lord,

13 Jesus then cometh, and taketh bread, and giveth them, and fish likewise.
14 This is now *the third time that Jesus shewed himself to his disciples, after that he was risen from the dead.
15 So, when they had dined, Jesus saith to Simon Peter, Simon, son of Jonas, lovest thou me more than these? He saith unto him, Yea, Lord: thou knowest that I love thee. He saith unto him, Feed my lambs.

13 ing that it was the Lord. Jesus cometh, and taketh the 1 bread, and giveth them, and the fish likewise.
14 This is now the third time that Jesus was manifested to the disciples, after that he was risen from the dead.
15 So when they had broken their fast, Jesus saith to Simon Peter, Simon, son of 2 John, 3 lovest thou me more than these? He saith unto him, Yea, Lord; thou knowest that I 4 love thee. He saith

a See ch. 20: 19. 26.——1 Or, loaf....2 Gr. Joanes.   See ch. 1: 42, margin....3 4 Love, in these places, represents two different Greek words.

they would doubtless have sought to have many things explained, and perhaps confirmed, by his word, if they had not been restrained by a sense of awe which made familiarity impossible. He only spoke; they were silent. Not a word thus far, according to the record of John, had any one of them addressed to him, except the monosyllable, "No," in answer to his question. (Ver. 5.)

13. Jesus then cometh, and taketh bread, and giveth them, and fish likewise. Then, should be omitted from the first clause, as it is wanting in the earliest manuscripts. (א B C D L X et. al.). Before **bread and fish,** the definite article should be inserted, as in the Revised Version. For thus it is written in the original, and there is no reason why the English Version should not here be strictly conformed to the original. It was "the bread" and "the fish" already spoken of which he gave to them. The expression, **Jesus cometh,** implies that he was not standing close beside the food when he invited the disciples to take their breakfast. (See ver. 12.) But now he acts the part of a gracious and friendly host, giving probably to each one of them his portion of the food.

14. In saying that this was **the third time that Jesus shewed himself** (or, *was manifested*) **to his disciples,** John speaks of the disciples as a body. For, if we include appearances to individuals, he has himself described three, which took place in Jerusalem, and therefore this would be the fourth. But, one of these appearances was to Mary Magdalene, while two of them were to the assembled disciples. Clearly enough he associates this manifestation of himself to a group of his disciples with the two similar manifestations in Jerusalem, and does not put in the same category his appearance to Mary.

In Luke 5: 1-11 (comp. Matt. 4: 18-22; Mark 1: 16-20), there is an account of a miraculous draught of fishes, which has been supposed by some identical with the one before us. But the events described in this narrative are different in all essential points from those mentioned by Luke. "(1) Those took place in the early part of Christ's ministry; these, after his resurrection. (2) Luke speaks of two boats; John, of but one. (3) Luke says that James and John were not in the same boat with Peter; John virtually says they were. (4) Luke says their net broke; John says the net did not break. (5) Luke declares that two boats were filled with the fishes taken; John asserts that the fish were not taken into the boat at all. (6) Luke represents Peter as falling at the feet of Jesus and beseeching him to depart; John represents him as plunging into the sea to come to Christ as quickly as possible. (7) Luke relates that Jesus called Peter to become a fisher of men; John, that he directed him to feed his sheep. (8) Luke declares that Christ was in the boat; John asserts that he was on the beach. Other minor differences may be passed over in silence, for these establish beyond a doubt the distinctness of the two miracles." (See the writer's work on "The Miracles of Christ," etc., p. 44.)

15-23. JESUS RESTORES PETER, AND SPEAKS OF JOHN.

15. The conversation between Jesus and Peter was in presence of the other disciples. This was suitable, if not morally necessary. For, having boasted in their hearing of his unconquerable faithfulness—whatever others might do, and having afterwards, in a public and cowardly manner denied the Saviour, it was fitting that his reproof and restoration should be witnessed by some of them. Such a reproof and restoration, so searching, and yet kind; so thorough, and yet gentle; were a lesson never to be forgotten by those present, and were worthy a conspicuous place in the Gospel which reveals to us the very "heart of Christ." Accordingly, after the disciples had breakfasted (not *dined*), **Jesus saith to Simon Peter, Simon, son of Jonas,**

16 He saith to him again the second time, Simon, *son of Jonas, lovest thou me?* He saith unto him, Yea, Lord; thou knowest that I love thee. *a* He saith unto him, Feed my sheep.

16 unto him, Feed my lambs. He saith to him again a second time, Simon, *son* of 1John, 2*lovest thou me?* He saith unto him, Yea, Lord; thou knowest that I 3love thee. He saith unto him, Tend my

a Acts 20: 28; Heb. 13: 20; 1 Pet. 2: 25; 5: 2, 4.——1 Gr. *Joanes.* See ch. 1: 42, margin....2 3 *Love,* in these places represents two different Greek words.

lovest thou me more than these? Instead of **Jonas,** the Revised Version has *John* and is supported in making this change by the larger part of the early manuscripts. More important, however, is it to remark, that Jesus does not here use the new and honorable name, Peter, in addressing his most conspicuous disciple. There would have been too deep a sarcasm in applying that designation now. For sincerity, not sarcasm, is called for when an offender is to be restored. So the firm and wise and loving Master goes back to the old name, and thus reminds his follower, without a touch of bitterness, that his recent conduct is inconsistent with his new name. To call him *Peter,* a *Rock,* in the face of conduct which seemed to prove him fickle as the wind, would be fearful irony; to call him *Simon, son of John,* was sincere reproof. It is also noticeable that the word **lovest,** (ἀγαπᾷς), employed by Jesus in his question, denotes a high moral regard and attachment, in distinction from warm personal affection. The latter was not counted worthless by Christ, but the former was what he specially sought in his followers. He expected to be honored and loved in view of his divine character, with an intelligent, voluntary appreciation. Such a love springs from the very source of spiritual life in the soul, and is, in the language of Jesus, "a well of water, springing up into everlasting life." It is an expression, not of impulse or natural affection, but of the whole moral personality in its purest action. Such a love ought, then, to overcome fear, and lead to the noblest self-sacrifice. Clearly, then, Peter had not manifested such love in his conduct; will he claim to possess it now? Notice also the words, **more than these.** They are charged with an allusion to the past. For Peter had said, with boastful assurance, on the evening before Jesus was delivered up: "If all shall be offended in thee, I will never be offended," and, "Even if I must die with thee, I will not deny thee." (Matt. 26: 33, 35, (Rev. Ver.; comp. John 13: 37.) In other words, taking exception to his Master's prediction:

"All ye shall be offended in me this night," he had asserted that, if all the rest should be made to stumble by anything that might be done or suffered by Jesus, his integrity would remain firm; his fidelity to Christ would be unshaken. Alas, within a few hours, he had fallen lower than any of them, and had openly denied the Lord. Would he now claim to have more true love for Jesus than these, his fellow-disciples? Never was a more searching reproof uttered in simple words. The least was said that could be said, and yet the most was said that could be said. And what was the answer? **Yea, Lord, thou knowest that I love thee.** A truthful answer, no doubt. A submission of the case to Christ's own knowledge, with a virtual confession that he had not known himself. But at the same time he is sure that Jesus must certainly see in his heart a warm personal attachment, if not the high moral affection to which he had referred. For, in his answer, Peter uses the word (φιλέω), which denotes personal affection. It was well; and the Lord saith unto him: **Feed my lambs.** These words assign to Peter the work of a Christian shepherd, who is called to lead the lambs of the flock into green pastures. And the word *lamb,* may be understood to refer to the still weak and immature members of Christ's flock. Feeding, rather than controlling, is the idea of the verb.

16. Jesus repeats the same question a second time, omitting, however, the words, **more than these.** For Peter's answer to his first question had shown that this disciple no longer thought his own love stronger than that of his fellow disciples; and therefore the Lord does not repeat his allusion to his great disciple's spiritual egotism and vanity. The second response of Peter is a simple repetition of his first; and is followed by the command. **Feed my sheep;** or, more precisely, *shepherd my sheep.* There is some authority for a Greek word, meaning *little sheep,* in place of the word that means *sheep.* But it is hardly sufficient to warrant a change in the text. The principal consideration in its favor is the fact that it is an uncommon word, while that

JOHN. [Ch. XXI.

17 He saith unto him the third time, Simon, son of Jonas, lovest thou me? Peter was grieved because he said unto him the third time, Lovest thou me? And he said unto him, Lord, *a* thou knowest all things; thou knowest that I love thee. Jesus saith unto him, Feed my sheep.
18 *b* Verily, verily I say unto thee, When thou wast young, thou girdedst thyself, and walkedst whither thou wouldest: but when thou shalt be old, thou shalt stretch forth thy hands, and another shall gird thee, and carry *thee* whither thou wouldest not.

17 sheep. He saith unto him the third time, Simon *son* of [1] John, [2] lovest thou me? Peter was grieved because he said unto him the third time, [3] Lovest thou me? And he said unto him, Lord, thou knowest all things; thou [4] knowest that I [3] love thee. Jesus saith unto him, Feed my sheep.
18 thee. Jesus saith unto him, Feed my sheep. Verily, verily, I say unto thee, When thou wast young, thou girdedst thyself, and walkedst whither thou wouldest; but when thou shalt be old, thou shalt stretch forth thy hands, and another shall gird thee, and carry thee whither thou wouldest not.

a ch. 2:24, 25; 16:30....*b* ch. 13:36; Acts 12:3, 4.——1 Gr. *Jonnes.* See ch. 1:42, margin....2 3 *Love,* in these places, represents two different Greek words....4 Or, *perceivest.*

for sheep is very common; and it is easier to suppose a change from an uncommon to a common word than the reverse.

17. Again the third time, Jesus repeats his question; but now with an important variation. For he substitutes the verb used by Peter, denoting warm personal affection, for the higher word previously employed by himself. It is this change which appears to have grieved Peter; for by it Christ seemed to call in question the genuineness of his personal devotion. If Peter's grief had arisen from the repetition of the question a third time, John would naturally have assigned to the **third time** an emphatic position in the sentence, **Peter was grieved because he said unto him the third time, Lovest thou me?** But he did not; and we are therefore forbidden to emphasize that expression. Moreover, the change of his own word, lovest, for the word persistently chosen by Peter, is an adequate and obvious explanation of the apostle's grief. His answer is now strengthened--**Lord, thou knowest all things; thou knowest that I love thee.** The verb which is translated **knowest,** in the last clause, is stronger than that which is translated by the same word in the preceding clause. To mark, if not to express, the distinction between them, the latter may be rendered, as in the margin of the Revised Version, *perceivest.* By his perfect knowledge Jesus must see, or perceive, the love which his disciple now feels for him. Jesus accepts the answer, and says to Peter, **Feed my sheep.** The verb feed, is the same as that used in verse 15—Feed my lambs. And if the word "lambs," in that verse refers to weak, immature Christians, the word "sheep," in this verse, must denote persons who are more advanced in Christian life. But there is no evidence that apostles were included among them; much less is there any evidence that Peter was now reinstated in a sort of governmental primacy over all that believe in Christ. All that was said to him on this occasion was said, in other words, to Paul, and to the rest of the apostles. The special reason, however, for saying it to Peter at this time, was the fact of his amazing fall—after which it could not have been easy for him to believe that the Lord would trust him as before, and allow him to resume the leading place which he had held among the apostles.

18. Verily, verily, I say unto thee, etc. The connection of this verse with the preceding is obvious. Having committed anew to Peter his life-work, as an apostle, Jesus solemnly refers to the personal issues of that work. It would lead him in a path not chosen by himself, and to an end which nature always dreads. In earlier days Peter had been self-reliant, and perhaps self-willed. He had been prompt in deciding, strenuous in action, preferring always to lead rather than to be led. But the future would be unlike the past. What was possible then, will be impossible hereafter. The time will come when he will feel the need of direction—when he will in old age stretch forth his hands (as a blind man) for guidance, and when he will be girded by another, and carried whither he would not. Then he will not, as in former years, choose his own way. Faithfulness to his Lord will involve self-denial and martyrdom. There seems to be no special obscurity in this figurative language, unless it be found in the clauses, **stretch forth thy hands, and another shall gird thee.** But the former, when applied to an old man, must naturally be understood as reaching out the hands either for support or for guidance. The writer admits that he has seen it done so often by his blind grandfather with a view to obtaining guidance, that this seems the more natural meaning; per-

CH. XXI.]   JOHN.   417

19 This spake he, signifying *by what death he should glorify God. And when he had spoken this, he saith unto him, Follow me.
20 Then Peter, turning about, seeth the disciple *b* whom Jesus loved following; which also leaned on his breast at supper, and said, Lord, which is he that betrayeth thee?
21 Peter seeing him saith to Jesus, Lord, and what *shall* this man *do?*
22 Jesus saith unto him, If I will that he tarry *c* till I come, what *is that* to thee? follow thou me.

19 Now this he spake, signifying by what manner of death he should glorify God. And when he had spoken this, he saith unto him, Follow me. Peter, turning about, seeth the disciple whom Jesus loved following; who also leaned back on his breast at the supper, and said, Lord, who is he that betrayeth 21 thee? Peter therefore seeing him saith to Jesus, 22 Lord, ¹ and what shall this man do? Jesus saith unto him, If I will that he tarry till I come,

a 2 Pet. 1: 14....*b* ch. 13: 23, 25; 20: 2,....*c* Matt. 16: 27, 29; 25: 31; 1 Cor. 4: 5; 11: 26; Rev. 2: 25; 3: 11; 22: 7: 20.——¹ Gr. *and this man, what?*

haps to one who has never had this early experience, the other reference may appear more probable. The only other tenable sense is that of stretching forth the hands to receive the manacles of a prisoner; but this would have seemed to require the passive, as officers of the law do not usually wait for prisoners to reach out their hands, but lay hold of them and apply the fetters themselves. The latter expression, **another shall gird thee**, was probably chosen for the sake of the contrast which it affords to, **thou girdedst thyself.** Girding oneself, denotes voluntary preparation for action; being girded by another, denotes, in this case, enforced preparation for death.

19. **This spake he, signifying by what death he should glorify God.** The Revised Version is more exact: *Now this he spake, signifying by what manner of death he should glorify God.* There is no sufficient reason for calling in question this statement of the sacred writer, or indeed for asserting that he has not referred to the deeper spiritual sense of the Saviour's words. It must first be proved that the deeper, spiritual sense spoken of is clearly present in the words of Christ. But this explanation does not require us to suppose, with some of the Christian Fathers, that the Saviour's language pointed to crucifixion as the manner of Peter's death. It is enough to see in his words a prediction of the violent death of Peter; though we do not wish to call in question the tradition that he was crucified. **And when he had spoken this, he saith unto him, Follow me.** The next verse implies that this was spoken as Jesus began to move from the place, and that Peter literally followed him, for a short distance, at least. Whether the bodily act was or was not the shadow of a spiritual act, to which the words of Jesus pointed, is not wholly certain; but such a reference is probable.

20. **And now, as the two were going away** from the group of disciples, **Peter, turning about, seeth the disciple whom Jesus loved, following.** It might have been expected that John would follow Jesus whenever decorum permitted. But in this instance he did not intrude upon his Lord's privacy with Peter, but allowed a considerable interval between himself and them. **Which also leaned on his breast at supper, and said, Lord, which is he that betrayeth thee?** (13: 25.) "In the emphatic three-fold reference to this disciple's intimacy with Jesus, we see most naturally the reason why he considered himself at liberty to follow, although Jesus had called upon no one but Peter to do this."—*Weiss.* "John was sure that nothing could pass between Jesus and Peter which needed to be concealed from himself."—*Godet.* This is the real ground for his referring to the expressions of Peter's love to him.

21. **Peter** (read *therefore*, as in Rev. Ver.), **seeing him saith to Jesus, Lord, and what shall this man do?** More briefly: *Lord, and this man, what?* That is, what of him? Of his work, and the manner of his death? Possibly the latter was specially in his mind. For, as the last words of Jesus had foreshadowed Peter's violent death, he may have been thinking of that more than of the work that would go before it. And his thoughts respecting himself may have determined the direction of his inquiry concerning John. This suggestion is favored by the answer of Christ, which appears to assume that Peter had in mind the death of John. The idea that Peter's question sprang from jealousy is unworthy of serious attention. Peter and John were faithful friends, and the question of the former respecting the latter, needs no explanation beyond what is afforded by the circumstances of the hour.

22. **If I will that he tarry till I come, what is that to thee?** These words of

23 Then went this saying abroad among the brethren, that that disciple should not die: yet Jesus said not unto him, He shall not die; but, If I will that he tarry till I come, what *is that* to thee?
24 This is the disciple which testifieth of these things,

23 what *is that* to thee? follow thou me. This saying therefore went forth among the brethren, that that disciple should not die; yet Jesus said not unto him, that he should not die; but, if I will that he tarry till I come, what *is that* to thee?
24 This is the disciple who beareth witness of these

Christ certainly imply his control over the duration of the apostles' lives. And if the great forces of nature were subject to his will in such a manner that neither pestilence nor famine, neither human prejudice nor passion, could defeat his purpose in regard to the apostles, it is easy to believe that he is "Head over all things to the church." The number of our days is with him. Amid the great forces of the universe Christ rules. Peter must have been profoundly moved by this assumption of authority in the realm of natural life, as well as in that of spiritual things, unless he had been previously convinced of his Lord's true Sonship to the Father, and supremacy over the world. Again, the words of Christ speak of his "coming," as an event certain in the future. But not in the immediate future. To think of the Day of Pentecost, is wholly out of the question. For Jesus had already spoken of Peter in language that foreshadowed his martyrdom in old age, while this passage implies that he would not remain till the Lord's coming. And when, in connection with this, Christ suggests the possibility of John's continuing in the flesh until he should come, an impression that his coming is somewhat remote is unavoidable. We may, therefore, conclude that none of the apostles, save John, expected to witness the coming of their Lord, without seeing death. But if the words of Jesus, though hypothetical, and not to be interpreted as a declaration of his will and a prediction concerning the life of John, are thought to point in a certain direction, and to render it probable that Jesus meant to preserve the life of John until his coming— that coming must be looked for between the death of the other apostles and that of the beloved disciple, and must have been fulfilled in the destruction of Jerusalem, regarded as the type of a greater coming and judgment at the end of the world. (But see Note on ver. 23.) **Follow thou me.** The pronoun **thou** is emphatic. And it is difficult to avoid giving a broad sense to the word **follow,** in this command—a sense so broad as to include the suffering of a cruel death, as well as a life of true devotion to God and patient service of mankind. For this broader and deeper sense grows out of the context, and presents itself to the reader's mind as the only sufficient meaning for the place.

23. Then went this saying, etc. Better, as in the Revised Version: *This saying, therefore, went forth among the brethren, that that disciple should not die.* The word *therefore,* is preferable to **then,** as a translation of the Greek connective. The saying that sprang out of Christ's remark, and was diffused among the brethren, was an inference; but a natural one, provided Christ was to come but once, and all the Christians then alive were to be changed, without tasting death, as Paul distinctly taught. (1 Cor. 15:51, 52.) This, we may assume, was the general belief of Christians; there is no ground for asserting that Paul differed from others on this point. Circumstances led him to speak of it more fully than it was treated by other apostles, but all held the same view. Yet the inference, **that that disciple should not die,** is plainly regarded by the sacred writer as illegitimate; but to show that it was illegitimate he simply repeats again the very words of Jesus. Those words were hypothetical, dependent on an *if.* Again, they said nothing about not dying, but only spoke of life prolonged till a certain event should take place. For some reason John does not tell his readers, whether he does or does not expect to die—whether he does or does not recognize any event in the past as the coming referred to by Jesus. We feel in reading this verse, that he did not regard the Lord's saying as any proof that he would not die; but if he believed that the coming referred to took place at the fall of Jerusalem, we are surprised that he has given us no hint of so important a fact. Indeed, his silence on this point makes us doubt whether the fall of Jerusalem was ever more than a faint type of the greater coming which was principally spoken of by Christ and his apostles.

24, 25. CONCLUDING STATEMENTS ABOUT THIS GOSPEL.

24. If we suppose this verse to have been

and wrote these things: and ᵃ we know that his testimony is true.

25 ᵇ And there are also many other things which Jesus did, the which, if they should be written every one, ᶜ I suppose that even the world itself could not contain the books that should be written. Amen.

things, and wrote these things: and we know that his witness is true.

25 And there are also many other things which Jesus did, the which if they should be written every one, I suppose that even the world itself would not contain the books that should be written.

a ch. 19: 35; 3 John 12.... *b* ch. 20: 30.... *c* Amos 7: 10.

---

written by John, it is a strong statement that the disciple just referred to (ver. 21-23) is the one who is bearing witness by this Gospel, who wrote these things by which he is bearing witness, and who is certain, from his personal knowledge, of their truth. With this view of the passage, John speaks of himself in the third person, to which there is no objection worth naming. His modesty leads him thus to speak. And the same feeling leads him to say we know, in the last clause, instead of *I know*. Meyer supposes that he speaks "*out of a consciousness of fellowship with his readers, no one of whom, as the gray-haired apostle rightly assumed, would doubt the truth of his testimony.*" On the other hand, Weiss believes that this verse was written by some one representing the Ephesian elders. "It is self-evident that 'the we,' can be only such persons as have lived in fellowship with John, and as have authority enough with the readers to whom the Gospel went out to secure its reception through their solemn testimony to its authorship and credibility: hence the Ephesian elders have been thought of as the writers of this verse." A third view is possible, namely; that the addition made by the Ephesian elders is only the last clause—**and we know that his testimony is true.** "In this case the appended words are to be regarded as the almost involuntary expression of their confidence in, and admiration of, one whose Gospel differed so much from the earlier Gospels, that some may have doubted how it would be received."—*Schaff.* The strongest reason for believing that this clause, (or, the whole verse), was inserted by some one besides the Evangelist, is the change from the third person in the earlier parts of the verse, to the first person in the last clause; and this change is as naturally explained by supposing the insertion to begin with **and we know,** as by supposing it to begin with the verse.

25. And there are also many other things which Jesus did, etc. Again, as in 20: 30, the Evangelist reminds his readers that his narrative is an incomplete record of the Lord's ministry—a selection from a great treasure-house, which seems to him inexhaustible. **The which, if they should be written every one, I suppose that even the world itself could not contain the books that should be written.** A hyperbolical statement, intimating the boundless variety and richness of the Saviour's teaching by word and deed, and suggesting that a complete record of the same would fill the world too full of books. And surely the Evangelist was correct in his judgment. Much as we may regret the brevity of the Gospels, when we are seeking to make a complete picture of the Lord's life on earth—there are ample grounds for believing that for the supreme ends of religious impression we have enough. Thus closes this wonderful Gospel, whose depths of wisdom and love will never be fathomed by the sons of earth.

APPENDIX.

BAPTISM AS RELATED TO REGENERATION AND FORGIVENESS.

John 3: 5 is one of a few passages on which men have founded the doctrine of baptismal regeneration. Indeed, it has probably been appealed to oftener than any other text of Scripture in support of that doctrine. But with it have been associated Titus 3: 5; 1 Peter 3: 21; Acts 2: 38; 22: 16; and Eph. 5: 26. These passages may be divided into two classes. (1) Those in which baptism is expressly named: Acts 2: 38; 22: 16; and 1 Peter 3: 21; and (2) those in which it is perhaps referred to: John 3: 5; Titus 3: 5; and Eph. 5: 26. Let us begin our study with the first class, wherein the ordinance is distinctly named. In neither of these passages is baptism represented as a means of regeneration—*i. e.*, of the work of the Holy Spirit in giving a new life to the soul. (a) The first of them reads as follows: "*Repent, and be baptized every one of you in* (or, *upon*) *the name of Jesus Christ, unto the remission* (or, *forgiveness*) *of your sins.*" (Acts 2: 38. Rev. Ver.) Here repentance and baptism are represented as leading to the forgiveness of sins. We understand repentance to be a voluntary turning of the soul from the exercise of unbelief to the exercise of belief, and from a paramount love of self and sin to a paramount love of God and holiness; while baptism is the prescribed symbol, sign, or expression of that inward change. The two are, therefore, properly united in our thought; but one as the essential, inward change, and the other as a divinely required confession or sign of that change. This view of the relation of baptism to repentance or faith is confirmed by the 41st verse below: "*They that gladly received his word were baptized.*" But there is no hint in these verses of any connection between baptism and regeneration by the Spirit of God; no suggestion, even, that the change called repentance was conditioned on the rite of baptism. (b) The second passage is a part of what Ananias said unto Paul in Damascus, after the latter had received his sight, and had been assured that he would be a witness for Christ unto all men, thus: "*Arise, and be baptized, and wash away thy sins, calling on the name of the Lord.*" (Acts 22: 16.) Of course there is no such thing possible as a literal washing away of sins. A removal of sins from the soul by bathing the body in water is absurd. But there is such a thing as forgiveness of sins; and this may be described figuratively as washing them away, so that henceforth the soul may be "clean" from the guilt or stain of sin. Dr. Hackett remarks, "that this clause (*and wash away thy sins*) states a result of the baptism in language derived from the nature of the ordinance. It answers to *unto the forgiveness of sins*, in 2: 38—*i. e.*, submit to the rite in order to be forgiven. In both passages, baptism is represented as having this importance or efficacy, because it is the sign of the repentance and faith which are the conditions of salvation." A similar use of language appears in the Old Testament. For in Lev. 4: 20, 26, 31, 35; 5: 10, 16, forgiveness of sin is promised as a result of the proper sacrifice for sin; while in Lev. 16: 19, 30, the presenting of the sin-offering is said to "cleanse" the people from sins. To forgive sins and to cleanse from sins were, therefore, substantially equivalent expressions. And let it be observed that Ananias adds an expression, *calling on his name*, (Rev. Ver.), which agrees perfectly with the view that baptism involves the idea of prayer for the forgiveness of sins. If baptism really signifies the change

APPENDIX. 421

of inward life, called "repentance toward God and faith toward the Lord Jesus Christ," it surely represents the candidate as entering for the first time upon a life of prayer for pardon and peace. (c) The third passage is more difficult; yet we believe it is in perfect accord with the two already considered. But we are satisfied with neither the Common nor the Revised Version of the text. It may, however, be translated as follows: *Which also now saveth you in its antitype—baptism, (not the putting away of the filth of the flesh, but the earnest request of a good conscience unto God), through the resurrection of Jesus Christ.* We give to the word (ἐπερώτημα) variously translated *answer, inquiry, seeking, earnest seeking, requirement*, the meaning *request*, or *earnest request*, because the verb (ἐρωτάω) signifies to ask a question, or to ask a favor—*i. e., to question, or to request*, and because the compound verb appears also to have both these senses, though slightly modified in use. Hence, the noun (ἐπερώτημα), which sometimes means a question asked, or a demand made, may naturally signify a *request made*. Grimm proposes to add another definition, namely, *strong desire;* because a feeling of desire is implied in the motions of interrogating or of demanding. But the form of the noun points rather to a request made than to the feeling which might lead to making it. Now we have seen that "calling on his name," or prayer, is associated by Ananias with baptism, while "forgiveness of sins" is represented by Peter as a result of the beginning of spiritual life, signified by baptism. But in this passage, baptism itself is spoken of as an embodied request or prayer unto God. And what can be truer than this, if it is a symbol of repentance, that is to say, of a change of mind and heart, if it is a sign and figure of entering into a new life? Is not the first motion of faith a beginning of actual trust in God, through Christ, for the forgiveness of sins? And is not this trust an implicit and earnest request for that forgiveness? Baptism, therefore, saves, because it stands for and means genuine reliance, for the first time, upon the mercy of God in Christ, and, indeed, an earnest request for pardon: it expresses the act of the soul in turning to God, committing itself to God, and seeking his grace.

If now we continue our study by looking at the other class of passages cited above, to-wit, those in which Baptism is not expressly named, we shall see that one of them (a) Eph. 5: 26, repeats the idea of "cleansing"—(*i. e.*, from sins) which, as has been shown, is sometimes a figurative expression for forgiveness of sins. The passage is rendered as follows in the Revised Version: *Even as Christ loved the church and gave himself up for it; that he might sanctify it, having cleansed it by the washing* (margin, *laver,*) *of water with the word.* Let the reader observe (1.) That "cleansing" seems to be distinguished by the apostle from "sanctifying." This accords with the view that it refers to the forgiveness of sins upon repentance, rather than to the implanting of a holy principle of life and sanctification in the soul. The two acts are doubtless co-incident in time, but are distinguishable in fact and thought. (2.) That here, as in the passages already examined, baptism—in case that is meant by "the laver of water,"—is used as a sign or symbol of conversion, and is spoken of as securing that which is secured by conversion—that is, by the turning of the soul to God for pardon and peace. In other words, the sign is here put for the thing signified; the ritual act of confession is put for the spiritual act which it represents. (3.) That an expression is added, *with the word*, or, *in the word*, which directs attention to the dispensation or element in which this cleansing or forgiveness is accomplished. That dispensation or element is *the gospel*—the word of divine grace in which sinners find light and peace. It is surely needless to justify this meaning of the expression, but we will refer to a few passages where it is illustrated—*e. g.*, Rom. 10: 8, 17; Eph. 6: 17; Heb. 6: 5; 1 Peter 1: 23. It is probably never used to denote the formula of baptism. (4) That the "cleansing by the laver of water" may be a simple figure of speech, founded on the bridal lustrations practiced in the East—the whole church of Christ being thought of as his bride. We do not accept this as the interpretation most likely on the whole to be correct, but it is certainly intelligible and in harmony with the context. At all events, there is nothing in this passage to show that Paul conceived of baptism as the medium in and through which divine life is conveyed by the Holy Spirit to the soul.

There remain two passages in which alone baptism seems to be connected with the work of the Holy Spirit in regeneration, viz.: Titus 3: 5, and John 3: 5. (b) The passage in Titus is thus translated by the Revisers: *But according to his mercy he saved us, through the washing* (or, *laver*) *of regeneration and renewing of the Holy Ghost.* As we understand the passage it might be literally translated, *through a laver of regeneration and a renewing of the Holy Ghost:*—"a laver of regeneration" referring to the inception of the new life by the work of the Spirit, and "a renewing of the Holy Ghost" referring to the preservation and development of the life, already implanted, by the same Spirit. But whether "a laver of regeneration," means a laver which belongs to regeneration, as its prescribed emblem and expression, or whether regeneration itself is figuratively called a laver of regeneration because in and by it the soul is cleansed, is not perfectly clear. If this passage could be interpreted by itself, without regard to other statements, we should be ready to adopt the latter view as correct, and say that there is here no reference to baptism. But bearing in mind the other passages, we accept the former view as probably correct, and believe that Paul had in mind baptism as representing and confessing the divine change called regeneration. Hence he teaches that men are saved by an outworking, obedient life, given and preserved by the Holy Spirit. (c) The other passage, John 3: 5, has been examined in the Commentary; but we may properly add a few remarks in this place. (1) There can be no reference in this passage to Christian baptism in distinction from John's baptism. For neither this Gospel nor any other gives us reason to think that Christ had yet administered the rite by the hands of his disciples, or had imparted to it any spiritual efficacy which it had not when administered by John. If then he meant to speak in language intelligible to Nicodemus, he must have referred either to John's baptism, or to a well-understood figurative sense of the term water He could not have referred to a rite that would begin to be used after two or three years. (2) As an expression, being "born of water and of Spirit" is clearly not synonymous with being "born of the Spirit" by means of water. For by the former the relation of these two sources of the new life to each other is not pointed out, while by the latter it is definitely stated. Taking the two sources separately, we may say that being "born of water" (baptized), must signify being cleansed from sins or forgiven; while being "born of Spirit" cannot signify less than being ingenerated, if we may use the word, with a new and holy principle of life by the Spirit of God. It is not, therefore, surprising that Jesus alludes to baptism in the briefest manner, while he dwells with special emphasis upon the work of the Spirit. (3) We do not hesitate to say that it is irrational to think of "water" as holding the same relation to the new birth, as that held by the Holy Spirit. A material substance cannot be supposed to effect a moral change. It may naturally enough *signify* a moral or spiritual change, but that is all. Dead matter cannot be a spring of moral power to the soul. And it is almost equally difficult to conceive of it as a physical medium of the Spirit.

Having shown that the principal texts on which men have founded the doctrine that the work of the Holy Spirit in regeneration is mediated by the water of baptism, need not be supposed to teach that doctrine, we will now look at certain representations of Scripture which are manifestly inconsistent with that doctrine. And we shall assume, for the sake of brevity, that repentance towards God, and faith in the Lord Jesus Christ, are just as truly fruits of the Spirit, beginning with regeneration, as is genuine love to God or one's neighbor. (Compare 1 John 5: 1 with 1 John 4: 7.) The representations of Scripture to which we refer, are such as these: (a) John the Baptist not only considered repentance, and, indeed, "fruits worthy of repentance," if not also faith in the coming Messiah, to be possible before baptism, but to be suitable prerequisites to it. (See Matt. 3: 6-8; Mark 1: 4, 5; Luke 3: 3, 8, 13, 14, 18; Acts 19: 4; and compare John 4: 1.) (b) The apostles, after receiving the gifts of the Spirit on the Day of Pentecost, taught the same thing as to repentance and faith in Christ going before baptism. (Acts 2: 38, 41; 8: 12, 35-38; 9: 15-18; 16: 14, 15, 31-34.) (c) Peter looked upon the extraordinary gift of the Spirit to Cornelius, his kinsmen, and near friends, as conclusive evidence that they might properly be baptized. (Acts 10: 24, 44-48.) (d) Paul represented the word of the cross, or the preaching of Christ crucified, in distinction from the administering of baptism, as the power of God unto salvation. (1 Cor.

1: 17, 18, 21-24.) (c) Paul affirmed that in Christ Jesus he had begotten the Corinthian Christians, through the gospel, (1 Cor. 4: 15), after saying a little before that he had baptized only a very few of them. (1 Cor. 1: 14-16.) These passages make it certain that, according to the teaching of John, of Christ, and of his apostles, the function of baptism is not to *originate* the new life of faith, but to *represent* the origin of it; to portray and confess the entrance of a human soul, through repentance and faith, produced by the Spirit of God, in the light of divine truth, upon a life of consecration and obedience. It is an ordinance that takes the mind of a believer back to the moment of conversion, that he may confess before men the change which then took place, by the grace of God, in his spiritual state. It is the specific, the prescribed, the significant rite, by which he signifies that he has ceased to live in unbelief, and has begun to live in faith and obedience. If any one thinks it unimportant, because it is concerned in the *manifestation* rather than in the *origination* of the new life, let him ponder the language of Paul: "If thou shalt confess with thy mouth, Jesus as Lord, and shalt believe in thy heart that God raised him from the dead, thou shalt be saved." (Rom. 10: 9, Rev. Ver.); or the words of James: "Show me thy faith apart from *thy* works, and I by my works will show thee my faith," and "as the body apart from the spirit is dead, even so faith apart from works is dead." (James 2: 18, 26, Rev. Ver.); or the saying of Christ himself: "Every one therefore who shall confess me before men, him will I also confess before my Father which is in heaven." (Matt. 10: 32, Rev. Ver.) If it can be said with Tertullian, that "a sound or vigorous faith is sure of salvation" (*fides integra secura est de salute*), it can also be affirmed, that "vigorous faith" works by love, and leads to obedience. If there can be no doubt as to the salvation of the penitent robber, without baptism, there can be as little doubt of his willingness to obey Christ in every practicable manner. Baptism, then, is a very definite and important act of obedience to Christ, and withal a very clear confession of divine truth; but it is prerequisite to salvation only as obedience to the known will of Christ is prerequisite.

www.ingramcontent.com/pod-product-compliance
Lightning Source LLC
Chambersburg PA
CBHW022105290426
44112CB00008B/559